The Theory of Public Choice–II

The Theory of Public Choice–II

Edited by
James M. Buchanan and
Robert D. Tollison

ANN ARBOR
THE UNIVERSITY OF MICHIGAN PRESS

We are grateful to the various authors and publishers for their cooperation in allowing us to reprint their papers. We would also like to thank Anna Tollison, without whose efforts the project should have surely foundered.

Published in the United States of America by
The University of Michigan Press and simultaneously
in Rexdale, Canada, by John Wiley & Sons Canada, Limited
Manufactured in the United States of America
1990 1989 1988 1987 5 4 3 2

Library of Congress Cataloging in Publication Data
Main entry under title:

The Theory of public choice—II.

Rev. ed. of: Theory of public choice. 1972.
Includes bibliographies and index.
1. Finance, Public—Addresses, essays, lectures.
2. Social choice—Addresses, essays, lectures.
I. Buchanan, James M. II. Tollison, Robert D.
HJ192.T47 1984 330 83-23323
ISBN 0-472-10040-8
ISBN 0-472-08041-5 (pbk.)

Contents

1 Introduction

Public Choice, 1972–82

Robert D. Tollison

In 1972, the University of Michigan Press published *The Theory of Public Choice,* a collection of papers edited by James M. Buchanan and myself. The volume sold well, and the comments of reviewers were encouraging. The *Economist* reported that "it would be wrong to dismiss gleans of insight on grounds that they fail to illuminate everything at once. The economics approach is stimulatingly different and if pursued with due modesty provides a useful challenge to political scientists."[1] Ursula Hicks noted that "this book is essentially a manifesto of the 'Virginian School' of Economics. . . . The whole approach is so (relatively) new that it is very useful to have them [the papers] all brought together in this way, so that their interrelation can be appreciated."[2] James E. Meade stressed that "for a number of years some economists have been working on the assumption that . . . both in spending their income in the market place and in casting their votes in the political arena citizens have been motivated by the unredeemed selfishness of 'economic man' . . . any economist who seeks a suggestive survey of what can be achieved by 'positive applied' work in this field . . . may usefully turn to this volume."[3]

The reviewers were right to stress the promise of public choice. Though many of the foundation works in the field, such as Buchanan and Tullock's *Calculus of Consent,* had been published in the early 1960s and before, the "movement" was just gathering steam in the early 1970s. The first classes of graduate students (many of them trained by Buchanan at the University of Virginia) had taken their places in the profession, and started to try to survive in academia by applying and expanding public choice principles. As Buchanan and I emphasized in 1972, public choice was a new entrant on the academic landscape: "The 'theory of public choice' remains on the threshold of development, but to those who seek both 'realism' and 'relevance' in their science, who seek informed and impartial 'involvements,' these preliminary essays may be suggestive of the extensive scope for research in a subdiscipline that will remain open-ended."[4] The young field of inquiry had a toehold in the profession; how would it fare?

In introducing a 1980s sequel to *The Theory of Public Choice,* it seems appropriate to try to answer this question from the perspective of approximately ten years later. To my knowledge public choice has no chronicler, no Boswell, and I do not pretend to that role in what follows. (I might add parenthetically that the growth of public choice is a topic worthy of a good history.) I have simply sought to pull together enough information to convey a general impression of the course of public choice over the past ten years. My review will be parochial, with an emphasis on the contributions of the "Virginian School" of political economy, both because I consider myself to be a member of this school and because I know it best. I offer my apologies in advance for omissions of other important developments and individuals.

I begin with the growth of the journal of the Public Choice Society, *Public Choice*. *Public Choice* started out as a publication called *Papers on Non-Market Decision Making,* which had no subscriptions and was simply sold. In 1966, *Papers* sold about 300 copies. *Papers II* and *Papers III* were published in 1967 and again sold about 300 copies. Over time, the back issues market for all of the early issues of *Papers* and *Public Choice* has been strong, so that a good many more than 300 copies of the early issues have been sold. In 1968, the journal changed its name to *Public Choice,* and began to be a regular journal with a subscription rate of about 350. Over the intervening years, it has grown to a subscription rate of about 1,400, of which about 350 are library and the others individual subscriptions. Martinus Nijhoff Publishing took over publication of *Public Choice* in 1978, and currently publishes it regularly. The journal appears to have a sound commercial footing.

In 1973, an effort was made to accommodate the more mathematical members in the society by appointing Peter Ordeshook as mathematics editor, with an allocation of one issue a year. In 1976, he was replaced by Kenneth Shepsle who, in turn, was replaced by Peter Aranson in 1980.

Gordon Tullock, of course, was a cofounder (with Buchanan) of *Public Choice* and the Public Choice Society, and continues to serve as the senior editor of the journal. Other members of the editoral board include: Peter Bernholz, Duncan Black, Kenneth Boulding, Steven Brams, James M. Buchanan, James S. Coleman, Anthony Downs, Francesco Forte, John Harsanyi, Melvin J. Hinich, Gerald Kramer, Richard G. Niemi, William A. Niskanen, Mancur Olson, Charles R. Plott, William A. Riker, and Akihito Udagawa.

The Public Choice Society began as an informal group headquartered at the University of Virginia called the Committee for Non-Market Decision Making. Buchanan and Tullock were cofounders of the group, and others in attendance at early meetings of the committee included John Rawls, James Coleman, Duncan Black, William Riker, Roland McKean, and Vincent Ostrom. In 1968, the group changed its name to the Public Choice Society. Membership in the society has grown to a present number of about eleven hundred scholars. Past presidents of the Public Choice Society include: Buchanan, Tullock, William Riker, Charles Plott, Vincent Ostrom, Mancur Olson, Otto Davis, James Coleman, Gerald Kramer, and John Ledyard. The president as of this writing is Elinor Ostrom of Indiana University.

There is a very active European Public Choice Society which started under the presidency of Peter Bernholz of Basel, Switzerland, about 1973. Originally, meetings were held every second year, but now every year, and the attendance at the most recent meeting in Poitiers, France, was about ninety. Charles Rowley has also served as president of the European section, but he resigned recently because he is moving to the United States. He is being replaced by Jean-Dominique Lafay of Poitiers. A special Spanish section of the Public Choice Society was formally launched in 1981. There is also a Japanese Public Choice organization which publishes its own journal. Akihito Udagawa is more or less in charge of this activity.

One point should be made about these empirical details—they undoubtedly understate the growth of interest in public choice. The reason for this is that many scholars, especially young ones, use the library or their professor's copy of the journal. So details of subscription and membership rates tend to understate the range of professional following of public choice.

On the general point of whether the society's growth is a "lot" or a "little," I would tend to say "a lot." To go from nothing to a steady-state revealed preference of fourteen hundred subscriptions in less than fifteen years, and *not* to be a regionally based academic group but rather a national organization with active counterparts in Japan and Europe, represents a remarkable achievement.

Of course, the impact of public choice is not revealed by these details; it resides in the impact of the ideas of public choice scholars. It is to this issue that I now turn.

The amount of public choice literature has grown rapidly. I would judge that now most important public choice research is not published in *Public Choice,* but in the major journals of economics and political science.[5] Moreover, the diversity of the scholarly backgrounds that are attracted to public choice makes it difficult to keep track of the growth of the literature. Fortunately, there are a number of sources of good bibliographies. Mark Pauly published an early bibliography of public choice literature in *Papers on Non-Market Decision Making.*[6] More current sources include the publication of public choice reading lists by Eno River Press, and the bibliography in Dennis Mueller's recent survey book on public choice.[7] Beyond these fairly accessible sources, there is a well-known "underground" bibliography circulated privately by Thomas Borcherding of Claremont Graduate School. Borcherding's bibliography is the most extensive and current source of public choice literature of which I know. I might add that he has always been willing to share his list and to accept suggestions for additions.

In this same vein it should also be noted that public choice has attained a niche in the *Journal of Economic Literature*'s classification system for economic writing. The classification falls under "General Economic Theory" and is listed as "025 Social choice; bureaucratic performance." The fact that the profession provides a convenient means to keep up with current research in the area is an impressive sign of the general scientific acceptance of public choice.[8]

What I have been covering to this point might be termed the straight empirical facts about the growth of public choice in scholarly circles. A follow-up question concerns the degree to which public choice has trickled down from the rarified atmosphere of the scientific journals to have a broader educational influence. Has public choice made it to the textbooks? Has public choice influenced public policy? These are heavy questions, and I stress again that my answers to them will only be suggestive of general developments.

The dent made by public choice in textbooks is large and growing. This process started in public finance textbooks, which until recently had basically been devoted to old-fashioned principles of taxation, with very little attention paid to modern developments in public choice theory. Today the tide is running in the other direction. More attention is paid in public finance textbooks to explaining why government does what it does than to normative tax principles. Books are increasingly oriented to a public choice approach, and virtually no major textbook comes without substantial sections devoted to public choice analysis. In sum, public choice has changed the way public finance (both undergraduate and graduate) is taught, no mean feat in a subdiscipline with as long and entrenched a history as public finance.[9]

In the highly competitive world of introductory textbooks, entries stressing a public choice perspective have appeared, and the commercial success of these books indicates that students and instructors are interested in the public choice approach. The best example from economics is Gwartney and Stroup's *Economics: Private and Public Choice.*[10] This is an introductory economics textbook with a public choice emphasis, which by all accounts ranks among the best-sellers in this market. This book and others indicate the growing viability of public choice in the undergraduate classroom.[11]

This is a brief, too brief, look at the impact that public choice has had on the literature of economics and political science. It is not meant to be extensive but to suggest a pattern of influence and evidence. There are, of course, many other ways to measure the intellectual impact of public choice. For example, public choice scholars such as Buchanan and Tullock are among the most often cited scholars in the social sciences. This is an important index because it measures the degree to which research is *used* by other scholars. In this sense citations are a better indication of professional success than, for example, sheer numbers of publications, and in this regard public choice scholars are generally among the most successful members of their professions.

The influence of public choice has also spread beyond scholarly circles. Of primary importance in this regard is the practical application of public choice in the movement in the United States toward tax and other types of limitations on government. This is not to take credit for the work of political entrepreneurs who have advanced tax and spending limitation and balanced budget proposals, but surely the intellectual precursors of such proposals are scholars such as Buchanan and, much earlier, Wicksell.[12]

Nor is this to argue that public choice scholars have sought an active role in public affairs. The vast majority have not, and their influence comes as a by-product of their scholarly work. There are, nevertheless, a number of individuals who have risen to prominent positions in government and who have also made useful and important contributions to public choice research.

James C. Miller III, chairman of the Federal Trade Commission, and William A. Niskanen, a member of the President's Council of Economic Advisers, are outstanding examples of public choice scholars in government service.[13]

I have discussed the direct influences of public choice on the ideas of scholars and policy makers. The indirect influences are perhaps even more important. Many scholars, journalists, politicians, and intellectual leaders generally may never have heard about "public choice," as such, but their way of thinking about politics, government, and governmental process has been affected. In a very real sense "public choice" provides the intellectual-analytical-empirical foundations for the increasingly pragmatic, realistic, and hard-nosed appraisal of political alternatives that describes general public attitudes in the 1980s.

Finally, it is important to note that although interest in public choice in the United States is great, it is a fair guess to say that it is greater in Europe. As noted earlier, there is a European Public Choice Society, and public choice seems to have captured the imagination of popular writers and young scholars in Europe. In his widely distributed book that surveyed new developments in economics, *Demain le Capitalisme,* Henri LaPage devoted a whole chapter to public choice.[14] These developments may be explicable by the fact that European countries and the European community generally are struggling with issues that are more nearly constitutional in nature. Public choice, with its emphasis on an equitable framework within which to conduct day-to-day government, is thus more relevant to European issues. This point, for example, applies with great force to Spain.

So public choice has fared well over the past decade, and we are pleased to bring out a second installment of readings which illustrate some of the reasons for this success. We have tried to pull together an interesting collection of public choice work over this period. We do not outline the contents of the volume here because the organization of the volume is straightforward and self-explanatory. Undoubtedly, we have missed papers and have been more or less "Virginian" in our selections. As the old saying goes, however, if it ain't broke, don't fix it! *Public Choice I* was received well; we hope the same fate awaits *Public Choice II.*

We launch our volume with the following sentiment: "Indeed, it is precisely because it deals with some of the oldest and toughest questions a community faces, that public choice attracts so many fine scholars. And for this reason, one can remain optimistic about the field's future growth and development."[15]

NOTES

I am grateful to James M. Buchanan and Gordon Tullock for help in preparing this essay. The usual caveat applies.

1. *The Economist,* August 5, 1972, 50.
2. Ursula Hicks, "Problems of Public Choice," *Finanzarchiv* 31 no. 2 (1972): 363–66.

3. James E. Meade, "Review of *Theory of Public Choice*," *Economic Journal* 82 (December 1972): 1423–25.
4. Robert D. Tollison, "Involved Social Analysis," in *The Theory of Public Choice: Political Applications of Economics*, ed. James M. Buchanan and Robert D. Tollison (Ann Arbor: University of Michigan Press, 1972), 7.
5. I would note, however, that many papers that are now widely cited in the literature have appeared in *Public Choice*. Tullock's paper on federalism is a good example. See Gordon Tullock, "Federalism: Problems of Scale," *Public Choice*, Spring 1969, 19–29.
6. Mark Pauly, "Bibliography of Recent Work in Non-Market Decision Making," *Papers in Non-Market Decision Making II* (Charlottesville: Thomas Jefferson Center for Political Economy, 1967), 105–18.
7. *Economics Reading Lists and Course Outlines*, compiled by Edward Tower (Durham, N.C.: Eno River Press, July 1980); and Dennis Mueller, *Public Choice* (Cambridge: Cambridge University Press, 1979), 271–88.
8. Indeed, public choice was the subject of a major review article published by this journal. See Dennis C. Mueller, "Public Choice: A Survey," *Journal of Economic Literature* 14 (June 1976): 395–433. Mueller's article was the basis for his subsequent book (*Public Choice*) published by Cambridge University Press as a part of its series on Surveys of Economic Literature. Also see A. Allan Schmid, "Theory of Public Choice: A Review Article," *Journal of Economic Issues* 8 (June 1974): 519–24; and Victor P. Goldberg, "Public Choice–Property Rights," *Journal of Economic Issues* 8 (September 1974): 555–79.
9. A leading example of "new wave" public finance texts is Richard E. Wagner, *The Public Economy* (Chicago: Markham, 1973). This book is now out of print, but Wagner is presently working on an expanded version to be published by Little, Brown.
10. James D. Gwartney and Richard M. Stroup, *Economics: Private and Public Choice*, 2d ed. (New York: Harcourt, Brace, Jovanovich, 1980).
11. At the advanced undergraduate level a number of specialized books have appeared that feature a public choice approach. See, for example, Ryan C. Amacher, Robert D. Tollison, and Thomas D. Willett, eds., *The Economic Approach to Public Policy* (Ithaca: Cornell University Press, 1976). For a review of public choice developments in the textbooks, see William C. Mitchell, "Textbook Public Choice: A Review Essay," *Public Choice* 30, no. 1 (1982): 97–112.
12. See the various papers by Buchanan in this volume; and Knut Wicksell, "A New Principle of Just Taxation," reprinted in *Classics in the Theory of Public Finance*, ed. Richard A. Musgrave and Alan T. Peacock (New York: St. Martin's Press, 1958). Also see Richard E. Wagner and Robert D. Tollison, *Balanced Budgets, Fiscal Responsibility, and the Constitution* (San Francisco: The CATO Institute, 1980).
13. See, for example, James C. Miller III, "A Program for Direct and Proxy Voting in the Legislative Process," *Public Choice* 7 (Fall 1969): 107–13; and Niskanen's widely acclaimed *Bureaucracy and Representative Government* (Chicago: Aldine, 1971).
14. Henri LaPage, *Demain le Capitalisme* (Paris: Librarie Generale Francaise, 1978). This book has now been translated into English; see *Tomorrow, Capitalism* (Lasalle, Ill.: Open Court Publishing Co., 1982).
15. Mueller, *Public Choice*, 270.

2 Public Choice, circa 1980

Politics without Romance: A Sketch of Positive Public Choice Theory and Its Normative Implications

James M. Buchanan

In this essay, I propose to summarize the emergence and the content of the "theory of public choice," or, alternatively, the economic theory of politics, or "the new political economy."[1] This area of research has become important only in the decades after World War II. Indeed in Europe and Japan, the theory has come to command the attention of scholars only within the 1970s; developments in America stem from the 1950s and 1960s. As I hope that my remarks here will suggest, the theory of public choice is not without antecedents, and especially in the European thought of the eighteenth and nineteenth centuries. Ecclesiastes tells us that there is nothing new under the sun, and in a genuine sense, such a claim is surely correct, and especially in the so-called social sciences. (I am reminded of this every week when I see my mathematically inclined younger colleagues in economics rediscovering almost every wheel that older economists have ever talked about.) In terms of its impact on the realm of prevailing ideas, however, "public choice" is *new*, and this subdiscipline that falls halfway between economics and political science has turned around the thinking of many persons. If I am allowed to use Thomas Kuhn's overly used word here, we can, I think, say that a new *paradigm* has been substituted for an old one. Or, to go somewhat further back, and to use Nietzsche's metaphor, we now look at some aspects of our world, and specifically our world of politics, through a different window.

My primary title for this essay, "Politics Without Romance," was chosen for its descriptive accuracy. Public choice theory has been the avenue through which a romantic and illusory set of notions about the workings of governments and the behavior of persons who govern has been replaced by a set of notions that embody more skepticism about what governments can do and what governors will do, notions that are surely more consistent with the political reality that we may all observe about us. I have often said that public choice offers a "theory of governmental failure" that is fully comparable to the "theory of market failure" that emerged from the theoretical welfare economics of the 1930s and 1940s. In that earlier effort, the system of private markets was shown to "fail" in certain respects when tested against the idealized criteria for efficiency in resource allocation and distribution. In the later effort, in public choice, government or political organization is shown to

First published in *IHS-Journal* 3 (1979): B1–11. © Physica-Verlag Ges.m.b.H., Seilerstätte 18, A-1010 Vienna/Austria.

"fail" in certain respects when tested for the satisfaction of idealized criteria for efficiency and equity. What has happened is that today we find few informed scholars who would try to test markets against idealized models. The private sector–public sector decision that each community must make is now more likely to be discussed in more meaningful terms, with organizational arrangements analyzed by comparisons between realistically modeled alternatives.

It seems to be nothing more than simple and obvious wisdom to compare social institutions as they might be expected actually to operate rather than to compare romantic models of how such institutions might be hoped to operate. But such simple and obvious wisdom was lost to the informed consciousness of Western man for more than a century. Nor is such wisdom today by any means universally accepted. The socialist mystique to the effect that the state, that politics, somehow works its way toward some transcendent "public good" is with us yet, in many guises, as we must surely acknowledge. And, even among those who reject such mystique, there are many who unceasingly search for the ideal that will resolve the dilemma of politics.

Especially at this early point, however, I do not want to appear to place too much emphasis on the normative implications of public choice theory. These implications can stand on their own, and they can be allowed to emerge as they will or will not from the positive analysis. The *theory* of public choice, as such, is or can be a wholly positive theory, wholly scientific and *wertfrei* in the standard meanings of these terms. The implications for the comparative evaluation of institutions, noted above, have to do with methods of making such comparisons, not with specific results. I do not want to commit the naturalistic fallacy, and I make no claim that public choice theory, any more than economic theory, can tell a community of persons what they "should" choose to do.

Definition

Let me now be somewhat more concrete and try to define "public choice theory" more directly. Such a definition can perhaps best be clarified by reference to economic theory, if only because the latter is more familiar. What is economic theory? It is a body of analysis that offers an understanding, an explanation, of the complex exchange process that we call "an economy." It is a body of analysis that allows us to relate the behavior of individual participants in market activity, as buyers, sellers, investors, producers, entrepreneurs, to the results that are attained for the whole community, results that are not within the purposes or the knowledge of the separate participants themselves (I should note here that Austria has a very proud and important heritage in the development of economic theory as I have here defined it, and I may say in passing that one of the most exciting and most encouraging developments within economics in the United States today is the observed resurgence of interest in "Austrian economics," and notably as among young research scholars.)

Public choice theory essentially takes the tools and methods of approach that have been developed to quite sophisticated analytical levels in economic theory and applies these tools and methods to the political or governmental sector, to politics, to the public economy. As with economic theory, the analysis attempts to relate the behavior of individual actors in the governmental sector, that is, the behavior of persons in their various capacities as voters, as candidates for office, as elected representatives, as leaders or members of political parties, as bureaucrats (all of these are "public choice" roles) to the composite of outcomes that we observe or might observe. Public choice theory attempts to offer an understanding, an explanation, of the complex institutional interactions that go on within the political sector. I emphasize the word *complex* here, since the appropriate contrast to be made is with the approach that models government as some sort of monolith, with a being of its own, somehow separate and apart from the individuals who actually participate in the process.

Methodological Individualism

As my definition suggests, public choice theory is methodologically individualistic, in the same sense that economic theory is. The basic units are choosing, acting, behaving persons rather than organic units such as parties, provinces, or nations. Indeed, yet another label for the subject matter here is "An Individualistic Theory of Politics."

There is no formal connection between the methodological individualism that describes formal public choice theory and the motivations that are attributed to persons as they behave in their various public choice capacities or roles listed above. It would be possible to construct a fully consistent and methodologically individualistic theory of politics on the romantic assumption that all persons in their political roles seek only to further their own conceptions of some "common good," and with utter and total disregard for their own more narrowly defined self-interest. Such a theory would not escape problems of reconciling differing persons' differing conceptions of just what defines "common good." But testable propositions might emerge from such a theory, and empirical work might be commenced to test these propositions.

But most of the scholars who have been instrumental in developing public choice theory have themselves been trained initially as economists. There has been, therefore, a tendency for these scholars to bring with them models of man that have been found useful within economic theory, models that have been used to develop empirically testable and empirically corroborated hypotheses. These models embody the presumption that persons seek to maximize their own utilities, and that their own narrowly defined economic well-being is an important component of these utilities. At this point, however, I do not want to enter into either a defense of or an attack on the usefulness of *homo economicus,* either in economics or in any theory of politics. I would say only, as I have many times before, that the burden of proof should rest with those who suggest that wholly different models of man apply in the political and the economic realms of behavior. Logical consistency suggests that, at least initially, we examine the implications of using the *same* models in different settings.

As I have already noted, we commence with individuals as utility maximizers. And, for present purposes, we do not need to specify just what arguments are contained in a person's utility function. We can, at this stage, allow for saints as well as sinners. In one sense, we can simply define a person in terms of his set of preferences, his utility function. This function defines or describes a set of possible trade-offs among alternatives for potential choice, whether the latter be those between apples and oranges at the fruit stand or between peace and war for the nation.

Once we begin analysis in terms of preference or utility functions, we are led almost immediately to inquire about possible differences among persons. Since there seems to be no self-evident reason why separate persons should exhibit the same preferences, it seems best to commence with the presumption that preferences may differ. Within economic theory, such differences present no problem. Indeed, quite the opposite. If one person places a relatively higher value on apples as compared with oranges than another person, an exchange opportunity is presented. Both persons can gain utility by trade. Indeed this trading to mutual advantage is what economic theory is all about, no matter how esoteric its modern practitioners may make it seem to be in its detail.

Political Exchange

By any comparison with politics, economic theory is *simple*. The process of "political exchange" is necessarily more complex than that of economic exchange through orderly markets, and for two quite separate reasons. In the first place, basic "political exchange," the conceptual contract under which the constitutional order is itself established, must precede any meaningful economic interaction. Orderly trade in private goods and services can take place only within a defined legal structure that establishes individuals' rights of ownership and control of resources, that enforces private contracts, and that places limits on the exercise of governmental powers. In the second place, even within a well-defined and functioning legal order, "political exchange" necessarily involves *all* members of the relevant community rather than the two trading partners that characterize economic exchange.[2]

The two levels of "political exchange" provide a somewhat natural classification for two related but separate areas of inquiry, both of which fall within the corpus of public choice. The first area of inquiry may be called an "economic theory of constitutions."[3] This theory has historical antecedents in the theory of social contract, and it also has modern philosophical generalization in the work of *Rawls* (1971). The second area of inquiry involves the "theory of political institutions" as these might be predicted to work within a constitutional-legal structure. The subject matter incorporates theories of voting and voting rules, theories of electoral and party competition, and theories of bureaucracy.[4]

The Economic Theory of Constitutions

As I have stated, this aspect of modern public choice theory is closely related to an important strand of ideas in traditional political theory or political philosophy, namely, the theory of the social contract or compact. The whole discussion here is directly relevant to the classic set of issues involving the *legitimacy* of political order. What gives legitimacy to governments, or to governors? What rights can some men possess to rule over other men?

At some basic philosophical level, the individualist must reject the notion that any such "rights of governance" exist. In this sense, I have often called myself a philosophical anarchist. Nonetheless, we are obligated to look squarely at the alternative social order that anarchy would represent, and without the romantic blinders that putative anarchists have always worn, then and now. And we look to Thomas Hobbes, whose seventeenth-century vision becomes very appealing to those of us who live in the late twentieth century. Hobbes described the life of persons in a society without government, without laws, as "solitary, poor, nasty, brutish, and short." In this Hobbesian perspective, any person in such a jungle would value security to life and property so highly that any contract with a sovereign government would seem highly beneficial. The person would agree to abide by the laws laid down by the sovereign, even if he recognizes that there were essentially no limits that could be placed on the sovereign's use of these laws for its own exploitative purposes.

Montesquieu, John Locke, and the American Founding Fathers were more optimistic than Hobbes in their conception of constitutional contract as potentially binding on the activities of government. And I think that a reading of history will, to an extent at least, bear out their conception. Governments have been limited by constitutions, and part of the Western heritage to this day reflects the eighteenth-century wisdom that imposed some limits on governmental powers. But the nineteenth- and twentieth-century fallacy in political thought was embodied in the presumption that electoral requirements were in themselves sufficient to hold government's Leviathan-like proclivities in check, the presumption that, so long as there were constitutional guarantees for free and periodic elections, the range and extent of governmental action would be controlled. Only in the middle of this century have we come to recognize that such electoral constraints do not keep governments within the implied "contract" through which they might have been established, the "contract" which alone can give governments any claim to legitimacy in the eyes of citizens.

The theory of constitutions that makes up a central part of public choice represents, in part, a return to the eighteenth- as opposed to the nineteenth- or twentieth-century perspective. The theory raises questions about how governments may be constrained, and about how governments should be constrained. What should governments be allowed to do? What is the appropriate sphere of political action? How large a share of national product should be available for political disposition? What sort of political decision structures should be adopted at the constitutional stage? Under what conditions and to what extent should individuals be franchised?

These questions, and many others like them, clearly depend for answers on some positive, predictive analysis of how different political institutions will operate if, in fact, they are constitutionally authorized. An informed, and meaningful, theory of constitutions cannot be constructed until and unless there exists some theory of the operation of alternative political rules.

Postconstitutional Politics

In a postconstitutional setting, with a defined legal order, there will remain opportunities for mutually advantageous "political exchanges." That is to say, after the conceptualized constitutional "contract" has established what has been variously called the "protective," "minimal," or "night-watchman" state, there are still likely to be efficiency-enhancing complex trades among all persons in the community. The "productive state" may emerge to provide "public goods," goods that are nonexcludable as among separate beneficiaries and that may be more cheaply produced jointly than separately.

How should the complex political exchanges be organized so as to insure that all beneficiaries secure net gains in the process? Voluntaristic trade akin to the pairwise matching of buyers and sellers that characterizes private-goods market exchange may not be possible. A role for governmental action is suggested, but how are government decisions to be made and by whom? By what rules? And how might various rules be predicted to work?

The theory here, as it has developed, has involved two distinct types of questions. First, it has attempted to look at how differing individual preferences over joint outcomes are reconciled, or might be reconciled. That is, how do groups of persons reach collective decisions under differing procedural rules? This type of theory has not been concerned with government, as such. In effect, it is a theory of *demand* for government goods and services without an accompanying theory of *supply*. The second, and more recent, development has addressed the quite different set of questions relating to the behavior of persons who are themselves charged with powers of governance, with supplying the goods and services that might be demanded by the citizenry. It will be useful to summarize the strands of postconstitutional political analysis separately.

Theory of Voting Rules

We may commence with the work of *Black,* who asked the simple question: How do committees reach decisions under simple majority voting rules?

Building on only bits and pieces of precursory work by Condorcet, Lewis Caroll, and a few others, *Black* was led to analyze the properties of majority voting, and he discovered the problem of the majority cycle, the problem that has occupied perhaps an undue amount of attention in public choice theory. There may exist situations where no single one of the possible alternatives for choice can command majority support over all other alternatives, despite the consistency of the preference sets of all members of the choosing group. In such a cyclical majority setting, there is no stable group decision attainable by majority rule; the group cannot make up its collective mind; it cannot decide.

Simultaneously with *Black,* and for a different purpose, *Arrow* was examining the desirable properties of a "social welfare function," and he was attempting to determine whether such a function could ever be constructed from a set of individual orderings. He reached the conclusion that no such function satisfying minimally acceptable properties could be found, and for basically the same reasons that *Black* developed more closely in connection with majority voting rules. *Arrow*'s work is not narrowly within what we might call the "public choice tradition," since he was, and is, concerned not with how institutions work but the logical structure of collective or social choice. Nonetheless, it was *Arrow*'s work that exerted a major influence on the thinking of social scientists; his work was taken to have demonstrated that government cannot work, if work here is defined in terms of the standard economist's criteria for consistency in choice. Collectivities in which individual preferences differ cannot, a la *Black,* make up their collective or group mind. And, a la *Arrow,* such groups cannot be assigned an ordering that will array all possible outcomes that is itself both consistent and reflective of individual orderings. Since the 1950s, since *Arrow* and *Black,* social choice theorists have explored in exhaustive logical and mathematical detail possible ways and means of escaping from the implications of the *Arrow* impossibility theorem, but they have had little or no success. "Social choice theory" has itself become a major growth industry, with an equilibrium not yet in sight.

Let me return to the work of *Black,* who, when confronted with the prospect of majority rule cycles, discovered that under certain configurations of preferences such cycles would not arise. If the alternatives for collective choice can be arrayed in such a fashion that individual orderings over these alternatives are single-peaked, for all voters in the group, there will be a unique majority outcome, one that will defeat any other outcome in a series of pairwise majority votes. This outcome or option will be that one which best satisfies or which is most preferred by the voter who is *median* among all voters, with respect to preferences over the options. The conditions required for single-peakedness are plausibly applicable in situations where the alternatives for collective choice are reducible to quantitative variations along a single dimension, for example, proposed amounts of public spending on a given public service. Consider a school board or committee of three members, one of whom prefers high spending on education, one of whom prefers medium spending, and the third of whom prefers low spending. So long as the high spender prefers medium to low spending, and so long as the low spender prefers medium to high spending, majority voting within the three-member committee will produce a stable medium spending outcome.

This tendency of majority voting rules to produce determinate outcomes that correspond to the preferences of the median voter under certain conditions has led to many studies, both analytical and empirical, notably in public finance applications of public choice, and particularly with reference to the budgetary decisions made in local governments. Median-voter models break down, however, even with simple budgetary allocation problems, when more than one dimension is introduced. If voters, or members of a committee, consider simultaneously several issues or dimensions, such as, say, spending on education and spending on police, the cyclical majority problem returns. And, related to this return, the multiplicity of dimensions allows for vote trading and "logrolling," the analysis of which has been important in public choice theory from its inception.

As I have already noted, the theory of voting and voting rules sketched here in summary is not a theory of government or of politics at all. It is, instead, a theory or set of theories about how groups of persons reach some decision or choice on what might be *demanded*, by the group, from some supplying agent or agency. Implicitly, the analysis proceeds on the presumption that the goods or services demanded are supplied passively and that the motivations of suppliers may be neglected. It is as if all collective decisions are somehow analogous to the decision made by a group meeting in a closed room about the setting for the thermostat, the presumption being that, once a joint decision is made, the heating or cooling system will respond automatically and passively to the demands placed on it.

Representation and Electoral Competition

Once we so much as move beyond the simple committee or town-meeting setting, however, something other than the passive response of suppliers must be reckoned with in any theory of politics that can pretend to model reality. Even if we take only the single step from town-meeting democracy to representative democracy, we must introduce the possible divergence between the interests of the representative or agent who is elected or appointed to act for the group and the interests of the group members themselves.

It is at this point that electoral competition, as an institution, plays a role that has some similarities with that played by market competition in the economy. In the latter, the principle of consumer sovereignty prevails if sellers are sufficiently competitive. At the idealized limit, no single seller can exercise any power over buyers. But to what extent does a system of electoral competition generate comparable results? To what extent is voter sovereignty analogous to consumer sovereignty? There are major differences that should be recognized, despite the underlying similarities. Persons or parties that seek to represent the interests of voters compete for approval or favor much in the manner as the sellers of products in imperfectly competitive markets for private goods and services. But politics differs categorically from markets in that, in political competition, there are mutually exclusive sets of losers and winners. Only one candidate or party wins; all others lose. Only one party is the governing party. One way of stating the basic difference here is to say that, in economic exchange, decisions are made at the margin, in terms of more or less, whereas in politics, decisions are made among mutually exclusive alternatives, in terms of all-or-none prospects. The voter may be disappointed when his candidate or party or policy proposal loses in a sense that is not experienced in market exchange.

At best electoral competition places limits on the exercise of discretionary power on the part of those who are successful in securing office. Reelection prospects tend to keep the self-interests of politicians within reasonable range of those of the median voter, but there is nothing to channel outcomes toward the needs of the nonmedian voting groups.

Theory of Bureaucracy

Even if we ignore the possible divergencies between the interests of legislative representatives, as elected agents of the voters, and those interests of the voters themselves, we remain without an effective model of government because we have not accounted for the behavior of those persons who actually *supply* the goods and services that are provided via governmental auspices. Voters elect members of legislatures or parliaments. Members of legislatures, through coalitions or through parties, make selections among various policy alternatives or options. But the implementation of policy, the actual process of government, remains with persons who hold positions in the bureaucracy. How do these persons behave? How are the conflicts between their own interests and those of the voters reconciled?

Recent developments in public choice theory have demonstrated the limits of legislative control over the discretionary powers of the bureaucracy. Modern government is complex and many-sided, so much so that it would be impossible for legislatures to make more than a tiny fraction of all genuine policy decisions. Discretionary power must be granted to bureaucrats over wide ranges of decision. Further, the bureaucracy can manipulate the agenda for legislative action for the purpose of securing outcomes favorable to its own interests. The bureaucracy can play off one set of constituents against others, insuring that budgets rise much beyond plausible efficiency limits.

Increasingly, public choice scholars have started to model governments in monopoly rather than competitive terms. Electoral competition has come more and more to be viewed as competition among prospective monopolists, all of whom are bidding for an exclusive franchise, with profit maximizing assumed to characterize the behavior of the successful bidder. Governments are viewed as exploiters of the citizenry, rather than the means through which the citizenry secures for itself goods and services that can best be provided jointly or collectively. Both the modern analysis and the observed empirical record suggests that governments have, indeed, got out of hand.

Can Leviathan Be Limited?

The rapidly accumulating developments in the theory of public choice—ranging from sophisticated analyses of schemes for amalgamating individual preferences into consistent collective outcomes, through the many models that demonstrate with convincing logic how political rules and institutions fail to work as their idealizations might promise, and finally to the array of empirical studies that corroborate the basic economic model of politics—have all been influential in modifying the way that modern man views government and political process. The romance is gone, perhaps never to be regained. The socialist paradise is lost. Politicians and bureaucrats are seen as ordinary persons much like the rest of us, and "politics" is viewed as a set of arrangements, a game if you will, in which many players with quite disparate objectives interact so as to generate a set of outcomes that may not be either internally consistent or efficient by any standards.

I do not want to claim, or to be taken to claim, too much for the contribution of public choice theory in turning attitudes around here, in being responsible for the paradigm shift. For social scientists, for scholars and intellectuals, the availability of an alternative model of political process probably has been of some considerable importance. But for members of the general public, the simple observation of failure on the part of governments to deliver on their promises, these failures have been much more important in modifying attitudes than any set of ideas or any ideology.

I noted earlier that the fallacy of nineteenth- and twentieth-century political thought lay in an implicit faith that electoral constraints would alone be sufficient to hold the Leviathan-like proclivities of government in check. The experience in Western nations since World War II has exposed this fallacy for what it is. And we are now seeking to reimpose constitutional limits on government over and beyond those exercised through democratic electoral constraints. At least we are trying to do so in the United States. Beyond minimal efforts, I am not sure that there is a comparable movement at work in Europe. It seems to me highly doubtful that this objective can be successfully accomplished. Having come to command shares in national income or product that were undreamt of, even in the most roseate of the early democratic socialist predictions, modern governmental bureaucracies will not relinquish their relative positions in society without struggle.

Nonetheless, the effort is being made and will be made. In America, 1978 was the year of Proposition 13, when the voters of California turned back, by a two to one margin, the growth of government spending and taxing. This event sent political shock waves throughout the Western world. The United States is now (1979) inundated with various proposals, at all levels of government, designed to limit the expansion of governmental powers. "Bridling the passions of the sovereign"—this eighteenth-century slogan has resurfaced to command political respectability.

I have indicated that developments in public choice theory may have been in some small way influential in generating this shift in attitudes toward bureaucracies, politicians, and government. But the question remains as to what contribution public choice theory might make in the face of the developing distrust of traditional political institutions. It is here that the economic theory of constitutions, discussed earlier as a part of public choice analysis, becomes relatively the most important area of emphasis. Western societies face a task of *reconstruction;* basic political institutions must be reexamined and rebuilt so as to keep governments as well as citizens within limits of tolerance. But we are approaching a period when critical diagnosis is not enough. Criticism alone can generate chaos, whether this be in the form of gradual breakdown or in the form of violent disruption. The reconstructive reform in our institutions can be accomplished without revolution of either the left or right, but this path toward the future requires that the public come to understand the limits of change as well as the value. Zealotry in the cause of antipolitics, antigovernment, anti-institutions movements can result in a drift toward anarchistic terror, the jungle against which Hobbes warned us all. We must indeed keep the "miracle" of social order clearly in our mind as we seek ways and means of reforming arrangements that seem to have got out of hand. I think that public choice theory offers an analytical setting that allows us to discuss genuine reconstruction in our constitutions that may be made without major social costs.

NOTES

1. For an earlier, and differently organized, discussion, see *Buchanan* 1978. For a more technical survey, see *Mueller* 1976.
2. For a development of the distinction between political exchange at the constitutional and the postconstitutional levels, see *Buchanan* 1975.
3. The development of such a theory was the primary purpose of the book that I wrote jointly with *Tullock* 1962.
4. In modern public choice theory, the theory of voting rules commences with *Black* (1958). The theory of electoral or party competition stems largely from the work of *Downs* (1957). The theory of bureaucracy in its modern sense was first developed in *Tullock* (1965).

REFERENCES

Arrow, K. *Social Choice and Individual Values.* New York: John Wiley, and Sons, 1951.

Black, D. *Theory of Committees and Elections.* Cambridge: Cambridge University Press, 1958.

Buchanan, J. M. *The Limits of Liberty.* Chicago: University of Chicago Press, 1975.

______. "From Private Preferences to Public Philosophy: The Development of Public

Choice." In *The Economics of Politics,* edited by Arthur Selden, pp. 1–18. London, 1978.

Buchanan, J. M., and Tullock, G. *The Calculus of Consent.* Ann Arbor: University of Michigan Press, 1962.

Downs, A. *An Economic Theory of Democracy.* New York: Harper and Row, 1957.

Mueller, D. "Public Choice: A Survey." *Journal of Economic Literature* 14, no. 2 (1976): 395–433.

Rawls, J. *A Theory of Justice.* Cambridge, Mass.: Harvard University Press, 1971.

Tullock, G. *The Politics of Bureaucracy.* Washington, D.C.: Public Affairs Press, 1965.

Public Choice: A Survey

Dennis C. Mueller

Public choice can be defined as the economic study of nonmarket decision making, or, simply the application of economics to political science. The basic behavioral postulate of public choice, as for economics, is that man is an egoistic, rational, utility maximizer.[1] This places public choice within the stream of political philosophy extending at least from Thomas Hobbes and Benedict Spinoza, and within political science from James Madison and Alexis de Tocqueville. It is separated from much of this earlier work on politics, however, by its use of the analytic tools of economics (see, however, Black 1958, 156–213; Buchanan and Tullock 1962, 307–22; Haefele 1971; and Ostrom 1971).

Indeed, public choice's development as a separate field has been largely within the last three decades and in response to issues and needs arising elsewhere in economics. Starting with Bergson's 1938 article (1969) and spurred by Arrow's 1951 book (1963) a large literature has grown exploring the properties of social welfare or social choice functions.[2] It focuses on the problems of aggregating individual preferences to *maximize* a social welfare function or to satisfy some set of normative criteria. This research on optimal methods of aggregating preferences has naturally spurred interest in the properties of *actual* procedures for aggregating preferences via voting rules, i.e., in public choice. The problem of finding a social choice function satisfying certain normative criteria turns out to be quite analogous to establishing an equilibrium under different voting rules. Thus, both Arrow's study (1963) of social welfare functions and Black's seminal work on committee voting procedures build on the works of de Borda (1781), Condorcet (1785), and Dodgson (1876). We discuss the most directly relevant parts of the social welfare function literature as part of normative public choice in Part Two.

The second development in economics fostering interest in public choice has been the work on market failures, again stemming from papers appearing in the forties and fifties. This work centers on establishing conditions for efficient allocation in the presence of market failures and leads directly to the study of nonmarket procedures for revealing individual preferences in these situations. The public choice approach to nonmarket decision making has been (1) to make the same behavioral assumptions as general economics (rational, utilitarian man), (2) often to depict the preference revelation process as analogous to the market (voters engage in exchange, citizens exit and enter clubs), and (3) to ask the same questions as traditional price theory (Do

First published in *Journal of Economic Literature* 14, no. 2 (June 1976): 395–433.

equilibria exist? Are they stable? Pareto efficient?). This part of the literature resembles positive economics so closely, that it is referred to here as positive public choice, although parts of it have normative implications. Positive public choice is reviewed in Part One.

Public choice and public expenditure theory share an ancestry in the work of the "Continental" writers on public finance (see Musgrave and Peacock 1958). Of particular importance here are the papers by Lindahl (1919) and Wicksell (1896). Lindahl's paper has had the greatest influence on public goods theory; Wicksell's on public choice and public finance. Wicksell's view of government as a quid pro quo process of exchange among citizens underlies Buchanan and Tullock's *Calculus of Consent* (1962) and much of the positive public choice literature. Musgrave's (1959) influential separation of government activity into allocation and redistribution decisions is directly traceable to Wicksell. In Part Three, we argue that this Wicksellian distinction constitutes the natural conceptual boundary between positive and normative public choice.[3]

Not surprisingly, given this background, many contributors to public choice have worked in or started from public finance. Despite this overlap, the amount of work on the interface between public choice and public finance remains small,[4] and little is said about it in this survey.

Along with the above intellectual developments, interest in public choice has undoubtedly been stimulated by the actual growth of the public sector. Between 1946 and 1974 total government (federal, state, and local) purchases of goods and services as a percentage of GNP in the United States increased from 13 to 22 percent, total government receipts as a percentage of national income from 28 to 40. Regardless of the normative properties of the collective choice process, the mere magnitude of the public sector warrants study of its decision rules.

Part One: The Positive Theory of Public Choice

The Reasons for Collective Choice

Probably the most important accomplishment of economics is the demonstration that individuals with purely selfish motives can mutually benefit from exchange. If *A* raises cattle and *B* corn, both may benefit by exchanging cattle for corn. With the help of the price system, the process can be extended to accommodate a wide variety of goods and services.

Although often depicted as the perfect example of the beneficial outcome of purely private, individualistic activity in the absence of government, the invisible hand theorem presumes a system of collective choice comparable in sophistication and complexity to the market system it governs. For the choices facing *A* and *B* are not merely to trade or not, as implicitly suggested. *A* can choose to steal *B*'s corn, rather than give up his cattle for it; *B* may do likewise. But, unlike trading, stealing is at best a zero sum game. What *A* gains, *B* loses. If stealing, and guarding against it, detract from *A* and *B*'s ability to produce corn and cattle, it becomes a negative sum game. While with trading each seeks to improve his position and both end up better off, with stealing the selfish pursuits of each may leave them both worse off.

The example can be illustrated with strategy Matrix 1. Square 1 gives the allocations when *A* and *B* trade and refrain from stealing, square 3 when they steal and trade. Both are better off when they both refrain from stealing, but each is still better off if he alone steals (squares 2 and 4). Both may be induced to adopt the dominant stealing strategy with the outcome square 3. Once there, both can become better off by tacitly or formally agreeing not to steal, providing the enforcement of such an agreement costs less than they jointly gain from it.

Matrix 1.

B→ *A*↓	Does not steal	Steals
Does not steal	1 *A*(10-cattle, 9-corn) *B*(8-cattle, 6-corn)	4 *A*(6-cattle, 5-corn) *B*(10-cattle, 9-corn)
Steals	2 *A*(10-cattle, 10-corn) *B*(5-cattle, 3-corn)	3 *A*(7-cattle, 5-corn) *B*(7-cattle, 5-corn)

The agreement against stealing is necessary to achieve Pareto optimality. More generally, the collective act of establishing and enforcing laws and property rights is undoubtedly a necessary precondition for a system of voluntary exchange (Bush and Mayer 1974; Buchanan 1975*a*). Problems of collective choice exist in all but a purely Hobbesian, anarchistic society and are coterminous with the existence of recognizable groups and communities.

A judicial system is a Samuelsonian public good in "that each individual's consumption leads to no subtraction from any other individual's consumption of that good" (Samuelson 1969*a*). Nearly all public goods, whose provision requires an expenditure of resources, time, or moral restraint, can be depicted with a strategy box analogous to Matrix 1 (Runciman and Sen 1965; Riker and Ordeshook 1973, 296–300). National defense is the collective provision of protection against external threats; laws and their enforcement against internal threats; fire departments against fires. Replace stealing with paying for an army, or a police force, or a fire department, and the same strategy choices emerge. Each individual is better off if all contribute to the provision of the public good than if all do not, and each is still better off if he alone does not pay for the good.

A pure public good is characterized by indivisibilities in production or jointness of supply and the impossibility or inefficiency of excluding others from its consumption, once it has been supplied to some members of the community (Musgrave 1959, 9–12, 86; Head 1962). The joint supply characteristic creates the potential gain from a cooperative move from square 3 to square 1. Given jointness of supply, a cooperative consumption decision is necessary to provide the good efficiently. If it took twice as many resources to protect *A* and *B* from one another as it does to protect only one of them, collective action would be unnecessary. The failure of the exclusion principle to apply provides an incentive for noncooperative individualistic behavior, a gain from moving from square 2 or 4. The impossibility of exclusion thus raises the likelihood that purely voluntary schemes for providing a public good break down. Together the properties of public goods provide the raison d'être for collective choice. Jointness of supply is the carrot, making cooperative-collective decisions beneficial to all; absence of the exclusion principle the apple tempting individuals into independent noncooperative behavior.

Matrix 1 depicts the familiar and extensively analyzed prisoner's dilemma. Despite the obvious superiority of the cooperative nonstealing outcome to the joint stealing outcome, the dominance of the stealing strategies ensures that nonstealing does not constitute an equilibrium. Nonstealing can be assured only through a joint, enforceable agreement. Such an agreement can be reached informally, through repeated plays of the game. Player *A* may induce player *B* not to steal, by not stealing himself. *A* can enforce this agreement by indicating by word or deed that he will begin to steal as soon as *B* does. By so tying his behavior to *B*'s, the strategies reduce to a choice between cells 1 and 3, and the cooperative solution can emerge.

The appearance of cooperative solutions in prisoners' dilemma games has been found in experimental studies to depend on the number of players, and number of plays of the game (Siegel and Fouraker 1960; Sherman 1971). When the number of other players is small, it is easier to learn their behavior and predict whether they will respond to cooperative strategy choices in a like manner. It is also easier to detect noncooperative behavior and single it out for punishment, thereby further encouraging the cooperative strategies. When numbers are large, some players can adopt the noncooperative strategy, and either not be detected, since the impact on the rest is small, or not be punished, since they cannot be discovered or it is too costly to the cooperating players to punish. Thus, voluntary compliance with behavioral sanctions or provision of public goods is more likely in small communities than large (Buchanan 1965*b*). Reliance on voluntary compliance in large groups leads to free riding by many individuals bringing about the under or nonprovision of the public good (Olson 1965).

In the large, mobile, heterogeneous community a formal statement of what behavior is mutually beneficial (e.g., how much each must contribute for a public good) may be needed, for individuals even to know what behavior is consistent with the general welfare. Given the incentives to free ride, compliance may require the implementation of individualized rewards or sanctions (Olson 1965, 50–51, 132–35).

Thus, democracy, formal voting procedures for making and enforcing collective choices, is needed by communities of only a certain size and impersonality. The family makes an array of collective decisions without ever voting; a tribe perhaps only occasionally. A metropolis or nation-state must make a great number of decisions by collective choice processes. Small stable communities may elicit voluntary compliance and contributions for collective decisions by merely publicizing them. Larger, more impersonal communities must establish formal penalties for asocial behavior and levy taxes (penalizing nonpayment) to provide for public goods.

The game theoretic underpinning of public choice, as represented by the prisoners' dilemma, and the different possibilities for arriving at the cooperative solution to this game have important implications for the selection of a set of democratic rules by a community as will become apparent as we examine the properties of these rules.

Public Choice in a Direct Democracy

This section explores the properties of various voting rules. These rules can be thought of as governing the polity itself, as when decisions are made in a town meeting or by referendum, or an assembly or committee of representatives of the citizenry. If the latter is assumed, the results can be strictly related only to the preferences of the representatives. The relationship between citizen and representative preferences is taken up later.

The Unanimity Rule

As we have seen, formal voting procedures are needed to provide public goods due to the incentives for violating voluntary, informal agreements—free riding. Since *all* can benefit by conforming to the cooperative solution to the prisoners' dilemma, the obvious voting rule for public goods would seem to be unanimous consent.

Although all consume a public good, not all benefit to the same degree. A classic problem of public expenditure theory has been the description of processes for revealing individual preferences for public goods. Following Lindahl (1958), a number of writers have described variants of a Walrasian tâtonnement process for providing public goods.[5] One can easily formulate these procedures into a public choice process. Consider a world with two persons and one public good. Let figure 1 depict the mapping of A and B's indifference curves from the private-public good space into public good–tax space (Johansen 1963). A's share of the public good's costs is measured upward along the vertical axis, B's share from top downward. A_1 and B_1 are A and B's utilities in the absence of any public good. For a specific quantity of public good, lower indifference curves imply lower tax shares and hence higher utility levels. If A_1 and B_1 intersect, the two individuals are better off under some sets of tax share–public good combinations. The tangency points for their indifference curves form a contract curve (CC^1) mapping the Pareto-possibility frontier (bounded by the zero public good level utilities implied by the initial endowments) into the public good–tax share space.

Now consider the following public choice process. An impartial observer proposes both a pair of tax shares for $A(X)$ and $B(1-X)$ and a quantity of the public good, Q_1. If this combination (F) falls within the eye formed by A_1 and B_1, both individuals prefer purchasing this quantity of public good at the

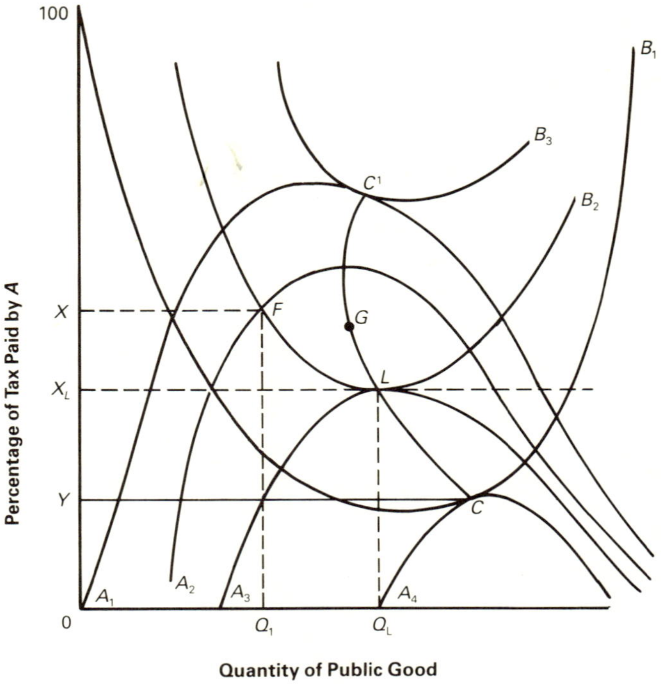

Fig. 1

given tax shares to no public good at all. Both will vote for it, if they vote sincerely. F now becomes the status quo decision and new tax share–quantity pairs are proposed. When a combination falling within the eye formed by A_2 and B_2 is hit upon, it is unanimously preferred to F. It now becomes the status quo and the process is continued until a point on CC^1, like G, is obtained. Once this occurs no new proposal can be unanimously preferred, i.e., can make both individuals better off, and the social choice has been, unanimously, made.

Under a slightly different procedure the Lindahl equilibrium can be achieved (see Escarraz 1967 and Slutsky 1975). Suppose for tax shares X and $(1-X)$, the voters are asked to vote on all possible pairs of public good quantities. If both voters agree on a quantity of the public good that they prefer to all others at these tax shares, it is *the* unanimous collective choice. This will occur only if the two individuals' indifference curves are tangent to the tax line from X at the same point. If no such Q is found for this X, a new X is chosen and the process repeated, until an X and Q are found which defeat all proposed quantities for the given X. This occurs in figure 1 at L, the Lindahl equilibrium for the X_L and Q_L combinations.

The length and shape of the contract curve is determined by the initial endowments (determining A_1 and B_1) and the individual preferences. If the second voting procedure is selected, the equilibrium attained (L) will be independent of the specific sequence of tax–public good proposals (assuming L is unique). In contrast, given initial endowments and preferences, the final choice under the first procedure, G, is entirely dependent upon the order of public good–tax share proposals. Unless G and L happen to coincide, the equilibrium at G would be one in which both voters would prefer a different quantity of public good given their tax shares. Each is thus somewhat "frustrated" in that he is consuming either too much or too little of the public good *at his tax price for it.* If this were thought unfortunate, one would prefer the second procedure leading to the Lindahl equilibrium at which all indifference curves are tangent to the tax shares line. On the other hand, if one preferred to have the entire range of the contract curve capable of selection by the voting process, one would prefer the first. As McGuire and Aaron have shown (1969), however, no normative significance can be attached to any particular set of tax shares.

The unanimity rule leads to Pareto-preferred public good quantities and tax shares and is the *only* rule certain to do so, a feature that led Wicksell (1958) and later Buchanan and Tullock (1962) to endorse it. Two main criticisms have been made against it.

First, a groping search for a point on the contract curve might take considerable time (Black 1958, 146–47; Buchanan and Tullock, 1962, chap. 6). The loss in time by members of the community in discovering a set of Pareto-optimal tax shares might outweigh the gains to those who are saved from paying a tax share exceeding their benefits from the public good. An individual, who was uncertain over whether he would be so "exploited" under a less than unanimity rule, might easily prefer such a rule rather than spend the time required to attain full unanimity. The second objection to a unanimity rule is that it encourages strategic behavior (Black 1958, 147; Buchanan and Tullock 1962, chap. 7; Barry 1965, 242–50; Samuelson 1969*b*). If A knows the maximum share of taxes B will assume rather than go without the public good, A can force B to point C on the contract curve, by voting against all tax shares greater than Y. All gains from providing the public good then accrue to A. If B behaves in the same way, the final outcome is dependent on the bargaining strengths of the two individuals. The same is true of other Lindahl-type equilibria.[6] Bargaining can further delay the attainment of the agreement as each player has to "test" the other's willingness to make concessions.

One also might object to an unanimity rule on the grounds that even if attained, the equilibrium depends on the bargaining abilities and risk preferences of the individuals (Barry 1965, 249; Samuelson 1969*b*). Such a criticism implicitly contains the *normative* judgment that the proper distribution of the gains from cooperation should *not* be distributed according to the individuals' willingness to bear risks. One can easily counter that they *should.* An individual who votes *against* a given tax share to secure a lower one risks under a unanimity rule not having the good provided at all. Voting in this manner expresses a low preference for the public good in much the same way as does voting against the tax share because it "truly" is greater than the expected benefits. Someone not willing to vote strategically might be said to value the public good higher. We return to the question of how the gains from cooperation *ought* to be shared in Part Two.[7]

The Optimal Majority

The above considerations suggest that the time required to pass a bill increases with the size of the majority required to pass it. At one pole stands unanimity under which any individual can block any agreement until he has one with which he is satisfied. At the other, each decides the issue alone, and no delay need occur as with a pure private good.

With a less than unanimous majority required to pass an issue, the possibility exists of individuals being worse off as a result of an issue's passage. If the issue is of the public good–prisoners' dilemma variety and there exist reformulations that could secure its unanimous approval, a less than unanimity rule can be said to impose a cost on those made worse off by the issue's passage. This cost is the difference in utility levels actually secured and those that would have been secured under unanimity (Buchanan and Tullock 1962, 63–91; Breton 1974, 145–48). The optimal rule is thus the one for which the expected gain in utility from redefining the bill to gain one more supporter just equals the expected loss in time from doing so.

Since these costs are likely to differ from issue to issue, one does not expect one voting rule to be optimal for all issues. *Ceteris paribus,* when opinions differ widely or information is scarce, large amounts of time may be required to reach consensus; and if the probable costs to opposing citizens are not too high, all might favor a less than full unanimity rule—if the identity of those bearing the costs was unknown *ex ante*. Issues for which large losses can occur are likely to require higher majorities, e.g., Bill of Rights–type issues (Buchanan and Tullock 1962, 111–16).

Majority Rule

The method of majority rule requires that at least the first whole integer above $n/2$ support an issue before it can be imposed on the community. Nothing we have said so far indicates why it should be the most frequently encountered voting rule. Indeed, a full treatment of majority rule requires a description of both its normative and positive properties. A number of the most recent and persuasive defenses of majority rule have been openly normative (e.g., May 1952; Downs 1961; Leibenstein 1962; Barry 1965, 312–16; Baumol 1965, 43–44; Rae 1969; and Taylor 1969). In discussing majority rule, therefore, we consider both its normative and positive properties. Since Rae's arguments are most compatible with the discussion here, we focus on them.[8]

Rae approaches the question of choosing a decision rule in the same way as Buchanan and Tullock, from the point of view of an egoistic individual uncertain of his future tastes and position, and asks what rule minimizes the chances of a person supporting an issue that fails *and* opposing an issue that passes. The rule that accomplishes this automatically maximizes the converse of these twin goals. The only rule that does so is the majority rule as Rae (1969) and Taylor (1969) prove.

If each issue promises an equal (or on average equal) change in utility, plus or minus, for each individual, this theorem becomes a plausible reason for an egoist, uncertain over future position, to favor majority rule. This equal intensity assumption is made explicitly by Rae (1969, 41, n. 6) and is implicit in other arguments favoring majority rule. The opposite assumption, that the losses of those opposing a decision by the majority may be greater than the losses of the majority when a nondecision is imposed by the minority, underlies the arguments against majority rule. This latter position arises from a view of the public choice process as one of revealing preferences for public goods. If the issue to be decided is one of providing a public good and if it is possible to devise a tax share–quantity combination that improves everyone's welfare, then it must be possible to obtain unanimous consent. If unanimity is not feasible, the issue must involve more than merely the attainment of allocative efficiency, i.e., it must involve redistributive considerations, and this takes it out of the set of decisions typically discussed by the positive public choice economists from Wicksell to the present in their discussions of the unanimity rule.[9] If one only seeks allocative efficiency through the provision of public goods, unanimity must be possible given enough time and in the absence of continually disruptive bargaining, and we are back to the cost of imposing a decision on some–cost of decision time trade-off. In the absence of these decision costs an individual need never support a pure public good issue that failed, or oppose one that passed. All issues that involve only allocative efficiency would eventually pass, and the normative significance of the Rae-Taylor theorem disappears.

Thus, if the Rae-type defense of majority rule does not rest entirely on considerations of time and bargaining costs, it must implicitly consider decisions with both allocative or redistributive aspects, or distributive aspects alone. Indeed, the assumption that the individuals opposing a bill have as much to lose from its passage as those favoring it have to gain seems most plausible with respect to a simple redistributive bill. But why this should be true for a bill to build a school or penalize theft seems unclear. As a rule for achieving a *net* redistribution of wealth majority rule, supported by the egalitarian assumption that the utility losses of the opponents equal the gains of the proponents, seems quite plausible. It is this difference in perspective that I think is at the heart of the debate over majority and unanimity decision rules.

Unfortunately, if majority rule is limited to choosing among points lying on some generalized Pareto frontier, a second problem arises: that of cycling.

Cycling

The possibility that an equilibrium does not exist under majority rule was recognized two hundred years ago by de Borda (1781) and has been a major focus of the public choice literature beginning with Black (1948) and Arrow

TABLE 1

	Issues						
Voters	X		Y		Z		X
1		>		>		<	
2		>		<		>	
3		<		>		>	
Community		>		>		>	

(1963). Consider the following three voters with preferences over three issues as in table 1 (> implies preferred). Each voter has transitive preferences, but the community does not. Pairwise voting leads to an endless cycle. Majority rule can select no winner nonarbitrarily.[10]

If *X, Y,* and *Z* are sequentially higher expenditures on a public good, then voters 1 and 3's preferences can be said to be single-peaked in the public good–utility space (see fig. 2). Voter 2's preferences are double-peaked, however, and herein is the cause of the cycle. Change 2's preferences so that they are single-peaked, and the cycle disappears.

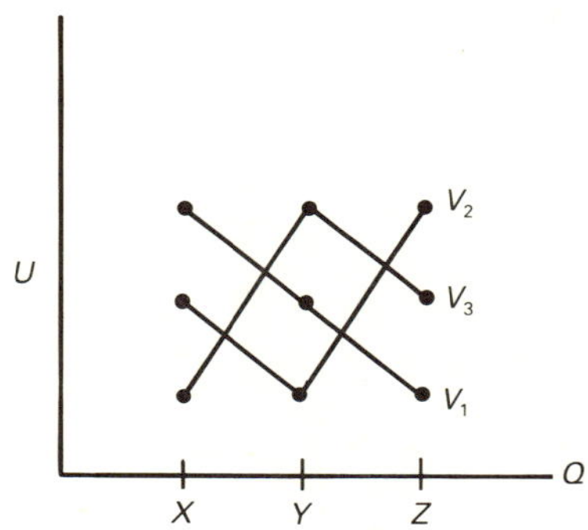

Fig. 2

One of the early important theorems in public choice was Black's proof that majority rule produces an equilibrium outcome when voter preferences are single-peaked (1969).[11] If voters' preferences can be depicted along a single dimension, as with an expenditure issue, this equilibrium lies at the peak-preference for the median voter. Figure 3 depicts the single-peaked preferences for five voters. Voters 3, 4, and 5 favor *m* over any proposal to supply less. Voters 3, 2, and 1 favor it over proposals to supply more. The preference of the median voter decides.

If all issues were unidimensional, multipeaked preferences of the type depicted in figure 2 might be sufficiently unlikely that cycling would not be much of a problem. In a multidimensional world, however, preferences as in

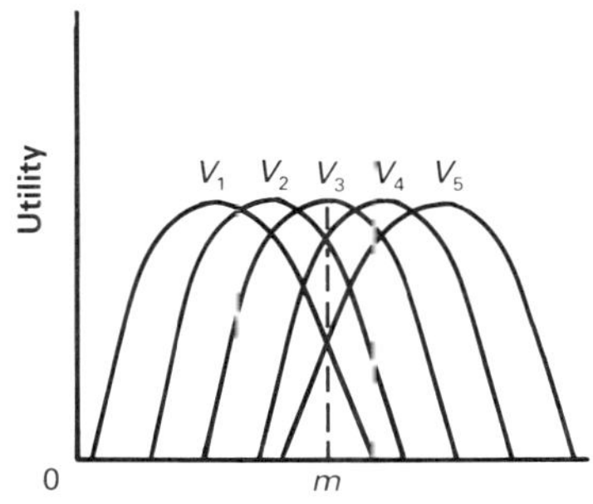

Fig. 3

table 1 seem quite plausible. Issues *X, Y,* and *Z* might, for example, be votes on whether to use a piece of land for a swimming pool, tennis courts, or a baseball diamond. Each voter could have single-peaked preferences on the amount to be spent on each activity, and a cycle could still appear over the issue of the land's use.

A great deal of effort has been devoted to defining conditions under which majority rule yields an equilibrium Returning to figure 3, we can see, somewhat trivially, that *m* emerges as an equilibrium because the other voters are evenly "paired off" against one another regarding any move from *m*. This condition has been generalized by Plott, who proved that a majority equilibrium exists if it is a maximum for one, and only one, individual and the remaining even number of individuals can be divided into pairs whose interests are diametrically opposed (1967). This condition is obviously too restrictive to be very comforting.[12]

A second stream of literature has attempted to establish equilibrium conditions by placing restrictions on the preferences of the individuals voting as the single-peakedness condition does.[13] Not all of this literature is particularly relevant to public choice, since the conditions proposed often do not lend themselves to straightforward interpretations as single-peakedness does, nor is it clear that they can be plausibly assumed to exist in reality.[14] One of the most relevant contributions is that of Kramer (1973). He makes the same assumptions about individual utility functions as usually encountered in economics, that they are quasi-concave and differentiable, and proves that "the only obvious condition on individual preferences which will ensure single-peakedness in two or more dimensions is the condition of complete unanimity of individual preference orderings" (1973, 295; see also Craven 1971; and Slutsky 1977*b*).

And so we return to a unanimity condition. Recalling that what we seek at this stage of the discussion is a voting rule to reveal individual preferences on public goods, the options would appear to be as follows. A unanimity rule might be selected requiring a, perhaps infinite, number of redefinitions of the issue until one that benefited all citizens was reached. While each redefinition might, in turn, be defeated until a point on the Pareto-possibility frontier had been reached, once attained no other could command a unanimous vote against it, and the process would come to a halt. The number of times an issue must be redefined before a passing majority is reached can be reduced by reducing the size of the majority required to pass an issue. While this "speeds up" the process of obtaining the *first* passing majority, it slows down, perhaps indefinitely, the process of reaching the *last* passing majority, i.e., the one that beats all others. For under a less than unanimity rule, some voters are made worse off; this is equivalent to a redistribution of wealth from the opponents of a measure to its proponents. But, as with any pure redistribution measure, it is generally possible to redefine an issue transferring the benefits among a few individuals and thus obtain a new winning coalition. The Plott "perfect balance" condition ensures an equilibrium under majority rule by imposing a severe equal intensity assumption on the distribution of preferences, which ensures that any redefinition of an issue always involves symmetric and offsetting redistributions of the benefits, leaving the winning coalition intact. The Kramer "identical utility functions" condition defines the condition under which a redefinition of an issue is certain not to produce any redistribution effects.

The redistributive characteristics of less than unanimity rules explain the similarities between the proofs and conditions establishing a social welfare function and majority rule equilibria (or the impossibilities thereof). Both flounder on their inability to choose among Pareto-preferred points, i.e., to handle the question of redistribution (see Sen 1970, chaps. 5, 5*).

Out of the frustration of seeking formal proofs for the existence of majority rule equilibria, a large number of studies have explored, using simulation techniques, the probabilities that cycles would occur in practice. If all possible preference orderings are assumed to be equally likely, the probability of a cycle occurring is very high.[15] As one introduces single-peakedness assumptions (Niemi 1969; Tullock and Campbell 1970) or assumes simply that some rankings are more likely than others (Williamson and Sargent 1967), the probability of cycles occurring declines.

Logrolling

When voter preference intensities on each issue are not the same, the gains of a winning majority may be less than the minority's losses. To avoid this, "intense minorities" may engage in logrolling or vote trading.[16]

TABLE 2

	Issues		
Voters	*X*	*Y*	*Z*
A	−2	−2	−3
B	5	−2	6
C	−2	5	−1

To understand the process, consider table 2. Each column gives the utility changes to three voters from an issue's passage; defeat produces no change. Assume first that only issues *X* and *Y* are being decided. If each is decided separately by majority rule, both fail. Voters *B* and *C* have much to gain from *X* and *Y*'s passage, however, and can achieve this if *B* votes for *Y* in exchange for *C*'s vote for *X*. Both issues now pass to *B* and *C*'s mutual benefit.

The existence of beneficial trades requires a nonuniform distribution of intensities. Change the two 5's to 2's and *B* and *C* gain nothing by trading. The equal intensity condition that guarantees majority rule's optimality would then also be satisfied, and it is this situation that proponents of majority rule have typically had in mind.

The numbers, as presented, depict the situation usually envisaged by logrolling's proponents. Without trading, the majority tyrannizes over the relatively more intense minority on each issue. Through vote trading these minorities express the intensity of their preferences, just as trading in private goods does, and thus improve the community's net welfare.

This result depends crucially on the total potential gains from voting being positive. Change the 5's to 3's or the -2's of *A* to -4's, and the same trades emerge as before. The sum of utilities for the community with trading is then negative, however. The pattern of trades depends only on the *relative* intensities of preferences of the voters. Since exchange increases the likelihood of the participants winning on their relatively more important issues, it tends to increase their realized gains. These increases *can* increase the utility gain for the entire community. Trading also imposes externalities on the nontraders, however (Rothenberg 1969, 215; Taylor 1971, 344; Riker and Brams 1973). If these are negative and large, they can outweigh the gains to the traders.

Tullock's argument that majority rule *with trading* can lead to too much government spending is of this type (1969). Let *X* be a road for farmer *B*, *Y* a road for *C*. If the gross gains to a farmer from an access road are 7 and the cost of 6 is shared equally, we have the figures of table 2. With these costs and benefits, total welfare is improved by logrolling. But a bill promising a gross gain of 5 at a cost of 6, equally shared, also passes. Such a bill lowers community welfare by excessively constructing new roads. The problem arises because under majority rule the two bills involve both allocation (the construction of roads with gross benefits of 5 at costs of 6) and the redistribution of wealth from *A* to *B* and *C*, and the latter is sufficient to pass them.

One important difference separating logrolling's critics and proponents is their views as to whether voting is a positive or negative (at best zero) sum game. If the latter, the game is obviously bad to begin with, and anything that improves its efficiency worsens the final outcome. The examples logrolling critics usually cite are tariff bills, tax loopholes, and pork barrel public works. The best a community can hope for is the defeat of all these issues. The obvious reform is to eliminate logrolling (Riker and Brams 1973).

Logrolling's proponents usually use parks, schools, defense, and other public goods as examples of issues and view vote trading as a potential method for better revealing preference intensities and establishing an equilibrium. They suggest reforms to improve the trading process (e.g., by introducing fungible votes) and/or eliminate its potentially negative side effects by restricting the issue set, in order to remove zero and negative sum games (Tullock 1969; Coleman 1966*a*; 1967; 1970; Haefele 1971; Mueller, 1971; Mueller, Tollison, and Willett 1975).

Logrolling can also be plagued by cycling, however. Indeed, when issues are decided in pairs, the same preference orderings that make trading attractive make cycles possible (Park 1967; Bernholz 1974*b;* 1974*c*). If Z is added to the issues in table 2, the preference orderings become nearly the same as in table 1, and an intransitive social ordering exists ($X=Y>Z>X$). The only condition under which a potential logrolling situation cannot produce a cycle is when a unanimity rule is imposed (Bernholz 1973). Logrolling is also vulnerable to strategic behavior (Mueller 1967).

The problems of cycling and strategic behavior are reduced if informal vote trading via forming coalitions is replaced with either formal markets for exchanging fungible votes (Coleman 1966*a*, 1966*b*; Mueller 1967; Wilson 1969; Mueller, Philpotts, and Vanek 1972) or by point voting, in which each voter allocates a stock of votes over the issue set (Musgrave 1959, 130–31; Coleman 1970; Intriligator 1973; Mueller 1973). In the former case, the cycling problem is replaced by the possibility of multiple or nonstable vote-price equilibria[17]; under point voting it disappears entirely. The *normative* properties of an equilibrium rest on the ethical justification of the voting process itself, the initial distribution of votes, choices of issues, etc. (Mueller 1973), as also is true of equilibria reached under private goods trading.[18] Both vote trading and point voting are vulnerable to individual strategic behavior, which can limit their attractiveness as procedures for revealing individual preferences (Philpotts 1972; Mueller 1973).[19] Wilson's proof that, under certain assumptions, a citizen's optimal vote-trading strategy is "sincere" voting is comforting in this regard (1969).

General Fund Financing

The most straightforward method for allowing voters to reveal their preferences for public goods would be to present each issue along with a tax formula for financing it, a procedure recommended by Wicksell (1958). While some expenditures are financed by "earmarked" taxes, most are financed out of general revenue.[20] For expenditures of this type, it is more realistic to view the voter as confronting two decisions: (1) the allocation of the total budget among competing expenditures and (2) the total budget's size. Replacement of direct voting on individual issues with this two-step procedure sufficiently complicates the decision process, however, so as to remove the direct relationship between voter preferences and the voting outcome. In general, one cannot predict the relationship between the level of government expenditures that would result under an earmarked taxing formula and under general fund financing. Nor can one predict, under general fund financing, the effect on expenditures of a change in voter preferences. The possibilities of indeterminate logrolling and strategizing also exist (Buchanan 1963; Goetz 1968). The work in this area brings into serious question the possibility of adequately revealing individual preferences on public expenditures when general fund financing is employed.

Public Choice in a Representative Democracy

The presence of intermediaries between the citizen and the outcome of his vote raises new issues about the characteristics and efficiency of the voting process. The public choice approach assumes that representatives, like voters, are rational, economic men bent on maximizing their utilities. The latter is tied to their being elected, or more formally to their vote plurality over other candidates.[21] Downs was the first to explore the implications of these assumptions, and the literature has developed around and from the framework he built (1957).

While many of the ideas in public choice have been developed in the context of a model of committees, the committees in mind are often assemblies of representatives, the coalitions parties. Many of the conclusions and problems discussed above carry over into the area of representative democracy. Thus, the median outcome, cycling, and logrolling all reappear.

The Median Voter

Harold Hotelling first presented a median voter theorem as an outcome of two-party representative democracy (1929).[22] Hotelling depicted political opinion as lying along a single liberal-conservative dimension. If everyone votes for the candidate closest to his favored position, then the candidate choosing the optimal position of the median voter wins. The logic of the argument is the same as that demonstrating the victory of the *issue* favored by the median voter, for as Hotelling depicts it, there is only one issue to be decided: how far to the left or right the winning candidate will be.

The assumptions underlying the theorem are so unrealistic (one issue dimension, all individuals vote, two candidates) that it naturally led to extensive examination of the consequences of relaxing them. Two reasonable assumptions about abstentions are that: (1) candidate positions can be too close together to make voting worthwhile (indifference), and (2) the nearest candidate may still be too far away (alienation). Alienation raises the cost of moving away from a voter and pulls the candidate toward the peak of the voter distribution. If the distribution is unimodal and symmetric, alienation has no effect. If it is single-peaked and skewed, the optimal strategy is pulled toward the mode (Comanor 1976). If the distribution is multipeaked, alienation *can* move the optimal strategies of the two candidates toward the separate modes. But, if weak, it also can either leave the median outcome unchanged or produce no stable set of strategies (Smithies 1941; Downs 1957, chap. 8; Davis, Hinich, and Ordeshook 1970; McKelvy 1975). A spreading out of candidates may also occur if elections are in two steps: competition for nomination within parties and then competition among parties. To win the party's nomination, the candidate is pulled toward the party median; the need to win the election pulls him back toward the population median. A Cournot strategy game results with equilibria generally falling between the party and population medians (Aranson and Ordeshook 1972; Coleman 1971, 1972).

The implications of relaxing the single-dimension assumption of the Hotelling-Downs model have been exhaustively examined.[23] The results of the previous section concerning the instability of majority rule equilibria carry over directly. The problem a candidate faces choosing a multidimensional platform that defeats all other platforms is the same as finding an issue in multidimensional space that defeats all other issues. To establish such equilibrium strategies, one must introduce highly restrictive assumptions, including single-peakedness (see Rae and Taylor 1971; Riker and Ordeshook 1973, chap. 12); when equilibria exist, they are at the mean (Davis, Hinich, and Ordeshook 1970, 439–43).

One can combine the assumptions of multimodal distributions and alienation, and envisage a candidate presenting a platform of extreme positions on several issues and winning the support of a sufficient number of minorities to defeat another candidate taking median positions on all. When this happens, a minority that supports a candidate for the position he takes on a couple of key issues, regardless of his position on others, is essentially trading away its votes on the other issues (Downs 1957, 132–37; Tullock 1967*a,* 57–61; Breton 1974, 153–55).

Unfortunately, the tendency for logrolling to produce cycles persists. Consider, again, the voter preferences in table 2. Suppose that two candidates vie for election on the three issues. If the first takes a position in favor of all three, the outcome that maximizes the net utility gains for all voters, he can be defeated by a candidate favoring any two issues and opposing the third, say (PPF), since two of the three voters always benefit from an issue's defeat. PPF can be defeated by PFF, however, and PFF by FFF. But all three voters favor PPP over FFF, and the cycle is complete. Every platform can be defeated.[24]

In a single election candidates cannot rotate through several platforms, and cycling is not likely to be evidenced. Over time it can be. To the extent incumbents' actions in office commit them to the initial platform choice, challengers have the advantage of choosing the second, winning platform. Cycling in a two-party system appears as the continual defeat of incumbents (Downs 1957, 54–62).[25]

Multiparty Systems

An important determinant of the number of parties is the mode of representation (Rae 1967; Tullock, 1967*a,* 144–49). A candidate guarantees himself a seat in a single member district by capturing 50 percent of the vote. This forces candidates to appeal to broad groups of voters and adopt positions near the median. If several representatives can be chosen from a district, candidates can "win" with fewer votes. Multiple representation thus allows for the existence of several parties.

Intuitively, one expects candidates in a multiparty system to spread out, and much of proportional representation's appeal comes from the expectation that they do (Downs 1957, chap. 8; Tullock 1967*a*, chap. 10; Mueller, Tollison, and Willett 1975). The lure of the center is sufficiently strong, however, so that the stability of a set of spatially separated strategies cannot be demonstrated (Hinich and Ordeshook 1970, 785–88). Full analysis of multiparty systems requires a game-theoretic approach, and has still to be developed (but see Lindeen 1970).

One interesting application of game theory is Riker's theory that all single and multiparty systems converge to two coalitions of equal size (1962). It assumes that politics is a zero sum game, as would occur, e.g., if all issues involved basically zero sum redistributions of wealth. In such a game, the optimal strategy is to allow the opposing coalition to be as large as possible, while remaining a losing-paying coalition. Under majority rule this implies two coalitions of equal size.

If one views collective choice as a process for revealing preferences for public goods, Riker's depiction of politics as a zero sum game would seem to be highly restrictive, for it implies that there are no *net* benefits from the passage of any bill, or the formation of any coalition. The theory has more apparent applicability, however, if one views politics as a dynamic process of redefining issues and coalitions. Suppose, reversing the steps presented above, a polity started with a public-good issue defined so that all participants benefit and unanimity could be forthcoming. If, however, only a simple majority were required to pass a bill, nearly half of the votes would be "wasted." It would be advantageous to some to redefine the bill so that others paid more for the good, and one could envisage a continual redefinition of the issue so as to benefit an ever-shrinking winning coalition until the coalition was just large enough to win. If this process consisted solely of changing the cost shares of the bill, allocational efficiency would be preserved, and only the distribution of income would be changed. If the transfers were made by expanding the quantity of the public good, forcing the losing coalition to cover a disproportionate share of the costs, one has Tullock's overexpenditure argument (1969, 1970). If the transfers are made by adding additional public-good bills as riders, with the losers again paying a disproportionate share of the costs, one has the Riker and Brams inefficient logrolling argument (1973). Thus, when issues and coalitions can be continually redefined, majority rule may convert positive sum prisoners' dilemma games into zero sum games, making Riker's analysis more general than first might appear. Combining the tendency of majority rule to result in redistribution with the median voter theorem leads to Director's Law, that redistribution in a democracy is from the tails of the income distribution to its center (Stigler 1970; Tullock 1971*b*).

The Behavior of Voters

When a consumer purchases a private good in the market his "dollar vote" leads directly to the desired end. When a voter "purchases" a public good, however, the result of his vote is dependent on the actions of other voters and, in a representative democracy, on the process of representation. These differences create the potential for a large discrepancy between the behavior usually assumed of consumers and that characteristic of voters.[26]

Two aspects of citizen behavior have received considerable attention: information gathering and direct participation. The latter can range from simply voting to running for office. The voter's decision function can be represented as follows:

$$R = BP - C + D. \tag{1}$$

Where

R = the voter's reaction (vote, gather information),
B = the potential public-good benefits from the action,
P = the probability these benefits accrue if the action is undertaken,
C = the action's cost, and
D = private benefits complementary to the action.

(Refer to Downs [1957, chaps. 11–14], Tullock [1967*a*, 110–14], and Riker and Ordeshook [1968]; and for a critique see Barry [1970, 13–19].)

In terms of information gathering, B represents the potential gain from picking the *best* candidate, P the probability that the citizen's choice matters, C the cost of gathering the information, and D its extra benefits (psychic income, status with peer group). Although B and P may change as information is acquired, it is plausible to assume they soon become constant. If D diminishes on the margin and C increases, then the utility from gathering political information is maximized by equating its marginal private benefits and cost. Political information's likely impact on election results does not affect its acquisition (Tullock 1967*a*, chaps. 6 and 7).

Similar arguments have been made about voting. If P is the probability of a single vote being decisive, then it obviously must be very small in a large constituency. To the extent that two-party competition brings candidate positions together, elections are close, raising P, but lowering the benefits from the best candidate's winning (B). Thus, B and P vary inversely and their product is probably small, implying again that participation's private returns and costs dominate. For most people the outcome of an election is a public good and political participation is vulnerable to free riding (Olson 1965, 86, 159–67). The greater participation rates of high income and high education groups may be explainable on these grounds (Frey 1971; Russell, Fraser, and Frey 1972; Tollison and Willett 1973). The higher turnouts in close elections suggest that the lefthandside variables are also important, however (see Riker and Ordeshook 1968; Barzel and Silberberg 1973; and Rosenthal and Sen 1973).

On some issues a voter's benefits from electing one candidate over another may be very high. Tariffs, tax loopholes, and a nearby bridge are examples of bills with large benefits for some voters. The costs of acquiring information about these bills is typically low. Thus, the probability of a citizen's voting for a candidate who supports issues promising special, narrow benefits for him may be much greater than for a candidate who supports "general interest" legislation with equal total benefits for the citizen (Olson 1965, 141–48). This reinforces incentives to form coalitions of minorities, each lured to the polls by promises of legislation with special interest to them (Downs 1957, chaps. 12 and 13; Tullock 1967*a*, 122–23, 142). It can lead to overexpenditures on special interest bills (Tullock 1970), and underexpenditures on general interest legislation (Downs 1960).

Deciding the Quantities of Quasi-Public Goods

For pure public goods, characterized by both nonexcludability and jointness of supply, a collective *voice* process for revealing preferences is required to achieve Pareto efficiency. For private goods, the entry and exit of buyers and sellers suffices. Between the poles of pure public and private goods lie a range of *mixed* goods, which one intuitively expects are most efficiently allocated by a mixture of exit and voice processes (Hirschman 1970).

Voting-with-the-Feet

We examine first the consequences of dropping the joint-supply (economies of scale) property. Consider a public good with no production costs: the proportion of tulips in the public square (bulbs are free). If the dimensions of the polity coincide with the population, the preference revelation problem persists. Assume more than one polity can exist, however. Within any polity all must consume the same public good (flower bed), but there are no spillovers between communities. With this *limited* degree of exclusion, people can reveal their preferences by moving into the community providing the most desirable fraction of tulips. Considering only the whole percentile options, 101 communities suffice to achieve Pareto optimality. No ballots need be cast. All preferences are revealed through the silent voting-with-the-feet of individuals exiting and entering communities, a possibility first noted by Tiebout (1956).

The Tiebout model rests on a number of extreme assumptions (Buchanan and Wagner 1970; Buchanan and Goetz 1972; McGuire 1972; Oates 1972; Pestieau 1974). It is not clear, for example, how the initial options are presented to "voters," without some central auctioneer who establishes communities and informs the population of them, an assumption contradicting the decentralized spirit of the model (Pauly 1970; McGuire 1972). More serious are the consequences of introducing a second public good: the proportion of oaks in the square. This issue's resolution requires further separation of individuals into groups of identical preferences, now with respect to *both* flowers and trees. The number of communities needed to ensure Pareto optimality leaps to 101 squared. If the number of public goods is very large, one reaches a solution in which the number of communities equals the size of the population. Each community-individual becomes a polity with a basket of public-private goods (garden, woods) tailored to his own tastes (Pestieau 1974).

Voting-with-the-feet achieves Pareto optimality by grouping individuals together in polities of homogeneous tastes. In the extreme, it satisfies Kramer's severe homogeneity of indifference map condition (1973; McGuire 1974), through the imposition of a silent unanimity rule. It can realistically be assumed to come close to satisfying this goal when, relative to the size of the population, (1) the number of public goods is small, and/or (2) the number of distinct preferences for combinations of public goods is small. Since *the* task of public choice is the revelation of (differing) individual preferences for public goods, voting-with-the-feet, in part, solves the public choice problem by significantly limiting its scope.

The Theory of Clubs

Assume next that exclusion is possible, but addition of a new member lowers the average costs of a good, i.e., there are economies of scale. If average costs fall indefinitely, optimal club size is the entire population, and the traditional public good problem exists. If they eventually rise, either because scale economies are exhausted or from the additional costs of crowding, an optimal club smaller than the population may exist.

Buchanan was the first to explore the efficiency properties of voluntary clubs using a model in which individuals have identical tastes for public and private goods (1965*a*). This assumption is important. As in the Tiebout model, it is inefficient to have individuals with differing tastes in the same club, for then some must consume a quantity of public goods different from that which would maximize their welfare. At a Pareto optimum each club has a membership with homogeneous tastes, and a unique public good quantity and club size exists at which the marginal benefits a club member receives from adding another equals the additional costs the extra member brings (Buchanan 1965*a;* McGuire 1974).

If the population is large relative to optimal club sizes, efficient allocation of these quasi-public goods through the voluntary association of individuals of homogeneous tastes can be envisaged. In such an equilibrium, each individual receives the same benefits as other members of his club, since efforts to discriminate will induce exit and formation of new clubs. If optimal club sizes are large relative to the population, discrimination is possible, and stable equilibria may not exist. With an optimal club size of $\frac{2}{3}$ of the population, for example, only one such club can exist. If it forms, those not in it have incentives to lure members away by offering disproportionate shares of the benefits gained from expanding the smaller club. But, the remaining members of the larger club have incentives to maintain club size and can attract new members by offering the full benefits of membership in the big club. No stable distribution of club sizes and benefits need exist (see Pauly 1967, 1970). Analytically the problem is identical to the cycling problem confronted earlier. The two farmers forming a winning majority constitute an optimal sized club, but the farmer left out has an incentive to try to form an optimal club too.

We thus are brought to a conclusion similar to the voting-with-the-feet model: The voluntary formation of clubs to allocate public goods is efficient only when the optimal club size is relatively small, i.e., when the quasi-public goods have a limited degree of publicness. Despite this qualification, the voluntary formation of clubs is at least *conceptually* a more promising means for revealing individual preferences for public goods than voting-with-the-feet, for it does not require geographic proximity of club members.

Voting-with-the-Feet in the Presence of Jointness of Supply

When public goods are produced with economies of scale, it is even more unlikely that individual mobility suffices to achieve Pareto optimality. It is then necessary that there be "just the right number of individuals" with identical preferences to satisfy the optimality conditions for each public good.

Pareto optimality in a global sense requires that the incremental change in net benefits to the community an individual joins equal the incremental loss to the community he leaves

$$\sum_{i=1}^{n} \Delta U_A^i = \sum_{i=1}^{m} \Delta U_B^i . \tag{2}$$

The change in utility of the nth individual to join community A is his total utility from being in A (U_A^n), just as his loss from leaving B is his total utility in B, U_B^m. Equation (2) can thus be written as

$$U_A^n + \sum_{i=1}^{n-1} \Delta U_A^i = U_B^m + \sum_{i=1}^{m-1} \Delta U_B^i . \tag{3}$$

In a world of pure competition without market failures, the marginal product of an individual is the same in all activities and areas, and the welfare of others is not affected by his location. All ΔU^i are zero except for the moving individual, and he naturally locates in his most favored community. With public goods present, the ΔU^i for individuals in a community are positive for an additional entrant, as its total costs get spread over a larger number of individuals. A new entrant thus confers positive externalities. With crowding, he can produce negative externalities. In either case, since the individual compares only his utility levels in the two communities and ignores the marginal effects of his move on others (the ΔU^i's in A and B), voting-with-the-feet does not, in general, produce Pareto optimality.[27]

Pareto optimality can be achieved through a combination of voting-with-the-feet and ballot. If the externalities for community A from in-migration were positive, it could offer a subsidy to newcomers equal to

$$\sum_{i=1}^{n} \Delta U_A^i ,$$

and levy an identical tax on out-migration. If B did the same, all individuals would be forced to internalize the external costs their moving entailed, and Pareto efficiency would be obtained (Buchanan 1971; Buchanan and Goetz 1972). Alternatively, a central authority could levy taxes and offer subsidies equal to the $\Sigma\Delta U^i$ terms (Flatters, Henderson, and Mieszkowski 1974; McMillan 1975).

While these alternatives have identical efficiency outcomes, they differ both in spirit and equity properties. The former weds Tiebout's decentralized voting-with-the-feet with the theory of exclusive clubs to produce a decentralized solution to the population allocation problem. The enacting of such taxes and subsidies by local communities immediately provides communities favored by natural characteristics, population size, income, etc. with a valuable property right, which they exercise by taxing individuals outside of their community (*i.e.*, those who would have entered in the absence of the tax subsidy scheme). The centralized solution vests the entire population with a property right in both communities and achieves allocational efficiency by taxing *all* members of the favored community to subsidize the disfavored community. In either case, the problems of ballot voting to reveal individual preferences again arise once the assumption of homogeneous preferences is dropped.

Despite these problems and qualifications, voting-with-the-feet provides a useful, perhaps essential substitute for the ballot, for those whose intensity of preference is significantly misstated by the latter.

The Theory of Revolution

When neither the ballot nor the feet constitute adequate modes of expression, there is still Chairman Mao's barrel of the gun. Given its role in real world politics, one might expect more to be said about revolutions than has been. Gordon Tullock has, however, gotten the discussion underway (1971*a*, 1974). He proposes to explain a revolutionary's behavior with a model resembling the one used to explain voter behavior. If R is a potential revolutionary's reaction, B the new government's public good benefits (possibly negative), P the probability that the individual's participation brings about success, D the private gains from participating in the revolution, and C the private costs, we have equation (1′).

$$R = BP + D - C \tag{1′}$$

If R is positive he participates in favor of the revolution, if negative against it. Since R can take on any value, the equation can also explain the degree of participation.

As with voting, one assumes that the typical citizen considers the fruits of the revolution a public good and the probability of affecting the outcome near zero and then makes his decision on the basis of the private gains and risks of participation. For most, this calculation will lead to apathy or occasional participation in a large rally; for a few, to commitment with the hope of a high position in the new regime.

While there are problems in extending the public choice paradigm to the study of revolutions, the theory fills an analytic gap in the literature. In a closed polity, an individual is always in danger of being "exploited" or "tyrannized" by a majority or minority of his fellow citizens. His choices in such situations are: to continue to rely on voice in the hope that outcomes change; to seek a new polity by migration; or to create a new one by revolution.

Empirical Public Choice

An increasing amount of attention has been devoted in recent years to testing various hypotheses from the public choice literature. This work generally explores what might literally be called "political economy," i.e., the two-way causality between dollars and votes. One set of models focuses on the determinants of campaign expenditures and their immediate effects (Crain and Tollison 1976). There is now empirical evidence that dollars do buy votes (Palda 1973; Welch 1974). A second set of models tries to explain the level of the vote or government popularity as a function of what it does in office. So far these studies have related government popularity chiefly to macroeconomic variables, e.g., unemployment and inflation rates (Goodhart and Bhansali 1970; Kramer 1971; Frey and Garbers 1972; Miller and Mackie 1973; Crain, Deaton, and Tollison 1975).

Turning the causality around, one can try to explain the choice of government policy, level of expenditure, and level of economic activity by the desire to win votes. The median voter hypothesis was one of the first used to explain government expenditures (Barr and Davis 1966; Davis and Haines, Jr. 1966), and a number of studies have either tested or employed this hypothesis (Kasper 1971; Borcherding and Deacon 1972; Bergstrom and Goodman 1973; Pommerehne and Frey 1975). More generally, Wright (1974) and Nordhaus (1975) have linked government macro policies and aggregate economic activity to party efforts to be reelected. The logical extension of this work is a full "politico-econometric" model integrating the economic and political "sectors" of society (Frey and Lau 1968; Frey 1974). Initial attempts to estimate one such model give promising results (Frey and Schneider 1975).

This recent empirical work undoubtedly represents but the tip on an emerging iceberg. Space does not allow adequate review of even this tip, however. Fortunately, most of it is ably covered in the Frey and Schneider survey (1975).

Part Two: Normative Theories of Public Choice

While one can speak of *the* positive theory of public choice based upon economic man assumptions, one must think of normative *theories* of public choice. For there are many views of what the goals of the state *should be* and how to achieve them. This potential multiplicity of views has been the focus of much criticism by the positivists, who have argued for a "value free" discipline. For the bulk of economics, it might be legitimate to focus on explanation and prediction and to leave to politics the explication of society's goals. For the study of politics itself, in toto, to take this position is less legitimate. Thus the interest in how the basic values of society are expressed through the political process arises. The challenge normative theory faces is to develop theorems about the expression and realization of values, based on generally accepted postulates, in the same way that positive theory has developed explanatory and predictive theorems from the postulates of rational egoistic behavior.

Rawls's Theory of Justice

One of the most ambitious normative theories of choice is that of John Rawls (1971). His theory rests on the same rational, egoistic man assumptions as public choice and explicitly eschews assuming altruism (pp. 183–92).

Rawls compares participation in society with participation in a game of chance. Each individual is born to a generation, culture, social system, family, and set of personal attributes that largely determine his happiness. If he accepts this information as given, social choice consists entirely of attempts to reach the Pareto frontier and of struggles for position along it—the subject matter of Part One. If position in society is by chance, however, the distribution of these assets and resulting happiness may be arbitrary or unfair. By posing life as a game of chance, Rawls argues that individuals ought to adopt the position of a potential entrant rather than their actual positions, and consider the social institutions and distribution of assets that would emerge if actual positions were unknown. The establishment of just institutions rests in part, therefore, on determining what information is *morally* relevant to a participant in the social contract uncertain of his specific position. To answer this question, individuals are asked to step behind a *veil of ignorance* and shed all knowledge of a specific nature (pp. 136–42). From this *original position,* they choose the rules and institutions that constitute the social contract (pp. 11–22). Since specific information about individuals is missing, the contract cannot favor any one individual or group. The rules are fair. From this springs the important notion of *justice as fairness.*

Rawls extends this idea to derive two principles as the core of the social contract: (1) "Each person is to have an equal right to the most extensive basic liberty compatible with a similar liberty for others" (p. 60), and (2) "social and economic inequalities are to be arranged so that they are both (a) to the greatest benefit of the least advantaged and (b) attached to offices and positions open to all under conditions of fair equality of opportunity" (p. 83). The second involves a lexicographic ordering of states of the world according to the utility levels (primary goods bundles) of the worst-off citizens. Rawls also argues that the two principles themselves are lexicographically ordered, the first over the second (pp. 150–61, 175–83, 541–58). Not surprisingly perhaps, given economists' fondness for trade-offs, these principles have come under attack.[28]

What is important to the theory of public choice, however, is not the principles Rawls arrives at, but the process by which he gets there (Buchanan 1972). To the extent that the ideas of justice as fairness, the original position, etc. have intuitive appeal, individuals might be led to make decisions as if they were behind a veil of ignorance. Rawls's theory as a contribution to normative public (social) choice thus has the potential of achieving the unanimous agreement sought in much of the literature. And Rawls, in responding to his critics, has focused on justifying the process by which the principles are derived, more so than on the principles themselves (1974*a*, 1974*b*).

The Constitution as a Social Contract

Buchanan and Tullock draw a distinction between the constitution, containing the basic decision rules of the polity, and the day-to-day decisions made (1962). The basic rules are assumed to change infrequently. Thus, in making a constitutional choice, an individual selects a rule that affects his welfare for a long time. He is, therefore, *assumed* to be uncertain about the impact of the rule upon him because he is uncertain about his specific position, tastes, etc., in the future. Buchanan and Tullock thus assume, as a behavioral postulate, that individuals choose constitutional rules (out of rational self-interest, given the uncertainty surrounding these long-run choices) by placing themselves in the envisaged positions of all future citizens (1962, 78–80, 95–96). They describe a process of constitution making quite analogous to Rawls's description of the social contract's formation. Although the tone of Buchanan and Tullock is clearly positivist, while Rawls's is normative, the similarities between the two approaches are so strong that they could be combined. That is, if one accepts Rawls's notion of justice as fairness and the Buchanan-Tullock assumption that individuals actually would make constitutional choices by weighing their impacts on all because of rational self-interest under uncertainty, actual constitutions formed under unanimity rules become just political contracts.

The degree to which individuals will evenly weigh the impact of a constitutional choice on all future citizens is obviously an open question. The long-run nature of these decisions certainly moves the individual calculus in this direction. A fully equal weighing of future utilities is doubtful, however, for it is difficult to envisage individual uncertainty over color of skin, sex, native tongue, and so on. On the other hand, to the extent that institutionalized discrimination is greatest against individuals with these easily recognizable characteristics, one has indirect evidence that just (nondiscriminatory) rules are chosen when real uncertainty over positions exists.

If there is not sufficient uncertainty at the constitutional stage to produce just rules, one might ask how the required uncertainty might be introduced into the process. While some possibilities come to mind (Mueller 1973;

Mueller, Tollison, and Willett 1975), the question has not received much attention. Indeed, despite its obvious importance in the theory of public choice, the constitutional stage itself has been essentially neglected. This is a pity, in my opinion, for it remains the most likely place both to obtain or approach the elusive unanimous agreement and to achieve an ethical underpinning to what otherwise are essentially amoral processes of collective choice.

The Constitution as a Social Welfare Function

J. C. Harsanyi has also discussed the ethical appeal of assuming individuals are uncertain over future positions (1953, 1969; see also Vickrey 1945, 1960; Leibenstein 1965). Building on a paper by John Marcus Fleming (1952), Harsanyi proved that if both individuals and social preferences satisfy the von Neumann and Morgenstern-Marschak postulates, and if each individual is indifferent between two states of the world implies social indifference between the states, then social welfare W is a weighted sum of individual utilities.

$$W = \sum_{i=1}^{n} a_i U_i . \tag{4}$$

This theorem is interesting in itself, for it creates a theoretical justification, from fairly weak postulates,[29] for the individualism and utilitarianism that underlie both the public choice and social welfare function literatures. Without a way to determine the a_i's, however, equation (4) is too general to be of much value. This welfare function can be given an ethical content if individuals choose the weights by assuming they have an equal probability of being any other individual in the society, i.e., of being in his position, having his utility function, etc.[30] Such an equal weighting would emerge if individuals were uncertain about future tastes and positions, and if they adopted the principle of insufficient reason to assign probabilities. Again this uncertainty could be artificially created by mentally assuming a place in Rawls's original position, or be real, due to the long-run nature of the decisions affecting social welfare. In either event, the equiprobability assumption achieves the same uniformity of opinion and unanimity of choice that Rawls and Buchanan and Tullock achieve by the use of uncertainty. And, it allows the reinterpretation of the social contract and constitution as discussed in these works as collective choice embodiments of a social welfare function.[31]

Real Valued Social Welfare Functions

Having introduced social welfare functions, let us consider directly their relationship to public choice. We start with the Bergson-Samuelson social welfare function

$$W = W(z_1, z_2, \ldots),$$

where W is a real valued function of all variables (z_i's) that might affect social welfare (Bergson 1969; Samuelson 1947). The z_i's and W are chosen to represent the ethical values of society or of the individuals in it (Samuelson 1947, 221). The objective is to define a W and set of z_i's and the constraints thereon to yield meaningful first and second order conditions for a maximum W. The social welfare function literature has adopted the same assumptions about consumers, production functions, etc., that underlie the bulk of economics and public choice (Bergson 1969; Samuelson 1947). Add to these the Pareto postulate, and a set of *necessary* conditions for the maximization of W is derived, which limit social choices to points along the generalized Pareto frontier. The collective choice process by which these conditions are fulfilled is not considered in the social welfare function literature.

To answer the knotty question of how one selects among the various possible Pareto points, additional assumptions are needed. And, it would appear, these must implicitly or explicitly involve cardinality and interpersonal utility comparisons (Bergson 1938; Lerner 1944; Samuelson 1947, 1967; Sen 1970, 123–25; Harsanyi 1975). These in turn imply the introduction of value judgments or ethical postulates, and the possibility arises of there being as many social welfare functions as individuals in the community. This specter led most contributors to the "new welfare economics" to eschew interpersonal comparisons and confine their attention to deriving necessary conditions for a welfare maximum, to delineating the set of Pareto points.

To choose among these requires a set of ethical beliefs shared by the community, which converts the many possible social welfare functions into one (Little 1957). We have discussed attempts to accomplish this via the introduction of uncertainty over position. We turn to an alternative approach.

Arrow's Axiomatic Social Welfare

Postulates and Logic of the Proof

Kenneth Arrow began his search for a social welfare function by stating five axioms, which he argued every social welfare function should obey (1963).[32] These axioms reflect both value judgments and assumptions of individual and collective rationality. Together, they express some of the basic postulates underlying individualism, utilitarianism, and consumer-citizen sovereignty. Viewed in the context of public choice, these axioms might be regarded as stating the basic value judgments of the community as imbedded in the social contract or constitution (Arrow 1963, 104–5; Kemp and Asimakopulos 1952). Briefly stated, they are:[33]

1. Unlimited Domain. All possible orderings of individual preferences are allowed.
2. The Pareto Postulate.
3. Transitivity. The social welfare function gives a consistent ordering of all feasible alternatives.
4. Nondictatorship. No individual enjoys a position such that whenever he

expresses a preference between any two alternatives and all other individuals express the opposite preference, his preference is always preserved in the social ordering.

5. Independence of Irrelevant Alternatives. The social choice between any two alternatives shall not be affected by preferences over any other alternatives.

The theorem states that no social welfare function satisfies these five postulates. The logic of the proof runs as follows: The unlimited domain assumption allows any possible constellation of ordinal preferences. When a unanimously preferred alternative does not emerge, some method for choosing among the Pareto-preferred alternatives must be found. The independence assumption restricts attention to the ordinal preferences of individuals for any two issues when deciding those issues. But, as we have seen in our discussion of majority rule, it is all too easy to construct rules that yield choices between two alternatives, but produce a cycle when three successive pairwise choices are made. The transitivity postulate forces a choice among the three, however. The social choice process is not to be left indecisive (Arrow 1963, 120). But with the information at hand (individual ordinal rankings of issue pairs) there is no method for making such a choice that is not imposed or dictatorial.

Relaxing the Postulates

The theorem's significance rests upon the weakness of its postulates. Most individuals will want to place more stringent normative constraints on the social choice process, and yet the above five postulates are already too severe. To avoid the impossibility result, even these must be relaxed.

Space precludes a complete review of all modifications of the postulates that have been made to produce either possibility theorems or new impossibility results.[34] Instead, we focus on modifications of particular relevance to public choice.

Relaxing unanimity and nondictatorship seems hardly worth discussing if the ideas of individualism and citizen sovereignty are to be maintained (but, see Little 1952). Nevertheless, the popularity of elitist theories of collective choice from Plato to the present indicates the attractiveness to many of abandoning this postulate. Worthy of special mention here is Hobbes's defense of monarchy. For Hobbes, there was one issue upon which all preferences are identical: life under anarchy was terrible and inferior to life under a unanimously accepted dictator. If one made the other postulates part of the Hobbesian contract, one might construct a new defense of autocracy. And, of course, in practice the dictatorial solution to the uncertainties and deadlocks of social choice is very popular.

Transitivity can be relaxed, at the cost of a degree of arbitrariness or indecisiveness in the choice process. One might simply declare society indifferent to all choices along the Pareto frontier.[35] Any choice among them will be arbitrary, but perhaps fair. In practice, such rules favor the status quo, although there is no reason why they must (Arrow 1963, 118–20). The status quo could be introduced as a choice along with new proposals with an equal likelihood of being chosen. Such a rule contains one set of implicit value judgments concerning the likely gains and losses from change; rules favoring the status quo contain another. If there is more general agreement concerning these decision rules than for transitivity, the problem is solved (Kemp 1954).

We have already discussed a number of collective choice results that rely on a restricted domain assumption. Single-peakedness ensures that majority rule produces an outcome, namely the median, and single-peakedness along with the other four assumptions produces a social welfare function. In the context of a public choice process, single-peakedness implies strict restrictions on both the rules by which issues are selected and on the voters who decide them (Slutsky 1977*b*). Issues must be of the one-dimensional variety—the number of guns, the number of school books; the voters cannot simultaneously consider both the number and kind of books. And their preferences must be single-peaked in this one dimension. If fate provides voters of this type, these issues can be resolved by majority rule without violating the other axioms, although we are still left with a plethora of multidimensional issues to resolve in some other way. If some individuals have multiple peaks, they must somehow be isolated and excluded from the community, or an impossibility result can emerge. More generally, ways of restricting membership in the polity to those with sufficiently homogeneous or complementary preferences to avoid the impossibility result can be considered. The theories of clubs and voting-with-the-feet describe processes by which such groups might form. In the absence of externalities across clubs (local communities), and perfect mobility, free entry, etc., such a process might avoid the Arrow problem. But, as we have seen, when spillovers exist, some decisions must be made by the aggregate population, and the impossibility problem will appear here, even when "solved" in the smaller ones. In such circumstances homogeneity of preferences can be brought about only if individuals adopt, or already have, a common set of values (Bergson 1954). Appeals to reason, *a la* Kant, or uncertainty, a la Rawls and Harsanyi, are along these lines.

The independence axiom eliminates the possibility of strategic misrepresentation of preferences. When a social choice process is not perversely responsive to an individual's ranking of x and y, and depends on only his and other rankings of x and y, he can do no better than state his true preferences between them. If the outcome on x and y also depends on his ranking between y and z, however, he may be able to benefit from misstating one set of preferences if it increases his chances of winning on the other. This need not worsen the outcome of the social choice process, e.g., as when positive-sum-game logrolling occurs. But it might. And, it does introduce an element of uncertainty and dependency on bargaining abilities that might be considered undesirable. The independence axiom excludes these possibilities.[36]

This axiom is stronger than it perhaps appears, and its relaxation provides a number of ways out of the paradox. By limiting the choice among any subset of issues to the information on individual rankings for the issues in that subset, it rules out all information with which one might cardinalize and interpersonally compare utilities (Sen 1970*a*, 89–91). Indeed, it was the desire to establish a welfare function that was not based upon interpersonal utility comparisons that first motivated Arrow (1963, 8–11, 109–11). Once it is abandoned or relaxed, a number of voting rules can be considered. One is the rank order method of voting first discussed by de Borda (1781).[37] Here the alternatives are allocated points, inversely to their rankings in individual preferences, and the alternative with the most points wins. Logrolling, literal vote trading, and point voting can reveal individual intensities on issues and can have attractive normative properties when restrictions are placed on the issues admitted to the decision set. These procedures are excluded by the independence axiom since their outcomes are dependent upon the specific (and full) set of issues proposed. Thus, abandonment of the independence axiom raises the importance of the process that selects the issues to be brought to a vote in a way its acceptance does not.

From a public choice perspective, relaxation of either the independence or unrestricted domain axioms appear to be the most appealing ways out of the paradox. Each in turn raises questions as to what issues are to be decided, who is to decide, and of those who decide, which preferences shall be weighed. Such choices directly or indirectly involve interpersonal utility comparisons and must rest on some additional value postulates, which if explicitly introduced would imply specific interpersonal utility comparisons. The latter cannot be avoided (Bergson 1969, 1954; Hildreth 1953; Kemp and Asimakopulos 1952; Sen 1970*a*, 123–25).

Part Three

Normative and Positive Theories of Public Choice Compared

Rules for collective decision are needed, quite simply, because people live together. Their mere grouping into circumscribed geographic areas creates the potential and necessity for collective action. Some collective decisions can benefit all individuals involved; other decisions benefit some and harm others. These two categories correspond to the familiar distinction between moves from off the Pareto frontier to points on it, and moves along the frontier or to allocation and redistribution. Positive public choice, as positive economics, is most pertinent to decisions in the first group; normative welfare theory to decisions within the second.

The work on real-valued welfare functions indicates that if only the Pareto postulate is introduced, "normative" and positive theory lead to the same marginal conditions defining allocations along the Pareto frontier. The Arrow-type theorems imply further that to choose from among these allocations using a consistent, nondictatorial social choice rule, either restrictions must be placed on the preference domain or postulates introduced that directly allow interpersonal utility comparisons, i.e., value judgments must be introduced.

As David Hume pointed out long ago, propositions concerning values cannot be derived from factual observations alone (1941; Sen 1970*a*, 56–64). Some intuitive conceptualization of right and wrong, of acceptable and unacceptable, is required. Thus, efforts to introduce values into collective choice in a nonarbitrary way become a search for a community's shared notions of justice and morality. Indeed, a community might easily be defined in terms of these shared values. Individualism, the Pareto postulate, the Arrow axioms, justice as fairness, and the golden rule are all essentially intuitive value statements, or notions of morality and justice. The social welfare function, or contract, or constitution embody and reflect these values.

Normative theory starts with the community and attempts to derive propositions based on its collectively held values. Treating the community as an "organic" body, as *the* starting point, follows logically from the necessity of there being a commonly held set of values for there to be any community. While consensual agreement on the underlying value postulates may be necessary, there is no logcial reason why unanimity must emerge from this consensus as the social choice rule. Indeed, when choices are to be made from points along the Pareto frontier, unanimity cannot be the collective choice rule. The redistributive property of all less-than-unanimity rules thus makes them the logical choice for selecting among Pareto-efficient allocations. The downplaying of the unanimity rule in the normative literature is thus explained.[38]

If normative theory studies processes for revealing commonly held values regarding interpersonal utility comparisons, positive public choice studies processes for revealing intrapersonal utility comparisons. For the bulk of the positive literature analyzes the implications of various collective decision rules given individual preferences and (often implicitly) a common value system. Thus, positive public choice focuses on decision making at the parliamentary or legislative stage under rules and values established in the constitution.

Given its focus on the revelation of *individual* preferences, much of positive public choice is implicitly, and sometimes explicitly as in the work of Buchanan and Tullock, in the contractarian tradition. If one starts with the individual, before the collective can be analyzed, it must, at least conceptually, be formed. The issues of which individuals make up the collective, what questions it can resolve, and what rights remain with the citizen must be faced. The positive literature's contractarian approach explains its emphasis on unanimous consent and Pareto optimality. If the polity is a union of individuals who, conceptually, have the option of not joining, then unanimous agreement on basic choices is required. But unanimity can only be achieved under individualistic—egoistic—assumptions for Pareto moves. Thus, Pareto efficiency and unanimity become ineluctably linked. In a voluntary association of individuals, unanimity is, potentially, always possible; all moves are latently Pareto-efficient.

The differences in starting points also explain the different approaches to the status quo apparent in the two literatures. The positivist works within a set of fixed rules and value consensus, and favors maintenance of the existing rules in the absence of clearly expressed preferences for change. The welfare theorist attempts to define the rules to be imbedded in an ideal (perhaps new) constitution and sees no reason to give previous rules preference.

The way constraints on the issue set are introduced is also revealing. When assumptions about the value consensus and domain of choice are made explicit in the positivist literature, they come at the beginning of the discussion. Given these assumed constraints, the positivist often evinces a lack of concern in, or downplays the importance of, the impossibility theorems (as, for example, Tullock 1967*b*). Sen's impossibility theorem (1970*b*) is disturbing to a positivist, only in that it presumes that one individual's preference that another read a book the latter thinks distasteful would even enter into the social choice process (Ng 1971; Peacock and Rowley 1972; Bernholz 1974*a*). The social welfare function texts, on the other hand, begin with an unlimited domain assumption and work back to consider restrictions on the set of admissible preferences, after deriving their impossibility results (Arrow 1963, 74–91; Vickrey 1960; Sen 1970*a*, 166–86). The suggestion that basic agreement on some ends must be part of the collective choice process comes after the exploration of the infeasibility of not assuming such consensus.

This contrasting of perspectives is an attempt to clarify the apparently differing conclusions and emphasis of the two approaches. It also may explain the interest in Rawls. For Rawls's theory is at once individualistic-contractarian and overtly normative. The unanimous agreement of all citizens for all time becomes *the* social preference ordering of the community, through the homogenization of tastes that occurs as individuals pass through the veil of ignorance into the original position, in the same way Harsanyi derives a unique-unanimous social welfare function.[39]

In closing this comparison, some paradoxes and unresolved questions must be noted. Although the bulk of the positivist-contractarian literature discusses decision making within an agreed social contract or constitution, the process by which this agreement is reached is almost never discussed. Buchanan and Tullock's book, subtitled the *Logical Foundations of Constitutional Democracy*, devotes only a few pages to the constitutional stage and here argues the plausibility of assuming unanimity due to uncertainty over future positions (1962). Buchanan's recent book, although devoted to the social contract, does not discuss the *process* by which actual constitutions are drawn (1975*a*).

Nor does the social welfare function literature discuss how agreement is expressed on basic values, even though, under the present interpretation at least, this literature is directly concerned with the functional embodiment of these values. Quite to the contrary. Barry (1965, 242–45) and Samuelson (1969*b*) are openly critical of unanimity, even when applied to the constitutional stage. Arrow accepts an interpretation of the social welfare function as a constitution, but seems not to feel it is literally agreed upon by citizens. Instead, he sees the implications of the social welfare function research as guiding ethically neutral public officials when making policy decisions (1963, 107). But this interpretation reopens all of the old questions of value judgments, interpersonal utility comparisons, etc., that the new welfare economics sought to avoid. Given Arrow's own results, it is clear that the policy maker cannot easily find a decision rule consistent with an obviously agreed upon set of normative axioms. New axioms must be found. But what (who?) guides the policy maker in this search, the economist? Unless there is a general consensus over the policy maker's or economist's choice of value postulates, the spectre of multiple social welfare functions reappears. But can the policy maker, or economist, determine if a consensus exists, and what it is, if it is not somehow literally expressed?

It is fitting that we close with this query. For the basic challenge facing a community is achieving a consensus or the dilemma of decision making in its absence. Public choice has shed light on these issues, but much remains to be done. The positive literature is riddled with demonstrations of the instability, inefficiency, or irrationality of various voting outcomes; the normative literature with impossibility proofs. But this should be neither surprising nor particularly discouraging. Indeed, it is precisely because it deals with some of the oldest and toughest questions a community faces, that public choice attracts so many fine scholars. And for this reason, one can remain optmistic about the field's future growth and development.

NOTES

1. For detailed justification of this postulate in the study of voting see Downs 1957, 3–20; Buchanan and Tullock 1962, 17–39; and Riker and Ordeshook 1973, 8–37. Schumpeter's early use of the postulate also should be mentioned (1950). One of the curiosities of the public choice literature is the slight *direct* influence Schumpeter's work appears to have had. Downs claims that "Schumpeter's profound analysis of democracy forms the inspiration and foundation for our whole thesis" (1957, 27, n. 11), but cites only one page of the book (twice), and this is in support of the economic man assumption. Most other work in the field makes no reference to Schumpeter.
2. For surveys see Sen (1970*a*) and Fishburn (1973).
3. This division of the literature also corresponds to a difference in views of the state as either an "organic" entity, or a union of individuals engaged in a quid pro quo exchange. The distinction was clearly drawn, and the subsequent development of the literature anticipated, in 1949 by Buchanan in an article that builds on Wicksell. See also Buchanan's article (1975*b*, n. 10).
4. Exceptions are Buchanan's book (1967) and articles by Greene (1970) and Klevorick and Kramer (1973). The general topic is reviewed and Wicksell's influence emphasized by Buchanan (1975*b*).
5. For a survey of this literature see Milleron (1972).
6. See Musgrave (1959, 78–80). The most rigorous discussion of this is by Drèze and de la Vallee Poussin, who show that honest revelation of preferences is a

minimax strategy (1971). With less conservative strategists, honest revelation of preferences cannot be assured.

7. At least two normative proposals for sharing these gains are dependent on the bargaining or risk preferences of the individuals (see Nash 1950 and Braithwaite 1955).
8. However, Rae explicitly rules out the legitimacy of such a comparison (1969, 43).
9. "If any public expenditure is to be approved, . . . it must generally be assumed that this expenditure as such . . . is intended for an activity useful to the whole of society and so recognized by all classes without exception. If this were not so . . . then I, for one, fail to see how the latter can be considered as satisfying a collective need in the proper sense of the word" (Wicksell 1958, 89). Black limits his discussion of unanimity to international agreements, where redistribution (other than of the Hochman and Rodgers Pareto-efficient kind [1969]) is out of the question (1958, 140–55). Buchanan and Tullock are positivist in approach.
10. See Sen's discussion (1970*a*, 68–77) of May's theorem (1952). May's theorem is more in the spirit of the Arrow welfare function taken up later.
11. Kramer has offered a rigorous proof (1972), and Slutsky an existence theorem based on a generalization of the result to more than one dimension (1977*b*). Kramer and Kelvorick establish a similar result for local optima (1974).
12. Although when buttressed by additional assumptions, it may become more plausible. See Tullock 1967*b*; Arrow 1969; and Simpson 1969*b*.
13. For the most general statement of single-peakedness type conditions see Sen 1966.
14. This literature is surveyed in Inada 1969; Sen 1970*a*; Plott 1971; and Taylor 1971. Slutsky examines the necessary and sufficient conditions for majority rule consistency and relates then to the collective choice process (1977b).
15. See Garman and Kamien 1968; Niemi and Weisberg 1968; and Demeyer and Plott 1970. This literature is reviewed by Niemi (1969) and Riker and Ordeshook (1973, 94–97).
16. The most extensive treatment of logrolling is by Buchanan and Tullock (1962). See also Tullock 1970.
17. Robert Wilson has explored the existence of an equilibrium with logrolling using a game-theoretic framework (1971*a*, 1971*b*).
18. The normative properties of vote trading can be enhanced by redistributing the initial stocks of votes in a manner analogous to redistribution of private wealth (Mueller, Tollison, and Willett 1974).
19. Simple majority rule can be too, however. A voter who thought that sincere voting would produce an undesirable, majority winner might misstate his preferences so as to produce a cycle, trusting to chance, or a known procedure, to break the cycle in a more favorable way (Taylor 1968; Farquharson 1969; Riker and Ordeshook 1973, 97–99).
20. Buchanan was the first to compare the properties of general fund and earmarked tax schemes (1963). His work has been extended by Goetz (1968); Goetz and McKnew (1972); and Browning (1975).
21. Other assumptions have been used, e.g., vote maximization, but plurality maximization yields either the same or superior results (Hinich and Ordeshook 1970).
22. Hotelling's article could be regarded as *the* pioneering contribution in public choice. It is both a direct application of economics to a political process and a clear intellectual antecedent of both Downs's and, more indirectly, Black's work. The argument is also found in Bowen's classic paper (1969).

23. In addition to the single dimension assumption, the whole spatial approach to political issues has been challenged on methodological grounds (Stokes 1963). This literature is admirably reviewed and partially defended by Ordeshook (1974).
24. Haefele argues that *two-party* representative democracy both avoids cycles and maximizes voter utility gains (1971). The argument rests on questionable assumptions, however. Haefele depicts representative democracy as strategic manuevers between essentially monolithic parties. Their search for an optimal platform is described by a set of rules, which essentially seeks out the maximum possible utility gain, and not by a goal of winning. Haefele can thus conclude, from a matrix similar to table 2, that PPP is a stable winning platform (1971, 358–62). I cannot see, however, why a party seeking victory would not choose PPF in response to another's PPP.
25. Defeating the incumbent party appears so easy that Wittman assumes parties are able to look beyond merely maximizing their votes and choose strategies that maximize their *expected* utility from being in office (1973).
26. Differences in behavior caused by the different nature of the *choices* facing voters and consumers were first discussed by Buchanan (1954).
27. See Buchanan and Wagner 1970; Buchanan and Goetz 1972; McMillan 1975; and Flatters, Henderson, and Mieszkowski 1974.
28. See Arrow 1973; Barry 1973; Alexander 1974; Dasgupta 1974; Klevorick 1974; Mueller, Tollison, and Willett 1974; Mueller 1974; Musgrave 1974; Sen 1974; and Harsanyi 1975*a;* for a defense, Buchanan 1976.
29. See, however, Diamond 1967; Wilson 1968; Sen 1970*a*, 142–44; and Harsanyi's reply (1975*b*).
30. The issue of how cardinal utilities can be measured is also raised. See Harsanyi 1955; 1975*b;* Little 1957; Vickrey 1960; Sen 1970*a;* and Goodin 1975. The importance of actually measuring cardinal utilities has probably been overstressed. If one thinks of interpersonal comparisons as being made to form a social contract or constitution, then the choices are of basic principles and rules (e.g., freedom of speech) and thus involve fundamental wants and values common to all.
31. The Harsanyi welfare function has been criticized by Pattanaik (1968) and Sen (1970*a*), on the same grounds as its utilitarian predecessors, for not taking into account the distribution of utilities over all individuals. This criticism has been challenged in Mueller 1973; Mueller, Tollison, and Willett 1974; and Harsanyi 1975*b*.
32. Arrow's definition differs from the Bergson-Samuelson definition of a social welfare function (1963, pp. 23–24).
33. For full statements of the axioms and proof, see Arrow (1963) and Sen (1970, 33–46). Vickrey presents a slightly different, easy to follow proof (1960).
34. Sen (1970*a*), Pattanaik (1971), and Fishburn (1973) all survey and extend this literature in important ways. See also Riker 1961; Rothenberg 1961; Arrow 1963, chap. 8; and Taylor 1971.
35. The weakest modification of this form is to replace transitivity with acyclicity; *i.e.* $(xPy \text{ and } yPz) \cdot (xRz)$. But this too introduces some arbitrariness (Sen 1970; 47–55).
36. Vickrey's speculation that immunity to strategy and the independence axiom are logically equivalent (1960, 517–19) has been rigorously proved by Gibbard (1973) and Satterthwaite (1975). For additional discussion of this axiom see Bergson 1954; Hansson 1973.

37. This voting procedure is consistent with a possibility theorem, a weaker statement of the independence axiom, and the other four Arrow axioms (Ray 1973).
38. Arrow 1963, 119–20; Barry 1965, 323–24; Baumol 1965, 43–44; Samuelson 1969*b;* Sen 1970*a,* 24–26.
39. Some criticisms of Rawls are also revealing. Buchanan (1972), the positivist-contractarian, objects to Rawls's extension of his theory of the social contract *process* to define actual outcomes of the process in terms of principles of justice. Welfare theorists Arrow (1973), Sen (1970*a,* 135–46; 1974), and Harsanyi (1975*a*) criticize only the form the principles take.

REFERENCES

Alexander, S. S. "Social Evaluation through Rational Choice." *Quarterly Journal of Economics* 88, no. 4 (November 1974): 597–624.

Aranson, P. H., and Ordeshook, P. C. "Spatial Strategies for Sequential Elections." In *Probability Models of Collective Decision-Making,* edited by R. G. Niemi and H. F. Weisberg. Columbus: Merrill, 1972.

Arrow, K. J. *Social Choice and Individual Values.* Rev. ed. New York and London: Yale University Press, 1963.

———. "Tullock and an Existence Theorem." *Public Choice* 6 (Spring 1969): 105–11.

———. "Some Ordinalist-Utilitarian Notes on Rawls's *Theory of Justice.*" *Journal of Philosophy* 70, no. 9 (May 1973): 245–63.

Arrow, K. J., and Scitovsky, T., eds. *Readings in Welfare Economics.* Homewood, Ill.: Irwin, 1969.

Barr, J. L., and Davis, O. A. "An Elementary Political and Economic Theory of the Expenditures of Local Governments." *Southern Economics Journal* 33, no. 2 (October 1966): 149–65.

Barry, B. M. *Political Argument.* London: Routledge and Kegan Paul; New York: Humanities Press, 1965.

———. *Sociologists, Economists and Democracy.* London: Collier-Macmillan, 1970.

———. *The Liberal Theory of Justice.* London: Oxford University Press, Clarendon Press, 1973.

Barzel, Y., and Silberberg, E. "Is the Act of Voting Rational?" *Public Choice* 16 (Fall 1973): 51–58.

Baumol, W. J. *Welfare Economics and the Theory of the State.* 2d ed. Cambridge, Mass.: Harvard University Press, 1965.

Bergson, A. "On the Concept of Social Welfare." *Quarterly Journal of Economics* 68 (May 1954): 233–52.

———. "A Reformulation of Certain Aspects of Welfare Economics." *Quarterly Journal of Economics* 52 (February 1938): 310–34. Reprinted in *Readings in Welfare Economics* (Arrow and Scitovsky 1969, 7–25).

Bergstrom, T. C., and Goodman, R. P. "Private Demands for Public Goods." *American Economic Review* 63, no. 3 (June 1973): 280–96.

Bernholz, P. "Logrolling, Arrow Paradox and Cyclical Majorities." *Public Choice* 15 (Summer 1973): 87–95.

———. "Is a Paretian Liberal Really Impossible?" *Public Choice* 20 (Winter 1974*a*): 99–107.

———. "Logrolling, Arrow-Paradox and Decision Rules—A Generalization." *Kyklos* 27 no. 1 (1974*b*): 49–62.

———. "The Paradox of Voting and Logrolling Are They Logically Equivalent?" Mimeographed. June 1974*c*.

Black, D. "The Decisions of a Committee Using a Special Majority. *Econometrica* 16 (July 1948): 245–61.

———. *The Theory of Committees and Elections*. Cambridge: Cambridge University Press, 1958.

———. "On the Rationale of Group Decision Making." *Journal of Political Economy* 56 (February 1948): 23–34. Reprinted in *Readings in Welfare Economics* (Arrow and Scitovsky 1969, 133–46).

Borcherding, T. E., and Deacon, R. T. "The Demand for the Services of Non-Federal Governments." *American Economic Review* 62, no. 5 (December 1972): 891–901.

Bowen, H. R. "The Interpretation of Voting in the Allocation of Economic Resources." *Quarterly Journal of Economics* 58 (November 1943): 27–48. Reprinted in *Readings in Welfare Economics* (Arrow and Scitovsky 1969, 115–32).

Braithwaite, R. B. *Theory of Games as a Tool for the Moral Philosopher*. Cambridge: Cambridge University Press, 1955.

Breton, A. *The Economic Theory of Representative Government*. Chicago: Aldine, 1974.

Browning, E. K. "Collective Choice and General Fund Financing." *Journal of Political Economy* 83, no. 2 (April 1975): 377–90

Buchanan, J. M. "The Pure Theory of Government Finance: A Suggested Approach." *Journal of Political Economy* 57 (December 1949): 496–505.

———. "Individual Choice in Voting and the Market." *Journal of Political Economy* 62 (August 1954): 334–43.

———. "The Economics of Earmarked Taxes." *Journal of Political Economy* 71 (October 1963): 457–69.

———. "An Economic Theory of Clubs." *Economica* 32, no. 125 (February 1965*a*): 1–14.

———. "Ethical Rules, Expected Values, and Large Numbers." *Ethics* 76 (October 1965*b*): 1–13.

———. *Public Finance in Democratic Process*. Chapel Hill: University of North Carolina Press, 1967.

———. "Principles of Urban Fiscal Strategy." *Public Choice* 11 (Fall 1971): 1–16.

———. "Rawls on Justice as Fairness." *Public Choice* 13 (Fall 1972): 123–28.

———. *The Limits of Liberty: Between Anarchy and Leviathan*. Chicago: University of Chicago Press, 1975*a*.

———. "Public Finance and Public Choice." *National Tax Journal* 28, no. 4 (December 1975*b*): 383–94.

———. "A Hobbesian Interpretation of the Rawlsian Difference Principle." *Kyklos* 29, no. 1 (1976): 5–25.

Buchanan, J. M., and Goetz, C. J. "Efficiency Limits of Fiscal Mobility: An Assessment of the Tiebout Model." *Journal of Public Economics* 1, no. 1 (April 1972): 25–43.

Buchanan, J. M., and Tollison, R. D., eds. *Theory of Public Choice*. Ann Arbor: University of Michigan Press, 1972.

Buchanan, J. M., and Tullock, G. *The Calculus of Consent*. Ann Arbor: University of Michigan Press, 1962.

Buchanan, J. M., and Wagner, R. E. "An Efficiency Basis for Federal Fiscal Equalization." In *The Analysis of Public Output,* edited by J. Margolis, pp. 139–58. New York: National Bureau of Economic Research, 1970.

Bush, W. C., and Mayer, L. S. "Some Implications of Anarchy for the Distribution of Property." *Journal of Economic Theory* 8, no. 4 (August 1974): 401–12.

Coleman, J. S. "Foundations for a Theory of Collective Decisions." *American Journal of Sociology* 71, no. 6 (May 1966*a*): 615–27.

______. "The Possibility of a Social Welfare Function." *American Economic Review* 56, no. 5 (December 1966*b*): 1105–22.

______. "The Possibility of a Social Welfare Function: Reply." *American Economic Review* 57, no. 5 (December 1967): 1311–17.

______. "Political Money." *American Political Science Review* 64, no. 5 (December 1970): 1074–87.

______. "Internal Processes Governing Party Positions in Elections." *Public Choice* 11 (Fall 1971): 35–60.

______. "The Positions of Political Parties in Elections." In *Probability Models of Collective Decision-Making,* edited by R. G. Niemi and H. F. Weisberg. Columbus: Merrill, 1972.

Comanor, W. S. "The Median Voter Rule and the Theory of Political Choice." *Journal of Public Economics* 5, no 1 (January-February 1976): 169–77.

Crain, W. M., and Tollison, R. D. "Campaign Expenditures and Political Competition." *Journal of Law and Economics* 19 (April 1976): 177–88.

Crain, W.; Deaton, T.; and Tollison, R. "Electoral Outcomes and Macroeconomic Variables: Is There a Discernable Relation?" Mimeographed. Texas A & M University, 1975.

Craven, J. "Majority Voting and Social Choice." *Review of Economic Studies* 38, no. 2 (April 1971): 265–67.

Dasgupta, P. "On Some Problems Arising from Professor Rawls' Conception of Distributive Justice." *Theory and Decision* 4, no. 3–4 (February-April 1974): 325–44.

Davis, O. A., and Haines, G. H., Jr. "A Political Approach to a Theory of Public Expenditure: The Case of Municipalities." *National Tax Journal* 19 (September 1966): 259–75.

Davis, O. A.; Hinich, M. J.; and Ordeshook, P. C. "An Expository Development of a Mathematical Model of the Electoral Process." *American Political Science Review* 64, no. 2 (June 1970): 426–48.

de Borda, J. C. "Mémoire sur les Elections au Scrutin." *Historie de l'Academie Royale des Sciences,* 1781.

de Condorcet, M. *Essai sur l'application de l'analyse a la Probabilité des Decisions Rendues à la Pluralisté des voix.* Paris: 1785.

Demeyer, F., and Plott, C. R. "The Probability of Cyclical Majority." *Econometrica* 38, no. 2 (March 1970): 345–54.

Diamond, P. A. "Cardinal Welfare, Individualistic Ethics, and Interpersonal Comparison of Utility: A Comment." *Journal of Political Economy* 75, no. 5 (October 1967): 765–66.

Dodgson, C. L. "A Method of Taking Votes on More than Two Issues." Written 23 February 1876. Reprinted in *The Theory of Committees and Elections* (Black 1958, 224–34).

Downs, A. *An Economic Theory of Democracy.* New York: Harper and Row, 1957.

———. "Why the Government Budget Is Too Small in a Democracy." *World Politics* 12 (July 1960): 541–63.

———. "In Defense of Majority Voting." *Journal of Political Economy* 69 (April 1961): 192–99.

Dreze, J. H., and de la Vallee Poussin, D. "A Tâtonnement Process for Public Goods." *Review of Economic Studies* 38, no. 2 (April 1971): 133–50.

Escarraz, D. R. "Wicksell and Lindahl: Theories of Public Expenditure and Tax Justice Reconsidered." *National Tax Journal* 20 (June 1967): 137–48.

Farquharson, R. *Theory of Voting*. New Haven: Yale University Press, 1969.

Fishburn, P. C. *The Theory of Social Choice*. Princeton: Princeton University Press, 1973.

Flatters, F.; Henderson, V.; and Mieszkowski, P. "Public Goods, Efficiency, and Regional Fiscal Equilization." *Journal of Public Economics* 3, no. 2 (May 1974): 99–112.

Fleming, J. M. "A Cardinal Concept of Welfare." *Quarterly Journal of Economics* 66 (August 1952): 366–84.

Frey, B. S. "Why Do High Income People Participate More in Politics?" *Public Choice* 11 (Fall 1971): 101–5.

———. "The Political-Economic System: A Simulation Model." *Kyklos* 27 no. 2 (1974): 227–54.

Frey, B. S., and Garbers, H. "Der Einfluss wirtschaftlicher Variabler auf die Popularität der Regierung." *Jahr. Nationalökon. Statist.* 186, no. 4 (April 1972): 281–95.

Frey, B. S., and Lau, L. J. "Towards a Mathematical Model of Government Behaviour." *Z. Nationalokon.* 28 (1968): 355–80.

Frey, B. S., and Schneider, F. "On the Modeling of Politico-Economic Interdependence." *European Journal of Political Research* 3 (December 1975): 339–60.

———. "An Econometric Model with an Endogenous Government Sector." Mimeographed. Konstanz, 1975.

Garman, M. B., and Kamien, M. I. "The Paradox of Voting: Probability Calculations." *Behavioral Science* 13 (July 1968): 306–17.

Gibbard, A. "Manipulation of Voting Schemes: A General Result." *Econometrica* 41, no. 4 (July 1973): 587–602.

Goetz, C. J. "Earmarked Taxes and Majority Rule Budgetary Processes." *American Economic Review* 58, no. 1 (March 1968): 128–36.

Goetz, C. J., and McKnew, C. R., Jr. "Paradoxical Results in a Public Choice Model of Alternative Government Grant Forms." In *Theory of Public Choice* (Buchanan and Tollison 1972, 224–35).

Goodhart, C. A. E., and Bhansali, R. J. "Political Economy." *Political Studies* 18, no. 1 (March 1970): 43–106.

Goodin, R. E. "How to Determine Who Should Get What." *Ethics* 85 (July 1975): 310–21.

Greene, K. V. "Some Institutional Considerations in Federal-State Fiscal Relations." *Public Choice* 9 (Fall 1970): 1–18.

Haefele, E. T. "A Utility Theory of Representative Government." *American Economic Review* 61, no. 3 (June 1971): 350–57.

Hansson, B. "The Independence Condition in the Theory of Social Choice." *Theory and Decision* 4, no. 1 (September 1973): 25–49.

Harsanyi, J. C. "Cardinal Utility in Welfare Economics and in the Theory of Risk-Taking." *Journal of Political Economy* 61 (October 1953): 434–35.

______. "Cardinal Welfare, Individualistic Ethics, and Interpersonal Comparisons of Utility." *Journal of Political Economy* 63 (August 1955): 309–21. Reprinted in *Readings in Welfare Economics* (Arrow and Scitovsky 1969, 46–60).

______. "Can the Maximin Principle Serve as a Basis for Morality: A Critique of John Rawls's Theory." *American Political Science Review* 69, no. 2 (June 1975*a*): 594–606.

______. "Nonlinear Social Welfare Functions." *Theory and Decision* 6 (August 1975*b*): 311–32.

Head, J. G. "Public Goods and Public Policy." *Public Finance* 17, no. 3 (1962): 197–221.

Hildreth, C. "Alternative Conditions for Social Orderings." *Econometrica* 21 (January 1953): 81–94.

Hinich, M. J., and Ordeshook, P. C. "Plurality Maximization vs. Vote Maximization: A Spatial Analysis with Variable Participation." *American Political Science Review* 64, no. 3 (September 1970): 772–91.

Hirschman, A. O. *Exit, Voice, and Loyalty*. Cambridge, Mass.: Harvard University Press, 1970.

Hochman, H. M., and Rodgers, J. D. "Pareto Optinal Redistribution." *American Economic Review* 59, no. 4 (September 1969): 542–57.

Hotelling, H. "Stability in Competition." *Economic Journal* 39 (March 1929): 41–57.

Hume, D. A. *Treatise of Human Nature*. Oxford: Oxford University Press, 1941.

Inada, K. "The Simple Majority Decisions Rule." *Econometrica* 37, no. 3 (July 1969): 490–506.

Intriligator, M. D. "A Probabilistic Model of Social Choice." *Review of Economic Studies* 40, no. 4 (October 1973): 553–60.

Johansen, L. "Some Notes on the Lindahl Theory of Determination of Public Expenditures." *International Economics Review* 4, no. 3 (September 1963): 346–58.

Kasper, H. "On Political Competition, Economic Policy, and Income Maintenance Programs." *Public Choice* 10 (Spring 1971): 1–19.

Kemp, M. C. "Arrow's General Possibility Theorem." *Review of Economic Studies* 21, no. 3 (1954): 240–43.

Kemp, M. C., and Asimakopulos, A. "A Note on 'Social Welfare Functions' and Cardinal Utility." *Canadian Journal of Economics and Political Science* 18 (May 1952): 195–200.

Klevorick, A. K. "Political Constraints on Contractual Redistribution: Discussion." *American Economic Review* 64, no. 2 (May 1974): 152–61.

Klevorick, A. K., and Kramer, G. H. "Social Choice on Pollution Management: The Genossenschaften." *Journal of Public Economics* 2, no. 2 (April 1973): 101–46.

Kramer, G. H. "Short-Term Fluctuations in U.S. Voting Behavior, 1896–1964." *American Political Science Review* 65, no. 1 (March 1971): 131–43.

______. "Sophisticated Voting Over Multidimensional Choice Spaces." *Journal of Mathematical Sociology* 2, no. 2 (July 1972): 165–80.

______. "On a Class of Equilibrium Conditions for Majority Rule." *Econometrica* 41, no. 2 (March 1973): 285–97.

Kramer, G. H., and Klevorick, A. K. "Existence of a 'Local' Cooperative Equilibrium in a Class of Voting Games." *Review of Economic Studies* 41, no. 4 (October 1974): 539–47.

Leibenstein, H. "Notes on Welfare Economics and the Theory of Democracy." *Economic Journal* 72 (June 1962): 299–319.

———. "Long-Run Welfare Criteria." In *The Public Economy of Urban Communities*, edited by J. Margolis, pp. 39–51. Baltimore: Johns Hopkins University Press, 1965.

Lerner, A. P. *The Economics of Control*. New York: Macmillan and Co., 1944.

Lindahl, E. "Just Taxation—A Positive Solution." Translated from the German in *Classics in the Theory of Public Finance* (Musgrave and Peacock, 1958, 168–76).

Lindeen, J. W. "An Oligopoly Model of Political Market Structures." *Public Choice* 9 (Fall 1970): 31–37.

Little, I. M. D. "Social Choice and Individual Values." *Journal of Political Economy* 60 (October 1952): 422–32.

May, K. O. "A Set of Independent, Necessary and Sufficient Conditions for Simple Majority Decision." *Econometrica* 20 (October 1952): 680–84.

McGuire, M. C. "Private Good Clubs and Public Good Clubs: Economic Models of Group Formation." *Swedish Journal of Economics* 74, no. 1 (March 1972): 84–99.

———. "Group Segregation and Optimal Jurisdictions." *Journal of Political Economy* 82, no. 1 (January–February 1974): 112–32.

McGuire, M. C., and Aaron, H. "Efficiency and Equity in the Optimal Supply of a Public Good." *Review of Economic Statistics* 51, no. 1 (February 1969): 31–39.

McKelvey, R. D. "Policy Related Voting and Electoral Equilibrium." *Econometrica* 43, nos. 5–6 (September–November 1975): 815–43.

McMillan, M. L. "Toward the More Optimal Provision of Local Public Goods: Internationalization of Benefits or Intergovernmental Grants?" *Public Finance Quarterly* 3 (July 1975): 229–60.

Miller, W. L., and Mackie, M. "The Electoral Cycle and the Asymmetry of Government and Opposition Popularity." *Political Studies*, 21, no. 3 (September 1973): 263–79.

Milleron, J. C. "Theory of Value with Public Goods: A Survey Article." *Journal of Economic Theory* 5 (December 1972): 419–77.

Mueller, D. C. "The Possibility of a Social Welfare Function: Comment." *American Economic Review* 57, no. 5 (December 1967): 1304–11.

———. "Fiscal Federalism in a Constitutional Democracy." *Public Policy* 19, no. 4 (Fall 1971): 567–93.

———. "Constitutional Democracy and Social Welfare." *Quarterly Journal of Economics* 87, no. 1 (February 1973): 60–80.

———. "Achieving the Just Polity." *American Economic Review*, 64, no. 2 (May 1974): 147–52.

Mueller, D. C.; Philpotts, G. C.; and Vanek, J. "The Social Gains from Exchanging Votes: A Simulation Approach." *Public Choice* 13 (Fall 1972): 55–79.

Mueller, D. C.; Tollison, R. D.; and Willett, T. D. "The Utilitarian Contract: A Generalization of Rawls' Theory of Justice." *Theory and Decision* 4, no. 3/4 (February–April 1974): 345–67.

———. "On Equalizing the Distribution of Political Income." *Journal of Political Economy* 82, no. 2 (March–April 1974): 414–22.

———. "Solving the Intensity Problem in a Representative Democracy." In *Political Economy and Public Policy*, edited by R. Amacher, R. D. Tollison, and T. D. Willett. Ithaca, N.Y.: Cornell University Press, 1975.

Musgrave, R. A. *The Theory of Public Finance*. New York: McGraw-Hill, 1959.

______. "Symposium: Rawls' *A Theory of Justice:* Maximin, Uncertainty, and the Leisure Trade-Off." *Quarterly Journal of Economics* 88, no. 4 (November 1974): 625–32.

Musgrave, R. A., and Peacock, A. T., eds. *Classics in the Theory of Public Finance.* New York: St. Martin's Press, 1958.

Nash, J. F. "The Bargaining Problem." *Econometrica* 18 (April 1950): 155–62.

Ng, Y. K. "The Possibility of a Paretian Liberal: Impossibility Theorems and Cardinal Utility." *Journal of Political Economy* 79, no. 6 (November–December 1971): 1397–1402.

Niemi, R. G. "Majority Decision-Making with Partial Unidimensionality." *American Political Science Review* 63, no. 2 (June 1969): 488–97.

Niemi, R. G., and Weisberg, H. F. "A Mathematical Solution for the Probability of the Paradox of Voting." *Behavioral Science* 13 (July 1968): 317–23.

Nordhaus, W. D. "The Political Business Cycle." *Review of Economic Studies* 42, no. 2 (April 1975): 169–90.

Oates, W. E. *Fiscal Federalism.* New York: Harcourt Brace, 1972.

Olson, M., Jr. *The Logic of Collective Action.* Cambridge, Mass.: Harvard University Press, 1965.

Ordeshook, P. C. "The Spatial Theory of Elections: A Review and Critique." Presented at the ECPR Workshop on Participation, Voting, and Party Competition. Strasbourg, 1974.

Ostrom, V. *The Political Theory of a Compound Republic.* Blacksburg, Va.: Public Choice Society, 1971.

Palda, K. S. "Does Advertising Influence Votes? An Analysis of the 1966 and 1970 Quebec Elections." *Canadian Journal of Political Science* 6, no. 4 (December 1973): 638–55.

Park, R. E. "The Possibility of a Social Welfare Function: Comment." *American Economic Review* 57, no. 5 (December 1967): 1300–1304.

Pattanaik, P. K. "Risk, Impersonality, and the Social Welfare Function." *Journal of Political Economy* 76, no. 6 (November–December 1968): 1152–69.

______. *Voting and Collective Choice.* Cambridge: Cambridge University Press, 1971.

Pauly, M. V. "Clubs, Commonality, and the Core: An Integration of Game Theory and the Theory of Public Goods." *Economica* 54, no. 135 (August 1967): 314–24.

______. "Cores and Clubs." *Public Choice* 9 (Fall 1970): 53–65.

Peacock, A. T., and Rowley, C. K. "Pareto Optimality and the Political Economy of Liberalism." *Journal of Political Economy* 80, no. 3 (May–June 1972): 476–90.

Pestieau, P. "The Optimality Limits of the Tiebout Model." Mimeographed. Ithaca, N.Y., 1974.

Philpotts, G. "Vote Trading, Welfare, and Uncertainty." *Canadian Journal of Economics* 5, no. 3 (August 1972): 358–72.

Plott, C. R. "A Notion of Equilibrium and Its Possibility Under Majority Rule." *American Economic Review* 57, no. 4 (September 1967): 787–806.

______. "Recent Results in the Theory of Voting." In *Frontiers of Quantitative Economics,* edited by M. D. Intriligator, pp. 109–27. Amsterdam: North-Holland, 1971.

Pommerehne, W., and Frey, B. S. "Two Approaches to Estimating Public Expenditures." Mimeographed. Konstanz, 1975.

Rae, D. W. *The Political Consequences of Electoral Laws.* New Haven: Yale University Press, 1967.

______. "Decision-Rules and Individual Values in Constitutional Choice." *American Political Science Review* 63, no. 1 (March 1969): 40–56.

Rae, D. W., and Taylor, M. "Decision Rules and Policy Outcomes." *British Journal of Political Science* 1 (January 1971): 71–90.

Rawls, J. *A Theory of Justice.* Cambridge, Mass.: Harvard University Press, Belknap Press, 1971.

______. "Some Reasons for the Maximin Criterion." *American Economic Review* 64, no. 2 (May 1974*a*): 141–46.

______. "Reply to Alexander and Musgrave." *Quarterly Journal of Economics* 88, no. 4 (November 1974*b*): 633–55.

Ray, P. "Independence of Irrelevant Alternatives." *Econometrica* 41, no. 3 (September 1973): 987–91.

Riker, W. H. "Voting and the Summation of Preferences: An Interpretive Bibliographical Review of Selected Developments During the Last Decade." *American Political Science Review* 55, no. 4 (December 1961): 900–911.

______. *The Theory of Political Coalitions.* New Haven and London: Yale University Press, 1962.

Riker, W. H., and Brams, S. J. "The Paradox of Vote Trading." *American Political Science Review* 67, no. 4 (December 1973): 1235–47.

Riker, W. H., and Ordeshook, P. C. "A Theory of the Calculus of Voting." *American Political Science Review* 62, no. 1 (March 1968): 25–42.

______. *An Introduction to Positive Political Theory.* Englewood Cliffs, N.J.: Prentice-Hall, 1973.

Rosenthal, H., and Sen, S. "Electoral Participation in the French Fifth Republic." *American Political Science Review* 67, no. 1 (March 1973): 29–54.

Rothenberg, J. *The Measurement of Social Welfare.* Englewood Cliffs, N.J.: Prentice-Hall, 1961.

______. "The Process of Group Choice in a Legislative Context." In *La Decision: Aggrégation et Dynamique des Ordres de Preference,* edited by G. T. Guilbaud, pp. 205–24. Paris: Centre National de la Recherche Scientific, 1969.

Runciman, W. G., and Sen, A. K. "Games, Justice and the General Will." *Mind,* October 1965, pp. 554–62.

Russell, K. P.; Fraser, J.; and Frey, B. S. "Political Participation and Income Level: An Exchange." *Public Choice* 13 (Fall 1972): 113–22.

Samuelson, P. A. *Foundations of Economic Analysis.* Cambridge, Mass.: Harvard University Press, 1947.

______. "Arrow's Mathematical Politics." In *Human Values and Economic Policy,* edited by S. Hook. New York: New York University Press, 1967.

______. "The Pure Theory of Public Expenditures." *Review of Economic Statistics* 36, no. 4 (November 1954): 387–89. Reprinted in *Readings in Welfare Economics* (Arrow and Scitovsky 1969*a,* 179–82).

______. "Pure Theory of Public Expenditure and Taxation." In *Public Economics,* edited by J. Margolis and H. Guitton, pp. 98–123. New York: St. Martin's Press, 1969*b*.

Satterthwaite, M. A. "Strategy-Proofness and Arrow's Conditions: Existence and Correspondence Theorems for Voting Procedures and Social Welfare Functions." *Journal of Economic Theory* 10, no. 2 (April 1975): 187–217.

Schumpeter, J. A. *Capitalism, Socialism, and Democracy.* 3d ed. New York: Harper and Row, 1950.

Sen, A. K. "A Possibility Theorem on Majority Decisions." *Econometrica* 34, no. 2 (April 1966): 491–99.

———. *Collective Choice and Social Welfare.* San Francisco: Holden-Day, 1970*a*.

———. "The Impossibility of a Paretian Liberal." *Journal of Political Economy* 78, no. 1 (January–February 1979*b*): 152–57.

———. "Rawls versus Bentham: An Axiomatic Examination of the Pure Distribution Problem." *Theory and Decision* 4, no. 3/4 (February–April 1974): 301–9.

Sherman, R. "Experimental Oligopoly." *Kyklos* 24, no. 1 (1971): 30–49.

Siegel, S., and Fouraker, L. E. *Bargaining and Group Decision Making: Experiments in Bilateral Monopoly.* New York: McGraw-Hill, 1960.

Simpson, P. B. "On Defining Areas of Voter Choice: Professor Tullock on Stable Voting." *Quarterly Journal of Economics* 83, no. 3 (August 1969): 478–90.

Slutsky, S. "Equilibrium Under Plurality Voting." Mimeographed. Cornell University, 1975.

———. "A Characterization of Societies with Consistent Majority Decision." *Review of Economic Studies* 44 (June 1977*a*): 211–25.

———. "A Voting Model for the Allocation of Public Goods: Existence of an Equilibrium." *Journal of Economic Theory* 14 (April 1977*b*): 299–325.

Smithies, A. "Optimum Location in Spatial Competition." *Journal of Political Economy* 49 (June 1941): 423–39.

Stigler, G. J. "Director's Law of Public Income Redistribution." *Journal of Law and Economics* 13, no. 1 (April 1970): 1–10.

Stokes, D. E. "Spatial Models of Party Competition." *American Political Science Review* 57, no. 2 (June 1963): 368–77.

Taylor, M. J. "Graph Theoretical Approaches to the Theory of Social Choice." *Public Choice* 4 (Spring 1968): 35–48.

———. "Proof of a Theorem on Majority Rule." *Behavioral Science* 14 (May 1969): 228–31.

———. "Review Article: Mathematical Political Theory." *British Journal of Political Science* 1 (July 1971): 339–82.

Tiebout, C. M. "A Pure Theory of Local Expenditures." *Journal of Political Economy* 64 (October 1956): 416–24.

Tollison, R. D., and Willett, T. D. "Some Simple Economics of Voting and Not Voting." *Public Choice* 16 (Fall 1973): 59–71.

Tullock, G. *Toward a Mathematics of Politics.* Ann Arbor: University of Michigan Press, 1967*a*.

———. "The General Irrelevance of the General Impossibility Theorem." *Quarterly Journal of Economics* 81, no. 2 (May 1967*b*): 256–70.

———. "Problems of Majority Voting." *Journal of Political Economy* 67 (December 1959): 571–79. Reprinted in *Readings in Welfare Economics* (Arrow and Scitovsky 1969, 169–78).

———. "A Simple Algebraic Logrolling Model." *American Economic Review* 60, no. 3 (June 1979): 419–26.

———. "The Paradox of Revolution." *Public Choice* 11 (Fall 1971*a*): 89–99.

———. "The Charity of the Uncharitable." *Western Economic Journal* 9, no. 4 (December 1971*b*): 379–92.

______. *The Social Dilemma: Economics of War and Revolution.* Blacksburg, Va.: Center for Study of Public Choice, 1974.

Tullock, G., and Campbell, C. D. "Computer Simulation of a Small Voting System." *Economic Journal* 80, no. 317 (March 1970): 97–104.

Vickrey, W. S. "Measuring Marginal Utility by Reactions to Risk." *Econometrica* 13 (October 1945): 319–33.

______. "Utility, Strategy, and Social Decision Rules." *Quarterly Journal of Economics* 74, no. 4 (November 1960): 507–35.

Welch, W. P. "The Economics of Campaign Funds." *Public Choice* 20 (Winter 1974): 83–97.

Wicksell, K. "A New Principle of Just Taxation." *Finanztheoretische Untersuchungen.* Jena, 1896. Reprinted in *Classics in the Theory of Public Finance* (Musgrave and Peacock 1958, 72–118).

Williamson, O. E., and Sargent, T. J. "Social Choice: A Probabilistic Approach." *Economic Journal* 77 (December 1967): 797–813.

Wilson, R. "The Theory of Syndicates." *Econometrica* 36 (January 1968): 119–32.

______. "An Axiomatic Model of Logrolling." *American Economic Review* 59, no. 3 (June 1969): 331–41.

______. "A Game-Theoretic Analysis of Social Choice." In *Social Choice,* edited by B. Lieherman. New York: Gordon and Breach, 1971*a.*

______. "Stable Coalition Proposals in Majority-Rule Voting." *Journal of Economic Theory* 3, no. 3 (September 1971*b*): 254–71.

Wittman, D. A. "Parties as Utility Maximizers." *American Political Science Review* 67, no. 2 (June 1973): 490–98.

Wright, G. "The Political Economy of New Deal Spending: An Econometric Analysis." *Review of Economic Statistics* 56, no. 1 (February 1974): 30–38.

3 Recent Contributions to Public Choice Theory and Methods

Towards a Tax Constitution for Leviathan

Geoffrey Brennan and James M. Buchanan

In this essay we analyze *constitutional* choice among tax institutions under a specified set of political assumptions. That is to say, we examine an individual's choice among tax rules and tax instruments when it is known that such institutions, once selected, will remain in being over an indeterminately long sequence of budgetary periods, and in a setting in which the individual is presumed to be unable to predict with precision what his own position will be at any particular moment in this postconstitutional sequence.[1] Our analytical framework differs from that which informs much of the conventional wisdom in a normative tax theory as well as from that which has informed much of the Wicksell-inspired, public choice alternative.

Neoclassical normative tax theory is, in all essential respects, institutionally vacuous.[2] Abstract normative criteria for a 'good' tax system are derived in response to the problem posed by the requirement to raise some exogenously determined amount of revenue for governmental use within a single time period. Emphasis is placed on the familiar efficiency and equity characteristics of alternative tax instruments. Within this traditional perspective, the influence of the tax instrument chosen on the amount of revenue demanded or required is neglected or obscured by the "equi-revenue" comparison within which the whole analysis is conducted. In a constitutional setting, by contrast, such possible feedback effects over a sequence by budgetary periods must be explicitly considered: the interdependencies between the form of tax institutions and the revenue demands placed on these institutions cannot be ignored. And, of course, predictions of such relationships will necessarily be embodied in the individual's choice. In this essay, we shall introduce an institutional model within which these interdependencies assume critical importance.

Modern public choice theorists have already gone some way toward incorporating these effects of tax instruments on public goods supply into the analysis of constitutional choice.[3] Almost exclusively, however, the public choice model of constitutional fiscal choice has embodied the assumption, explicit or implicit, that postconstitutional or in-period budgetary decisions conform to the public goods demands of the median voter or his representative in a legislative assembly. Our analysis differs critically from this in that we substitute the model of a revenue-seeking Leviathan for the demand-driven and essentially passive government characteristic of early public choice analysis.

First published in *Journal of Public Economics* 8 (1977): 255–73.

The norms for taxation suggested by the analysis seem to accord more closely with some of the empirically observed attitudes of the taxpaying public than those which emerge from either of the alternative paradigms. Furthermore, the institutional model is in apparent consistency with a large, rapidly growing and uncontrollable public sector. This is in dramatic contrast with the implied setting from which the traditional reform suggestions emerge, a setting that retains residues of the classical economists' assumption of nonproductive public expenditures along with the implicit notion that the governmental share in national product is severely limited. Our model is also sharply at variance with the naively optimistic public choice perspective which incorporates the productiveness of a possibly large public sector but which does not allow for a supply-side influence on fiscal outcomes.

This essay is intended to be a contribution to the ongoing discussion of real-world tax reform, rather than an exercise in deriving the logical properties of yet another set of arbitrarily selected assumptions. Indeed, in some sense, the point of departure for our discussion is the observation that tax reform is a quasi-constitutional exercise. Tax institutions are usually intended to be moderately permanent features of the political framework: they set the context within which in-period decisions about public goods supply are made. Furthermore, the major tax reform process (say of the Carter type in Canada, or the British Royal Commissions) is perhaps more like an attempt at a genuinely "constitutional convention" than any other common aspect of political life (at least in the public finance specialists' experience).

Once this is acknowledged it becomes natural to think of devising tax institutions by appeal to the constitutional calculus of the typical taxpayer-voter rather than by reference to abstract ethical norms. On the other hand, it should be borne in mind that tax reform is *not* the full constitutional arrangement envisaged for example in *The Calculus of Consent*[4]; the mandate is necessarily much more restricted. For this reason, although we acknowledge the possibility of nontax institutions which might perform a similar role to the tax rules we discuss and perhaps do so more efficiently, we do not consider such alternatives here.[5] To do so would be to move outside our basic tax reform orientation.

The central structure of the institutional model is set out in section 1. In section 2, we examine the choice of an individual as he compares a comprehensive and a noncomprehensive tax base as well as alternative rate structures within these. The analysis is extended to many tax bases in section 3, and to a many-person setting in section 4. Finally, in section 5, the discussion of the paper is related to commonly held views on tax reform.

1. Government as a Revenue-Maximizer Subject to Constitutional Tax Constraints

As Knut Wicksell noted, no persons would approve the imposition of taxes, either at a constitutional or a postconstitutional stage of decision, unless they expect to secure some benefits from the goods and services that they predict will be financed from the revenues collected. Taxes are coercive instruments that allow governments to levy charges upon persons without any corresponding individualized expression of current willingness to pay. Furthermore, in postconstitutional stages of decision, political consent through the action of legislative representatives will not, typically, be extended to more than a simple majority of the citizenry.

What is a reasonable model of postconstitutional fiscal decision making by governments, a model that might be appropriate in informing the constitutional-stage choice among fiscal instruments? Perhaps at one period in history, it may have seemed reasonable to rely on the operation of majority rule in legislatures to hold governmental fiscal activities in bounds. And majority rule models remain in both the analysis of median-voter behavior and in popular discussion of democracy. Confronted with public sectors of modern scope, and with bureaucracies that demonstrably possess power quite apart from specifically legislated authority, the democratic-limits model of governmental fiscal constraint seems to become increasingly naive. A more acceptable model would seem to be one in which the political-bureaucratic process, as it is predicted to operate postconstitutionally, involves the maximization of revenues within the tax constraints imposed in the fiscal constitution.

This is what might loosely be termed a model of "Leviathan." The citizenry has no effective or operational control over government, once established, beyond the constraints that are imposed at the constitutional level; in-period or postconstitutional fiscal decisions are made entirely by the budget-maximizing or revenue-maximizing politician-bureaucrat.[6] The model here is in several respects similar to the "monopoly" or "noncooperative" state theories developed by earlier continental writers, notably some of the Italian fiscal theorists.[7] These monopoly-state conceptions, however, assume that the governmental powers have emerged from some coercive seizure of the state apparatus at some period in history. By contrast, in our model government is voluntarily established by general agreement in a constitutional contract among potential taxpayers–beneficiaries.[8] The problem faced by persons in such a setting involves securing and insuring the benefits of governmentally provided goods and services (including the enforcement of contracts and claims to property titles, without which market trading would hardly be feasible), while avoiding vulnerability to exploitation by the Leviathan-like institutions that may be uncontrollable once they are established.

Many different types of constitutionally derived constraints are conceivable, and these need not be mutually exclusive. Here we focus on the subset embodied in the tax system. In doing so, however, we assume that there exist some effective constraints on the disposition of tax revenues. Specifically, we assume that the uses of tax revenues must include the financing of at least some goods and services that cannot be provided noncollectively. Without this assumption, as previously noted with reference to Wicksell's statement, a constitutional contract establishing a coercive tax-levying authority could not be assumed to have emerged.

Our stylized constitutional setting is characterized by the further, and familiar, assumption that each person has well-defined predictions about the aggregate level and the distribution of incomes and consumption patterns in all postconstitutional periods, but that he possesses no knowledge about his own future position within the distribution or about the characteristics of his own taste pattern. This general, nonindividualized, knowledge is sufficient for him to make some estimate, within broad limits, both of the "efficient" levels of budgetary outlay on public goods, and of the aggregate revenues to be obtained under alternative tax systems. Since the individual remains ignorant concerning his own predicted income or tastes, he cannot identify a cost share for himself under any particular tax system. He cannot, therefore, predict whether, in-period, he might prefer a larger or a smaller public-goods quantity than that which he predicts to be "efficient" for the whole community. Thus, each individual rationally prefers institutions that will generate the "efficient" quantity, $\bar{G}$, given an independent estimate of the costs of provision. The actual level of outlay on desired public goods and services is given by

$$(G) = \alpha \cdot R, \tag{1}$$

where α is the predicted proportion of tax revenue spent on the desired budgetary component, and R is aggregate tax revenue. Throughout this discussion, the value of α is taken to be exogenous, by which we mean that it is fixed by the operation of constraints other than those incorporated in the tax system.[9] As we have indicated, α is such that

$$1 > \alpha > 0. \tag{2}$$

Hence, the outlay on desired public goods and services is some direct function of total revenue raised, and the problem that the individual faces at the constitutional stage is to organize tax arrangements so that the revenue raised, when adjusted by α, will yield roughly the quantity of public goods and services estimated to be "efficient," at the given estimated net costs—costs that will, of course, be dependent on the value of α.

Thus, R will be chosen so that

$$\alpha \cdot R = \bar{G}. \tag{3}$$

The characteristic assumption of our Leviathan-type model is that, in each postconstitutional budgetary period, the government will attempt to maximize total revenue collections (and hence total spending), within the constitutionally appointed tax regime—that is,

$$R = R^*(b, r), \tag{4}$$

where R^* is the maximum revenue that can be raised from the tax regime, and is a function of b, the tax base, and r, the allowable rate structure. Formally, then, the problem facing the individual is to select b and r so that

$$R^*(b,r) = \frac{\bar{G}}{\alpha}. \tag{5}$$

What this implies in terms of the desired tax constitution is elaborated in ensuing sections.

2. Tax Base and Tax Rate Constraints in a Simple Model

Initially, we restrict the analysis to a single individual who is assumed to be exercising his constitutional choice between only two potential definitions of the tax base—the one fully "comprehensive," the other falling short of this. We relax these assumptions later, but at this stage the simplification is convenient. It is immaterial for our argument precisely what the noncomprehensive base is, and whether the tax is levied on the "uses" or the "sources" side (that is, whether it is an "income" or an "expenditure" tax). Let us suppose, however, that the noncomprehensive base is money income from labor effort in the market, and that the comprehensive base includes this money income and also the money equivalent of the individual's nonmarket production of valued end products; in other words, the comprehensive base is full income. The question we examine is whether the person would prefer a tax constitution that embodies the comprehensive base over the one that restricts the base to money income.[10]

The situation is depicted in figure 1. The indifference curves, labeled with i's, indicate the individual's preferences as between money-income earn-

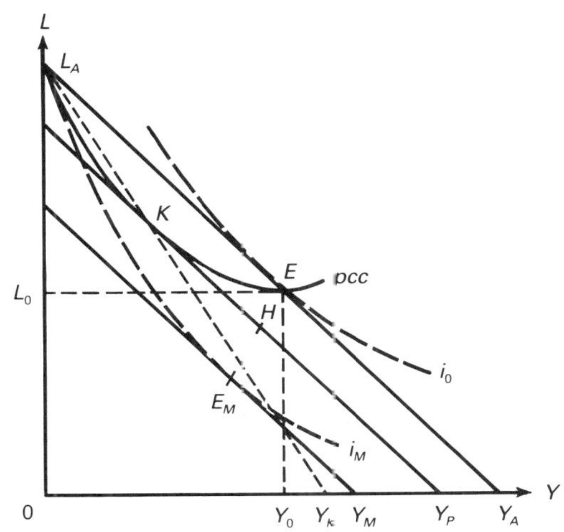

Fig. 1

ing activity Y, and, say, leisure activity L. These preferences exhibit the standard properties.[11] The pretax situation is characterized by a relative price between L and Y reflecting the productivity of income earning activity; the initial equilibrium is at $E(Y_0, L_0)$ on i_0.

Consider now the prospect that the individual would face here if the government should be granted access to the fully comprehensive tax base. In this event, the individual would be exploitable up to the full limits of his potential earning ability, over and above some minimal subsistence. Apart from this minimal limit, all of the "income equivalent," OY_A, is potentially available for governmental use. The government could levy a lump-sum tax that appropriated the individual's *maximum* potential earnings, beyond the subsistence level.[12]

Since it is inconceivable that anyone could ever anticipate an "efficient" public-private sector mix that would require all potential income above subsistence for governmental purposes, it seems clear that a potential taxpayer–beneficiary would *not* select the comprehensive tax base at the constitutional level if he predicts postconstitutional governmental behavior of the type that we have postulated. He will seek to impose constitutional constraints on the fisc, on the ability of the government to tax. He can do so, in our simple case, by allowing the government to levy an income tax only on the ordinary sources of earnings. This constraint, alone, will reduce the potential maximum revenue collections of government drastically—from OY_A to Y_MY_A in figure 1. Clearly, if the government imposes a tax on money income the revenue from which exceeds Y_MY_A, then the individual will be better off if he ceases to earn income at all; if he switches to L_A. If limited to the money-income base, the government can secure revenues up to this maximum limit, Y_MY_A, only by levying an "ideally" structured *regressive* tax, in which the rate for each level of Y is equal to the slope of i_m. This involves creeping down i_m to the maximum revenue equilibrium at E_m, allowing the taxpayer a minute slice of surplus to ensure only that the position E_m is actually preferred to L_A.

Recognizing this prospect, the taxpayer may wish to impose the further constitutional constraint that the income tax should not be regressive in its rate structure. This would clearly be the case if the money-income base, along with the predicted value for α and the revenue-maximizing regressive rate structures, should be predicted to generate outlays on desired public goods and services in excess of the efficient levels of provision. If, for example, the government should be required to stay within a rate structure that is at least *proportional*, it would be effectively confronted with a locus of potential equilibria along the individual's price-consumption curve for varying "prices" of Y, depicted by L_AKE in figure 1. The revenue-maximizing arrangement in this case occurs at the point where a line drawn parallel to L_AY_A is tangent to the price-consumption curve, as indicated by K, with the associated revenue-maximizing proportional rate of tax being, Y_kY_A/OY_A. The precise characteristics of this case, and the analytic resemblance to familiar results in price theory, can be isolated by appeal to the corresponding partial equilibrium diagram in figure 2.[13]

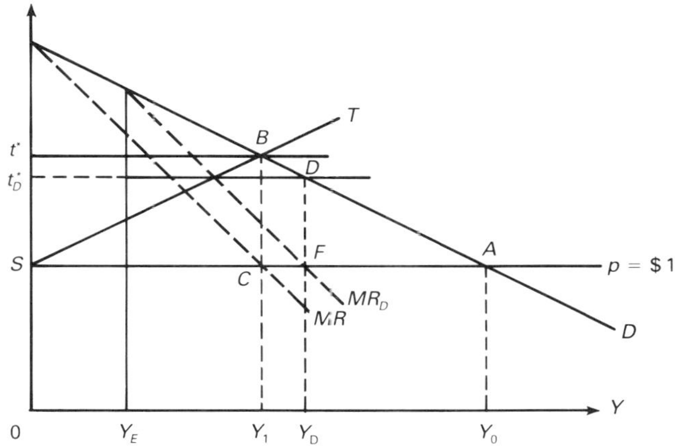

Fig. 2

The curve *DD* in figure 2. indicates the individual's demand for the income-yielding activity; this might be derived from a preference mapping exhibiting the properties depicted in figure 1. Confronted with the requirement that it must levy a proportional tax, what tax rate will the revenue-maximizing government impose? The question is obviously analogous to that asked of the monopolist who will seek to maximize profits, with the same answer. We derive a "marginal revenue" curve, *MR* in figure 2, and the maximum revenue is given where this cuts the horizontal dollar-price line (the marginal cost line), determining a post-tax equilibrium at Y_1.

This construction reveals the precise analogy between our model of postconstitutional governmental process and monopoly theory—in an analytic as well as a conceptual sense, our model is appropriately called a "monopoly theory government." The revenue-maximizing tax rate, t^*, can be derived as follows:

$$R = tY_1, \tag{4}$$

$$Y_0 - Y_1 = Y_0 \cdot \eta t, \text{ since } \eta = \frac{-\Delta Y}{Y_0} \Big/ \frac{\Delta P}{P}, \tag{6}$$

where R is government revenue; t is the proportional tax rate and equals $\Delta P/P$

$$\therefore R = tY_0(1 - \eta t), \tag{7}$$

$$\frac{\partial R}{\partial t} = Y_0(1 - 2\eta t). \tag{8}$$

Setting (8) at zero, we have

$$t^* = \frac{1}{2\eta}, \tag{9}$$

and, substituting t^* in (7), we have

$$R^* = \frac{Y_0}{4\eta} . \tag{10}$$

Hence, as we might expect, maximum revenue is directly related to the initial size of the taxable base, and inversely related to the value of the elasticity.

As we have indicated, the revenue raised from the given base under a *proportional* tax is less than that which might be raised from the same base under an ideally *regressive* rate structure. We are led to ask what might be the influence of a *progressive* rate structure here. The revenue-maximizing government will have no incentive to shift from the equilibrium proportional rate to any rate structure that embodies progression, since this latter would imply increasing rather than declining marginal rates of tax. The revenue effect can be demonstrated most easily by thinking of the simplest of all progressive rate structures, one that involves only two marginal rates, with the first rate being zero. Consider such a structure, sometimes called a *degressive* one, where income over some initial range to Y_E is wholly exempted from tax. With this additional constraint, the revenue-maximizing proportional rate on remaining units of income falls and total revenue collections fall correspondingly.

To show this, note that under a degressive structure,[16]

$$R = t(Y_1 - Y_E)$$

$$= tY_0\left[1 - \eta t - \frac{Y_E}{Y_0}\right] ,$$

$$\frac{\vartheta R}{\vartheta t} = Y_0\left[1 - 2\eta t - \frac{Y_E}{Y_0}\right] ,$$

and

$$t_D^* = \left(1 - \frac{Y_E}{Y_0}\right)\frac{1}{2\eta} \text{ which is } < \frac{1}{2\eta} , \tag{11}$$

and

$$R_D^* = \frac{(Y_0 - Y_E)^2}{4\eta Y_0} \text{ which is } < \frac{Y_0}{4\eta} . \tag{12}$$

In terms of figure 2 it is clear not only that the revenue-maximizing degressive structure postulated generates less total revenue than the revenue-maximizing proportional tax, but also that the excess burden is smaller. Under proportionality, the excess burden is measured in figure 2 by the area *ABC*. Under the postulated degressive structure, excess burden falls to *ADF*.

Not all forms of progression yield this result for the change in excess burden. For example, a linear progressive rate schedule (of the form shown by the line *ST* in figure 2) [15] will yield the revenue-maximizing *marginal* rate that is equal to the proportional revenue-maximizing rate, with the same posttax equilibrium at Y_1. Note that, in this case, the total revenue obtained under progression is a constant share of that which would be obtained under proportionality where the marginal rate levied at income Y_1 would be applied over the entire income range. Thus, under the rate structure, *ST*, total revenue raised under progression is one-half that raised under proportionality. But the excess burden in the two cases is identical.

It may be useful to summarize the basic argument of this section. We have observed that the constitutional decision-making calculus of the potential taxpayer–beneficiary, operating under an expectation of a Leviathan-like postconstitutional fiscal process, involves his opting for institutional devices that will limit the revenue-raising potential of the tax system. We have explored two ways that might accomplish this. One is by limiting the size of the tax base—increasing the comprehensiveness of the tax base will be, beyond some point, clearly undesirable. The other is by imposing a constitutional requirement that some degree of progressiveness be incorporated in any rate structure. This "defense of progression" is completely different from any to be found in normative tax theory. It stems both from the constitutional perspective within which our whole analysis is developed, and from the unconventional, but highly plausible, assumptions we have made about the predicted workings of the political process. The argument does *not* spring from assumed risk aversion on the part of individuals behind the veil of ignorance, from Rawlsian maximin theorems, or from the more familiar "vertical equity" norms.[16]

3. Maximum Revenue and Excess Burden

To this point, we have restricted analysis to the simple setting in which the individual chooses between two potential tax bases and among rate structures on these bases. Generally, however, the potential taxpayer at the constitutional stage will have the option of considering many possible base and rate structures, all of which might be estimated to raise roughly the desired level of revenue, G/α, when exploited to the maximum-revenue potential. Retaining the single-person perspective, is there any reason to expect a constitutional preference for any particular method?

Presumably, the potential taxpayer will prefer that arrangement from among the set that will minimize net efficiency loss or excess burden. We may focus initially on the proportional rate case, and assume that the "demand curves" are linear over relevant ranges. In this setting it is interesting to observe that when maximum revenue is obtained from a source, the excess burden is a fixed proportion of revenue raised. For,

$$\begin{aligned} W &= \tfrac{1}{2}t(Y_0 - Y_1) \\ &= \tfrac{1}{2}t(Y_0\eta t), \end{aligned} \tag{13}$$

where W is the excess burden or efficiency loss generated by the tax. Substituting t^* in (13), we have

$$W = \frac{Y_0}{8\eta} = \tfrac{1}{2}R^*. \tag{14}$$

Consequently, given the assumption of linear "demand schedules," any two bases which yield the same maximum revenue under proportional rate structures will involve identical excess burdens, independently of the size of the base or of the elasticity. Given proportionality, then, the maximum revenue potential becomes the dominant choice criterion—excess burden tends to become irrelevant.

Once we admit progression into the analysis, excess burden may once again assume a role. Suppose, for example, that the choice is to be made between a proportional tax on commodity (or income source) A, and a tax on commodity (or income source) B, that yields identical maximum revenue under a *linear progressive* tax schedule. In this case, the excess burden generated will be larger under the latter, and in the assumption of our geometrical model, will be exactly two times that in the former. This result stems from the fact that, under linear progression, maximum revenue and the corresponding excess burden are identical. Of course, not all forms of progression exhibit this property. Specifically, for the type of degressive structures analyzed in equations (11) and (12) the relation indicated in (14) holds. In this sense, a persuasive case can be made for degression over other types of progressivity. It is also clear that, with the relevant equal-yield comparison made (that based on maximum potential revenue), a proportional tax and a degressive tax are equivalent on strict efficiency or excess-burden grounds, while either tax is preferable to other forms of a progressive tax.

This result, which indicates that many progressive rate structures generate more excess burden than the equi-yield proportional tax, is not at variance with our conclusion earlier to the effect that a constitutional requirement of progression may be one way of insuring a restriction on the total level of governmental outlay through the limits imposed by the rate structure. We are simply observing here that, compared with equi-income reductions in the tax base, if these possibilities should exist, then progression may be an inefficient means of accomplishing this restriction.

Finally, it may be useful to make a technical comment on the methodology of tax analysis. One feature of the discussion in this section is our usage of one variety of an "equi-revenue" technique of comparison. These equi-revenue comparisons, however, involve separate base-rate combinations that yield the same *maximum* revenue. It is only within this stringently restricted subset of possible tax arrangements that we have permitted the application of the equal-revenue methodology, and that we have applied excess-burden criteria, appropriately derived from the constitutional perspective. Strictly speaking, even this limited use of the equi-revenue comparison is questionable, because *all* of the separate dimensions of tax selection (maximum revenue yield, excess burden, and such "equity" effects as intrude) are aspects of the same general constitutional choice. It seems clear, however, that given our model of postconstitutional political process maximum revenue potential will be the predominant issue in the selection of tax institutions.

4. One Among Many

So far our discussion has been cast in terms of a single individual's choice calculus. This need not be nearly so restrictive as it might appear, particularly since we have examined choice in a constitutional setting, where the chooser is not expected to know just what his own position will be in postconstitutional periods. Nonetheless, we have neglected the problems that arise when the individual recognizes that, regardless of what his own position will be, he will be one among many taxpayers, with differences among persons in both tax base and in preferences.

We may first consider whether or not our earlier results concerning tax base limitations will hold in this setting. We may look at a simple two-person illustration. In figure 3, we assume that the two persons, *A* and *B*, will earn an equal amount of money income and in the pretax or no-tax equilibrium, Y_0. (Recall that, under our constitutional-stage assumptions the individual will know only that the two persons *A* and *B* will have the characteristics depicted; he will not know which of the two positions he will, himself, occupy.) The persons are predicted to differ substantially, however, in their response to the imposition of a tax on the limited or money-income base, with leisure (or other valued end products) exempted from tax. The differential responsiveness is indicated by the slopes of the "demand curves" for money income, as shown by D_A and D_B.

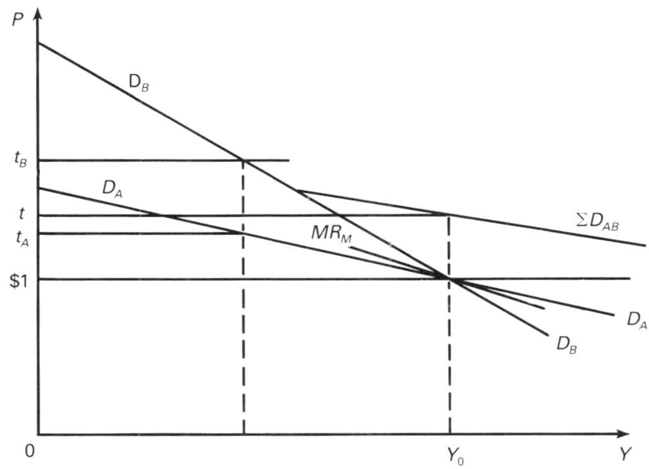

Fig. 3

The first point to be noted here is that so long as any responsiveness at all is predicted, the argument for the noncomprehensive base developed earlier holds without qualification. Each of the two persons whose preferences are depicted in figure 3 will be protected against the exploitation potential of government that would be present under full-income as opposed to money-income taxation.

Let us now examine the revenue-maximizing government's predicted tax behavior in this two-person situation. If the government could treat A and B separately and differentially, and if it could levy a proportional tax on each (but not a regressive tax), it would impose a tax rate of t_a on A and the higher rate, t_b, on B. Such differential treatment would clearly allow scope for the extraction of more revenue from the community than would be possible if the government were required to levy the *same* proportional rate on each person. The revenue-maximizing uniform rate, t, is determined in figure 3 where the "market" marginal revenue curve, MR_m, cuts the dollar price line, with "price" set at the intercept of the vertical drawn from this intersection and the aggregate "demand curve" ΣD. This rate is such that $t_a < t < t_b$. The fact that revenue collections under the revenue-maximizing discriminatory rate structure (t_a, t_b) exceed those under the uniform rate, t, suggests a further means of constitutionally restricting the revenue proclivities of Leviathan: by imposing the constraint that tax schedules be *uniform* over persons. Such an argument for *uniformity,* which is related to but different from the more familiar "horizontal equity" norm, has not, to our knowledge, been developed anywhere in normative tax theory.[17]

The construction in figure 3 can also be used to illustrate a proposition that seems at variance with that reached in models which assume institutional fixity. In the conventional framework, the behavior of individuals within the structure of given tax institutions is analyzed, and any attempt on the part of one person or group to avoid or to reduce tax payments, through recourse to nontaxable sources or uses of income, is interpreted as imposing an *external diseconomy* on less responsive taxpayers.[18] Behavior in reducing tax liability generates costs for others in the community by making higher rates or tax and/or lower rates of public spending necessary than would otherwise be required.

Consider the same issue in our constitutional framework. An individual seeks to limit the revenue potential of Leviathan, while remaining uncertain as to his own position. In this case, he is benefited by the knowledge that at least some taxpayers will be able to reduce tax liability by shifting to nontaxable sources (uses) of income. This may be shown easily in figure 3. Compare the revenue-maximizing uniform rate, t, with that rate which would be revenue-maximizing if the two taxpayers were predicted to be equally responsive in the manner indicated by D_b. The uniform rate would, of course, rise to t_b, with a higher revenue potential. To the extent, therefore, that a person at the constitutional-choice level can predict that some members of the set of taxpayers will be able to shift to nontaxable sources (uses) in postconstitutional periods, his concern about the exploitative possibilities of Leviathan is correspondingly reduced.

Finally, we want to consider whether or not our earlier results concerning the relationship between progression and maximum revenue hold in the many-person setting. It is perhaps intuitively appealing to suggest that the results might not hold, since if low-income persons should have particularly high elasticities of demand for leisure, it seems as if it might be revenue-maximizing to levy lower rates of tax on their incomes while, at the same time, levying higher rates on incomes above such limits. Progression offers one means of making this sort of discrimination, while preserving uniformity.

Once more we begin with the simple two-person case, and for simplicity suppose that for any positive tax rate individual B has higher income than individual A. Under the uniform-schedule restriction, will progression always yield less revenue than proportionality? We may answer this question by examining the revenue-maximizing uniform rate schedule in our two-person case. Only if this schedule is progressive will proportionality raise less revenue than progression. To check this, let us suppose that the tax rate, t_a, is imposed on all incomes over the range from zero to Y_a^1, and rate t_b on all additional income. In this case, total revenue, R, is given by:

$$R = 2t_a Y_a^1 + t_b(Y_b^1 - Y_a^1), \tag{16}$$

where Y_i^1 is individual i's equilibrium income in the presence of taxation. Now we use the result

$$Y_i^1 = Y_i^0(1-\eta_i t_i) \text{ for } i = a\ b, \tag{17}$$

where Y_i^0 is individual i's equilibrium income in the absence of taxation, and η_i is i's elasticity of demand over the range Y_i^0 to Y_i^1, and define γ so that

$$\gamma = \frac{Y_b^0}{Y_a^0}, \tag{18}$$

to obtain

$$R = Y_a^0[2t_a(1-\eta_a t_a)+yt_b(1-\eta_b t_b)-t_b(1-\eta_a t_a)]. \tag{19}$$

By maximizing R with respect to t_a and t_b, we determine $\hat{t}_a$ *and* $\hat{t}_b$ and can examine the ratio

$$\frac{\hat{t}_a}{\hat{t}_b} = \frac{4\gamma\eta_b + \eta_a(\gamma - 1)}{4\eta_a(\gamma - 1) + 2\eta_a}. \tag{20}$$

Clearly, the revenue-maximizing rate structure is progressive only if (19) is less than unity in value; or if

$$\eta_b < \frac{\eta_a(3\gamma - 1)}{4\gamma} . \tag{21}$$

Since $\gamma \geqq 1$, we know that

$$\tfrac{1}{2} < \frac{3\gamma - 1}{4\gamma} < \tfrac{3}{4}. \tag{22}$$

Thus, if there were no particular reason to assume that high-income receivers have lower demand elasticities than low-income receivers, we would expect (20) to be violated. In this case, the conclusion derived in our one-person model would carry over: progression would involve a revenue loss. But, it is also quite clear that (20) may hold; and in the case where η_a is significantly larger than η_b (by no means implausible), then the "right" degree of progression *could* generate more revenue than the revenue-maximizing proportional rate. The "right" degree of progression (from the revenue-maximizing government's perspective) does not, however, seem likely to be large. For example, it can be shown that the maximum revenue derived from linear progression of the type examined above (i.e., a rate schedule of the form $m = \beta \cdot Y^1$) is always less than that generated by the maximum revenue proportional structure.[19]

5. Tax Limits and Tax Reform

As our analysis has suggested, the tax base and tax rate constraints imposed on governments at the constitutional level should, ideally, be such as to allow for the financing of some roughly efficient bundle of public goods and services. The danger of allowing governments access to revenue-raising instruments that will generate budgets in excess of these requirements is central to our whole model. We should, however, recognize that errors can be made in the opposing direction, that the constitutional tax constraints might, through time, prove to be overly restrictive. In this case, postconstitutional pressures will surely arise for escape through constitutional-style adjustments designed to widen the bases and to allow for more flexible rate structures, to move generally from specificity toward comprehensiveness. Empirically, it will always be difficult to distinguish between genuine constituency demands for a relaxation of such tax constraints, and the ever-present demands of the revenue-seeking politicians-bureaucrats. For the latter group, and their spokesmen, efforts will tend to be directed toward "loophole closing," toward increasing the number of sources that may be taxed. "Tax reform" advocacy on the part of the "bureaucratic establishment" will tend to be centered on "tax base erosion." Indeed one indirect test of the empirical validity of our model of political process lies in the observed lack of reformist concern about relative rates of tax within existing tax law limits. This offers some evidence to the effect that the revenue limits are indeed being approached.

In the discussion of proposed tax base changes the attitude of the traditional normative tax theorist and the members of the taxpaying public perhaps differ more sharply than anywhere else. Our analysis is helpful in "explaining" the attitudes of the taxpayers. For example, they are likely to react negatively and emphatically to proposals to move toward taxation on the basis of full income, as, for example, by including the imputed rental values of owned residences in the base for the personal income tax. The normative tax theorist, who advocates such inclusion always from reasoning based on equal-yield comparisons, responds to the taxpayers by arguing that overall rates of tax may be lowered simultaneously with the proposed widening of the base. But the taxpayers may be implicitly, but correctly, rejecting the equal-yield postulate, in their predictions that *any* widening of the tax base must open up further taxing possibilities for a revenue-seeking government.

Illustrations might easily be drawn from recent American fiscal experience. For example, in the early 1960s, a proposal was widely discussed which sought to replace part of the corporation income tax with a broad-based value-added tax. The proposal was quickly rejected, no doubt in part for the reasons suggested: it may have been predicted that, ultimately, the rates of value-added tax would reach heights that would greatly exceed those required to recover revenue forgone under the corporate income tax. In fact, of course, almost any widely advocated tax change tends to be justified in terms of its greater "efficiency" or its greater fairness springing from the extension of the tax base. And as our analysis indicates, if our perception of postconstitutional political processes bears any relation to reality at all, it is precisely on such grounds that the change should be rejected!

We have, in broad and general terms, examined the basic issue of tax-base comprehensiveness in a constitutional-choice perspective, as opposed to the standard economists' perspective which is limited to single-period alternatives informed by familiar in-period efficiency criteria. We should emphasize, however, that our analysis does not involve a rejection of the efficiency norm, as properly understood. The rational person, who tried to predict his own position as a future taxpayer and as a beneficiary of public goods and services, will try to carry out some efficiency-like calculus in arriving at his choices among fiscal institutions at the constitutional stage, in the prediction that these institutions, once chosen, will remain as quasi-permanent features of the economic-political environment. As our analysis indicates, what is efficient at this level of choice may not be coincident with those institutions that seem to be efficient in the more restricted choice models usually discussed by fiscal theorists.

Our results depend critically on the assumed predictions about the properties of the political process. We have introduced a model of government as a revenue maximizer limited by the tax constraints imposed in the constitution. This model is not to be confused with any one of the following models: the all-powerful government, subject to no constitutional constraints whatever; the benevolent and omniscient government, which provides the ideally efficient in-period quantities of public goods and "prices" these efficiently; the majority-rule democracy that makes fiscal decisions about public goods supply reflecting the preferences of the median voter—at least as traditionally conceived.

Each one of these alternative models of government (along with other variants not listed), as well as the one we have introduced in this paper, can be used to "explain" certain features of the institutional reality that we observe. Our claim is limited; the analysis based on the constitutionally constrained but revenue-maximizing government seems congruous with some fiscal institutions in existence that do command deference as "constitutional" elements, while at the same time the analysis seems consistent with many public, as opposed to academic, attitudes toward central issues in tax reform.

To the extent that our analysis does succeed in "explaining" both the institutions in existence and prevailing attitudes toward changes in these institutions, the contribution is positive. We should emphasize, however, that we are not primarily concerned with drawing a contrast between the "what is" of fiscal reality and the "what ought to be" that is contained in the traditional normative discussions of tax reform. Our analysis may well have a higher degree of positive explanatory content than the familiar alternatives. But our discussion is grounded squarely on a normative model of constitutional decision making. Tax-base comprehensiveness is a reform objective that is almost never questioned in the traditional treatments. This paper suggests, first, that tax-base comprehensiveness may be rejected in a normative constitutional-choice calculus under certain political assumptions, and secondly, that elements of the observed fiscal structure may well reflect this normative framework.

NOTES

We are grateful to members of the Public Choice Seminar at Virginia Polytechnic Institute, and in particular our colleague, E. G. West, for helpful comments on an earlier version.

1. In the limit, we may assume that the individual is in some Rawlsian "original position" and behind the "veil of ignorance." (John Rawls, *A Theory of Justice* [Cambridge: Harvard University Press, 1971].) We do not need to impose such rigid requirements, however, for the constitutional setting to be relevant. Somewhat more plausibly, we may assume only that the individual is highly uncertain about his own future position. Cf. James M. Buchanan and Gordon Tullock, *The Calculus of Consent* (Ann Arbor: University of Michigan Press, 1962).
2. We would include under this rubric the recent "optimal taxation" literature, virtually all of which is explicitly set in this framework. For a useful summary, see David F. Bradford and Harvey S. Rosen, "The Optimal Taxation of Commodities and Income," *American Economic Review* 66 (May 1976): 94–101.
3. Notably by James M. Buchanan in his book, *Public Finance in Democratic Process* (Chapel Hill: University of North Carolina Press, 1967). The relationship is implicit in Knut Wicksell's whole analytical framework. See Knut Wicksell, *Finanztheoretische Untersuchungen* (Jena: Gustav Fischer, 1896).

4. Buchanan and Tullock, *The Calculus of Consent.*
5. One such possibility is that of explicit constitutional limits on the proportion of national product available for public use (or on maximum rates of tax)—the national analogue of the recent tax limitations proposals in California and Michigan. It is worth noting in passing, that restrictions on maximum rates would tend to cause Leviathan to aim at comprehensiveness, which restrictions on revenue as a proportion of GNP would not do. In so far as comprehensiveness is viewed as desirable in such a context, this might be seen as suggesting a case for rate restrictions rather than revenue restrictions. Because such policy options lie outside the range of those typically available in the standard tax reform exercise, we do not focus on them here. The ensuing discussion is conducted on the (practically relevant) assumption that such explicit rate and/or revenue constraints are not operative. (Of course, restrictions on nontax means of securing bureaucratic surplus (use of laws, commandeering without compensation, etc.) would be required, both in the case of tax liability and in our discussion, to ensure that the fiscal constraints are operative.)
6. There are evident similarities between our model and that developed by William Niskanen. See his *Bureaucracy and Representative Government* (Chicago: Aldine, 1971).

   We should note that the assumption of the revenue-maximizing politician is not inconsistent with the assumption that the politician is constrained by the political process. In the absence of effective constraints on the domain of public spending, or on the government's ability to redistribute private goods among voters, majoritarian democracy may simply involve "maximum" transfers from minority to majority, along with or independently of the provision of genuinely public goods. Our discussion is, however, *phrased* largely in terms of a "monopoly" government in which revenue maximization arises from the utility maximization of the partially unconstrained politician-bureaucrat rather than from the democratic political process itself.
7. For a summary of the Italian contributions, see James M. Buchanan, *Fiscal Theory and Political Economy* (Chapel Hill: University of North Carolina Press, 1960), especially pp. 24–74.
8. It is perhaps necessary to add the comment that the relevance of our analysis does *not* critically depend on whether or not governments have been, in fact, established in such a manner. The object of the contractarian exercise is to develop acceptable criteria for normative evaluation.

   In this respect, the model resembles that which is familiar to economists in their analysis of the granting of franchises to monopoly enterprises.
9. Interesting questions arise if we allow the revenue yield to vary with α. In particular, there is the possibility of choosing tax institutions so as to constrain the disposition of revenues as well as the aggregate level. These are issues which we take up in a subsequent article.
10. The basic conclusions hold equally for the case in which full "neutrality" is precluded, and the choice must be made between the narrower base and the "second-best" alternative, in which different goods are taxed at different rates according to their complement-substitute relationships with leisure (the question of interest in most of the recent "optimal taxation" literature). Our argument is thus equally with "optimal tax" and "comprehensiveness" proponents.
11. By the assumptions of our model, the individual cannot predict his precise preference pattern as between money-income–earning and alternative activity in

postconstitutional periods. All that is required for our analysis here is that these preferences are predicted to be standard.

12. It should perhaps be emphasized that the "comprehensive" *tax* is levied on the income side only: the surplus which accrues to the bureaucrat-politician, the excess of revenue collections over public spending (as distinct from the bureaucrat's *income*, more narrowly conceived), is assumed to lie outside the coverage of the tax system. This assumption can be rationalized in a variety of ways, depending on the particular conception of Leviathan that one adopts. In the simple conception of "Leviathan" as the ruling class or monarch, the assumption is tantamount to allowing the king not to pay taxes. In a dominant majority conception, the comprehensive tax may be presumed to fall on all income, but not to fall on the special benefits, transfers, etc., that accrue to the majority coalition as a result of disbursement of the total revenue.

13. The construction in figure 1 can be used to show how the constitutional-choice setting under our political assumptions transforms the familiar excess-burden argument in favor of the general or comprehensive-base tax. A solution at point K, in the neoclassical argument, is demonstrated to be inferior to that which might be attained with a comprehensive-base or general tax that will yield the *same* revenue, producing an ideal solution at some point like H in figure 1. This argument presumes, however, that the government once empowered to levy the general or comprehensive-base tax will, in fact, restrict its attempts to raise revenue to the collections dictated by the equi-yield comparison.

The partial equilibrium version, based on the Marshallian demand curve construction, can be used to illustrate the revenue-maximizing regressive structure, but by virtue of income effects will indicate a different rate structure than that derived from i_m. For similar reasons, the area under the demand curve does not accurately reflect consumer surplus; nor does the standard welfare triangle accurately reflect the welfare loss, or at least will do so only when the income-consumption curve E_mHE in figure 1 is a horizontal line. In what follows, we set such problems aside as being of no particular relevance to our discussion.

14. A diagrammatic derivation of this result can be indicated by drawing a new MR curve, MR_D, over the range where the nonzero proportional rate is to be applied—as in figure 2, with the maximum revenue rate being t^*_d.

15. That is, one in which the marginal tax rate, m, is given by $m = \beta Y^1(m)$, where Y^1 is equilibrium income in the presence of tax and β is some constant.

16. The existence of these is not inconsistent with our model. Constitutional preferences for progression as such may exist, and will merely complement the arguments posited here.

17. It is interesting to note that in this model no constitutional rationalization for "horizontal equity" as traditionally conceived emerges. A Rawlsian maximin rule, or generalized risk aversion, might generate a case for reducing the expected variance of the posttax, postexpenditure income distribution in postconstitutional periods, but neither involves a specific, independent desire to tax those with identical pretax incomes identically. By contrast, in the more familiar model of constitutional choice in which the median voter's preference is decisive at the postconstitutional level, horizontal equity norms may be desired as a means of limiting distortions in public goods supply. A tax rule which levies burdens only on a small proportion of the population could be expected to generate levels of public goods supply which are significantly different from the optimum. In our

model, however, the median voter is essentially irrelevant and horizontal equity norms are simply subsumed by "vertical equity" ones.

18. For an explicit discussion in such an externality setting, see James M. Buchanan, "Externality in Tax Response," *Southern Economic Journal* 33 (July 1966): 35–42.
19. This essay is restricted to an analysis of the opportunities of imposing limits on the revenue-collecting potential of Leviathan through constitutional constraints on tax bases and tax rates. This would not, of course, be the only objective of an ideal "fiscal constitution," even if we remain within tax-side questions. To the extent that Rawlsian-like precepts of justice enter into the constitutional calculus, or even the more utilitarian motives of insurance and/or protection, a requirement that general public goods be financed at least partially by the imposition of progressive income taxes may emerge from conceptual agreement among all parties. In this context, our analysis may be viewed as complementary through its implication that progression may, independently, impose its own revenue limits.

Towards a Theory of Yes-No Voting

Roger L. Faith and James M. Buchanan

The formal theory of majority rule voting has dealt almost entirely with the unique selection of a single candidate(s) or motion(s) from a set of alternatives greater than two. The analysis presumes that there is only a single group or collective decision to be made, a single "election," or a single "proposition."[1] This orthodox conceptual setting for collective choice is necessary to generate the possibility of the cyclically rotating, and hence disequilibrium, set of outcomes on the one hand and for the median-voter–dominated equilibrium outcome on the other. If the number of alternatives in the choice set is limited to two, simple majority rule voting yields unambiguous results provided only that we assume an odd number of voters with each voter assumed to have strictly ordered preferences. In the orthodox voting model setting, few problems of analytical interest seem to arise in the single pairwise choice between two alternatives, for example, between approval and disapproval of a proposition.

When the voting population is presented with a whole set of independent propositions, however, each one of which is to be resolved by simple "yes-no," "up-down," or "approve-disapprove" majority voting, questions of considerable analytical interest do arise. To our knowledge no one has discussed or investigated the analogues and contrasts between yes-no voting and the conventional, multi-alternative, majority rule voting. The relative neglect of the properties of yes-no voting under majority rule is itself puzzling since many real-world collective choice institutions formally operate in this way. Examples that come to mind include zoning boards, referenda, and initiatives; in several states judges are reelected on a yes-no basis.

The Basic Model

The institutional setting we wish to analyze is one in which there are several propositions to be settled by simple majority rule. The propositions are characterized by dichotomous choice—yes or no—and counterproposals are not permitted.[2] The propositions are independent in the sense that none, some, or all may be approved as a result of the voting process. There is no technological or consumptive complementarity or mutual exclusivity among propositions. With respect to voters, we assume they vote without strategic considerations. Vote trading or other mechanisms by which differences in preference intensities are resolved are precluded here. Each voter makes his or

First published in *Public Choice* 37, no. 2 (1981): 231–45.

her own subjective evaluation of each proposition being voted upon. Note that this assumption does not preclude representation, where an individual voter acts as an agent or "representative" of some constituency or even for some special interest group.

For purposes of exposition let us initially consider a board of zoning appeals made up of three members. Their job is to vote, yes or no, on separate requests for zoning variances. Several requests are allowed to accumulate before any voting occurs, say, before the regular monthly meeting of the board. Suppose that six different, and independent, requests for zoning variances are placed on the agenda facing the three-person board.

As a first step, assume that the individual evaluations (or subjective benefit-cost computations) of the different requests for variance are such that all board members ordinally rank the six requests in the same way. This does not mean that evaluations for all six proposals are identical over all three members in some cardinal sense—the precise benefit-cost ratios need not be equal. If such a level of "objectivity" could be reached, no decision problem would arise and all members would agree unanimously on the number and identity of proposals to be approved. Equivalence of ordinal rankings means only that if each member were asked to rank or array the six proposals according to his/her subjective estimates of benefits and costs, the three rankings would be the same. This assumption of equivalent ordinal ranking does not tell us anything about how many proposals are looked upon favorably or unfavorably by the individual voters. Two voters could have the same ranking with one voter approving all proposals while the other voter approves none.

A hypothetical set of ordinal rankings is illustrated in figure 1 where the rows represent the six requests, numbered 1 through 6, and the columns represent the three voters, *i*, *j*, and *k*. The vote of each member is either yes (Y) or no (N) on each request as it comes under consideration.

	i	*j*	*k*
1	Y	Y	Y
2	Y	Y	Y
3	Y	Y	N
4	Y	N	N
5	N	N	N
6	N	N	N

Fig. 1

Analogues and Contrasts to Conventional Majority-Rule Voting Models

The three board members, illustrated in figure 1, differ in the number of requests approved. Member *i* votes yes on two-thirds of the requests, *j* votes yes on one-half of the requests, and *k* votes yes on only one-third of the requests. Stated alternatively, the three voters or board members differ along what we might term the "proclivity to affirm" or "yea-saying" dimension.[3] If the six proposals are generically equivalent, e.g., all requests for zoning variances are to allow the development of separate and unrelated entrepreneurial projects, the underlying dimension might be classified on some scale of optimism-pessimism about the potential productivity of the projects. For other kinds of proposals, the underlying dimension might fall along ideological lines such as "liberal-conservative." Member *i* tends to evaluate benefits highly and costs minimally, while member *k* estimates costs highly and benefits minimally. Member *j* falls somewhere in between.

Under majority rule voting, requests 1, 2, and 3 will be approved while requests 4 through 6 will fail to secure the requisite majority of yes votes. This set of outcomes, not coincidentally, is precisely that set of outcomes desired by member *j*. In a very real sense, *j*'s decision-making status is the same as that of the median voter in conventional voting models where a single alternative is to be selected from a set of mutually exclusive alternatives and where individual preferences are single-peaked. In yes-no voting the analogue to the single-peakedness is the equivalence of the ordinal rankings of the separate propositions across all voters. The board member whose position is median on the "proclivity to affirm" dimension tends to dominate the results. The difference between this median voter and the conventional one is that here *median* is not defined with reference to the evaluation of a set of separate mutually exclusive alternatives from which one is to be selected. Rather *median* is defined with respect to the relative frequency of favorable votes cast in a set of independent proposals. The relationship between the median-voter construction in conventional models and that introduced here can be illustrated by a modification of our example. Consider a school board facing separate proposals for spending on six new schools, each costing $1 million. Voter *i*, in our construction, will approve four such proposals, voter *j* three, and voter *k* two. But note that this example might be translated into a single-election, conventional model by introducing the total budget dimension, in which case voter *j*, who prefers the $3 million outlay, will dominate the result.

It is, however, highly restrictive to assume that the ordinal rankings of the separate projects are identical over all board members, perhaps even more restrictive than to assume single-peakedness in preferences for all voters in the conventional majority rule voting models. Since the benefit-cost calculus must in any case be highly subjective, it seems apparent that the ordinal rankings would probably differ across voters or board members. How would this affect our median-voter result? As we shall see shortly, interpersonal differences in ordinal rankings need not make our "proclivity to affirm" dimension lose all of its descriptive or predictive value.

Under nonidentical ordinal rankings, the comparisons of our model of yes-no voting with the model of majority rule voting in the absence of single-peakedness are both interesting and complex. A characteristic feature of the latter voting model is the absence of any stable equilibrium. In contrast, our model of yes-no voting always yields a stable and unique voting outcome. Despite variation in the ordinal rankings across voters, one need only count up the number of yes votes cast on each proposal to see if a proposition is or is not approved. There will always be a definitive number of proposals approved; the voting process terminates. But will the median voter, the person who approves the median number of proposals, still dominate the proceedings? In general, the answer is negative. That is, there is an analogue between our model of yes-no voting on several issues and the cyclical majority model in terms of the loss of direct correspondence between the preferences of the median voter and the actual set of emergent outcomes.

Despite the fact that there will be a unique set of outcomes given *any* set of individual evaluations, one cannot predict, in advance, that these outcomes will correspond to those desired by the board member who is median in terms of our "proclivity to affirm" scale. However, the median voter does not lose all correspondence with the voting outcome, at least for a variety of different distributions of "proclivities for yea-saying" among voters. In the conventional model with a majority rule cycle, by contrast, the voter with median preferences is no more likely to get his preferences satisfied than any other voter within the range of cyclical results. Median preferences are, of course, hard to define in the cyclical or rotating majority case, but for the sake of comparison we may say that along some dimension measured independently of the voting process, the median voter is defined as the one whose *first preference* is median with respect to the first preference of other voters. As the voting outcomes rotate among the possible outcomes, no voter is more successful than others in the relevant set of achieving his/her most preferred outcome.

Yes-No Voting Power Indices

Having claimed that in yes-no voting the person with median "proclivities to affirm" has, in most cases, a greater likelihood of having his/her preferences satisfied than his/her counterparts, the question of interest is under what conditions is our claim valid? How likely is the median voter to have his/her preferences satisfied vis-à-vis other nonmedian voters?[4]

As mentioned above, given any pattern of ordinal rankings or propositions by the members of the voting group, a definitive set of outcomes results. And by association, some members' own preferences over the defined set of propositions correspond more closely with the set of outcomes than others. There is, of course, no reason to assume that the voter with the greater number of issues resolved in his/her favor is more "satisfied" in some utility sense. Such an implication would, of course, require an assumption about the intensities and interpersonal comparabilities of individual preferences.

We can, however, in some expected sense identify that voter who will have the greatest number of issues resolved in accord with his/her own preferences. (We shall, largely for purposes of expositional economy, refer to the relative positions of voters along such an "ability to get preferences satisfied" scale as "power," but the restricted meaning of this term should be kept in mind.) Consider again the example illustrated in figure 1. In order to ascertain voter *i*'s chance of having his/her way on each of the six issues, we assume, without loss of generality, that the six issues are numbered in accordance with *i*'s subjective benefit-cost ratios with issues 1 through 4 having benefit-cost ratios greater than one and issues 5 and 6 ratios less than one. We do not specify the ordinal rankings for voters *j* and *k,* but we retain the "proclivity to affirm" parameters for these two voters at one-half and one-third. Given any conceivable evaluation of the propositions by voters *j* and *k,* the probability of any given proposal securing majority approval *given that* i *votes yes* is .67. The probability of a given issue not passing *given that* i *votes no* is .83.[5] The *power index* for voter *i* can now be defined as the number of times *i* votes yes multiplied by the probability of majority approval plus the number of times *i* votes no multiplied by the probability of majority disapproval. Hence, in the current example the power index for *i* is $(4 \times .67) + (2 \times .83) = 4.34$. Similar calculations for voters *j* and *k* yield power indices of 4.67 and 4.34 respectively. Note that, as claimed earlier, voter *j,* the person with the median proclivity to approve propositions, has the highest power index.[6]

The most straightforward interpretation of the power index is that it measures the expected number of propositions to be resolved in a particular voter's favor. That is, over repeated votes taken on the same set of six propositions by the same three voters with fixed preferences, voters *i, j* and *k* can expect to have 4.34, 4.67, and 4.34 propositions, respectively, resolved in accord with their preferences. In order to compare and contrast indices when the number of proposals vary, we can "normalize" by dividing the power indices by the number of propositions yielding power indices of .72, .78, and .72 respectively. These numbers are interpreted as the expected fraction of group decisions resolved in the three voters' respective favors.

To see how the power index changes and the effect on the median voter's influence when the parameters of the model change we shall initially hold the number of voters fixed at three. Let N equal the number of propositions under consideration, and V_i, V_j and V_k equal the number of yes votes that voters *i, j,* and *k,* respectively, are expected to cast when presented with N independent propositions. Thus, V_i/N equals the probability of voter *i* voting yes on a given proposal. Further, assume that $V_i > V_j > V_k$. Generalizing the formulation presented above for the simple case, the power indices (PI) of the three voters can be written:

$$PI(i) = \frac{1}{N}[V_iV_j + V_iV_k - V_jV_k + N(N - V_i)]$$

$$PI(j) = \frac{1}{N}[V_iV_j + V_jV_k - V_iV_k + N(N - V_j)] \qquad (1)$$

$$PI(k) = \frac{1}{N}[V_iV_k + V_jV_k - V_iV_j - N(N - V_k)].$$

It follows that:

$$PI(j) - PI(k) = (2V_i - N)(V_j - V_k)/N \tag{2}$$

and that given $V_i > V_j > V_k$,

$$PI(j) - PI(k)\{\gtreqless\}0 \text{ if } V_i\{\gtreqless\}N/2. \tag{3}$$

Further, it follows that:

$$PI(j) - PI(i)\{\gtreqless\}0 \text{ if } V_k\{\gtreqless\}N/2. \tag{4}$$

From conditions (3) and (4) we see that the median voter has the highest power index if

$$\frac{V_i}{N} > \frac{1}{2} > \frac{V_k}{N}.^7 \tag{5}$$

Thus, in the three-voter case, the power of the median voter depends solely on the "proclivities to affirm" of the two extreme voters. The example illustrated in figure 1 where $V_i/N = .67$ and $V_k/N = .33$ satisfies the above condition and, as we saw, voter j has the highest power index. It also follows from (3) and (4) that if either of the inequalities in (5) is an equality the median voter shares the highest power index with that voter whose "proclivity to affirm" is not equal to one-half. For example, if $V_i = 3$, $V_j = 2$, and $V_k = 1$, implying that $V_i/N = \frac{1}{2}$, the power indices of i, j, and k are 4.16, 4.83, and 4.83, respectively; while if $V_i = 5$, $V_j = 4$, and $V_k = 3$, implying that $V_k/N = \frac{1}{2}$, the power indices are 4.83, 4.83, and 4.16 respectively. Finally, it follows from (3) and (4) that if all voters have "proclivities to affirm" greater (less) than one-half, the voter with the highest (lowest) proclivity has the highest power index. These relationships hold regardless of the absolute difference between any two voters' proclivity to "yea-say."

Before illustrating the effect of adding more voters, some simple comparative statics can be derived for voter i from conditions (1).[8] For greater generality we make no assumptions regarding the relative magnitudes of V_i, V_j and V_k.

$$\frac{\Delta PI(i)}{\Delta V_i} = \frac{V_j}{N} + \frac{V_k}{N} - 1, \tag{6}$$

$$\frac{\Delta PI(i)}{\Delta V_j} = \frac{V_i}{N} - \frac{V_k}{N}, \tag{7}$$

$$\frac{\Delta PI(i)}{\Delta N} = \frac{V_jV_k - V_i(V_j + V_k)}{N^2 + N} - 1 \tag{8}$$

Equation (6) states an increase in one's own "proclivity to affirm" will increase one's power index if the sum of the affirming proclivities of the remaining voters is greater than one and contrariwise. If the sum of the other two voters' proclivities to affirm is greater than one, then, on average, these voters prefer that a proposal will pass. Thus, an increase in *i*'s desire to see more propositions passed will be reinforced with an expectation of favorable votes from the remaining voters, increasing *i*'s power index. On the other hand if the voters on average tend to disapprove propositions, an increase in voter *i*'s approval proclivity is a move away from the majority position and hence will reduce his power index. Equation (7) states that an increase in the "proclivity to affirm" of another voter increases (decreases) *i*'s power index if the remaining voter is less (more) likely to vote affirmatively than the voter *i*. If voter *i* is more prone to voting yes than voter *k*, then *i*'s power index will rise with an increase in *j*'s proclivity to affirm which reinforces *i*'s preferences relative to *k*'s. If $V_k > V_i$ then an increase in V_j reinforces voter *k*'s preferences relative to *i*'s, and *i*'s power index will fall. Finally, equation (8) states that an increase in the number of propositions increases or decreases one's power index depending upon the distribution of proclivities among the three voters.

Consider now an increase in the number of voters from three to five. The power index for each of the five voters is calculated in a similar manner as for three voters. In this expanded case, how does the median voter's power index compare to that of the remaining four voters?

For the sake of brevity, let us compare the median voter, voter *k* in the five-voter model, with the two voters who tend to be less prone to vote yes than *k*, voters *l* and *m*. In table 1, we illustrate a hypothetical case of five voters voting on ten propositions, their respective voting proclivities and resulting power indices. Note that once again the median voter is, in one sense, more "powerful," and because of the symmetric distribution of probabilities, the pairwise extreme voters on either side of the median voter have identical indices. Letting V_i, V_j, V_k, V_l, and V_m represent the expected number of yes votes to be cast on a set of *N* propositions for voters *i, j, k, l,* and *m* respectively, it follows that:

$$PI(k)\{\gtreqless\}PI(l) \text{ if } 2N(V_iV_j + V_lV_m + V_jV_m)\{\gtreqless\}N^3 + 4V_iV_jV_m, \tag{9}$$

and

$$\mathrm{PI}(k)\{\gtreqless\}PI(m) \text{ if } 2N(V_iV_j + V_iV_l + V_jV_l)\{\gtreqless\}N^3 + 4V_iV_jV_m, \tag{10}$$

A little arithmetic reveals some interesting properties. Suppose that voter *m* approves no proposition so that $V_m = 0$. Conditions (9) and (10) reduce to:

TABLE 1. Power Indices—5 Voters and 10 Propositions

Voter	Proclivity to Vote Yes	Power Index
i	.7	6.59
j	.6	6.89
k	.5	7.01
l	.4	6.89
m	.3	6.59

$$PI(k)\{\gtreqless\}PI(l) \text{ if } \frac{V_iV_j}{N^2}\{\gtreqless\}\tfrac{1}{2}, \tag{11}$$

and

$$PI(k)\{\gtreqless\}PI(m) \text{ if } \frac{V_iV_j}{N^2}\{\gtreqless\}\tfrac{1}{2} - \frac{V_l(V_i + V_j)}{N^2} + \frac{2V_iV_jV_l}{N^3}. \tag{12}$$

Assuming $V_i > V_j > V_k > V_l > V_m$, condition (11) says that the median voter's power index is greater than that of the relative negativist (voter l, as opposed to extreme negativist, voter m) if and only if the *product* of the relative and extreme affirmist's proclivities to affirm is greater than one-half. Consider the maximum value V_i can undertake, 10 (as there are only ten propositions). Then V_j must equal 6 or greater to give voter k, the median, a greater power index than l. This also implies via condition (12) that if $V_l = 0$ voter k dominates voter m. This result follows from our previous analysis of the three-voter case. If $V_i = 10$ and $V_m = 0$, then i and m cancel each other out leaving only three voters to determine the outcome.[9] In this case, voter j becomes the extreme affirmist and by our earlier result for three voters, the now-median voter dominates if V_j is greater than $N/2$, which is true when $V_j = 6$. Now suppose that $V_l = 1$ while $V_m = 0$. Condition (12) says if V_i assumes its maximum value, 10, V_j need only be equal to 5 for voter k to dominate voter m. Again, we can interpret this as saying voters i and m pair off. However, now that voter l is slightly more prone to vote yes, his affirming counterpart, voter j, need not be as affirmative in order for the median to have the highest power index. Hence, whether the median will have the highest power index depends on the *aggregate* "proclivity to vote yes" of the pairs of voters on either side of the median voter. For example, in the case where $V_m = 0$ and $V_l = 0$ any sum of expected yes votes equal to or greater than 16 will give voter k the most power. When $V_l = 1$, this sum drops to 15. Finally, as in the case of three voters, if all voters have a probability of voting yes (no) less than .5, then the absolute negativist (affirmist) dominates. These properties are illustrated in figure 2 where power indices for various distributions of voting proclivities are displayed. It should be obvious that if the

						i	*j*	*k*	*l*	*m*
Distribution of	10	4	2	1	0	1.24	4.89	8.59	8.78*	8.76
expected number	10	5	2	1	0	1.49	4.89	8.69*	8.69*	8.49
of yes votes	10	5	3	1	0	1.99	6.69	8.29*	8.29*	7.99
for voters *i, j,*	10	6	2	1	0	1.76	4.89	8.79*	8.59*	8.24
k, l, m	9	7	2	1	0	2.80	4.72	8.82*	8.56	8.16
	8	8	2	1	0	3.79	3.79	8.83*	8.55	8.14
	4	3	2	1	0	6.36	7.32	8.24	8.97	9.57*
	5	4	3	2	1	6.07	6.88	7.58	8.08	8.38*
	7	6	5	4	3	6.29	6.90	7.01*	6.90	6.29
	9	7	5	3	1	5.71	6.91	7.56*	6.91	5.71

Fig. 2. Power indices—5 voters and 10 propositions. Asterisk indicates highest power index for a given distribution.

orders of the distributions are reversed, the power indices will be in reverse order.

Generalized Information

Suppose that there is no information about individual proclivities to vote yes but there is general information about the whole group of voters. That is, only the proclivity of the *population* of voters to vote yes on a given proposition is known. Obviously, the notion of a particular voter with the median proclivity to vote yes vanishes. Some properties of the voting outcomes may, however, still be examined under these assumptions. For example, let there be a committee of seven voters casting 'yes' or 'no' votes on five independent proposals. Further, assume that the population proclivity to affirm is known, historically perhaps, to be .6 for the group. The probability of any proposal passing is the sum of the probabilities of getting exactly four yes votes, exactly five yes votes, exactly six yes votes, and exactly seven yes votes.[10] In the current example, this totals to .727. Notice the difference obtained here. The proportion of yes votes in the population over *all* issues in the set is .6. These votes, for lack of sufficient reason, can be thought of as randomly distributed across the five voters and the five issues. The probability that any *given issue* will obtain a majority exceeds the population probability that a *given vote* will be yes.

Table 2 shows probabilities of passage of a single proposition for alternative values of number of propositions to be voted on and number of voters when the general proclivity to vote yes is two-thirds. Fixing the number of propositions and the *proportion* of yes votes, an increase in the number of voters increases the probability of a proposal passing. On the other hand, increasing the number of propositions reduces (and apparently more slowly) the probability of any one proposition passing. Intuitively, as the number of voters becomes large given the number of propositions to be considered and

TABLE 2. Probability of a Given Proposition Passing for Various Numbers of Voters and Propositions and a Group Proclivity to Vote Yes of .67

Number of Propositions	Number of Voters			
	3	5	7	9
3	.773	.831	.871	.900
6	.755	.808	.847	.876
9	.748	.800	.838	.866
12	.747	.798	.836	.865

the group proclivity to affirm, the probability of any given proposal securing majority approval approaches 1(0) if the general proclivity to affirm is greater (less) than .5. This is because the random sample of votes drawn from the population approaches the population size and hence the expected number of yes votes in the sample will be close to the fraction of yes votes in the population. If this fraction is greater than one-half, a proposal will have majority approval.[11] On the other hand, as the number of propositions becomes large given the number of voters and the average proclivity to affirm, the probability of any given proposal passing approaches the average proclivity to affirm since one is drawing a sample of fixed size from an ever-increasing population.

An extension of this model is "casting lots" where there is a fixed number of yes votes in the group. There is no specific information on the number of yes votes held by each voter (cf. note 6). Assuming the yes votes are distributed randomly across voters and issues, the probability of any single issue passing remains the same as before. However, the probability of passage for subsequent proposals contingent on the passage of prior propositions falls as yes votes, or lots, are "used up" in passing the prior propositions. For example in our seven voter–five proposition case where there was a .6 group proclivity to affirm, let there be a total of 21 yes votes randomly distributed through the population of votes. In this case, the probability of any one proposal passing is .727 as before. The probability of any second proposal passing given one proposition has already passed is .687, and the probability of any third proposal passing given two have passed is .454. Table 3 lists the conditional probability of passage for all five propositions. The average probability for the set of five propositions is .482 which can be interpreted as the expected fraction of propositions under consideration that will pass given the voting scheme outlined above. Table 4 reports the expected fraction of propositions passed under the casting lots model for some selected voter-proposition combinations when 60 percent of the votes are yes votes. Table 5 reports expected fraction of propositions passed for the five voter–five proposition case given various percentages of yes votes in the total number of votes cast on all propositions.

TABLE 3. Probability of a Proposition Passing Conditional upon All Prior Propositions Have Passed—7 Voters and a Group Proclivity to Affirm of .6

Proposition	Probability of Passage
1st	.727
2d	.687
3d	.454
4th	.359
5th	.181

TABLE 4. Expected Fraction of Propositions Passed when There Is a .6 Group Proclivity to Affirm

Voters	Propositions
3	.355
5	.429
7	.482
9	.491

TABLE 5. Expected Fraction of Propositions Passed under Various Group Proclivities to Affirm Given 5 Voters and 5 Propositions

Number of Yes Votes in Total Votes Cast on All Propositions (in percentage)	Expected Fraction of Propositions Passed
10 (40%)	.091
15 (60%)	.429
20 (80%)	.922

As we saw earlier, the expected fraction of proposals passing, for a given percentage of yes votes in the population, rises with the number of voters and falls with the number of propositions. Not surprisingly, the expected passage rate increases with the percentage of yes votes in the population and appears to do so at an increasing rate.

Concluding Remarks

In conventional majority rule voting models, a weakening of the information concerning individual voter preference orderings effectively rules out any analysis of the voting outcomes. In the model of yes-no voting presented here, information assumptions can be progressively weakened without removing all of the model's predictive content.

We saw that when the rank ordering of the separate proposals are known and identical across voters, a unique outcome results and that this outcome exactly matches the median voter's preferred outcome. When ordinal rankings are assumed to differ among voters, majority rule voting still yields unique and stable results while the equivalence between the outcome and the median voter's preferences is weakened but not lost. That is, when the only information available is each voter's probability of voting yes, the voting outcome, under many circumstances, more closely corresponds to the preferences of the median voter than for any other voter. Finally, we considered the case where the only information is the voting group's aggregate likelihood to vote yes. Here, the median voter has no meaning and all that can be said is that the expected number of propositions passed by the group depends on the number considered, the number of voters, and the group proclivity to vote yes.

It should be pointed out that the results reported here are preliminary. Our arguments have been made by reference to specific examples rather than by formal theorems and proofs. One possible way of generalizing our model is to construct a large-scale computer simulation of the model under various information assumptions in order to discover the properties of the model when there are large numbers of voters and issues.[12]

Elsewhere (1981), we argued that the allocation of resources and the potential for economic growth will be affected differently when disputes over property are resolved privately or collectively by majority rule. When such disputes are resolved by yes-no voting such as deciding upon zoning variances, our analysis of yes-no voting outcomes becomes both relevant and important. It is interesting to speculate on the reasons for the relative analytical neglect of the voting institutions discussed here, which, as we have noted, are descriptive of frequently observed collective choice situations. Attention may have been concentrated on the single-election setting primarily because of the underlying motivation to answer questions concerning the 'rationality' or 'irrationality' of collective choice, questions that have been presumed to have normative or evaluative content. In straightforward yes-no majority rule voting on a proposition, there is a unique result. The question of "collective rationality" that has preoccupied public choice and social choice theorists simply does not arise. But the absence of this particular "rationality" question does not make the positive analysis of yes-no voting either uninteresting or unimportant, perhaps even for normative questions of institutional-constitutional design.

NOTES

We should like to thank our colleagues Geoffrey Brennan and Joseph Reid for helpful suggestions on earlier drafts of this paper, and Janet Faith, Richard Carter, and David

Laband for their research assistance. Finally, we thank Akira Yokoyama of Josai University for saving us from some mathematical errors.

1. We use the term *proposition* here rather than *issue* in order to avoid confusion with the treatment of multi-issue space in public choice analysis. In the latter, candidates, party platforms, and voters' ideal positions are described by vectors that employ several issue dimensions. But the analysis is directed toward the selection of a single candidate (a list), or platform, in a single election. Our analysis, by contrast, explicitly examines a bundle of "elections," or "group choices," each one of which is presented as a single yes-no proposition.
2. One might interpret this as a setting of an agenda by an exogenous actor. The voters themselves do not offer new proposals for consideration. Some of the recent work on agenda manipulation where voters are presented with only two options may readily be brought within our framework of analysis. See, for example, Romer and Rosenthal (1978), Mackay and Weaver (1978), and Denzau, Mackay, and Weaver (1981).

   An alternative interpretation is that the costs of communicating and enforcing compromise proposals are prohibitively high. This may particularly be the case when the issue is largely an emotional one such as the legalization of marijuana, the development of nuclear power, or the adoption of capital punishment. In other cases, the amount of wealth at stake simply may be insufficient to induce the affected party (or parties) to make expensive counterproposals.
3. This requires that propositions are defined such that "yes" has a consistent meaning. For example, a yes vote "to grant a zoning variance" is equivalent to a no vote "to not grant a zoning variance." We shall assume henceforth that propositions are worded so that affirmation is always denoted by a yes vote.
4. From both an empirical and practical viewpoint this question of correspondence of preferences with outcomes is interesting. Consider an individual board member. If every voting member had an established history or known frequency of voting yes or no on single issues drawn from a certain broadly defined set, then one might be able to predict the probable outcome of each vote. For a hypothetical board member, such information would be important particularly if he were new to the board and were trying to figure out on which proposals his vote would be most highly weighted in the outcome (cf. Badger 1972). By extension, a set of citizens searching for a person to represent them in some governmental body would want to know which of the candidates would have the most "power" to deliver legislation preferred by the constituency. In a rough sense, one might scan the voting proclivities of the current members of the legislative body and the proclivities of the candidates so as to decide upon the most effective candidate. The same may hold true within legislative bodies, like Congress, where newly elected representatives must be assigned to existing committees and subcommittees. In this case, the impact of one representative's purely random voting (a reasonable assumption if there is no prior information on the new representative) on the committee outcomes would be taken into account by the party leader in assigning legislators to committees.
5. If voter i votes yes on a proposition, then to secure majority approval it is required that either j or k or both vote yes. The probability that j will vote yes on any given proposition, that is for a randomly selected ordering of j's preferences, is .5. For voter k this same probability is .33. As there are 3 pairs of votes from j and k

which in conjunction with i's yes vote will result in a majority—yes-yes, yes-no, no-yes—the probability of approval is $(\frac{1}{2}\cdot\frac{1}{3}) + (\frac{1}{2}\cdot\frac{2}{3}) + (\frac{1}{2}\cdot\frac{1}{3}) = .67$. To obtain a majority no, the necessary possibilities are yes-no, no-yes, and no-no; and the probability of majority disapproval given i votes 'no' is $(\frac{1}{2}\cdot\frac{2}{3}) + (\frac{1}{2}\cdot\frac{1}{3}) + (\frac{1}{2}\cdot\frac{2}{3}) = .83$.

6. An alternative voting model is to allocate each voter a fixed number of yes votes to cast over all propositions in the set. The probability of a subsequent proposal passing given a prior proposal has passed will then decrease since some yes votes are "used up" in passing the earlier one. Calculating probabilities in such an analytical setting is extremely time-consuming. For example, if there are five voters and six propositions, to calculate the probability of the sixth proposal passing given the first five have passed for just one voter requires over ten hours of computer execution time! Thus as a model with any empirical content along the lines suggested in note 4, this alternative formulation would be inappropriate. On the other hand, the probabilities discussed in the paper can be easily calculated.
7. This result is analogous to the "pairing off" condition for majority rule equilibrium with the median preference dominating. See Plott (1967). However, as expression (5) shows, in our model median dominance also requires that the extreme voters do not both have proclivities greater than one-half.
8. Since we are dealing with discrete changes in the parameters differential calculus is inappropriate for determining sensitivities. Thus, average rates of change are used where all changes in the independent variables are unit changes.
9. See note 7 above.
10. Letting L = total votes cast (voters times propositions), R = number of yes votes in L, D = number of voters, and k = number of yes votes in a random sample of D votes, the probability of getting exactly K yes votes on a given proposal is given by the hypergeometric probability:

$$k = \frac{\binom{D}{K}\binom{L-D}{R-k}}{\binom{L}{R}}$$

See Feller (1957, 42).

11. This result, in a somewhat different context, has been obtained by Kazmann (1973) and Grofman (1975).
12. In a sense our efforts are at a stage analogous to that of Tullock and Campbell (1970) who used simulation techniques to determine the probability of the occurrence of majority rule cycles as the number of voters and number of candidates change.

REFERENCES

Badger, W. W. "Political Individualism, Positional Preferences, and Optimal Decision-rules." In *Probability Models of Collective Choice*, edited by R. Niemi and H. Weisberg. Columbus: Merrill, 1972.

Buchanan, J. M., and Faith, R. L. "Entrepreneurship and Internalization of Externalities." *Journal of Law and Economics* 24 (April 1981): 95–111.

Denzau, A. T.; Mackay, R. J.; and Weaver, C. L. "On the Initiative-Referendum Option and the Control of Monopoly Government." In *Tax and Expenditure Limitations*, edited by Helen Ladd and T. N. Tideman, pp. 191–221. Washington, D.C.: Urban Institute Press, 1981.

Feller, W. *An Introduction to Probability Theory and Its Applications*. Vol. 1, 2d ed. New York: Wiley, 1957.

Grofman, B. "A Comment on 'Democratic Theory': A Preliminary Mathematical Model." *Public Choice* 21 (Spring 1975): 99–103.

Kazmann, R. G. "Democratic Organization: A Preliminary Mathematical Model." *Public Choice* 16 (Fall 1973): 17–26.

Mackay, R. J., and Weaver, C. L. "Monopoly Bureaus and Fiscal Outcomes: Deductive Models and Implications for Reform." In *Policy Analysis and Deductive Reasoning*, edited by G. Tullock and R. Wagner. Lexington, Mass.: D. C. Heath, 1978.

Plott, C. R. "A Notion of Equilibrium and Its Possibility under Majority Rule." *American Economic Review* 57 (September 1967): 787–806.

Romer, T., and Rosenthal, H. "Political Resource Allocation, Controlled Agendas, and the Status Quo." *Public Choice* 33 (Winter 1978): 27–43.

Tullock, G., and Campbell, C. D. "Computer Simulation of a Small Voting System." *Economic Journal* 80 (March 1970): 97–104.

Political Resource Allocation, Controlled Agendas, and the Status Quo

Thomas Romer and Howard Rosenthal

Economic analysis requires modeling political as well as market resource allocation. Voting institutions, in particular two-candidate majority rule elections and voting on motions, have been a primary focus of recent analytical developments. In the case of a single good to be allocated politically, standard assumptions lead to "single-peakedness" of voter preferences over the set of alternatives. When, in choosing between a pair of available alternatives, every voter votes for his preferred alternative, the allocative equilibrium is the "Condorcet point" or political allocation most desired by the median voter (Bowen 1943, Black 1958, Riker and Ordeshook 1973).

This result concerning the dominance of the median voter's ideal allocation depends importantly on the nature of competition in the allocation process. In the context of the political allocation of economic goods, the "median voter" outcome is typically justified on the basis of an underlying—but usually unmodeled—process of political competition between two candidates for elective office, wherein the dominant strategy for each candidate is to offer to provide the level of public spending that corresponds to the median voter's ideal expenditure.

Such a view of equilibrium under majority rule (when equilibrium exists) may be very unrepresentative of political processes. Many such processes, particularly those related to collective expenditure determination, may be more appropriately characterized as ones in which some group has the power to make a proposal to the voters, and thereby set the agenda. This group, which we call the agenda *setter*, by having monopoly power over the proposal placed before the electorate, can confront the voters with a "take it or leave it" choice. Because "competitive" substitutes to the setter's proposal are not offered, the median voter cannot simply "hold out" until the Condorcet point is proposed.

When the setter has monopoly power, voters are forced to choose between the setter's proposal and the status quo or fallback position. The status quo is the situation that prevails if voters reject the setter's proposed alternative. The rule determining the status quo or fallback position is generally specified by law, and is not subject to the setter's control. Examples of fallback positions are zero expenditure and the previous year's expenditure.

To provide some structure for this monopoly type of process, we analyze a simple model of collective expenditure determination with agenda-setting

First published in *Public Choice* 33, no. 4 (1978): 27–44.

behavior. This model corresponds quite closely to the situation in many local jurisdictions where some collective expenditures are determined through the interaction of citizen-voters and a committee or a bureau charged with the provision of public services. Typically, the bureau/committee formulates a proposal for the coming period's expenditures. This budget proposal is then subject to approval or defeat in a referendum of the jurisdiction's residents.[1]

In this article, we are concerned with a single vote on a tax expenditure decision. We thus do not consider dynamic, sequential aspects of the political process, nor do we investigate logrolling and coalition formation. Voters are characterized as behaving individualistically, making voting decisions independently of others. Decisions are made in a world of certainty, so that we do not deal with questions arising from incomplete turnout and lack of information about voter preferences. Neglecting these aspects of the problem does not mean we feel they are unimportant. Rather, our intention is to explore the implications of agenda control per se, leaving to future work the further elaboration of the basic structure.[2]

To focus as sharply as possible on the role of the setter, we characterize the setter as having a preference for the largest feasible expenditure. The justification for this view of bureaucratic motivation is explored in detail by Niskanen (1971, chap. 4; 1975). Although there has been some criticism of the budget-maximizing assumption when applied to bureaucrats in general (see, for example, Breton and Wintrobe 1975 and Margolis 1975), we find this characterization of setter behavior particularly appropriate for the situations that concern us here. The setter in public expenditure referenda is typically an interested professional, such as a school superintendent, who may quite sincerely believe that provision of the service supplied by his agency is important for the community's welfare. Consequently, he would value incremental units of supply quite highly. A setter, of course, may also find direct personal satisfaction (pecuniary and nonpecuniary in source) from being in charge of an agency with a large budget. It may be argued that neither altruism nor private incentives need make the setter literally a budget maximizer. While acknowledging and agreeing with this contention, we do not believe that introduction of complicating factors—structuring the problem in terms of maximizing the "discretionary budget" or maximizing a setter's utility function, some of whose arguments depend positively on budget size—would provide significantly greater analytical insight in this context. We are interested primarily in exploring the implications of the expenditure-maximizing assumption, since it highlights quite sharply the importance of the setter.[3]

Although an expenditure-maximizing setter obviously prefers a level of supply higher than that desired by the median voter, to pass the proposed expenditure under majority voting, the setter needs the approval of at least half the voters. We are particularly interested in the way that the level of supply that the voters approve depends on the status quo position. We show that the status quo point strongly affects the allocation. In other words, the institutional structure or historical background—the determinants of the status quo or fallback position—are very important to the outcome of the expenditure election. We obtain the seemingly perverse and paradoxical result that a large majority of the voters may be better off and allocative efficiency may be more nearly achieved when the setter can impose some tax *without voter approval* than when the setter requires voter approval for all taxes. The reason for this is that, in effect, zero taxes also means zero expenditure. The setter can then use his monopoly power over the agenda to threaten the voters with facing the consequences of zero expenditure if they fail to approve a high level of expenditure. We also show that the setter has a more complex problem than simply choosing a proposal that induces a "yea" vote by a uniquely defined "median" voter, even in the context of a single election with full turnout and perfect information for the setter.

We begin by characterizing the behavior of voters and setter. Comparative statics of changes in the status quo are analyzed and illustrated with discussions related to educational finance and public works expenditures. In a more speculative vein, we also comment briefly on possible implications of using zero-base budgeting in an environment where expenditure-maximizing setters are active. The article concludes with indications for the direction of future investigation.

Analytical Framework

The Individual Voter[4]

We deal with a set $N = \{1, 2, \ldots, n\}$ of voters. Each voter $i \epsilon N$ has a strictly quasi-concave preference function $U^i(C^i, G^i)$, defined over all pairs of goods (C, G) and nondecreasing in (C, G). C^i represents i's consumption of a bundle of private goods and G^i his consumption of a collectively provided good. This good may be a pure public good, a private good, or some mixed good. Its essential characteristic is that it is financed collectively and allocated politically. The relationship between collective expenditures (in units of private consumption good) E and i's consumption G^i is given by:

$$G^i = f^i(E).$$

We take $f^i\ (E)$ to be increasing and weakly concave. It follows that

$$u^i\ (C^i, E) \equiv U^i\ [C^i, f^i\ (E)]$$

is strictly quasi-concave and nondecreasing in (C^i, E).[5]

Supply of the collective good is financed from (e.g., local) taxes and, possibly, from other (e.g., state or federal) revenue sources. We define a tax structure as a rule that determines, given the level of expenditure E, the tax payments of each voter i. For a given tax structure, each collective expenditure level is associated with some maximum feasible private consumption for each voter.

The status quo for voter i is represented by a (C^i, E) pair that we call q^i. This is a point associated with some constitutionally prescribed "reversion rule" that specifies the level of expenditure (and the reversion tax structure) that occurs if a proposed alternative is voted down.

For a given tax structure, the alternatives to the status quo impose a constraint

$$C^i \leqslant T^i (E) \tag{1}$$

on voter i. The function T^i is determined by the way taxes are apportioned among the voters and the availability of outside revenue. We assume that T^i is nonincreasing and weakly concave for all voters. Individual utility maximization implies that, for given E, (1) will hold with equality. Letting A^i denote the *set of alternatives to the status quo* facing voter i, we have:

$$A^i = (C^i, E) : C^i = T^i (E). \tag{2}$$

The utility for voter i of alternative collective expenditure is given by

$$V^i (E) \equiv u^i [Y^i (E), E]. \tag{3}$$

A straightforward consequence of our assumptions about the utility functions and alternative sets is:

LEMMA 1. V^i *(*E*) is single-peaked in* E. *Specifically,* V^i *(*E*) is strictly increasing for* $0 \leqslant E \; H \; \bar{E}^i$ *and strictly decreasing for* $E > \bar{E}^i$, *for all* $i \in N$, *where* $\bar{E}^i$ *is the voter's "most-preferred" or* ideal expenditure given T^i.

Any proposal by the setter (other than the status quo) implies a point in A^i for each voter. If the financing of the status quo involves the same tax structure as the financing of alternatives to the status quo, then $q^i \in A^i$ for all i. If, on the other hand, in proposing a change in total expenditure from the status quo, the proposing body or *setter* is constrained to using a different financing structure, then q^i may not be in the set of alternatives.[6]

Individuals are asked to vote "yea" or "nay" on a proposed expenditure E. If the status quo for voter i is q^i, then he votes "yea" on the proposed alternative if

$$V^i (E) \geqslant u^i (q\text{i}).$$

Otherwise, he votes "nay." (We arbitrarily—and unimportantly—assume a "yea" vote in the case of indifference between the proposal and the status quo.)

LEMMA 2. *Let* $B^i(q^i_0) \subseteq A^i$ *designate the set of proposals voter* i *approves when status quo is* q^i_0 *and* $B^i(q^i_1) \subseteq A^i$ *designate the set of proposals approved when the status quo is some different point* q^i_1. *If* $u^i(q^i_1) \geqslant u^i(q^i_0)$, *then* $B^i(q^i_1) \subseteq B^i(q^i_0)$.

This follows directly from our assumptions about $u^i(\cdot)$ and A^i. The lemma is illustrated in figure 1. With point q_0 on contour I^0 the voter will support any expenditure level between E_1 and E_4. For q_1 on contour I^1, only expenditures between E_2 and E_3 would be supported. Note also that for status quos such that $u^i(q^i) > V^i(\bar{E}^i)$, $B^i(q^i)$ is empty. (This is the case with q_+ in fig. 1.)

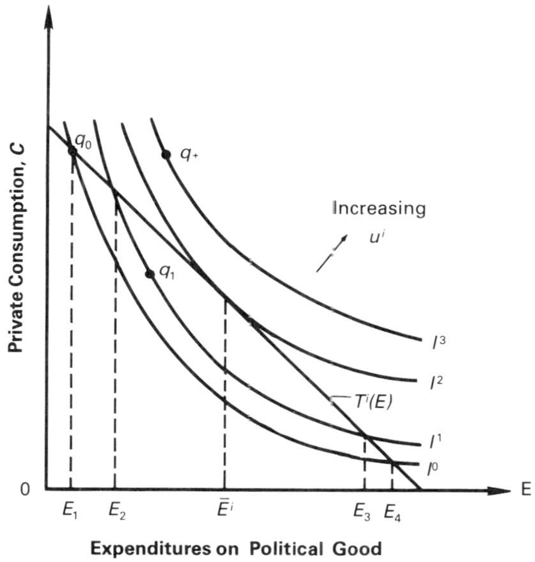

Fig. 1. Decision making for individual voter

The Setter's Behavior

The setter or group making expenditure proposals is assumed to know voters' preferences. For a given expenditure proposal E, define $b_i(E) = 1$ if voter i votes "yea" and $b_i(E) = 0$ if "nay." Then the setter's objective is to

$$\text{maximize } E \qquad \text{subject to } \sum_{i=1}^{n} b_i(E) > 0.5n. \tag{4}$$

The rest of this article considers how changes in the status quo affect the solution of this maximization problem. In particular, we are concerned with how the solution changes with increases in the status quo level of expenditure.

Changes in the Status Quo Expenditure: Some Comparative Statics

Let $Q = \{q^1, q^2, \ldots, q^n\}$ be the set of status quo points under a given fallback rule, and let $E(Q)$ denote collective expenditures when the status quo is Q.

DEFINITION. *An alternative expenditure* E' *is* viable *against a status quo* Q *if:*
(a) the number of voters for whom $V^i(E') \geq u^i(q^i)$, $i \in N$, *is greater than* $0.5n$; *and*
(b) $E' > E(Q)$; *i.e., the setter prefers* E' *over* $E(Q)$.

The setter's problem is trivial for status quos without viable alternatives: stick with the status quo. The more interesting cases involve status quos which do have viable alternatives. Our discussion therefore focuses on these cases.

Dominant Status Quo Points

DEFINITION. *A status quo* $Q_0 = \{q_0^1 \ldots, q_0^n\}$ dominates *another status quo* $Q_1 = \{q_1^1, \ldots, q_1^n\}$ if $u^i(q_0^i) \geq u^i(q_1^i)$ *for all* $i \in N$, *and* $u^i(q_0^i) \geq u^i(q_1^i)$ *for some* $i \in N$.

Proposition 1. *Consider two status quos* Q_0 *and* Q_1, *each with at least one viable alternative. Let the solution to the setter's problem (4) be* $E^*(Q_0)$ *when the status quo is* Q_0 *and* $E^*(Q_1)$ *when the status quo is* Q_1. *If* Q_0 *dominates* Q_1, *then* $E^*(Q_0) \leq E^*(Q_1)$.

Proof.
1. Consider some proposal E' such that when the status quo facing voter i is q_0^i, he votes in favor of E'. By Lemma 2 and dominance of Q_0 over Q_1, this voter will vote "yea" on E' when the status quo is q_1^i.
2. Now suppose that $E^*(Q_0) > E^*(Q_1)$. By the above argument, at least as many voters would vote "yea" on $E^*(Q_0)$ when the status quo is Q_1 as when the status quo is Q_0. Thus $E^*(Q_1) < E^*(Q_0)$ cannot be a solution to (4) when the status quo is Q_1. Therefore $E^*(Q_0) \leq E^*(Q_1)$.

Discussion
As our definition of dominance did not depend on the actual expenditure levels associated with the status quo points, Proposition 1 holds even in the

somewhat paradoxical case where the expenditures are less for the dominated status quo than for the dominating status quo. If it is dominated, the lower status quo expenditure leads the setter to a higher approved budget. Of course, since higher status quo expenditures will not always dominate lower status quo expenditures, it is important to analyze the response of the solution to (4) to higher status quo expenditures in the absence of dominance. The next section looks at an important case that usually will not involve dominant status quos.

Status Quo Points in the Alternative Set

We now turn to the situation (common in practice) where the status quo and alternatives involve the same tax structure; that is $q^i \in A^i$ for all $i \in N$. Analysis of this case depends critically on how the status quo expenditure is located relative to the median of voters' ideal expenditures.

Status Quo Expenditure Greater than or Equal to Median Ideal Expenditure

Let F (E) denote the proportion of the voters who, given T^i, have ideal expenditures $\bar{E}^i$ less than or equal to E. Define the "median" ideal expenditure $\bar{E}^m$ as the largest expenditure such that F $(\bar{E}^m) < 0.5$. If the level of expenditure associated with the status quo is not less than $\bar{E}^m$, then the status quo is the best that the setter can do. No expenditure *greater* than the status quo would be preferred to the status quo by a simple majority of voters, and hence there is no expenditure viable against the status quo.

Status Quo Expenditure Less than Median Ideal Expenditure

The more interesting condition involves status quo expenditure levels less than the median ideal expenditure. For this condition, we show that there is a *negative* relationship between the level of expenditure that solves the setter's problem—which we call the *approved level*—and the status quo level, even in the absence of dominance. This result is formalized in the following proposition.

> PROPOSITION 2. *Let* Q_0 *and* Q_1 *be two distinct status quos such that* $q^i_0 \in A^i$ *and* $q^i_1 \in A^i$ *for all* $i \in N$. *Let* E^* (Q_0) *and* E^* (Q_1) *be the approved expenditures when the status quo expenditures are, respectively,* E (Q_0) *and* E (Q_1). *Suppose that* E $(Q_1) < E$ $(Q_0) < \bar{E}^m$. *Then* E^* $(Q_1) \geqslant E^*$ (Q_0).

To prove Proposition 2, we first develop an additional lemma.[7]

> LEMMA 3. *Consider status quos such that* $q^i \in A^i$ *for all* $i \in N$. *For a proposed expenditure greater than a given status quo expenditure, the number of votes in favor of the proposal* cannot decrease *as the status quo expenditure is* decreased.

Proof. Let $E(Q_1) < E(Q_0) < E_0$. Since $q^i \in A^i$ for all $i \in N$, V^i gives voter i's ranking of all collective expenditures, including the status quo. From the single-peakedness of V^i, we must have $V^i[E(Q_0)] > V^i(E_0)$ and/or $V^i[E(Q_0)] > V^i[E(Q_1)]$. If i votes for E_0 against $E(Q_0)$, then $V^i(E_0) \geqslant V^i[E(Q_0)]$, so $V^i[E(Q_0)] > V^i[E(Q_1)]$. Thus, $V^i(E_0) > V^i[E(Q_1)]$ and the voter must vote for E_0 against $E(Q_1)$.

Proposition 2 then follows by noting:

1. The setter will never offer a proposal lower than the status quo expenditure.
2. Assume $E^*(Q_1)$ solves (4) for $E(Q_1)$ and suppose that $E^*(Q_0) > E^*(Q_1)$ solves (4) for $E(Q_0) > E(Q_1)$. But then, from Lemma 3, $E^*(Q_0)$ would get at least as many votes against $E(Q_1)$ as against $E(Q_0)$, implying that $E^*(Q_1)$ is not a solution to (4) for $E(Q_1)$. The contradiction implies that $E^*(Q_1) \geqslant E^*(Q_0)$.

Other Status Quo Points

A more explicit consideration including private consumption bundles as well as expenditure levels allows us to develop a somewhat more general result which includes Proposition 2 as a special case. We consider changes in status quo expenditures such that status quo points lie on or above the $C^i = T^i(E)$ locus for each voter. We generalize Lemma 3 to:

LEMMA 3′. *Let* Q_0 *and* Q_1 *be two distinct status quos, with collective expenditures* $E(Q_0)$ *and* $E(Q_1)$*, respectively, and* $E(Q_0) > E(Q_1)$*. Let* C_0^i *and* C_1^i *be the private consumption of voter* i *under status quos* q_0^i *and* q_1^i*, respectively. Suppose that*

$$C_1^i \geqslant T^i[E(Q_1)] \text{ for all } i \in N \tag{5}$$

$$C_1^i - C_0^i \leqslant T^i[E(Q_1)] - T^i[E(Q_0)] \text{ for all } i \in N \tag{6}$$

Consider a proposed expenditure E' (which allows voter i to obtain $(T^i(E'), E') \in A^i$) such that $E' > E(Q_0) > E(Q_1)$. Then the proposal E' cannot receive more "yea" votes when $E(Q_0)$ is the status quo expenditure than when $E(Q_1)$ is the status quo expenditure.

Remark. Condition (5) requires that the status quo point q_1^i lie on or above the alternative locus.
Condition (6) states that the tax cost to voter i of the increase in expenditure from $E(Q_1)$ to $E(Q_0)$ under the status quo (i.e., $C_1^i - C_0^i$) be no greater than would be the tax cost of such a change under the alternative tax structure [i.e., $T^i(E(Q_1)) - T^i(E(Q_0))$]. Note that conditions (5) and (6) together imply that $C_0^i \geqslant T^i[E(Q_0)]$ for all $i \in N$.

Proof of Lemma 3′. Consider three exhaustive cases:

1. If $u^i(q^i_1) \geqslant u^i(q^i_0)$, then $V^i(E^1) < u^i(q^i_0)$ and voter i will vote *against* E' under both status quos. This follows from the conditions of the lemma, the concavity of $T^i(E)$, and the strict quasi-concavity of preferences (for details, see appendix).
2. If $u^i(q^i_0) > u^i(q^i_1) > V^i(E')$, then voter i will vote *against* E' under both status quos.
3. If $u^i(q'_0) > u^i(q^i_1)$ and $u^i(q^i_1) \leqslant V^i(E')$, then voter i will vote *for* E' when the status quo is q^i_1, and vote *either for* or *against* E' when the status quo is q^i_0.

Consequently, E' cannot get more "yea" votes against $E(Q_0)$ than against $E(Q_1)$. This establishes the lemma.

With Lemma 3′ and arguments similar to those used to demonstrate Proposition 2 we can prove the following:

PROPOSITION 2′. *Consider two distinct status quos* Q_0 *and* Q_1, *each with at least one viable alternative, and satisfying conditions (5) and (6). Suppose that proposal* $E^*(Q_0)$ *solves (4) when the status quo is* Q_0 *with status quo expenditure* $E(Q_0)$, *and proposal* $E^*(Q_1)$ *solves (4) when the status quo is* Q_1 *with status quo expenditure* $E(Q_1) < E(Q_0)$. *Then* $E^*(Q_1) \geqslant E^*(Q_0)$.

Discussion and Examples

The crucial feature of the allocation process we are examining is the existence of "barriers to entry" in the formulation of alternatives. The ability to control the agenda gives the setter a monopoly power which he can exploit to an extent that depends on the status quo. By facing the voters with a "take it or leave it" choice, the setter exercises a threat over the voters. The worse the status quo, the greater this threat and, consequently, the greater the gain to the setter from being able to propose the alternative. The remainder of this article is devoted to elucidation and amplification of our results as they apply to a variety of situations.

A Potential Test of the Model

A number of states use referenda to determine public school budgets. In the state of Oregon, or example, local school district budgets and their implicit tax rates must be approved by the voters annually if the board's proposal exceeds a statutory amount that can be levied without going to the voters. Simplifying somewhat, this statutory maximum expenditure is given by

$$E(Q) = (\text{BASE})(1.06)^{t-1916} \qquad [sic]$$

$E(Q)$ is, in effect, the status quo expenditure for the local school district, and status quo points lie in the set of alternatives. BASE is a number directly related to the district's expenditure in the year 1916, and t is the current calendar year. Since BASE varies widely across districts, so does E (Q). Moreover, E (Q) is independent of current expenditures, and is outside the setter's control. Provided single-peakedness is satisfied—which is likely where there are few private or parochial alternatives to public education—our results would predict that, *ceteris paribus*, current expenditures should be less in districts that had substantial tax base in 1916 than in the many districts that have low BASE and hence must face the voters with a low E (Q)—in many cases E $(Q) = 0$—each year.

Under the "competitive" assumption, variations in the status quo should not affect the outcome of a referendum. An econometric model that takes into account demographic and socioeconomic factors and explicitly incorporates the variations in the status quo would provide an empirical test of our hypotheses. We are currently engaged in developing such a test.[8]

Example: Public Works Expenditures

As an illustration of some of the properties of the controlled agenda process, consider a highway department that proposes to replace an existing bridge with a new structure. Any construction of a new bridge involves destruction of the old facility. The new bridge would be paid for out of a special assessment. The existing bridge yields utility u^i (q^i) to voter i. Suppose an expenditure-maximizing bureau were to submit an expenditure proposal to the voters. Our example focuses on the relationship between the quality of the old bridge (as measured by the status quo utilities) and the approved expenditure on the new structure.

We consider a "community" with three voters, with preferences over new expenditures given by V^1 (E), V^2 (E), and V^3 (E), respectively (see fig. 2). For simplicity, we arbitrarily assume a utility scale such that u^1 $(q^1) = u^2$ $(q^2) = u^3$ (q^3), for all the status quos under consideration. Increasing $u(q)$ then implies moving to a status quo that dominates the previous status quo.[9]

In figure 2, we measure utility on the vertical axis and expenditure on the horizontal axis. With status quo utility u_0, for example, the largest expenditure that voter 1 would approve is E_0^1. Any higher expenditure would leave him worse of than he is with the status quo. E_0^1 would not, however, be approved by a majority, since with status quo utility u_0, both voters 2 and 3 would vote *against* E_0^1. In fact, the highest expenditure that will pass against u_0 is E_0^2, the largest expenditure acceptable to voter 2.

The heavy black line in the figure is the graph of the solution to the setter's problem (4) as a function of the status quo. In accord with the results of the previous section of this article ("Changes in the Status Quo Expenditure"), the approved expenditure decreases as status quo quality increases. For status quo values above u_4, no positive amount of new expenditure would be approved. (The discontinuities that occur at status quo values u_3 and u_4 are a consequence of the small number of voters. With many voters, the plot of approved expenditures will usually be "close" to continuous.)

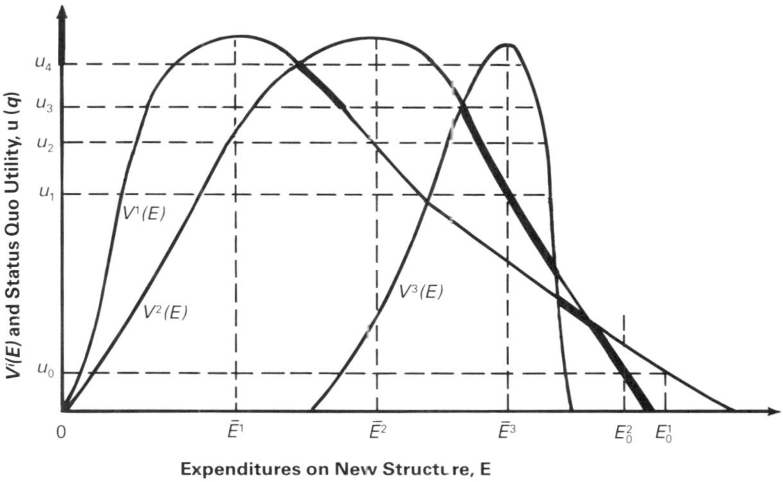

Fig. 2. Approved expenditure and status quo utility. Heavy line shows approved expenditure.

In contrast to the outcome of this controlled agenda process, standard cost-benefit analysis suggests that, provided that the new bridge has positive net benefits (treating as a cost the loss of the utility provided by the old bridge), the optimal scale of the new bridge should be independent of the value of the old bridge. Note also that, for status quo values below u_1, the approved expenditure is such that the voters would unanimously prefer a reduction in expenditure, under the tax/financing arrangements for the new project. (For status quos below u_1, expenditure $\bar{E}^3$ (which happens to be voter 3's ideal expenditure is preferred unanimously to any $E > \bar{E}^3$.)

This example also points out that the voter whose preferences are decisive for the setter depends on the status quo. As the heavy solution line indicates, at low levels of the status quo voter 2 is decisive. As the status quo improves, first voter 1, then voter 3, then voter 2 again, and finally voter 1 again become decisive. Consequently, the critical role Niskanen (1971, chaps. 13–14) and others ascribe to the "middle demand group" (or, in general, voter with median ideal point) is misleading in this context, and would arise only as a result of special forms ascribed to the V^i (E) functions.

In the usual majority rule situation, the median voter does, of course, have a central role. In our example, if there is no status quo alternative, and the "competitive" process is operating, majority rule leads to an expenditure of $\bar{E}^2$, that most desired by voter 2. Even with a status quo, this level, if proposed, would be selected as long as the status quo for each voter is not better than u_2. At status quo just above u_2, voters 1 and 3 both prefer the status quo to $\bar{E}^2$ and would combine to defeat $\bar{E}^2$. In fact, cyclical majorities arise and a Condorcet equilibrium fails to exist until the status quo value passes u_4. At this point, the status quo is a Condorcet winner.

If decisiveness is a valued attribute of choice mechanisms, the example illustrates a general advantage of controlled agendas over competitive majority rule. Even though preferences are single-peaked in expenditure, the presence of a status quo point will frequently suffice to rob competitive majority rule of an equilibrium, whereas the controlled agenda always creates a decision.

Agendas Controlled by High Demand Groups

The agenda may not actually be controlled by an expenditure maximizer but by the group with the highest ideal point.[10] If this group is the setter and can pass a budget beyond its ideal point, given single-peakedness, it can also pass its ideal point. Consequently, we may reformulate (4) as

$$\max E$$

$$\text{subject to } E \geqslant \bar{E}^h \qquad (4')$$

$$\text{and } \sum_{i=1}^{n} b_i(E) > 0.5n$$

where $\bar{E}^h$ is the most preferred level of expenditure for the voter with the highest ideal expenditure.

This modification to the objective function only trivially modifies the solution. The solution to the public works example in figure 2 is voter 3's ideal point, $\bar{E}^3$, for status quo utility less than u_1. For greater status quo utility, the previous solution applies.

Implications for "Zero-Base Budgeting"

Going beyond our formal structure, we note that although public projects are rarely built by voters, they are frequently undertaken by legislatures using a Niskanen-type review process. If proposals for an agency's budget are controlled by a high-demand group, our results suggest that the agency may well prefer a reversion rule which makes the status quo fairly low. In the absence of a careful review mechanism in which low- and moderate-demand groups have the opportunity to enter the policy formulation process, lower status quos will tend to lead to higher approved expenditures.

Responding to what appears to be widespread concern over the level of public spending by the U.S. government, pending congressional legislation aims to institute a new review process for federal expenditures. This process would require "authorizations of new budget authority for Government programs and activities at least every five years [and would] establish a procedure for zero-base review and evaluation of Government programs and activities every five years."[11] The major purpose of such legislation—referred to, with varying degrees of precision and vividness, as "zero-base review," "zero-base budgeting," or "sunset legislation"—is, of course, to eliminate unnecessary and outdated programs. Most critics of the legislation, while agreeing with its goals, have focused on the enormity of the reviewing task and on the undesirability of having programs such as national defense or the federal judiciary system go to a zero base pending review.

Drawing on our results, we suggest, in addition, that for many programs whose continuation is deemed desirable, zero-base review and—even more so—zero-base budgeting may tend to increase the monopoly power of the agencies. This seemingly perverse outcome is particularly likely if, swamped with the newly instituted review process (or by crises such as Vietnam or Watergate), congressional committees become lax with respect to appropriations for activities whose budgets a majority would be unwilling to have go to zero. The threat of a zero budget actually occurring for cases when this event would be a very bad outcome (a low-ranked status quo) may then work to the advantage of an expenditure-maximizing bureau (whose motto in this case may well be "*reculer pour mieux sauter*"). As long as agenda-setting power remains with the agencies, for important areas of public spending a nonzero reversion rule would therefore prove to be a more effective way to control the size of the budget.

Concluding Remarks

The need for further elaboration of this basic model is indicated by the importance of referenda and direct voting from Berkeley to Berne and by the likelihood that there is more than a grain of truth in Niskanen's idea that high-interest groups control agendas in legislatures. While the efficiency properties of controlled agendas may indeed be troubling, it is not clear that other democratic procedures, such as conventional majority rule, are always preferable. Moreover, controlled agendas appear (like dictators, beneficient and otherwise) to minimize decision costs.

Our model of political resource allocation focuses on the effects of monopoly power in the form of controlled agendas. As in other monopoly situations, it would certainly be in the interest of some groups to devote resources to attempt to reduce the extent of monopoly power. In particular, low demand groups would make significant gains if they could attenuate the power of a high-demand setter. The incentive to form low- and moderate-demand coalitions is certainly present, though such coalition formation may be very costly—especially if the barriers to entry are high. A most interesting extension of our analysis would be a kind of "imperfect competition" model of the political resource allocation process which recognizes the role of agenda setters and allows for some competition for that position. Would such a process approach, as its dynamic equilibrium, the "median voter" allocation? Or would some of the setter's monopoly power be preserved?

To answer these questions requires further explicit modeling of the political allocation process. Incorporating imperfect information and uncertainty, as well as sequential elements, are necessary steps toward the characterization of equilibrium.

Appendix: Elaboration of Step 1 of Proof of Lemma 3′

$$\text{Let } \lambda \equiv \frac{E' - E(Q_0)}{E' - E(Q_1)}, \text{ so that } \lambda E(Q_1) + (1 - \lambda)E' = E(Q_0).$$

From concavity of T^i:

$$T^i[E(Q_0)] \geqslant \lambda T^i[E(Q_1)] + (1 - \lambda)T^i(E'),$$

so that

$$T^i[E(Q_0)] - T^i[E(Q_1)] \geqslant (1 - \lambda)T^i(E') - (1 - \lambda)T^i[E(Q_1)] \quad \text{(A1)}$$

Using (6):

$$C_0^i - \lambda C_1^i - \{T^i[E(Q_0)] - T^i[E(Q_1)]\} \geqslant (1 - \lambda)C_1^i$$

and (A1):

$$C_0^i - \lambda C_1^i - \{(1 - \lambda)T^i(E') - (1 - \lambda)T^i[E(Q_1)]\} \geqslant (1 - \lambda)C_1^i$$
$$\Rightarrow C_0^i - \lambda C_1^i - (1 - \lambda)T^i(E') \geqslant (1 - \lambda)\{C_1^i - T^i[E(Q_1)]$$
$$\geqslant 0 \quad \text{(A2)}$$

i.e.: $C_0^i \geqslant \lambda C_1^i + (1 - \lambda)T^i(E')$, and therefore:

$$u^i(q_0^i) = u^i[C_0^i, E(Q_0)] \geqslant u^i[\lambda C_1^i + (1 - \lambda)T^i(E'), E(Q_o)] \quad \text{(A3)}$$

From strict quasi concavity of u^i:

$$u^i[\lambda C_1^i + (1 - \lambda)T^i(E'), E(Q_0)] > \min \{u^i[C_1^i, E(Q_1)], u^i[T^i(E'), E']\}$$

i.e.:

$$u^i[\lambda C_1^i + (1 - \lambda)T^i(E'), E(Q_0)] > \min [u^i(q_1^i), V^i(E')] \quad \text{(A4)}$$

By assumption:

$$u^i(q_1^i) \geqslant u^i(q_0^i)$$

This, together with (A3) and (A4), implies:

$$u^i(q_0^i) > V^i(E')$$

NOTES

We thank M. Harris, J. Lave, S. Salop, and participants in workshops at the Board of Governors of the Federal Reserve and at Queen's University for helpful comments.

1. In the area of public education alone (the most important item of collectively provided goods at the local level), Holcombe (1975) lists twenty-two states in the United States that require a referendum process to determine local school taxes and budgets.
2. In addition to public expenditure processes characterized by direct referenda, the controlled agenda framework is an appealing model for voting on California-style popular initiatives, where there are significant costs to generating new alternatives. We also suggest, following Niskanen (1971), that setters may play an important role in legislative voting, although we recognize that legislative processes may differ significantly from referendum voting in the extent of opportunities for logrolling, coalition formation, and generating new alternatives.
3. An important question arises when the proposing party is an elected board rather than a civil service bureau. One might contend that the desire for reelection might not lead the board to make expenditure-maximizing proposals. Yet it might just as well be argued that the personal investment of time and money needed to obtain reelection to the board results in the board being drawn only from high-interest individuals. If this is the case, an entry barrier may allow board members to disregard the threat of challenge from low-interest individuals. Another possibility is that the board members maximize the budget subject to an upper bound, either as a hedge on reelection or as an expression of personal preference. As we indicate in the "Discussion and Examples" section, the analysis is not materially affected by taking the setter as the group or person with the highest ideal expenditure, rather than actually expenditure maximizing.

   Oblique support for viewing the setter as a budget-maximizing entrepreneur comes from evidence, presented by Edwards (1977), that managers of private firms operating in a regulated industry behave as expense maximizers. Edwards also finds that increasing monopoly power intensifies expense-preference behavior.
4. The assumptions that lead to Lemma 1 are by now standard in the literature. We develop them mainly as a convenient way of indicating the notation that will be followed in the paper.
5. If G is a pure public good, $G^i = E$. For publicly provided private goods, such as socialized health care, a simple formulation would be $G^i = a_i E$ with $0 < a_i < 1$, where a_i represents individual i's perception of his "benefit share."
6. This might be the case if, for example, the status quo involves different amount of outside financing than would be available under the proposed alternative.
7. The suggestions of an anonymous referee helped abbreviate the proof of Lemma 3.
8. For an attempt to test the "competitive" model, see Inman (1978).
9. The assumption of equal utilities for a given status quo enables us to carry on the discussion using only one diagram. It is by no means necessary for the results we are illustrating. In the current context, what matters is that voters agree on the ranking of status quos.

10. This assumption is used in Niskanen's model (1971, chap. 14).
11. The quote is from the title of a prominent recent legislative document of this type, S.2925, the "Government Economy and Spending Reform Act of 1976."

REFERENCES

Black, D. *The Theory of Committees and Elections.* Cambridge: Cambridge University Press, 1958.

Bowen, H. R. "The Interpretation of Voting in the Allocation of Economic Resources." *Quarterly Journal of Economics,* November, 1943.

Breton, A., and Wintrobe, R. "The Equilibrium Size of a Budget-Maximizing Bureau: A Note on Niskanen's Theory of Bureaucracy." *Journal of Political Economy,* February, 1975.

Edwards, F. R. "Managerial Objectives in Regulated Industries: Expense-Preference Behavior in Banking." *Journal of Political Economy,* February, 1977.

Holcombe, R. G. "A Public Choice Analysis of Millage Issue Elections for Financing Public Schools." Ph.D. diss., Virginia Polytechnic Institute and State University, 1975.

Inman, R. P. "Testing Political Economy's 'As If' Proposition: Is the Median Voter Really Decisive?" *Public Choice,* Summer, 1978.

Margolis, J. "Comment [on Niskanen]." *Journal of Law and Economics,* December, 1975.

Niskanen, W. *Bureaucracy and Representative Government.* Chicago: Aldine-Atherton, 1971.

Niskanen, W. "Bureaucrats and Politicians." *Journal of Law and Economics,* December, 1975.

Riker, W., and Ordeshook, P. *An Introduction to Positive Political Theory.* Englewood Cliffs, N.J.: Prentice-Hall, 1973.

A New and Superior Process for Making Social Choices

T. Nicolaus Tideman and Gordon Tullock

This essay describes a new process for making social choices, one that is superior to other processes that have been suggested. The method is immune to strategic maneuvering on the part of individual voters. It avoids the conditions of the Arrow theorem by using more information than the rank orders of preferences, and selects a unique point on or "almost on" the Pareto-optimal frontier, one that maximizes or "almost maximizes" the consumer surplus of society. Subject to any given distribution of wealth, the process may be used to approximate the Lindahl equilibrium for all public goods.[1]

These are strong claims, and it is therefore only sensible to begin by pointing out that the process will not cure cancer, stop the tides, or, indeed, deal successfully with many other problems. As far as we know, all existing social choice processes are subject to exploitation by suitably designed coalitions. This process is no exception. In addition, as in all democratic voting processes, voters are undermotivated to invest time and effort in a comparative evaluation of alternatives. The motives they are given for making sensible decisions are somewhat stronger than those for persons engaging in voting under majority rule, but voters will be asked to do more in the way of expressing their preferences than simply saying yes or no. Therefore, it is not clear whether the lack of an incentive to vote is more or less of a handicap for this process than it is for ordinary voting processes.

The process may be described most generally as a demand-revealing process. It relies on what might be called an incomplete compensation mechanism that appears to have been first described by Vickrey (1961) in the context of optimum counterspeculation policy for a socialist economy. The essence of the mechanism is that each person is paid for the benefit (or pays the costs) of his actions, but no one is charged (or credited) as required for budget balance. Vickrey showed that it would be possible to motivate individuals to reveal their true supply and demand schedules for a private good by paying each person the net increase in the sum of the producer and consumer surpluses of other persons in the market that resulted from the supply or demand schedule that the one person reported. Vickrey noted that there would be a problem of financing such a system, since it would generate a deficit. He did not discuss the potential application of such a system to public goods.

Two persons who were unaware of each other's work or Vickrey's

Reprinted from *Journal of Political Economy* 84 (December 1976): 1145–60, by permission of The University of Chicago Press.

discovered the applicability of a similar compensation mechanism to the problem of motivating individuals to reveal their true demands for public goods. The first to publish was Edward Clarke (1971, 1972), whose papers until now have made very little impact on the economics profession. The lack of impact can be attributed partly to the nature of the idea that Clarke put forward, which is counterintuitive to almost any welfare economist, and partly to Clarke's difficult writing style. The second person was Theodore Groves. In one paper (1973) he offered a mathematically rigorous treatment of a procedure like Vickrey's for allocating scarce private goods within an organization. More recently Groves and Loeb (1975) published a procedure isomorphic to Clarke's for selecting the optimal quantities of public goods. Our objectives here are to provide a clear explanation of the demand-revealing process as it applies to public goods and to extend the understanding of the process on several fronts.

While, as Bowen (1943) showed, majority rule is efficient if the intensity of voters' preferences is distributed symmetrically, the demand-revealing process does not require for its efficiency any restriction on the distribution of intensities of voters' preferences. Unlike the voting processes proposed by Thompson (1965), Dreze and de la Vallee Poussin (1971) and Tideman (1972), the demand-revealing process requires no special beliefs on the part of voters. Basically, it provides an environment in which each voter is motivated to reveal his preferences correctly. This is accomplished by the use of a special—indeed, bizarre—tax mechanism which rewards truthful presentation of preferences and penalizes concealment or falsification.

In order to explain the process, we start not with the problem with which Clarke's first paper dealt, the choices of the optimal amount of a single-dimensional public good, but with the simpler case of a choice among discrete options, which Clarke's second paper discussed cryptically. For simplicity, we shall start with two alternatives, which may be conceived of as two policies or two candidates. We shall then show how the process can be extended to more than two options. Having introduced the subject with these simple examples, we shall then turn to the choice of the optimal amount of a public good.

Choice between Two Options

Suppose that a collective choice must be made between two options, designated *A* and *B*. The rule we describe involves asking each individual to state which option he prefers and the amount of money he is willing to pay to secure his preferred option instead of the other. We shall show shortly why he would have an incentive to respond truthfully. In table 1, we show the "votes" of each of three voters for the two options. Option *A* is worth a total of $70 to the persons who prefer it and is chosen by the rule because *B* is worth less to its proponent.

We now turn to why the voter is motivated to correctly state his preferences. There is a "Clarke tax" to be levied, and, as we said before, it is a

TABLE 1. Aggregating Preferences for Two Options (in dollars)

Voter	Differential Values of Options	
	A	*B*
1	30	0
2	0	60
3	40	0
Total	70	60

bizarre tax. We inquire with respect to each voter what the outcome would have been if he had not voted. For example, if voter 1 had not voted, then the outcome would have been that alternative *A* would have received \$40 total and alternative *B* \$60; hence; alternative *B* would have won. We charge voter 1 \$20, the amount necessary to bring the "votes" for *A* up to equality with the "votes" for *B*. By the same line of reasoning, voter 3 pays a tax of \$30. Voter 2 pays no tax because his vote did not change the outcome. Note that, had voter 1 understated his preference for *A* by an amount less than \$10, he would have paid exactly the same tax as he did. If he had understated his preference for *A* by more than \$10, *B* would have been selected. And voter 1 would prefer having *A* at the price of \$20 to having *B*. Similarly, if a voter overstates his preferences, either the overstatement makes no difference in what is selected or what he pays or else (e.g., if voter 2 said *B* was worth \$100 to him) he changes the result by his action and pays more for his choice than it is worth to him.

To describe the decision rule generally, define S_A as the sum over all voters who state a preference for *A* over *B* of the amounts they offer to pay to have *A* instead of *B*. Define S_B similarly. The collective choice rule will be to choose *A* if $S_A > S_B$, choose *B* is $S_B > S_A$, and flip a coin to decide if $S_A = S_B$. The incentive to respond truthfully is generated by a "Clarke tax," a rule that a voter must pay a portion of his offer if and only if his vote changes the outcome. Any voter who changes the outcome must pay $(S_A - S_B)$, calculated without his vote. In the case of a tie that is decided by a coin toss, every voter on the side that wins the toss is regarded as having changed the outcome. If the result without a person's vote is a tie, he pays nothing.

In effect, this rule gives each voter the choice of (1) leaving the outcome where it would be without his vote or (2) changing it at a price of the reported net loss to other voters. If the value to a voter of his preferred outcome is less than the net value of the alternative to others, then he prefers (1), which occurs if he responds truthfully. If his value is greater than the aggregate net value to others, then he prefers (2), which again is what occurs upon a truthful response. If his value exactly balances the net value reported by others, then he is indifferent between the two possibilities, and we flip a coin if he responds truthfully. A nontruthful response cannot benefit the respondent, and it carries a risk of making him worse off than he would have been with the truth. If he understates his value, he may pass up an opportunity to obtain the result he desires at an attractive price. If he overstates his value, he may wind up paying more than it is worth to him to have his choice.

To characterize the rule in terms of property rights, one might call it "entitlement to the consequences of one's abstention," since the result that occurs if a voter abstains costs him nothing; while if his vote changes the collective choice, he must pay. This has a certain family resemblance to majority rule, where the voter's only entitlement is to what a majority of persons other than himself want, except that, if all others tie, he can decide the issue.

Any money collected from voters in this system must be wasted or given to nonvoters to keep the incentives correct. If voters received the money collected, the possibility of increasing their shares would distort their incentives. However, if the revenue were simply divided equally among all voters, the effective distortion would be minimal if there were more than 100 or so voters; with a large number of voters, it is most likely that no one vote will change the outcome, so that in most cases no taxes for voting will be collected. We will discuss the significance of the lack of budget balance in more detail in the context of decisions about continuous variables.

A serious problem in all voting systems is the weakness of the incentive to vote. The demand-revealing process is no exception. The only wholly instrumental reason for a person to vote is the possibility that his vote will be decisive. Failure to vote carries a risk of passing up a chance to alter the outcome at a favorable price, but the probability of being decisive is usually small enough so that people might still reasonably conclude that voting is not worth the effort. Even if people do decide to vote, they are normally not motivated to give any serious study to their vote in collective decision processes, because the probable gain from acquiring further information or simply reflecting on the information already at hand is usually less than the cost. Thus, ill-informed voting is to be expected. The demand-revealing process is no exception to this general rule put forward by Downs (1957).

It may seem that a person who sustains a large loss when his preference is not followed deserves compensation, but this cannot be given without motivating an excessive statement of differential value. If a voter expected to lose, an offer to compensate his loss would motivate a statement from him of a larger loss. In regard to the uncompensated losses that are produced, the demand-revealing process is similar to majority rule. In the latter, every voter must live with the choice of the majority. His only opportunity to be decisive on the issue is if there is an equal number of other voters on each side. Similarly, in the demand-revealing process, every voter must live with a finding that the aggregate value placed by others on the alternatives is opposed to his own interest, provided that he is not willing to pay enough to give his preference the higher aggregate value.

It might be objected that the demand-revealing process would permit confiscatory action. If there is a proposal to tear down one person's house and make the site a park, and if others report a greater gain from the park than the occupant's loss, then the latter loses his property. The demand-revealing process would indeed have this confiscatory characteristic if there were no constitutional limits on the proposals that could be considered. In this respect, the system is again like majority rule, which has a similar confiscatory potential. It is reasonable to expect that people making collective choices by the demand-revealing process would desire constitutional restrictions that would limit the potential for overt redistribution. For instance, a proposal that a person's property be taken for a public purpose might be admissible only if he would be given reasonable compensation.

Choices among Several Discrete Options

We now show how a demand-revealing process operates when there are more than two discrete options. In table 2 there are three voters, indicated by numbers, and three options, indicated by letters. The numbers in table 2 have been obtained by simply adding a third option, *C*, to the two shown in table 1, while leaving the differential the voter is willing to pay for a choice between *A* and *B* the same as it was in table 1. The difference between the numbers associated with any two options is interpreted as the amount of money the voter is willing to pay to have the one option with the higher number instead of the other. Whether or not this is a legitimate interpretation will be discussed below.

It may be noted that the rank-order preferences generate cyclic choices when majority rule is used. To determine the collective choice by the demand-revealing process, we simply sum the columns and select the option with the

TABLE 2. Aggregating Preferences for Three Options (in dollars)

Voter	Differential Values of Options			Tax	Net Benefit of Voting
	A	*B*	*C*		
1	50	20	0	30	20
2	0	60	20	0	0
3	40	0	50	30	10
Total	90	80	70	—	—
	Total without Indicated Votes				
For 1: 2 + 3	40	60	70	—	—
For 2: 1 + 3	90	20	50	—	—
For 3: 1 + 2	50	80	20	—	—

highest total, which in this case is *A*. There is no cycle, nor could there be, although a tie would be possible.

The tax for each voter is calculated from the lower portion of table 2. For the tax on voter 1, add up the sum of the other individuals' votes. Option *C* would have been chosen with \$70. The tax on voter 1 would be \$70 minus \$40, or \$30, and voter 1 is better off by \$20 (\$50 − \$30) than he would have been by abstaining. Note that if he had understated his preferences enough to avoid being taxed, for instance, if he had reported that *A* only benefited him \$25, *C* would have been selected and voter 1 would have been worse off than he was by correctly presenting his preferences. In the case of voter 2, there is no tax because his vote does not change the outcome; and in the case of voter 3, there is a tax of \$30 (\$80 − \$50), and he obtains a net benefit of \$10 (\$40 − \$30). These taxes are fairly substantial, but that is because we have only a small number of voters. With many voters, the probability is high that the total tax would be relatively miniscule if not zero.

We next inquire whether the proposed method produces results that are "independent of irrelevant alternatives." If option *C* is dropped from the example in table 2, what difference would it make? Consider voter 1 first. He reports a differential value of \$30 for *A* over *B* in table 2. If *C* were dropped from consideration, voter 1 would no longer have to offer \$50 for *A* instead of *C*. He would be richer, and he might spend some of his additional wealth to increase his offer with respect to *A* instead of *B*, say, from \$30 to \$32. Such wealth effects could conceivably change the result.

We do not, however, think that this is what is normally meant by a dependence on irrelevant alternatives. Option *C* is relevant because its presence or absence affects the wealth of voter 1. If *A* owns a pizza den and is negotiating with *B* for its sale and *C* builds another pizza restaurant directly across the street, this will clearly affect the bargain between *A* and *B*. However, we do not think that it would be proper to say that this was a situation which "lacked independence of irrelevant alternatives." In view of the general controversies surrounding this particular criterion of the Arrow theorem, however, we should like to simply discuss the wealth effect in the demand-revealing process rather than attempt to clear up the linguistic problem.

To put the matter another way, when we insist that each voter arrange the options on a linear scale, so that the difference between the numbers on the scale for any pair of options represents what he is willing to pay to have one option instead of the other, we leave no room for wealth effects. It may be that voter 1's true willingness to pay is \$22 for *B* instead of *C* and \$32 for *A* instead of *B*, but only \$50 (rather than \$54), for *A* instead of *C*, because if he has to pay \$22 to get from *C* to *B*, he is poorer than if he starts at *B*. With his lower wealth, it is not irrational for him to be willing to spend only \$28 rather than \$32, at that point, to get from *B* to *A*. The linear scale does not permit voter 1 to report these wealth effects, so he compromises by reporting the values in table 2.

It might be proposed that voters be asked to report their preferences among all pairs so that wealth effects could be taken into account in the

TABLE 3. The Possible Cycle in Three Options (in dollars)

	A against *B*		*B* against *C*		*A* against *C*	
1	32	0	22	0	50	0
2	0	31	0	21	0	51

decision process. However, to do that would be to reintroduce a possibility of cycles. Consider the two voters shown in table 3.

Voter 1 has the preferences described earlier. Voter 2 has preferences in the opposite order, of approximately the same magnitude but with less nonlinearity from wealth effects. When the preferences are summed, we find a collective choice for *A* over *B* and *B* over *C*, but also for *C* over *A*. This problem of intransitivity might be resolved by applying some analytic device such as the "tournament matrix" described by Moon and Pullman (1970), but it is not clear how the Clarke tax would then be calculated. Furthermore, as long as there were cycles, there would be incentives for strategic misstatements. Therefore, it may be best to require each voter to submit a linearized statement of his preferences, letting him make the necessary approximations there. Then if he can guess which option would be selected without his vote, it will be in his interest to present comparisons with respect to that option truthfully.

A Simple Continuous Application

We now proceed with the specific case Clarke presented in his *Public Choice* article (1971). Assume there is some public good which can be purchased in any desired quantity. For the purpose of graphic ease, we assume that it is sold in units which cost \$1, no matter how many are purchased, so that the line at \$1/unit on figure 1 represents the social cost schedule for purchasing

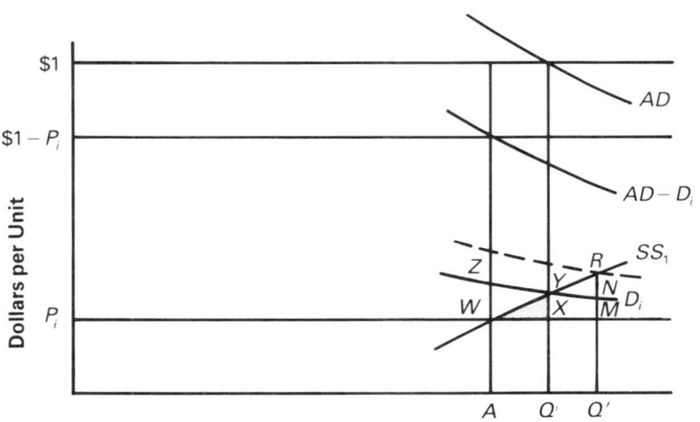

Fig. 1. The tax on a person whose benefit exceeds his assigned tax share

different quantities. The first stage in Clarke's process is to assign to each voter his share of the total cost. Let us temporarily assume this share is assigned arbitrarily, and for the *i*th voter the share is the line shown at P_i. Later we will discuss how it is possible to approximate the Lindahl condition in the allocation of these shares.

The voters are now asked to state their demand curves for the public good. Voter *i*'s curve is shown as D_i. These curves are then summed vertically to get the aggregate demand (aggregate willingness to pay) curve *AD*. The point where the sum crosses the cost curve, that is, the \$1/unit line, is the efficient quantity of public good to purchase. This is, of course, the Samuelson equilibrium and has many fine properties, although not as many as the Lindahl equilibrium, toward which we shall move shortly.

How do we motivate voter *i*, and indeed all of the other voters, to correctly reveal their true demand curves? The answer is by telling each voter he will be subject to a Clarke tax, calculated as follows. When all the ballots are received, the tax for voter *i* will be calculated by summing (vertically) the demand curves of all of the voters other than *i*, generating the curve $AD - D_i$, and finding the intersection between that curve and the line $\$1 - P_i$, which is the share of the tax cost that all voters other than *i* will pay. The intersection in figure 1 occurs at quantity *A*. This is the quantity of the public good that would be purchased if *i* reported a perfectly elastic (i.e., horizontal) demand schedule, identical to his cost share. Such a vote, offering to pay one's assigned share of whatever quantity others desire to purchase, is the analogue for continuous choices of abstaining in discrete choices. With voter *i* "abstaining," the revealed demand (of others) would intersect their share of cost at *A*, and *i*'s payment would be the rectangle to the left of *A* and below P_i. In order to compute *i*'s tax when he does not "abstain," we determine from the curve $AD - D_i$ the amount of compensation that voter *i* would have to pay to keep all other voters indifferent to any change from quantity *A*. The required compensation per unit at any quantity is the difference at that quantity between the total cost and the aggregate willingness of others to pay. We call the schedule of such amounts, calculated as $\$1 - (AD - D_i)$, a synthetic supply schedule. It can be thought of as the net marginal social cost of supplying *i* with additional units of the public good after allowing credit against the gross cost for the value of the good to others. This schedule is shown as line SS_i in figure 1. The schedule SS_i is a mirror image of $AD - D_i$. In this example, we assume that *i* has a higher willingness to pay than his cost share at *A*. This implies that the effect of including his demand is to increase the quantity. The intersection of the synthetic supply curve and *i*'s demand is at the quantity *Q*, and that is the optimal amount of the public good, because that is also the quantity where *AD* intersects the \$1 line.

The amount that would have to be paid to individuals other than *i* in order to make them indifferent to the move from *A* to *Q* is represented by the area under SS_i, while the gain to voter *i* is the area under his demand curve. Voter *i* pays a composite tax which is the standard payment if he abstained plus the

Clarke tax area under SS_i from A to Q. The total tax is equivalent to his assigned share of the cost of Q units of the public good (the rectangle to the left of line Q and below P_i) plus the shaded triangle WXY. The sum of such rectangles for all voters is enough to pay the total cost of the public good; the shaded triangle and corresponding amounts for other voters must be wasted or given to nonvoters to keep all the incentives correct.[2]

Suppose that voter i had misstated his demand curve in an effort to increase his net benefit. The benefit he has obtained from voting is the triangle WYZ. Clearly, stating his demand as less than it actually is would reduce the size of his triangle. On the other hand, if he stated his demand schedule as higher than it actually is, so that the quantity chosen would be, say, Q', his additional taxes would be $QQ'RY$ while his additional benefits would be only $QQ'NY$. He is best off correctly presenting his demand curve.

It must be mentioned that there is a very slight conceptual problem in the specification of these demand curves. Quantity demanded depends on income as well as price, and one determinant of a person's income is the Clarke tax he must pay. Since one person's Clarke tax depends on the demand curves specified by others, each person could logically say that he could not specify his demand curve until all others had done so. This is not a practical problem, however, because the Clarke tax, as we will show, is very small, and in most cases the uncertainty in the Clarke tax is very small, since it depends only on the elasticity of the aggregate willingness to pay of other voters, and in any event people can simply be directed to report demand curves that reflect their best guesses about their incomes.

In figure 2, we assume that j, given his tax share, wants less than that amount of the public good which the other voters would choose. As in figure 1, D_j represents his true demand for the public good, and quantity A represents the amount which would be purchased if he chose to abstain, that is, the

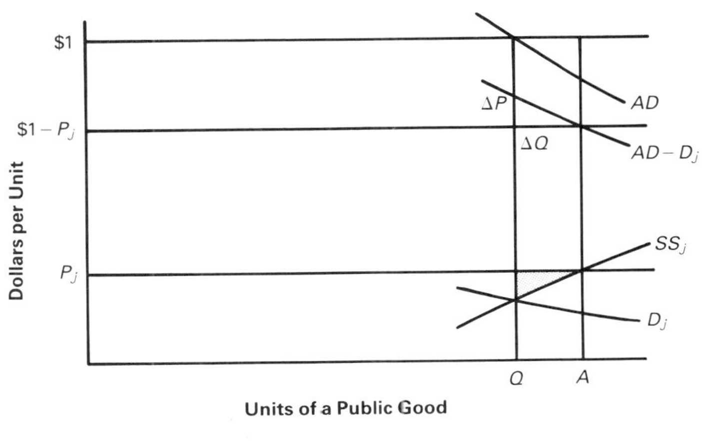

Fig. 2. The tax on a person whose benefit is less than his assigned tax share

point where the sum of the demand curves of all the other voters intersects the sum of their shares of the tax price. Line SS_j in this case, as in figure 1, represents the rate of compensation per unit which it would be necessary to pay the other voters to compensate them for any change from point A in the amount of the public good. To the left of point A, SS_j may be interpreted as the rate of reduction in taxes for j that can be granted while reducing the quantity of the public good and reducing taxes for others by the full amount of the loss of income that they experience. As in figure 1, this compensation is not actually going to be paid, but voter j will be taxed this amount.

Once again, the point of intersection between j's demand curve and the synthetic supply curve represents the optimal quantity of the public good, Q, which is also the quantity at which AD intersects the \$1/unit line. In this case, Q is less than would be chosen if voter j abstained. Voter j then pays a tax which is equal to the rectangle to the left of line Q and below his tax share, plus the shaded triangle. The rectangle is enough to pay his share of the cost of provision of the public good; the shaded triangle, once again, is wasted or given to nonvoters. We will leave to the reader the demonstration that the correct presentation of his demand curve will maximize his welfare under these circumstances. It is essentially the same as the demonstration for figure 1.

What is true for voters i and j is true for all voters. They are motivated by this peculiar tax procedure to present accurately their true demand curves. The motivation, however, represented by triangle WYZ in figure 1, would normally be very small, about the same as the area of the shaded triangle.

To see how small the Clarke taxes would be, note that the shaded triangle in figure 2 is a mirror image of the one with sides labeled ΔP and ΔQ. If the elasticity of $AD - D_j$ is η, then $\Delta Q = \eta Q \Delta P/(1 - P_j)$, so that the area of the triangle is $1/2\eta Q(\Delta P)^2/(1 - P_j)$. The denominator approaches 1 as the number of voters increases, so that if η is on the order of magnitude of 2, then each voter's Clarke tax is roughly $Q(\Delta P)^2$. The values of ΔP would be related to the number of voters (N); it would be implausible for the average value of $(\Delta P)^2$ to be greater than $1/N^2$. Thus, the typical voter, whose share of the resource cost is Q/N, has a Clarke tax on the order of magnitude of $1/N$ times his resource cost, and the sum of all Clarke taxes is on the order of magnitude of one voter's taxes. Thus, if the citizens of the United States were voting on the annual federal budget, the grand total of all the Clarke taxes charged would be in the neighborhood of \$2,000, or about one-thousandth of a penny per person.

As the triangles go to zero, the motivation for taking the trouble to present one's demand curve goes to zero. The method is cheat-proof and generates the socially optimal quantity of the public good when every voter maximizes his self-interest, but when N is large the Downs paradox is present: voters have almost no incentive to vote.

Since the excess revenues generated by the process are so very small, and certainly less than the administrative cost for any situation with more than a very small number of persons, the excess revenues deserve to be ignored.

This may be rather untidy, but it is normal in welfare economics to ignore the cost of reaching a decision. If the Clarke tax is considered as part of the cost of making the decision, then it should be ignored. Contrarily, if it is not ignored, the cost of the processes of reaching decision rules by other processes should also be included. We feel that our suggestion of simply wasting the extra revenue rather than searching for some complex budget-balancing process which might or might not achieve the same result is an important contribution. It is also one of the reasons why it is so hard for welfare economists (ourselves included) to feel at home with the process.

So far, we have generated the Samuelson equilibrium; we now indicate how the Lindahl equilibrium may be approximated. To this point, we have simply assigned the base share of the total expenditure for the individual in an arbitrary manner. Suppose that, instead of assigning it arbitrarily, we appoint someone to do this, with the stipulation that from his pay we are going to subtract some multiple of the sum of the triangles for all of the voters.[3] The person assigning the fixed shares would be motivated to try to minimize the triangles. In the limit, if he were able to perfectly achieve his goal, there would be no triangles and no loss; we would have a perfect Lindahl equilibrium, with each voter paying for public goods according to his marginal evaluation.

It is unlikely that the official allocating the shares could do this perfectly, but he might be able to do quite well with advanced econometric methods. It should be emphasized, however, that there is one piece of information he cannot use in assigning the tax share of any individual: that individual's performance on previous choices. The voter, in making his choices on each individual decision, must not be able to offset against the optimality conditions for that particular choice the prospect of changing his base tax share in the future, because this would motivate him to misstate his demand curve.

As in all voting methods, there is a possibility for coalitions to distort the result. In particular, consider the strategy for a coalition of N persons whose equal benefits are greater than their equal tax shares. In figure 3, the demand

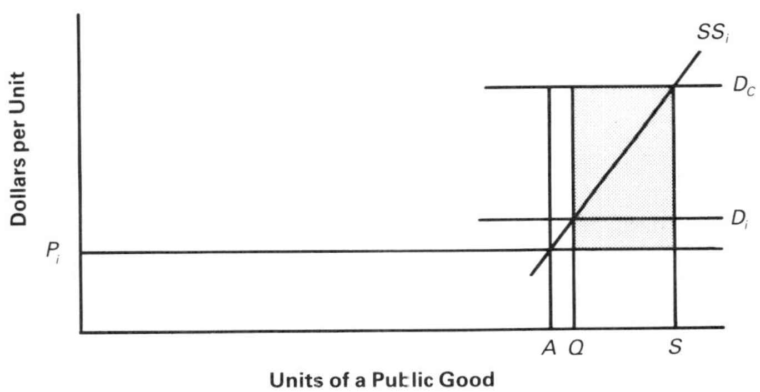

Fig. 3. The strategic calculation of a coalition

schedule of voter i, D_i, is shown as a horizontal line because changes in the height would generally be negligible over the range of potential effects he and his coalition could have. The higher line, D_c, represents the demand that i would express taking account of the benefit of $D_i - P_i$ that each member of his coalition would receive for each unit increase in the quantity chosen. The distance from A to S is N times as far as the distance from A to Q, where the outcome would have been moved by an honest vote. With N persons in the coalition voting this way, the effect is to move the choice $N(N - 1)$ times the distance from A to Q, compared with honest voting. The gross benefit of the coalition activity to each member, in terms of benefits not paid for by his standard tax share, is $N(N - 1)(D_i - P_i)(Q - A)$, which is the area of the shaded rectangle. Each member's extra tax from coalition activity, apart from his standard tax share, is that portion of the shaded rectangle that is below the synthetic supply schedule. Thus, the net benefit of coalition activity to each member is a triangle like that in the upper left corner of the shaded rectangle, the area of which is proportional to $(N - 1)^2$ and to $(D_i - P_i)^2$. Thus, the benefit of forming coalitions varies with the square of the errors in tax shares and with the square of the number of members minus one. Voters whose tax shares overstate their benefits have a similar opportunity to form coalitions that multiply the understatements of their demands.

In this example, we have assumed that the only thing chosen is the unidimensional quantity of one public good. One of the convenient characteristics of the demand-revealing process is that it is not necessary to restrain voting to one issue at a time. A multidimensional public good or several public goods or public goods *plus* candidates can all be dealt with simultaneously. In general, it is much harder to organize coalitions in cases where the choice is not unidimensional. This is not to say that it is impossible. Still, we suspect that the demand-revealing process is rather less susceptible to coalition distortion than most voting methods.

The extension of the voting method to choices for more than one good is straightforward if the chosen quantity of one public good has no impact on demands for other public goods. However, if the chosen quantity of some goods affects the demands for other goods, a simultaneous solution is needed. One could ignore the interactions in the choice procedure and rely on individuals to make estimates of the quantities of other goods that would be chosen in reporting their demand schedules, but any misestimates by voters would lead to unnecessary inefficiencies.

At a conceptual level, one could ask all voters to report their marginal valuation schedules for each good at every combination of quantities of other public goods, although the data problem if this were really attempted would be unmanageable. If it were not impossible to obtain and operate on the data, the identification of an equilibrium where the appropriate marginal conditions were all satisfied simultaneously would be essentially no different from calculating a competitive equilibrium for private goods. Groves and Ledyard (1975) developed the theoretical foundations of such a system in detail.

In later publications,[4] we propose to apply the process to a number of other problems such as income redistribution, badly behaved demand curves, and use as a welfare indicator. We will also discuss its practical application in realistic government structure. The purpose of this article, however, has been to explain the system and to demonstrate that it solves a number of problems previously thought to be unsolvable. The process does not violate the Arrow theorem, but it avoids the problems of the Arrow theorem by not meeting Arrow's assumptions. However, it seems to us that, if the Arrow theorem is considered as a result that suggests that a good voting process cannot be devised, then the real problem raised by Arrow is solved by this process.

NOTES

1. The method is also applicable to decisions about income and wealth redistribution, instead of leaving that issue aside in the conventional manner. It can be used to ensure the competitiveness of markets, and it provides a welfare criterion superior, in our opinion, to Pareto optimality. All of these matters must be deferred for later publication.
2. One possibility for avoiding waste would be for pairs of communities to agree to exchange their collections of these excess revenues.
3. Probably the best way of selecting the "tax setter" would be to solicit bids. Precautions against bribery would, of course, be necessary.
4. Mimeographed preliminary drafts are available on request.

REFERENCES

Bowen, H. R. "The Interpretation of Voting in the Allocation of Economic Resources." *Quarterly Journal of Economics* 58 (November 1943): 32–42.

Clarke, E. H. "Multipart Pricing of Public Goods." *Public Choice* 11 (Fall 1971): 17–33.

———. "Multipart Pricing of Public Goods: An Example." In *Public Prices for Public Products*, edited by S. Mushkin. Washington, D.C.: Urban Institute, 1972.

Downs, A. *An Economic Theory of Democracy*. New York: Harper and Row, 1957.

Dreze, J. H., and de la Vallee Poussin, D. "A Tâtonnement Process for Public Goods." *Review of Economic Studies* 38 (April 1971): 133–50.

Groves, T. "Incentives in Teams." *Econometrica* 41 (July 1973): 617–33.

Groves, T., and Ledyard, J. "Optimal Allocation of Public Goods: A Solution to the 'Free Rider Problem.'" Discussion paper 144. Center for Mathematical Studies in Economics and Management Science, Northwestern University, May 1975.

Groves, T., and Loeb, M. "Incentives and Public Inputs." *Journal of Public Economics* 4 (August 1975): 211–26.

Moon, J. W., and Pullman, N. J. "On Generalized Tournament Matrices." *SIAM Review* 12 (July 1970): 389–94.

Thompson, E. "A Pareto Optimal Group Decision Process." *Papers on Non-Market Decision Making* 1 (1965): 133–40.

Tideman, T. N. "The Efficient Provision of Public Goods." In *Public Prices for Public Products*, edited by S. Mushkin. Washington, D.C.: Urban Institute, 1972.

Vickrey, W. "Counterspeculation, Auctions, and Competitive Sealed Tenders." *Journal of Finance* 16 (May 1961): 8–37.

An Economic Theory of Mutually Advantageous Issue Linkages in International Negotiations

Robert D. Tollison and Thomas D. Willett

There has been considerable interest in recent years on both a practical and a scholarly level in the question of issue linkages in international negotiations. While interest in linkage is not new in international affairs, what seems different is the explicit stress put on linkages as a negotiating device, that is, making trade-offs explicit among issues. Most of the highly publicized cases of proposed issue linkages appear to have been motivated by attempts of individual countries or groups of countries to extend their dominant bargaining or veto power in one particular issue area into other areas so as to achieve maximum advantage from their whole array of international interactions, for example, the possible threat of U.S. troop withdrawals as a way to influence German international financial policies, and the attempts by OPEC to link oil discussions to other international economic issues.[1] Indeed, as a referee of this paper pointed out, the general, albeit uninformed, view has been that linkages usually exacerbate problems rather than help to resolve them.

In this article we stress the existence of an additional rationale for linkage that relies upon mutual interest. Drawing on the economic theory of exchange, we consider the use of issue linkages to facilitate the completion of a greater number of mutually beneficial agreements among nations. Our purpose is not to deny the importance of the traditional rationales for issue linkages, but rather to spell out some of the implications of our mutual benefit rationale. We hope that this will prove a fruitful step toward developing a more general theory of issue linkages which integrates and extends both types of considerations.

Our approach differs from many examples of economic analysis in that we explicitly focus upon distributional considerations. Often in the economics literature attention is focused on attaining maximum aggregate economic efficiency or potential welfare to the neglect of distributional considerations. While for many types of domestic policies this may be a reasonable simplification, for many international issues it clearly is not. Consider, for example, a change in macroeconomic policies which might benefit another country greatly, but which would cause moderate harm to the country initiating the policy change. Even though to most observers the gain to the one country seems much greater than the loss to the other, the harmed country has no direct interest in adopting the policy which would maximize potential welfare between the two countries. The economist's answer to this dilemma is that the

First published in *International Organization* 33 (Autumn 1979): 425–49.

country which would have a large prospective gain should bribe the country which would be harmed with sufficient compensation so that it too would enjoy an overall gain. In practice, however, the economist's direct bribe is extremely unlikely to be politically feasible. Through the formal or informal linking of issues, however, the possibility emerges of indirectly paying compensation through positions taken in other negotiations.

Although well understood by many negotiators, the use of issue linkages to secure international agreements, which would otherwise be frustrated because of distributional effects, does not appear to have been emphasized. In a recent paper William Wallace has discussed many facets of issue linkages and outlined a major project that Chatham House is undertaking that will examine how major Atlantic countries attempt to link different issue areas in their foreign relations.[2] Wallace outlines some of the pertinent factors such as the level of government-to-government contact, the capacity of top political leaders to absorb information on issues, and a number of other institutional considerations that in his view influence the process of issue linkage among governments. He does not, however, consider issue linkages as a method of overcoming distributional obstacles to the provision of international cooperative actions, nor to our knowledge has this been emphasized elsewhere in discussions of international issue linkages other than in our own preliminary sketch of the beginnings of a theory of optimal negotiations.[3]

A major conclusion of our analysis is that linkage will be more important where the distribution of benefits from agreement is highly skewed toward one (or a few) countries. In this case linkage of issues with offsetting distributional patterns can help promote agreements which otherwise might go unconsumated because of distributional effects. The converse of this proposition is also interesting in that linkage will not be important where the distribution of benefits from agreement is fairly even across countries. Some additional qualifications and extensions of the analysis will be discussed.

The Mutual Advantage Approach to Issue Linkages

Our purpose in this section is to introduce the reader to some of the concepts and terminology that will be employed in the subsequent analysis. This discussion, as well as the later analysis, will be presented in terms of single-actor models and will assume that negotiators are efficient representatives of their countries' interests. We are aware that this approach has certain limitations, but we will defer consideration of these complications and qualifications. For the present we take the view that the analysis of policies on the basis of single-actor models of economic self-interest can offer useful insights if applied with due respect for the complexities of particular situations.

Consider a simple case of bargaining between two representative individuals in figure 1. There are two individuals and two commodities. To give the model a flavor of international negotiations, one might think of the two individuals as diplomats-negotiators and the two commodities as issues on

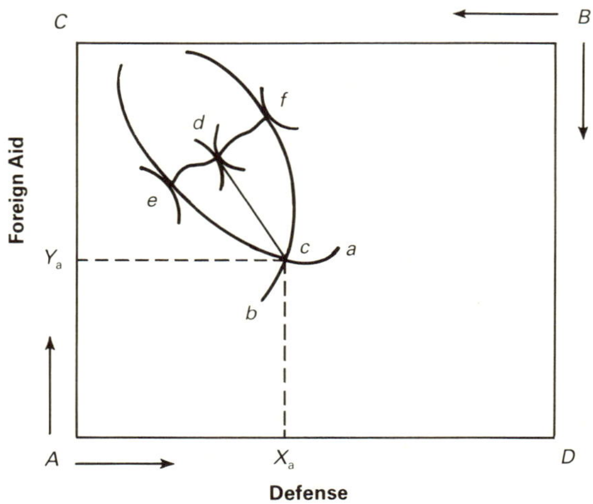

Fig. 1. Exchange between negotiators

which the diplomats seek to reach an agreement. For example, the two issues could be expenditures to support a common defense alliance versus expenditures for a foreign aid program which the two countries jointly provide for a third country. The model assumes by construction that there is a fixed amount of expenditures to support the two issues over which agreements can be negotiated. Thus, $AD = CB$ represents the level of expenditure necessary to fund the defense alliance, and $AC = DB$ is the expenditure level required, say, to fund a capital development project under the joint foreign aid program. One might think of these magnitudes as allocations for such potential joint projects given in the government budget of the country of each negotiator.

The curves denoted by a and b are the indifference curves of the two negotiators. Each point on these curves represents a combination of expenditures on the two issues that provide negotiator *A* and negotiator *B* with the same level of satisfaction as measured by some utility index. A whole family of such curves for each negotiator can be derived, though we only utilize one for each negotiator in the discussion here. It is important to recognize that negotiator *A*'s indifference curves are read from the southwest origin at *A* and negotiator *B*'s are read from the northeast origin at *B*. Thus, increases in negotiator *A*'s satisfaction (i.e., higher indifference curves) are represented by northeastward movements, and increases in welfare for negotiator *B* are read by southwestward movements. A higher indifference curve for a negotiator in this setting simply means a more preferred locus of benefits from the two joint projects.

Consider negotiations between the two diplomats starting at point c in the diagram. Negotiator *A*, whose position is read from the southwest corner of the box, is originally endowed with AX_a units of contribution to the common defense program. Negotiator *B*, whose position is read from the northeast corner of the box, is endowed with the remainder of the fixed amounts of contributions to the two joint activities, that is, with X_aD units of defense expenditures and Y_aC units of foreign aid expenditures. We want to analyze negotiations or agreements emanating from *c* and simply accept the fact for the moment that the two countries somehow arrived at *c*—i.e., at what will turn out to be an unsustainable position. The football-shaped area, viewed from point *c*, represents the potential gains from agreement confronting the negotiators. This follows since movements from *c* into that area place *both* negotiators on higher indifference curves. The area of potential gains from agreement is bounded by the two indifference curves which intersect at *c* since neither negotiator would accept a bargain that lowered his original level of satisfaction as given by indifference curves *a* and *b*, respectively. Movements into the football-shaped area depend upon the terms of trade or "price" at which the two negotiators might trade off between the two issues, and their immediate problem is to reach agreement on what the terms of trade will be. For example, if negotiator A were a very superior bargainer, he might be able to obtain an agreement to move to f where negotiator *B* is no better off than in the absence of trade. Negotiator *B*, of course, could perhaps obtain a point such as *e* if he were a very superior bargainer. In general, however, bargaining will take place along some intermediate vector such as *cd* where the gains from agreement between the two issues are split between the two negotiators.

Bargaining will take place until the gains from agreement are exhausted, which occurs at points where the indifference curves of the two negotiators become tangent. Tangencies of the two sets of indifference curves exhaust mutually agreeable trades since this implies that both negotiators place the same subjective trade-off on one issue relative to the other. When all such tangencies within the football-shaped area are connected, such as *ef*, the result is called a contract curve, because agreements will predictably end up along such a relation where the gains from agreement are exhausted. The exact point on the contract curve at which a given agreement is reached is where the terms of trade line and the two indifference curves are tangent, i.e., the price at which the negotiators can trade is equal to the subjective evaluations that they place on the two issues. In the example in figure 1, negotiator *A* trades off increased expenditures on the foreign aid program for reductions in the support of the defense alliance, while *B* trades off in the opposite direction. The basis for such an agreement could reside in the comparative advantage of country *A* in providing the capital development project in the foreign aid program versus the comparative advantage of country *B* in providing the joint defense expenditures, where both countries share common objectives in these areas.

Several other points in this simple example are worth keeping in mind. It should be clear that where one ends up in such an exercise is not independent of where one starts. The original endowments of resources define the limits of mutually agreeable negotiations, and for purposes of this discussion these were determined somehow outside of the model, e.g., some countries have more resources that others. The influence of such differences on negotiations is not a trivial problem, but we will defer consideration of such problems until the next section.

Movements to the contract curve may be thought of as welfare-enhancing for both countries, or as positive-sum or Pareto-superior, in that both parties are made better off by such agreements.

Once on the contract curve, mutually acceptable agreements are no longer possible. Moving along a contract curve means that one negotiator must give up more on *both* issues to the other negotiator. This is an example of zero-sum trade since one party wins what the other gives up. Such agreements represent a situation of pure conflict.

Another category of agreement can be characterized as negative-sum in the sense that individuals would not voluntarily engage in such agreements, that is, the expected value of agreeing ("playing the game") is less than the individual's original endowment which could be retained by not agreeing. Normally, we would not expect negative-sum agreements to be quantitatively important in the two-person case since they are irrational for at least one negotiator. For example, Negotiator *A* would not voluntarily agree to a movement from c that placed him on a lower indifference curve than a, although, of course, the negotiator could be "coerced" into such a move through threats.

While such threat considerations can be quite important in some negotiations, they lie beyond the scope of our analysis. In our terminology our primary concern will be with the analysis of the factors that affect whether negotiations among countries reach the contract curve, that is, with the factors that promote positive-sum agreements among nations.

A Simple Model of Issue Linkages

As a means of exposition, we will consider the case of the production of military hardware in an alliance and illustrate how different cost functions can make agreements easier or more difficult to achieve where countries perceive an interest in having production located in their own country.[4] In figure 2 let Q_AQ_B equal the total amount of alliance hardware to be produced. Dollar values of costs (and later of benefits) are measured vertically. At Q_A all production is in country *A;* at Q_B all production is in country *B*.

Alliance Cost Conditions

If there are no economies of large-scale production, the cost curves would be horizontal lines such as CA_1 and CB_1 in figure 2.1. In the constant-costs environment country *B* is the low-cost producer, and the most economically efficient outcome would be for all production to take place in country *B*.

In figure 2.2 economies of scale are introduced. Country *B*'s quantity of production runs from left to right, and vice versa for country *A*. Economies of scale in this case are more pronounced in country *B*, and the least-cost alterna-

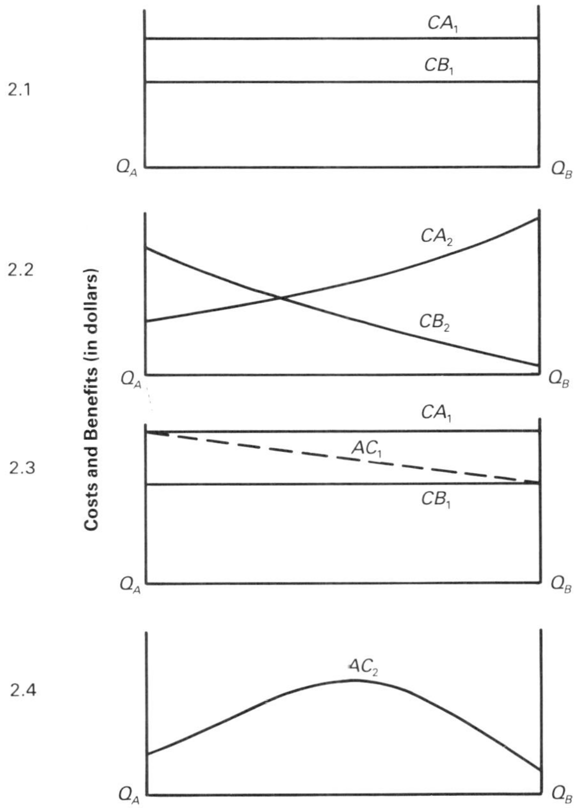

Fig. 2. Cost conditions and the distribution of production among alliance members

tive is again to produce all the alliance hardware in country *B*. But note that it would also be more efficient to produce all the hardware in country *A* rather than to divide production evenly between the two countries.

The results of dividing production between the two countries are illustrated in figures 2.3 and 2.4. In figure 2.3, which corresponds to figure 2.1, the cost (AC_1) of dividing production between the two countries rises continuously as a greater proportion of production is shifted to country *A*. This rate of increase (the slope of AC_1) will be greater, the greater is the difference in cost between countries *A* and *B*. In this case, as will be considered later, there is a constant trade-off between the total costs of production for the alliance and the distribution of the location of production among alliance members.

In figure 2.4, which corresponds to the case of economies of scale in both countries in figure 2.2, there is not a constant trade-off between costs and location of production, and the costs of dividing production fairly evenly between the two countries may be quite high—that is, maximum cost to the alliance for the hardware is obtained along the hump of the cost mountain given by AC_2.

Alliance Benefit Functions

It will now be useful to introduce a benefit function to our analysis.[5] Assume that the alliance output is a pure public good to both countries, that both countries perceive no positive or negative externalities from the production of alliance output in their own countries, and that they have agreed on the total quantity the alliance should provide (Q_AQ_B in the preceding diagrammatics) and the proportion of the total output each should buy (we will assume for convenience of exposition that each buys half). In such a case the decision on the location of alliance production is an easy one; all production will be located in the country which can produce the output at least cost, country *B* in our example.

Further, however, suppose that we drop the assumption of no perceived positive or negative externalities from the location of alliance production. In particular assume that for reasons of prestige, domestic employment, greater security if the alliance breaks up in the future, or similar reasons, the governments of country *A* and country *B* perceive considerable benefits from defense production being located in their countries. Their perceived benefit functions will have two arguments. The first argument is the general security benefit from the possession of defense output by the alliance, a benefit that is independent of the location of production and that is denoted by general utility curves (*GU*) in our subsequent analysis. The second argument is the specific benefits perceived from the location of defense production in their own country and is denoted by specific utility curves (*SU*) in our subsequent analysis. On the assumption that countries *A* and *B* derive the same level of general benefits from the production of the defense output, we may place each country's *SU* curve on the top of a common *GU* curve yielding the total utility curves (*TU*) in figure 3. If we assume that country *A* and country *B* are identical with respect to their perceived specific benefits as well, then the total benefit to *A* plus *B* will be constant with respect to the distribution of production (as given by the horizontal TU_{A+B} curve in fig. 3).

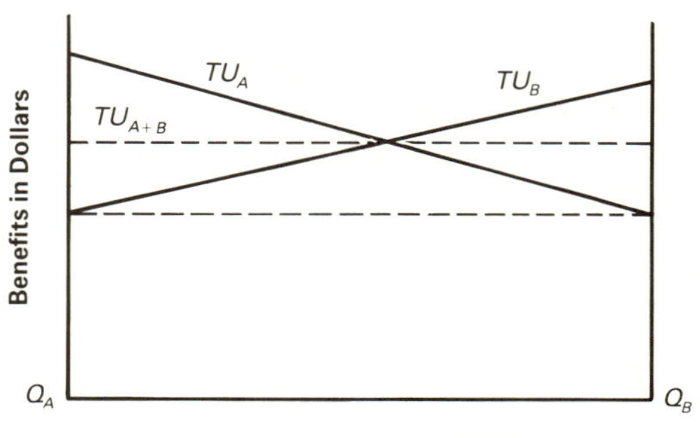

Fig. 3. Benefit functions and the distribution of production among alliance members

Probability of Agreement

Where costs are the same in the two countries, this benefit condition would make the allocation of production decision a constant-sum adversary game, and it would be likely that the outcome of such a game would be an agreement to product half of the alliance output in each country. But as long as an agreement on any allocation was reached, the solution would be efficient in the sense that the maximum potentially achievable net benefits (utility minus cost for country *A* plus country *B*) would be achieved. If costs are less in one country than the other (as in the construction of the various panels of fig. 2), the game would be positive-sum, although there would remain the linkage problem since the more efficient producer cannot compensate the less efficient one for the disproportionate location of production in the former's country.

As we stressed in our earlier discussion of negative-sum tactics in negotiations, there would still be some possibility that agreement would not be reached if each party unsuccessfully tried to bluff the other into granting a disproportionate share of the benefits. In such a bluffing game the country seeking to secure a disproportionate share of the benefits would balance the value of its additional gains (times the subjective estimate of the probability of its securing them) against the prospective net loss if agreement were not reached (again, times the subjective estimate of the probability of this occurring). In general we would expect that the probability of agreement would decline as the skewness of the resulting distribution of benefits increases. Thus in our example the probability of successful agreement, depending on the initial allocation offer by each negotiator, can be derived as in figure 4.

4.1

4.2

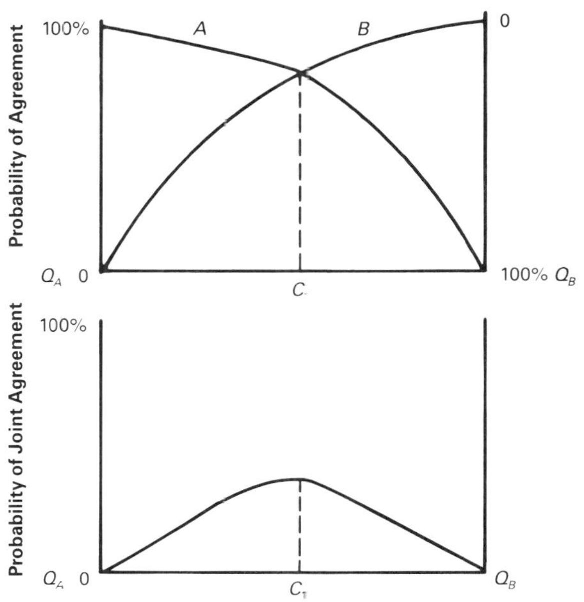

Fig. 4. Probability of agreement functions and the distribution of production among alliance members

Figure 4.1 gives the probability of agreement functions as viewed by each country, and figure 4.2 derives a probability of mutual agreement function from figure 4.1. The probability of successful agreement is therefore larger, the more even is the resulting distribution of benefits from agreement.

Given countries' basic risk-taking preferences and perceptions about their abilities to try to bargain with the other country, the likelihood that countries would take large chances of not agreeing would decrease as the size of the general benefits of the agreement increased and as the size of the specific utility from the distribution of alliance production decreased. In other words, the higher is the *GU* curve and the lower is the slope of the *SU* curve, the greater would be the chances of successful agreement.

The Ability to Make Side Payments

Where the specific benefits are important and the general benefits are low relative to costs, the odds of reaching successful agreement may fall drastically. Consider the following example where the general benefits from the

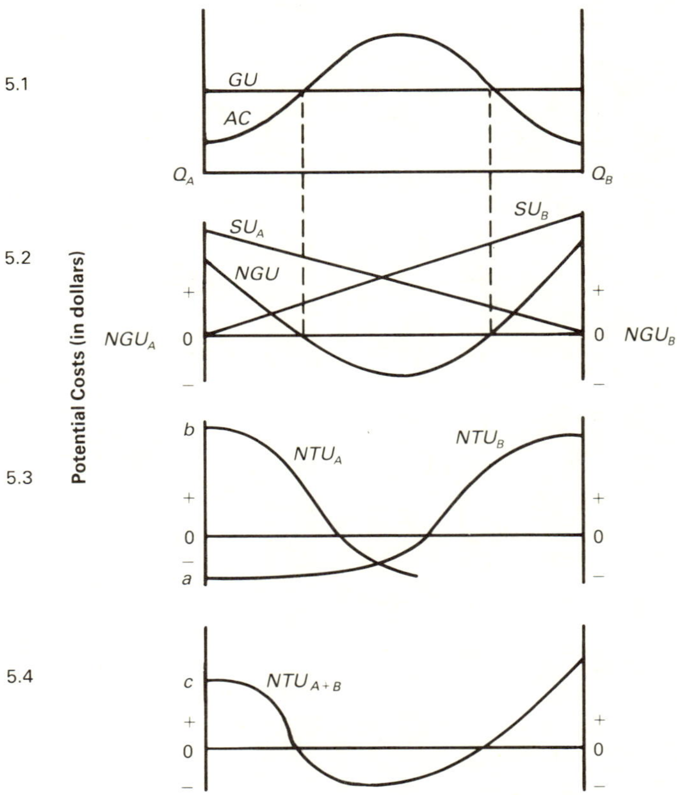

Fig. 5. The potential costs of the inability to make side payments

alliance are less than costs of production but specific benefits are quite sizeable. In figures 5.1 and 5.2 we present a new curve, which represents net general utility (*NGU*) after subtracting the cost of production at each alternative distribution of alliance production, Q_A through Q_B. In figure 5.2 we add the *SU* curve for each country, and in figure 5.3 we present the resulting net total utility (*NTU*) curves for each country. In this case there is a strong possibility that in the absence of side payments agreement will not be reached even though there is the possibility of large total benefits being generated by the alliance. Although there are large net total benefits to *A* and *B* combined from the provision of a large number of combinations of production allocations, there is no point at which *both A* and *B* have positive utility. As is indicated by the joint *NTU* curve in figure 5.4, considerable potential welfare will be forfeited because of the absence of terms which will mutually benefit both parties. Since $0b$ in figure 5.3 is considerably greater than $0a$ (in fig. 5.4 $0c = 0b - 0a$ in fig. 5.3), *A* could offer a side payment to *B* of an amount somewhere between $0b$ and $0a$ to have all production in *A*. Such a side payment would leave both *A* and *B* better off. Similarly, *B* could make such an offer to *A* to have all production in *B*. Thus even apart from the types of problems of failing to reach agreement because each party tries too hard to skew the proportion of mutual benefits heavily in its favor, in this example there is no way that both *A* and *B* can gain utility from an alliance in the absence of side payments. Thus if this is a one-shot negotiation in isolation, there is a strong possibility that it will fail.

A Major Principle of Linkage

As we have stressed, explicit side payments are usually very difficult to make in international political decision making. There is, therefore, considerable likelihood that direct side payments to reach agreements that would benefit both countries would not be feasible. In such a situation the best alternative may be to attempt to find another area of negotiations which has highly skewed benefits. Then by linking the two negotiations so that high benefits go to *A* in one area and high benefits go to *B* in the other, there may be a possibility to secure agreement in both negotiations in a way that brings benefits to both countries and brings the outcome much closer to the aggregate efficiency or potential welfare frontier.[6]

The easiest situation in this case would be where there were two important types of military hardware (planes and missiles) of roughly equal volume and with economies of scale which were independent of each other. Then it would be a fairly simple matter to reach agreement to produce all of one type of hardware in country *A* and all of the other in country *B*. It is doubtful that one could often find exact mirror-image conditions for such a linkage so that the limits of potential welfare could be obtained, but even roughly offsetting distributional patterns could increase substantially the odds of agreeing on linkages that would bring countries closer to the efficiency frontier.

Linkages and Information Costs

In searching for possible linkages to facilitate movements toward the efficiency frontier, it frequently may be necessary to seek agreements which cut across broad issue areas. In such a case the search for offsetting patterns of net benefits will be limited by the increased complexity of the negotiations and the increased difficulty for the officials attempting such linkages to have a good idea of what the costs and benefits in each issue area really look like. Thus, limits on information-processing ability at the level of top decision making will constrain the number and types of issues which can be effectively linked.

Consider the following example. Suppose a high-level official is debating a potential linkage to secure an agreement which he feels is worth 0*A* (evaluated in the official's own terms) to the other country in figure 6. The official's point estimate is that this concession would cost him only 0*B*. Since 0*B* is a smaller negative value than 0*A*, the expected value of this linkage would be positive. Suppose, however, that the official is quite uncertain about the actual outcome. Then *NTU* (*B*) is bounded by a range of possible outcomes, such as *NTU* (*C*) and *NTU* (*D*). The lower part of this range (*AD*) yields outcomes which are worse than 0*A*. The expected value of linkage in this range thus turns negative, and a risk-averse official might not therefore approve the linkage.

For such reasons some potential welfare will probably be traded off to achieve more balanced distributional effects where this is feasible within a particular issue area. Consider our original example with constant but different costs of production, but where the difference in costs is not too great. In figure 7.1 we combine the *SU* and *GU* schedules from figure 5 with the cost conditions in figure 2.1. In figure 7.2 we subtract the cost conditions to give the net benefit curves for countries *A* and *B*, respectively. Finally, in figure 7.3 we derive an aggregate potential welfare curve which reflects the net effect of the various production allocations between the two countries in figure 7.2.

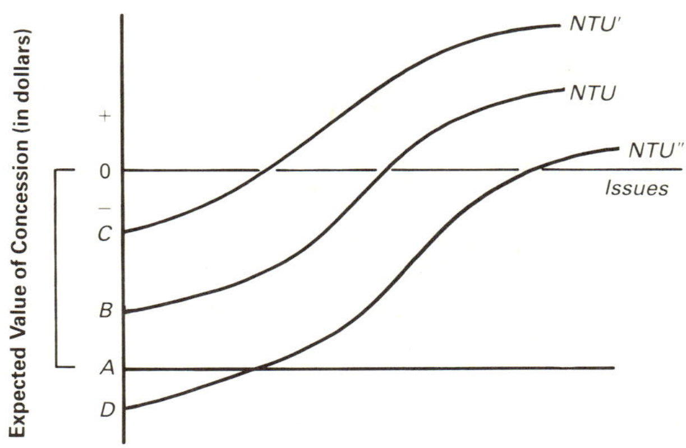

Fig. 6. Linkage with information costs and uncertainty

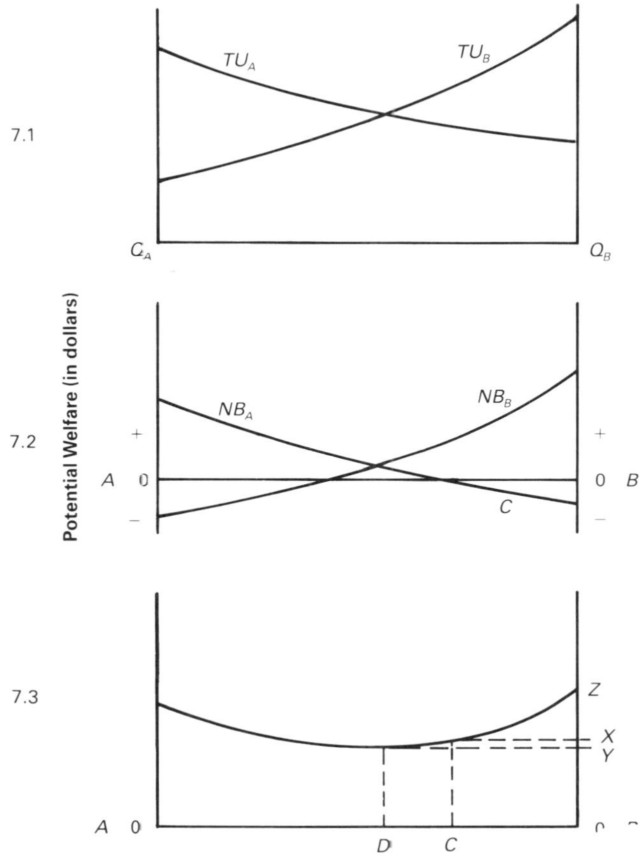

Fig. 7. The trade-off of production efficiency to obtain an agreement

In figures 7.2 and 7.3 it is clear that aggregate potential welfare is maximized by producing exclusively in *B*. In such a situation, however, the probability of unlinked agreement is zero, as country *A*'s net benefits are negative at that point. By shifting the production allocation to point *C*, one begins to get a positive probability of agreement at a cost of *XZ* of potential welfare. The probability of agreement would be maximized at a point near *D* with a cost of potential welfare of *ZY*.[7] So within a given issue area where it is difficult to find other areas of negotiations for linkage purposes, some potential welfare can be traded off in order to enhance the odds of an agreement.

Summary

This theory of optimal negotiations stresses the factors that influence the degree to which countries can obtain the benefits or potential welfare offered by collective agreements among themselves. Where there are constant or increasing costs for alliance hardware and cost differentials are not too great among countries, we find that collective agreements are facilitated without the need for linkages on the grounds that under such conditions one can obtain a balanced distribution of benefits by allocating alliance production fairly evenly among members with only a minimal efficiency cost.[8] Where there are substantial economies of scale in producing alliance hardware, however, the inability to make side payments in international relations will tend to frustrate the attainment of potentially beneficial collective agreements. This same type of problem also arises where the perceived benefits from having own-country production of alliance hardware are high. For these cases we stress the importance of linking issues in such a way that the cost or benefit skewness among the countries is offsetting. Linkage in this manner should promote potentially beneficial agreements. Information and other types of transaction costs will constrain this type of issue linkage to some extent. We thus generally expect that negotiators would be willing to trade off some amount of potential benefits from agreements close to their preferred positions in order to increase the likelihood of reaching an agreement in a given issue area.

Qualifications and Extensions

Our theory of issue linkages for mutual benefit is a new theory (we believe), and like most new ideas, it is subject to certain qualifications. The first task, therefore, is to present some of the qualifications and complications that accompany our analysis. Moreover, our statement of a mutual benefit theory of issue linkage is not likely to be the last word on the subject. We would thus also like to take the opportunity in this section to consider some possible extensions of our analysis. We begin by considering two qualifications—the relevance of single-actor models of economic self-interest for international negotiating processes and the impact that discontinuous policy options have in our theory—and then proceed to consider several possible extensions.

The Relevance of Single-Actor Models

As we have noted, our analytics are based on single-actor models and on the assumption that negotiators are efficient representatives of their countries' interests. While we feel that this is a reasonable approach to developing a general statement of our theory, we are quite aware of the limitations of such an approach in analyzing international negotiating processes.

Indeed, what constitutes individuals' and nations' conceptions of their self-interests is not a trivial question, nor will it be the same for all individuals and groups at all points in time. Both in terms of explaining behavior in international affairs and of designing "good" international institutions, it is desirable to know the weights placed by different actors on economic, political, social, and humanitarian objectives, and their views of how these are affected by alternative policy outcomes and institutional arrangements. Likewise, in many instances the objectives of negotiators and policy makers may differ from what might be judged from various perspectives to be the overall interests of the nations they represent. Indeed, there is frequently as much or more disagreement within than between countries about appropriate international policies. Our conclusion, then, is not that the assumptions of self-interested behavior are useless in explaining and predicting national behavior in the international arena, but rather that frequently one runs into trouble in attempting to explain the behavior of nations as if they were monolithic entities. In fact, nations are made up of many actors with varying stakes in international policy decisions, and we must frequently go further to explore the institutional framework within which decisions are made and carried out.

Within various nations, officials may develop particular interests of their own which cause them to pursue different outcomes from those which would be favored by the informed voter. A popular example is the negotiator whose personal reputation becomes so tied up in securing completion of a complex negotiation that by the final stages he becomes more concerned with seeing that an agreement is reached than that the contents of the agreement are in the interests of his country. Such divergences of interests between decision makers and voters may exist not just with respect to particular policies but also with respect to the overall amount of attention and resources devoted to international activities.[9] As will be discussed, such considerations are likely to make it more difficult to link issues successfully.

Analysis of actual policy making is further complicated by the fact that countries may frequently act on the basis of an "incorrect" view of the nature of the situation. A fascinating area of study is the way in which decision makers and negotiators obtain their views of "economic reality" and the processes by which these views are changed. Even if countries always followed their economic self-interest as they perceived it, their perception of economic self-interest may not always appear to be correct or invariant over time. Likewise, in many areas economically desirable outcomes may specifically be ruled out by overriding political or foreign policy considerations, or economic interests in one area may be sacrificed for what are judged to be greater gains in another area. The discovery that arguments are incorrect does not mean, of course, that those who were making them were necessarily deceived. Arguments, whether true or not, may be useful in negotiating, and an individual may know the correct argument, but ignore it for political purposes.

Again, however, such considerations do not render the analysis of policies on the basis of single-actor models of economic self-interest useless. Rather, they suggest that such tools must be applied with care and with due regard for the complexities of particular situations. The fact that countries do not always follow their economic self-interest as viewed by the external analyst does not preclude analyzing behavior from this perspective. Indeed, categorization of the types of instances in which countries do not follow their economic self-interests is an important avenue for study. So are the ways in which countries resolve conflicting economic interests of their own citizens.

In such instances the use of economic analysis offers insights, although it is not a magic guide to all of the intricacies of explaining and predicting outcomes of international economic deliberations.

Discontinuous Policy Options

A second way in which our earlier analysis must be qualified concerns the assumption in our theoretical model that negotiators face continuous policy options. In other words, it was assumed that a negotiator could trade a little more or a little less of each policy option in order to reach agreements. Any observer will note that this condition is not terribly descriptive of actual relations among governments. There is typically lots of discontinuity among policy options, and one often faces difficult all-or-none choices between policies (e.g., fixed versus flexible exchange rates). There thus may be a conflict in such cases between technical efficiency (i.e., reaching an agreement) and freedom to distribute the benefits from a positive-sum agreement.

The basic point to keep in mind in such a case is that discontinuities are likely to increase the importance of issue trades. The point here is analogous to how to divide the baby between separated parents. The child cannot be cut in half, and some sort of sharing mechanism must be arranged. The answer to this type of dilemma lies in searching for ways to make side payments. Issues on which reaching technically efficient agreements are difficult must be linked with other issues in order to make trade possible; they can be decided in isolation only at great costs in terms of failing to reach agreements. Returning to our alliance example, consider the issue of who makes airplanes for the defense alliance. Where there are large economies of scale in producing the airplane, it will be difficult to reach agreement on who gets the production contract, and linkage will be important under these conditions. Where there are no economies of scale in producing the airplane, one can obtain lots of equity at a small efficiency cost by distributing the production around the alliance countries. Linkage will be less important in such a case. The point, therefore, is to stress the importance of arranging for side payments through issue linkage where it is difficult to reach technically efficient agreements on an issue.

Linkage and the Aggregation of Issues

There are a number of aspects of our analysis that would appear to be fruitful areas for further research. The first concerns the relationship between issue linkage and the level of aggregation at which decisions among nations are discussed and implemented. This problem has become an increasingly important item of discussion in the literature. For example, in a well-known paper by Keohane and Nye, an operational distinction between intergovernmental and transgovernmental as two forms of communication between governments is stressed.[10] The former type of communication refers to the formal or traditional pattern of international diplomacy which flows through regular channels for coordinating foreign policy at high levels of government-to-government contact. The latter type of communication refers to contact between ministers and officials in governments without detailed clearance by high levels of the central government. The level at which negotiations take place, then, is the primary matter of concern in such a distinction. The question we pose is whether there are any general principles in our discussion of the theory of linkages that will enable some rough conjectures to be given to questions such as how many issues should be included in a decision-making package and at what level should governments negotiate in matters of international policy?

The main point that we wish to make in this regard is that where issues are well understood by negotiators, issue linkage and the aggregation of issues to be decided by top decision makers may be desirable for promoting agreements. This follows from the fact that more issues can be brought to bear in arranging for positive-sum trades in negotiations among governments. Thus attempts to reach agreement by negotiating on one issue at a time are likely to be frustrated because of the inability of participants to make side payments, and by aggregating issues and dealing with them at the highest levels of government, there is greater scope for indirect trades that will lead parties to efficient agreements. The basic idea here is similar to the way in which vote trading in legislatures can contribute to more efficient collective choices. We recognize that some observers disapprove of vote trading (''logrolling''), but recent contributions to the theory of public choice emphasize that vote trading in the appropriate institutional setting is a method for voters to obtain mutually beneficial bargains.[11]

It is clear that terminology such as ''the appropriate institutional setting'' is difficult to carry over to real world international negotiating processes. Factors such as external effects to parties who are not privileged to be a part of a negotiation—decision making, information costs (discussed below), intransitivities in voting outcomes, and so forth—may present formidable difficulties to the argument that vote trading within existing international institutional arrangements is an unmitigated good. The question of what is the appropriate institutional setting in the international context is therefore an important topic for further research.

The argument for vote or issue trading is not as strong where issues are not well understood by negotiators. For example, there may be no agreement on what is the best direction for policy to take. An excellent example of this condition would be discussions of fixed versus flexible exchange rates in the area of international economic policy. One can find scholarly and political opinion on both sides of this issue, and in such a case to link and aggregate issues at higher levels of decision making might be viewed largely as increasing the risk of making an agreement which will turn out to be disadvantageous, and as a result, might only intensify government-to-government conflict.[12] A variant of this example is where there is consensus among experts about the nature of the issues, but the issues involved are so complicated that higher-level officials can never spare the time to become well informed about the nature of the relevant trade-offs. Hence the complexity of the issues involved restricts the degree to which they can be linked and aggregated in some cases. In these circumstances government-to-government contact possibly could be handled at lower levels, and the work here would involve primarily the technical task of clarifying the nature of the issues for higher-level decision makers. Wallace, for example, outlines nicely some of the reasons why handling issues at a lower level might be appropriate.[13]

However, shifting the issue linkage problem in highly technical policy areas to lower levels of government opens the linkage process to yet other considerations. Domestic bureaucratic constituencies will have an important impact on the types of issues that can be successfully linked. For example, attempted linkages of certain policy areas may lead to disharmony among national bureaucrats. A pertinent example from the law of the sea negotiations would be the desire of U.S. defense officials for guaranteed freedom of transit through the world's straits relative to the interests of U.S. economic officials in promoting an efficient use of ocean resources. While the defense officials might be willing to trade off economic interests heavily to obtain their goal of unfettered ship transit, the economic officals are likely to place a much lower evaluation on the worth of freedom of transit relative to the case for efficient exploitation of ocean resources, and squabbling among bureaucracies will inevitably break out. The point is simply that domestic bureaucratic interests will affect the types of issue areas which can be successfully linked. In general, divergences in such interests will make linkage more difficult.[14]

So while the demands on high-level decision makers make it apparent that they will have little time to absorb information about the relevant trade-offs among highly technical issues, the relegation of these issues to lower levels of government-to-government contact opens the door to conflicting views among domestic bureaucracies as to what the proper policy should be. The level of aggregation at which decisions among nations are discussed and made thus involves some difficult trade-offs in practice. This is an area where scholars with expertise in particular policy areas can make useful contributions by examining the nature of these trade-offs in their particular areas of interest.

The Costs of Negotiating

Another important issue which was not directly considered in our theoretical presentation concerns the effect of the number of negotiators (both among and within countries) on negotiating processes. In other words what happens if we increase the number of effective decision makers in our analytical framework? The result is straightforward—increased decision costs. Where there are a given number of issues to be decided, the greater the number of decision agents the more difficult it will be to reach agreements. Thus debating international issues in large forums should tend to be a quite costly way of reaching collective agreements because, for example, the cost of keeping in touch with trade-offs on issues is increased immensely since there are more positions that have to be known in order to reach agreements. In general we expect that the greater the number of actors, the more difficult it should be to arrange linkages, so that each negotiator should be willing to accept greater deviations from the efficiency frontier to achieve a more balanced distribution of benefits within an issue area. This general rule, however, must be applied carefully in practice. For example, although there may be a large number of decision makers involved, where countries fall into blocs with similar interests, the process of bargaining and issue linkage should be facilitated.

We suggest as a basic principle to follow in this area that the number of actors involved in a negotiation be confined to those with well-defined stakes in the outcome. It makes little sense to give individuals votes on issues where the outcome does not affect them (positively or negatively). Normally in bargaining among governments where agreements are voluntarily reached and no country with a well-defined stake in the outcome is denied a voice, this condition should be roughly met. Countries without stakes in the outcome are not involved in the negotiations. In bargaining in international organizations, however, this condition may not be met. Each country often has an equal vote on an issue whether or not it has a positive or negative stake in the outcome. As will be discussed below, this not only increases decision costs dramatically, but also makes the possibility of capricious outcomes more likely. A considerable problem is where to draw the line when there are many countries with legitimate, but small, stakes in an issue. In such cases, there may be a strong conflict between the probability of securing agreement and the equitable representation of all affected parties. The scope for successful issue linkages should be greatest where the number of decision makers is small and where "voting power" is tailored to the underlying stakes of decision makers in the outcome.

Voting Rules

Another implicit assumption of our theoretical model was that both parties must agree before trades can be consummated. The implicit voting rule in such a case is unanimity. Unanimity will typically be the case where countries voluntarily enter into international negotiations since they can withdraw from agreements if they object to them. Yet in international organizations where some negotiations are carried out, the voting rule implicit in producing an outcome is rarely unanimity. In such a case the voting rule will influence the process of negotiations. At a very simple level the degree of restrictiveness will influence the level of decision costs for a given number of decision makers. A more restrictive voting rule thus increases the costs of reaching collective decisions will giving minorities greater protection against adverse outcomes. Our point in this context is that fewer issues will be successfully linked where it is relatively more costly to obtain agreements.

Voting rules also imply different distributions of political income. One nation–one vote is only a particular distribution of political power. Different countries have different stakes in different issues, and one nation–one vote is not necessarily tailored to these stakes. So even where there is an enforceable mechanism such as majority voting for international collective decision making, an optimal outcome is not guaranteed by this fact. Where voting power differs substantially from the distribution of potential costs and benefits to be derived from voting, collective outcomes may be both inequitable and inefficient. Attempts to skew the cost and benefits of outcomes by the majority of countries may result in the underprovision of the collective good in question.[15] Essentially, the provision of international public goods is a mixed-motive game with the scope for potential benefits to all countries from the provision of the public good yielding cooperative elements, the positive-sum aspect of the game, while the desire to minimize one's share of the cost of providing the public goods leads to competitive zero or negative-sum elements. Attempts at securing too great a share of the benefits run the risk of ending in failure of the good to be provided in sufficient quantities (or sometimes even at all). The prospect for underprovision in such circumstances is enhanced by the fact that it is usually far easier for nation states to withdraw from international agreements than it is for citizens to withdraw from the effective jurisdication of national political decisions. Thus, where the implicit weights on votes do not coincide with the stakes that countries have in issues, countries may tend to withdraw the consideration of those issues from forums where one man–one vote procedures apply.

Weighted voting would not be, however, a panacea. For one thing it is not necessarily an easy voting scheme to administer. The weights must be designed in an appropriate manner, and this problem can be complicated where countries' positions change over time and where there is wide variation in exactly what constitutes a country's "interest" on different issues. Even in international forums where voting processes are important, the feasibility of weighted voting depends to a large extent upon a stable pattern of interests over time.

The emergence of new issues of a discrete and important nature in international affairs should necessitate a great deal of flux and flexibility in arranging forums for the discussion of international issues. Thus, many negotiations tailored to underlying stakes and issues will be likely to take place outside of formal international organizations. While untidy, this may contribute to a more efficient pattern of international agreements because of the possibility of creating effective weights of voting power of participants which more closely approximate their interests in particular issues.

Summary and Conclusion

We have presented a theory of issue linkage for mutual benefit. Our theory stresses issue linkage as a means of overcoming distributional obstacles to international agreement where direct side payments among countries are not a politically feasible alternative. The mutual benefit theory contrasts with and supplements the traditional rationale for linkage in terms of extending one's leverage in one area of negotiations to other areas. Integration of these two approaches is not attempted in this paper, but we believe that it is an important task for future research on issue linkage.

The qualifications to our analysis that we stressed concerned the relevance of single-actor models of economic self-interest to international negotiating processes and the impact of discontinuous policy options on the process of issue linkage. We suggested several possible extensions of our analysis.

Some of our more important conjectures were that: (*a*) linkage and aggregation of issues should help to promote agreements where issues and the trade-offs among issues are well understood by top decision makers; (*b*) where there is fundamental disagreement about the proper policy, linkage and aggregation of issues should be less useful in promoting agreement among high-level decision makers; and (*c*) issue linkage should be less important in international forums where the costs of linkage are high due to large numbers of effective decision makers, either because of a large number of countries participating or because of multiple interests represented for each country.

We also briefly discussed the influence which voting rules can have on the difficulty of reaching international agreements and on the efficiency and equity of such outcomes. In our judgment such considerations of the appropriate institutional setting for vote trading or issue linkages represent an extremely important topic for further research.

We believe that our theory of issue linkage for mutual benefit offers a useful set of analytical tools in both a positive and a normative sense. In a positive spirit our analysis offers an explanation for issue linkages that do not seem to fit the traditional rationale of expanding one's bargaining power into other areas. In a normative sense our theory provides the beginnings of a framework within which the performance of international institutions in promoting cooperative actions among countries can be evaluated. In both respects we hope that the approach to issue linkages for mutual benefit begun in this paper can make useful contributions to the understanding and design of international negotiations and institutions.

NOTES

We are grateful to Robert O. Keohane and to two unidentified referees of this journal for useful comments on an earlier draft of this paper. The usual caveat applies.

1. See, for example, the discussion in Robert Keohane and Joseph Nye, *Power and Interdependence* (Boston: Little, Brown, and Co., 1977), and Branislav Gosovic and John Gerard Ruggie, "On the Creation of a New International Economic Order: Issue Linkage and the Seventh Special Session of the U.N. General Assembly," *International Organization* 30 (Spring 1976): 309–46.
2. William Wallace, "Issues Linkage Among Atlantic Governments," *International Affairs* (April 1976): 163–79.

3. See the section on "Towards a Theory of Optimal Negotiations," in Robert D. Tollison and Thomas D. Willett, "Institutional Mechanisms for Dealing with International Externalities: A Public Choice Perspective," in *The Law of the Sea: U.S. Interests and Alternatives*, ed. Ryan C. Amacher and Richard J. Sweeney (Washington, D.C.: American Enterprise Institute, 1976), pp. 97–100. Within the context of fiscal federalism this aspect of issue linkages is stressed in Albert Breton, "Public Goods and the Stability of Federalism," *Kyklos* 23, no. 4 (1970): 882–901. This rationale is also briefly alluded to, but not emphasized, in Keohane and Nye, *Power and Interdependence*, p. 122, where they mention that "reinforcing this [power] impetus toward linkage was the inclination, particularly of Third World majorities at international conferences, to link issues to secure satisfactory overall bargains."
4. Economists and other scholars have analyzed alliances from a public goods perspective. See especially Mancur Olson and Richard Zeckhauser, "An Economic Theory of Alliances," *Review of Economics and Statistics* 48 (August 1966): 266–79; idem, "Collective Goods, Comparative Advantage, and Alliance Efficiency," in *Issues in Defense Economics*, ed. Roland N. McKean, (New York: Columbia University Press, 1967), pp. 25–63; Norman Frolich and Joel A. Oppenheimer, "I Get By With a Little Help From My Friends," *World Politics* 23 (October 1970): 104–20; Bruce M. Russett and John D. Sullivan, "Collective Goods and International Organization," *International Organization* 25 (Autumn 1971): 845–65; Mancur Olson, "Increasing the Incentives for International Cooperation," *International Organization* 25 (Autumn 1971): 866–74; and William Loehr, "Collective Goods and International Cooperation: Comments," *International Organization* 27 (Autumn 1975): 421–43.
5. For convenience we make the hypothetical assumption that decision makers' evaluations of benefits and, later, of utilities can be expressed in dollar terms.
6. The latter terminology in the present context refers to the capture of the benefits of agreement by the two countries relative to the previous case in which the inability to make side payments led to a lack of agreement and to the loss of such potential benefits.
7. We defer considerations of the costs of decision making until the next section, but it should be apparent here that where *ZY* is small, the attempt to link issues may cost more than it is worth.
8. Although we did not analyze the increasing-costs case in the text, it is easy to understand how unlinked agreement is facilitated under these conditions. Namely, where the cost of alliance production arises monotonically in each country, the conflict between alliance efficiency and distributional effects dissipates, that is, the objective of maximizing potential welfare (a least-cost allocation of production) becomes more congruent with spreading production fairly evenly among countries.
9. There is considerable literature on this question emanating from a paper by Anthony Downs on "Why the Government Budget is Too Small in a Democracy," *World Politics* 12 (July 1960): 541–63. For a review of this literature, see R. C. Amacher, R. D. Tollison, and T. D. Willett, "Budget Size in a Democracy: A Review of the Arguments," *Public Finance Quarterly* 3 (April 1975): 99–121.
10. R. O. Keohane and J. S. Nye, "Transgovernmental Relations and International Organizations," *World Politics* 27 (October 1974): 39–62.
11. For a general discussion of this point with references to the literature, see D. C.

Mueller, R. D. Tollison, and T. D. Willett, "Solving the Intensity Problem in Representative Democracy," in *The Economic Approach to Public Policy*, ed. R. C. Amacher, R. D. Tollison, and T. D. Willett (Ithaca, New York: Cornell University Press, 1976), pp. 444–73.

12. Uncertainty over the proper direction for policy does not, however, imply that there will not be issue trades in any event.
13. Wallace, "Issues Linkage." We should stress, however, that this is a complicated problem and that under some circumstances linkage can be used to bring about agreement irrespective of poor understanding or of fundamental disagreements over proper policies. A helpful referee gives the following example. At the time of the Bretton Woods Conference the U.S. and U.K. disagreed particularly over the question of the role of discriminatory trading blocs in the postwar economic order. The U.S. linkage of Lend Lease and postwar credits to the dismantling of Imperial preferences helped bring about an agreement.
14. Two recent papers in *International Organization* are closely related to this theme. See Peter J. Katzenstein, "International Relations and Domestic Structures: Foreign Economic Policies of Advanced Industrial States," *International Organization* 29 (Fall 1975): 1021–34; and Raymond F. Hopkins, "The International Role of Domestic Bureaucracy," *International Organization* 30 (Summer 1976): 405–32.
15. This point has not yet been sufficiently recognized in discussion of the optimal provision of international public goods. For example, in their classic paper "An Economic Theory of Alliances," *Review of Economics and Statistics* 48 (August 1966): 266–79, Olson and Zeckhauser show how the failure to have collective agreements can result in the underprovision of international public goods, but fail to consider how in this model the ability to achieve optimality through binding international agreements would not be invariant to the voting rules adopted. For further discussion on this point, see Robert D. Tollison and Thomas D. Willett "International Public Goods and the Economic Theory of Alliances," in *The Challenge of Economic Interdependence: A Public Choice Perspective* (in progress). For recent discussions of the Olson-Zeckhauser model, see the references cited in note 4.

4 Applications

The Coase Theorem and the Theory of the State

James M. Buchanan

Things were really quite simple in the post-Pigovian world of microeconomic policy, a world characterized by possible divergencies between private and social marginal cost (or product). The classically nefarious factory might be observed to spew its smoke on the neighboring housewife's laundry, and in so doing impose costs that were not reckoned in its presumed strict profit-maximizing calculus. The remedy seemed straightforward. The "government" should impose a corrective tax on the factory owner, related directly to the smoke-generating output (or, if required, a particular input) and measured by the marginal external or spillover cost. Through this device the firm would be forced to make its decisions on the basis of a "socially correct" comparison of costs and revenues. Its profit-maximizing objective should then lead it to results that would be "socially optimal."

Things have not seemed nearly so simple since R. H. Coase presented his analysis of social cost.[1] Coase's central insight lay in his recognition that there are two sides to any potential economic interdependence, two parties to any potential exchange, and that this insures at least some pressure toward fully voluntary and freely negotiated agreements. Moreover, such agreements tend to insure the attainment of efficiency without the necessity of governmental intervention beyond the initial definition of rights and the enforcement of contracts. Applied to the example in hand, if the damage to the housewife's laundry exceeds in value the benefits that the firm derives from allowing its stacks to smoke, a range of mutual gain exists, and utility and profit-maximizing behavior on the part of the two parties involved will result in at least some reduction in the observed level of smoke damage, a reduction that can be taken to be efficient in terms of total product value. No governmental remedy may be called for at all, and indeed Coase argued that attempted correction by government might create inefficiency. Such intervention might forestall or distort the negotiations between the affected parties. As a further aspect of his analysis, Coase advanced the theorem on allocational neutrality that now bears his name. This states that under idealized conditions when transactions costs are absent and where income-effect feedbacks are not relevant, the allocational results of voluntarily negotiated agreements will be invariant over differing assignments of property rights among the parties to the interaction.

Much of the discussion since 1960 has involved the limitations of this theorem in the presence of positive transactions costs. In this setting, differing

First published in *Natural Resources Journal* 13 (October 1973): 579–94.

assignments of rights may affect allocative outcomes. Furthermore, the transactions costs barrier to voluntarily negotiated agreements that can be classified as tolerably efficient may be all but prohibitive in some situations, notably those that may require simultaneous agreement among many parties. The generalized transactions costs rubric may be used to array alternative institutional structures, with the implied objective being that of minimizing these costs.

My purpose here is not to elaborate these extensions and/or limitations of the Coase analysis, many of which have become familiar even if an exhaustive taxonomy of cases has not been completed. My purpose is almost the opposite. I want to extend the Coase analysis, within his assumptions of zero transactions costs and insignificant income-effect feedbacks, to differing institutional settings than those that have normally been implicitly assumed in the discussions of the neutrality theorem. This approach leads to the question: Why did Coase suggest that the Pigovian prescriptions might produce inefficient results? Or, to put this somewhat differently, why does the theorem of allocational neutrality stop short at certain ill-defined institutional limits? Why can it not be extended to encompass all possible institutional variations, variations that may be broadly interpreted as differences in the assignments of property rights? What is there in the implied Pigovian institutional framework that might inhibit the voluntary negotiations among parties, always assuming zero transactions costs? If the neutrality theorem holds, why should the political economist be overly concerned about institutional reform, as such?

There is a paradox of sorts here between the theorem of allocational neutrality, interpreted in its most general sense, and Coase's basic policy position. One implication of the theorem, so interpreted, would be that the thrust of classical political economy may have been misdirected. Adam Smith's central message points toward institutional reform and reconstruction as means of guaranteeing overall efficiency in resource usage, and, as noted, we can always interpret institutions as embodying specific property rights. Governmental authorities were to be stripped of their traditionally established rights to interfere in the workings of the market economy; or, stated conversely, individual traders were to be granted rights to negotiate on their own terms. The central theorem of classical economies might be summarized as the demonstration of the differences in allocational results under divergent institutional structures. I do not think that Coase would disagree with my statements here, and I think that he shares with me an admiration for Adam Smith and that Coase, too, places Smith's emphasis on institutional-structural reform above the modern policy emphasis on detailed and particularistic manipulation of observed results.

The apparent paradox may be resolved when we take account of the theory of the state or of government that is, perhaps surprisingly, shared by Adam Smith, Pigou, and Coase. My argument proceeds in several steps. First, it is necessary to distinguish carefully between property rights and liability rules. Second, I shall demonstrate that governmental or collective action, if conceived in the Wicksellian framework or model, does not modify the applicability of the neutrality theorem. Third, I shall show that government, conceived in a non-Wicksellian model, need not modify the applicability of the theorem, but that, in such case, property rights are explicitly changed with the introduction of governmental action. Finally, I shall suggest that the theory of government decision making implicit in both classical and neoclassical economics, and carried over in Coase's analysis, offers the source of the seemingly paradoxical limits on the neutrality theorem.

Property Rules and Liability Rules

In his basic paper, Coase did not carefully make a distinction between the assignment of rights to particular individuals and the rules determining the liability of particular individuals for damage that their behavior might impose on others. His example, the now familiar one of the interaction between the rancher and the farmer, was discussed in terms of alternative rules for bearing liability for damages. Either the rancher, whose cattle strayed onto the neighboring croplands, was liable for damages that the farmer might suffer, or he was not liable. If both cattle and grain were marketed competitively, the neutrality theorem showed that the same allocative outcome would be generated, regardless of which set of liability rules should be in existence. In the former case, the rancher, knowing in advance that he would be liable for damages caused by his straying animals, would include these payments as an anticipated cost in making his size-of-herd decisions. In the latter case, the farmer, knowing that he can collect no damages from the rancher (and that he must respect the property rights of the rancher to cattle), will find it advantageous to initiate payments to the latter in exchange for agreements limiting the size of herd, if indeed the value of crop damage at the margin exceeds the value of the additional grazing to the rancher.

Coase overlooked the fact that the institutional structure was significantly different in the two cases. In the second case, the shift toward an efficient outcome takes place through an ordinary market or exchange process, in which none other than the two parties need get involved. In the first case, however, as presented by Coase, there must be third-party interference by a "judge" to assess charges for damage that has been done. In the context of his discussions, this institutional difference does not matter, since the third party can, presumably, measure and assess damages with complete accuracy. The difference is nonetheless important in the more general setting. Consistency should have dictated that the first case be presented, not as one where the rancher was liable ex post for damages caused by his straying animals, but as one where the farmer held enforceable property rights in his croplands, rights that were inviolate except on his own agreement. In this framework, the rancher would have had to negotiate an agreement with the farmer in advance of any actual straying of cattle. This converts the institutional setting on this side into one that is parallel to the converse case. No third party, no judge, is required to intervene and to assess damages ex post.

We may define this setting as one in which property rules are established and enforced, as opposed to liability rules.[2] This setting calls direct attention to the motivation that both parties have to exploit the potentially realizable surplus by moving from the initial inefficient position. This setting also allows for an extension of the neutrality-efficiency theorem beyond those strictly objectifiable circumstances suggested to be present in the Coase example. If the precise degree of damage caused by external imposition is ambiguous, the third party must necessarily exercise his own best judgment in making a settlement. By contrast, if property rules are defined, with the necessity of prior agreement on the part of the potentially damaged party, the latter's own subjective assessment of potential damage becomes controlling in determining the range over which final outcomes may settle. This assessment is, of course, a better measure of actual value lost than the estimate made by any third party.

Wicksellian Unanimity

For our purposes, the specification that parties to an interaction are defined by property rather than liability rules facilitates relating the Coase theorem on allocational neutrality to the underlying conception of theory of government or of the State. In the simplest possible model, we may conceive of a polity that is limited in membership to the parties directly involved in the potential interaction. The interacting group can be made coincident in membership with the political unit. On this basis, we can interpret the "trades" among the parties as being analogous to collective or governmental decisions reached under the operation of a Wicksellian rule of unanimity.[3] Consider either the earlier factory-housewife example, or Coase's familiar rancher-farmer one. In either illustration, we can think of the two-party group as comprising the all-inclusive membership in the political community, in which case agreement between the two parties on any matter is equivalent to unanimous accord. Resort to third-party adjudication is impossible for the simple reason that no third party exists.

From this context, it becomes easier to conceive "the State" merely as the instrumental means or device through which individuals attempt to carry out activities aimed at securing jointly desired objectives. This is, of course, the traditional framework for all theories of social-contract origins of government. In this setting, all activities of the public sector are explained in exchange terms, even if it is recognized that the exchange process is significantly more complex than that which makes up the central subject matter of orthodox economic theory. There is at least no conceptual or logical necessity to think of "the State" as an entity that exists separate from and apart from citizens.

If we remain within the strict contractarian conception of collective action, where all decisions require unanimous consent by all members of the political community, and if we retain the assumption that transactions costs are absent, the Coase theorem on allocational neutrality may be applied beyond those limits within which it has normally been discussed. In this model, collective or governmental decision making remains equivalent to freely negotiated voluntary exchange. Hence, there is little or no cause for concern about "governmental intervention" as such, because any action that might properly be classified as "governmental" would not emerge unless all parties agree on the contractual terms.

Differences in the assignment of rights might, as in the standard simple exchange cases, generate differences in distributional outcomes, but the contractual process would lead to allocational results that are both efficient and invariant. Consider a classic example, that introduces what we may appropriately call collective or public goods, David Hume's villagers whose utility would be increased by drainage of a meadow. The neutrality theorem, applied to this example, demonstrates that an efficient and unchanged allocational result will emerge from freely negotiated contract whether the postulated initial position should be one in which individuals own separate plots of land through which the swampy stream flows or whether the whole meadow is defined as communal property, accessible to all parties. With an effective unanimity rule, and with zero transactions costs, the complex exchange that is required for efficiency would be worked out under any initial structure of individual rights. The sharing of the gross gains from trade among separate persons would, of course, be influenced by the particular property assignment in being. If the sharing of such gains modifies individual demands for the common good, at the margin, that is, if income effects are present, differing assignments can produce slight differences in allocational results, but, under the assumptions here, those results produced will continue to be efficient.

Simple Majority Voting

When the unanimity requirement for collective decisions is abandoned, governmental action no longer represents a complex equivalent of a voluntary exchange process.[4] If decisions that are to be binding over the inclusive group can be made by a subset of this group, there is no guarantee that a particular individual holds against the imposition of net harm or damage. Once his own contractual agreement to the terms of governmental or collective action is dropped as a requirement, an individual can no longer be certain that he will share in the gross gains that governmental action will, presumably, generate. From this it seems to follow that collective action, motivated by improvement in the positions of members of a decisive coalition smaller than the totality of community membership, need not produce results that are efficient, even with zero transactions costs.[5] Any nonunanimity voting rule, for example, that of simple majority voting, would seem to produce results that may be, in the net, inefficient.

The neutrality theorem is, however, more powerful than might be suggested by cursory attention to this example. Efficient outcomes will tend to emerge from the contractual process, even under less-than-unanimity voting rules for collective action, if the modified structure of property rights consequent on the departure from unanimity is acknowledged, and if individuals are allowed freely to negotiate trades in these rights. Economists have not fully incorporated the property rights structure of less-than-unanimity voting rules into their orthodoxy, and they tend to stop short of the extension of the neutrality theorem herein suggested.

Consider a situation in which individuals hold well-defined rights, which are acknowledged by all parties, and which are known to be enforceable without costs. If no collective action is undertaken, individuals trade such rights among themselves in simple exchanges, insuring mutuality of gain. If collective action is undertaken, but only on the agreement of all parties, mutuality of gain (or, at the limit, absence of loss) is insured. If this requirement is dropped, and individuals may be subjected to damage or harm through collective action, the value of their initial holdings is necessarily changed, again on the assumption of zero transactions costs. Individuals no longer hold claims that are inviolate against imposed reductions in value. A new and ambiguous set of rights is brought into being by the authorization of governmental action taken without the approval of all parties. Any potentially decisive decision-making coalition, a simple majority of voters in our example here, possesses rights to the nominal holdings of the minority. These rights are, in this instance, ambiguous because they emerge only upon the identification of the majority coalition that is to be decisive with respect to the issue under consideration for collective action. Once identified, however, members of the effective majority hold potentially marketable rights. These may be exchanged, directly or indirectly, and the contractual process will again insure that the efficient allocative outcome will be achieved, and that this will be invariant, given the appropriate assumptions about transactions costs and income effects.

We may illustrate this in a highly simplified three-person example. Consider a community that includes three men: A, B, and C. Collective decisions are to be made by simple majority voting. Initial holdings of units of an all-purpose and numerable consumption good are, let us say, 100 for A, 60 for B, and 30 for C. In this environment, let us suppose that a governmental project is proposed, one that promises to yield benefits of 30 units, distributed equally among the three persons. The gross costs of this project are, however, 40 units; clearly, the proposal is inefficient. Despite this, if B and C can succeed in organizing themselves into a majority coalition, and if they can impose the full tax costs of the proposal on A, they can make net gains. In this case, the results would appear as follows:

Person	Benefits	Costs	Net
A	10	40	−30
B	10	0	10
C	10	0	10

Once B and C are identified as the decisive members of the coalition, however, individual A can negotiate trades, or side payments, that will be mutually beneficial to all parties, and which will keep this inefficient outcome from being achieved. Individual A can, for example, offer either B or C a net gain of 15 units to join a different majority coalition that will disapprove the project. Or, if both B and C hold firm, they can exact from A a payment of 10 units for their agreement to withhold the project. The side payments, which must be allowed to take place under our assumption of zero transactions costs, will insure that all inefficient projects are forestalled, and, similarly, that all efficient projects will be carried out.[6]

The values to individuals of the ''property rights in franchise'' embodied in a majority-voting regime depend critically on the constitutional limits within which majorities are allowed to take collective political action. These values will also depend on the technological possibilities for potential coalition gains within the given set of constitutional constraints defined. Detailed exploration of these interesting and mostly unresolved issues would not be suitable in this paper. For present purposes, the points to be recognized are, first, that any departure from unanimity in collective decision processes modifies the structure of rights from that which is defined exclusively by private-sector claims and obligations, and, second, that even with this modified set of rights, the theorem on allocational neutrality remains valid within the required, and highly restricted, assumptions concerning transactions costs and income effects.[7]

Administrative Authority

In traditional economic policy discussions, the arguments for and/or against governmental intervention in the private sector rarely take place under explicitly defined models for collective decision making. For the most part, those who propose ''corrections'' to the outcomes of voluntary exchange processes, like those who oppose them, are content to treat governmental decisions as exogenous to the valuations of the persons in the economy itself. If, however, these arguments are interpreted consistently within any collective decision-making framework, the structure that can most readily be inferred is neither that of unanimity nor simple majority voting. The model of government that accords most closely with economic policy discussions is one in which authority to take collective action is vested in an administrator, a bureaucrat, an expert, who chooses for the community, presumably on the basis of his own version of the ''public interest,'' or, in technical economist's jargon, some ''social welfare function.''

It is useful, therefore, to extend our analysis of the theorem on allocational neutrality to this administrative decision model of public choice. Probably because the model is essentially implicit rather than explicitly postulated, little or no attention has been paid to the alternative means through which the single decision maker for the collectivity may be selected. Nor need this concern us here. Strictly speaking, the conclusions developed here follow whether the decision maker be divinely ordained, democratically elected, arbitrarily appointed, selected in competitive examination, or hereditarily determined.[8] I want to examine a model in which a single person has been empowered to make decisions for a whole community. This defines a specific structure of rights, an assignment, and the problem is to determine the allocative results that will emerge in comparison with those predicted under alternative structures. The first point to be noted is the same as that made with respect to simple majority voting. The delegation of decision-making power to the single person modifies the set of rights in existence, even prior to the onset of any imposed governmental action. The designated chooser for the community holds potentially valued claims that were nonexistent before he was constitutionally authorized to act.

Consider again Hume's drainage of the village meadow. Instead of operating through a rule of unanimity, we now assume that the village has empowered a single person to act on behalf of all persons in the group and, furthermore, it is acknowledged that his decisions will be enforced. Formally, it does not matter whether the decision maker is chosen from within or from outside the group. For expositional simplicity, however, we shall assume that he is selected from outside the village. We now assume that a drainage project, lumpy in nature, will yield symmetrically distributed benefits to villagers valued at 1000 units of the numeraire commodity. The project will cost a total of 800 units and the taxing institution requires symmetrical sharing. The project is clearly Pareto-efficient, and, as indicated earlier, under an operating rule of unanimity, the project will be undertaken, given our zero transactions costs assumption, and including all free-rider behavior under the transactions costs rubric. The question becomes: Would this project necessarily be selected by the single decision maker, the alternative structure of property rights under consideration?

It is illegitimate to assume that the single administrator knows the preferences of the citizens, or, even should these be estimated with accuracy, that he would necessarily embody individual values dollar-for-dollar in his own choice calculus. The administrator or bureaucrat will select the project if the costs that he bears are less than the benefits that he, personally, secures. But these costs and benefits are not, and cannot possibly be, those of the community of citizens. Apparently, there is nothing in this model to insure correspondence between the bureaucrat's choices and those results that are to be classified as efficient by orthodox economists' criteria. This suggests that the theorem of allocational neutrality breaks down.

If, however, we move beyond this naive model of administrative behavior, the applicability of the neutrality theorem may be restored. By acting in accordance with his own subjective evaluation, the bureaucrat may be failing to maximize the value of the property right that has been assigned to him constitutionally. To show this, let us assume that, naively, the decision taker decides against the project noted. In this decision, he deprives the citizenry of benefits valued at 1000 units and, at the same time, avoids the imposition of tax costs of 800 units on the community. In a setting with zero transactions costs, where large numbers can readily reach contractual agreements, the citizenry, as an inclusive group of taxpayer-beneficiaries, would be willing to offer side payments up to a total of 200 units to secure a change from negative to positive action on the project.[9] If the decision maker, the administrator or bureaucrat, uses these side payments, either indicatively or actually, to determine his final choice, the drainage project will be carried out. The theorem of allocational neutrality is apparently validated in this more sophisticated model for bureaucratic behavior. So long as the decision maker acts to maximize the potential rent on the property right delegated to him, the right to make the final decision for the whole community, the allocative result will be identical to that forthcoming under alternative rights structures, with, of course, the transactions-costs, income-effect assumptions postulated. As in all property assignment shifts, the distributional results may be quite different under differing assignments. If the bureaucrat maximizes the potential rent on his right to choose for the group, and, furthermore, if he collects this in the form of a personal side payment, there is an income transfer from members of the original group to the "outsider" selected as decision taker.[10]

Objection may be raised to rent maximizing as the appropriate norm for bureaucratic behavior, even if we neglect ethical considerations (these will be introduced in the next section). To postulate that the designated decision maker maximizes the potential side payments that he can receive from taxpayer-beneficiaries, as a group, implies that the decision maker, himself, is indifferent as among the choice alternatives that he places no personal evaluation on the differences among these opportunities available to him. If, in fact, the bureaucrat or administrator is external to the affected group of persons in the community, this assumption may seem plausibly realistic. If, however, he is chosen from within the community itself, his own evaluation must be taken into account. Whether the decision taker is selected from within or without the original group of members, his own evaluation can be, and must be, included in any correct assessment of costs and benefits.

We may return to the numerical illustration introduced above. Suppose that the gross benefits of the proposed drainage project, to all persons other than the decision taker, amount to 1000 units of a numeraire good (we may call these "dollars"), and that the gross costs, to all persons other than the decision taker, amount to 800. Suppose, however, that the decision maker, himself, places a monetary value of, say, 400 dollars on the "natural beauty" of the swampy and undrained meadow. Even should he be required to pay no part of the tax costs of the project, this 400 units of value necessarily becomes a component in the total opportunity cost of the drainage scheme. Under these conditions, the bureaucrat will refuse the proffered side payment of 200 units. The project will not be undertaken.

Does this result suggest that the theorem of allocational neutrality breaks down? The question of whether the decision taker is selected from within or without the initial membership of the group becomes critical at this point. If the selection is internal, the project is inefficient under the conditions suggested, and it will not be undertaken under any rights assignment. This is because the person's negative evaluation would be an input in any internal contractual negotiations that might produce an allocative outcome. In this case, the neutrality theorem remains valid. Suppose, however, that the bureaucrat is not in the initial group of members. In such case, his own personal evaluation of the project alternatives will not enter and will not affect allocative outcomes when the assignment of rights is limited to initial members. This decision maker's evaluation will, however, enter as a determinant when he is assigned the rights to choose for the group. The neutrality theorem would not hold valid under these conditions unless the decision maker should be, in fact, wholly indifferent as among the choice alternatives.

This result should not be at all surprising. The theorem on allocational neutrality, even under its restricted set of required assumptions, should hardly be expected to extend to rights assignments that embody differing memberships in the group. For fixed memberships, the theorem remains fully valid. Even when the decision maker is selected from outside, the theorem suggests that any change in rights assignments, once the additional member is included, among this new membership will produce identical allocational results.

The Theory of the State

It is possible to interpret both the policy implications of Coase's theorem on allocational neutrality and Pigovian corrective policy prescriptions in terms of the underlying conceptions, models, or theories of government. As the analysis above has suggested, under certain conceptions of governmental process neither Coase nor the Pigovians should have been greatly concerned about institutional change as means of generating allocative efficiency. If distributional considerations are neglected, and if decision makers for the community are chosen from within the group, the structure of rights will modify allocative outcomes only because of differentials in levels of transactions costs, provided that the decision takers are motivated by economic self-interest. The policy thrust of Coase's discussion is, however, to the effect that governmental or collective intrusion into the negotiation processes of the market economy tends to retard rather than to advance movement toward allocative efficiency. Conversely, the policy thrust of the whole Pigovian tradition is that governmental or collective intrusion into the market economy tends to be corrective of distortions and leads toward rather than away from those results that might satisfy agreed-on efficiency criteria.

The Pigovian model of the state may be examined first. The decision taker, the person or group empowered to impose the corrective taxes or subsidies, is presumed to act in accordance with rules laid down for him by the welfare economist. His task is that of measuring social costs and social benefits from alternative courses of action, a task that he is presumed able to carry out effectively. On the basis of such measurements, the decision taker is to follow the rules laid down, quite independently of the personal opportunity costs that he may face in refusing side payment offers. The Pigovian policy maker must be an economic eunuch. The idealized allocative results are, of course, identical with those that would emerge under a regime where the decision maker is wholly "corrupt" in the sense of strict maximization of the potential side payments or rents on his rights to make decisions. If he is expected to behave as a rent maximizer, however, there would be no need for elaborated and detailed instruction in the form of rules or norms, as derived from the theorems of welfare economics. Within this Pigovian conception, the decision maker for the group does not and/or should not maximize the rental value of the rights of decision that he is granted. This may be treated either as a positive prediction about bureaucratic behavior or as a normative proposition for bureaucratic behavior.

In the Coase conception,[11] an interpretation that is similar in certain respects seems to follow. If, in fact, governmental decision makers act as strict rent maximizers, the neutrality theorem suggests that there should be little or no concern about allocative results, per se. The evidence of such concern must, therefore, indicate some denial of the rent-maximizing behavioral hypothesis. Again, this may be taken as positive prediction or normative statement. The governmental decision maker, the bureaucrat, empowered to act on behalf of the group, either does not maximize rents on the rights that he commands or he should not do so on moral-ethical grounds. In either case, the Coase concern for allocational efficiency returns since the negotiating pressure toward optimality is removed once the decision-making power is shifted from the market to the public sector.

It is perhaps surprising to find common elements in the basic conceptions of political process held by the proponents of essentially opposing policy positions. But in both the Pigovian framework and in that imputed here to Coase, the governmental decision maker, either singly or as a member of a choosing group, is and/or should be "incorruptible." In this respect, the two conceptions of governmental process seem identical, despite the sharp differences in information possibilities attributed to the governmental authority in the two models. In the Pigovian tradition, the bureaucrat is both informed and incorruptible; in the Coase framework, he is ignorant and incorruptible.

Agreement on this "incorruptibility" characteristic of governmental decision makers, and indeed the introduction of the term *corruptible* in this familiar usage, suggests that there exist widely shared ethical presuppositions concerning the inalienability of the delegated rights to make collective choices. That is to say, some shift away from the unanimity rule for collective decisions may be accepted as necessary, with the accompanying acknowledgment that new and previously nonexistent "rights of decision" are brought into being, rights that have economic value that is potentially capturable by the subset of the citizenry empowered to take decisions on behalf of all. Such rights may, however, be considered to be inalienable; that is, the holder is not entitled to sell them or to exploit his possession of them through collection of personal rewards, either directly or indirectly.[12] It would be inappropriate to examine in detail here the validity of such ethical presuppositions, although this opens up many interesting and highly controversial topics for analysis.[13]

The existence of such presuppositions can scarcely be denied. The pejorative content of such terms as *vote trading, logrolling, political favoritism, spoils system, pork barrel legislation* all attest to the pervasiveness of negative attitudes toward even minor attempts on the part of possessors of political decision-making rights to increase rental returns. If these attitudes are sufficiently widespread, prohibitions against bureaucratic and political rent maximization may extend beyond the mere promulgation of ethical norms for behavior. The rewards and punishments that are consciously built into the governmental structure may be specifically aimed at making such rent maximization unprofitable for any person empowered to take decisions on behalf of the whole group. The designated bureaucrat who is assigned authority over one specific aspect of public policy may not be morally or ethically inhibited from accepting side payments. But he may face harsh legal penalties should he accede to monetary temptations. To the extent that these constitutionally determined constraints insure that the economic self-interests of governmental decision makers dictate behavior unresponsive to proffered side-payments (direct or indirect) it may be argued, almost tautologically, that any outcomes chosen for the community by the "incorruptibles" must be, by definition, classified as "efficient." This would produce the paradoxical conclusion that the conditions for efficiency depend critically on the institutional structure and that, even with unchanged personal evaluations, solutions which are deemed efficient under one set of institutions may be inefficient under another.

The avoidance of this paradox becomes possible if we are content to define as allocationally efficient only that set of possible outcomes that could emerge from the contractual negotiation process among persons in the community, on the assumption that no rights are inalienable. In this case, the introduction of inalienability in the rights of governmental decision takers clearly makes the theorem of allocational neutrality invalid. Under the highly restricted assumptions of zero transactions costs, any activity will be efficiently organized in the absence of governmental intervention, and, absent income effect feedbacks, the allocational outcome will be invariant over differing assignments of private and alienable rights. Under such conditions as these, it is the inalienability of rights that the shift to the public sector introduces which removes the guarantee that outcomes will be efficient, not the shift to governmental decision taking per se. If we avoid the apparent paradox in this manner, however, the implication is left that the constitutional shift of activities to the public sector is an almost necessary source of inefficiency. When other considerations are accounted for, however, this implication need not follow. When transactions costs are recognized, and especially when distributional implications are considered, efficiency "in the large" may dictate the governmental organization of activities along with the inalienability of the rights delegated necessarily to bureaucratic decision makers. There is no final escape from the requirements that each particular institutional change proposed must be examined on its own merits, on some case-by-case procedure, with the interdependence among separate organizational decisions firmly in mind.

NOTES

I am indebted to my colleagues Winston Bush, Dennis Mueller, and Gordon Tullock for helpful suggestions.

1. Coase, "The Problem of Social Cost," *Journal of Law and Economics* 3 (1960): 1–44.
2. This terminology is adopted from the discussion by Calabresi and Melamed, whose paper clarifies the distinction between these two. As they state, a property rule "is the form of entitlement which gives rise to the least amount of state intervention." See Calabresi and Melamed, "Property Rules, Liability Rules, and Inalienability: One View of the Cathedral," *Harvard Law Review* 85 (1972): 1089–146. See also Demsetz, "Some Aspects of Propery Rights," *Journal of Law and Economics* 9 (1966): 64–5.

   In a paper to be published, I have also called attention to the distinction between these two institutional arrangements, noting in particular the necessary resort to third-party action under liability rules. See Buchanan, "The Institutional Structure of Externality," *Public Choice* 14 (Spring 1973): 69–82.
3. Collective decision making under a rule of unanimity is associated with the name of Knut Wicksell in modern public finance theory analysis because he proposed institutional reforms that embodied unanimity in the reaching of tax and expenditure decisions. K. Wicksell, *Finanztheoretische Untersuchungen* (Jena: Gustav Fischer, 1896). The central portion of this work appears in English translation as "A New Principle of Just Taxation," in *Classics in the Theory of Public Finance*, ed., R. Musgrave and A. Peacock (New York: St. Martin's Press, 1959), pp. 72–118.
4. It is possible to use the analogue to voluntary exchange at the level of constitutional, as opposed to day-to-day choice. That is to say, we might analyze the selection of a political constitution, the rules for the reaching of collective decisions, under a postulated unanimity rule. It is then possible to derive a logical basis for nonunanimity rules from unanimous agreement at the constitutional level. This is the approach taken by J. Buchanan and G. Tullock in *The Calculus of Consent* (Ann Arbor: University of Michigan Press, 1962).
5. With zero transactions costs, any departure from unanimity voting rules for collective action would hardly be acceptable at the constitutional level. But this modification is introduced here for purposes of developing the exposition of the argument, not for descriptive relevance.
6. It is often erroneously argued that individuals with the superior economic power, A in our example, can exercise more influence in the formation of dominant

coalitions than individuals with inferior economic power, C in our example. If, however, C fully recognizes the exploitation potential available in the situation described, he can offer B precisely the same terms as those offered by A. In the basic arithmetic here, there is no more likelihood that the net gains from not undertaking the project, 10 units, will be shared by A rather than by B or C. In effect, the Von Neumann-Morgenstern solution set of imputations to the simple majority game becomes:

(5,5,0) (5,0,5) (0,5,5).

For an elaboration of this analysis, see, Buchanan and Tullock, *The Calculus of Consent,* chaps. 11 and 12.

7. In another paper, I have developed somewhat more fully some of the possible implications of the modified rights structure that majority voting rules embody. *See* Buchanan, "The Political Economy of the Welfare State," Center for the Study of Public Choice Research Paper No. 808231-1-8 (June, 1972). This paper was prepared for the Conference on Capitalism and Freedom, in honor of Milton Freidman, in Charlottesville, Virginia, October 1972; see Buchanan, "The Political Economy of Franchise in the Welfare State," in *Capitalism and Freedom: Problems and Prospects,* ed. R. T. Selden (Charlottesville: University of Virginia Press, 1975), pp. 52–77.
8. The method of selection may affect the motivation of the decision maker and, in this way, modify the likelihood that the behavioral hypotheses implicit in the orthodox conceptions will be corroborated.
9. In the numerical example, the potentially capturable rent seems to be 200 units because of the assumptions that both benefits and costs of the drainage project are shared symmetrically among all of the villagers. If these assumptions are relaxed, the decision maker can collect a larger sum in rent. His potential gain, will, in all cases, be the sum of the *larger* of the *positive* or the *negative* differences between benefits and costs, the sum being taken over all members of the community.
10. This modifies the standard economist's treatment of the distinction between allocational and distributional results. The latter may, for certain purposes, be neglected if the zero-sum aspects are confined to a stable group of "members." If, however, a new rights assignment, such as that discussed, generates distributional transfers outside the original group, the effects, for this group, are negative-sum. Applied to the realistic setting in which transactions costs are present, this suggests that a community may, under certain conditions, find it advantageous to put up with allocative inefficiency rather than to secure its removal at the expense of distributional transfers to delegated decision takers.
11. For an explicit statement of the Coase-Chicago position, see Demsetz, "The Exchange and Enforcement of Property Rights," *Journal of Law and Economics* 7 (1964): 21–2.
12. In "Property Rules, Liability Rules, and Inalienability," Calabresi and Melamed discuss the inalienability of rights at some length, and particularly they draw attention to several examples where inalienability is accepted.

The precise location of "inalienability" in the situation discussed may be questioned. In delegating decision-making authority to an agent, citizens may not be considered to be transferring the economic value inherent in the "right to choose." In this framework, it is the rights of the citizenry which are "inalienable" in some fundamental sense, and the agent could scarcely transfer a "right" which he does not possess. In my discussion, I have equated the empirically observed delegation of decision-making authority with an effective transfer of a valuable "right" which is then supposed to be "inalienable."

13. The ethical bases for such widely shared attitudes may be challenged when the economic analysis is carefully developed. In the case of marketing rights to make decisions for the community, the relative undesirability of the distributional results provide a sufficient reason for inalienability. Conceptually, the decision maker can capture *all* of the potential surplus from constitutionally authorized action. In this limit, those who presumably make the constitutional delegation of authority, the citizenry, find themselves with zero net gains from collective action. So long as the delegation of decision rights along with inalienability is predicted to generate positive net gains, the citizenry's economic position is enhanced. The possible inefficiency in the standard allocative sense is more than offset by the distributional gains.

The Political Economy of the Welfare State

James M. Buchanan

1. Pareto-Optimal Redistribution

In this paper I propose to examine carefully the implications concerning the voting franchise that are implicitly contained in the modern concept of Pareto-optimal income redistribution. This concept has been discussed at length in several papers in the late 1960s. I share some of the responsibility for generating this interest. In my early review of Musgrave's treatise,[1] I called explicitly for the derivation of a conceptual logic for redistribution that is on all fours with the logic for allocation in the public sector. It seemed inconsistent to me to adopt the stance of modern public finance theorists, exemplified by both Samuelson and Musgrave in somewhat different ways, who attempt to derive criteria for public-sector allocation from individualistic valuations but to reject these criteria for public-sector redistribution.[2] Hochman and Rodgers, in their much-cited paper, and Edgar Olsen, independently, responded directly or indirectly to my suggestion. They attempted to construct a "theory of income redistribution" or a "theory of transfers" on the basis of individual utility interdependence.[3] This "theory" is open to either positive or normative interpretation, as "explaining" what is observed to take place through the fiscal process or as indicating what should take place under a regime characterized by utility interdependence of the sort postulated. Implicit in either interpretation, however, is the limitation of membership in the "fiscal club" of donors or potential donors. *To the members of the donor group,* whose utility functions contain arguments for the income or utility levels of other persons who are poor, the transfer of income to the latter group becomes a purely "public" good. And because of the jointness and nonexclusion attributes, a case is established, prima facie, for cooperative action, whether this is organized voluntaristically or politically.

If collective action takes its organizational form via political or governmental process, however, implications for the voting franchise are raised at the outset. If, in fact, the political decision mechanism is to serve, even to some remote approximation, as a surrogate for the idealized collective-cooperative fiscal club of potential donors, the voting franchise must be restricted to potential taxpayers, to those whose utility functions contain or might contain arguments for the income levels of poorer members of the larger community. Those persons to whom income transfers are to be made cannot be

First published in *Capitalism and Freedom: Problems and Prospects,* edited by R. T. Selden (Charlottesville: University Press of Virginia, 1975), pp. 52–77.

allowed to participate in the collective decision concerning the extent of this transfer itself since their own private interest will, of course, be unidirectional.

Elementary Analytics

Consider a community of $n + 1$ persons, composed of n i's and a single j. Each of the i's ($i = 1, 2, \ldots, n$) has the same utility function, which contains an argument for the income of j, designated in an all-purpose consumption good which also is the numeraire,

$$U^i = U^i\,(Y^i, Y^j), \tag{1}$$

where the Y's represent all-purpose consumption goods. Since the Y^j enters the utility functions of all i's, and since it is nonpartitionable among the i's, it qualifies as a purely public good in the Samuelsonian sense. The necessary condition for efficiency is familiar,

$$\sum_{i=1}^{n} \frac{u^i Y^j}{u^i Y^i} = 1, \tag{2}$$

where the small u's refer to the partial derivatives of the utility function. This condition states that the summed marginal evaluations over all i's, evaluated in the numeraire, equals marginal cost, which is simply one, owing to the monetary dimensionality of Y^j.

The satisfaction of (2) may be but need not be accompanied by the fulfillment of (3),

$$\frac{u^i Y^j}{u^i Y^i} = \frac{1}{n} \text{ for all } i. \tag{3}$$

If (2) is met, the Pareto frontier is attained since there exists no means of shifting from this position so as to improve the position of any person without harming another. All gains from trade in the most inclusive sense are exhausted, and, even allowing for full side payments at zero transactions costs, there is no proposal for change that could command unanimous agreement of all parties.

Note, however, that this seemingly straightforward application of the standard norm for public-goods efficiency does not contain the evaluation placed on the income transfer by the potential recipient, j.[4] Since we are treating transfers of income or general purchasing power, it is clear that the marginal evaluation placed on a dollar's additional transfer by j will, at all levels, be a dollar, or

$$\frac{u^j Y^j}{u^j Y^j} = 1. \tag{4}$$

If we now incorporate this evaluation of j into the summation over all members of the community, the necessary condition for efficiency seems to become

$$\sum_{i,j=1}^{n+1} \frac{u^{i,j}Y^j}{u^{i,j}Y^i} = 1. \tag{5}$$

But (2) and (5) are not satisfied at equivalent levels of income transfer to j. In order to satisfy (5), the summed marginal evaluations over the i's alone must equal zero, or

$$\sum_{i=1}^{n} \frac{u^iY^j}{u^iY^i} = 0. \tag{6}$$

When (6) is met, there is no utility interdependence at the margin. Note that *both* (2) and (5) describe positions on the Pareto welfare surface. These positions do not, of course, exhaust the Pareto set. *Any* level of income transfer at or beyond that which satisfies (2) will produce a result that qualifies as a Pareto-optimal position. Once attained, there will exist no means of changing or shifting from any such position under an idealized unanimity rule, when *both* the i's and the j's are franchised.

If the evaluation of recipients is included, note that (5) is *not* a necessary condition for Pareto optimality. Summed marginal evaluations need not equal marginal cost. This apparent paradox arises from the particular nature of pure income transfers, and this nonuniqueness in outcomes makes the application of the standard tools difficult. For purposes of comparison, consider the collective or public provision of a lighthouse-type purely public good. In this latter instance, absent transactions costs and income-effect feedbacks, any departure from that allocation which satisfies the equivalent to (5) will set forces in motion that will return the system to the unique position where (5) is met.[5] No such equilibrating forces can emerge with pure income transfers because, despite a possible willingness of the donors, as a group, to offer amounts differing from a dollar for a dollar's change upward or downward in the amount of income transfer, such offer cannot be accepted by the recipient(s) since this total, also, must be computed as part of the transfer. In one sense, therefore, the condition defined by (5) alone is meaningless because, operationally, it is not different from any other among a subinfinity of positions.

By contrast, for the i's treated as a group, the members of which evaluate the transfer of income to j as a public or collective-consumption good, condition (2) is fully analogous to the orthodox efficiency norm in public goods provision. Any change from that position defined or described by the satisfaction of (2) will set equilibrating tendencies in motion that will shift the outcome back to the equilibrium position, provided, of course, that the restricted assumptions about transactions costs and income-effect feedbacks are maintained.

Public Choice Implications

The formal analysis is simple enough, but its implications for the problems of collective decision making must be examined. Three quarters of a century have passed since Knut Wicksell admonished his fellow economists for their failure to relate economic policy norms to the political setting within which policy takes place.[6] He accused economists of assuming that policy is made by an "enlightened and benevolent despot," whose criteria are those provided to him by pure-minded professors. Wicksell's strictures are almost wholly applicable in the current professional and quasi-professional discourse on income redistribution policy. The pros and cons of the various income maintenance plans, sometimes called negative income taxes, are discussed with little or no reference to the political choice process.[7] In this context, the preliminary attempts to develop criteria for politically implemented income redistribution from individual evaluations represent advance over the naiveté inherent in the invocation of external value norms. These attempts have remained seriously incomplete, however, because of the failure to relate the analysis directly ot the political decision mechanism, either that which is potential or in being.

In order to discuss this relationship systematically, it is useful to digress briefly and summarize the elementary methodology of the Pareto criterion itself. An initial or existing state of the economy is described by an imputation (assignment, allocation, distribution) of "goods" (positive and negative) among persons in the relevant community. In the normal case, individualized shares in total product are assumed to consist in full-fledged claims to the disposition of "goods" as their "owners" see fit, although behavioral limitations may be incorporated into the definitions without difficulty. Similarly, the "goods" are usually assumed to be fully partitionable among separate persons although, once again, the existence of joint and common ownership rights may be embodied in the appropriate definitions. In all cases, however, the imputation defines a structure of rights or claims that is presumed to be known with certainty. If individuals are informed about the qualities of the "goods" assigned to them, and if they are assumed to be rational utility maximizers, the private behavior of each person carries him to what we may call the nonexchange utility possibility frontier. That is to say, all gains from internal "trade" will be exhausted in the private or presocial behavioral calculus of individuals.

The Pareto criterion, whether applied to a classification of final positions, described by imputations of "goods" among persons, or to a distinction among changes from one position to another, is rooted in interpersonal or social *exchange*, the central institution that is analyzed variously in economic theory. Given any imputation, the Pareto criterion enables us to classify this into the nonoptimal or the optimal set.[8] If it is nonoptimal, it enables us also to classify proposed moves or shifts as efficient or inefficient. The criterion can be applied positively to the observation of behavior as well as conceptually on the presumption that individual utility functions are known. Individuals, endowed with initial imputations, are presumed to engage in simple or ordinary trades that will shift the system in the direction of the Pareto frontier, exploiting the potentially available surplus obtainable. The Pareto norm can be utilized to assess the results of such trades, but its potential usefulness is found largely in the location and isolation of possible complex trading arrangements that may not emerge from the simpler trading processes. These complex trading prospects may, and normally will, involve simultaneous agreement on the part of more than two parties, and they may include trades in the form of "agreements" to change the rules or institutions within which orthodox trading can take place.

The Donor Cooperative or Club

If this summary description of the Pareto criterion is provisionally accepted, what can be said about "Pareto-optimal income redistribution"? Commencing from some initial imputation, unilateral transfers in some numeraire good (income) might be observed to take place voluntarily if utility functions exhibit interdependence.[9] Some such transfers would take place under wholly independent behavior but, as noted, there may exist both jointness and nonexclusion attributes that suggest superior results from joint or cooperative action. Potential donors would, in this setting, organize and join a voluntary cooperative for the purpose of making transfers to those persons designated as being eligible for "charity." The latter would, however, remain external to the acting donor group or club, and these recipients would treat the transfers as purely gratuitous. They could scarcely be expected to participate in decisions concerning the amount of transfer they receive and, of course, their evaluation of the transfer will not directly influence the decision of the donors.

Within the cooperative donor group or club, decisions must be made on the amount of transfer along with the distribution of the costs among individual members. In aggregate terms, the necessary condition for efficiency is that defined by (2) above. In a setting without decision-making costs, the group would operate under some effective rule of unanimity. Condition (2) would be satisfied, along with that defined in (3) for a set of equal i's. If members of the donor club should differ in preferences for income transfers, the equivalent of condition (3) would, of course, involve differing marginal costs among members. Decision-making costs exist, however, and these become significant where groups must reach agreement. Hence, even in purely voluntary donor clubs members might acquiesce in agreed-on, nonunanimity decision rules. Departure from unanimity removes any assurance that the aggregative marginal condition for efficiency, defined in (2), will be satisfied, or that the individualistic marginal conditions, defined in (3) or its equivalent, will be fulfilled. The voluntary nature of the arrangement embodied in the right of any member to withdraw unilaterally insures, however, that each person secure net gains from his participation. That is,

$$\int_0^T \frac{u^i Y^j}{u^i Y^i} \geqslant 1, \tag{7}$$

for all i's, where T measures the amount of income transfer to j by the fiscal club of the i's.[10]

In this more comprehensive setting that does allow for decision-making costs, the level of income transfer from donor groups to recipients under a regime of voluntary cooperative groups might appropriately be designated as "Pareto-optimal." Conceptually, this seems to have been the organizational model assumed by several of those who have participated in the recent discussion.

Governmental Analogues to Voluntary Donor Cooperative

The observed institutional framework for much income redistribution is not voluntary; it is political or governmental. The analysis must somehow bridge the gap between voluntary and coercive organizational structure. How can analysis based on voluntary exchange, and utilizing the Pareto criterion, be extended to apply to political or governmental structure, since the latter must be, in its nature, coercive?

There are three institutions that would allow governmentally determined income transfers to be brought under orthodox Pareto norms, and to be treated *as if* such transfers emerged from voluntary fiscal clubs with only minor variants. In each case, we make the preliminary and necessary assumption that decisions are made democratically through some voting process in which many persons participate, directly or indirectly. This rules out authoritarian decision making on the part of governments.

Model I. In the first model, we can assume that a genuine rule of unanimity is operative, at least with respect to redistribution policy, and that all persons in the community have the voting franchise, both potential donors and potential recipients of transfers. The restrictiveness of unanimity may be relaxed sufficiently to allow for representative processes provided that the legislators selected represent all interests and that the unanimity requirement holds within the legislative assembly.

Commencing from an initial imputation of goods among persons, and with no voluntary redistribution, we may consider the results of an idealized decision process. It is clear that representatives of donors and recipients would agree on a level of income transfer that would satisfy condition (2) above. Proposals for additional income transfers beyond this level would be opposed by donor interests. Such extensions would, of course, be supported by representatives of recipient groups, as indeed would all proposals for additional transfers within meaningful limits. The political process would in this model accomplish essentially identical objectives as the cooperative or voluntary clubs organization discussed earlier. In practical fact, however, a political decision structure organized in that fashion would probably generate a lower level of total income transfer than the alternative regime of wholly voluntary fiscal clubs. In the latter, the voluntary participation feature would make individual donors more acquiescent in departures from effective unanimity as a means of allowing some reduction in group decision costs. In political organization, departures from unanimity would be more strongly resisted.

Model II. Consider now a second model in which politically determined income transfers might be discussed in an orthodox setting of Pareto optimality. If a regime of competitive governmental units exists, and if persons may shift membership among these at relatively little personal costs, each political unit may embody both an inclusive voting franchise and departures from an effective unanimity rule for collective choice while generating results that are akin to those broadly predictable under voluntary organization. This model is applicable, however, only in those situations where the utility interdependence, if such exists, involves members of the same "local" governmental jurisdiction. In this sort of setting, income redistribution takes on most of the properties of a "localized public good," and a Tiebout-like adjustment process places severe limits on the possible inefficiency that can emerge regardless of internal political decision rules.[11]

Model III. A third model is one in which the voting franchise is specifically limited to those who are actual or potential contributors or donors in the income-transfer system, that is, net taxpayers rather than net beneficiaries. In this model, those who receive income transfers are explicitly excluded from participation in the collective or governmental decisions that are concerned with either the level or the financing of the transfers. In this setting, income transfers to the "poor," treated here as an external group, can be analyzed as a purely public good whose benefits and costs are shared among members of the potential taxpayer, and hence voting, group in the community. If, among this restricted set of persons, an effective rule of unanimity prevails for collective decisions, a regime closely analogous to that of voluntary clubs exists, with the differences previously noted. If the costs of decision making suggest significant departures from unanimity, and if individual members of the group do not have available low-cost migrational alternatives, the moves or shifts in income distribution emerging from the political process may not be Pareto-superior. If, for example, a majority coalition among the potential taxpayer group desires to redistribute substantial income to the poor outside the voting group, at the expense of all potential taxpayers, the minority of the latter may suffer genuine fiscal exploitation. Nonetheless, the majority coalition need not act in such fashion, and the disenfranchisement of the transfer recipients removes the direct influence of those whose strictly private self-interest dictates extensions in transfers at all levels. Under such conditions, it seems plausible to treat observed political outcomes as indirect surrogates for something akin to genuinely voluntary transfers.

2. Property in Franchise

Observation tells us that none of the three models sketched briefly above describes the real world. What we do observe is politically determined redistribution of income at jurisdictional levels that guarantee high-cost migrational alternatives and under the operation of decision rules that are basically majoritarian rather than unanimitarian. We observe, furthermore, that transfer recipients are not excluded from voting and otherwise participating in politics, including the politics of transfer policy itself. In this realistic setting, the Pareto criterion must either be judged of relatively little value in analyzing transfers or it must be modified substantially from its standard application.

Recall our summary of the methodology of the Pareto norm. Individuals in the social group are described in terms of an imputation or assignment of "goods," with well-defined limits as to rights of disposition. The orthodox Pareto criterion assists in evaluating or in proposing changes that involve simple and/or complex "trades" in these assigned "goods" among separate members of the community. I now think that this traditional approach that has been taken by many political economists, including me, has been seriously deficient. The deficiency may be identified and discussed in terms of the problems considered in this essay.

Nominal and Real Claims

In the distributional setting as observed in the real world, "goods" are *not* partitioned among separate persons (families) in the well-defined sense that is implicitly postulated in the standard analysis. To indicate this, I propose to distinguish "nominal" and "real" imputations or assignments over final "goods," over rights to the use of "goods." What we may actually observe, at any moment, is a set of nominal rights, which may be defined by an imputation, which may or may not accurately map the initial position or basis from which simple and complex trades among persons must commence. Alongside and accompanying the set of nominal claims over "goods," there exists a *membership* right in the social group or community, which may or may not be accompanied by a *voting* right in group or collective decisions. Both the membership right and the voting right have economic value to the holders, an economic value that takes its meaning in terms of some contingent claim on the "common fund" of "goods" available in the whole community.

Membership rights and voting rights are separate, and, in some cases, the distinction is important.[12] But for our purposes these rights accompany each other; we simply assume that membership in the social group implies voting rights. What we observe, then, is a set of nominal claims, partitioned among persons and/or families in the group, along with universal and uniform voting rights (political equality) over all adults in the community. The latter rights take economic value in our model only through the indirect claims that they might represent over the total resource stock in the economy, all of which we assume is partitioned among persons in the nominal sense. For purposes of simplifying the analysis, we assume that there are no joint-consumption goods, no public goods of the standard variety.

Constitutional Restrictions

The value that a voting-membership right has for its holder depends on several things, including the allowable range for collective or political action. This will be defined by a political constitution, which may or may not be formally specified. We limit consideration in this paper to redistributional policy, and we specify the effective constitutional requirements to be as follows.

1. Income redistribution shall be general rather than discriminatory, and redistribution, if it occurs, must take the form of transfers from higher to lower income categories, with equalization as the limit.
2. No person in the recipient group who stands lower on the income scale before political redistribution shall secure less in total transfer than another who stands higher on the scale.
3. No person in the taxpaying group who stands lower on the income scale before political redistribution shall be taxed by a higher amount than another who stands higher on the scale.
4. Collective decisions are reached through simple majority voting.

These requirements seem plausible on their own account, as well as realistic if we confine attention to pure income transfer policy. Basically, these requirements state that arbitrarily composed political coalitions may not exploit minorities. "Regressive" and nondiscriminatory transfers as well as taxes are ruled out. Taken together, these requirements add stability to the expectations about redistribution policy, and they enable us to define more clearly the value of the membership-voting franchise.

No Production–No Utility Interdependence

I assume initially that there is no utility interdependence of the sort adduced to "explain" observed income transfers under the orthodox Pareto constructions discussed in section 1. In the absence of collective action, therefore, each person (family) retains all the "goods" under his assignment in the nominal sense. I assume, further, that agreed-on laws against theft are enforced perfectly. Finally, I assume in this model that the initial assignment of "goods" falls as manna with a distribution that is unchanging from one period to the next. "Goods" are not "produced" by human effort.[13]

Under the restricted conditions postulated, simple majority voting will generate an amount and type of income redistribution determined by the median income recipient acting to further his own position. His problem is one of simple maximization subject to the constitutional constraints imposed.

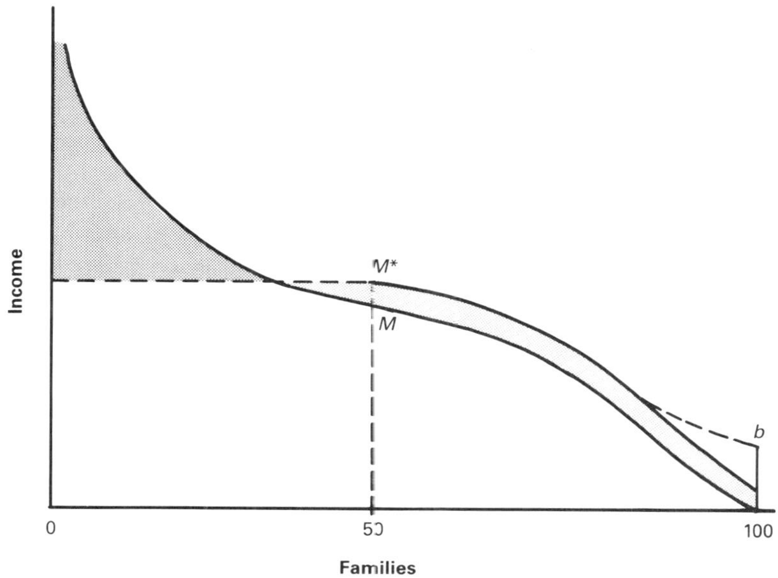

Fig. 1

In the no-production economy majority voting will tend to equalize all posttransfer incomes above and including the median and to equalize all positive transfers to persons below and including the median.

Figure 1 depicts family distribution in a community in a shape that is similar to that which describes distribution in the United States. The median is located at *M*. If, in fact, this pattern should describe a distribution in a no-production setting, and if the constitutional limits were those indicated, the posttransfer income distribution would be shown by the dotted curve. The transfer to the median family, measured by *MM**, would be maximized subject to the constraints suggested, including the necessity that the two shaded areas be equal in size, that is to say, that the transfer budget be balanced.

We may now look at the value of the voting franchise to a person along the income scale in this model. It is clear that the franchise has value only through its indirect influence on the location of the median voter. Disenfranchisement of, say, persons at the lower levels of income would shift *M* to the left on the diagram and the distance analogous to *MM** would be smaller. This would impose monetary costs on all transfer recipients, not only those who might suffer disenfranchisement as such. Similarly, disenfranchisement of persons at the upper end of the scale would shift the median to the right in the diagram. This would increase the amount of tax paid by each taxpayer, increase the number of taxpayers, increase the total amount of transfer, and increase the positive transfers received per recipient.

It may be noted from the construction of figure 1 that, in the conditions of this model, the median voter will be harmed by the disenfranchisement of voters at either end of the scale; he will suffer from any shift of the median. A shift to the right will equalize incomes at and above the new median, but this must be at a lower level. A shift of the median to the left will reduce the total tax revenue collections while simultaneously increasing the number of recipients. This must involve a reduction in the amount of transfer per recipient, and hence the amount received by the initial median voter. It will not, therefore, be to the direct interest of the established median voter, presumed here to be the median pretransfer income recipient, to extend or to limit the franchise asymmetrically. He will, of course, be indifferent as to symmetrical changes.

No Production with Utility Interdependence

The introduction of utility interdependence into this model will have less effect on the results than might have been anticipated. The preference of certain upper-income receivers for greater amounts of transfer than that emergent in the no-interdependence framework will have an effect similar to their own disenfranchisement. The effective median position shifts to the right, with the results indicated above. Note particularly that this sort of utility interdependence will not allow for the inverse discrimination represented by larger transfers to the lowest pretransfer income recipients so long as the effective median voter's preference does not exhibit a concern for the utility of those standing lower along the pretransfer income scale. There will be no flaring of the dotted curve upward as traced out by the extended segment shown by *b* in figure 1. If such a flaring is to be produced, this must arise because of utility interdependence of voters in median income ranges, at least if we confine analysis to this very simple political choice model.

Production without Utility Interdependence

The introduction of production will drastically change the model. Instead of "goods" being initially distributed as manna, we now assume that "goods" are produced exclusively by human effort, and that the initially generated distribution is the same as before. In this model, the amount of redistribution that becomes rational for the median-income recipient, and voter, will be directly dependent on the incentive effects that taxation will exert on those from whom funds are to be exacted politically. It will clearly be inefficient to levy more than a revenue-maximizing tax on any person. Hence, we should predict that the posttax distribution of income will reflect some inequality throughout the scale under the constitutional restrictions previously postulated. Figure 2 depicts the situation. The curved line indicates the pretransfer distribution of initially received incomes *after* income earning adjustments to the transfers have been made. The dotted curve indicates the posttransfer distribution.

As in the no-production model, the median voter faces a constrained maximization problem. He will try to maximize the net transfer to him, shown

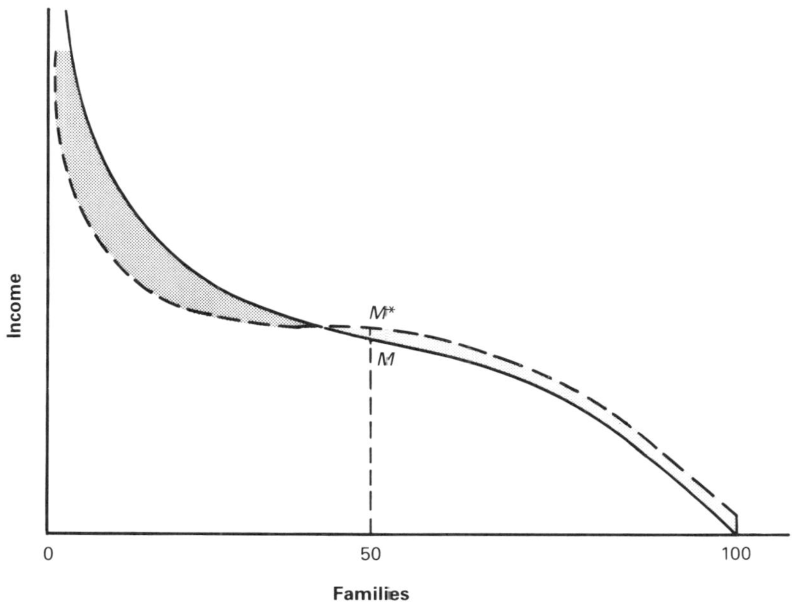

Fig. 2

by MM^*. Let us assume that the dotted curve over the net taxpayer group represents the strict revenue-maximizing locus. We want now to examine effects of a shift in the franchise as before. If persons at the lower extremities of the scale are disenfranchised, the median shifts to the left, as before, but note that this will have no effect on the total tax levied on those at the upper extremities of the scale. This is because these persons are, in all cases, being subjected to the revenue-maximizing tax. Shifts in the median will not, therefore, modify their final positions. In such case, however, these highest-income recipients will be totally indifferent as to whether or not they exercise their own franchise. The vote will have no value to them and they may be observed either to neglect the exercise of franchise or, more likely, to fulfill a presumed internal moral commitment by affecting to exhibit great concern for those at lower income levels.[14]

If this reaction on the part of the highest-income recipients is fully recognized by the median voter, however, this, in itself, will cause the latter to refrain from imposing taxes at the strict revenue-maximizing level. High-income recipients will be taxed at a level sufficiently below such limits as to insure their attention to the voting process. The potential upward mobility in the income scale that enters into the expectations of the median voter will also modify or mitigate against impositions of taxes at the revenue-maximizing limits.

In this model we should also note that changes in the location of the median voter along the income scale, brought about by voluntary voting abstention, utility interdependence, or explicit disenfranchisement, will not affect the net transfer to recipients at the lowest end of the scale nearly so much as in the no-production setting. Because the highest-income recipients are likely to be taxed at or near revenue-maximizing limits regardless of the location of the median, over broad middle ranges, this source of funds remains invariant. Shifts in the median will affect the transfer per recipient slightly, but the primary effect will be that of shifting the break-even position, where a person is changed from a net taxpayer to a net beneficiary of the transfer scheme.

Democratic Income Transfers and Pareto Norms

It is tempting to extend the majoritarian transfer models, to introduce further qualifications, and to modify the assumptions. All of this offers challenging subject matter for the application of the tools of public choice theory. My purpose here, however, is neither such elaboration nor defense of the particular models chosen. Rather it is to relate the basic majoritarian transfer process to the Pareto criterion framework within which income transfers were discussed in section 1. As noted, I now recognize a serious deficiency in the standard application of the Pareto norms, and I want to discuss this deficiency explicitly with reference to the models introduced here.

Orthodox procedure would classify the income transfers generated by the working of pure majority voting rules, or by any political process that may reasonably be described by this model, as being coercive in nature, and, as such, clearly violative of the Pareto criterion as the latter is applied to changes or moves among positions. That is to say, a pure majoritarian transfer of income under the constitutional restrictions suggested would qualify as a "nonsuperior" move. I now think that this is an overly restricted usage of the Pareto norm, even as applied to changes. As I have noted at several places, the Pareto criterion, strictly speaking, is applicable only when the nominal imputation of "goods" among persons represents accurately the "real" set of claims or rights of persons over the final disposition of these "goods." It is erroneous, however, to acknowledge a nominal imputation as "real" in a setting that allows for income redistribution under collective or governmental auspices.

Consider, for example, the position of a single high-income recipient. His nominal claim over the disposition of "goods" may be, relatively, very large indeed. But he secures (or earns) this nominal income in a polity (economy) that has extended universal and uniform suffrage to all its adult members. Furthermore, this recipient of the nominally high income cannot, by assumption, shift to alternative polities (economies) without undergoing major costs. In a very genuine sense, therefore, the high-income recipient does not possess a full-fledged "property right" to the "goods" over which his nominal income apparently gives him claim. By the very nature of their simple voting or potential voting membership in a polity (economy) that constitutionally allows income transfers to take place under collective aegis, *all* other members in the community hold a contingent claim on the "goods" purchasable by the nominal income of the person in question. Hence, to say that the recipient of a nominally high income actively opposes a majoritarian transfer policy that makes him a net taxpayer and that this behavior, in itself, reveals that the policy does not reflect a Pareto-superior move or change, tends to obscure the underlying nature or basis of the complex interaction that is involved here. The majoritarian transfer can be viewed merely as the working out of the "real" set of claims to income in the community, the revision in the nominal set of claims predictable under the political structure in being, which includes "property rights" in franchise. The observed opposition of the rich man to transfer policy is akin to that of the person who has to pay an obligation previously made. Since the nominal income is not "his" by any "real" rights of ownership in the first place, his opposition can hardly be adduced in evidence that the transfer is violative of a meaningful welfare norm. To the extent that such a transfer appeared to violate clearly the Pareto criterion, as applied to the orthodox sense, many economists have rejected the Pareto framework in application to the whole set of issues involving income redistribution. Having no alternative, many of those who reject the Pareto criterion have sought to introduce external ethical norms to apply to all redistribution policy.

My own work, as well as those who have advanced the analysis of so-called Pareto-optimal redistribution, has suffered in the opposite sense. Because political transfers seem to violate the standard Pareto norms, we have tended to opt out of any discussion and to say that nothing further can be constructed on the basis of individual evaluations. I now propose to modify this stance, and to do so in a substantial sense. Failure to carry out income transfer policy in a political setting such as that sketched out in the models above would represent a fundamental shift in the real assignment of rights, a shift in favor of those with the nominally higher incomes. Once the franchise has been extended to all adults, and once the constitution has allowed income transfers to take place collectively, the formal act of transfer becomes fully predictable from positive economic analysis. The basic property right inheres in the voting franchise, and the economic value of this franchise reflects the measure of the contingent claim to the incomes and wealth nominally imputed to individuals in the whole community.[15]

Pareto Optimality and the Status Quo

To this point, the income transfers from the nominally rich to the nominally poor that are predicted to occur under a democratic polity are derived from individual evaluations without normative content. The Pareto norms have not been utilized to evaluate these transfers, other than in the negative commentary suggesting their inapplicability. We may now, however, try to evaluate such redistribution in terms of the Paretian criteria. Is the institutional structure which embodies pure majoritarian transfers itself Pareto-optimal? Does there exist a means of changing this structure that is Pareto-superior; that is, does there exist any proposed change in constitutional-institutional rules that would, conceptually, command the assent of all members of the community?

At first glance, these questions may seem to reflect a return to the orthodox Pareto framework, which I have explicitly criticized. There is a major difference, however, which should be stressed. Paretian criteria have often been criticized because they lend support to the status quo. In a sense, this charge is correct, but my own response has always been that "we start from here," from the status quo, and, willy nilly, this constrains our analysis. The error in my own earlier methodological position has been my initial definition of the status quo, or starting point, in terms of a presumed imputation of "goods" among persons that ignores the political process in being and the genuine claims to "goods" inherent in this process.[16] This is properly to be regarded as much a part of the status quo as is any strictly defined nominal imputation. Having redefined the status quo, the Pareto criterion can be applied in the standard manner.[17]

It seems clear that any restriction on the voting franchise, once this has been universally extended, is nonoptimal; such a shift would harm some members of the community. Under universal franchise, we may then ask whether any of the constitutional constraints can be modified to the advantage of all parties. If we limit attention to income redistribution alone, and leave other collective activity out of account, there seems no apparent change that would qualify as Pareto-superior. If this is the case, the total regime as described can be classified as Pareto-optimal.

3. Impure Redistribution

The whole approach of section 2 may be questioned, however, as regards its descriptive accuracy. Can the political process that we observe in the real world be approximated in such models, even if we accept the necessity of extreme simplicity and abstraction? Presumably, little distortion is created by the assumptions of universal suffrage. Effective majority voting rules, even when the complexities of actual political decision making are acknowledged, seem broadly acceptable in the context of the discussion here. The presence of high-cost migrational alternatives can scarcely be challenged with reference to redistribution policy at the national government level.

More serious issues may be raised concerning the specific constitutional restrictions imposed on redistribution policy itself. We do not observe much "pure" income redistribution in the absence of collective provision of real goods and services. When the allocative role of the political sector is included in the analysis of distributional outcomes, quite different results may emerge. A more acceptable and alternative model would allow tax funds to be used (1) for financing publicly supplied or publicly subsidized real goods and services; or (2) for financing pure income transfers. In this setting, it may be to the advantage of the median voter–cum–income recipient to choose (1) rather than (2). This offers a means of escaping from constitutional restriction on regressively discriminatory transfers in the numeraire. While it may not be possible to discriminate in favor of the median voter by grants of larger absolute amounts of money than those offered to persons standing lower on the nominal income scale, the same purposes may be accomplished by choosing for public or governmental supply that set of real goods and services which is most highly valued by median voters. Once supplied, these goods and services may be available on equal terms to all members of the community, but the actual distribution of benefits, as valued, may be skewed dramatically toward middle income ranges.

This may be illustrated in figure 3. The curve Y_n, as before, depicts the nominal income distribution, after behavioral adjustments but before transfers. The curve Y_d represents the most preferred pure distributional scheme for the median voter under the constitutional restrictions imposed in section 2. The curve Y_p depicts the alternative curve of effective final distribution under the regime that allows for collective provision of real goods and services. Note that Y_p falls *along* Y_d over high income ranges, and *below* Y_d over low income ranges.

This alternative model of impure redistribution is in accord with the hypotheses advanced by Aaron Director, George Stigler, and Gordon Tullock, which suggest that the major beneficiaries of transfer policies are those in the median income ranges rather than the very poor. In neither of the basic models here do the "poor," as a group, possess decisive power via the

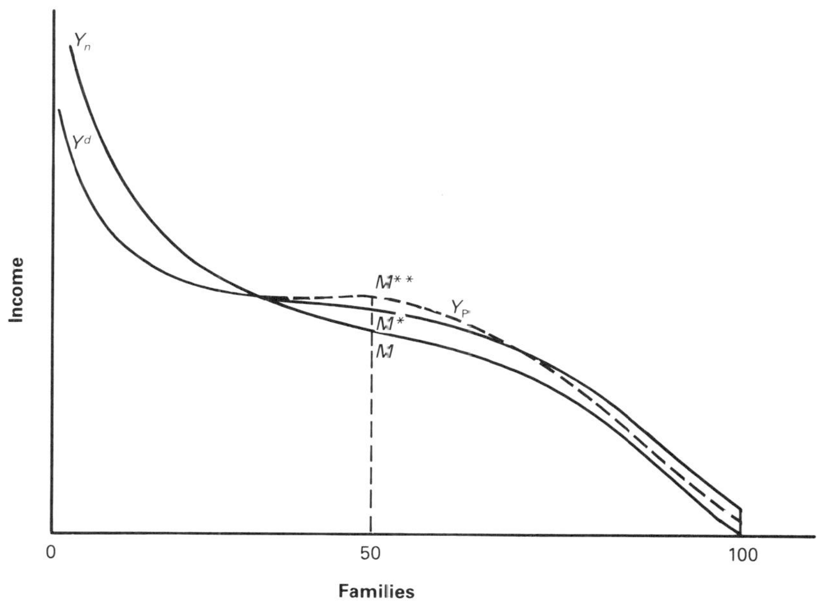

Fig. 3

voting process. Under a nondiscriminatory constitutional requirement, however, the very poor could do as well in terms of absolute pure transfers as median-income recipients. This outcome is circumvented to the extent that in-kind goods and services are offered governmentally that are differentially valued by the median voters. Public education, at all levels, seems to provide the example here.

4. Conclusions

Much of the confusion in the discussion of income redistribution stems from an inconsistency between our economic and our political attitudes. On the one hand, the ethics of capitalism suggest that the market earnings of resources become the property of the nominal owners, who may, presumably, dispose of these as they, personally, desire. They may, of course, elect to worry about their fellows, but in such an attitudinal framework "charity" is merely another consumption "good." Any politically determined transfer of income above minimal limits involves a coercive "taking." At the same time, however, the ethics of democracy suggest that restrictions on franchise are not to be tolerated. Few seem to have recognized the implications of the inconsistency between these value positions.

The inconsistency appears in its starkest form in redistribution policy, and it is the basis for the neoclassical dichotomy between allocation and distribution. Economists claim competence in defining and in identifying allocative efficiency, using as inputs the revealed (actually or conceptually) preferences (values) of individuals. They stop short when faced with distribution, and they often pull in external and nonindividualistic norms which they acknowledge to be less "scientific" than those introduced for the theory of allocation. Efficiency in allocation is defined to characterize a position where all of the potentially realizable surplus has been squeezed out of simple and complex trading arrangements. Essentially, this procedure is to describe the end point of a process, and economists have not carefully considered the starting point. Implicitly, they postulate an initial distribution of endowments and/or capacities among persons, and it is presumed that this imputation can be mapped directly into a set of final imputations of "goods" on the Pareto welfare surface. As noted, efforts have been made to bring this basic Pareto efficiency framework into the evaluation of distribution but without much success, largely because here too economists have not escaped from the inconsistency noted.

In this essay, I have tried to reconcile the inconsistency by going back to the starting point, and to call into question the orthodox definition of that imputation from which trade commences. If membership in a sociopolitical community carries with it a valued "right" of participation, this value must be somehow incorporated into any exhaustive partitioning of "potential goods" among persons, even if it is fully recognized that such value can, at best, be probabilistically estimated or determined. This procedure allows us, at least conceptually, to examine both allocation and distribution problems within a coherent analytical framework. The fact that the analysis, at all stages, becomes much more difficult, and perhaps less aesthetically satisfying, should not deter serious scholarship. Like it or not, we live in an environment where the workings and forms of capitalism are tempered by the workings and forms of majoritarian democracy.

NOTES

I am indebted to both Winston Bush and Gordon Tullock for comments.

1. "The Theory of Public Finance," *Southern Economic Journal* 26 (January 1960): 234–38.
2. In his now-classic formulation, Samuelson defined the necessary conditions for allocative efficiency with public-goods provision and then introduced a social welfare function to determine the final distribution. See Paul A. Samuelson, "The Pure Theory of Public Expenditures," *Review of Economics and Statistics* 36 (November 1954): 387–89. Musgrave was less willing to introduce external welfare norms to determine distributional outcomes, but his conceptual separation of the allocation and distribution branches of the budget suggested different normative principles. See R. A. Musgrave, *The Theory of Public Finance* (New York: McGraw-Hill, 1959.)
3. Harold M. Hochman and James D. Rodgers, "Pareto Optimal Redistribution," *American Economic Review* 59 (September 1969): 542–57; Edgar O. Olsen, "A Normative Theory of Transfers," *Public Choice* 6 (Spring 1969): 39–58. The Hochman-Rodgers paper stimulated several comments, both in criticism and in extension. See Paul A. Meyer and J. J. Shipley, "Pareto Optimal Redistribution: Comment," *American Economic Review* 60 (December 1970): 988–90; R. A. Musgrave, "Comment," *American Economic Review* 60 (December 1970): 991–93; R. S. Goldfarb, "Comment," *American Economic Review* 60 (December 1970): 995–96; Harold M. Hochman and James D. Rodgers, "Reply," *American Economic Review* 60 (December 1970): 997–1002; E. J. Mishan, "Welfare Economics and Pareto Optimal Redistribution" (Typescript, June 1971).
4. This has, of course, been recognized. Cf. W. C. Stubblebine, "Redistribution and Wicksellian Unanimity" (unpublished note, University of Virginia, 1962); George E. Peterson, *Welfare, Workfare, and Pareto Optimality,* Working Paper 1200–12 (Washington, D.C.: Urban Institute, December 1970).

   For simplicity, we assume that j is not concerned about the utility of the i's. That is, j's utility function is written $U^j = U^j(Y^j)$.
5. This is the collective or public goods equivalent of the Coase theorem. Cf. R. H. Coase, "The Problem of Social Cost," *Journal of Law and Economics* 3 (1960): 1–44. In the transactions-costs rubric we must, of course, here include free rider and preference revelation difficulties.
6. Knut Wicksell, *Finanztheoretische Untersuchungen* (Jena: Gustav Fischer, 1896). Major portions of this work are published in translation as "A New Principle of Just Taxation," in *Classics in the Theory of Public Finance,* ed. R. A. Musgrave and A. T. Peacock (London: Macmillan and Co., 1958), pp. 72–118. The relevant passages are found on pages 82–87.

7. There are notable exceptions of this generalization, among which are the contributions of both George Stigler and Gordon Tullock. See George J. Stigler, "Director's Law of Public Income Redistribution," *Journal of Law and Economics* 13 (April 1970): 1–10; Gordon Tullock, "Welfare for Whom?" *Il Politico* 33 (December 1968): 748–61, and "Charity of the Uncharitable," *Western Economic Journal* 9 (December 1971): 379–92.
8. For background discussion, see Ragner Frisch, "On Welfare Theory and Pareto Regions," *International Economic Papers* 9 (London: Macmillan, 1959): 39–92; and my "The Relevance of Pareto Optimality," *Journal of Conflict Resolution* 6 (December 1962): 341–54.
9. Transfers of specific goods, income-in-kind, might also occur. These are not discussed in order to keep the basic analysis simplified.
10. In a regime of competing fiscal clubs each member must secure net benefits at least equal to that available to him from membership in any other club.
11. For further discussion, see Mark Pauly, "Income Redistribution as a Local Public Good," *Journal of Political Economy* 81 (February, 1973): 35; and my "Who Should Distribute What in a Federal System," in *Redistribution Through Public Choice,* ed. H. Hochman and G. Peterson (New York: Columbia University Press, 1974): pp. 20–42.
12. It is clear, for example, that open and free international migration would stimulate massive migration into nations even if migrants were wholly excluded from the voting franchise. It is precisely the claims that such migrants might make on the "common funds" of the community that provides one of the rational arguments against open migration. See Leland Yeager, "Immigration, Trade, and Factor Price Equalization," *Current Economic Comment* 20 (August 1958): 3–8.
13. The model here, and indeed much of the discussion in this section, is influenced by Winston Bush. See his "Individual Welfare in Anarchy," in *Explorations in the Theory of Anarchy,* ed. Gordon Tullock (Blacksburg: Center for Study of Public Choice, 1972), pp. 5–18.
14. This explanation of the apparent charitable impulses of the very rich is akin to that offered for other groups by Gordon Tullock in his paper, "The Charity of the Uncharitable," (see note 7).
15. My own recognition of the basic point that the property-rights assignment takes place when the franchise is granted was, so far as I can tell, influenced by two sources. First, the discussion of W. C. Stubblebine, in a seminar on property rights, made clear that the presence of others in the social group must modify the environment for Crusoe, and this must be taken into account in any analysis. See his "On Property Rights and Institutions," in *Explorations in the Theory of Anarchy,* ed. Gordon Tullock (Blacksburg: Center for Study of Public Choice, 1972), pp. 39–50.

    Secondly, Nicolaus Tideman, in a seminar discussion in Blacksburg, Virginia, on 19 May 1972, advanced a proposal for using posterior probabilities as a means of getting around the revelation-of-preference problem in public goods settings. In this discussion, Tideman explicitly referred to the notion that, once choice alternatives are introduced for a vote, the property rights of those who hold differing positions on the alternatives have already been modified.
16. This modification in my own position brings me close to that expressed by Musgrave in his "Comment," cited above (note 3), on the Hochman-Rodgers paper. Musgrave suggested that "primary" redistribution occurs as a result of the

"social contact" within which political decision making takes place. He did not, however, attempt to modify the applicability of the Pareto norms. Furthermore, Musgrave's position, as expressed in his "Comment" seems at variance with the explicitly normative stance taken in his presentation of the three-part budget. In that part of their "Reply" relating to Musgrave's criticism Hochman and Rodgers also take a position similar in many respects to that developed here. However, they note at one point that "one cannot determine in welfare terms, whether the initial or market-determined distribution of income is satisfactory *until* Pareto optimal transfers have occurred" (p. 999). This inference is directly contrary to that which emerges from the analysis of this essay. Taking the "property in franchise" approach, we can say that the initial positions from which Pareto-optimal redistribution (defined in the Hochman-Rodgers sense) may take place cannot be established until the political or majoritarian redistribution has occurred.

17. In a discussion that is directly relevant to this essay, Alan T. Peacock and Charles K. Rowley criticize those who have developed models for Pareto-optimal redistribution on the grounds that the status quo starting point along with difficulties of securing unanimous agreement lend a conservative bias to the whole analysis, a bias that they consider contrary to liberal values. See "Pareto Optimality and the Political Economy of Liberalism," *Journal of Political Economy* 80 (May/June 1972): 476–90. Much of their criticism of the Pareto norms vanishes, however, under the reformulation suggested in this paper.

Tax Rates and Tax Revenues in Political Equilibrium: Some Simple Analytics

James M. Buchanan and Dwight R. Lee

Our purpose here is to analyze the tax rate–tax revenue relationship that figured prominently in the supply-side economics discussion which dominated macropolicy argument in the early 1980s, and to use standard utility-maximization to define the conditions for both taxpayer and political equilibrium. In order to simplify our exposition, we ignore the serious complexities involved in conceptualizing a single rate-revenue relationship in a tax system that incorporates many separate bases for taxation, along with many rates, including progressive rates on important sources. What is *the* rate of tax in the United States? We simply assume that this question may be satisfactorily answered.

In order to bring the analysis to the simplest possible level, we shall assume that there is only one well-defined base for taxation, and, further, that there is a single uniform rate of tax imposed on the generation or use of this base. We shall use a demand-theory construction throughout the analysis. We consider the behavior of the potential taxpayer as a potential "demander" of the tax base. This construction is self-evident if we think of the base as an ordinary commodity, say, beer. It is less familiar, but nonetheless fully appropriate, to think of the taxpayer as demanding units of income when he supplies resource inputs. With an income base for tax, it is, of course, possible to examine the taxpayer's behavior in supplying labor or other resources to produce the base. Most of the analysis of taxpayer response has taken this supply-side approach.[1] The two constructions are reciprocals of each other; they describe the same behavior and yield identical results.[2] Our demand-side approach, however, will enable us to draw on familiar propositions in orthodox demand theory that tend more readily to be overlooked when the supply-side approach is taken.

The first objective is to examine carefully the possible relationships between tax rates and tax revenues. There will be a direct and proportionate relationship when the base is invariant with changes in rate. In terms of familiar Marshallian coordinates, the direct and proportional rate-revenue relationship exists when the elasticity of the demand for base is zero throughout the range of possible tax rates.

In all normal conditions, we should expect that the "demand curve" for the base would be downsloping throughout the range of possible rates, there-

First published in *Economic Inquiry* 20 (July 1982): 344–54, Journal of the Western Economic Association.

by generating nonlinear relationships between rates and revenues.[3] With a pretax price assumed constant over quantities, the rate-revenue curve becomes fully analogous to the price-revenue curve derived from the standard downward sloping demand curve. Commencing with a zero tax rate, and then allowing this rate to increase incrementally, we can trace a range over which total tax revenues increase, reach a maximum, and then a range over which revenues decrease, until at some rate, revenues fall to zero. For simplicity in exposition throughout, we shall use linear relationships between price (including tax) and quantities demanded.

The second objective is to analyze the behavior of those who make decisions on rates of tax with the purpose of predicting the "equilibrium" position or location along the rate-revenue function. In particular, we seek to determine whether or not rational rate-setting behavior could generate a location characterized by an inverse relationship between tax rate and tax revenue.

A Model of Government

For our purposes, we do not need to choose among alternative public choice models of governmental decision making (median voter, bureaucratic dominance, agenda setter, benevolent despot, monopolist surplus maximizer, etc.). We require only that government's utility function contain two arguments, expenditures (revenues), and tax rates with expenditures (revenues) considered as "goods," and tax rates as "bads." Clearly, this minimal requirement fits the objective function of all governments. The ideal position would be one of being able to make expenditures, either to finance public goods and services or to secure private-personal gains (or some combination) without, at the same time, having to levy taxes on a recalcitrant citizenry. The worst possible position, by contrast, would be that in which governments found it necessary to levy onerous taxes without securing the advantages of the revenue collections from which to make public expenditures.

The second characteristic of our model for governmental behavior is somewhat more restrictive than the first, although it is surely realistic. We postulate that governmental decisions are made on the basis of a limited time perspective.

If politicians in office could, at the end of their tenure, effectively realize the capital value generated as a consequence of their decisions, the necessary uncertainty of political tenure need not affect the time horizon. Without marketability of the capital value (generated, for example, by a record of fiscal prudence) politicians have little motivation to consider consequences that extend beyond the expected period of tenure. Furthermore, and somewhat paradoxically, expected tenure actually may be increased by focusing on short-run considerations. The rational ignorance of voters makes it unlikely that they will understand the long-term consequences of current decisions or be able to assign political responsibility for these consequences once they arrive. The politicians who push for policies that generate near-term benefits probably increase their chances for reelection even if the long-run effects of these policies are decidedly negative. This short-sighted bias is intensified by the fact that the immediate advantages of policy often accrue to specific constituencies while the eventual costs are spread over an entire taxpaying public. When providing benefits for his constituency the politician is in much the same position as the exploiter of a common property resource. Not only will he and his constituents not pay all of the cost of exploiting the political process for their immediate gain, but if they refrain from this exploitation they cannot expect to gain a preferential claim on future benefits in exchange. The politician, much like the harpooner of blue whales, sees little advantage in taking a long-run perspective.

In the analysis to follow, we do not need to specify in any precise way what the time horizon of the political decision maker is. We require only that this horizon be shorter than that period of time that is necessary for taxpayers to make their full behavioral adjustments to changes in the rates of taxation.

The Rate-Revenue Analytics

We introduce a highly simplified geometrical construction, depicted in figure 1*A* and 1*B*. The abscissa is drawn at the level of the pretax price, which, for a money-income base is simply $1. In figure 1*A*, the heavily drawn curve D_L is defined as the truncated long-run demand curve for the base with "long-run"

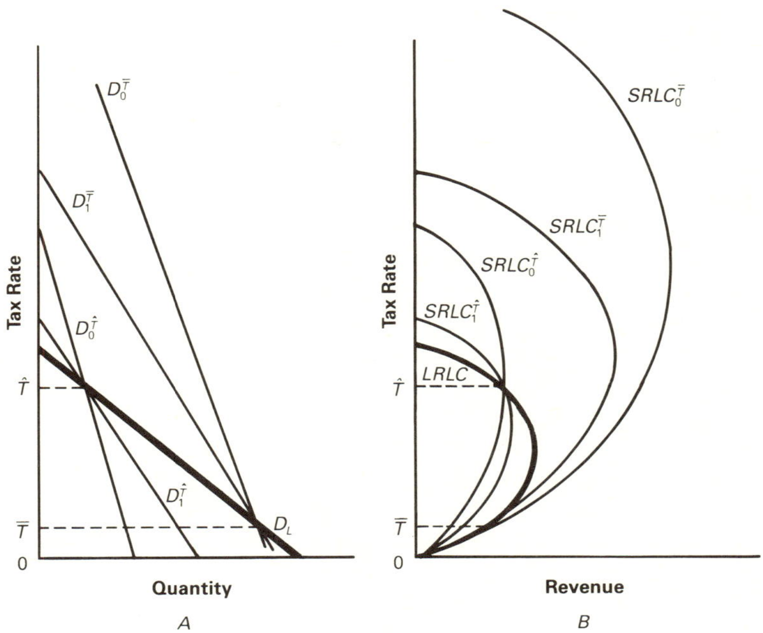

Fig. 1

being specifically defined to be a period sufficiently long to allow for full behavioral adjustment to each rate of tax on base, and for the attainment for the full institutional equilibrium subsequent to such behaviorial adjustment. In his work on the Swedish tax structure, Stuart (1979) has suggested that the calendar length of such a period, for Sweden at any rate, may be up to ten years. The short-run, long-run distinction clearly seems more important in the tax-adjustment context than it does when we are considering demands for ordinary commodities, in part at least because governments tend to levy taxes on those bases that are relatively immune to easy adjustment by potential taxpayers (as indeed they are advised to do by orthodox normative tax theorists).

The same relationship as that shown in the demand curve (heavily drawn) in figure 1*A* is traced out in figure 1*B* by the heavily drawn curve, *LRLC*, with total tax revenues being measured along the abscissa. The two end points of this curve correspond to the origin (at zero tax rate) and to the intercept of the demand curve in figure 1*A*, at which point the tax rate becomes sufficiently high so that, given time for complete adjustment, no base is demanded at all. If prices are converted to percentage rates, this intercept value may lie close to 100 percent, although it may readily fall below or even go above this level.

The heavily drawn demand curve in figure 1*A* and the heavily drawn rate-revenue curve (Laffer curve) in figure 1*B* depict taxpayer responses to alternative rates of tax after full adjustments have been made to each rate. In other words, these curves are necessarily long-run if taxpayer adjustments to rates are postulated to take time. Indeed, these curves define a unique relationship between rate and base, or rate and revenue, only if the full-adjustment stipulation is made. If we restrict taxpayer response to any period of time shorter than that required for full adjustment it becomes necessary to date the functional relationship between rate and base, or rate and revenue, and, in addition, to fix the initial rate to which full adjustments are assumed to have been made.

On figures 1*A* and *B*, assume that taxpayers have fully adjusted their behavior to the rate shown by $\bar{T}$. There will be a whole family of demand curves (figure 1*A*) and Laffer curves (figure 1*B*) that may be drawn through the initial position of taxpayer equilibrium, each one of which will incorporate a different period of adjustment that must be specifically defined. In figure 1*A*, the demand curve labeled, $D_0^{\bar{T}}$, depicts the current-period adjustment to alternative rates of tax, given that taxpayers have fully adjusted to $\bar{T}$ before any change. The demand curve, $D_1^{\bar{T}}$, depicts the adjustment after a single period of time. The Laffer curves, $SRLC_0^{\bar{T}}$ and $SRLC_1^{\bar{T}}$, are, of course, alternative depictions of the same relationships. Only two short-run curves are drawn although any number could be included.

The same exercise could be carried out for any initial rate to which taxpayers might be assumed to have been fully adjusted. One additional rate, $\hat{T}$, is included in figure 1. Note that at all rates of tax above that for which behavioral adjustments have been completed, more revenues will be generated in the short run than in the long run, whether revenues will increase in both cases, whether short-run revenues will increase and long-run revenues decrease, or whether both short-run and long-run revenues will decrease. Conversely, for all rates of tax below that for which behavioral adjustments have been completed, more revenues will be generated in the long run than in the short-run, whether short-run revenues will decrease and long-run revenues increase, or whether both short-run and long-run revenues increase, or whether both short-run and long-run revenues will increase.

Political Equilibrium

To derive the necessary conditions for political equilibrium, we must introduce the utility function for government itself, restricted by the stipulation that revenues are "goods" and taxes are "bads." This restriction allows us to depict government's preferences with ordinary indifference mapping on the same dimensions of figure 1. We do this in figure 2.

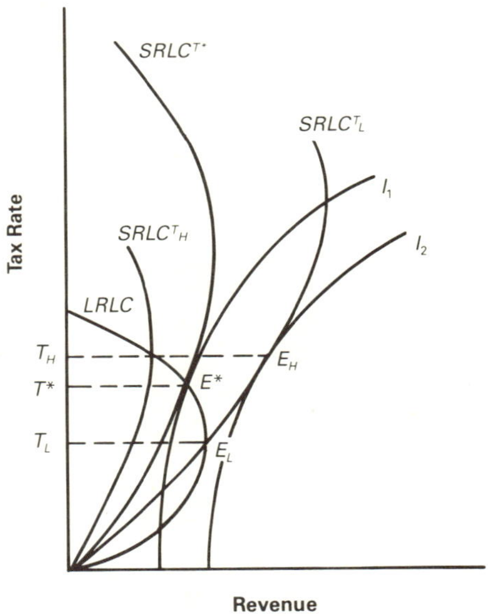

Fig. 2

The rate-revenue relationship defines the constraints within which governmental fiscal decisions are made. But it is necessary to specify carefully which particular rate-revenue relationship is relevant here. As noted earlier, the location of the rate-revenue function will depend on the initial tax-rate equilibrium to which taxpayers have adjusted and on the length of the time horizon incorporated in governmental decisions. The long-run or full-adjustment rate-revenue or Laffer curve will become the relevant constraint only if political decision makers adopt the long-term perspective. In all other cases, this long-run curve is irrelevant to decision making by government, although it continues to describe the locus of equilibrium positions for taxpayers, and, through this means, to constrain the ultimate location of the position that defines equilibrium both for government and for taxpayers.

The equilibrium conditions for the politicians will be defined by the equality of the trade-offs between tax rate and tax revenue in the government's utility function on the one hand and in the appropriate rate-revenue function on the other. If this equilibrium is also to represent the long-run equilibrium adjustment for the taxpayer, it must lie on the long-run Laffer curve. One such equilibrium position is that shown at E^* in figure 2. At E^*, with tax rate, T^*, political decision makers are in the required tangency position; they have no incentive to increase or to decrease tax rates. Taxpayers, on the other hand, have fully adjusted to the tax rate, T^*; they will not modify their behavior further as time passes.

Note that government could, if it desired, increase revenues in the short run; the relevant short-run rate-revenue curve is upsloping at E^*. (It is assumed that only one short-run curve is relevant between a change in the tax rate and full adjustment to that tax rate.) If government should be strictly revenue maximizing, E^* would not, of course, be a position of political equilibrium. In this case, political equilibrium would be attained only where the relevant rate-revenue curve becomes vertical at its intersection with the long-run curve.[4]

As the geometrical construction in figure 2 indicates, the position of equilibrium may be located either on the upsloping or the downsloping portion of the long-run rate-revenue curve. Only by chance would the position be at the maximum revenue position on the long-run relationship, and there is no analytical reason to predict precisely where the equilibrium position will be located. Note, however, that the equilibrium will always be below the maximum-revenue point on the short-term rate-revenue curve, so long as taxes are "bads" in government's utility function.

Consider the case where the tax rate to which long-term adjustment has been made is T_L, the rate which does generate maximum revenues per period after all taxpayer adjustment has been completed. Finding itself at E_L government will seek to increase the tax rate to T_H in order to attain position, E_H, on the short-run curve, $SRLC^{T}{}_{L}$, that passes through E_L and which defines the appropriate adjustments over the period of the government's planning horizon. The position, E_H, cannot be attained for longer than the short period so defined because it is not consistent with long-term taxpayer equilibrium. As time passes, and as adjustments are made, both in taxpayer behavior and in tax rates, government will (assuming convergence) shift to the position of sustainable equilibrium, E^*, with tax rate, T^*.

With different configurations of the indifference curves or the rate-revenue curves, equilibrium could, of course, be located somewhere along the upsloping portion of the long-run Laffer curve. We do not analyze this sort of equilibrium diagrammatically since the relevant necessary conditions are fully analogous to the position depicted in figure 2. We should note, however, that regardless of where sustainable equilibrium is located, the tax rate will be *above* that which would be chosen by a government whose time horizon is as long as the period required for taxpayers to make full adjustments to rate changes. It should also be evident that the longer the time horizon of government, even within the constraint that it remain shorter than the time for full adjustment, the closer will be the equilibrium tax rate to that which would characterize the rational behavior of the genuinely far-seeking government. We may summarize much of our analysis by stating that, so long as government is short-sighted, it will always seek to exploit to some degree the vulnerability of the taxpayer over the period between the change in tax rate and the attainment of full individual and institutional adjustment.

Convergence and Stability

The emphasis to this point has been to define the conditions for taxpayer and government equilibrium. We have simply presumed that the equilibrium will be attained, and we have neglected any analysis of the process through which the final position might be reached as well as the whole question as to whether convergence takes place at all. Without going into a detailed analysis of the dynamic features of the model and the stability conditions, some general observations can be made.

Assume that the government can adjust the tax rate once each period, and further that the government's concern is only with the current period while full private adjustment to a tax rate is not complete until the beginning of the period following its imposition. In this case it can be shown that the tax rate will oscillate around the political equilibrium rate, T^*, if the objective is simple revenue maximization (the indifference curves are vertical with respect to the horizontal axis).[5] When the tax rate enters the utility function as a bad, tax rates may oscillate around T^* early on, but will not necessarily continue to oscillate as T^* is approached. It is clear, for example, from the discussion of figure 2 that if the initial rate is below T^* at T_L, then the next period's rate will be above T^* at T_H. Once full adjustment to rate T_H has been made and the government is contemplating a new rate, $SRLC^{T_H}$ is the relevant short-run Laffer curve. It is reasonable to assume that the slope of $SRLC^{T_H}$ will be less positive (or more negative) at each tax rate than will the slope of any short-run Laffer curve to its right, and vice versa.[6] But one also expects that at each tax rate the indifference curves become steeper as we move left, reflecting a willingness to increase the tax rate more in return for a given increase in revenue when revenue is low than when it is high. Therefore the point of tangency between $SRLC^{T_H}$ and an indifference curve can occur either above or below T^*.[7] The possibilities for developing a general characterization of the tax rate time path appear limited and will not be attempted here.

Expectations

A more critical restriction on the analysis involves our neglect of expectations. We have implicitly assumed that taxpayers respond to rate changes in a passive sense; they expect any rate to be permanent. They do not, themselves, model the behavior of government in imposing these rates. The introduction of taxpayer expectations into the analysis has several interesting results that are apparently relevant to current tax policy debates.

If taxpayers model the tax-setting behavior of government correctly and if both taxpayers and government have available the same data on rate-revenue relationships, taxpayers will be able to predict the position of equilibrium and make their own behavioral adjustments accordingly. The possibly long sequence of adjustments through which response to rate changes take place will be foreshortened dramatically. Suppose, however, that in a rational expectations equilibrium, described by some position like E^* in figure 2, government should want to take on a longer time perspective than that which has characterized its previous behavior and which had been incorporated in the model of government held by taxpayers. Suppose government recognizes the additional revenue potential, in a long-run sense, available to it from tax-rate reduction, and that it seeks to exploit this. To government, this clearly should seem to be a net gain, since it should be able to secure additional revenues which will allow it to make additional outlays, while at the same time, rates of tax on the citizenry are reduced. Taxpayers should, seemingly, welcome this move toward rate reduction, since excess burdens would be lowered without any sacrifice in benefits available from public outlays.

The government may, however, find it difficult to move from E^* along the long-run Laffer curve in the manner that seems indicated. So long as taxpayers continue to model government as a short-run maximizer, they will not respond fully to a tax rate below T^*. Rather, they will incorporate only short-run considerations into their calculus and respond along curve $SRLC^T$ in figure 2. Taxpayers will reason that, if they respond fully to the rate cut below T^*, they will leave themselves again vulnerable to short-term exploitations as government returns to T^* or above. Therefore, a rate reduction will put the government on a lower indifference curve for a period that extends beyond the short run, and even a relatively far-sighted government will be unable to move down the long-run Laffer curve, LRLC in figure 2, from position E^*.

In order to generate shifts along the long-run Laffer curve, even in the long run, the government must convince taxpayers that tax rate reductions are permanent; in other words, they must, simultaneously with cuts in tax rates, get taxpayers to change their model of governmental behavior. If, however, taxpayers construct their model of governmental behavior on the basis of a developing historical record, there may be no readily available means of escape from the high tax dilemma. The straightforward shift in time perspective of government is not sufficient; government must, somehow, bind or commit itself in such fashion that taxpayers become convinced that a "new deal" has, indeed, arrived. It is at this point that the argument for *constitutional* commitment on rates of tax, or on other forms of fiscal limits, comes into force. The promised results of "Reagonomics" might, indeed, become possible with constitutional rate reductions; they seem unlikely to emerge in the expectational setting of 1982 when taxpayers remain highly skeptical of the willingness of government, in future years, to keep real tax rates at promised levels.

Conclusions

Our purpose has been almost exclusively analytical rather than empirical. We have shown how equilibrium positions along the "wrong side" of the rate-revenue relationship may be attained, without any violation of rationality precepts on the part of governmental decision makers, and, further, we have indicated why escape from the genuine dilemma that such positions represent might prove difficult. The analysis is, however, helpful in assessing the attempts to locate empirically the position of the United States fiscal structure in the early 1980s. It seems clear that, in the debates of 1981, those supply-side economists who argued in terms of Laffer curve effects were implicitly adopting a long-time perspective, whereas those economists who argued that location along the downsloping portion of the Laffer curve was highly unlikely were, again implicitly, thinking in terms of some short-time Laffer relationship.

The empirical studies that have been attempted have been largely based on studies of the elasticity of input response to changes in net returns. Much of this work seems inconclusive in judging the long-run impact of a tax cut on revenues. For example, in an effort to address this impact, Fullerton (1980) makes use of thirteen empirical investigations of labor supply elasticities. Of the thirteen studies all were cross sectional except two, leaving inconclusive any means of assessment concerning the completeness of the adjustments. All thirteen studies generated estimates based on uncompensated responses to changes in the return to labor. This is reasonable when, as in the cases in most of the studies, the response of particular subsets of the labor force is being investigated. However, when the response of the aggregate labor force is to be estimated, as it necessarily must be when considering the results of a general tax change, the more reasonable assumption is that at least some compensation takes place. What workers gain (lose) from a tax reduction (increase) will be offset to some degree by a reduction (increase) in benefits from governmental service.[8] To ignore this offset is to understate labor supply elasticity when leisure is a normal good.

It is also true that input supply elasticities will generally be smaller than the output elasticities that are of ultimate concern. The positive effect of an increase in the return to labor may not come primarily from the motivation it provides to work more hours, but from the motivation to work more productively. Labor supply elasticities fail to pick up the output effects that flow from human capital increases induced by an additional return to labor. This output effect is further enhanced through the symbiotic interaction that exists between a growing stock of human and physical capital.

The definitive empirical work remains to be done. Not only does such work call for the estimation of long-run input elasticities (where the long run may extend to a decade or more), but also for the inclusion of these elasticities into a model that recognizes the dynamic interactions and feedbacks that exist between inputs in the generation of measured output. The simple analytics we have presented here offer the challenges to those who would either refute or corroborate the claims of the Lafferites.

The thrust of the analysis does not depend at all on the empirical findings concerning the location of the United States tax structure on the long-run Laffer curve. As we have noted, so long as government makes its fiscal decisions on the basis of a time horizon shorter than that period required for full taxpayer adjustment to tax rate changes, observed tax rates will be higher than those that a far-seeking or "enlightened" government would impose. The "high tax trap" is only one of several critically important policy dilemmas that arise when there is an obvious discrepancy between the government's rate of discount and that rate that would be "efficient" in some long-run sense. Fortunately, economists are rapidly coming to be aware of the central features of these dilemmas and are now shifting their attention to the analysis of *rules* that will restrict the operations of ordinary politics.[9]

NOTES

We are indebted to our colleagues, Geoffrey Brennan, Nicolaus Tideman, Robert Tollison, and Gordon Tullock, for helpful suggestions on an earlier draft.

1. Specifically related to the Laffer-curve relationship, see Fullerton (1980). By contrast, in their recent book, Buchanan and Brennan (1980) utilize a demand-theory construction throughout their analysis.
2. For a discussion of the reciprocal nature of the demand and supply relationship, see Buchanan (1971).
3. In our construction, we apply the rate of tax directly to the base, with base defined in units of ultimate consumable "goods," whether a single commodity like "beer" or the bundle of commodities and services that the taxpayer might purchase with posttax income units. This procedure allows us to convert the percentage rate of tax readily into an increment to pretax price, and to utilize orthodox demand analysis straightforwardly. Note, however, that this construction differs from the standard definition of a tax "rate" under income taxation, which involves applying a percentage rate to the generation of base, *inclusive* of tax. In terms of a simple numerical example, if the pretax price of a unit of consumable goods is $1, a 10 percent tax, in our construction, becomes equivalent to a 10 cent addition to pretax price. In order to generate $1's worth of final consumable goods, the taxpayer would have to generate $1.10's worth of income including tax, to which a "rate"

of 9.09 percent would be applied to secure the 10 cents. Hence, a rate of 10 percent, in our construction, is equivalent to the lower rate of 9.09 percent on the inclusive base.

The distinction here is important with respect to the dimension in which responses to changes in rate are measured. Invariance in the generation of base, net of tax, in our construction, necessarily implies a positive relationship between rate and generation of base, defined gross of tax. More generally, and as our analysis in the text indicates, any range of adjustment over which the demand for base, net of tax, is inelastic definitionally implies a positive relationship between rate and base, gross of tax.

4. In a forthcoming elliptical note, we develop the analysis of equilibrium in this limited revenue-maximizing case. See Buchanan and Lee, "Politics, Time, and the Laffer Curve," *Journal of Political Economy* (August, 1982): 816–19.
5. This has been established and the conditions for convergence worked out in Buchanan and Lee (1981).
6. This will be true of all short-run Laffer curves when the short-run demand curves are vertically parallel to each other.
7. It is possible that a tangency occurs at the point where $SRLC^{T_H}$ intersects *LRLC* and thus there will exist multiple political equilibria. This multiple equilibria possibility does not exist in a strict revenue-maximizing model.
8. For a theoretical investigation of this consideration see Lindbeck (1980).
9. The "high tax trap" analyzed in this article is closely analogous to the "inflationary trap" generated by discretionary monetary policy in a setting where there is a recognized short-run trade-off between unemployment and inflation. Governments that respond rationally in the face of this short-run trade-off are led to policies that generate inflation which is undesired within the long-term perspective. And the difficulties involved in any escape from this inflationary trap are in many respects identical to those analyzed here. On the inflationary trap, see Kydland and Prescott (1977) and Barro and Gordon (1981).

REFERENCES

Barro, R. J., and Gordon, D. B. "A Positive Theory of Monetary Policy in a Natural-Rate Model." Mimeographed Paper, University of Rochester and National Bureau of Economic Research, 1981.

Buchanan, J. M., "The Backbending Supply Curve of Labor: An Example of Doctrinal Retrogression?" *History of Political Economy* 3 (1971): 383–90.

———, and Brennan, G. *The Power to Tax.* (Cambridge: Cambridge University Press, 1980).

———, and Lee, D. R. "The Simple Analytics of the Laffer Curve." *Working Paper,* Center for Study of Public Choice, VPI, Blacksburg, Va., September, 1981.

———. "Politics, Time, and the Laffer Curve." *Journal of Political Economy* 90 (August 1982): 816–19.

Fullerton, D. "On the Possibility of an Inverse Relationship Between Tax Rates and Government Revenues." Working Paper No. 467, National Bureau of Economic Research, April 1980.

Kydland, F. E., and Prescott, E. C. "Rules Rather Than Discretion: The Inconsistency of Optimal Plans." *Journal of Political Economy* 85 (1977): 493–91.

Lindbeck, A. "Tax Effects Versus Budgets Effects on Labor Supply." *Seminar Working Paper* No. 148, Institute For International Economic Studies, Stockholm, Sweden, July 1980.

Stuart, C. "Swedish Tax Rates, Labor Supply, and Tax Revenues." Natisnalokomiska Institutionen Lunds Universitet, Meddelande, 1979: 64.

A Rent-Seeking Theory of French Mercantilism

Robert B. Ekelund, Jr., and Robert D. Tollison

There are two traditions in studies of mercantilism. One tradition involves debunking mercantilist ideas and is best illustrated in the works of Adam Smith (1776) and Jacob Viner (1937). From this tradition we have received the standard interpretation that mercantilism was a confused collection of ideas about the relationship between power and wealth. We have no arguments with this standard interpretation of mercantilist doctrines. A second tradition consists of the study of historical practices in the mercantile economies, the best examples of which are various works by members of the German Historical School, especially Schmoller (1897). This tradition emphasizes the general thesis that mercantile policies were quite rational responses to the problems of nation-state building. While there are a few recent exceptions (e.g., Wilson 1967), most modern scholars have concentrated on the doctrinal fallacies of mercantilist writers.[1]

We view the primary emphasis on doctrinal fallacy as an unfortunate development because the positive analysis of mercantilist political economy hinted at by the German Historical School has never been undertaken. The central treatment in the literature on this subject remains the classic study by Heckscher (1934), the one writer on mercantilism who spans *both* of the above traditions. Heckscher's treatment, however, while historically copious, is in clear need of a modern reassessment. In the years since this study appeared, economic theory has been expanded to encompass such matters as political choice (Buchanan and Tullock 1962) and economic regulation (Stigler 1971), and it is important to reexamine the historians' analysis in light of these modern developments to see if their explanations of mercantilist political economy can be improved upon or altered in any important respects. Moreover, the historical experiences in these economies represent a valuable laboratory for the application of modern economic concepts.

Our purpose here is not to present a wholesale reinterpretation of all aspects of mercantilist political economy. Further, the idea that French mercantilism had a strong *fiscal* component is hardly new or original. The theme of mercantilism as "fiscalism" has, for example, been admirably treated by Wilson (1967, 495–573).[2] We have the more limited goal of developing a positive economic theory of the internal regulation of industry in mercantile France which supplements and expands the "state-building" interpretations found in Heckscher and in more recent literature. Our research is in the "polinomic" tradition recently called for by Davis (1980) and earlier by Lane (1958), in that it attempts to bridge the gap between economic policy and the economic motives of public and private actors in the political process of policy formation.[3]

We focus in this essay on French mercantilism for several important reasons. One is that we have analyzed the rise and fall of internal regulation in England elsewhere (Ekelund and Tollison 1980*a*, 1981).[4] Secondly, since we will draw heavily on Heckscher as a historical source and a repository of alternative hypotheses, it is useful to follow his lead in treating internal regulation in England and France separately (Heckscher 1934, 1: 135–325). We will, however, contrast the English and French experiences with internal regulation in a concluding section.

The most important reason for a separate treatment of the French mercantile experience is that it permits us to confront the explanations of economic historians for the two most important features of the French economy of the time: (1) the repressive and controlled internal economic structure, and (2) the very clear emphasis (bias?) upon luxury at the expense of basic productions, a characteristic of the French economy which is often said to have impeded the Industrial Revolution in France. To be sure there is some divergence of explanations among historians. The most celebrated historical interpretation of French mercantilism, however, that of Charles Woolsey Cole (1939, 1943), falls far short of providing a satisfying explanation of these two features of the French mercantile economy. Cole features Jean Baptiste Colbert, Louis XIV's indomitable finance minister, as the "Great Man" and prime mover of the French State for the seventeenth and eighteenth centuries. Further, Cole clearly and repeatedly expresses the view that Colbert's economic "reforms" were in the public interest, i.e., made in the interests of the French people. State building was the maximand for both the public interest and the glory of the monarch according to Cole.

While we do not dispute the details of these historical accounts of the French experience, we reject the "hero" and other major axioms of the historians and argue that positive economic theory offers a more plausible account of these developments. We shall argue that the French political and economic environment was conducive to the self-interested demand and supply of a massive system of economic regulation and that the success of this extensive intervention in the French economy impacted greatly upon French economic development up to the time of the Revolution. We shall argue further that the theory of economic regulation goes far in providing a plausible explanation for aspects of French mercantilism that have puzzled the historians, namely, the French mercantilists' response to innovations and their selective cartelization of industries. Thus, we do not offer our interpretation as a substitute for those of the historians, or even as an original interpretation of mercantilism as "fiscalism." Rather, we simply attempt to provide the basic organizing principles for a more satisfying analysis of several major features of the period.[5]

The discussion proceeds as follows. The rise of French mercantilism is explained in section 1 in terms of the relative efficiency of monopoly grants over taxation as a source of revenue for the French state. The highly effective system of enforcing the monopoly and cartel arrangements is discussed in section 2. The usefulness of analyzing French mercantilism as an example of efficient rent seeking is illustrated in section 3, with a discussion of the efforts of the French administrators to restrict the introduction of printed calicos in the textile industry. In section 4, an explanation of why the French mercantilists stressed luxury-oriented cartels is given. The costs of extending economic regulation to the rural sector are discussed briefly in section 5. Finally, some comparative observations are offered on English versus French mercantilist experiences with internal regulation in section 6.

1. A Theory of Monarchical Rent Seeking

The French monarchy sought revenue to finance its expenditures, and the term that we apply to this behavior is *rent seeking*. There were basically two sources of revenue available to the French administrators—taxation and grants of monopoly. Taxation was extensive in France at this time, as we shall see, and this aspect of revenue seeking has been covered extensively by the historians. The extensive use of monopoly grants to raise revenue came about during the time of Colbert who, under pressure to raise additional revenues for the king, found monopoly grants to be a more efficient form of rent seeking than taxation *at the margin*. Monopoly grants at the height of Colbert's administration became a *major* source of the French state's revenues.[6] The turn by Colbert to monopoly grants forms the basis of our interpretation of French internal economic regulation. For the present, however, let us review the difficulties that Colbert faced with taxation and then go on to analyze the relative efficiency of monopoly grants in the revenue-seeking context of Colbert's administration.

In the medieval and early mercantile period, the difficulty of taxing was related to such factors as the absence of data on transactions and the general ease of tax evasion. Moreover, taxation places the burden on state authorities to ascertain taxable values and to collect tax revenues. Though difficulties of tax collection and assessment and the ease of tax evasion explain the emergence of rent-seeking behavior in the early French economy, the even greater reliance on monopoly creation as a means to raise revenue in the age of Colbert (the hightime of French mercantilism) admits of further explanation. In addition to the still general technical difficulties of collection and assessment, Colbert, in 1661, faced the deeply entrenched interests of a fiscal bureaucracy and a fiendishly complex tax structure.[7] Colbert's hold on the king (Louis XIV) was a function of his ability to produce revenues, so that his first order of business (when he replaced Cardinal Mazarin as Louis's finance minister) was to attempt to circumvent an encrusted tax system, born of feudal and medieval traditions. At this, and in spite of his very considerable powers and machinations, he was an abject failure, as Cole clearly documents.

After several dictatorial revenue-getting measures, alienating a massive segment of the French financial community, Colbert attempted his great reform of the tax system.[8] First, Colbert attempted "reform" of the *taille reele,* a land tax that was the single largest revenue source of the state. But there were many, many exemptions based upon privilege, bribery, and tradition, so that Colbert's use of spies, seizures, and investigations of those claiming exemptions were to no avail. Next, owing to this failure, Colbert attempted to shift the incidence of taxation, reducing the *taille* from which so many claimed exemption, and drastically raising the *aides.* (The aides were an internal indirect tax on commodities at the wholesale and retail levels and tolls on river and road transportation, the collection of which was farmed.) But so corrupt and intimidating were the farmers of the *taille* that Colbert was again thwarted and nullified (Cole 1939, 1: 305–6).

Colbert's dilemma was the personal urgency of retaining the king's support in the face of an inability to increase revenues sufficiently through the tax system. Vested interests, coupled with the exigencies of an opulent court and the 1672 war with the Dutch, drove Colbert to "new" and "extraordinary" methods of acquiring funds (Cole 1939, 1: 307–12).

Colbert directed his rent-seeking efforts to the granting and enforcement of monopoly rights, and the French mercantile economy took on the form of a massive web of economic regulations administered by the central state. The creation of monopoly was a more efficient route to revenue because, unlike taxation where the state has to bear the costs of discovering taxable values, aspiring monopolists will reveal the value of monopolies to the authorities in their efforts to secure such grants from the state. State officials would not have to seek out estimates of the value of their enforcement services in the case of monopoly grants. Rather, monopoly seekers would come to them, and so long as the bidding for monopoly privileges was competitive, they would reveal to state authorities the underlying value of the monopoly rights. For this basic reason, then, the French mercantile state found it efficient to raise revenue by creating a highly monopolized economy.

Our concern in the remainder of this essay will be with showing how this rent-seeking-through-monopolization interpretation of French mercantilism can be applied to offer an appealing analysis of the main features of French economic behavior and development over this period. This is not to argue that historians have ignored the revenue-seeking aspect of French mercantilism. There is ample evidence in Heckscher (1934, 1: 179, 183) and other sources (Wilson 1967) about this aspect of French mercantilism. Historians, however, have tended to treat rent seeking as a manifestation of some greater mercantile objective, such as the balance of trade, rather than portraying it as a central element in an interpretation of the period. As we shall see, French administrators were very ingenious and intelligent rent seekers, and interpreting their behavior as a manifestation of efficient rent seeking offers a plausible route to a fuller understanding of the important episodes of economic regulation over the period.

Monarchical rent seeking in France, therefore, is reasonable explanation for the stress on the power of the state in French mercantilism. There were rent-seeking opportunities for the central state, and economic regulation in the form of cartel expansion and enforcement was the result. The form of this rent-seeking competition consisted of a monopolist (the state) providing cartel enforcement services, with the numerous "industries" throughout France bidding for these services. By presenting itself as the only agent in the process with an effective monopoly (i.e., on force), one can surmise that the French state was able to capture the monopoly rents inherent in the economic regulation of the economy. As we shall see in the next section, these rents were not entirely "pure profits," as considerable sums had to be spent on the administration and enforcement of the economic regulations.

2. Enforcement of Monarchical Rent Seeking

The administrative machinery set up by the French to provide cartel enforcement services is often admired as one of the greatest administrative accomplishments in the historical development of nation-states. We view this administrative machinery as a natural expression of efficient rent seeking—the enforcement system was an expression of a desire to maximize revenues from rent seeking.

The primary means through which the French monarchy provided cartel enforcement services was through paid civil servants (the *intendants*).[9] The authority of the *intendants* under Colbert was extensive. These officers were in charge of all other authorities in their administrative district and formed the link with the central authority in the administration of cartel enforcement activities. They judged many cases evoked by the Crown, organized and superintended tax collections, inspected and regulated industry, directed public education, and controlled the police and administration of troops and municipalities (Boulanger 1967, 344).

The fact that they were paid is important. As Becker and Stigler (1974) have demonstrated, higher pay is a means to control malfeasance in labor contracts where an element of "trust" is involved. This follows, for example, in the sense that there is a greater opportunity cost (actually, the loss of rents) to the official of losing his position by accepting bribes. Paid enforcement agents, then, may be interpreted as a primary means to control corruption and to insure uniform cartel enforcement across the country. Without a guarantee of honest and even enforcement the services of the state in this respect would have been less valuable, and we can view the *intendants* as an efficient means to enforce the economic regulations of French mercantilism.

The nature of the regulations to be enforced by the *intendants* was also an expression of efficient rent-seeking policies. The monarchy not only set up uniform price and wage controls and restricted entry into the local cartels with an apprenticeship system, but it also sought to provide protection against competition from within the cartels. This latter condition is especially important in the enforcement of eonomic regulation because licensed sellers within the cartel will otherwise compete away excess profits through output expansion.

The general characteristics of this aspect of cartel enforcement were impressive. The regulations were incredibly detailed, on the order of a substantial planned economy, and the details were tailored to restrict the various means by which firms could expand output from within the industry. Heckscher (1934, 1: 160–61) provides the following small example of the regulations.

> Regulation followed the course of production. In the first place, it contained specifications regarding the handling of raw material, especially wool and the methods of dealing with it and went on to deal with all the subsequent states of production, the most important of which were weaving and, especially dyeing. Amongst numberless others, we will single out as an example of the weaving regulations a special *reglement* of 1718 for Burgundy and four neighbouring districts. As the *reglement* itself puts it, these districts produced woolen goods for the use of the soldiers and the general public, so that it was by no means a luxury industry. The dimensions of the cloths were specified in 18 articles for each place separately. We will confine ourselves to quoting the first five rules.
>
> The fabrics of Dijon and Selongey were to be put in reeds $1\frac{3}{4}$ ells wide, a warp was to contain 44 × 32 or 1408 threads including the selvedges, and when it came to the fulling-mill, the cloth was to be exactly one ell wide. Semur in Auxois, and Axerre, Montbard, Avalon and Beaune were to have a warp of 43 × 32 or 1376 threads, the same width in the reed, and the same width of cloth when it left the fulling-hammer. Saulieu was to have the same width with 42 × 32 or 1340 (really 1344) threads, but it seems that the white and the more finely spun cloths were to have 74 × 32 or 2368 threads. Chatillon on the Seine and five other places were to have 1216 threads in a width of $1\frac{5}{8}$ ells with the same variation for white cloths. The *sardis* fabric, which was produced in Bourg en Bresse and various other towns was to have only 576 threads with reeds of one ell and a width of half an ell after fulling, etc., etc.

The control of this system of economic regulation rested with paid agents of the monarchy, and their means of control were extensive. There was widespread inspection of production, well-regulated measurement of outputs, various marking procedures whereby outputs bore the name of the producer, town marks, and so forth. Penalties for violating the regulations consisted in the confiscation and destruction of "inferior" output, heavy fines, public mockery of the offender, and ultimate loss of one's license to practice for continued offenses. What we see in the nature of the regulations is an extensive system of output restriction. Indeed, Colbert instituted a system of spies in each town who were to report cartel chiselers to the local *intendant*. Another purpose of the spies may have been to keep an eye on the *intendants*.

The French monarchy devised efficient means to enforce economic regulation on a large scale. Paying the local enforcement agents controlled malfeasance in the application of the regulations, which would have reduced the returns from monarchical rent seeking, and, moreover, the nature of the regulations governing cartel behavior appear to have been an efficient system of output control on a large scale.

3. Rent Seeking as a Useful Interpretation of French Mercantilism

Evidence for the usefulness of the rent-seeking theory as the principle explanation of internal economic policy is plentiful, although Heckscher and especially Cole ascribe such activity to other motives. Cole, particularly, views mercantile developments, and especially those instituted by Colbert, as initiated to provide a strong French state and economy that would be of public benefit for the people and of glory to the sovereign monarch (e.g., Cole 1939, 1: 301, 311–20, 329–30; 2: 141). Nevertheless, both Heckscher and Cole in their historical descriptions provide a great deal of evidence for the rent-seeking interpretation.

The General Dimensions of Rent Seeking under Colbert

As evidence of Colbert's "public service," we might look briefly at some of the cartels formed during his administration. After several unsuccessful attempts Colbert was able, in 1681, to form a tobacco monopoly that applied to the entire kingdom. The monopoly regulated all aspects of tobacco production, importation, manufacture, and sale. In spite of the heated opposition of consumers and retailers, revenues to the state multiplied rapidly—500,000 *livres* in 1681, 600,000 in 1683, to an annual 30,000,000 *livres* in 1789. Colbert oversaw the conduct of the postal monopoly which, after 1673, brought in 1,000,000 *livres* per year. United to the postal system in 1673, Colbert encouraged transport monopolies (covering coaches and certain water transportation), bringing more than 5,500,000 *livres* per year into the fisc by 1683. In 1674, Colbert forced all trades to form themselves into gilds, which then traded sums of money for statutes and regulations (Cole 1939, 1: 307–9).

Cole (1939, 1: 309) reports that some of Colbert's intrusions met with "unhappy results." In 1674, he levied a tax in the form of a fee for the "inspection and making" of tin and pewterware. A great opposition developed, however, because such utensils were used almost exclusively by common people.

A still more familiar rent-seeking expedient was employed by Colbert when he farmed coinage rights to a syndicate of capitalists for 630,000 *livres* in 1674. Colbert's nephew, Desmarets, and his agent, Bellinzani (in charge of managing the cartel), were bribed into silence by gifts, while the monopolists struck off 26,000,000 four-*sous* pieces, far in excess of that permitted by contract, and reduced the fineness of coins by a twelfth. Colbert ignored the enormous profits, however, since, as Cole reports (1939, 1: 310), "the syndicate assisted him in certain financial operations."

Examples of such cartelizing and monopoly-creating activity by Colbert and other French administrators could be multiplied exponentially over the mercantile period. Cole and other historians have maintained that through all of Colbert's measures ran a "keynote of economy," that Colbert "knew how hard it was to raise adequate funds, how necessary was money for the glory of the king and the strength of the state" (1939, 1: 311). The modern economist has another explanation. Aside from Colbert's own incentives, which were certainly not selfless, a better and more plausible explanation for the economic structure of mercantile France is that its institutions permitted rent-seeking behavior of a predictable type.

The Matter of Calicos

The alternative rent-seeking explanation, however, rests upon firm support, for it enables the interpretation of historical episodes that otherwise appear to be highly irrational. The outstanding example in this regard concerns the attempt by the state to prevent the production, import, or consumption of printed calicos and other cotton goods in France.

The implications drawn by the two leading mercantile historians of this episode are very noteworthy. Heckscher (1934, 1: 170–75), terming the prohibitions an "attack on innovations," outlined the lengths to which cartel managers went to achieve these goals.

> It is estimated that the economic measures taken in this connection cost the lives of some 16,000 people, partly through executions and partly through armed affrays, without reckoning the unknown but certainly much larger number of people who were sent to the galleys, or punished in other ways. On one occasion in Valence, 77 were sentended to be hanged, 58 were to be broken upon the wheel, 631 were sent to the galleys, one was set free and none were pardoned. But even this vigorous action did not help to attain the desired end. (P. 173)

Heckscher sees this episode as an irrational attempt by the administrators to stifle innovation.

Cole, likewise, regards calico legislation as an "aberration of French policy" and as merely "one of a number of instances in which the French government tried to restrict or arrest the forces of technological, industrial or commercial change" (1943, 177). Both Cole and Heckscher miss the point of this episode by failing to consider the implications of calicos for the costs of enforcing economic regulations in the textile industry.

The French textile industry (silk, linen, and wool productions) was the object of intense cartelization long before the time of Colbert, although Colbert cartelized these areas with renewed vigor (Cole 1943, 132–237). Private traders and the East India Company, which was created by Colbert in 1663–64 (See 1927, 157–74), were responsible for the import of printed calicos into France. No attempt was made by Colbert (who died in 1683) or by his successor Seignelay (not Colbert's son but 39 percent owner and president of the East India Company) to bring calicos under the umbrella of regulation. Before 1681, moreover, the Huguenots, already relegated to the role of second-class citizens, manufactured, within guilds, imitation calicos that were consumed largely by the poor.

In 1681, a "boom" occurred in calico demand causing guild leaders of the wool, cloth, silk, and linen industries to complain to local *intendants* of unfair competition and unemployment within their ranks. The response was a ban in 1686 on the domestic production and import of calicos. After the absolute ban in 1686, a number of "deals" took place whereby the king earned rents and the East India Company was permitted exclusive but very limited importation rights. Regulation of varying degrees of exclusiveness and severity took place between 1686 and 1700, with an absolute ban between 1700 and 1753, although a good deal of smuggling undoubtedly took place over the entire period since the demand for calicos was strong and growing (Cole 1943, 164–77).

The question that economic historians have been at pains to answer concerning this episode relates to the extent of the enforcement and policing of the ban against printed calicos. Punishment was extreme, though perhaps less extreme than that described by Heckscher (Scoville 1960). Enforcement was extended to a prohibition after 1700 against the wearing of calicos in France. But was this policy actuated by "irrational" motives or as a "mindless attack on innovations," as Cole and Heckscher have argued? These arguments simply fall short by failing to consider the implications of the calicos for the managers of French economic regulation. Two basic points are relevant in this regard.

As noted above, the cartel managers had to contend with the reaction of the producers of calico substitutes (the wool, cloth, silk, and linen producers). Calico production would have encroached upon these markets, and it is no mystery why these producers sought to ban the production of calicos.

The reaction of the producers of substitutes, however, does not explain why calicos were *banned*. Given the inherent rents in regulating the production of calicos, it seems reasonable to expect that the French administrators would have found a way to capture these rents and at the same time nullify the producers of substitutes (side payments?). The answer to this part of the puzzle lies in the fact that management of economic regulation is less costly when the industry produces a homogeneous product. The price, entry, and output controls of French mercantilism could be more effectively implemented where cloth of uniform colors and sizes was produced. Indeed, uniformity was extreme in the incredibly detailed regulation of the French textile industry (Cole 1939, 2: 156–58; 1943, 48).

The printed calicos presented a threat of no small importance to the French textile cartel—product differentiation. These colored cloths raised costs to the regulatory managers because product differentiation opened the door to nonprice competition. Even where the cartel price is controlled and where there are extensive controls on entry from without and within the industry, the introduction of printed calicos would have meant that licensed calico firms could have competed for expanded market shares through quality (pattern and choice) competition. Such nonprice competition would have dissipated excess profits within the cartel, an outcome which was in the interest of neither the regulatory managers nor the regulated firms (Stigler 1968).

For these two basic reasons, then, the reaction of producers of substitutes and the difficulty of regulating nonprice competition, the response to calicos may be viewed as a highly rational expression of efficient rent seeking and not as a mindless attack on innovation. Numerous other examples could be drawn from Cole, Heckscher, and various other sources to illustrate the usefulness of the rent-seeking theory in interpreting French internal regulation. The example of printed calicos is sufficiently dramatic, however, to illustrate the power of the rent-seeking interpretation.

4. Luxury-Oriented Cartels and French Economic Development

One of the most perplexing problems associated with French mercantile history is related to the very apparent encouragement of luxury industries with protective cartels and the clear neglect of certain basic industries such as iron and wood products. (By "neglect" we simply mean a failure to cartelize, protect, and encourage.) This feature of French mercantile policy has figured prominently in the stock-in-trade explanation of the historians for the tardiness of industrialization in France.

An example is the French economic policy toward iron production. The managers of economic regulation offered no cartel services for this industry. Heckscher (1934, 1: 198–99) describes the situation.

> There is no lack of contemporary statements to the effect that the usual type of French economic policy tended to obstruct the development of iron production. For instance, the head of an iron works wrote, "Glass manufacturers, manufacturers of genuine procelain and faience, cloth manufacturers, embroidery concerns, silk and gold-lace production, all enjoy every possible privilege and exemption; iron manufacturers alone have no advantages, and yet they cater for real needs while the others serve only luxury and comfort."

The important question is *why* did the French administrators seek rents primarily by cartelizing luxury industries? The traditional answers are distinctly unsatisfying, and we believe that positive economic analysis offers an alternative, noncompeting, and better explanation.

Traditional Explanations

Let us first consider two traditional explanations. First, there is the luxury-consumption argument. In this case the French monarch and aristocracy are seen as the major demanders of luxury goods. They therefore had a direct interest in regulating the quality of their purchases. As examples, one could look at the tobacco monopoly and tapestry manufacture, the latter a good example of a totally state-directed cartel (Cole 1939, 2: 287). Unfortunately, in these two cases and many others this argument ignores the fact that basic materials were also demanded by aristocrats (certainly indirectly as luxury items) and that, *ceteris paribus,* cartel managers could have earned rents by cartelizing *any* industry, basic or otherwise.

A second line of reasoning, congruent with the luxury-consumption argument, is that import substitution should be prevented for luxury productions. Indeed, most of the goods imported to France were luxury goods. In this argument luxury cartels were formed to "expropriate" rents from foreigners. The lace industry provides a clear example of protectionist cant ("protect domestic employment") to support baser motives.[10] Certainly, this could have been one of the reasons—especially when combined with the luxury-demand argument—for the establishment of luxury-directed cartels. It would give substance, moreover, to the so-called mercantile policy of importing raw materials and exporting finished goods; the "Balance of Labor" axiom of mercantilism. However, it is not clear on the basis of the import-substitution argument why the directors of French mercantilism would have not wanted to be independent in all productions or why rents could not have been earned by cartelizing raw materials production or other inputs such as steel.

Rent-Seeking Explanations

We feel that the rent-seeking model provides the basis of a good explanation of this important aspect of French mercantilism, and three points are fundamental in this respect.

First, certain basic production was not cartelized because the government itself was a major demander of industry output. For example, we find some interesting instruction regarding the supply of wood to the navy in Colbert's *Lettres* to an official.

> The purchase of forests to be managed at the expense and under the care of his Majesty could never be advantageous, and there are grounds for astonishment that you should make such a proposition, which is subject to so many inconveniences which are so easy to see that it should not even be thought of.
>
> If there are forests for sales in Provence and Dauphine you must stimulate the merchants to purchase them, and make bargains with them to supply all sorts of wood to the navy at the best price possible. (Cole 1939, 1: 350)

The government did not offer cartel services to certain basic industries—especially those involved in the production of goods demanded by government—but rather acted as a monopsonist in these cases, buying lumber and other basic inputs at the best terms available. Iron and other basic inputs were consequently left unregulated. Moreover, to the extent that this monopsonistic behavior extracted rents from producers of basic commodities which would otherwise have been used for expansion or innovation, a linkage can be established between the rent-seeking theory and the retardation of French industrial growth.

A second reason for luxury-oriented cartels is that raw materials and basic industrial suppliers, located mainly in the countryside, were competitive suppliers of inputs to the cartelized luxury industries located in cities and towns. The Crown was receiving regulatory rents from the latter industries, and in principle the Crown's receipts would have been the *same*, regardless of whether the cartel tax was levied on the raw-material or finished-goods stage of production. In other words, to cartelize basic input suppliers and then force cartelized luxury goods producers to pay cartel prices for inputs would have been redundant. Regulatory profits would have been the same had monopoly existed at any point in the production chain (Stigler 1951).

Figure 1 illustrates the demand and cost functions for some luxury good, let us say fine furniture. Assume that both wood and furniture producers are constant-cost industries and that MC_F represents all the costs of producing furniture, save lumber costs. Clearly, if both industries were competitively organized, the price and quantity of furniture would be *OC* and Q_C, respectively. If lumber producers are cartelized, they can restrict output and charge a price *OG*, equal to the cost of production of furniture (MC_F), plus the monopoly price of lumber (*BG*). In this way cartel managers can extract *CGHI* in rents from lumber producers. However, if furniture manufacturers are orga-

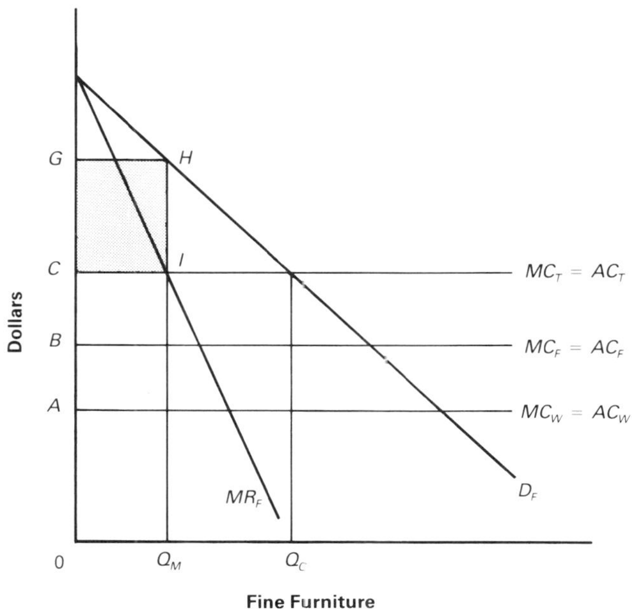

Fig. 1

nized by government into a cartel and lumber producers are left unregulated, the *same* rents, *CGHI*, could be extracted from the regulatory system. That is, furniture producers would restrict output and charge a price *OG*, equal to the cost of production of wood (MC_W), plus the monopoly price of furniture (*AG*). To the French cartel manager, then, it would have made no difference in terms of regulatory profits where the cartel was located, assuming only that organization, policing, and enforcement costs were identical. This brings us to a third point.

In general, a profitable cartel requires successful enforcement and policing so that competition does not erode profits. But in mercantile France, nonluxury industries tended to be located away from towns, presenting the problem of rural regulatory enforcement. Rural economic regulation was virtually impossible because the opportunities to cheat on cartel arrangements in a vast rural sector were numerous. By contrast, regulation of a luxury industry agglomerated in cities was far less costly to the regulatory authorities. Organizational and enforcement costs impacted on the industries that would be cartelized in the sense that basic industry and raw materials production were simply too costly to organize in this fashion.

Thus, monopsony, efficient rent seeking, and enforcement costs provide a plausible explanation for the so-called bias toward luxury cartels. Such a regulatory scheme was rational and readily understandable, given the economic incentives facing the French regulatory managers. It seems undeniable that such a pattern of rent seeking would impact dramatically on the pattern and pace of French economic development.[11]

5. The Absence of Regulation in the Rural Sector

Rural industry was a thorn in the side of the French regulatory managers. This resulted primarily from the fact that it was not efficient for the administrators to attempt to effect a detailed control of rural production. Several aspects of this process are of interest, however.

The original intent of the regulatory managers was to cartelize the whole country on the model of the guilds, but it should come as no surprise that they found it uneconomic to extend the guild model to the countryside. As Heckscher (1934, 1: 210–11) observes,

> It may safely be said that not only did the attempt to create gilds in rural areas fail almost completely, but the inefficiency of the innumerable regulations diminished in proportion to the distance from towns which had gild organization. There is a sufficiency of official data to confirm this, especially in the 18th century. The rural population obstinately opposed all state encroachment, even to the extent of offering personal violence to agents of the administration.

Other forces besides enforcement costs also pushed for lax enforcement of the regulations in the countryside. Perhaps the most important additional pressure came from certain municipal entrepreneurs who wanted to be able to procure the benefits of lower-cost, rural labor. Consider Heckscher on this point: "This was partly due to the already mentioned antagonism between the municipal entrepreneurs and their workers inside the cities, because the state sided with the entrepreneurs in their endeavours to exploit the less 'class-conscious' rural population with its lower wage standards" (1934, 1: 211).

A de facto free trade zone existed in the French countryside due to rising marginal costs of extending and enforcing the system of regulation and as a result of pressures from municipal entrepreneurs. This unregulated sector checked the power of the monarchical cartel and created generalized pressures toward competition. We would agree with Heckscher who concludes along these lines, "the French government did seek to apply the general rules to rural areas but they always had to yield to the impossibility of enforcing them" (1934, 1: 212).[12]

6. Conclusion

The parallels and contrasts between English and French internal economic regulation are remarkable. English regulation was motivated by the same rent-seeking forces as in France. Yet the English monarchy set up an inefficient means of enforcing monopoly rights. They chose to rely on *unpaid* justices of the peace and suffered the consequences of a corrupt and unstable pattern of local regulatory enforcement. The countryside was also an unregulated sector in England which, when coupled with the inefficient enforcement system, resulted in the long-run demise of local regulation. Moreover, there developed in mercantile England a heated competition between the Crown and Parliament over which institution had the right to supply monopoly rights (and legislation in general) and to collect the consequent rents. This competition manifested itself in various forms, such as competing judiciaries, and ultimately led to the victory of Parliament after a protracted civil war. However, once it had the right to supply monopoly rights, Parliament, for a variety of reasons, was unable to consolidate this power in such a way as to enact and sustain monopoly privileges. Free enterprise came to England, then, as an unintended consequence of the rise of representative democracy.

The French experience is a remarkable contrast to the case of England. As we have suggested, Louis XIII and especially Louis XIV were masters at cartel creation and enforcement. The administrative genius of a Colbert, coupled with the vast power of the Crown to impose absolute authority, are the proximate explanations for the incredibly vast and detailed centralized system of French mercantilism of the seventeenth and early eighteenth centuries. The forms of rent seeking in mercantile England and France were quite the same, but the difference lay in the power to implement and to police the underlying regulations.

The ultimate question, of course, which cannot be answered here, revolves around the origins of the particular sets of institutions which we find in sixteenth-, seventeenth-, and eighteenth-century England and France. That institutions were rapidly changing in both countries over this period is manifest, but it is clear that important checks (respecting the power to tax, for example) were imposed upon English monarchs as early as the thirteenth century, whereas such checks were not binding in the French case until the eighteenth century. An obvious point, then, is that crucial constraints upon the power to enforce economic regulations differed greatly between France and England.

It has not been our intention here, however, to present a broad social theory of why English and French institutional patterns differed over the mercantilist era or to argue that the rent-seeking interpretation supplants all others. Rather, accepting institutions as given, we have analyzed French mercantile policies and events in positive economic terms. We have shown that modern contributions to the theory of economic regulation provide us with plausible explanations for episodes which historians unsatisfactorily attribute to other causes.

NOTES

1. Two excellent papers on the doctrinal fallacies and growing liberalism in the writings of English mercantile pamphleteers are Chalk (1951) and Grampp (1952). Doctrinal development in French mercantile economic thought is treated in Cole's 1931 essay (reprint, 1969).
2. Wilson, in particular, clearly elucidates a fiscalist interpretation of mercantilism and is especially clear in his interpretation of English developments (1967, 521, 571). He argues, in the matter of the decline of French mercantilism, that the attack on mercantile institutions was partly the result of activity by merchants "left out" of the benefits of regulation and partly the result of liberal philosophers. We would, in our own approach, emphasize the former explanation, expanding it with a consistent modern theory of cartel formation and public choice with endogenous politicians.
3. While Heckscher was a superb scholar, many critics of his great work pointed to a grave (they thought) omission in it—the total absence of "economic actors." Economic historians, especially, were distressed that he presented a very generalized treatment of economic policy with a cohesive economic doctrine unaffected by economic events (Marshall 1935; Heaton 1937; Coleman 1957). Coleman, for example, argued that Heckscher posited no political process through which "unifying" policies were supposedly made. We suggest a means for building the political process into the analysis of mercantilism in this essay.
4. From our studies of English mercantilism we have also developed a new hypothesis concerning the origins of the modern corporation. See Ekelund and Tollison 1980*b*. In addition to the "demand-for-capital" explanation for the emergence of the corporation, we argue that economic efficiency demanded tradable stock shares to avoid the difficulties associated with hereditary successions of ownership.
5. French economic historians are not, of course, a monolithic entity. We have relied upon well-known English sources, such as Cole and Heckscher, to develop our

analysis. Indeed, the major contributions to an analysis of French mercantilism have been made in English-language presentations (see, for example, Wilson's bibliography, 1967, 615–16). Another English source that should be mentioned is Nef (1940). The interested reader may wish to consult Cameron (1970) for an excellent collection of essays and sources on French economic history by French scholars.

6. Crude calculations from Cole (1939, 1: 304–9) suggest that the revenue from only three monopolies (tobacco, coinage, and postage) amounted to one-half of all state revenues at roughly the midpoint of Colbert's administration (1670). Such regulations were only part of an elaborate system of interrelated cartel enforcement and revenue collection.
7. See Cole's enumeration of the *nineteen major* internal duties and taxes levied within and without five French provinces between 1304 and Colbert's attempted reform of 1664 (Cole 1939, 1: 420–27).
8. Institution of the *Chambre de Justice* by edict in 1661 permitted Colbert to try hundreds of financiers for "abuses" dating back to 1635. In this act, amounting to a legal exaction of tribute, Colbert raised over 100 million *livres*, some of which was used to buy back offices that had been sold. In addition, Colbert "revised" the *rentes*—government bonds and other obligations issued before Louis XIV's majority—by cutting the government's payment on the obligation by one-third. By decree of the *Chambre* or by royal edit, more than 8 million *livres* per year were saved for the state in this manner (Cole 1939, 1: 301–10). In spite of these once-and-for-all ministrations to Louis's budget, the demands were well ahead of Colbert's ability to supply funds in this manner. The attempted abolition of the hereditary features of certain offices as well as the farming of certain taxes by open bidding were also of no avail.
9. Although there is nothing analogous to an independent judiciary in mercantile France, there were the independent and powerful high courts, the *parlements*. In contrast to the *intendants*, positions in these courts were typically purchased and passed on within a family. We view this process as a means of rent protection, that is, individual monopolists bought these positions as a form of insurance against adverse rulings by the cartel enforcement agents of the king.
10. In May 1665, a royal proclamation was issued establishing monopoly privileges for the manufacture of lace in order to prevent "the export of money and to give employment to the people" (Cole 1939, 2: 239). In return for rents from lace manufacturers, the state enforced the cartel, forbidding anyone other than the franchisees from making lace. In order to discourage smuggling and cheating, more edicts were required—the wearing of foreign lace was prohibited after 1667.
11. We do not wish to become involved here in the heated discussion over whether French economic growth "stagnated" over the period or whether France ever went through an Industrial Revolution: see Roehl's (1976) proposed resolution of the matter, for instance. However, certain features of our "cartel" interpretation may be relevant to this question. It seems clear, for instance, that the unwillingness to tamper with profitable cartels retarded the introduction of certain kinds of technology, but that, once introduced, the government tended to capture the rewards from innovation. Looms, for example, were invented early in the seventeenth century, but they were principally used for producing silk stockings. When the technology began to be applied to the manufacture of woolen and linen goods, the reaction of the hand-knitters (an industry which Colbert was fostering at the

time) was entirely predictable. By decree, in 1680, Cobert outlawed the use of looms on any article except silk. But the users of the new technology were powerful enough to pressure the government in 1684 to give them their own protective legislation contravening the order of 1680. All sorts of offensive and defensive restrictions followed with the government trying to take rents from both sides (Cole 1943, 177–79). Such rent-taking within cartels must have taken a toll on the profitability of new technology, reducing the rewards for invention and innovation with predictable effects upon economic growth. Still other kinds of cartels, which must have suppressed creativity, were Colbert's monopoly creations in the fine arts and academics, e.g., in the teaching of arts and sciences (Cole 1939, 1: 314–19).

12. We have argued that the form of internal French mercantilism was well structured—it was essentially the cartelization and rent-expropriation of industry based upon the guild model of restrictions. But we have oversimplified the process somewhat by failing to note that the power to seek rent at the provincial and local levels was, over the entire mercantile period, the object of competition between two opposing factions, the judiciary or *parlements* in cities and provinces and the Crown and its agents—ministers, *controleurs*, and *intendants*. (Though the judicial system of France was more complex over the period, we adopt the term *parlements* as a simplification.) The conflicts engendered between the Crown and *parlement* over the power to seek enforcement rents impacted upon the decline of the monarchy and upon the manner of the Ancient Regime's end. Monarchical mercantilism in France declined contemporaneously with this struggle, but the struggle was not over the legitimacy of cartel formation or rent seeking. It was simply a contest over the locus of rent-seeking power, and in this respect is very analogous to the decline of English mercantilism.

REFERENCES

Becker, Gary, and Stigler, George J. "Law Enforcement, Malfeasance, and Compensation of Enforcers." *Journal of Legal Studies* 3 (January 1974): 1–18.

Boulanger, Jacques. *The National History of France*. Vol. 4, *The Seventeenth Century*. Edited by Dr. Funck-Brentano. New York: AMS Press, 1967.

Buchanan, J. M., and Tullock, Gordon. *The Calculus of Consent*. Ann Arbor: University of Michigan Press, 1962.

Cameron, Rondo, ed. *Essays in French Economic History*. Homewood, Ill.: Irwin, 1970.

Chalk, A. F. "Natural Law and the Rise of Economic Individualism in England." *Journal of Political Economy* 59 (August 1951). 330–47.

Cole, Charles W. *Colbert and a Century of French Mercantilism*. 2 vols. New York: Columbia University Press, 1939.

______. *French Mercantilism, 1683–1700*. New York: Columbia University Press, 1943.

______. *French Mercantilist Doctrines Before Colbert*. New York: Octagon Books, 1931, reprint ed. 1969.

Coleman, D. C. "Eli Heckscher and the Idea of Mercantilism." *Scandinavian Economic History Review* 5 (1957): 3–25.

Davis, L. E. "It's a Long Road to Tipperary, or Reflections on Organized Violence,

Protection Rents, and Related Topics: The New Political History.'' *Journal of Economic History* 40 (1980): 1–16.

Ekelund, R. B., Jr., and Tollison, Robert D. ''Economic Regulation in Mercantile England: Heckscher Revisited.'' *Economic Inquiry* 18 (October 1980*a*): 567–99.

______. ''Mercantilist Origins of the Corporation.'' *The Bell Journal of Economics* 11 (Autumn 1980*b*): 715–20.

______. *Mercantilism as a Rent-Seeking Society*. College Station: Texas A&M University Press, 1981.

Grampp, W. D. ''The Liberal Element in English Mercantilism.'' *Quarterly Journal of Economics* 66 (November 1952): 465–501.

Heaton, H. H. ''Heckscher on Mercantilism'' *Journal of Political Economy* 45 (1937): 370–93.

Heckscher, Eli. *Mercantilism*. 2 vols. Translated by Mendel Shapiro. London: George Allen and Unwin, 1934.

Lane, F. C. ''The Economic Consequences of Organized Violence.'' *Journal of Economic History* 18 (1958): 401–17.

Marshall, T. H. ''Review of Heckscher's *Mercantilism*.'' *Economic Journal* 14 (1935): 716–19.

Nef, John U. *Industry and Government in France and England, 1540–1640*. New York: Russell and Russell, 1968; first published, 1940.

Roehl, Richard. ''French Industrialization: A Reconsideration.'' *Explorations in Economic History* 13 (1976): 233–81.

Schmoller, G. *The Mercantile System*. New York: Macmillan, 1897.

Scoville, Warren C. *The Persecution of Huguenots and French Economic Development, 1680–1720*. Los Angeles: University of California Press, 1960.

See, Henri. *Economic and Social Conditions in France During the Eighteenth Century*. New York: Alfred A. Knopf, Inc., 1927.

Smith, Adam. *The Wealth of Nations*. Cannan edition. New York: Random House, 1937.

Stigler, G. J. ''The Division of Labor is Limited by the Extent of the Market.'' *Journal of Political Economy* 59 (1951): 185–93.

______. ''Price and Non-Price Competition.'' *Journal of Political Economy* 76 (1968): 149–64.

______. ''The Theory of Economic Regulation.'' *Bell Journal of Economics and Management Science* 2 (Spring 1971): 3–21.

Viner, Jacob. *Studies in the Theory of International Trade*. New York: Augustus M. Kelley, 1967, first published, 1937.

Wilson, C. H. ''Trade, Society and the State.' In *The Cambridge Economic History of Europe*, vol. 4. Edited by C. H. Wilson and E. E. Rich. Cambridge: Cambridge University Press, 1967.

The Backward Society: Static Inefficiency, Rent Seeking, and the Rule of Law

Gordon Tullock

In my youth, I spent some time in China. I was deeply impressed by the fact that a group of very energetic and intelligent people did not seem to be producing very much and hence had a very low living standard. A careful inspection turned up two obvious reasons for their relative poverty. First, there was a very large number of economic institutions which promoted inefficiency—government-sponsored monopoly, for example. Numerous and detailed regulations which not only created monopolies but sharply reduced efficiency were also very common. Second, the principal economic activity of the more intelligent and better-educated citizens was not actually producing things but attempting to achieve rents of one sort or another or at least to avoid exploitation by achieving the favor and special consideration of the government. It was obvious that this activity, although personally profitable, was socially unproductive.

The purpose of this essay is to examine much the same model of a backward society in a more rigorous and formal way. The first of these two reasons, the existence of widespread government-sponsored monopoly and detailed regulations of an inefficient character, has, of course, been discussed by economists since Adam Smith. I propose to call these the *static inefficiencies* of the economy and I shall begin with a discussion of them.

After having dealt with the static inefficiencies I propose to turn to the activity of getting a monopoly or getting some other government favor, i.e., rent seeking. Lastly, I shall briefly discuss one of the reasons that Western states have been able, at least in the past, to keep these phenomena in check. This is what is commonly called "rule of law," although if the reader continues with the article that far he will find that in my opinion this is something of a misnomer.

Turning then to the static inefficiencies, all economists are aware of the fact that local monopolies generate inefficiency in economy. It has recently been realized that the traditional analysis in which the welfare triangle was depicted as the real social cost of monopolies is inadequate. There is also the resource investment devoted to acquiring monopoly and this is a further and generally larger social waste.[1] I propose, however, to leave this second activity, the seeking of monopoly, until I turn to the third section of the paper and currently discuss only the static inefficiencies that come from the existence of monopolies.

These inefficiencies have been measured in a number of modern economies and, in general, the verdict is that the net loss, i.e., the welfare triangle, is not all that great. I have no quarrel with these measurements although, of course, they are subject to detailed criticism, but in the poorer part of the world the situation is much more severe. There, monopolies are much more common and in consequence the situation in which there are several monopolies, all of which affect the single production process but which are not themselves coordinated, is fairly common.

This situation of several monopolies in series is much worse than a single monopoly. This has been known since Adam Smith. Not only is it inefficient from the standpoint of the economy as a whole, it is inefficient from the standpoint of the individual monopolies who have a very strong incentive to coordinate their activities. As in medieval Europe, however, the political situation is such that such coordination is normally not possible. The reader will recall, for example, that the Industrial Revolution occurred in areas which were not officially cities in order to escape the power of the guilds.

In the Third World, in addition to the natural problems of such coordination under these conditions, there is another difficulty. The government as a whole tends to regard any even reasonably large organization as something which requires careful attention and, in general, which must pay very large amounts of graft. Under the circumstances, amalgamation, even on an informal level, is likely to attract the attention of the government, and the resulting costs may well be greater than the benefits.

In addition to creating small monopolies all over the place, governments very commonly engage in regulations which, from a standpoint of production, are essentially arbitrary. The emperor Claudius rewarding the inventor of a number of devices for reducing the labor input in construction, then prohibiting the use of the devices because they would cause unemployment, is but one of the innumerable examples which any student of the area can find. Indeed, simply contemplating our Occupational Safety and Health Administration (OSHA) or Environmental Protection Agency regulations will give a very large number of examples.

In my opinion, detailed investigation of such regulations and their effects is worthwhile, but we will simply assume that they raise the cost of production. The fact that the regulations are continuously changing adds another cost in that there is very significant risk involved in engaging in business in this kind of unpredictable environmental change. Discussion of this, however, will be put off until later when we discuss rent seeking and rent avoidance.

Let us consider the condition of the society in which these traditional economic inefficiencies exist but in which there is no rent seeking, i.e., no resources are put into attempting to achieve government-granted monopoly, to change regulations in your favor, or to protect yourself against these activities. The first thing to be said is that there would be a very considerable waste but there would be no dynamic waste in the sense of resources invested in attempting to make society less efficient for private gain.

Everyone would be adjusting optimally to a peculiar environment. There might be a prohibitive tariff on the import of automobiles and one guild might have a complete monopoly on the manufacture of ball bearings for automobiles, but there will be efficient adjustment to the conditions. The situation would be very much the same as if natural barriers such as expensive raw materials or backward technology were causing difficulty. Human energy would be devoted solely and specifically to efficient production subject to these hazards.

Suppose, for example, that a monopoly has been given to an enterprise which is not the lowest-cost producer, or regulations require the use of a relatively inefficient production technique. In both cases, the society will be poorer than if these regulations did not exist but economic adjustment to them is exactly the same as if the permitted producer were the owner of a unique natural resource or if the more efficient methods of production have not yet been discovered. The waste would be a static but not a dynamic waste. Resources would be devoted to improving efficiency given the conditions and not to reducing efficiency, as they are under rent seeking.

No doubt the traditional economic writing was correct in pointing out that these inefficient institutions were indeed both inefficient and important. The fact that energy, capital, and invention, are devoted toward efficient production under this system, however, even if that production is production under handicap, does make it quite different from a rent-seeking society. There are at least two cases of societies which came close to, although they did not perfectly fit, this condition.

The British government in the sixteenth century, like other governments in Europe, had an elaborate set of economic regulations which were continuously changed. This led to large investments in courting the favor of the king, and for that matter Parliament, in efforts to get monopolies. Thus, in 1620 or thereabouts a very inefficient set of legislation was on the books.

Beginning with Charles I's difficulties with Parliament, however, the government of England was substantially paralyzed on the economic front for twenty years. Cromwell had his difficulties, too, and after the Restoration and even more after the glorious revolution, the government of England did relatively little to bring this antique legislation up to date. In consequence, all the inefficiencies remained but rent seeking did not occur. This was, of course, a period of very considerable progress, although much faster progress was made later, partly because the regulations literally became obsolete, i.e., there was no longer anything for them to apply to, and partly because as a result of the Smith-Bentham revolution the bulk of them were repealed.

Note that it is not true there was no rent seeking or that this was a government conspicuous for honesty. Indeed, it was generally regarded as one of the most corrupt in Europe. The king, who was responsible for actually running the government, got his bills through Parliament more or less by bribery, and the bribery consisted almost exclusively in offering rents in the form of appointments or monopolies to individual members of Parliament. But although this is the way the government ran, it was not a major phenomenon. Most Englishmen were little, if at all, affected by it except insofar as part of their taxes went to pay for these bribes. Rent seeking was a major activity on the part of a very small minority of people, but for the bulk of the population it was irrelevant. The total cost was trivial over the economy as a whole, and it did not cause any inefficiency in the bulk of the economy.

My second example is colonial United States. The colonies inherited from England a set of detailed economic regulations, and on the whole made efforts to enforce them. They did not, however, expand them or change them very much and with time they fell into disuse. This was also a period of rapid growth in the colonies. Thus, this kind of static waste, although certainly important and worth both study and vigorous criticism, is not inconsistent with a fairly rapid growth. What happens, in essence, is that the growth comes from a lower base but it can be quite rapid. Needless to say, this is no argument against getting rid of such unfortunate institutions. Each time you get rid of them there is a spurt of additional growth which comes from eliminating inefficiency added on to the regular growth pattern.

Let us now turn, however, to the situation in which energy in society is devoted not to just making the best of a bad deal, but attempting to make the deal worse because there are profits for individuals under those circumstances. This, of course, is rent seeking, a subject upon which a great deal has been written.[2] A brief outline of the rent-seeking argument will serve as background for further discussion. Figure 1, therefore, is the classical rent-

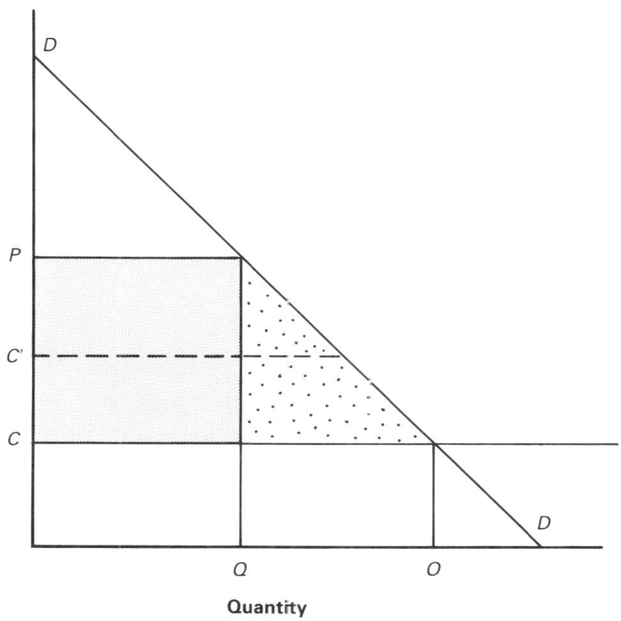

Fig. 1

seeking diagram. We have some product which can be produced at cost *C* and for which there is a demand shown by *D*. Quantity *O* would be produced at the price of *C* in a competitive market. Suppose, however, it is possible to get a monopoly either by private efforts or through government intervention. The monopoly will now charge price *P* and sell *Q* units, making a profit equal to the rectangle. The traditional argument was that the social cost of such an activity was not the shaded rectangle, which was simply a transfer from the customers to the owners of the monopoly, but the stippled triangle, which represented a net deadweight loss. This argument is not really accurate and its inaccuracy was apparently known by Adam Smith[3] but was largely forgotten by economists until I revived it.[4] Roughly speaking, the argument which we now call the rent-seeking argument is simply that getting a monopoly whether by influencing the government or by getting it privately is essentially a competitive industry. Resources will therefore flow into the activity of getting the monopoly and will continue their flow until the present discounted value of the resource investment equals the present discounted value of the monopoly, taking account of risk. Thus, the shaded rectangle is not a transfer from the customers to the monopolist, but something which the monopolist has obtained by investment of resources and, hence, is a net social waste as well as the stippled triangle. Thus, the waste of monopoly is much greater than the traditional argument would imply.

So far I have not said anything very much about the cost of creating a monopoly. It is quite probable, however, that it is in fact not the same as the present discounted value of the shaded rectangle over the future. This problem is discussed in greater detail in my article, "Efficient Rent Seeking."[5]

Note that it is not only monopoly which has these characteristics. Any activity which transfers a rent from one person to another or which creates a rent for someone has this characteristic. Thus, policemen are permitted to accept small bribes from traffic offenders. Their activity may well prevent traffic offenses just as readily as would a court fine. It will, however, lead people into investing resources into becoming policemen and thus lead to waste unless the sum of the policeman's basic wage, plus his expected bribe, is the amount necessary to attract appropriate quality people into police activities.

Note that not only are people interested in obtaining this kind of rent, but they will also defend it because its removal costs them something. Further, people from whom the rent is extracted may, if possible, organize to fight against the creation of the rent. Thus, the total resources involved in the fight for and against the rent can have a value greater than the present discounted value of the shaded rectangle.

So much for the foundations of rent seeking. There are several factors which must be admitted to modify the above reasoning. The first of these I will call the public interest cover and the second the public good problem. Beginning with the public interest cover, economists normally like to assume that everybody is perfectly informed and behaves rationally. It is hard to examine the special interest legislation of governments, however, without realizing that there are certain elements of irrationality in it. It should be kept in mind that the average citizen is not motivated to be particularly well informed about government but he is motivated to vote in accordance with what he knows. A special interest, therefore, if it wishes to get legislation through Congress which will injure the average man but benefit the special interest group, will have to cover their intentions well enough that a rather casual newspaper reader will not realize what is happening.

This cover normally takes two forms. The first, of course, is simply lying, i.e., false statements are made about what will happen. In some cases, as for example the worry about unemployment if we do not put on protective tariffs, the falsity of the false statement may not even be recognized by the person who makes it. But, in any event, whether it is consciously or deliberately a falsehood it is certainly untrue. But simple falsehood is less important than the other methods of covering up the special interest legislation. The second thing that usually must be done is to design the special interest intervention in such a way that it looks as if it is devoted to public interest.

As a general rule, from a welfare standpoint, simply giving the special interest group cash money raised by taxes is superior to whatever intervention they are arguing for. They can get more money for the same cost to the customer-taxpayer.

The reason this method is almost never used is that it would be too obvious. It is necessary to fool the average man, at least to a small extent, and hence a method of transferring funds to the special interest which is less efficient must be adopted. This means that there is always an inherent element of inefficiency in these special interest transfers. We can show this on figure 1 by assuming that the particular method of transferring power to the special interest raises its cost in some way and hence that it wastes C' per unit of production. Thus its monopoly gain is only half what it would be if it had not adopted the inefficient production technique.

There are many cases in which monopolies or at least some monopoly power are conferred by regulations on production which do raise cost while at the same time restricting competition. An obvious case is the restrictions on the practice of medicine in the United States which require that people either get no medical advice at all or buy high-quality medical advice even though whatever is wrong with them might well be treated by a less skilled practitioner. When the Carnegie Foundation funded the drive for the present arrangements with respect to medicine they gave as objectives improving the quality of medical care and providing the doctors an income suitable for their status in society. They could have reached the second without the first and everyone would have been better off. It would have, however, been a little too blatant and hence would not have gone through the legislature.

Anyone with any knowledge at all of government activity in these areas must realize that this kind of thing is very, very common. The waste costs are presumably very large, although they are offset in part by a reduction in the total amount of rent-seeking activity. Unfortunately, as we shall see below, this is not as much of a saving as one might hope.

If the voter-consumer is to be kept fooled, it is also important that various special interest groups whose interests are at least partially contrary to the interest group pushing for the particular bit of special interest legislation not inform the voters. This is usually accomplished by buying them off, by splitting part of the monopoly profits with them. This normally also involves various special rules which are inherently inefficient.

Thus, rent-seeking activity, in addition to a direct waste from efforts to achieve rent normally in the real world, will lead to considerable waste in that inefficient production methods are required as a sort of disguise. Note once again that this does not necessarily increase total waste because it lowers the total value of the monopoly and hence the amount of rent seeking which will be involved.

Another basic restriction on rent seeking under these terms is more significant and tends to make rent seeking much less common than it otherwise would be. This is a problem of the public good.[6]

In general, it is very hard to organize large groups to press the government not to take action because individual members of the groups are aware that their contributions make relatively little difference in the success, or lack of success, of pressure group activities. Thus, each individual is likely to refuse to participate or to participate at a quantity which is much below his actual interest in the matter.

The result of this public good characteristic is that a great many interest groups are not organized or if they are organized are relatively ineffective. This means that many opportunities for generating monopoly profits or other special benefits out of government activity are ignored simply because it is too hard to organize a pressure group.

Unfortunately, and this is a point which has been made by many economists, the defense against specialized pressure group activity also suffers from this kind of a public good problem and, hence, also tends to be underprovided. The result is that since, in general, special interest groups tend to spread the damage of their activity over a much larger group than they benefit, there is a good deal of fairly large scale special interest activity. Further, as pointed out by Wagner,[7] the professional politicians may act as entrepreneur for these pressure groups with the result that the individual is called upon to do nothing except to vote in his own interest. Much waste can follow.

Still, what we do observe is that it is hard to get large pressure groups organized and that the number of such groups is not gigantic and the total cost is as a necessity low. Suppose, for example, that the dry cleaners would like to have a law passed prohibiting entry of other new dry cleaners and, hence, permitting them to charge higher prices. Perhaps the law will provide that there is some restriction on the quality of dry cleaning and that a board of dry cleaners are to enforce this and they will, of course, decide that dry cleaning which is cheap, as can be seen from its price, is below standard and should be abolished.

In this law, if enacted, there undeniably will be a loss from the monopoly, but this will be a static loss in the terms of our previous discussion. The actual resources invested in generating this particular monopoly are apt to be very much less than its value simply because a great many of the dry cleaners will choose to free ride on a minority. Indeed, Mancur Olson's book would have argued that the pressure group would have had to be organized around something like a technical journal for dry cleaners. It would simply charge a little more for its subscriptions than the actual cost of producing the journal and then use the additional fund for lobbying.

Thus, the cost of the rent seeking in this case is apt to be quite small even though once the monopoly has been organized the total social cost may be very large. As long as we confine ourselves to consideration of these cases in which large numbers of people have to be brought together in order to lobby for the generation of rent, the actual costs in rent seeking are apt to be relatively minor for the economy as a whole and, hence, the net waste from rent seeking will tend to be small. This does not mean the problem is not important because the monopolies or other inefficiences generated can be very expensive indeed for society. But the costs are in the more traditional field which we have chosen to denominate "static." The "dynamic" costs of rent seeking are relatively modest.

As the number of people who are involved in the effort to achieve a given rent goes down, however, the practicality of free riding on other people's activity declines. Therefore, although a fairly small privilege of some sort would tend to inflict only modest costs on a society once it is established, the rent-seeking activity necessary to get it may be a very significant addition to that cost.

Suppose, for example, that a minor change in the tariff is proposed which will benefit only one company because that is the only company producing the particular minor product in the United States, and it is unlikely that anyone else will move in even if it becomes quite profitable. It is clear that enactment of this particular tariff change will have only a very modest effect on the total economy, although, of course, that effect will be completely negative. It is also clear, however, that the single company has motives to invest funds in rent seeking and that there is no way it can free ride. Under the circumstances, although the total static cost is small, the dynamic cost, i.e., the rent-seeking cost, is apt to be fairly close to the present discounted value of the gains which they made over the years to the individual company.[8] Suppose we are contemplating two types of government restrictions. One is a single measure for the benefit of wheat farmers which will cost the country a billion dollars a year. The farmers, being a hard group to organize, will put not more than, let us say, fifty million into lobbying for it, The static cost is great but the rent-seeking cost is small.

Let us contrast that to a large bundle of individual privileges offered to individuals or corporations which sum up to about the same amount. Here we would have a static loss once again of a billion dollars a year but the dynamic cost, the cost of rent seeking, might go up to somewhere on the order of ten billion dollars. That is the present discount value of the monopoly at a 10 percent interest rate. Clearly this collection is far more expensive than the single monopoly.

With smaller amounts of money invested in rent seeking in our public good case, it is less likely that lobbying will be effective. The ten billion in small lobbying activities is far more likely to get this large collection of small rents than is the fifty million to get a single very large rent.

It should be pointed out that the farmers may get their rent through another form of pressure. They may simply vote for whichever candidate offers the best deal. This makes the politician himself the entrepreneur, but note that there is once again a large cost here. The farmers are voting with respect to only one issue, i.e., how much they will get out of the government on this project. Their lack of concern for the other issues may lead to a very significant cost. If each pressure group votes only in terms of benefiting itself, the cost to society of this is the loss of the supervision over the government which voters can provide. In a way, the farmers pay for their rent by granting large grants to other people which hurt them. The cost may turn out to be larger than the benefit even from that standpoint, but of course they don't notice this.

In any event, information is not free and it is unlikely that politicians will be as good at organizing this kind of pressure group as a professional lobbyist would be. Thus, although some "public good" pressure group activity and rents will be generated by congressional entrepreneurs, the amount will be smaller than would be generated if somehow or other the members of the pressure group could be organized. The worst of all possible arrangements would be to provide the farmers with the right to pass special taxes by majority votes among themselves for the purposes of maintaining lobbies in Washington. But note that that is what we are beginning to do with respect to local governments. A local government is capable of putting a tax on its own citizens for the purpose of maintaining a lobby in Washington and as time goes by more and more of them are doing so. This, with respect to special privileges for geographic areas, gets around the free rider and public good problem and hence probably leads to a very large and very wasteful investment in rent seeking.

What we have been saying so far, then, is that the static inefficiences in the economy which come out of rent-seeking activity are relatively independent of the way in which the rent is created. If the beneficiaries are numerous with the result that there is a great deal of free riding and avoidance of contribution, then it is less likely that the rent will be created. But once it is created it is just as bad as if it were created in the other way. Small privileges, on the other hand, affect only a very few people and are individually less costly although they may add up to very large sums over the whole collection.

In any case, there is an additional dynamic cost becaue normally a great deal of resources compared to the size of the rent will be invested in the rent seeking because it is not possible to free ride on the activities of others. Thus, once the government is so organized that the small benefits, particularly individual benefits, are available, one anticipates that first a great deal of resources will be put into getting them and second, as a consequence of this large investment in resources, a great many of them in fact will be obtained. The picture that I saw in China was of a very large number of local monopolies and special administrative rules together with overpaid government officials on the one hand, and a very large investment of individuals in getting possession of these various rents on the other. That is what could be expected.

In the present-day world the invention of the corporation permits "individuals" to be quite large, and it may be that one of the reasons for existence of large corporations is the fact that their very size permits them to avoid the free rider problem. In a way, the stockholders of a large corporation are a collective group who have the right to put taxes on themselves for the purpose of lobbying in Washington. This is true but that is not the way it goes in terms of bookkeeping. The management simply allocates some of its resources to maintaining a Washington office or bribing a congressman, but the effect is the same.

As a result of this line of reasoning we can see that if most laws are broad laws covering many people, there is apt to be very little in the way of rent seeking and probably lower static inefficiency than would otherwise develop. This was the situation in England in the eighteenth and nineteenth centuries and the United States in the same period and this, of course, was also the period during which those two countries achieved their immense economic predominance. It turned out that their basic ideas were catching and the Industrial Revolution and modern capitalism spread from them.

Today, we seem to be in the middle of a retrogression. Our laws are immensely lengthy and detailed, they are frequently changed, and they are subject to administrative discretion which permits specialized interests, even very small ones, to get a positive return on investments in rent seeking. This development has, of course, been accompanied by a general decline in the relative growth rate in both England and the United States, although I would not like to argue that it is the sole reason for that development.

It is notable that those countries which have been growth leaders in the period since World War II have all in one way or another been areas where rent seeking activity of this particular nature has been severely restrained. Specifically, they have all been countries where the export trade is of very great importance. In general, it is not possible for a government of, let us say, Sweden, to give any particular rents to someone who sells most of his products to South Africa.

It should be noted, however, that in Sweden, the economists classify the economy into two parts, the export trade, which in Sweden makes up almost half the economy, and what they call the sheltered areas where there is little or no competition with foreigners. In the latter, rent seeking has had a major role and that part of the economy is extremely inefficient. I am told the same is true in Switzerland, although there have been no formal studies in the matter. I suspect we would find it true also in Japan.

The common market has had much to do with forcing European countries out of the rent-seeking mode. Elimination of most tariffs between European countries deprived the governments of control over their own markets in many areas. The Brussels organization has devoted its time almost exclusively to attempting to make up for this by establishing cartels but, except in agriculture, it has always failed because there is always at least one country that can do better under competitive conditions than it could under a monopoly dominated by the other countries. This explains the very rapid growth in the post–World War II period of those countries whose economy is dominated by the export trade.

If I am right about this, we have coming up a nice test for the hypothesis. England is moving into the common market and in fact is now in with the result that a number of English industries are in very severe trouble and others—for example, hotels and the service trades—are booming. If my hypothesis is correct, the net effect over time is almost certainly going to be an increase in the rate of growth in England even though it is going to be very painful to those people who find it necessary to shift from one occupation to another.

The economy of the United States, fortunately, is large enough that foreign trade does not dominate its activities. To a large extent, our prosperity in the nineteenth century came from the fact that the federal government was relatively inactive, like the Brussels EEC, and the states found themselves in a situation where the export trade (to other states) drove their economy. They might not be shipping too much to Germany, but they were shipping a good deal to Nebraska. The states, then, were prevented from developing a rent-seeking economy by much the same things that are bringing it under control in Europe. Unfortunately, this changed. The federal government developed far, far more control and in fact began organizing cartels for the states, with the result that rent seeking became much more prosperous. I would guess that the same development will occur in Europe with time, but as one who wishes Europe well, I hope it takes a very long time.

To continue with remarks on the present American situation, however, although we have had an immense body of detailed regulations, the bulk of them are general in the sense that they cover the whole United States, and tend to be written in Washington. This kind of regulation is subject to a great deal less in the way of rent seeking than local regulations covering specific companies or individual plants. The reason, quite simply, is that there usually are at least two or three different enterprises covered by each part of the regulations and it is rare that their interests are exactly coincident. Thus there is some free riding and some internal fighting within the group who might want a regulation.

Another advantage is that our present regulation is essentially a very recent development. The length of the federal register is increasing exponentially and this rapid increase seems to have proceeded more rapidly than the institutional structure for rent seeking can develop. The massive expansion in development of specialists in Washington who know who is writing the section on safety requirements for tennis shoes, know him well, and know how to provide that he receives some (indeed 90 percent) of the gain if the regulation is written in such a way as to produce a rent for someone, is not yet developed. Indeed, as far as I can see, the payoff system, which was so important in the countries where rent seeking has been going on for a long time, is still very much in its infancy in the United States. In general, the bureaucrats and politicians who write these regulations receive only the most modest and indirect payoffs from the people who benefit from them.

Thus, although we are moving in the direction of a rent-seeking society, we have by no means reached it. We have an immense amount of static inefficiency as a result of government creation of monopolies or restrictive regulation. Rent seeking, however, is still only a rather minor part of our economy. Unfortunately, the trends point toward more and more rent seeking. Unless something is done to stop these trends we may end up in the same situation as the backward societies I have described.

This brings me, finally, to the rule of law. Giving the words rather unusual meaning, I am going to discuss the use of a jury as the primary enforcement mechanism.

Those who have read my previous work[9] know that I do not like juries. I think that they tend to make mistakes, do not necessarily understand the evidence, and, in particular, do not carry out the law if they do not feel that it is "just." I don't propose to withdraw any of these statements as to the use of the jury in the enforcement of the law but I gradually come to the conclusion that although the jury is a bad method of enforcing the law it may have a desirable economic effect. Note, I am not arguing that we could not get these desirable effects by other means. My point is simply that historically the use of the jury was one of the major reasons for rent seeking being relatively unimportant in England and the United States. It is notable that most regulations in the United States and England today are enforced by techniques which avoid juries.

Consider the situation in England in 1700 and suppose that an English Parliament or king had decided to enact the kind of detailed economic regulations which were then dominant in France. A person who was alleged to have violated these regulations would have had the right of jury trial. The prospects that a jury would convict and send to prison that man for violating the rule which they had never heard of before and which in any event seemed of rather dubious moral value were very low indeed. In order to have rent seeking, we have to have an immensely detailed set of rules which more or less by definition most people will not know exist and which will, in general, have very little moral weight behind them. Juries simply do not enforce such rules with any degree of regularity.

Recently, OSHA, which had had a specific rule as to the height at which a fire extinguisher must be placed on a wall, rescinded this rule and permitted factories and other installations to have some variance in the height of their fire extinguishers. Suppose that OSHA, from the beginning, had been compelled whenever it felt that some factory was violating the rule on the height of fire extinguishers to take that factory before a jury. In the first place, the government attorney would probably have refused to make a fool of himself by presenting a case. If they did present the case, however, they would find extreme difficulty getting convictions. It would not be true they couldn't get any. Juries are highly unpredictable but they wouldn't get very many and after a while, the regulation would in essence be repealed even though it remained on the books because no one would go through the frustrating business of trying to convict people of the crime of placing a fire extinguisher at the wrong height on the wall. The administrative state requires an economical and efficient way of enforcing its regulations and the jury is emphatically not such a mechanism.

Note, however, that the reason the jury is not such a mechanism is that it does not necessarily carry out the law. I earlier said that I was going to use a somewhat odd definition of "rule of law" and I have surely done so. What actually happens is that the law, although not totally ignored by the jury, is regarded by most juries as less important than other matters, one of which is their own basic code of morality. This means that reforms and improvements in the law are almost impossible under a jury system, but it also means that the jury system prevents the development of detailed regulations of the sort which are necessary to produce large-scale rent seeking. The rent-seeking society must have some method of enforcing its laws other than by trial by jury. Of course, it does. In modern times even the English-speaking people have worked out techniques for avoiding any necessity of presenting regulatory matters of this sort to a jury.

Thus, the fact that from 1650 to 1900 England depended primarily on juries for enforcing the law, as did the United States until recently, may well have had the accidental by-product of making it impossible to have a highly detailed set of economic regulations. In a way, I am arguing that the development of a jury was probably unfortunate from the standpoint of the legal system of England and the United States but very fortunate indeed from the standpoint of development of their economy. It provided, rather by accident, a barrier to the development of the kinds of detailed administrative regulation which was so prevalent in most of the rest of the world.

Needless to say, I do not argue that the jury is the only or the best barrier against detailed economic regulation. In particular, the jury carries with it the very large cost that desirable changes in the law are as hard to get through as undesirable ones. It also carries a large cost in that it very commonly does not understand the evidence and hence simply makes wrong decisions. It does, however, in the areas where it operates, make detailed economic regulations unenforceable and hence makes people relatively unconcerned with their content. This eliminates rent seeking.

It can be seen that the particular interpretation of "rule of law" which I have been using implies that a lot of the success in England and the United States was essentially an accidental by-product of an institution adopted for other reasons and which, in my opinion, is relatively inefficient for the objectives toward which it formally points. We should not be too surprised. We cannot yet predict everything that happens in history and we still have many areas where apparent accident and random behavior are of great importance. Thus, the English-speaking people, rather by accident, got out of the rent-seeking society and began the Industrial Revolution before anyone understood what a good economic system was. I would hope that we will not have to depend on historical accident to make our economic progress in the future. We can avoid the rent-seeking society by consciously deciding not to have the kind of government which promotes rent seeking. This is better than to abort monopolies by an inefficient enforcement mechanism.

NOTES

1. Gordon Tullock, "The Welfare Costs of Tariffs, Monopolies and Theft," *Western Economic Journal* 5 (June 1967): 224–32.
2. James M. Buchanan, Robert D. Tollison, and Gordon Tullock, eds., *Toward A Theory of the Rent-Seeking Society* (College Station: Texas A&M University Press, 1981).
3. E. G. West, "The Burdens of Monopoly: Classical Versus Neoclassical," *Southern Economic Journal* 44, no. 4 (April 1978): 829–44. He has a superb discussion of Smith's view on the matter.
4. Gordon Tullock, "The Welfare Costs of Tariffs, Monopolies, and Theft," *Western Economic Journal* 5 (June 1967): 224–32.
5. In *Toward a Theory of the Rent-Seeking Society*, pp. 98–112.
6. The discussion here will owe much to Mancur Olson, *The Logic of Collective Action* (Cambridge, Mass.: Harvard University Press, 1965), and to my own "Cost of Transfers," *Kyklos* 24 (1972): 629–43. Also see E. K. Browning, "On the Welfare Cost of Transfers," *Kyklos* 27 (1974): 374–77, and my reply to Browning, "More on the Welfare Cost of Transfers," *Kyklos* 27 (1974): 378–81.
7. Richard Wagner, "Pressure Groups and Political Entrepreneurs," *Papers On Non-Market Decision Making* 1 (1966): 161–70.
8. But, once again, see my "Efficient Rent Seeking," in *Toward a Theory of the Rent-Seeking Society*.
9. *The Logic of the Law* (New York: Basic Books, 1971), and *Trials on Trial: The Pure Theory of Legal Procedures* (New York: Columbia University Press, 1980).

Boom and Bust: The Political Economy of Economic Disorder

Richard E. Wagner

Politics and Macroeconomic Management

Adam Smith noted in 1776 that "What is prudence in the conduct of every private family can scarce be folly in that of a great kingdom." The classical economists generally believed that principles of sound business practice were equally appropriate for a family and for government, and this belief dominated public opinion until a generation or so ago. Thrift led to prosperity, profligacy to poverty. Borrowing, especially to finance consumption, would destroy wealth, and so should be avoided by any prudent person or government. The classical economists recognized that fluctuations in economic activity were possible, but they also recognized that these fluctuations would set in motion self-correcting forces that would restore the normal condition of full employment. This self-correcting property came to be known as Say's Equality, which can be summarized by the statement that in a free economy supply creates its own demand.[1] There is no basis for a fear that consumers will be unable to buy what producers offer for sale, for the act of production entails the earning by consumers of the income necessary to buy what is produced. Moreover, saving creates no problem, for it does not represent a reduction in demand. Rather it represents only a shift in the object of demand from consumer goods to capital goods. Within this classical perspective, what government should do to promote prosperity was to avoid profligacy, which would result from deficit finance, and the injection of sources of economic instability into the economy, which would result, for instance, from such interferences in the pricing process as the control of prices and the inflation of the supply of money.

Say's Equality explained why the idea of a paradox of thrift was invalid, and it did this nearly two centuries before the paradox became part of the folklore of Keynesian economic management. According to this paradox, saving could actually cause impoverishment, and it was spending for consumption that became the path to prosperity. This paradox to thrift, which informed the Keynesian program for economic management that has dominated postwar policy, held that the spontaneous coordination of economic activities within a market order cannot be relied upon to proceed in a smooth and stable manner. An economy may be plagued by prolonged unemployment

First published in *Journal of Libertarian Studies* 4, no. 1 (Winter 1980): 1–37.

or buffeted by cycles of prosperity and depression. A market economy will not be a reliable guarantor of prosperity because, as an implication of the paradox of thrift, self-correcting forces cannot be depended upon to restore full employment. Substantial unemployment is as likely as full employment, the Keynesian perspective held.[2] In light of the unrealiability of the self-correcting or automatically adjusting forces of the market, the assurance of prosperity was seen as a necessary task for macroeconomic management by government. Only government, it was argued, could assure prosperity, and it could do that by expanding or contracting the rate of aggregate spending so as, ideally, to promote approximate stability in or constancy of spending over time.

Postwar macroeconomic policy has been based on two main presumptions. One is that unemployment reflects an inadequacy of aggregate demand, as reflected by the paradox of thrift. The attention given to the Phillips-curve trade-off between inflation and unemployment follows naturally from this first presumption. The other main presumption is that the process of public policy formation will work as well as can be expected to promote economic stability. The tools of economic policy will be put to the best use possible, limited only by such things as irreducible ignorance, unavoidable error, or unforeseen events. As will be explained below, both of these presumptions are inappropriate to an understanding of the relations between economic conditions and government policy. With respect to economics, the common-perspective macroeconomic management suffers from the holistic approach it takes toward its phenomena. The focus on such economic aggregates as the percentage of the population unemployed and the change in some index of prices obscures rather than facilitates analysis of the sources of prosperity and depression. For instance, as explained below, the common perspective leads to an erroneous treatment of inflation and recession as being alternatives for choice, instead of both being a product of monetary disorder.

With respect to politics, the common approach to macroeconomic policy reflects a failure to recognize the possible inconsistency between the type of macroeconomic policy required to promote prosperity and the type of policy that is consistent with electoral success in a democracy. In large measure it has been tacitly assumed either that politicians will act selflessly to promote economic stability or that their own political survival will require them to act to promote such stability. Consequently, our historical pattern of economic instability is attributed to mistakes in policy, and most certainly not to the rational pursuit of political gain within an existing institutional order characterized by, among other things, government monopoly over money. Herschel Grossman, in reviewing the contributions of James Tobin to macroeconomics, clearly described this failure of economics to treat seriously the relation between politics and macroeconomic policy. While particular references were to Tobin, Grossman was speaking of economists in general when he noted:

> Tobin presumes that the historical record of monetary and fiscal policy involves a series of avoidable mistakes, rather than the predictable consequences of personal preferences and capabilities working through the existing constitutional process by which policy is formulated. Specifically, Tobin shows no interest in analysis of either the economically motivated behavior of private individuals in the political process or the behavior of the government agents who make and administer policy.[3]

Recognition that public policy emerges from a political process has rarely been incorporated into macroeconomic analysis. Should the electoral interests of an incumbent party be advanced more effectively through policies that create instability than through policies that promote stability, the promotion of stability is unlikely to be pursued. Quite recently, there has emerged considerable interest in the possibility that in pursuing their political interests politicians might use their monetary and fiscal powers to promote economic disorder. There are two related lines of analysis on this topic. One stresses the inflationary bias of existing democratic institutions.[4] There is a political bias toward budget deficits, and these deficits will in turn induce a more rapid creation of money than would have resulted in their absence. The other line of analysis focuses on the possibility that governments may act deliberately to create economic instability.[5] Government may act to promote business cycles rather than dampen them, thereby giving rise to what has been referred to as a political business cycle. Pursuit of this line of analysis explains why there are strong grounds for suggesting that macroeconomic ills are a by-product of democratic politics, at least so long as government possesses a monetary monopoly and is large enough to produce macroeconomic consequences through its policies.[6] Both lines of investigation explain why there is no necessary congruence between democracy and prosperity. Existing democratic processes may be plagued by institutions that bring about a negative-sum destruction of wealth. The extent to which this will happen will depend heavily on the incentives provided by and the knowledge produced within a particular institutional order. So long as the interests of politicians are promoted more effectively through actions and policies that are negative-sum than through actions that are positive-sum, we should expect such negative-sum action and policies to dominate the political process.

Economic Conditions and Political Success

To continue in office, an incumbent politician must secure more votes than a challenger. Policies are instruments that politicians have to assist them in maintaining their incumbency. It is reasonable to view politicians as designing policies so as to enhance their electoral support.[7] This is not to say that politicians care only about reelection. They may very well choose to pursue various ideological beliefs, even though doing so may diminish their probable electoral support. But it is rare that ideological belief would be pursued at the cost of reelection. As the likelihood of reelection weakens, it becomes increasingly likely that policies will be chosen for their ability to enhance the odds of reelection rather than for their congruity with ideological beliefs.

Budgetary policy can be used to influence the electoral prospects of incumbent politicians. Consequently, the budgetary outcomes that emerge from within a democratic system will be shaped by the incumbent party's anticipation of the electoral gains and losses from different taxing and spending programs. In general, expenditure programs are vehicles to secure political support, while the taxes necessary to finance those programs will by themselves diminish political support. If the government operates within a balanced-budget constraint, any proposal for expenditure must also entail a proposal for taxation to finance the program. The ability to engage in deficit finance severs this link between spending and taxing. It then becomes possible to enact expenditure programs without having to raise taxes; the incumbent party can pursue the vote-increasing ability of expenditure programs without having to bear the vote-decreasing burden of taxation. Deficit finance enhances the ability of politicians to use budgetary policy to strengthen their electoral prospects. While borrowing implies future tax payments to amortize the debt, there are a variety of reasons why people will regard borrowing as less costly than tax finance. Hence, borrowing will lose less political support than the equivalent amount of taxation.[8] Political success will be promoted by deficit finance because, in contrast to a balanced budget, it appears to politicians and citizens as a less costly way of providing expenditure programs.

Numerous observers have suggested that a systematic relationship exists between general economic conditions and political success. In particular, it has been widely suggested that such macroeconomic variables as the rates of inflation, unemployment, and growth of real per capita income can influence the electoral prospects of the incumbent government. On the basis of such relations, it has often been suggested that democratic processes will tend to produce policies designed to influence macroeconomic variables so as to enhance the prospects of reelection.[9] While democratic governments may be prone to deficits and inflation (with the inflation resulting from the response of the central bank to the deficits), they are also prone to economic fluctuations, due not to "natural" conditions but to the pursuit of electoral success.

Several efforts have been made to assess empirically and to understand conceptually the use by governments of what is commonly called macroeconomic policy for purposes of electoral gain. In several different studies, Bruno Frey and Friedrich Schneider have examined the relation between the common macroeconomic variables and the popularity of incumbent politicians in West Germany, the United Kingdom, and the United States.[10] They found that incumbents become less popular as rates of inflation and unemployment increase, while they become more popular as the rate of growth in real per capita consumption increases. These findings would appear to suggest that general economic conditions can influence the probable electoral success of incumbent politicians. The second element of their analytical framework is the effort of the incumbent party to influence these macroeconomic variables so as to enhance their electoral prospects. This can be done, they suggest, by using government expenditure programs to do such things as, among others, increase transfer payments and employment in the public sector.

Frey and Schneider used survey measures of actual popularity as an indicator of the political implications of macroeconomic circumstances. In contrast, most other authors have used some measure of actual electoral support, typically the number of votes received or seats won in an election. It might be thought that a measure of actual support would be the preferable approach because it is an objective, ex post indicator of how well the incumbent party actually fared, and this objective indicator can in turn be related to objective measures of the macroeconomic variables at the time of the election. However, what is relevant for political conduct, or for any rational conduct, is the ex ante belief about the relation between possible courses of action and probable subsequent success. Measures of popularity are one such forward-looking indicator, though they are by no means a complete description of an incumbent's belief about anticipated future success. They do, however, relate to the states of mind of incumbents before an election, which is what is relevant for action, and not to the results of the election, which is irrelevant for action. For reasons explained below, there is a sound basis for suggesting that the common focus on macroeconomic conditions obscures much of what is essential about the relation between economic policy and political success. For this reason, there is little to be gained from a detailed consideration of different possible measures of electoral success.

Besides differing in the measure of success, these studies have differed in the particular variables that have been found to be significant in determining electoral success. Gerald Kramer, for instance, found that the share of the popular vote going to the incumbent party in congressional elections varied positively with the rate of change in real income and negatively with the rate of inflation, but found the rate of unemployment to be insignificant.[11] Allan Meltzer and Marc Vellrath also found two of the three variables used by Frey and Schneider to be significant in explaining the division of the vote, only these were the rate of unemployment and the rate of inflation.[12] Moreover, Meltzer and Vellrath examined voting in presidential elections, although congressional elections were examined by Francisco Arcelus and Allan Meltzer.[13] Ray Fair found that only the rate of growth of real income had a significant impact on the outcome of presidential elections.[14] George Stigler, similarly, found only one variable to be significant in determining election outcomes, the rate of inflation. He, however, examined only congressional elections and, moreover, on conceptual grounds suggested that aggregate variables should generally be unimportant as determinants of political success.[15]

What is important, of course, is not whether incumbents were actually able to strengthen their electoral prospects through manipulating macroeconomic variables, but whether they believed that they could strengthen their prospects by such manipulation. To the extent that politicians possess such beliefs, efforts at macroeconomic manipulation will be timed with an eye to the occurrence of elections. On this account, Yoram Ben-Porath found that during the 1952–1973 period, per capita consumption in Israel increased significantly more rapidly in the years close to an election than in the years immediately following an election. He suggested that this difference in consumption resulted from polities chosen to enhance electoral prospects.[16] This finding might suggest that politicians believe that the timing of peaks and troughs in employment will influence their survival prospects. Similarly, Edward Tufte found evidence for politically induced cycles in nineteen of the twenty-seven democracies he surveyed.[17] These cycles were characterized by a more rapid rate of growth in real income before elections than after elections. There are, of course, numerous differences in particular details among the various empirical studies that have been undertaken. Nonetheless, what is important and relevant here is the central proposition that the incumbent government will attempt to use economic policy to serve its political purposes. Just how such an electorally motivated policy will take place, and just what will be the character of its economic consequences is, however, something that remains to be examined.

A Basis for Politically Induced Economic Disorder

It is a short step from a belief on the part of the politicians that economic conditions will affect their electoral prospects to a presumption that the incumbent party will conduct economic policy in such a way as to improve the electoral prospects of its members, at least if they feel threatened by the forthcoming election. It is a simple matter to move from this presumption to an elementary description of how an incumbent party can enhance its electoral prospects through the deliberate creation of economic instability. Numerous efforts have been made to develop such a description of what has come to be called a political business cycle.[18] This cycle can be described quite simply within a Phillips-curve framework. The various analytical efforts contain two main elements: the impact of inflation and unemployment upon voter support for the incumbent party and the ability of the incumbent party to influence rates of inflation and unemployment.

As for voters, it is assumed that inflation and unemployment are both evaluated negatively. This is in keeping with the empirical evidence described above and the two pertinent variables described by the Phillips-curve framework. The preferences of voters are assumed to be described by the indifference curves illustrated in figure 1. The most preferred outcome is assumed to lie at the origin, in which there exists neither inflation nor unemployment. Consequently, the curve i_1u_1 represents a higher rate of voter approval than the curve i_2u_2, and so on. For instance, i_1u_1 might represent, say, 56:44 odds that the representative voter will support the incumbent party, while i_2u_2 represents, say, 52:48 odds, with the odds of any voter supporting the incumbent party declining as the macroeconomic variables move in a northeasterly direction as described by figure 1.

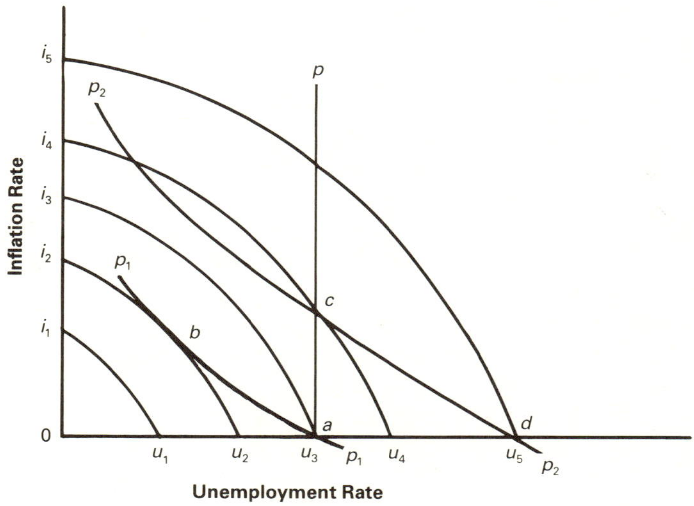

Fig. 1

The possibility of a politically induced business cycle exists so long as the economy is properly characterized as facing a Phillips-curve trade-off that differs between the short run and the long run. For convenience of illustration, figure 1 describes a Phillips curve that is vertical in the long run. At the same time, the economy faces the short-run trade-offs described by the configuration of *pp* curves. The incumbent party can, it is also assumed, choose that combination of inflation and unemployment it most prefers. As figure 1 is constructed, the optimal choice of inflation and unemployment in the long run is described by the corner solution at *a*. Within this framework, it is easy to see how a politically induced business cycle could increase the incumbent's electoral prospects. Suppose the incumbent party is able to pursue an inflationary policy that reduces unemployment in the short run, with the outcome being the attainment of a state described by *b*. If this is done in the interval before the election, the odds that the representative voter will support the incumbent party will have been increased from that implied by i_3u_3 to that implied by i_2u_2, say, for illustration, from 48:52 to 52:48.

In the typical discussions of Phillips-curve trade-offs, unemployment declines because employers mistake the general rise in prices for a relative rise in the particular prices of their products. As employers come to anticipate the inflation correctly, they will cut back on their willingness to hire people. Inflation will be able to stimulate employment only in the short run while anticipations about future prices are incorrect. As these anticipations become correct, inflation will lose its ability to stimulate employment. Consequently, the natural rate of unemployment, described by the long-run Phillips curve, *p*, will be attained again. Inflation will have reduced unemployment only temporarily, and ultimately the economy will come to be characterized by *c*. The temporary reduction in unemployment will have been purchased at the price of a permanent inflation of prices. Should the economy be kept stable at *c*, the representative voter is less likely to support the incumbent party than he was either before the initial inflation, when the economy was at *a*, or just before the election (after the inflation had begun but before anticipations had adjusted), when the economy was at *b*. The level of voter satisfaction is lower at *c*, i_4u_4, than it was at *a*, i_3u_3, let alone when the economy was at *b*, i_2u_2.

The incumbent party could wait until the next election came near, and then increase the rate of inflation, hoping to move the economy along the short-run Phillips curve p_2p_2 in such a way as to achieve some increase in the odds of electoral success. Within the framework described by figure 1, however, it would be more effective to pursue a deflationary policy in advance of the next election. This policy would initially force the economy to contract along the short-run Phillips curve p_2p_2 to *d*. The party's popularity will then decline still further, as indicated by the movement to i_5u_5. But as people come to anticipate correctly the change in inflation, the short-run Phillips curve will shift downward to p_1p_1 until *a* is attained once again, which completes an electoral cycle. An inflationary policy, described by the movement from *a* to *b*, is instituted before the election to gain voters. The long-run erosion of the party's electoral support that is done by the permanent inflation described by *c* is eliminated by incurring still greater disfavor by pursuing a deflationary policy, described by the movement to *d*, after the election, but well in advance of the next election. And when the next election draws near, the incumbent party stands ready to repeat the cycle.

Within this common analytical framework, the dichotomy between short run and long run reflects voter myopia. In evaluating politicians, voters weight recent experiences more heavily than more distant experiences. In this setting, a macroeconomic policy that provides for a constant rate of unemployment or inflation over the entire electoral period will be less successful in achieving political support than a stop-and-go policy that contracts the economy shortly after an election and expands it shortly before the next election. Unemployment is raised immediately after an election to combat the inflation that follows the stimulatory policies applied before the election. And as the next election approaches, unemployment is lowered in an effort to buy votes, although this policy will generate inflation after the election. This analytical framework typically yields a stable business cycle that has a period equal to the length of the election period. While such stability emerges from the mathematics of the analysis, the political value of such macroeconomic manipulation would seem likely to decline as it becomes more regular because regularity would strengthen the ability of voters to discern such manipulation.[19] Raising this last point is, however, getting ahead of the line of development that seems to provide the clearest exposition. What seems valuable about the recently developing literature on the political business cycle is that it reflects a realization that politicians will use policy to promote their ends, along with a recognition that the promotion of instability will dominate the promotion of stability if the former contributes more strongly to political success. The common approach to the political business cycle is characterized by its aggregative approach to its subject matter. A less aggregative approach, both to the process of policy formation and to the understanding of the economic consequences of such policies, can be exceedingly valuable. Such an alternative approach can deepen our understanding both of the impact of economic conditions and policies upon political success and of the economic consequences of such politically motivated policies.

The Fictive Character of Macroeconomic Policy

The standard literature on the political business cycle is constructed within a Phillips-curve framework, in which politicians pursue their interests by seeking to influence such macroeconomic variables as rates of unemployment and inflation. The value of this focus on aggregate or macroeconomic variables is questionable. Suppose there is some inverse statistical relation between, say, the rate of unemployment and a measure of votes received by, or popularity of, an incumbent party. Other things being equal, this evidence might show a 55 percent chance of electoral success when the unemployment rate is 5 percent, and only a 45 percent chance of success when the unemployment rate is 10 percent. Just because this aggregate relationship can be detected, however, does not mean that the aggregate, Phillips-curve framework captures the essence of the phenomena under examination. The reduction in unemployment increases the total amount of working time within the population. However, this increase is not distributed uniformly among the population, but rather is concentrated among particular people. The success of the policy results not because of the general or aggregate increase in working time, but because of the concentration of this increase on particular beneficiaries. The votes of particular individuals have, in effect, been bought by government expenditure. This interpretation suggests that the phenomena must be understood microeconomically in terms of the relation between policy and the incomes of particular people. To the extent that an inverse relation exists between the unemployment rate and the degree of support for the incumbent party, it is because a rise in unemployment indicates a reduction in real income for particular people, and these people will be less likely to support the incumbent party because they blame their loss of income on that party.

The common distinction between macroeconomic variables and policies and microeconomic variables and policies does not seem very helpful in promoting our understanding of the relations between politics and economic activity. A policy that reduces the rate of unemployment increases the electoral support for the incumbent party because it provides income gains for particular people. The success of the policy must be understood in terms of its impact upon individuals and their real incomes, and not in terms of its impact upon some aggregate measure of unemployment. A useful distinction between a class of phenomena referred to as macroeconomic policy and another class referred to as microeconomic policy must be grounded in something firmer than just the number of digits in the price tag, which is all there seems to be to the common distinction. The only distinction that seems capable of offering such a grounding, at least within the context of politics and prosperity, is a distinction between policies that discriminate among people and those that do not. Only the former type of policy would seem to have political value within a majoritarian democracy.

Price levels and unemployment rates dominate discussions of macroeconomic policy and business cycles. Yet these variables have little to do with understanding economic policy because these variables are incapable of addressing the distributional focus that dominates policy formation in democratic governments. Changes in the rate of unemployment are significant precisely because different people are affected differently. An increase of 1 percent for one year in the rate of unemployment does not mean that all people are employed 2.5 days less during the year. A 1 percent reduction for one year in the rate of unemployment will not increase each person's work year by 2.5 days. The increased employment will be concentrated on particular people, and these people will be the primary beneficiaries of the policy to lower the rate of unemployment. There would be no political purpose to a policy that affected everyone indiscriminately. Discrimination among people is the essence of majoritarian democracy, and such discrimination can be understood only by getting behind the general or nondiscriminatory concern with the rate of unemployment.

It is the same with reference to the price level, the rate of growth of which is these days referred to as the rate of inflation. What is called the level of absolute prices (the price level) has nothing to do with rational political action. Political action is concerned with achieving desired changes in the structure of prices. Any change in the level of prices that may happen to result because of a resort to money creation is an incidental by-product of the effort to change the structure of prices.

Again, discriminatory policies will dominate nondiscriminatory policies in a majoritarian democracy. A simple majority rule game can illustrate this point. Suppose a government is to distribute $90 in its effort to gain support. Whether this money comes from taxation or from money creation is irrelevant for the point being illustrated. In a three-person model, easily generalizable to *n* persons, one possible policy would be the nondiscriminatory

$$p_1 = (30, 30, 30).$$

With majority rule, there would be numerous policies that would provide larger benefits to a winning coalition. One such policy would be

$$p_2 = (45, 45, 0).$$

A program that dispersed benefits in a nondiscriminatory fashion would be defeated by one that discriminated among people. Discrimination, what may be called tax-transfer policies, will, in a setting of majoritarian democracy, dominate nondiscrimination.[20] Political action is not aimed at altering something called total spending. It is aimed at altering the distribution of incomes through changing market prices. Any changes in total spending that may result are simply a by-product of the process of inducing these changes in market prices of products and factors.

While it is possible to conceive of a truly macroeconomic (i.e., nondiscriminatory) policy, there is probably no such thing in practice. What are commonly referred to as macroeconomic policies always affect the structure of relative prices and thereby the distribution of income. Whether tax reduction is to be regarded as a microeconomic or a macroeconomic policy is generally viewed as a matter of how big the reduction is to be, as well as what type of taxes are reduced and what rhetoric is used to rationalize the policies. Regardless of the amount or form of tax reduction, or what is said by way of promoting it, however, tax reduction cannot be considered a macroeconomic policy, for its very essence is a discrimination among people in a political search for gain. Some will advocate the reduction of personal income taxes; others will advocate the reduction of corporate taxes. Among the former, some will advocate across-the-board reductions and others that the reduction be concentrated in the lower brackets; still others will advocate the reduction of taxes on capital appreciation. It is the same with government expenditure. Numerous programs of equal aggregate magnitude could be proposed, but what would determine their political fate would not be their aggregate magnitude, but their impact upon the real incomes of a decisive coalition. Similarly, the process of money expansion confers new money balances on particular people. There is no indiscriminate or proportional increase in all money balances. In all of these instances, policies may lead to increases in the absolute price level. The inflation, however, can be understood only by looking behind the change in the average level of prices to the change in the distribution of income or the structure of prices, for it is this type of change that affects political success. If politicians were truly concerned with macroeconomic variables, they would be indifferent among all policies of the same aggregate magnitude. That they are not indifferent is, of course, readily apparent when it is realized that the debates about so-called macroeconomic policy take place not over the size of the policy but over the specific design or content of the policy, i.e., over the distributional impact of the policy. Political success is mainly achieved through discriminatory policies, and this success depends on achieving transfers of income through policy, which in turn requires changes in the pattern of prices in favor of those whose political support is sought. Controversy about macroeconomic policy revolves not around how much to increase aggregate spending or how much to raise the price level, but around how to transfer wealth to a favored clientele, with the macroeconomic language serving simply as a smokescreen to obscure the essential nature of the vote-buying process.

A reasonable approach to politics and business cycles must be based on the presumption that human conduct is purposive and forward-looking, in politics as well as in economics.[21] As part of this approach, financial policies are regarded as resulting not by accident, but from the rational actions of people in light of the knowledge and the incentives produced within particular monetary institutions. Money is created and inflation results because of the incentives that characterize a particular monetary institution.[22] A prominent feature of the prevailing system of monetary order is the effective nationalization of money and credit. Those who control this system can certainly be expected to use their control over money and credit to pursue their interests.[23] The nationalization of money and credit—in conjunction with the nonneutral character of monetary disturbance, which is explained below—leads to the political generation of economic disorder.[24]

The nationalization of money and credit has not been advocated because it allows government to promote the interests of those who dominate the political process, with the resulting instability a necessary by-product. Such advocacy or apologetics is based on some hypothetical gains in economic efficiency. As compared with a commodity standard, a fiat system of monetary organization holds out the promise of a potential social saving. With a commodity standard, specific commodities must be produced and then used for monetary purposes. A fiat system obviates the need for this type of production. Pieces of paper can serve as substitutes for the gold or other commodities that would serve as money under a commodity standard, so it is argued. The social saving is possible because the commodities that otherwise would have been tied up in money stocks can be used for other purposes under a fiat standard. The adoption of a fiat standard offers the potential of an outward shift in the production capabilities within the economy. The services formerly supplied by the money commodity, and which require the dedication of stocks of that commodity to serve as money, can now be supplied costlessly through government fiat, at least in principle.

A rationalization for state monopoly over money should, however, never be confused with an explanation of the essential properties of state monopoly. A statement about the desirable conduct of a monetary monopoly generally has little bearing upon actual conduct. It is contrary to reason and to history to expect that a monopoly position will fail to be exploited for the benefit of those in a position to do so. It is the very costlessness with which fiat money can be created which creates the potential for monetary abuse when money is nationalized. There is a substantial cost of producing gold or silver, but with a fiat standard it is possible to produce claims to real resources at nearly zero cost. Counterfeiting becomes a profitable activity, one that the state customarily tries to reserve for its own use. An ounce of gold can be mined and exchanged for a television set. Alternatively, someone could simply print up $400 worth of currency to trade for the television. The temptation to counterfeit is understandable, whether it is done by private citizens or by the state. By counterfeiting, a private citizen can gain control over resources without having to provide a valuable service in return. It is the same with counterfeiting by government, only the power to collect taxes means that government is already able to gain control over resources without having to provide a valuable service in return. The money creation still helps the incumbent party, because it enables the party to buy the support of a favored clientele, who benefit from the money expansion, without having to impose vote-losing taxes in the process.

Government monopoly over money is typically advocated on the presumption that monetary order is a public good. This presumption implies that monetary order must be provided by government because the process of market competition will not bring about an efficient provision of monetary order. Yet there is a considerable history of the provision of money through the competitive market, with the effectiveness of such provision casting grave doubt upon the public-good rationalization for state monopoly over money.[25] Instead of being an agency for the provision of a public good, a central bank seems more reasonably seen as an agent for cartelizing a banking system that otherwise would be competitive. The member banks gain from the formation of this cartel, as the members of any cartel gain from the cartel's formation. It is the government that makes this cartel possible, and which enforces the cartel, so it too would share in the gains from the monopolization of money and credit. A fractional reserve banking system allows such a sharing of the gains from cartelization, with the government's share in the gain varying directly with the reserve requirement.

After the cant of political language is blown away, politics reduces essentially to designing policies that take from some citizens to give to others, with those who control the government claiming a brokerage commission in the process.[26] Within this context, it is clear that the nationalization of money and credit gives those who control government an additional instrument to use in promoting their interests. The power to do this resides, of course, in the office itself, and not in the holder of that office. Within a commodity standard, an increase in the benefits promised to one set of citizens necessarily requires a decrease in the benefits promised to (or disposable incomes left with) another set, for this is how the increased benefits must be paid for. Government monopoly over a fiat standard, however, severs this link between passive and negative benefits. It now becomes possible to enact or expand a program designed to benefit one set of citizens without having to curtail a program designed to benefit another set or having to increase taxes. Positive promises can be made without negative offsets, for the excess of desire to spend over the means to pay for such spending can be bridged through money creation.

Money Creation, Inflation, and Price Distortion

A reasonable understanding of political conduct must be based on the presumption that politicians act rationally to use their means to attain their ends. For the most part, the attainment of these ends requires their presence in office. The means to attain these ends are their ability to create policies which can then be financed through money creation as well as through taxation. Nondiscriminatory policies will be ineffective policies within the majoritarian political setting presently in existence. There will be no political gain from the promotion of policies that secure proportionate increases in prices across the board. Such gain is possible only if some prices increase relative to others. This change in relative prices could well be accomplished within an environment in which prices are rising generally. But it could also be accomplished within an environment of overall price stability. The presence or absence of inflation is nonessential to what is actually happening—the shift in the pattern of relative prices. If the shift in prices takes place through money creation, the average level of prices will rise as a result. This rise in average level, however, is not the object of the policy, but only a by-product of the real object—the shift in the structure of prices, i.e., the redistribution of income.

A focus on relative prices is more consistent with a presumption of rational political conduct than is a focus on the absolute price level; and it leads to a quite different, more accurate understanding of the economic consequences of vote buying through the government's manipulation of money and credit. Recognition that a regime of generally rising prices is simply a smokescreen that hides the variation in the pattern of relative prices fits in nicely with recognition of the nonneutral character of monetary change.[27] Monetary expansion will, of course, increase total spending, as is assumed in the standard literature on the political business cycle; the monetary value of output or income will increase as a result of the creation of additional money. What is of primary importance, however, is the change in the pattern of prices that results from such monetary creation. Inflation, or generally rising prices, is characterized by a change in the pattern of prices; prices do not all increase proportionately at the rate of increase of prices in general.[28]

Recognition that monetary expansion will change the pattern of prices has a long history in economics, and includes such prominent authors of the past as Richard Cantillon, Henry Thornton, Knut Wicksell, and Ludwig von Mises. The reason for the change in the pattern of prices is easy to understand. The newly created money is created by someone, either by an indivdiaul or by a collection of individuals acting under the cover of government. In the former case, such episodes of money creation are called counterfeiting; in the latter, they are called something like public policy actions. The economic impact is the same in either event. The newly created money resides initially with those who create it. As these people spend this money, those who receive it will in turn find an excess demand for their products and services. This excess demand leads to rising prices for these products and services. Eventually, the newly created money will become diffused throughout the economy, and the general level of prices will be higher than it was before the money creation. What is of central importance, however, is that there is a temporal sequence to the receipt of the new money, and that the initial recipients are favored over those who occupy later positions in the chain of transactions.

For instance, the government might create a program of subsidies for certain types of energy-saving expenditures, perhaps operating through a tax credit. The initial recipients of the new money would be those who made the approved expenditures. In turn, the demand for insulation and thermal glass will increase; prices will rise and output will expand. Retailers who sell insulation and thermal glass will gain from the higher than previously anticipated rate of buying, as will manufacturers as new orders are placed. These beneficiaries will in turn spend their incomes on such other things as the consumption goods they prefer, diffusing the newly created money in the process. A point will be reached in the chain of transactions where, beyond that point, people will lose more in terms of the higher prices they pay for what they buy than they gain in terms of the higher prices they get for what they sell. At earlier points in the chain of transactions, the reverse is true; people gain more from the higher prices of what they sell than they lose from the higher prices they pay for what they buy. The inflation will ultimately mean a higher price for canned tuna, along with everything else. For the seller or producer of thermal glass, the gain from rises in the prices of the sources of income will exceed the loss from rises in the prices of the uses of income. For the tuna fisherman or packer the reverse will be true. And herein lies the essence of all counterfeiting, whether done by individuals or by government: wealth—control over resources—is transferred to those who counterfeit, or occupy positions in the chain of transactions close to the counterfeiter; and is transferred away from those relatively distant in the chain of transactions. The change in the pattern of prices brought about by this counterfeiting will, moreover, be a source of economic disorder.

Economic Disorder through Money Creation

With respect to politics and business cycles, it is the inflation-induced shifts in the pattern of relative prices, and its consequences, which are the primary phenomena to be examined.[29] Any variation in the price level is, even though a consequence of the money creation, just a by-product of the political effort to alter the structure of relative prices. While rational political action will aim to change the structure of relative prices and not simply the level of absolute prices, the resulting modifications in the structure of relative prices will inject disorder into the pattern of economic activity. How this disorder comes about can perhaps be seen most clearly by considering the actual process of money creation.[30] Money is created not directly by the Treasury's printing of currency, but indirectly through the Federal Reserve System's increasing its ownership of Treasury debt. Much confusion results because of our institutional confounding of money creation and borrowing.[31] In principle, borrowing results from actions of the Treasury, while money creation results from actions of the Federal Reserve. In practice, the distinction is not so neat.

To begin, assume that government neither borrows nor creates money. The ability of individuals to borrow is limited by the willingness of people to lend. People who save choose to relinquish their control over resources now in exchange for repayment of principal and interest at some later time. Repayment is made by borrowers or investors, and what makes this repayment possible is the yield on the investment. The rate of interest indicates the rate of return to savers from lending, but it is also the price of borrowing. Consequently, the higher the rate of interest, the greater the amount of saving, but the less the desired amount of borrowing. Figure 2 can be used to illustrate this point, as well as to show the impact of government borrowing. The demand for loans on the part of investors is described by *D*, and the supply of loans by savers is described by *S*. In the absence of government borrowing and money creation, figure 2 indicates that saving and investment would be equal to $100 billion annually, with an 8 percent rate of interest.

When a government deficit is financed through the Treasury's borrowing from private citizens, the demand for loans will increase to *D′* in figure 2.

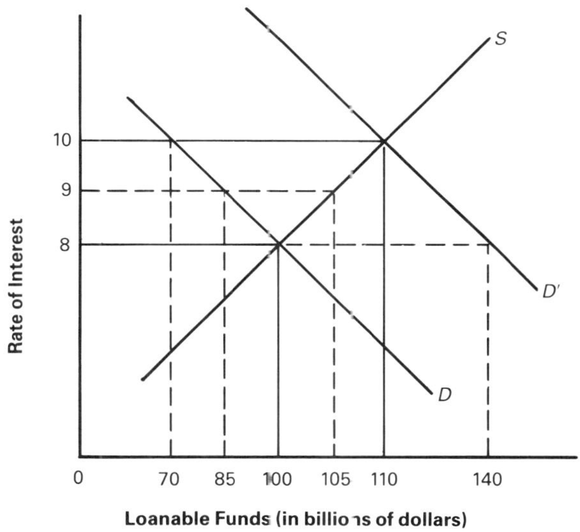

Fig. 2

Suppose the government runs a $40 billion deficit. The $140 billion of desired borrowing exceeds the $100 billion of desired saving at the 8 percent rate of interest. The excess demand for loans will lead to a rise in the rate of interest, owing to the competition among borrowers for funds. As the rate of interest rises above 8 percent, some potential borrowers will curtail their desire to borrow. This process of reduction in the amount of loans must continue until the excess demand for loans disappears.

The rise in the rate of interest due to this competition among borrowers does two things. First, it reduces the amount the borrowers wish to borrow. They might wish to borrow $100 billion at an 8 percent rate of interest, but only $85 billion at 9 percent. Second, the rise in the rate of interest will increase the desire of people to save, increasing it to, say, $105 billion at a 9 percent rate of interest. The rate of interest will continue to rise until the amount of loans demanded equals the amount supplied. Suppose the rate of interest rises to 10 percent before this equality is attained, in which event the amount of saving is $110 billion. Government will borrow $40 billion of this total; private citizens the remaining $70 billion. The $40 billion budget deficit will have crowded out $30 billion of private investment, for private borrowing will have been reduced from $100 billion to $70 billion.[32]

As noted above, a budget deficit that is financed by borrowing from private citizens is true borrowing, which is to be distinguished from the so-called borrowing that is really money creation. But if the Federal Reserve System increases its ownership of Treasury debt, money creation will have occurred instead. This process of money creation is referred to as debt monetization, for it describes the conversion of government debt into money through the mechanics of our Federal Reserve System. The impact is the same as if the Treasury had simply printed money to finance the excess of its expenditures over its revenues. There is, it should be noted, no automatic, mechanical connection between government borrowing and money expansion. Even in the absence of government borrowing, the Federal Reserve System could increase its ownership of outstanding government debt, thus causing an expansion of the stock of money. And despite government borrowing, the Federal Reserve System could keep its ownership of government debt unchanged, as noted above. Yet there is a good basis for connecting government borrowing to monetary expansion.

In the absence of debt monetization, government borrowing will, as explained above, place an upward pressure on interest rates and therefore crowd out private investment. There will be political gains from some resistance to this crowding out. The Congress will have chosen the budget deficit because a majority of its members believe that deficits strengthen their political support. The political gains from deficit finance vary directly with the degree of diffusion of the costs of deficits over the population. A cost of $10 billion spread over 100 million people will generally provoke less opposition than the same cost spread over only one million people. To the extent that budget deficits are financed by genuine government borrowing, the costs of deficit finance will be concentrated upon the investors who are crowded out. In contrast, money creation would diffuse the cost more generally among the population. Therefore, deficit finance accompanied by money creation will typically evoke less opposition than deficit finance in the absence of money creation. To the extent that congressional interests are reflected in the actions of the Federal Reserve Board, budget deficits will result in money expansion. Debt monetization would offset some of this rise in interest rates through its ability to counteract some of the crowding out.[33] Moreover, the interests of the banking system will generally operate in the same direction of supporting debt monetization.

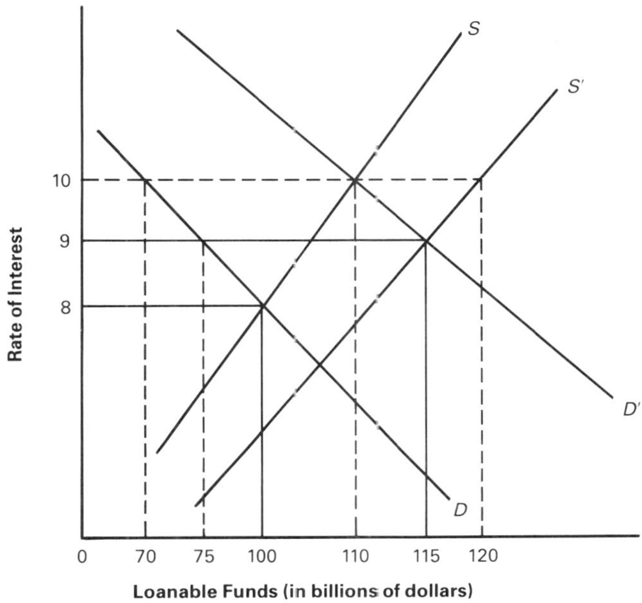

Fig. 3

With debt monetization, the supply of loanable funds is no longer limited to what people save. If $10 billion of money is created through debt monetization, the amount of lending, continuing with the above illustration, can rise to $120 billion, as illustrated by figure 3. With $40 billion of government borrowing, $80 billion will now be available for private borrowing. However, at a rate of interest of 10 percent, people will not be willing to borrow $80 billion privately. As shown by *D*, they will be willing to borrow only $70 billion. The money creation has produced an excess supply of loanable funds, which will produce a downward pressure on the rate of interest. To illustrate the argument, suppose the rate of interest falls to 9 percent. Saving will now be $105 billion, which when added to the $10 billion of money creation gives a total supply of loanable funds of $115 billion. With $40 billion being used to finance the government's budget deficit, $75 billion remains available for private investors. As a result of the debt monetization, the amount of crowding out was reduced from $30 billion to $25 billion. Debt monetization reduces the extent of crowding out because the inflation in the stock of money is used to provide the resources necessary to finance the additional private investment. The money creation reduces the real value of the existing stock of money; this erosion of value provides the means for reducing the extent of the crowding out.[34]

Monetary expansion allows the amount of borrowing to exceed the amount of saving. The rate of interest at which these two quantities would be equal is the natural rate of interest. Money creation drives the market rate of interest below this natural rate. This divergence can best be understood as a lowering of the price of using more time- or capital-intensive forms of production. The process of production in an economy can be characterized as containing vertical and horizontal dimensions. Milk and ice cream in a grocery store are consumer goods ready for purchase. Milk and ice cream at a distributor are producer goods, though ones of relatively low order, because they are close in time to final consumption. Raw milk at a dairy is a producer good of a high order, for it would be still further removed in time from final consumption. And a new barn and milking equipment would be producer goods of higher order yet, for each would represent milk and ice cream still further removed in time from final consumption.

Monetary expansion will lead to a lengthening of the structure of production; resources will shift, in effect, from producing milk and ice cream to producing refrigerators and milking equipment. A simple example can show how this is so. In the absence of money creation, there will be some pattern of production that is consistent with the rate of interest in the economy. Suppose, to keep the arithmetic simple, that wine may be aged either one or two years before sale, and that the rate of interest is 10 percent. Simple principles govern the equilibrium prices for the two types of wine, as well as the division of output between these two types of wine. If it is anticipated that one-year wine will earn $110 per barrel, two-year wine will be produced only if it is anticipated to return $121 per barrel. If the anticipated price of two-year wine is less than this amount, production will concentrate on one-year wine. And if the anticipated price of two-year wine exceeds $121, two-year wine will be produced instead of one-year wine. The more of any one good offered for sale, the lower the price it will command; and this principle of demand will lead to a distribution of output between the two types of wine. Resources devoted to these two methods of producing wine will tend to be apportioned such that the present values of the anticipated future yields will be the same. If, for instance, people anticipate a greater present value from investing in the longer, more capital-intensive method of producing wine, resources will shift to this method from the less capital-intensive method of production.

Suppose the rate of interest falls below 10 percent as a result of money creation. (Actually, the money creation will increase nominal interest rates because of the addition of an inflation premium. Nonetheless, the money creation will still leave the market rate of interest below the natural rate, and as long as this pattern of divergence obtains, the inflation premium will itself be of no consequence, and so can be ignored for ease of exposition.) Investment in the more capital-intensive, two-year wine will now become relatively more profitable. With the 10 percent rate of interest, the present value of either investment is $100, with this equality of present values being a necessary condition for equilibrium. The fall in the rate of interest causes a divergence in the anticipated present values of the two types of investment. With a 5 percent rate of interest, the present value of wines becomes $104.76 and $115.24 respectively. The reduction in the rate of interest has increased the attractiveness of investing in the two-year wine. More generally, it increases the attractiveness of investing in more time- or capital-intensive forms of production.

This resultant lengthening of the structure of production is, however, inconsistent with the underlying data of wants, resources, and knowledge to which an economy is always adapting. It would have been different had the added investment taken place as a result of an increased willingness of people to save. Otherwise, the process of capital goods expansion will reverse itself. The money creation leads to a shift in the structure of production away from consumer goods and lower-order producer goods into higher-order producer goods. This structure of production is consistent with a setting in which people wish to consume less and save more. Only no such change in preference has taken place when the fall in the rate of interest results from money creation. In this case the increased investment is financed not by saving, but by what can be called "forced saving," with this description indicating that there has been involuntary transfer of resources to entrepreneurs who receive loans from those who lose real wealth through the reduced value of their money balances. With the production of consumer goods decreasing relative to that of producer goods, in conjunction with no greater desire of consumers to save, prices of consumer goods will start to rise in response to shortages of these goods. A self-reversal will set in motion: the capital goods boom will turn into a capital goods bust. The process of expansion that is set in motion by the money creation will reverse itself automatically, unless the inflation accelerates. Without this acceleration of inflation, much of this increased investment will turn out to be unprofitable. As these investments are scrapped or put to different uses, economic contraction will result. Excess capacity will arise as capital becomes unemployed. But labor will become unemployed as well. Both types of unemployment result from the previous inflation.

The money expansion creates an artifical economic high by leading people to make investments that will turn out to be unprofitable. In the absence of perfect foresight, there will always be some investments that will turn out unprofitably. What money creation does, however, is to increase the volume of such mistaken investments. As people subsequently revise downward their estimates of profitability and take corrective action, economic contraction will result. Such contraction is necessary to correct these previous mistakes, and this recession is implied by the previous inflation. The decision to have the inflation in the stock of money actually implies a simultaneous decision to have a subsequent recession; the inflation, and the momentary prosperity it may entail, cannot be created without burdening the future with a recession.

The Boom-and-Bust Sequence

The common approach to economic policy is based on the presumption that there is a trade-off between inflation and unemployment and that boom (inflation) and bust (recession or unemployment) result from changes in aggregate spending, changes that can be offset by countercyclical government policy. Within this Phillips-curve framework, recession is characterized by unemployment and excess capacity, and these can be offset by policies that increase total spending.[35] Inflation is characterized by an excessive demand placed on labor and industrial capacity, and this excessive demand can be offset by policies that decrease total spending. The Phillips-curve framework seems deceptively appealing at first glance, possibly because of its stark simplicity. If the economy becomes overheated (inflation), the task of policy is to cool it down by reducing the amount of spending. If the economy becomes sluggish (recession), the task of policy is to quicken the pace of activity by increasing the amount of spending. This standard framework sees inflation and recession as inversely related, with both magnitudes contemporaneously controllable through public policy. But if the problem of economic management were truly as simple as this Phillips-curve framework implies, it would seem impossible to understand our recent experience. Conversely, our recent experience would seem to attest to some fundamental inadequacy in the mechanistic framework of aggregate demand management.

In this common framework, a nation is portrayed as able to choose a desired combination of inflation and unemployment.[36] As noted above, however, inflation and unemployment are not options for choice, for a nation does not have the ability to choose a combination of the two at a particular time. Obviously, at any time there is both a rate of inflation and a rate of unemployment, simply as a matter of historical observation. But these two variables are not contemporaneously chosen and inversely related; rather they are directly related in a sequence of cause and effect. Today's unemployment is a result of yesterday's inflation, and today's inflation will cause tomorrow's unemployment. A recession becomes a necessary price of the political activities that produced the inflation in the first place.[37] Reallocations of labor must take place before the economy's structure of production will once again reflect the underlying data to which the economy adapts. The mistakes that resulted because people responded to the nonsustainable price signals generated by inflation must be worked out before the economy can return to normalcy. Recession is an inherent part of the recovery process.

What if the government attempts to counteract the economic contraction by further money creation? With a sufficiently strong injection of money, the contractionary forces can be offset—temporarily. But inflation cannot accelerate indefinitely. When the inflation, or even just its acceleration, ceases, contraction will result. Only, the longer the inflation is allowed to accelerate before the recession is faced, the greater will have become the distortion in prices and in the pattern of investment in the economy. A dilemma results by attempting to resist the contraction. Resistance increases the amount of distortion in the economy. But resistance cannot continue indefinitely. The longer the period of resistance before the monetary expansion is brought under control, the stronger will be the subsequent economic contraction. Once it is recognized that inflation breeds recession, it is easy to see why it is possible to confront rising prices along with unemployment. This situation, called stagflation, is nothing new or mysterious. It is a natural outgrowth of inflation; in particular, of attempting to resist or counteract by further money expansion the recession that was made necessary by the initial inflation.[38]

What About Exogenous Sources of Disorder?

Recognizing that economic policy is to some extent shaped by the desire for political success and that inflation contributes to economic disorder leads to a realization that such disorder is an endogenous feature of our present institutional order. Yet there are exogenous sources of disorder as well, and it might be thought that an activist policy is necessary to offset these types of disorder. It might even be thought that the sufferance of monetary sources of disorder is a reasonable price to pay for having a government with the ability to offset such exogenous sources of disorder. The desirability of government monopoly over money, in conjunction with related institutional arrangements, would seem, in other words, to be ultimately an empirical matter of the relative strengths of the endogenous and exogenous sources of disorder.

For instance, sudden reductions in food production below anticipated amounts can bring on recession. So can oil embargoes or increases in oil prices. All these events, and many more, diminish the production possibilities open to an economy and disrupt the network of production relations. It was estimated that the 1973–74 oil embargo reduced employment by 500,000 and was responsible for the decline in gross national product of $10 to $20 billion in the first quarter of 1974. With a lower rate of output in the economy, the average level of prices will rise, unless the stock of money has declined as well. Rising prices and unemployment can result simultaneously from exogenous forces that either destroy part of the production of particular commodities or reduce their availability.

But what is the role of policy in the face of such exogenous disturbances? Monetary expansion cannot offset these disturbances: it will not substitute for the food or oil that was lost—we cannot eat currency, and our cars will not run on government bonds. These losses are irretrievable. Such exogenous changes necessarily leave us less wealthy than we were previously. The best that can be hoped for is that the transition to a new pattern of economic relations will come about as smoothly as possible. Money creation in response to such exogenous disturbances will not, however, smooth the transition to a new pattern of economic activity. Indeed, they will make this transition more difficult. This nonmonetary disturbance will necessitate a readjustment in the network of economic relations. Changes in the pattern of prices as a result of changes in such things as resource availabilities facilitate that readjustment. Monetary expansion cannot assist in the process of the readjustment of prices. On the contrary, it will create further, nonsustainable shifts in prices, in addition to the shifts made necessary by the exogenous disturbance. The price distortion resulting from the exogenous disturbance will be compounded by the distortion resulting from the monetary expansion. The process of economic readjustment will have been made more difficult by the monetary expansion.

Cycles and the Anticipation of Policy

The process of economic policy formation has been typically portrayed as something that works as well as possible to promote economic stability, only sometimes the exogenous shocks can prove difficult to overcome. Still, the tools of economic policy will be put to the best use possible, limited only by ignorance (on the part of economists), error (a bad set of survey data), or unforeseen events (recalcitrant Arabs). Any contribution of policy to the creation of economic disorder, therefore, will be a result of accident or error. There would be nothing systematic about the process of making economic policy that generates economic disorder. Contemporary scholarship, however, has begun to deepen our understanding of the bias toward economic disorder that characterizes the prevailing institutional order through which policy emerges.

It would be easy to construct a model of the political business cycle by emending the standard literature to account for a relative price focus and the nonneutrality of money. The economy would be stimulated before an election, only now it would be recognized that stimulation means that particular people have received the newly created money. The expansionary process during the preelection period could be traced out, and the distribution of gains and losses examined. The boom phase could be described by a relatively simple model, and this description would not differ greatly from the common story about the expansion phase of the political business cycle. The collapse would, of course, be described differently. The collapse would no longer result from a conscious decision by politicians to deflate after the election. Instead, a decision to inflate before the election would imply a subsequent collapse after the election, with both boom and bust being inseparable components of a unified economic process. While the description of the bust phase would differ from the typical description, the process of bust could retain the same simplicity as found in the standard approach. Consequently, the complete boom-and-bust sequence would be timed so that the bust would occur optimally (from the perspective of the incumbent party) after the election, leaving plenty of time to manufacture another boom before the next election.

Such a model, however, would seem incapable of capturing the inherent complexity of economic life, and it is this complexity that creates so much scope for the disorder that results from monetary manipulation. The common models of political business cycles always describe situations well under control. There are booms before an election and collapses afterwards, all of this taking place regularly and within safe bounds. These models are largely based on what might be called hot-air economics: an economy is like a balloon, and the problem of economic manipulation is simply one of adjusting the air pressure according to the proximity of the next election.[39]

Historically, of course, cycles have not represented such easily controlled phenomena as the models make them appear. Once it is recognized that an economy is quite unlike a balloon, but is actually a complex network of human anticipations, it becomes apparent that it is impossible to know the full consequences of money creation, or of any other change in policy. All that can be known are some general outlines of those consequences. The regularity and controllability of cycles disappears, and it becomes possible for the cyclical process to get out of control in the sense that the easy assurance of what is to come is replaced by a pervasive uncertainty.[40] An incumbent government may counterfeit to strengthen its electoral prospects. However, the collapse that is implied by this action cannot be nicely timed, and it may even begin before the election. Out of desperation, the government may work the printing presses even harder, yet the boom may not set in until after the election, when there is a new government. Politicians can certainly be depended upon to seek their interests, which will include the resort to counterfeiting when monetary institutions permit it Economic instability will result from such money creation, though this process of boom and bust will not be simple and easily controlled.

Some people have objected to the idea of a political business cycle, not because they see inherent complexity in economic life and hence an inherent unpredictability in all efforts at economic manipulation, but because they see economic life as extraordinarily simple and easy to control. From this type of perspective, the political business cycle would seem to be grounded in myopia; people vote for a candidate who gives them something before an election which he takes away afterwards, and yet they persist in repeating this cycle.[41] Within the Phillips-curve framework, the political business cycle would indeed seem to be grounded in a presumption of voter myopia. Rather than discard the idea of politically generated instability, it may be more sensible to discard the Phillips-curve framework. This framework, after all, characterizes an economy as consisting of one commodity, an aggregate of indistinguishable output, and it treats all people as identical, for differences among persons are inessential for the model. With this view of reality, it seems quite natural to conceptualize an economy as something like a balloon, which in turn would indeed make the presence of a political business cycle a matter of myopia.

Stated differently, the presence of politically induced economic instability should indeed be attributed to myopia if the understanding of reality held by people conforms to that described by figure 1. But if people universally possessed this interpretation of reality, it would be impossible to understand why government monopoly over money is permitted in the first place. That the monopoly over money is allowed to continue, i.e., that the negative-sum institution is allowed to persist, is evidence that people do not uniformly share the interpretation of reality described by figure 1. Although the interpretation described by figure 1 does convey the idea that policy is used to pursue electoral purposes, it is wrong in the details of that process and in the description of the consequences that follow.

In a market setting, those who possess the correct interpretation of reality and act on it will profit from their action and, in the process, convey some benefit to others. In politics, however, what matters generally is what most people commonly believe to be so, and there is no way for those who think differently to test their contrary belief. Suppose, for instance, that the supply of food has been nationalized. Before the election people are allotted daily rations of steak, vegetables, and wine, but after the election they subsist for a while on beef bouillon, vegetable soup, and grape juice. Is it evidence of myopia if someone votes for the incumbent party? It would be so only if that person has an interpretation of reality that says that the government is manipulating the supply of food so as to cause the alternating periods of famine and plenty. People who think this way are, of course, unlikely to support the incumbent party. Alternatively, those who do support the incumbent party are likely to have a quite different interpretation of reality. They could, for instance, think that the government is doing its best to react to such exogenous forces as continuing changes in the birth rate among insects.

The greater the complexity of economic life, the greater the number of possible interpretations, and, *ceteris paribus*, the greater the likelihood that erroneous interpretations will dominate in politics, in contrast to the market. In a market setting, rational action is largely a matter of responding to a question of "what." Thus, as food supplies become more variable, people will come to carry larger inventories of food. No knowledge of the reason for the variability is necessary for rational action. In contrast, rational choice in politics is largely a matter of responding to a question of "why." It is essentially a matter of choosing among different hypotheses—in the illustration at hand, choosing among different hypotheses on the reason for the recurring periods of famine and plenty. This greater complexity of political choice is compounded by an inability to gain from any investment in knowledge. In a market setting, a person can gain by storing food during the boom periods; it is a simple task to profit directly from knowledge. In a political setting, however, even if a person has acquired knowledge about the more complex question of "why," there is no way that he can profit from his knowledge because a change in policy will take place only after a majority of people have come to the same conclusion. Consequently, it is rational to be considerably more ignorant about general political matters than about matters of market choice.

There is certainly no point in basing an explanation of economic phenomena upon a presumption that people will fail to take advantage of the profit opportunities available to them. Much economic analysis has, however, done exactly this.[42] But it is inappropriate to jump from this truism to a proposition that politicians cannot use the government's nationalization of money and credit to promote their ends. Such an effort to do so may well backfire, as noted above; but in bringing in these notions of the essential complexity of economic life, we are getting into issues that cannot be treated within any of the analytical frameworks that are grounded in an essential simplicity of economic life. To take advantage of profit opportunities is, of course, a trivial matter in the typical approaches found in this literature. In turn, the making of errors by entrepreneurs can only be ascribed to stupidity, much on the order of making mistakes in arithmetic computations.

Matters are seen differently when the essential complexity of economic life is taken into account. Entrepreneurial error can become quite prevalent. Saying this is not, it should be noted, the same as saying that continual repetition of the same set of antecedents will elicit the same entrepreneurial mistakes. It would seem silly to attribute such denseness to entrepreneurs. But how many trials are required for the cognitive faculties to bring about a change in inference as to the need for change in economic action? A typical entrepreneurial career will span about ten presidential elections. Also, circumstances will never be the same in all relevant respects but one, the change in government policy.

Most importantly, the very ability of those who control government to accomplish their ends depends largely upon their ability to create entrepreneurial error. Policy is concerned primarily with creating rents for a favored clientele, paid for by taking—directly through taxation or indirectly through counterfeiting—from those not so favored. Political entrepreneurship, within our present institutional order, consists of finding ways to promote such transfers and to capture a brokerage commission or finder's fee in the process. To use the same method of theft repetitively would not be effective political entrepreneurship, for the victims would come to develop better ways of protecting themselves. Of course, the more complex the economic reality, the less rapidly will victims come to make the correct inference and take evasive action; so the amount of rent that could be captured from repetitive policy would be larger than in a less complex economy.

Nonetheless, political entrepreneurship will be designed to foster entrepreneurial error, so predictability in policy would be contrary to a requirement of rational political entrepreneurship. And it is just as necessary to assume rationality in politics as it is to assume it in the market. To have politicians act systematically in enacting their policies is to presume that they will fail to take advantage of the profit opportunities open to them.[43] Recognition that entrepreneurs are just as rational in the public sector as they are in the private sector, in conjunction with recognition of the essential complexity of economic life, leads to a recognition that there is no conflict between an assumption of rationality and the continual governmental injection of sources of instability into the economy. This becomes particularly apparent once it is seen that the particular channels through which the new money enters the economy will affect the outcome. Episodes of money creation are not homogeneous—each one is different, and, so, each will entail different patterns of resource transfer as well as different patterns of subsequent economic reaction. It is not enough to act on the basis of a presumption of a relation between monetary expansion and the increase in the measured price level. What must be formed is a presumption of a relation between monetary expansion and changes in the structure of prices. Moreover, monetary expansion may take place in a variety of ways, each way having a different effect upon the structure of prices. While numerous episodes of monetary expansion can all have the same effect upon the aggregate price level, each particular episode will nevertheless differ in its effect upon the structure of prices.

Disorder and the Problem of Waste in Economic Life

Inflation and recession are inseparable consequences of the pursuit of political interest in the context of government monopoly over money. The discoordination of interdependent plans as a result of government counterfeiting constitutes the business cycle. Once the analytical focal point is shifted from cyclical fluctuations in such aggregate variables as price levels and unemployment rates to the coordination of interdependent plans, however, the basis for looking at the business cycle as a distinct phenomenon seems to erode. In the division of labor among economists, it is customary to link business cycles with monetary manipulation, and resource misallocations with a variety of taxes and regulations: two distinct phenomena linked with two distinct classes of government action. This very way of thinking about business cycles as something different from resource misallocation seems to suggest a reluctance to totally give up notions of the neutrality of money and the dichotomization of the pricing process. Such thinking is one aspect of the presumption that macroeconomic policy is to be distinguished from microeconomic policy on the basis of the price tag of the policy. Within the rigorously applied subjectivism and methodological individualism pursued here, it would seem inadmissible to distinguish cycles from resource misallocations, because the two do not constitute independent phenomena.[44]

What makes for a successful economy? Is it a stable level of employment, even if that level is defined as full employment? In such an economy, there would obviously be no fluctuations in employment. But should such an economy be necessarily considered successful? To illustrate, consider a Hayekian-type cycle in which the structure of production lengthens at first, then subsequently shrinks. The shrinkage of the structure of production is normally associated with rising unemployment. But there is no reason why this must be so. It is certainly possible to postulate a frictionless world in which people who were laid off in the capital goods industries immediately found employment in the consumer goods industries. Or some more complex pattern of reemployment could be described. Yet such a constancy in the rate of unemployment should hardly be taken as a sign of a successful economy. The economy would be plagued by waste, which in this instance would be the divergence between the wants that could have been satisfied in the absence of a change in the structure of production and the wants that were actually satisfied.[45] In the process of lengthening and then shortening of the structure of production, what could have been produced had the malinvestments not been made is lost forever. Mistakes cannot be corrected costlessly, even though labor may be fully employed in the process of correcting those mistakes. Someone who spends two hours cleaning a carpet, only to knock over a bucket of dirty water, making it necessary to clean the carpet again, is fully employed for four hours, not two. Yet the second cleaning represents waste, for what could have been done with those second two hours had the bucket not been spilled has been lost forever. Wastage of what could have been produced to satisfy human needs, had the monetary expansion not discoordinated individual plans, is also a cost of that expansion even though the rate of unemployment may have remained unchanged. And even if unemployment does result, the waste caused by money creation will be understated if only the change in unemployment is brought under consideration.

Waste is an inherent aspect of economic life, for there will never be perfect coordination among people's plans. The difference between perfect coordination and the best attainable degree of coordination can be called the natural rate of waste. Different institutional orders will entail different degrees of waste, and an "ideal" institutional order will entail the natural rate of waste. A comparison between two economies is illustrated by figure 4. The

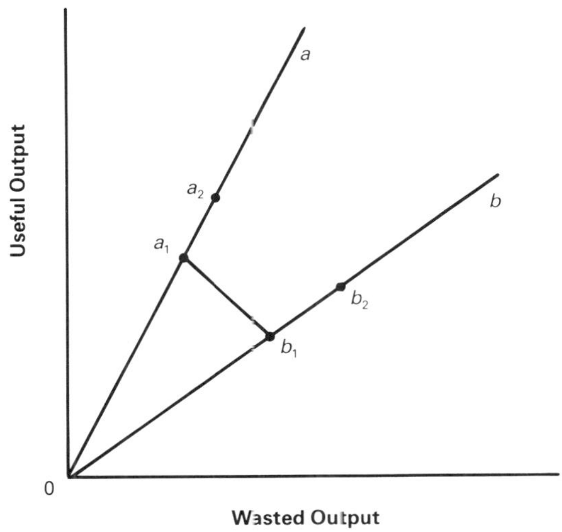

Fig. 4

economy characterized by the production ray *a* operates within an ideal institutional order, and is characterized by the natural rate of waste. The economy described by the production ray *b* has a higher proportion of waste to useful output. With respect to the subject of this essay, economy *b* represents the effect of government monopoly over money, where the output mix has shifted toward more effort being devoted to making and rectifying malinvestments.

It might be thought that such waste could be detected through the national income accounts, either as a lower level of national income or as a slower rate of growth. Neither seems possible, however, and the problems confronted in attempting to do so are the same as those that are confronted in efforts to compare the sizes and growth rates of economies.[46] The way that these accounts are constructed, resources devoted to the correction of error are valued equivalently with resources devoted to other production. If the economies described by a and b are equal in all other relevant respects, the one described by b_1 will have the same measured national income as the one described by a_1, though the extent that economy b falls short of economy a's ability to satisfy human wants is indicated by the line segment a_1b_1, which would have a slope of minus one. Differences in measured rates of growth would not seem likely to be discernible either. There is no reason why technological progress would necessarily be any slower with regard to the correction of malinvestment than it would be for other economic activities. There would seem to be no systematic basis for economy b not moving from b_1 to b_2 at the same rate that a moves from a_1 to a_2. Measures of national income and rates of growth might not differ, yet the economy with institutions that promote waste would have a lesser ability to fulfill human wants.

The assessment of economic performance is a matter of ethics, not economics, so waste cannot be assessed independently of a normative judgment. This, of course, is, equally true in engineering. By virtue of the law of conservation, all engines are necessarily 100 percent efficient. To say that an engine is less than perfectly efficient requires a normative judgment that separates the output into useful or desired output and waste. A pump that moves water uphill to a house can be said to be less than 100 percent efficient only as a result of someone's having judged that such things as the water lost in transit and the heat dissipated in the pump house are unwanted and hence represent waste. It is the same with society.[47] At the end of a day, twenty-four hours have been lived through, and it cannot be otherwise. Each instant of time can in principle be accounted for in an accounting system. This time might be spent chopping down trees. It might be spent just lying under a tree. Or it might be spent smashing in store windows. It could also be spent in filling out government demands for information. For each moment of time, there would necessarily correspond an output that represents the use of that time. In only a fraction of those moments would some material traces be created to remain behind, but always there would be, by definition, some use made of that time. The efficiency of an economy cannot be judged without placing some valuation upon different uses of time, any more than the efficiency of an engine can be judged without placing some valuation upon different transformations of energy. By extension, unemployment cannot be said necessarily to worsen economic performances. For instance, what if the unemployment results from layoffs in the cadre of government regulators and inspectors? The decrease in regulation would free people privately to engage in truly productive activity rather than in make-believe and even destructive work made necessary by regulation. Or what if the unemployment resulted among physicians and nurses, due to a sudden cessation of automobile accidents?

A Concluding Summary

Macroeconomic theory has tended to look upon government as having the function of keeping stable what would otherwise be an unstable economy. Once it is recognized that macroeconomic policy emerges from within a political process, it quickly becomes apparent that the politically rational conduct of public policy may actually amplify rather than dampen business cycles. When recognition of the nonneutral character of monetary disturbance is combined with an awareness of the patterns of rational political action, it becomes possible to understand more clearly just how existing institutional arrangements contribute to economic instability.

To focus on aggregate variables, however, is to miss the essence of the process being examined. Political manipulation revolves around individual rather than aggregate variables. Cycles are a by-product of the efforts of politicians to buy votes through monetary manipulations that bring about changes in the structure of relative prices. When unemployment is addressed, it is through specific programs to increase the real income of particular people, not through generalized increases in aggregate demand. There may well be changes in what are called macroeconomic variables, but the reasons for these changes, as well as their nature, must be understood microeconomically. Additionally, the waste resulting from the changes in plans due to monetary manipulation is an important consequence of this manipulation, and this waste will remain largely undetected by rates of unemployment. A thorough application of the methodologically individualist perspective leads to a realization that the business cycle does not constitute an independent phenomenon, but is rather one aspect of the problem of waste in human affairs. At the most general level, what is of interest is the relationship of different institutional orders to the waste of human life.

State monopoly over money, as created by the Federal Reserve Act, strengthened over the past half century, and culminating in the repudiation of the gold convertability of the dollar in 1971, was not supposed to contribute to economic instability. But a growing body of literature suggests that it has, and explains why it has had this effect. The pursuit of political gain in conjunction with an institutional setting of state monopoly over money contributes to economic instability and more generally to waste—a lessened ability of an economy to satisfy people's wants. Politicians cannot be expected to stop being politicians; they will continue to promote policies and seek reelection—it can be no other way. What can be altered, however, is the nature of the monetary order within which politicians pursue their ends. By taking a variety of steps to remove money from the category of a nationalized industry, the ability of the ordinary vicissitudes of politics to promote economic disorder would be lessened.[48] Without such steps, we can expect to remain plagued by disorder. The denationalization of money and the restoration of competition in banking and in the supply of money will not, of course, remove all sources of economic disorder, but a gigantic first step in the right direction will have been taken.

NOTES

1. For a recent analysis of this perspective, see W. H. Hutt, *A Rehabilitation of Say's Law* (Athens: Ohio University Press, 1974).
2. For a description of these contrasting perspectives, see Axel Leijonhufvud, "Effective Demand Failures," *Swedish Journal of Economics* 75 (March 1973): 27–48.
3. Herschel I. Grossman, "Tobin on Macroeconomics: A Review Article," *Journal of Political Economy* 83 (August 1975): 845–46.
4. For an examination of this bias within an American context, see James M. Buchanan and Richard E. Wagner, *Democracy in Deficit: The Political Legacy of Lord Keynes* (New York: Academic Press, 1977). This analytical framework is extended to a British context in James M. Buchanan, John Burton, and Richard E. Wagner, *The Consequences of Mr. Keynes,* Hobart Paper no. 78 (London: Institute of Economic Affairs, 1978).
5. For a recent survey of this literature, both conceptual foundations and empirical evidence, see Bruno S. Frey, "Theorie und Empire Politischer Konjunkturzyklen," *Zeitschrift für Natiönalokonomie* 36, no. 1 (1976): 95–120. Early statements of the possibility of a political business cycle are contained in Johan Akerman, "Political Economic Cycles," *Kyklos* 1, no. 2 (1947): 107–17; and Michael Kalecki, "Political Aspects of Full Employment," *Political Quarterly* 14, no. 4 (1943): 322–31. Kalecki's thinking on this topic is examined in George R. Feiwel, "Reflection on Kalecki's Theory of Political Business Cycle," *Kyklos* 27, no. 1 (1974): 21–48.
6. On some topics, though within a somewhat different perspective than found in most of the literature, see Richard E. Wagner, "Economic Manipulation for Political Profit: Macroeconomic Consequences and Constitutional Implications," *Kyklos* 30, no. 3 (1977): 395–410; and idem, "Politics, Monetary Control, and Economic Disruption," in *Models of Political Economy,* ed. Paul Whiteley (London: Sage, 1980), pp. 201–20.
7. Anthony Downs, *An Economic Theory of Democracy* (New York: Harper and Row, 1957), inspired a voluminous literature.
8. Some evidence on this point is developed in W. Mark Crain and Robert B. Ekelund, Jr., "Deficits and Democracy," *Southern Economic Journal* 44 (April 1978): 813–28.
9. A few items among many are Bruno S. Frey, "Politico-Economic Models and Cycles," *Journal of Public Economics* 9 (April 1978): 203–20; Bruno S. Frey and Lawrence J. Lau, "Towards a Mathematical Model of Government Behavior," *Zeitschrift für Natiönalokonomie* 28 (November 1968): 355–80; Lawrence J. Lau and Bruno S. Frey, "Ideology, Public Approval, and Government Behavior," *Public Choice* 10 (Spring 1971): 21–40; Howard S. Bloom and H. Douglas

Price, "Voter Response to Short-Run Economic Conditions: The Asymmetric Effect of Prosperity and Recession," *American Political Science Review* 69 (December 1975): 1240–54; Susan J. Lepper, "Voting Behavior and Aggregate Policy Targets," *Public Choice* 18 (Summer 1974): 25–43; Assar Lindbeck, "Stabilization Policy in Open Economies with Endogenous Politicians," *American Economic Review* Proceedings, 66 (May 1976): 1–19; and W. Mark Crain, Thomas H. Deaton, and Robert D. Tollison, "Macroeconomic Determinants of Tenure in the U.S. House of Representatives," *Atlantic Economic Journal* 6 (July 1978): 79–83.

10. Their general framework is presented in Bruno S. Frey and Friedrich Schneider, "On the Modelling of Politico-Economic Interdependence," *European Journal of Political Research* 3 (December 1975): 339–60. See also idem, "An Empirical Study of Politico-Economic Interaction in the United States," *Review of Economics and Statistics* 60 (May 1978): 174–83; and idem, "A Politico-Economic Model of the United Kingdom," *Economic Journal* 88 (June 1978): 243–53. Simulation studies within this general framework are presented in Bruno S. Frey, "The Politico-Economic System: A Simulation Model," *Kyklos* 27, no. 2 (1974): 227–54; and Friedrich Schneider, "Politisch-okonomische Könjunkturmodelle: Ein Simulationsmodell," *Schweizerische Zeitschrift für Volkswirtschaft und Statistik* 110 (September 1974): 519–49.
11. Gerlad H. Kramer, "Short-Term Fluctuations in U.S. Voting Behavior, 1896–1964," *American Political Science Review* 65 (March 1971): 131–43.
12. Allan H. Meltzer and Marc Vellrath, "The Effects of Economic Policies on Votes for the Presidency: Some Evidence from Recent Elections," *Journal of Law and Economics* 18 (December 1975): 781–98.
13. Francisco Arcelus and Allan H. Meltzer, "The Effect of Aggregate Economic Variables on Congressional Elections," *American Political Science Review* 69 (December 1975): 1232–39.
14. Ray C. Fair, "The Effect of Economic Events on Votes for President," *Review of Economics and Statistics* 60 (May 1978): 159–73.
15. George J. Stigler, "General Economic Conditions and National Elections," *American Economic Review*, Proceedings, 63 (May 1973): 160–67.
16. Yoram Ben-Porath, "The Years of Plenty and the Years of Famine-A Political Business Cycle?" *Kyklos* 28, no. 2 (1975): 400–403.
17. Edward R. Tufte, *Political Control of the Economy* (Princeton: Princeton University Press, 1978).
18. In addition to the literature already cited on the political business cycles, see William D. Nordhaus, "The Political Business Cycle," *Review of Economic Studies* 42 (April 1975): 169–90; C. Duncan MacRae, "A Political Model of the Business Cycle," *Journal of Political Economy* 85 (April 1977): 239–63; and Paul Mosley, "Images of the 'Floating Voter': or, The 'Political Business Cycle' Revisited," *Political Studies* 26 (September 1978); 375–94.
19. Robert J. Gordon, "The Demand For and Supply of Inflation," *Journal of Law and Economics* 18 (December 1975): 807–36.
20. This is one of the central themes of James M. Buchanan and Gordon Tullock, *The Calculus of Consent* (Ann Arbor: University of Michigan Press, 1962). For a comparison between the market order and majoritarian politics on this point, see Ludwig von Mises, "The Clash of Group Interests" in *The Clash of Group Interests and Other Essays*, ed. Richard M. Ebeling (New York: Center for Libertarian Studies, 1978), pp. 1–12.

21. A concise statement of this presumption is William H. Meckling, "Values and the Choice of the Model of the Individual in the Social Sciences," *Schweizerische Zeitschrift für Volkswirtschaft und Statistik* 112 (December 1976): 545–60.
22. Some interesting observations on developing a political economy of inflation are contained in Karl Brunner, "Comment" (on Robert J. Gordon's "The Demand for and Supply of Inflation"), *Journal of Law and Economics* 18 (December 1975): 837–57.
23. With respect to central banking in relation to government policy, see, for example, Keith Acheson and John F. Chant, "The Choice of Monetary Instruments and the Theory of Bureaucracy," *Public Choice* 12 (Spring 1972): 13–24; idem, "Bureaucratic Theory and the Choice of Central Bank Goals," *Journal of Money, Credit, and Banking* 5 (May 1973): 637–55; and William P. Yohe, "Federal Reserve Behavior," in *Crisis in Economic Theory*, ed. William J. Frazer (Gainesville: University of Florida Press, 1974), pp. 189–200.
24. Though neglected in the literature on the political business cycle, a seminal treatment of how politics is responsible for business cycles is contained in Ludwig von Mises, *The Theory of Money and Credit* (original ed. 1912; London: Jonathan Cape, 1934).
25. See Benjamin Klein, "The Competitive Supply of Money," *Journal of Money, Credit, and Banking* 6 (November 1974): 423–53; and Lawrence H. White, "Free Banking in Scotland Prior to 1845," manuscript, University of California at Los Angeles, 1979.
26. Murray N. Rothbard, *Power and Market*, 2d ed. (Kansas City: Sheed Andrews and McMeel, 1977). On proprietorship as a quite different basis for organizing a community, see Spencer H. MacCallum, *The Art of Community* (Menlo Park, Calif.: Institute for Humane Studies, 1970).
27. This nonneutral character is what Gottfried Haberler referred to as the monetary overinvestment theory of the business cycle, as contrasted with the purely aggregative, monetary theory of the cycle. See Gottfried Haberler, *Prosperity and Depression*, 3d ed. (London: George Allen and Unwin, 1958). A different comparison of these perspectives can be found in Robert E. Lucas, Jr., "An Equilibrium Model of the Business Cycle," *Journal of Political Economy* 83 (December 1975): 1113–44. The reasons for the nonneutral character of monetary disturbance are summarized in Friedrich A. Lutz, "On Neutral Money," in *Roads to Freedom*, ed. Erich Streissler, et al. (London: Routledge and Kegan Paul, 1969), pp. 105–16.
28. For an empirical examination of price changes under inflation, showing not only that some prices will increase more rapidly than others, but also that these price changes will be highly skewed rather than symmetrically distributed, see Daniel R. Vining and Thomas C. Elwertowski, "The Relationship between Relative Prices and the General Price Level," *American Economic Review* 66 (September 1976): 699–708.
29. While the nonneutral character of monetary disturbance has been discussed by many authors, the seminal statement of interest for the topic of this study is contained in Friedrich A. Hayek, *Prices and Production*, 2d ed. (London: Routledge and Kegan Paul, 1935); and idem, *Monetary Theory and the Trade Cycle* (New York: Harcourt Brace, 1932). Hayek's work on economic coordination is portrayed in Gerald P. O'Driscoll, Jr., *Economics as a Coordination Problem: The Contributions of Friedrich A. Hayek* (Kansas City: Sheed Andrews and McMeel, 1977).

30. For another exposition of the material covered in this section, though developed for a somewhat different purpose, see Robert D. Tollison and Richard E. Wagner, *Balanced Budgets, Fiscal Responsibility, and the Constitution* (San Francisco: Cato Institute, 1980).
31. This confounding of borrowing and money creation is described in James M. Buchanan and Richard E. Wagner, *Public Debt in a Democratic Society* (Washington: American Enterprise Institute, 1967)
32. For an analysis of crowding out, see Keith M. Carlson and Roger W. Spencer, "Crowding Out and its Critics," *Federal Reserve Bank of St. Louis, Review* 57 (December 1975): 2–17.
33. For discussions of the connection between rising interest rates and monetary expansion, see Raymond E. Lombra and Raymond G. Torto, "The Strategy of Monetary Policy," *Federal Reserve Bank of Richmond, Monthly Review* 61 (September–October 1975): 3–14; and Susan R. Roesch, "The Monetary-Fiscal Mix through Mid-1976," *Federal Reserve Bank of St. Louis, Review* 57 (August 1975): 2–7.
34. The increase in prices due to the monetary expansion will also lead to an upward shift in rates of interest. Figure 3 does not account for this inflation premium, but the analysis could easily be modified to do so. The result would be a more complicated narrative, with no change in the essential point of the analysis. This point is discussed in Gerald P. O'Driscoll, Jr., "Rational Expectations, Politics, and Stagflation," in *Time, Uncertainty, and Disequilibrium,* ed. Mario J. Rizzo (Lexington, Mass.: D. C. Heath, 1979), pp. 153–76.
35. A. W. Phillips, "The Relation Between Unemployment and the Rate of Change in Money Wage Rates in the United Kingdom, 1869–1957," *Economica* 25 (November 1958): 283–99. A survey of different perspectives toward the Phillips curve is presented in Thomas M. Humphrey, "Changing Views of the Phillips Curve," *Federal Reserve Bank of Richmond, Monthly Review* 59 (July 1973): 2–13.
36. This theme is developed in Paul A. Samuelson and Robert M. Solow, "Analytical Aspects of Anti-Inflation Policy," *American Economic Review,* Proceedings 50 (May 1960): 177–94.
37. For an application of this line of analysis to the Great Depression, see Murray N. Rothbard, *America's Great Depression,* 3d ed. (Kansas City: Sheed and Ward, 1975).
38. On stagflation, see Gerald P. O'Driscoll, Jr. and Sudha R. Shenoy, "Inflation, Recession, and Stagflation," in *Foundations of Modern Austrian Economics,* ed. Edwin G. Dolan (Kansas City: Sheed and Ward, 1976), pp. 185–211.
39. Hot-air economics is compared with the alternative discussed here in Wagner, "Economic Manipulation for Political Profit."
40. For a related argument, though from a somewhat different perspective, that an economy, while normally stable, can get out of control, see Axel Leijonhufvud, "Effective Demand Failures."
41. See, for instance, Bennett T. McCallum, "The Political Business Cycle: An Empirical Test," *Southern Economic Journal* 44 (January 1978): 504–15. For careful examinations of the rational-expectations framework from which such reasoning as this stems, see Gerald P. O'Driscoll, Jr., "Rational Expectations and Entrepreneurship," manuscript, New York University, 1978; and idem, "Rational Expectations, Politics, and Stagflation."
42. This is pointed out in, for instance, Robert J. Barro, "Rational Expectations and

the Role of Monetary Policy,'' *Journal of Monetary Economics* 2 (January 1976): 1–32; and Robert E. Lucas, Jr., ''Econometric Policy Evaluation: A Critique,'' in *The Phillips Curve and Labor Markets,* ed. Karl Brunner and Allan H. Meltzer (Amsterdam: North-Holland, 1976), pp. 19–46.

43. A similar conclusion, though in illustration of a somewhat different point, is presented in Andrew Schotter and Gerald P. O'Driscoll, Jr., ''Why Rational Expectations May Be Impossible: An Application of Newcomb's Paradox,'' manuscript, New York University, 1978.

44. For a brief survey of some of the main conceptual difficulties with macroeconomics, see Ludwig M. Lachmann, *Macro-economic Thinking and the Market Economy* (London: Institute of Economic Affairs, 1973).

45. W. H. Hutt, ''The Concept of Waste,'' *South African Journal of Economics* 11 (March 1943): 1–10.

46. For a careful treatment of this topic, see G. Warren Nutter, ''On Economic Size and Growth,'' *Journal of Law and Economics* 9 (October 1966): 163–88.

47. See, for instance, Frank H. Knight, ''What is 'Truth' in Economics?'' in idem, *On the History and Method of Economics* (Chicago: University of Chicago Press, 1956), p. 164.

48. For one consideration of the types of steps that could be taken, see Friedrich A. Hayek, *Denationalization of Money* (London: Institute of Economic Affairs, 1976).

5 Empirical Public Choice

The Political Economy of Political Philosophy: Discretionary Spending by Senators on Staff

James T. Bennett and Thomas J. DiLorenzo

With respect to expenditures from the public purse, politicians play two roles: first, in conjunction with other members of the legislative body, they vote on a wide variety of appropriation measures and, second, in order to carry out their official duties, each politican is allocated a fixed amount of public funds for specific purposes to spend at his own discretion. Although considerable attention has been given to the maximizing behavior of politicians in the voting process in the economics literature, no one, to our knowledge, has investigated the expenditures of public funds under the direct control of politicians.[1] This paper attempts to alleviate this deficiency by investigating the expenditures for staff by U.S. senators in fiscal year 1978. In section 1, a brief discussion is given of senate staff spending and budgets; the hypotheses are developed in section 2 and are tested in section 3. The last section contains the conclusions and policy implications.

1. Budgets and Spending for Senate Staffs

In the U.S. Congress, a number of official allowances are provided to each member. Funds are allocated for hiring employees, travel, telephone expenses, stationery, and so forth. The analysis herein is concerned with the budgets and expenditures for staff, because the allocation for this purpose (1) is largest; (2) cannot be transferred to other uses or legally taken as income (a strict rule against nepotism prohibits hiring anyone with a familial relationship closer than second cousin); and, (3) cannot be carried over from one fiscal year to another. Also, detailed data are available.[2] Each senator's authorized allowance for administrative, legislative, and clerical assistance in fiscal year 1978 was determined by state population, as shown in table 1. In addition, each senator was also permitted to spend $149,286 for legislative assistance on committees. Although the levels of authorized staff allowances vary widely with population, it is apparent that, overall, economies of scale are believed to exist with respect to staff allowances. Salary restrictions are the only constraints placed on the senator's discretionary allocation of the staff budget: one employee's annual salary cannot exceed $49,941; eight others cannot exceed $47,500; and all other employees cannot exceed $30,807 per year. Staff are employed for a variety of purposes: to assist with legislative matters

First published in *American Economic Review* 72, no. 5 (December 1982): 1153–61.

TABLE 1. Authorized Staff Allowances for U.S. Senators, Fiscal Year 1978

Population (in millions)	Allowance	Population (in millions)	Allowance
<2	$481,331	≥10 < 11	$716,537
≥2 < 3	495,293	≥11 < 12	757,349
≥3 < 4	528,995	≥12 < 13	788,495
≥4 < 5	572,263	≥13 < 15	828,495
≥5 < 7	607,705	≥15 < 17	867,971
≥7 < 8	644,937	≥17 < 19	907,709
≥8 < 9	664,627	≥19 < 21	937,423
≥9 < 10	685,391	≥21	967,137

Source: U.S. Congress, *Congressional Handbook* (Washington, D.C.: U.S. Government Printing Office, 1977), p. 22.

(legislative aides), to respond to constituents' complaints and inquiries (case workers), to deal with the media (press aides), to operate area offices in the home state (state assistants), and to supervise the coterie of clerks, interns, typists, secretaries, and assorted factotums associated with a senatorial office. In general, the staff serves as the politician's "right hand" in performing the duties of public office.[3] By serving constituents and dealing effectively with the media, staff members can significantly influence the likelihood of their senator's reelection.

There is a broad consensus that the utility of an incumbent politician is enhanced by reelection (see, for example, Fiorina and Noll 1978). Given that staff services can contribute to the senator's standing with constituents which can influence voters, economic logic (and common sense) dictates that virtually all of the allocation for staff would be spent by every senator. This is not the case, however. In table 2, the ten senators who returned the largest percentages of their staff allocations are compared to the ten with the smallest percentages. For each senator, political party is reported along with three measures of the "conservativeness" of political philosophy: the Americans for Democratic Action (ADA), the American Conservative Union (ACU), and the AFL-CIO labor union scorecards which tally for each senator the percentage of "correct" votes.

Measures of political philosophy are included in table 2 because the difference in philosophy between individuals in either of the two spending extremes is striking. On the average, the senators who returned the highest percentage of their staff budgets are significantly more conservative than the most "profligate" politicians, regardless of the indicator of political philosophy.[4] Without exception, the top ten spenders are Democrats, but only four of the most frugal belong to that party. Each group differs considerably from the mean percentage returned by all 96 senators, 15.1 percent.[5]

From an economic perspective, the wide variation in the proportion of staff budget returned to the Treasury among senators is consistent with utility-

TABLE 2. The Ten Senators with the Smallest and the Largest Percentages of Unspent Staff Budgets Returned to the Treasury in Fiscal Year 1978 with Party Affiliation, Home State, and Three Measures of Conservative Ranking

Smallest Proportion Returned					Largest Proportion Returned				
		Conservative Ranking					Conservative Ranking		
Senator (party, state)	Percentage Returned	ADA	AFL-CIO	ACU	Senator (party, state)	Percentage Returned	ADA	AFL-CIO	ACU
Anderson (D, MN)	0.0	65	13	0	Scott (R, VA)	62.2	90	84	97
Clark (D, IA)	0.0	10	12	3	Zorinsky (D, NE)	53.1	75	72	73
Gravel (D, AK)	0.0	30	19	10	Pearson (R, KS)	50.2	70	61	14
Riegle (D, MI)	0.2	15	8	5	Burdick (D, ND)	42.5	45	16	24
Hart (D, CO)	0.2	35	20	5	Byrd (I, VA)	41.4	90	88	92
Haskell (D, CO)	1.4	50	24	8	Stafford (R, VT)	40.0	45	30	17
Melcher (D, MT)	1.8	55	26	24	Young (R, ND)	36.7	95	77	72
Stone (D, FL)	2.5	75	49	38	Chafee (R, RI)	32.2	45	46	22
Durkin (D, NH)	3.2	35	9	13	Randolph (D, WV)	29.8	70	25	32
Culver (D, IA)	3.8	15	11	3	Stennis (D, MS)	29.6	90	78	59
Mean	1.3	38.5	19.1	10.9	Mean	41.8	71.5	57.7	50.2
Standard deviation	1.45	22.24	12.22	11.70	Standard deviation	10.69	20.28	26.50	32.03

Source: U.S. Congress. Senate. *Report of the Secretary of the Senate*, 1978a, 1978b.

maximizing behavior only if utility, *ceteris paribus,* is enhanced by frugality with public funds, i.e., some senators must derive satisfaction from returning funds to the public purse. In general parlance, politicians who oppose "excessive" government spending are considered conservatives. Thus, an interesting hypothesis is whether a senator who is viewed as conservative in making collective decisions is also conservative in the management of taxpayer's money under his direct control. Or, equivalently, *ceteris paribus,* a conservative who practices what he preaches publicly should be parsimonious and should return a greater proportion of staff allocation unspent. In short, are conservatives fiscally conservative?

2. Determinants of Spending on Staff

Although indicative, the information shown in table 2 on staff expenditures does not apply to all senators, but only to those in the highest and lowest extremes. Further, factors other than political philosophy influence the proportion of budget spent on staff, and these factors must also be taken into account. These include the socioeconomic characteristics of the senator's constituents, the characteristics of the senator himself, and various dimensions of the political market served by the senator.

Since the total amount of staff appropriations available to each senator depends upon the population of the senator's home state, the variable of interest is the proportion of staff budget returned to the Treasury, R/B, where R = unused staff allowance, and B = staff budget. The model estimated by ordinary least squares to test the hypothesis that conservatives are fiscally conservative with regard to staff spending is shown in equation (1).

$$(R/B)_i = \alpha_0 + \sum_{j=1}^{5} \beta_j C_{ij} + \sum_{j=1}^{12} \gamma_j S_{ij} + \sum_{j=1}^{3} \delta_j P_{ij} + e_i \qquad (1)$$

where

C_{ij} = vector of characteristics of senator i;
S_{ij} = vector of socioeconomic variables pertaining to the senator's constituency;
P_{ij} = vector of variables controlling for various dimensions of the senator's political market; and
e_i = random error term.

The independent variables are defined in table 3. To determine whether the proportion of staff funds unexpended is related to a senator's conservative or liberal leanings in making collective decisions, an indicator of each senator's political philosophy is required. Four are considered in this study: the Americans for Democratic Action (ADA), the American Conservative Union

TABLE 3. Factors Determining Proportion of Staff Budget Unused

Variable	Expected Sign	Definition
ADA	+	Americans for Democratic Actions' measure of conservatism
AFL-CIO	+	AFL-CIO's conservatism measure
ACU	+	American Conservative Union's conservatism measure
PARTY	+	Dummy variable for political party = 1 if Republican, 0 if Democrat
TEN	+	Number of years in office
REELECT	−	Dummy variable = 1 if senator faced reelection in 1978, 0 otherwise
COM	−	Number of committee memberships
CHAIR	?	Number of committees chaired
AREA	−	Square miles in the senator's state
DIST	−	Distance from Washington, D.C. (miles to the state capitol)
POPCH	?	Percentage population change
URBAN	−	Percent urban population
NONW	−	Percent nonwhite population
FAM	−	Number of families
HSGRAD	−	Percentage of high school graduates
YCAP	−	Income per capita
POOR	−	Percentage of families living in poverty
VET	−	Number of veterans
UNEMP	−	Unemployment rate
OVER65	−	Percentage of population over 65 years of age
W	?	Dummy variable = 1 if western state, 0 otherwise
S	?	Dummy variable = 1 if southern state, 0 otherwise
NC	?	Dummy variable = 1 if north central state, 0 otherwise
C		Constant

(ACU), and the AFL-CIO labor union scorecards which tally for each senator the percent of "correct" votes in the view of each organization, and political party. Political party is a dummy variable which takes the value of one for a Republican senator and zero for a Democrat.[6] The ACU index rates "ultraconservatives," e.g., Helms and Laxalt, at 100 and "ultraliberals," e.g., Inouye and Case at 0. The ADA and AFL-CIO ratings, as might be anticipated, rank liberals at 100 and conservatives at 0. To make these three rankings consistent measures of conservatism, the ADA and the AFL-CIO ratings were subtracted from 100.[7] It is interesting that, with the exception of political party, all four measures of conservatism are highly related, as shown by the matrix of simple pairwise correlation coefficients in table 4. Thus, even

TABLE 4. Simple Correlation Coefficients among Four Measures of Political Conservatism

Rating	ACU	ADA	AFL-CIO	Party
ACU	1.0	0.878	0.908	0.590
ADA	—	1.0	0.880	0.508
AFL-CIO	—	—	1.0	0.634
Party	—	—	—	1.0

among these diverse organizations, there appears to be a general consensus regarding which senators are liberals and which are conservatives.

A priori, it is expected that the larger the number of committees on which a senator serves (COM), the smaller the percentage of staff budget that is returned to the Treasury. Different committees deal with different types of legislation which should require more assistance and expertise from legislative specialists. With regard to the number of committee chairmanships, (CHAIR) two forces are at work simultaneously.[8] A committee chairman in the Senate wields enormous power in directing (or obstructing) the course of large numbers of bills submitted to the committee for consideration. Such responsibilities might be expected to require substantial staff resources which could create a drain on the chairman's staff budget. However, some committees and many investigative subcommittees have permanent staffs, e.g., the Joint Economic Committee and the Majority Policy Committee, which a shrewd chairman might be able to, at least partially, commandeer for his own purposes. Thus, it is not clear that the number of committee chairmanships will either increase or decrease the percentage of staff budget returned.

The anticipated sign of the committee chairmanship variable is further complicated by the fact that the tenure of senators may play an important role independent of whether a given senator has acquired sufficient tenure to chair a committee. But, since committee chairmanships are assigned almost exclusively on the basis of tenure, the years ot tenure (TEN) and the number of committee chairmanships are interrelated. (The simple correlation coefficient between TEN and CHAIR is .572.) Senators who have enjoyed a long tenure in office are better known to their constituents than freshman senators, and in some cases, have become almost political institutions in themselves. Therefore, for such senators, less staff effort should be required for the principal objective of most staff activity: the reelection of the senator. Moreover, senators with many years in office have acquired clout in dealing with the bureaucracy and their staffs have gained valuable experience in resolving the problems of constituents. Other things equal, a staff member in the office of a senator with long tenure should be more effective than in the office of a junior senator. An economic interpretation of this is that "older" incumbents have already invested in the production of "political information"—information regarding what benefits they have bestowed upon their constituents. Competing political entrepreneurs or younger incumbents who may have yet to prove how productive they are require more staff effort to convey information regarding the quality of their (political) product. Thus, just as older, established firms in an industry (e.g., Holiday Inn) have an advertising advantage over newer firms (e.g., Travelodge) due to their past service record, older incumbents have an advantage over younger ones in the form of a higher level of "output" per staff member.

The binary variable REELECT, which takes the value 1 if the senator's seat was contested in the election of 1978, is included to determine if different staff spending behavior occurs among senators who stood for reelection in

1978. Political expedience would dictate that the allocated staff budget could provide useful resources for the campaign.

The volume of constituent services may also be affected by the number of families to be served, whether the state is rapidly growing in population, the degree to which the state is urbanized, the level of education, and the income levels of constituents. A concentration of retired and elderly individuals may create demands from constituents to resolve disputes arising from such problems as Social Security payments, veteran's benefits, and Medicare claims. A disproportionate number of poverty program recipients could increase the need for staff services to untangle the red tape associated with welfare and unemployment benefits. As shown in table 3, ten variables appear in the model (POPCH through OVER65) to capture demographic and socioeconomic factors that may influence the spending for staff services.

The physical characteristics of the senator's state, i.e., his political "marketplace," also influence the requirements for staff, for offices are maintained in the home state to provide direct contact with constituents. As state area increases, more offices and staff should be required to provide convenient access and effective service. Distance from Washington, D.C., to the state capitol is also included in the model. For senators far removed from their constituents, staff provide a substitute "presence" for the senator; a senator whose state is very close to the nation's capital may supplement state office staffs with personnel from the office at the Capitol. Geography and topography also play a role in serving constituents. For example, the distribution of population is important. A large state may have population clustered in a small number of urban centers (e.g., Nevada), whereas the distribution of population may be far more dispersed in others. A mountainous state (e.g., Colorado) may have a number of population centers, but these may not be easily accessible from a central location. Moreover, a given senator's supporters may reside predominately in one section of the state and political prudence might dictate that state offices would be most advantageously deployed in only certain areas. These factors are difficult to quantify, but regional variables are a reasonable way to capture some of the effects, for they tend to occur on a regional basis. Mountainous states are located primarily in the West, as are states with populations mostly clustered in a small number of urban centers. States which, in 1978, had one senator rated as a liberal and the other as a conservative are also regionally concentrated in the West and South: Alabama, Alaska, Arizona, California, Idaho, Kansas, North Carolina, Oklahoma, and Texas. In such states, there is a greater likelihood that political support is concentrated in certain geographic areas than in states where both senators share the same political philosophy. The coefficients of the three regional dummy variables which appear in the model measure the difference between the average percentage of unspent staff funds for senators in each region relative to the average returned by senators in the Northeast, the omitted region.

The expected signs of the factors influencing the proportion of the staff budget returned unspent to the U.S. Treasury are summarized in table 3. In some cases, the signs are indeterminate a priori because diverse and offsetting influences come into play. Our principal concern is the ideology variables and, because other factors may also influence decisions regarding staff expenditures, this analysis is suggestive rather than exhaustive.[9]

3. Empirical Findings

The empirical results are reported in table 5, where the estimated coefficients, their associated t-statistics (in parentheses), the coefficient of determination, R^2, and the F-statistic are displayed for each of the regressions which employs a different measure of conservatism to estimate equation (1). Overall, the empirical results for the four regressions are quite similar, which is not surprising given that the four measures of conservatism are interrelated. The independent variables explain about half of the variation in the proportion of staff allocation returned to the Treasury by individual senators. The F-statistics indicate that the predictive power of the equations is significantly different from zero at better than the 99.9 percent level of confidence. The results generally confirm the hypothesis that conservatives return a larger percentage of staff budget than liberals. Each one-point increase in the index of conservatism increases the percentage of staff budget returned to the Treasury by .166 to .219, depending upon the index of conservatism employed. The regression which contains PARTY as the measure of conservatism indicates that Republican senators, on average, returned 9.6 percent more of their staff budgets than did Democrats, all other things equal.

Apparently, there is no significant difference in the percentage of staff budget returned by senators whose seats were contested in 1978 and those whose seats were not. One interpretation of this finding is that incumbents are hesitant to increase staff spending from public funds when they campaign for reelection because their opponent may claim foul play or use evidence of increased staff on the public payroll during an election year as a campaign issue. Alternatively, campaign contributions for incumbent senators may provide adequate resources to hire staff for the campaign, particularly when the role of volunteers is taken into account.

As expected, committee service produces a drain on staff resources, for the estimated coefficients indicate that for each additional committee on which a senator serves, about 4.6 to 5.7 percent less of the staff allotment is returned, depending upon the measure of conservatism used. Committee chairmen appear to be able to divert substantial resources to their own uses, for chairmen return between 6.9 and 10.9 percent more of their staff budgets, *ceteris paribus,* than do senators who do not serve as committee chairmen. Although statistically insignificant, the coefficients for the tenure variable, TEN, are positive, which indicates that with increased length of service, staff effectiveness may increase so that the legislator can conserve on public funds for staff.

TABLE 5. Estimated Coefficients of Equation (1): Percentage of Staff Budget Unused by Individual Senators in Fiscal Year 1978

Independent Variable	Measure of Conservatism							
	ADA		AFL-CIO		ACU		Party	
Constant	−4.686	(−0.132)	17.558	(0.511)	1.726	(0.049)	22.189	(0.619)
Conservatism measure	0.219*	(4.192)	0.200*	(4.545)	0.166*	(4.135)	9.550*	(3.560)
TEN	0.196	(1.178)	0.194	(1.188)	0.256	(1.550)	0.101	(0.567)
REELECT	0.187	(0.075)	1.032	(0.430)	0.380	(0.153)	1.098	(0.436)
COM	−5.419**	(−3.295)	−5.668*	(−3.505)	−4.567**	(−2.739)	−5.621**	(−3.328)
CHAIR	8.258***	(2.557)	9.191**	(2.853)	6.910***	(2.186)	10.853**	(2.964)
POPCH	0.386	(0.221)	0.577	(0.338)	0.291	(0.167)	1.459	(0.812)
AREA	−0.052***	(−2.486)	−0.049***	(−2.385)	−0.048***	(−2.305)	−0.039****	(−1.826)
URBAN	−0.109****	(−1.698)	−0.105	(−1.653)	−0.110****	(−1.710)	−0.107	(−1.617)
NONW	−0.190	(−0.722)	−0.260	(−0.999)	−0.152	(−0.580)	0.083	(−0.306)
FAM	−0.005	(−0.730)	−0.001	(−0.907)	−0.001	(−0.929)	−0.001	(−1.296)
HSGRAD	−0.108	(−0.303)	−0.379	(−1.074)	−0.246	(−0.689)	−0.197	(−0.540)
YCAP	0.006***	(2.345)	0.007**	(2.655)	0.006***	(2.352)	0.006****	(2.170)
POOR	0.124	(0.210)	0.035	(0.060)	0.230	(0.387)	0.223	(0.366)
VET	0.749	(0.548)	0.185	(0.138)	0.826	(0.602)	−0.802	(−0.559)
UNEMPL	−0.297	(−0.436)	−0.656	(−0.984)	−0.548	(−0.807)	−0.655	(−0.941)
DIST	−0.001	(−0.367)	−0.001	(−0.487)	−0.0001	(−0.005)	−0.002	(−0.828)
OVER65	−0.118	(−0.164)	0.315	(0.447)	0.161	(0.225)	0.611	(0.816)
W	−5.401	(−0.923)	−4.482	(−0.791)	−6.397	(−1.075)	−1.564	(−0.269)
S	−1.973	(−0.395)	−4.056	(−0.816)	−4.024	(−0.793)	−0.968	(−0.189)
NC	−2.862	(−0.699)	−5.202	(−1.269)	−3.729	(−0.903)	−2.554	(−0.608)
R^2	0.481		0.498		0.479		0.452	
$F_{(19,71)}$	3.479		3.720		3.443		3.097	

*, **, ***, **** denote significance at the 0.001, 0.01, 0.05, 0.10 level, respectively.

With respect to the socioeconomic variables, POP, POOR, VET, and YCAP were all found to be positive, but only YCAP was statistically significant. The remaining eight socioeconomic variables exerted a negative influence on the percentage of staff budget unused by senators, but only AREA and URBAN were significant. The coefficients for the regional dummy variables were all found to be negative but insignificant.

These empirical results generally confirm the main hypothesis regarding the politician's utility-maximizing behavior: Conservative politicians apparently derive greater utility from returning funds unspent to the Treasury than do liberals.

5. Summary and Conclusions

A legislator plays two roles in making decisions about expenditures from the public purse: First, as a participant with other legislators in voting on appropriation bills, and, second, as an individual whose decisions are decisive in spending public monies allocated for specific purposes for his own use. This essay investigates the economic behavior of individual senators in the spending of staff budgets in order to determine if a relationship exists between a politician's political philosophy in collective decision making and his expenditures for staff.

Staff services and the level of funds returned to the Treasury were viewed as arguments in the politician's utility function. It was hypothesized that, other things held constant, one would expect conservatives who publicly eschew "excessive" government spending to gain greater utility by returning larger proportions of their staff allocations than "free-spending" liberals. An empirical model was developed to test the hypothesis that conservatives, *ceteris paribus,* do in fact return a larger proportion of their staff allocations unspent than do liberals. Four measures of conservatism were employed, and the empirical results were generally invariant to the indicator of political philosophy: Senators who are conservative in making collective decisions are also fiscally conservative in spending public funds under their direct control. In contrast to the well-worn dictum of Governor George Wallace, there is, indeed, more than "a dime's worth of difference" between liberals and conservatives. The average senator receives an annual staff budget of slightly less than three-quarters of a million dollars, $712,670. Based on the ADA estimates shown in table 5, an ultraconservative (ADA = 100) would spend about $156,787, or 22 percent less on staff than an ultraliberal (ADA = 0).

This is the first study of which we are aware that addresses the economic behavior of politicians in spending public funds under their direct control. Additional research in a number of related areas would yield fruitful results in terms of a better understanding of the behavior of politicians and political institutions. For example, it would be interesting to determine whether different behavior is observed when public money provided to politicians is more "substitutable" with the politician's income, e.g., travel funds. A second interesting issue is whether politicians at state and local levels of government follow the same patterns of behavior as those at the national level. Third, an improved specification of the role of political staffs is needed in terms of services to constituents. Research on these issues, among many others, would improve our understanding of the political economy.

NOTES

The authors gratefully acknowledge research support provided by the Sarah Scaife Foundation and the Earhart Foundation.

1. See, for example, empirical work by Danielson and Rubin (1977) and by Silberman and Durden (1976). Examples of theoretical contributions are those made by Buchanan and Tullock (1962).
2. The Secretary of the Senate is required by Section 105 of Public Law 88–454, approved August 20, 1964, to report periodically a full statement of receipts and expenditures of the Senate. The reports, issued semiannually, list every voucher paid, even for expenditures less than one dollar. The salary paid to each staff member is also given by name.
3. At times, congressmen may place individuals on the public payroll to provide services of a more "private" sort, e.g., the widely heralded working relationship between Elizabeth Ray and Congressman Wayne Hayes.
4. A t-test for the difference between the means of each of the three measures of conservatism indicated at the 0.0005 level of significance or better that the ten who spent the lowest proportion of their budget allocation were more conservative.
5. Four senators were omitted from the analysis because they served only partial terms during fiscal year 1978; Humphrey (Minnesota), McLellan (Arkansas), Metcalf (Montana), and Allen (Alabama). The sample size is 96.
6. Senator Harry Byrd of Virginia labels himself an independent, but was considered a Republican, because he dropped his affiliation with the Democratic party. In a comment on Silberman and Durden 1976, Kau and Rubin (1978) employ both party and ADA rankings as a "measure of ideology."
7. Actually, the AFL-CIO reports the number of "right" (R) and the number of "wrong" (W) votes by each senator. An index was generated by calculating the proportion of "right votes," i.e., $R/(R + W) * 100$.
8. Only one senator, Claiborne Pell (Rhode Island), served as the chairman of more than one committee. He chaired the Joint Committee on Printing and the Committee on Rules and Administration.
9. The empirical results reported in table 5 are representative of a wide range of models estimated using a variety of functional forms and incorporating various additional regressors. For example, the percentage of the popular vote received by the senator in the most recent election was included to test whether those senators who won by a small margin spent more on staff; an attempt was also made to capture the ideology of voters as measured by the presidential votes in each state. The findings, in terms of the magnitudes and significance levels of coefficients, were basically invariant to such permutations and combinations. There is, of course, no measure of either the quality or quantity of staff services. Moreover, in state offices, salaries may reflect the cost of living which also varies from region to region, and even among cities in the same state.

REFERENCES

Buchanan, James M., and Tullock, Gordon. *The Calculus of Consent.* Ann Arbor: University of Michigan Press, 1962.

Danielson, Albert L., and Rubin, Paul H. "An Empirical Investigation of Voting on Energy Issues." *Public Choice* 31 (Fall 1977): 121–28.

Fiorina, Morris P., and Noll, Roger G. "Voters, Bureaucrats and Legislators: A Rational Choice Perspective on the Growth of Bureaucracy." *Journal of Public Economics* 9 (April, 1978): 239–54.

Kau, James B., and Rubin, Paul H. "Voting on Minimum Wages: A Time-Series Analysis." *Journal of Political Economy* 86 (April, 1978): 337–42.

Silberman, Jonathan I., and Durden, Gary C. "Determining Legislative Preferences on the Minimum Wage: An Economic Approach." *Journal of Political Economy* 84 (April, 1976): 317–29.

Tullock, Gordon. *Toward a Mathematics of Politics.* Ann Arbor: University of Michigan Press, 1967.

U.S. Congress. Senate. *Report of the Secretary of the Senate from October 1, 1977, to March 31, 1978.* S. Doc. 92–102, 95th Cong., 2d sess., 1978*a*.

———. *Report of the Secretary of the Senate from April 1, 1978, to September 30, 1978.* S. Doc. 95–131, 95th Cong., 2d sess., 1978*b*.

Regulators as an Interest Group

W. Mark Crain and Robert E. McCormick

Modeling the regulatory process as a scheme for wealth redistribution is no longer a novelty. Indeed, the view that the basic stake involved is a transfer of wealth has been central to recasting the paradigm of economic regulation. This article falls within that analytical tilt, but with three extensions that we shall summarize at the outset.

We formulate a model of political decision making in the context of price-entry regulation which explicitly treats regulators as one of the interest groups seeking to capture wealth transfers.[1] This treatment has only been implicitly integrated (if at all) into previous formulations, most of which stress the rivalry among other interest groups in the polity (for example, producers versus consumers) in vying to achieve benefits or to mitigate losses. Regulators, politicians, and producers have thus been depicted as bedfellows more than adversaries, squaring off against consumers or other producers in the political-regulatory process.[2] Regulators in our model aspire to get a piece of the action beyond the simple election or reelection aims that have motivated the decision-making problem as previously specified (for example, Peltzman, 1976). The incorporation of an underlying wealth-maximizing goal to regulators amounts to adding a common denominator to the interest group theory of regulation and to emphasize that regulators—qua interest group—constitute an important third party that must be reckoned with if we are to accurately portray the gains and losses of the political redistribution of wealth. Stated differently, from the standpoint of the n-1 nonregulator interest groups who find it economical to vie for transfers through the regulatory process, the total wealth which is redistributed may not be a zero sum game. Regulators in our model constitute an interest group, not differently motivated than other interest groups, who seek to achieve positive payoffs from the rechanneling of wealth through the political-regulatory process.

The second purpose of the article is to expand on the generality of a first principle suggested by Stigler (1971) and formally reiterated by Peltzman (1976): that the "political equilibrium will not result in the monopoly or cartel maximizing price" (p. 223). Our model suggests that this principle is not only independent of campaign or organizational costs (Peltzman's message), but it also holds when extraelection means such as bribes and conflicts of interest are influential factors in regulator decision making.

The third objective is to compare the impact of different institutional settings on a variety of regulatory outcomes. For example, in light of our analytical model we reexamine a paradox previously posed by Stigler (1972, 161):

> The simultaneous granting of regulatory benefits and levying of taxes poses an obvious question: if the industry has sufficient political power to obtain a state-supported cartel, why cannot the industry avoid becoming the object of selective excise taxation?

Finally, we offer some empirical evidence on our extended version of the interest group approach to regulation, and we offer evidence that the organization form of regulatory commissions affects regulated rates of return and prices.

The Model

There are three homogeneous groups—producers, consumers, and regulators—seeking benefits and avoiding losses from regulation. The regulators or political decision makers provide these gains and losses by setting regulated prices and the amount of tax (if any), together with control over entry. Each of the individuals in these groups is assumed to be a wealth maximizer, and each seeks to use the political process to do so.

The Regulator's Goal: Majorities versus Taxes

The choice problem is formulated from the standpoint of the regulator, whose wealth depends upon election as well as extraelection payoffs. This regulator seeks to maximize

$$W = W(M, T), \tag{1}$$

where

W = regulator's wealth,
M = size of electoral majority, and
T = all costs, legal or illegal, *broadly defined* to include taxes, bribes, campaign contributions, and so forth which might be imposed on regulated industries.

The taxes argument is general and includes all costs stemming from government regulation including, for example, campaign contributions. It also includes taxes paid to government general funds, some of which may be captured by the regulator through his budget share. T may also represent bribes from producers which are directly pocketed by the regulator. The T argument is any cost paid by the regulated industry associated with political influence. In the cases that follow the exact types of cost included in the argument will be made explicit. W_M and W_T (throughout the article subscripts refer to partial derivatives) are both greater than zero.

How Majorities are Gained and Lost

M is a majority-generating function which depends upon three factors: consumer support, producer support, and the acceptance of bribes or illegal contributions. This function is specified as

$$M = M(P,R,T) \tag{2}$$

where P is the producer's regulated price and R is producer return, net of taxes. Lower prices mean greater consumer support in elections whereas higher returns translate into more electoral support from producers, so $M_P < 0$, $M_R > 0$, and we assume that the marginal rate of substitution is diminishing.

The sign of M_T is more complex since it depends on the exact type of tax. When a regulator accepts taxes in the form of *illegal* bribes or contributions, we assume that voters are alienated so that his probability of election is reduced or that his probability of being removed from office is increased, so $M_T < 0$. Of course, there may be other more costly risks through legal sanctions such as fines or jail terms. For our purposes it is sufficient to enter the negative effects of bribes through the wealth reduction associated with losing political office. The *acceptance* of a *legal* contribution does not change a politician's election prospect. When the T argument represents taxes paid into the general fund, two possibilities are plausible. If voters perceive that these taxes increase bureau size and salaries, then industry taxation is an opportunity cost to the general taxpayer, and $M_T < 0$. Alternatively, when regulators substitute industry taxes for personal taxes of voters, then the politician's election prospect is enhanced; here $M_T > 0$.

Legal and Illegal Taxation

The range of taxes and bribes is determined by the profit frontier in the individual industry. Thus the exogenous demand and cost conditions in the industry combined with the net returns to the producer group place a constraint on the range of potential taxes, which is expressed as

$$R = \pi - T. \tag{3}$$

The returns to the producers are the industry profits, π, less taxes, bribes, and contributions, T. This means that profit changes, holding producer returns constant, will have a positive effect on the potential tax base, while changes in producer returns, holding profits constant, will be negatively related to tax receipts.

The untaxed profit function is given by demand and costs,

$$\pi = \pi(P,C), \tag{4}$$

where C is operating cost (excluding all costs included in T). We make the standard assumption $\pi_P \leq 0$, $\pi_{PP} < 0$, and $\pi_C < 0$.

Discussion and Summary

The constraint imposed in (3) together with (4) has several implications. First, movements along any profit function due to price changes are trade-offs of producer for consumer support. These Peltzman-style price adjustments cause profits to change which then must be split between R, producer returns, and T, gains to the regulator. Second, at any chosen price there is a division of the profits between the industry, R, and the regulator, T. The regulator also faces a Niskanen-style trade-off between direct financial support for his bureau versus political support from producers.

We stress again that the similar treatment of bribes and taxes in this formulation is primarily to simplify the notation and manipulations. Bribes, taxes, and contributions could be entered as separate arguments into the wealth function without altering the major results. It is useful, however, to view contributions as a purely privatized tax system which may be levied on producers or consumers without the legal or statutory authority of the state. The only difference between taxes and bribes or contributions in our formulation is that since bribes and some contributions are illegal, an additional cost is imposed on the regulators' probability of acquiring or retaining his office.

The impact of an illegal inducement on the regulators' wealth is straightforward. In the case of a tax or special fee on producers, the link to regulator's wealth stems from the expansion of the regulatory agency.[3] However, the assumption in our model does not require budget-maximizing behavior but only that there are gains to the regulator/legislator from larger tax receipts. For example, apart from the familiar Niskanen-Tullock type arrangements, the link between tax receipts and regulator wealth might be thought of as providing the politician more autonomy (Landes and Posner 1975). Alternatively, larger agency budgets may offer expanded opportunities for hiring campaign workers or for paying off old election favors; for example, the patronage or spoils system argument developed in Stigler (1971) and Demsetz (1977).

Finally, we note that the distinction between conflicts of interest and taxes or bribes is simply that the interest conflicts or revolving doors are analogous to a profit-sharing arrangement between producers and the regulators and, as such, will not increase producer expenses.[4] Bribes or taxes, on the other hand, will reduce the aggregate level of producer returns, *ceteris paribus*. This in turn will reduce campaign support by the producers. The regulator thus faces a profit possibilities frontier for various industries, and his choice problem is one of trading off these profit possibilities between building a majority of electoral support versus direct pecuniary gains from taxes, bribes, campaign contributions, or conflicts of interest.

The regulator's indirect wealth function is formed in (5) by substituting equations (2)–(4) into equation (1).

$$W = W\{M[P,\pi(P,C)-T,T],T\} \tag{5}$$

The Regulator's Decision Variables and Choices

The decision maker maximizes W by controlling price and choosing a tax. The first order conditions for a wealth maximum with respect to P and T are

$$W_M(M_P+M_R\cdot\pi_P) = 0 \tag{6}$$

and

$$W_M(-M_R+M_T) + W_T = 0. \tag{7}$$

Equation (6) depicts changes in the regulator's wealth as he moves along the profit frontier by changing price, whereas equation (7) picks up the wealth effect of changing the tax for a particular point on the profit frontier (given a constant regulated price). In effect (7) measures the pure producer burden of a tax in the sense that increases in the gains to the regulator squash the producer returns function below the profit frontier at every price.

Comparative Regulator Behavior: Three Cases

Born to Run

For illustrative and comparative purposes, we first examine the outcome of this decision problem for the case where the regulator's only goal is election or reelection. This is the situation formally modeled by Peltzman (1976) and can be treated as a special case of our formulation. With the possibility of bribery, taxation, and conflicts of interest eliminated, all profits accrue to producers as returns. That is, assuming no taxes, (6) yields the solution

$$\pi_P = [W_M\cdot(-M_P)]/[W_M\cdot(M_R)], \tag{8}$$

which is identical to the result obtained by Peltzman (1976) using similar assumptions and a slightly different formulation of the optimization problem. Since $(-M_P)$ and M_R are both positive, the important conclusion which emerges from the strict majority maximization objective is that $\pi > 0$; which means that the political equilibrium will not yield that price which maximizes producer returns which, in this initial case, are equal to profits. In Peltzman's words,

> even if a single economic interest gets all the benefits of regulation, these must be less than a perfect broker for the group would obtain. The best organized cartel will yield less to the membership if the government organizes it than if it were (could be) organized privately. This principle is independent of organization or campaign costs, but rests on the heed the political process must pay to marginal opposition. (Peltzman, 1976, p. 217)

In other words, pure producer-protection ($\pi_P = 0$) can only be predicted in the majority maximization case (equation 8) if there is no consumer opposition to price increases, which would require that $M_P = 0$.

If $W_M = 0$ and election/reelection is not valued by the regulator, the outcome is unpredictable, which reflects one limitation of the strict majority maximization approach. This drawback presents an obvious dilemma; as regulators become more removed from elective politics (for example, closer to the end of their careers as elected officials) do their choices vis-à-vis prices, taxes, and producer returns become systematically biased toward producer profit maximization?[5]

One advantage of the objective function postulated in (5) is that we can evaluate this critique of the strict majority maximization approach. To reiterate, the solution presented in (8) for majority maximization is only a special case that can be broadened to examine more general versions of the regulator's objective function. In the cases below we explore the limits to the generality of this first principle, posit several additional principles, and investigate how the various interest groups fare under different regulatory settings.

Beyond Majority Generation: Conflicts of Interest and Revolving Doors

We now consider the outcome of the regulator's choice problem when his decision is influenced by a conflict of interest in addition to an election aim. Specifically, we now postulate that the decision maker is a member of the regulated group and so his wealth depends directly upon π. In the simplest conflict of interest case, we assume that there are no costs stemming from government, no taxes, no bribes, nor any campaign contributions. This means that the regulator's general objective function (equation 1) reduces to $W = W(M,\pi)$. The regulator values larger majorities, and he is simultaneously a member (present or future) of the regulated producer group, but this membership imposes no cost on the producer group. The solution in this setting is

$$\pi_P = [W_M \cdot (-M_P)]/[W_m \cdot M_R + W_\pi], \tag{9}$$

where W_π is the extent of the conflict, as it is the regulator's pro rata share of producer group's returns. The sign of π_P in (9) obviously depends upon the values of W_M, $-M_P$, M_R, and M_π which are all positive.

The surprising result in (9) is that $\pi_P > 0$, or that profit-maximizing prices will not emerge even in the presence of conflicts of interest, or profit sharing between the producer group and the regulator. This means that even if the regulator has direct claim to a share of the profits of the producer group which he regulates, the price he selects in maximizing his wealth is not the price which would coincidentally maximize producer profit. It is worth emphasis that this result in (9) does *not* depend on the possible illegality of conflicts of interest. Even if it is not feasible to police laws against conflict of interest and revolving doors, π_P is predictably positive.

Comparing this result in (9) with the strict majority maximizing solution in (8), we see that (for given values of W_M, M_R and M_P) π_P will be smaller, regulated prices higher, and producer returns greater in the conflict of interest case than in the simple majority maximization case. In effect, the conflict of interest (or the potential for profit sharing) has raised the price of heeding consumer opposition.

Equation (9) offers a continuous characterization of the distance between the wealth-maximizing choice of the regulator and the top of the profit hill. This distance, for a given majority-generating function, depends upon the extent of the regulator's interest conflict or the discounted present value of his pro rata share of producer profit. While the regulator would be willing to trade off some degree of majority support or risk of defeat in exchange for his pro rata pecuniary share of the producer profit, the principle enumerated by Peltzman holds so long as election/reelection has a positive contribution to the regulator's wealth at the margin, that is, $W_M > 0$. Unlike the solution presented in (8), however, for the case of conflicts of interest if $W_M = 0$, the predictable solution (from equation 9) is that $\pi_P = 0$ or that producer returns are maximized when the regulator does not seek reelection. This suggests that "lame duck" regulators are more attractive targets for profit-sharing offers from producer groups.[6]

Given the existence of conflicts of interest, when concern for generating a majority of voter support becomes a less important objective with respect to the wealth of regulators, the more nearly regulated prices will approach profit-maximizing levels. The degree of concern for the support of an electoral majority is presumably established by numerous institutional factors; for example, the appointment of regulatory commissioners versus direct election by constituents, term lengths, mandatory limitations on succession rights, entry barriers in the competition to obtain regulatory offices, and simply approaching the end of a career in elective politics.[7]

Two additional insights are offered by the solution to the conflict of interest case presented in equation (9). First, regulators are more likely to establish profit sharing or conflict arrangements with those producer groups who can offer relatively more electoral support. This is because of the feedback effect of increased profits on regulator wealth through $W_M M_R$, that is, regulator wealth is not only increased through higher profits because of the sharing arrangement (W_π), but also because higher profits mean more electoral support from the cohorts in the producer group. While profit sharing unambiguously results in a reduction in majorities (relative to the no-conflict case, in equation 8), this reduction is dampened since more producer support will be forthcoming. The greater the incremental level of producer support, M_R, the smaller is the wealth loss through W_M for a given level of profit sharing. Stated in the reverse, a larger (absolute) share of producer returns would be required of less politically powerful producer groups (and hence they would be less likely to go along with the sharing arrangement) in order to compensate the regulator for his relatively greater losses in terms of electoral support. This means that for any given value of W_M, as the electoral strength of a producer group increases, the more attractive it becomes for a conflict of interest type involvement with regulators. Second, equation (9) suggests that the recent proposals to impose a longer time period between employment as a regulator and subsequent employment in the related industry (that is, the revolving door effect) have predictable implications. As W_π must be discounted further into the future its present value falls thus increasing π_P, which means that prices would tend away from their profit-maximizing levels toward the competitive level.

The Effect of Taxes, Contributions, and Bribes

We now examine the regulator's decision problem when his wealth may be enhanced indirectly through general taxation (and hence budgetary expansion) or directly through the collection of campaign contributions or bribes from producers in exchange for higher prices. To avoid unnecessary complications we do not permit any conflicts of interest. The combination of equations (6) and (7) again allows us to express the solution to the regulator's optimization problem as

$$\pi_P = [W_m \cdot (-M_P)]/(W_M \cdot M_T + W_T). \tag{10}$$

In the case of bribes especially, but also illegal campaign contributions, M_T may be larger than in the simple case of taxes. There may be cases, when all tax revenues accrue to the state treasury or when the campaign contributions are legal, that correspond to $M_T = 0$, or, perhaps, even when M_T is positive. In this second case some voters will *encourage* a regulated-monopoly solution with all rents taxed away, as this will reduce or substitute for their own tax liabilities. This result paves the way for a perverse regulatory outcome. Politically weak producer groups may be the target of regulation. By cartelizing the industry, price is raised above marginal cost and a regulatory rent is generated which subsequently can be taxed away to provide the state or the regulators with added revenue. This will be most perverse where the consumers of this good are also politically inept.[8]

Hence we expect not only small, powerful producer groups to be the subject of regulation but large, weak industries as well. If M_T is sufficiently negative, that is, if there is large voter opposition to bribes or contributions (or, more precisely, if $W_M \cdot M_T + W_T = 0$), then the solution to equation (10) is undefined, and we cannot predict what the regulator will do. As M_T becomes less negative, then π_P grows, which indicates that price is falling. This means that if voters are less alienated by overfed bureaucracies than they are by an equivalent level of industry expenses on bribes and campaign contributions, then we predict that industries which bribe or make campaign contributions will have higher product prices than industries that pay the same amounts in taxes, even if *all* these taxes support bureaucracy, other things the same. Of course, if voters are generally not concerned with the honesty of their elected officials, then they will see a dollar spent on bureaucracy in the same light as a dollar spent on bribes or on campaigning. In this event M_T is not influenced by the taxes-bribes issue, and equation (10) is the same for both cases. This last situation suggests that stricter laws or tighter enforcement of existing laws governing illegal activity among regulators will not necessarily affect their wealth decisions as might first be imagined, but that such laws would increase the attractiveness of levying general taxes.

More generally, this provides a clear rationale for why regulators who have the power to regulate prices and entry would also seek to acquire taxation authority over the regulated industry—the regulators could never be worse off and could obviously be made better off. Perhaps not so obvious, however, are the related inferences from our model concerning the incentive for merging or coordinating the price-setting authority with the power to set tax rates and the type of tax that will be employed. First, consider a situation where tax revenues are raised by other than lump-sum charges (per unit or ad valorem taxes for example). If taxes and prices are fixed independently, the gains to the regulator will be lower than when they are solved simultaneously, as in our formulation. This means that for any given tax, if the firm is allowed to optimize with respect to the price variable, this price will, in general, diverge from that price which the wealth-maximizing regulator in our model would have set.

Consider the example in figure 1. As a reference point, suppose the optimal solution from the standpoint of the regulator who can fix price and the tax rate is to select price p^0 and tax rate t, yielding a tax revenue of T. Compare this solution to one which arises when the regulator can set tax rates but does not have price setting authority. Given tax rate t, in the absence of a regulated price, the monopoly firm or cartelized industry would choose price p^2, which would result in total tax receipts of T' less than T.[9] A more realistic variation of this point is where two separate governmental units (for example, the legislature and a regulatory commission) have each been delegated the independent authority to control one decision. Without cooperation and trade, the separate objective functions or targets of the respective units are likely to result in a nonoptimal (from the separate regulators' wealth- or vote-maximizing view) solution. In short, there is a potential gain to governmental decision-making units from merger, that is, for one political unit to assume authority for setting both tax and price.[10] By the same argument, we would predict that where these decisions have not been merged or coordinated tax revenues are more likely to be raised by lump sum charges or fees rather than by per-unit taxes.

A final word on the tax and bribery solutions from (10). Note that when either $W_M = 0$ or $M_P = 0$ (that is, when regulators do not seek election/reelection or when consumers do not influence elections), the profit-maximizing price will be set. In the former case (when $W_M = 0$), all profits would be extracted through bribes, contributions, or taxes. In the latter case, $M_P = 0$ and $W_M > 0$, the profits would be split between producer returns and

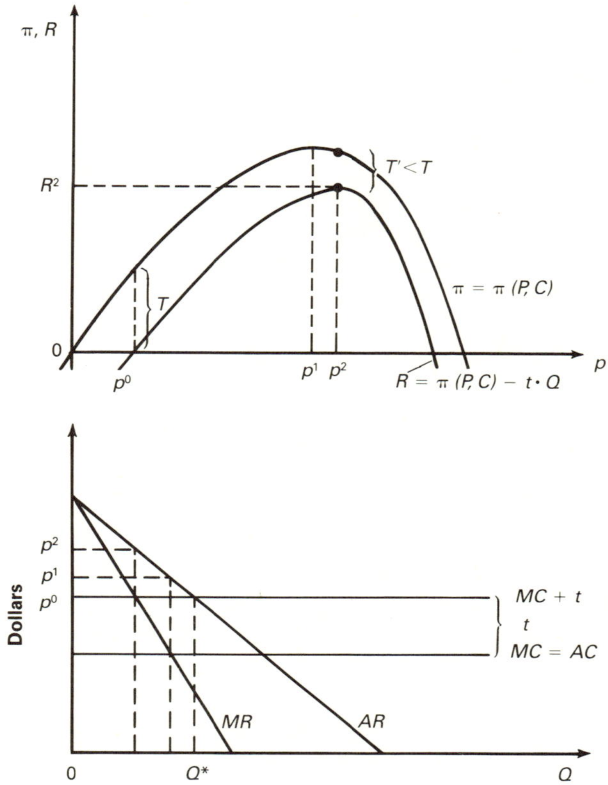

Fig. 1. t = tax rate; p = price; T = tax revenue; R = regulated price

tax revenues. The former case is of interest because it is precisely analogous to the Tullock (1967) and Posner (1975) rent-seeking models of monopoly regulation. The Tullock and Posner models suggest that the cost of obtaining or maintaining a monopoly will be roughly equal to the expected profit of being a monopolist (Posner 1975, 809). This special case, where $W_M = 0$, is especially interesting because of the nature of the rent-seeking costs or excess burden of the regulation. Because the monopoly rents are all taxed away, there is no lobbying or rent-seeking behavior to acquire the monopoly privilege.[11] To repeat the earlier discussion, the regulators select a politically weak industry to regulate, cartelize, and tax. Having taxed away all the monopoly rents, the rent-seeking costs will only be those expended by nonproducers in quest of the tax revenues. We reiterate our earlier suggestion that a two-on-one perspective of the regulatory process may be misleading.

As a final note on the general perspective, postregulatory employment through the revolving door technique is one convenient "tax" method used by regulated industries to compensate politicians for service rendered. To the extent that these individuals are paid in excess of their marginal products, a tax is being levied on the industry and the revolving door effect reduces to a legal means of influencing the regulatory outcome in the same fashion as bribes or campaign contributions.

Some Evidence

In support of our theory we present evidence from two different regulatory settings. Namely, we examine the effects of the institutional structure of public utility commissions on rates of return and prices of regulated gas and electricity producing firms across states in the United States. A straightforward implication of our model equation (8) is that when election or reelection becomes a less important aspect of the regulator's optimization problem, his choices will tend to favor higher regulated prices—and hence an upward movement along the profit or tax frontier—which will be divided in some proportion between higher producer returns and higher tax revenues or bribes.

There are two different procedures for choosing members of public utility commissions across states. Most states allow the governor or the legislature to appoint the members of public utility commission, but in a few states these regulators are chosen by a direct election of the registered voters. Table 1 lists the states, their method of appointment, and the allowable rates of return for electric utilities in 1966–67. Data for several states are missing due

TABLE 1. Rates of Return for Electric Utilities: 1967

State	Rate of Return	State	Rate of Return
	Regulators Chosen by Direct Election		
Arizona	6.5%* (5–8%)	Montana	5.3%
Georgia	6.0	Oklahoma	6.125 (6–6.25)
Louisiana	6.0	Tennessee	6.0
	Regulators Chosen by Governor or Legislature		
Alaska	7.0%	New Hampshire	6.5% (6–7%)
California	6.26 (5.75–6.76%)	Ohio	5.75 (5.5–6.0)
Colorado	6.35	Pennsylvania	5.9
Connecticut	6.0	Rhode Island	6.0
Delaware	6.5	Utah	6.15
Hawaii	6.5	Vermont	6.11
Idaho	6.1	Virginia	6.375 (5.75–7)
Illinois	5.85	Washington	6.1
Maryland	6.25	West Virginia	6.25 (6–6.5)
Michigan	6.425 (6–6.85)	Wisconsin	6.0
Nevada	6.85 (6.7–7.0)	Wyoming	5.6

Source: State Utility Commissions 1967.

Note: Data in parentheses are the range of legally prescribed rates of return. Where such a range was presented, we chose the midpoint as our datum.

to the reporting procedures. We cannot determine if missing data are strictly missing data or if it represents the absence of rate of return restrictions.

The first hypothesis is that where regulators are selected (appointed by legislature/governor) rather than elected, rates of return, rate bases, and profits will be higher. Consumer-voter input to the price-setting process is less direct since the regulators are one step removed from elections.[12] In other words, when regulators are selected as opposed to elected, $-M_P$ and W_M will be closer to zero, and regulated producer returns will be predictably higher. The mean rates of return for utilities in directly elected and legislatively/gubernatorially selected states are 5.99 and 6.22, respectively. The test statistic is $t=1.45$, which is significantly different from zero at the 10 percent level using a one-tailed test.[13] We interpret this difference in rates of return as supportive of the argument that when regulators are appointed, as opposed to elected directly, the relative importance of consumer-voter opposition to regulated prices is diminished and, hence, we would expect to observe higher returns in the regulated firms.[14]

We also have data for 1980 allowed rates of return.[15] For the appointed states the average allowed rate of return is 14.38 percent. On the other hand, the elected commissions allowed an average of 13.89 percent return on equity. The t-statistic is 1.42 which is significant at the 10 percent level using a one-tailed test.[16]

Stigler and Friedland (1962) and Jarrell (1978) have examined the impact of regulation on electricity prices. Peltzman (1971) has compared the pricing practices in public versus privately owned utilities, and Meyer and Leland (1980) have predicted unregulated prices to assay the effectiveness of regulation. However, none of these studies examines the differential impact on prices as the method of selecting regulators varies. As we noted earlier there should be an inverse relationship between regulated prices and the importance attached to election/reelection by the regulator. For this reason we reiterate our hypothesis that in states where public utility regulatory commissioners are chosen in a general election we will observe cheaper prices.

The means of average price, average residential price, and average industrial price are reported in table 2 by each class of regulatory commission, appointed and elected for 1967. We observe that average residential prices of electricity are marginally statistically significantly lower in the states with directly elected regulators. Overall, prices and industrial prices are lower, but not in a statistically reliable sense.

For gas prices we find that overall price, industrial price, and residential price are all lower in states with directly elected regulators. Deleting Texas and Louisiana from the sample, with appointed and elected commissions respectively, does not alter the results. However, these results should be interpreted with caution. Factors other than commission selection influence price, and although the averaging technique may take account of such differences, there can remain systematic effects correlated with commission selection which may account for these results. For example, in the case of natural gas, transmission costs can drastically affect price.

TABLE 2. Average Prices: 1967

	Average Price				
	Appointed Commissions	Elected Commissions	F-Statistics (= variances)	t-Statistics (= means)	N
	Electricity Prices				
Overall	1.69¢/kwh	1.58¢/kwh	1.49	0.73	48
Industrial users	1.43¢/kwh	1.36¢/kwh	1.66	0.51	36
Residential users	2.32¢/kwh	2.07¢/kwh	1.25	1.56*	12
	Natural Gas Prices				
Overall	0.927$/MMBTU	0.439$/MMBTU	25.61**	4.13**	48
Industrial prices	0.699$/MMBTU	0.372$/MMBTU	30.61**	4.00**	36
Residential prices	1.30$/MMBTU	1.01$/MMBTU	1.76	1.46*	12

*Significant at the 10 percent level, one-tailed test.
**Significant at the 1 percent level, one-tailed test.

To control for the other factors that might systematically affect price we used the following three-equation model of electricity price, gas price, and commission selection:

$$P_E = a_0 + a_1 COMM + a_2 P_G + a_3 YPC + a_4 POP + a_5 CAP + a_6 FC + a_7 LF + a_8 EXP + u_1 \quad (11)$$

$$P_G = b_0 + b_1 COMM + b_2 P_E + b_3 YPC + b_4 POP + b_5 RES + u_2 \quad (12)$$

$$COMM = c_0 + c_1 P_E + c_2 P_G + c_3 YPC - c_4 POP + c_5 DEN + c_6 SIZE + c_7 RATIO + u_3 \quad (13)$$

where

P_E = log of the average price of electricity,
P_G = log of the average price of natural gas,
$COMM$ = dummy variable, 0 if appointed, 1 if elected,
YPC = log of income per capita,
POP = log of population,
CAP = log of installed electric generating capacity per plant,
FC = log of net fuel cost per kwh produced,
LF = log of load factor (generation/capacity),
EXP = absolute value of export ratio,
RES = log of proven natural gas reserves,
$SIZE$ = log of size of state legislature,
$RATIO$ = ratio of house to senate size, and
u_1, u_2, u_3 = error terms.

Equation (11) posits that the price of electricity is a function of the method of commission selection; the price of a substitute, natural gas; income per capita and population as demand shifters; and capacity, fuel cost, load factor, and exports as supply shifters. Capacity per plant will measure the effect of economies of scale that may exist. Fuel cost and load factor control for input costs and exports measures the effect of selling to out-of-state voters. Higher load factors imply higher operator capital utilization and hence lower prices. Higher exports are expected to be associated with higher prices because local regulators are less concerned about the welfare of foreign-disenfranchised consumers.[17] Equation (12) predicts that the price of natural gas is a function of the method of commission selection, the price of electricity, income, population, and a proxy for the cost of natural gas transportation. Presumably natural gas reserves are negatively correlated with transportation costs. Hence we predict that the sign on this coefficient will be negative.

Equation (13) argues that not only does the method of commission selection affect regulated prices, but that the level of utility prices also affects how the state determines the institution to regulate prices. In those states with high prices consumers demand more control over the regulatory process. Consequently we expect that the higher the natural gas and electricity prices the more likely a state is to have elected regulators. Of course, if competition or other forces are already assuring low prices then consumers have little demand to control the price-setting process. It is sort of like the question of do neighborhoods with many locks have high or low crime rates. This makes the signs on the prices of electricity and natural gas ambiguous. Income, population, density, and institutional factors are also included. Larger legislatures are more likely to have elected commissions because large legislatures have bigger organization and control costs. The same explanation suggests that high-ratio states are more likely to have elected regulatory commissions.[18]

Simultaneous estimation of the system allows us to capture all of these effects jointly.[19] The three-stage-least-squares estimates of equations (11) and (12) are reported in table 3.[20] The results are mixed.[21] Commission selection is not significantly associated with electricity prices, but elected commissions are systematically related with lower natural gas prices. The F-statistic on the equality of the *COMM* coefficient across the two price equations is 7.04 which is significant at the 1 percent level. This suggests that the impact of commission selection is not the same for electricity and natural gas which is not surprising since the producer and consumer groups are different in the two cases.

Summary and Conclusions

In this article we attempt to merge the theory of bureaucracy with the theory of regulation. The results hold new predictions about the pattern of regulation. For example, producer groups who offer politicians strong electoral support (for example, by sharing the gains with labor who in turn vote accordingly)

TABLE 3. Electricity and Natural Gas Price Regressions (3SLS estimates)

Variable	Parameter Estimate	Standard Error	t-Ratio	Approx. PROB > |t|
		Electricity Price Equation		
INTERCEPT	−1.767434	1.520818	−1.1622	0.2522
COMM	0.056568	0.076037	0.7440	0.4614
LINGASP	0.157450	0.064463	2.4425	0.0192
LNYPC	0.414136	0.196099	2.1119	0.0412
LNPOP	0.103181	0.039016	2.6446	0.0117
LNCAPP	−0.161547	0.039718	−4.0674	0.0002
LNFC	0.156240	0.037391	4.1786	0.0002
LNLF	−0.249336	0.171811	−1.4512	0.1547
ABSEXP	0.254314	0.102272	2.4866	0.0173
		Gas Price Equation		
INTERCEPT	1.267385	2.664008	0.4757	0.6367
COMM	−0.36457	0.131403	−2.7744	0.0082
LNP	0.552940	0.170877	3.2359	0.0024
LNYPC	0.240028	0.356512	0.6733	0.5045
LNPOP	−0.00156447	0.053704	−0.0291	0.9769
LINGASRES	−0.040751	0.008333991	−4.8897	0.0001

Sources: Edision Electric Institute, *Statistical Yearbook*, 1967. *State Utility Commissions*, 1967. *Statistical Abstract of the U.S.*, 1968. *Book of the States* 1968.

are preferred over producer cartels who only offer bribes. In addition, we observe a strong theoretical propensity for the regulatory process to house its taxing and control functions under one roof. And finally, in the Tullock and Posner rent-seeking models of political behavior the regulated industry is taxed the total benefit of regulation. However, in our model this result is only predicted if politicians do not seek election or reelection.

Practically speaking, we found some evidence that direct election of regulators rather than appointment is associated with lower prices and rates of return for regulated natural gas and electricity prices.

NOTES

We are grateful to Mike Bradley, Harold Demsetz, Gregg Jarrell, C. M. Lindsay, Richard Smith, Robert Tollison, Jerry Zimmerman, participants in the Law and Economics Workshop at UCLA, and the Applied Economics Workshop at the University of Rochester for helpful comments. Partial financial support was provided by the Center for Study of Public Choice, Virginia Polytechnic Institute, and the Center for Research in Government Policy and Business, University of Rochester. The first draft of this paper was dated June, 1978.

1. This modified approach is suggested by Hirshleifer (1976) in his critique of Peltzman's (1976) model.
2. Stigler (1972, 162–63), for example, portrays this perspective: "Our theory of industry-acquired regulation predicts that the regulatory body will have the character of trustworthy bureaucracy rather than the dangerous potentialities of competitive politics."
3. The connection between the size of an agency's budget and regulator wealth (broadly defined to include pecuniary and nonpecuniary income) has, of course, received extensive analytical and empirical attention. The most familiar examples of this analytical tradition are Niskanen (1971) and Tullock (1965). Some empirical evidence is presented in Crain and Tollison (1976).
4. Stigler (1972) offers some interesting data and additional discussion of the prior and subsequent occupations of the personnel of regulatory commissions. The influence of finite terms of office, and hence the problem of postgovernment employment, has been addressed in Hilton (1972) and Eckert (1973). See also McCormick and Tollison (1981, chap. 5), and Horne (1982).
5. This principle of regulation has not dodged previous criticism, also stemming from the simplifying one-dimensional goal of majority maximization in its roots. For example, Hirshleifer (1976, 241) argues that

   > (I)f wealth is the ultimate goal, majority maximization can only be an instrumental and partial aim. The politician should be willing to accept some risk of defeat in exchange for a sufficient direct or indirect monetary payment.

6. Note, however that the "lame duck" effect may also influence demand for regulator outcomes by special interest groups. As the expected tenure in office of the regulator falls, the expected durability and hence the present value of that regulator's influence may also decline. The importance of long-term durability on the present value of special interest legislation is the central theme of Landes and Posner (1975).
7. This analysis reiterates the importance of mechanisms for controlling the behavior of governmental officials such as discussed in Becker and Stigler (1974) and Barro (1973).
8. For example, they live and vote outside the political jurisdication. For more on this point see Maloney, McCormick, and Tollison (1982).
9. Obviously, if this industry is comprised of a number of firms who cannot privately cartelize output, then price will be p^0 and tax revenues T.
10. Ehrlich and Posner (1974) reach a similar conclusion from a different perspective.
11. To be sure they can rent seek to acquire the tax revenues.
12. In this context we are implicitly assuming that there is an agency cost between elected politicians and their bureaucratic servants. Without this loss of control, voters would through the election of legislators and governors de facto elect the public utility commissioners. Whether there exists an organizational and control problem between legislators and bureaucrats is, of course, an empirical issue. We assume that one exists, which grants a degree of independence to the regulator. The tests that follow are in fact tests of the joint hypothesis that an agency problem exists and that regulators insulated from election tend to favor higher prices.
13. If Montana is deleted from the "elected" data set, then the means are not statistically different. This test is based on the assumption of equal variances across groups. The F-statistic testing the hypothesis of equality is 1.75, suggesting that the variances are equal.

14. Several states either do not have a public utilities commission or relegate that function to some other bureau in the state. Theoretically and empirically, we align those states with the states where the commissioners are appointed either by the legislature or the governor.
15. Saloman Brothers, Stock Research, Industry Analysis, February 17, 1981, reports "recently allowed return on equity" rulings by state regulatory commissions.
16. Again, we have assumed that the variances are equal. The F-statistic is 1.06.
17. See Peltzman (1971), Taylor (1975), Jarrell (1978), and Maloney, McCormick, and Tollison (1982) for further discussion of these variables.
18. See Crain (1979) and McCormick and Tollison (1981, chap. 5) for a detailed discussion of the impact of legislative size and ratio on similar institutional variables.
19. *3SLS* estimation is not efficient because the *COMM* variable is discrete. However, logit estimation of the *COMM* equation separately suggests that this problem is not serious. All the coefficients have the same sign except electricity price, and none change significance levels.
20. Estimates of the *COMM* equation are available on request.
21. Deleting the commission equation does not alter the basic result although the significance of *COMM* in the gas equation is reduced to the 10 percent level.

REFERENCES

Barro, Robert T. "The Control of Politicians: An Economic Model." *Public Choice* 14 (Spring 1973): 19–42.

Becker, Gary S., and Stigler, G. J. "Law Enforcement, Malfeasance, and Compensation of Enforcers." *Journal of Legal Studies* 3 (January 1974): 1–18.

Council of State Governments. *Book of the States, 1967–68*. Chicago: Council of State Governments, 1968.

Crain, W. M. "Cost and Output in the Legislative Firm." *Journal of Legal Studies* 8, no. 3 (June 1979): 507–22.

Crain, W. M., and Tollison, R. D. "State Budget Sizes and the Marginal Productivity of Governors." *Public Choice* 27 (Fall 1976): 91–96.

Demsetz, Harold. "The Growth of Bureaucracy." Unpublished paper presented at Public Choice Society Meetings, New Orleans, 1977.

Eckert, R. D. "On the Incentives of Regulators: The Case of Taxicabs." *Public Choice* 14 (Spring 1973): 83–99.

Edison Electric Institute. *Statistical Yearbook of the Electric Utility Industry for 1967*. New York, 1968.

Ehrlich, I., and Posner, R. "An Economic Analysis of Legal Rulemaking." *Journal of Legal Studies* 3, no. 1 (January 1974): 257–86.

Hirshleifer, J. "Comment." *Journal of Law and Economics* 19, no. 2 (August 1976): 241–44.

Hilton, G. W. "The Basic Behavior of Regulatory Commissions." *American Economic Review Papers and Proceedings*, May, 1972, pp. 47–54.

Horne, C. H. "Regulations, Regulators, and Intra-Industry Transfers: The Federal Home Loan Bank Board, a Case Study." Ms. 1982.

Jarrell, G. A. "The Demand for State Regulation of the Electric Utility Industry." *Journal of Law and Economics* 21 (October 1978): 269–95.

Landes, W., and Posner, R. "The Independent Judiciary in an Interest-Group Perspective." *Journal of Law and Economics* 18, no. 3 (December 1975): 875–901.

Maloney, M.; McCormick, R.; and Tollison, R. "Exporting Economic Regulation." Working paper, Center for Economic Research, Clemson University, 1982.

Meyer, R. A., and Leland, H. C. "The Effectiveness of Price Regulation." *Review of Economic and Statistics* 62, no. 4 (November, 1980): 555–66.

McCormick, R. E., and Tollison, R. D. *Politicians, Legislation, and the Economy: An Inquiry Into the Interest Group Theory of Government.* Boston: Martinus–Nijhoff, 1981.

Niskanen, W. A. *Bureaucracy and Representative Government.* Chicago: Aldine Atherton, 1971.

Peltzman, S. "Pricing in Public and Private Enterprises: Electric Utilities in the United States." *Journal of Law and Economics* 14, no. 1 (April 1971): 109–47.

______. "Toward a More General Theory of Regulation." *Journal of Law and Economics* 19 (August 1976): 211–40.

Posner, R. A. "The Social Cost of Monopoly and Regulation." *Journal of Political Economy* 83 (August 1975): 807–27.

Statistical Abstract of the U.S. Washington: Government Printing Office, 1976.

Stigler, G. J. "The Theory of Economic Regulation." *Bell Journal of Economics and Management Science* 2, no. 1 (Spring 1971): 3–21.

______. "The Process of Economic Regulation." In G. J. Stigler, ed., *The Citizen and the State.* Chicago: University of Chicago Press, 1975, pp. 145–66.

Stigler, G. J., and Friedland, C. "What Can Regulators Regulate?" *Journal of Law and Economics* 5 (October 1962): 1–16.

Taylor, Lester D. "The Demand for Electricity: A Survey." *Bell Journal of Economics* 6, no. 1 (Spring 1975): 74–110.

Tullock, G. "The Welfare Costs of Tariffs, Monopolies, and Theft." *Western Economic Journal* 5 (June 1967): 224–32.

Tullock, G. *Politics of Bureaucracy.* Washington, D.C.: Public Affairs Press, 1965.

Politico-Economic Models and Cycles

Bruno S. Frey

Politico-economic models study the *mutual interaction* of the economic and the political sectors of society concentrating on the relationship between consumer-voters and government. The influences of the economy on the polity and of the polity on the economy are treated in an *explicit* and for the most part formal fashion, making it possible to test the theories *empirically*.

This article does not deal with models which are not intended for empirical testing (such as Rothenberg 1965; Morris and Giral 1969). Neither are median-voter models discussed because they assume that the revealed preferences of the electorate are automatically implemented by an anonymous, noninstitutional political sector (see Pommerehne 1978).

The basic idea of a politico-economic model is that the voters' evaluation of government performance, and therefore a government's chance of staying in power, depends substantially on economic conditions; and that the government in turn seeks to manipulate the economy in order to stay in power and to maximize its utility (e.g. by putting ideological programs into action).

This general relationship between the two actors and the two sectors may be represented as in figure 1. The evaluation function captures the influence of

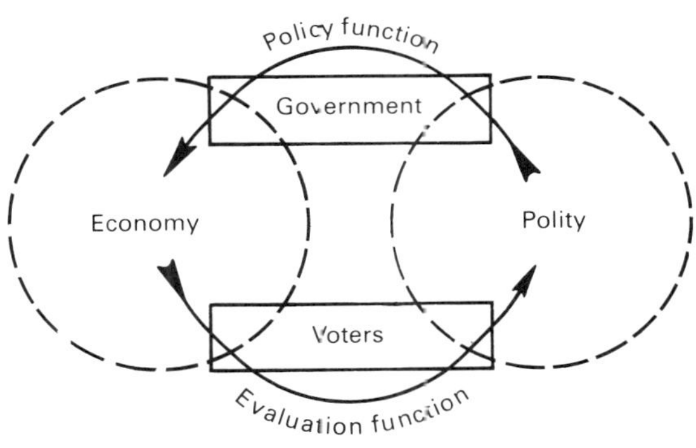

Fig. 1

the economy on the polity through the voters, and the policy function captures the influence of the polity on the economy through government.

This article discusses the main assumptions concerning the *building blocks* used in politico-economic models, namely the actors and the type of

First published in *Journal of Public Economics* 9 (April 1978): 203–20.

economic and political system considered (sec. 1). On this basis some *representative models* using them are sketched and some empirical results are presented (sec. 2). Section 3 outlines (yet) nonformalized models extending the analysis in more general directions. The concluding section offers some comments on the potential of, and prospects for, this line of research.

1. The Main Building Blocks

Politico-economic models are composed of various building blocks about which different assumptions can be made. Of prime importance are the particular utility function, time perspective, and information processes by both government and voters, as well as the characteristics of the *economic* and *political* sectors.

1.1. Voters

Voters are assumed to be rational. They evaluate the government's past and expected future performance on the basis of the state of the economy, supporting another party (the opposition) if they are dissatisfied. The effect upon the polity is measured by the government's (or parties') current *popularity* index (as regularly collected, e.g., by Gallup or National Opinion Poll) or *election* results. Due to the public good effects involved, individual voters have little incentive to become fully informed and may, therefore, behave like "satisficers" (see Kramer 1971).

The various approaches proposed differ strongly with respect to the arguments included in the *consumer-voters' utility function*. Due to differences in the political indicators (popularity index or election results), and other data, in the period and area covered in the specification of the functions and statistical procedures, there is mixed empirical evidence about which (if any) economic variables exert a statistically significant political influence. It may be argued that with rational voters *no* macroeconomic variable has any effect (see Stigler 1973; and Arcelus and Meltzer 1975 for U.S. congressional elections). These studies have, however, been severely criticized on theoretical and empirical grounds (Okun 1973; Goodman and Kramer 1975).

Various authors find that general economic conditions are reflected by one variable only—the growth of disposable income (Tufte 1975; Fair 1975), or the rate of unemployment (Mueller 1970; see the critique by Hibbs 1974). The most common result is to have two arguments in the voters' utility function, usually the rate of unemployment and of inflation (the earliest study being by Goodhart and Bhansali 1970). For American presidential elections it has been found that a Democratic presidential candidate's vote share is positively influenced by an increase in the rates of unemployment and inflation (and negatively by a rise in transfers). The reverse is found to hold for a Republican presidential candidate (Meltzer and Vellrath 1975). The explanations offered for these results are, however, rather ad hoc.

If the popularity and election functions are carefully specified, particularly taking into account shifts due to noneconomic effects, there is evidence that in countries dominated by two major parties all three macroeconomic variables (rate of unemployment, inflation, and growth of disposable income) are statistically significant (for the United States see Goodman and Kramer 1975; Frey and Schneider 1978*a;* for other countries see Frey and Schneider 1978*a*, 1978*b*, 1979). Other indicators for the state of the economy may also be of importance, such as real share prices which reflect changes in wealth as well as expectations about the future course of the economy (Niskanan 1975).

From the point of view of public economics it is particularly interesting to know whether government's fiscal activity *directly* affects its popularity and election success (rather than indirectly through its effect on the macroeconomic variables discussed above). An increase in public transfers (to private households) has a positive effect on the government's political position (Tufte 1974). This is implicitly accounted for in all studies taking (the growth of) *disposable* income as a determinant. It is also suggested that the growth rate of real per capita federal spending over the election period has a highly significant *negative* effect on the vote share of the presidential candidate of the incumbent party in the United States, 1896–1972. What is less surprising is the fact that the growth rate of real per capita federal tax revenue also has a highly significant negative effect (Niskanen 1975). More sophisticated assumptions about the particular way economic conditions affect voters have also been made. Instead of the level, the *change* in economic variables, particularly the rate of unemployment (Lepper 1974) is introduced. It has been argued and empirically tested that economic variables exert a significant effect only if their level crosses a certain threshold; within it their effect is random (Frey and Garbers 1972). The proposition that government is 'punished' if economic conditions worsen, but does not benefit if they improve, has so far not been substantiated by empirical evidence [see the effort by Bloom and Price (1975) and the critique by Goodman and Kramer (1975)].

Widely divergent assumptions are also made about how quickly *voters discount the government's performance* in the past: The most extreme is to assume that only the current election year is considered. One study claims that—at least for the United States—this hypothesis is realistic (Fair 1975). The analogy to positive finite discounting of the future is to assume that past events have a geometrically declining weight in the voters' evaluation. Myopia is also present if voters only consider the current election term in their voting decision, even if constant weights are attached to each year.

1.2. Government

Government is taken to be a unit acting rationally. Some models consider government to be fully informed about the voters' reactions and about its chances of influencing the economy while others stress that it typically acts under lack of information. Politico-economic models consider parties as competing on the *vote market.* Parties and the government seek to maximize votes, plurality, or the vote share, either in absolute terms, as an expected number, or as a probability of exceeding a certain number. A related view is that governments maximize their probability of winning the next election.

The classical economic assumption of *utility maximization* (subject to constraints) is in *explicit* terms employed surprisingly little. It is informally used when changing weights of idealistic (or personal goals such as pecuniary gains or power) and of popularity goals over the term of office are assumed (Lindbeck 1976; Breton 1974).

A more precise formulation identifies the government's utility with "ideological" goals as stated, e.g., in party programs, or with long-run goals, and differentiates between *political* constraints (the need to be re-elected), *administrative* constraints (mainly brought about by the public bureaucracy) and *economic* constraints (the general structure of the economy, balance of the budget and of international payments) (Frey and Lau 1968; Attali 1972; Frey and Schneider 1978*a*, 1978*b*, 1979).

The party in power is usually taken to have a *time horizon* extending up to the next election. This assumption may be disputed: If a government is confident of winning the next election it would be irrational not to include (at least) the following term into the time horizon. The next legislative period is of no interest (though possibly later ones) only if the government is absolutely sure of losing the forthcoming election.

1.3. Political Sector

Formal politico-economic models have so far considered parliamentary democracies, mostly taking the length of the election period as fixed. If it is variable a theory of election fixing is needed (see Frey and Schneider 1978*b* for the United Kingdom). There is, however, an identification problem here because it is no longer clear whether the economy is steered in view of elections, or whether elections are fixed in view of the state of the economy, or both (Lindbeck 1976).

One class of models assumes that competition between parties is of no relevance (the Marxist approaches), or that they even form a coalition *against* the electorate (Wittmann 1973). In general, politico-economic models assume some amount of competition. Government needs to win a sufficient number of votes in order to survive. More intensive political competition is implied if a reciprocal interaction between the parties (or the government and the opposition) is allowed for as in the path-breaking static party competition model by Downs (1957). Party competition in a dynamic context has so far not been amenable to analysis (an exception is Kramer 1975).

The best *current* indicator the government has to assess its future election chances is the popularity index. At election time it is the number of *votes* that counts. Under some constitutional arrangements there may, however, be a considerable difference between votes and *seats* in parliament received by the various parties (see Tufte 1973). In a political system with more than two parties and no majority party, the number of seats is not decisive in determining the government due to the many *coalition* possibilities which may arise. (For a calculation see Rae 1971.) The problem of going from votes to the selection of the government has so far not been taken into account by politico-economic models.

1.4. Economic Sector

Most politico-economic models are *partial* in the sense that they cover only a specific part of the economy. Most attention has been given to the trade-off between inflation and unemployment (extended Phillips curve). Few models have used a *complete macroeconometric* model of the economy.

2. Representative Models

The formal and (partly) empirically tested politico-economic models examined here rest upon the assumptions discussed in the last section—though in many different ways. Table 1 shows six representative models (identified by the name of their authors), arranged according to the assumptions made concerning the arguments in the *voters' utility function* and the *government's objective function.*

Table 2 shows an alternative arrangement of the same six models when the voters' and government's *time horizon* is taken into account. The govern-

TABLE 1. Assumptions about the Voters' and Government's Utility Functions

		Government's Objectives	
		Vote Maximization	Utility Maximization
Arguments in the voters' utility function	Growth	Fair (1975)	
	Inflation and unemployment	Nordhaus (1975) MacRae (1977) Lindbeck (1975, 1976)	
	Growth, inflation, and unemployment		Frey and Lau (1968) Frey and Schneider (1978*a*; 1978*b*; 1979)

TABLE 2. Assumptions about the Voters' and Government's Time Perspective

		Government's Time Horizon	
		Next Election	Infinite
Voters' rate of discount of the past (within an election period)	Complete (approx. current election year)	Lindbeck Fair	Frey and Schneider
	Positive, finite	Nordhaus	Frey and Lau
	No discounting	MacRae	

ment's time horizon is prospective, the voters' retrospective. These politico-economic models differ, of course, in other apsects, such as the degree of *information* and the *economic structure* assumed.

It is useful to deal simultaneously with the models of Nordhaus, MacRae, and Lindbeck, as they all are concerned with *government vote maximization* in the face of an inflation-unemployment trade-off (sec. 2.1). Fair's model also assumes vote maximization as the government's objective but includes a *complete macro model* of the economy (section 2.2). The models by Frey and Lau and Frey and Schneider are again discussed jointly; they also consider a complete model of the economy but explicitly assume that the *government maximizes its utility* (section 2.3).

2.1. Vote Maximization with an Inflation-Unemployment Trade-Off

A democratic system with a vote- (or plurality-) maximizing government knowing the voters' preferences over the course of many electoral regimes asymptotically approaches a *steady state equilibrium* on the long-run Phillips curve. Interpreting the aggregate vote function (depending on unemployment and inflation) as an individualistic social welfare function this democratic equilibrium may be compared with a benevolent dictator's policy representing the social welfare optimum. It may be shown that the two equilibria coincide only if the dictator's rate of time preference is infinite. Provided society does not completely discount the future, the democratic outcome is nonoptimal; there is higher inflation and lower unemployment than is socially desirable according to the social welfare function (Nordhaus 1975).

This result may be questioned. If a different but equally plausible assumption is made about the government's utility function different results follow. If, e.g., government is assumed to maximize the length of time which it can expect to remain uninterruptedly in power, the democratic outcome is not necessarily nonoptimal. A purely myopic policy is theoretically not a *general* characteristic of democracies (Frey and Ramser 1976).

The model may also be used to study *short-run behavior within* an election period, i.e., the *political business cycle* (Nordhaus 1975). Voters are assumed to have a decaying memory of the past and are concerned only with the current election period. The following typical cycle results. Immediately after an election victory the government undertakes a deflationary policy by increasing unemployment in order to combat inflation. Over the course of the election period unemployment is continuously reduced and reaches the purely myopic point at election time.

Voters' discounting of the past is not a necessary requirement for the creation of the cycle. Assuming no discounting over the election period it is still optimal for the government to generate a stable political business cycle equal to the election period. At the beginning of the term the economy moves toward a turnpike—which corresponds to the long-run welfare optimum of the voters—and before the election it moves away (MacRae 1977). This cycle is produced because a deflationary policy at the beginning of the election period constitutes an investment in the future (the Phillips curve is shifted inward due to a depression of inflation expectations), and the inflation following after the election date does not hurt the government because its time horizon is confined to the present election period.

The optimal election cycle produced by government is quite similar if it is assumed that the voters are sensitive not to the level but to *changes* in the rate of unemployment. At election time, the optimal point on the Phillips curve would be reached when the trade-off is near to the origin *and* unemployment has been *falling* before the elections. This would be achieved in the area between points *A* and *D*, e.g., at *E* in figure 2.

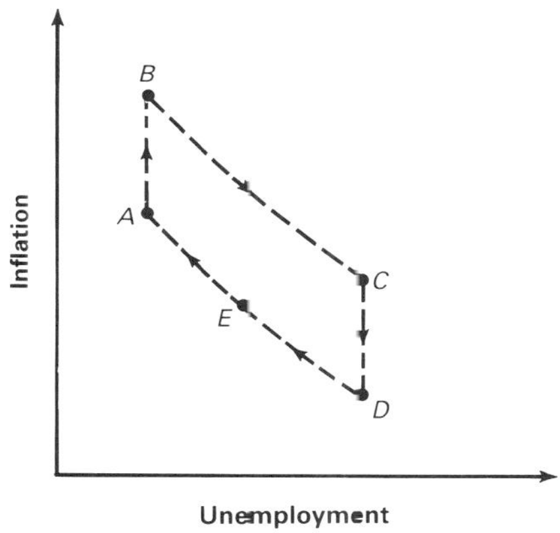

Fig. 2

A significant increase in inflation (shift of the trade-off from *A* to *B*) takes place only after the election has taken place. Immediately following the election a restrictive policy is pursued until about one year before the election. This increases unemployment (movement from *B* to *C*) and shifts the Phillips curve inward from *C* to *D* (Lindbeck 1975, 1976).

2.2. Vote Maximization in a Complete Macroeconomic Model

American presidential administrations are assumed (Fair 1975) to have a time horizon extending up to the next election and to act within the framework given by a medium-sized quarterly macroeconometric model. The instruments available to the president are the value of goods purchased by the government (in real terms) and the value of government securities outstanding (in current dollar terms). The government's goal simply consists of bringing about the maximum real growth rate of the economy in the election year because according to Fair's own econometric estimate American voters are myopic and interested in the real growth rate of per capita GNP, only.

Assuming complete knowledge of the economic structure, the optimal policy consists of bringing about a trough six to eight quarters before the elections, i.e., in the first three quarters of the preelection year. The most restrictive use of the fiscal policy instrument is one quarter earlier. This politically induced cycle enables an increase in the real growth rate of national income of about 20 percent in the election year.

This election year–induced real growth rate seems unbelievably high. The actual growth rate has indeed been much lower. American presidents have, therefore, missed the target derived in the model by far. The following explanations are offered (Fair 1975, p 29): The president may be restricted in his vote-maximizing policies by Congress and the Federal Reserve; the government may think that voters judge its performance by additional (or other) criteria; or the government may pursue non vote-maximizing goals.

Even if the question is left aside of what economic variables influence the electorate's choice (Fair's estimate is in conflict with the other studies mentioned above), these explanations are ad hoc, only. The main shortcoming of this approach is that an explicit model of politico-economic interdependence covering all the decision makers he deems relevant is missing.

2.3. Government Utility Maximization in a Complete Macroeconomic Context

Government may be assumed to maximize its utility by pursuing economic policies in accordance with its ideological views concerning the desirable state of the economy, e.g., the relative weight to be accorded to efficiency compared to equity. When voters evaluate the government's performance with geometrically declining weights toward the past, depending on the structure of the economy, it may be impossible to meet the reelection constraint. If, however, a feasible policy exists, it is optimal to create a *political business cycle* by pursuing an ideological policy at the beginning of the election period and to progressively adjust its actions so as to guarantee reelection (Frey and Lau 1968). Such a policy presumes full information on the part of government. More realistically, government is incompletely informed about the exact structure of economy, particularly when and how its policy instruments affect the economic variables entering the voters' utility function. As its existence depends on staying in power, government politicians devote most of their attention to meeting the reelection constraint. Its policy will, however, also be influenced by legal constraints and by the public bureaucracy's interest in continually expanding public outlays (see Davis, Dempster, and Wildavsky 1966) (administrative constraint) and by the limits set by the budget and the balance of payments (economic constraints).

A satisficing policy may proceed in the following way: If the government's current popularity (*POP*) is lower than the value considered necessary for reelection (*POP**), it will make an effort to increase its popularity with the voters. This will be the stronger, the larger the popularity deficit and the nearer the elections are because there is less and less time available to raise popularity sufficiently to be reelected. If its popularity is so high that reelection seems likely, government pursues an ideological policy: With respect to the budget, a right-wing party may be expected to reduce expenditures and a left-wing party to increase them, compared with the trend. (A simulation model comparing the effect of various government ideologies is provided in Frey 1977.) The model specifies the two interacting links between the economy and the polity shown in figure 1 in the following way:

a) The *evaluation function* measures the negative influence of the rates of unemployment and of inflation, and the positive influence of the growth rate of disposable real income (or consumption) on *government popularity*. Popularity also depends on political factors which are captured by a popularity level (specific to each government or party) and an autonomous depreciation variable, capturing noneconomic popularity losses (e.g., due to internal scandals and wars).

b) The *policy function* describes the use of economic policy instruments (especially *public expenditures*) by a utility-maximizing government. When there is a popularity "surplus" $POP_t \geqq POP^*$ (indicated by a dummy variable S being equal to one) government is free to pursue its ideology ID. ID depends on the dummy variable R (respectively L) taking the value 1 if a right-wing (respectively a left-wing) party is in power, otherwise it is zero, multiplied by squared popularity surplus $(POP_t - POP^*)^2$ to indicate the room available to act ideologically.

ID is thus defined as:

$$ID_t = [\beta_R \cdot R + \beta_L \cdot L](POP_t - POP^*)^2,$$

where β_R and β_L are parameters. According to a priori expectations, right-wing governments have the tendency to spend less, and left-wing governments to spend more, when they are free to act ideologically ($\beta_R < 0$, $\beta_L > 0$).

The government's need to raise its popularity "deficit" $POP_t < POP^*$ (indicated by $S = 0$) is reflected by the size of the squared deficit $(POP_t - POP^*)^2$ and by a variable TP giving the time passed since the last election, showing how much time the government has available to lift its popularity. In case of a popularity deficit, government is assumed to undertake an expansionary policy.

The administrative constraint is taken into account by introducing the lagged instrument use.

The policy equation reads in linear form

$$\begin{aligned} INSTR^i_{t+1} = {} & a_0 + a_1 INSTR^i_t + [a_2 \cdot ID]S \\ & + [a_3(POP_t - POP^*)^2 + a_4 TP] \cdot (1 - S) \\ & + \text{various economic constraints and cost factors} \end{aligned}$$

$INSTR^i$ refers to various government policy instruments ($i = 1,2, \ldots$) available, particularly public expenditures.

The popularity and policy functions have been *econometrically tested* with quarterly data for the United States, the United Kingdom, and Germany over the postwar period (Frey and Schneider 1978*a,* 1978*b,* 1979). Each model has, of course, been adapted to the special economic and political systems of each of these countries, e.g., that the balance-of-payments constraint is of little significance in the United States and Germany, but of great importance in the United Kingdom. For that reason, only those parameters of the regression estimates of the popularity and policy functions are presented here which are of prime interest for politico-economic cycles and which are (up to a point) amenable to intercountry comparisons.

Table 3 presents the estimated coefficients of the government's *popularity function.*

Table 3 suggests that economic variables do influence government popularity. While the rate of unemployment and inflation have a statistically (highly) significant effect, the influence of the growth of real disposable income is less well founded in the case of the U.S. and Germany.[1] The coefficients for the United States and the United Kingdom are of comparable magnitude; the British seem to politically resent unemployment somewhat more and inflation somewhat less than the Americans. The Germans appear to "punish" the government little when unemployment rises. They are—relative to other goals—more strongly opposed to inflation than both the British and the Americans. The growth of real disposable income has a positive effect of similar size on government popularity in all three countries.

The empirical estimates of the popularity functions indicate that a government which aims at increasing its popularity does well to pursue in the short run an *expansionary* policy which lowers unemployment and raises the growth of disposable income. Only a very rapid and immediate increase in the rate of inflation would prevent an increase in the government's popularity share. The governments of the three countries considered are aware of this possibility: According to the empirical estimates shown in table 4 governments increase public expenditures, i.e. pursue an expansionary policy,[2] if they have a popularity deficit.

Table 4 presents a selection of estimated coefficients of the *policy function* for the case of *exhaustive expenditures* (for transfer expenditures the results are similar). The parameters are (with two exceptions) statistically significant for all countries and in each case have the theoretically expected sign. The past level of expenditure has a large effect on its present level ($\hat{a}_1 > 0$), reflecting administrative constraints. The estimates support the hypothesis that a government pursues the more vigorously an expansionary policy the larger its popularity deficit ($\hat{a}_3 > 0$). They indicate that left-wing parties tend to spend significantly *more* than right-wing parties, i.e., that governments pursue ideological policies when they are confident of staying in power ($b_R < b_L$).

TABLE 3. Government Popularity Functions for Three Countries, Quarterly Estimates

		Economic Variables			Political Variables	Test Statistics		
Country	Period	Rate of Unemployment (%)	Rate of Inflation (%)	Growth of Real Disposable Income (%)	Popularity Level and Depreciation	Degrees of Freedom (d.f.)	$\bar{R}^2$	Durbin-Watson Coeff. (D.W.)
United States	1953: II–1975: II	−4.03 (−5.23)	−1.00 (−1.99)	0.52 (1.69)	Specific to each president	78	0.91	1.99
United Kingdom	1959: IV–1974: IV	−6.01 (−3.89)	−0.61 (2.65)	0.81 (2.88)	Specific to Labour and Conservative government	54	0.69	1.71
Federal Republic of Germany	1951: I–1975: III	−0.91 (−3.47)	−0.71 (−3.09)	0.43 (1.63)	Level: specific to each government coalition	96	0.96	1.91

Source: Based on Frey and Schneider (1978*a*; 1978*b*; 1979). The values for Germany have been reestimated using quarterly observations.

Note: In the case of the U.K. the dependent variable is the government popularity lead relative to the main opposition party. For the U.S. the rate of inflation is lagged by one quarter. For Germany the economic variables are measured as deviations from their value at the beginning of each election term. The figures in parentheses are t-values.

TABLE 4. Policy Functions for Three Countries, Quarterly Estimates

Country	Period	Government Policy Instrument (Dependent Variable, $t+1$)	a_0	Lagged Dependent Variable a_1	Popularity Surplus ($S = 1$) Ideology: Right-wing b_R	Left-wing b_L	Popularity Deficit ($S = 0$): Size of Deficit (squared) a_3	Time Passed Since Election a_4	Economic Constraints	Test Statistics: d.f.	$\bar{R}^2$	D.W.
United States	1953: II–1975: II	Civilian exhaustive expenditures	−0.45	0.64 (9.23)	Specific to each president		0.002 (2.49)	0.37 (3.39)	Budget	82	0.99	1.61
United Kingdom	1962: II–1974: IV	Consumption expenditures	−0.63	0.38 (2.08)	−0.003 (−1.43)	0.008 (2.17)	0.007 (2.10)	0.004 (2.21)	Budget, balance of	42	0.99	1.73
		Investment expenditures	0.53	0.32 (2.14)	0.004 (−1.74)	0.006 (2.03)	0.006 (2.29)	0.003 (2.14)	payments, cost factors	42	0.97	2.12
Federal Republic of Germany	1951: II–1975: IV	Exhaustive expenditures	−0.84	1.012 (27.68)	−0.012 (−2.91)	0.145 (2.79)	0.003 (3.49)	0.339 (2.94)	Budget, cost factors	86	0.99	1.74

Note: POP^* is taken to be 58 percent for the U.S. and 52 percent for Germany. For the U.K., popularity is substituted by government lead and the respective surplus and deficit is based on a $LEAD^*$ of −5 percent and is not squared. The right-wing parties are the Conservatives (U.K.) and the Christian Democratic Party (alone or in coalition with nonsocialist parties, F.R.G.); the left-wing parties are Labour (U.K.) and the Social Democratic Party (in coalition with the Free Democratic Party, F.R.G.), respectively. For the U.S., "ideologies" are identified with presidential administrations (for reasons of space the coefficients are not reproduced here). For a precise definition of variables and specifications see the sources given in table 3.

There is clear evidence for a *politico-economic cycle* in all countries: Exhaustive expenditures are increased before each election the government is not confident of winning (the coefficient a_4 referring to the time passed since the last election is highly significantly positive). There is thus, *ceteris paribus*, a tendency to embark on an expansionary policy before elections in order to increase popularity and election chances.

The good results of the econometric estimates of the popularity and policy functions for three different countries suggest that the model captures certain features of the underlying structure of politico-economic interdependence in industrialized democratic nations reasonably well. It must be stressed, however, that these models are highly simplified and that many important aspects are not considered.

3. Other Types of Models

The representative models discussed in the previous section have used different combinations of the building blocks presented in section 1. The models sketched in this section stress other aspects of politico-economic interaction by extending the building blocks in various directions. The two general aspects treated are new views of the *economic system* and of the *political system*. The models are (so far) informal; they are discussed here because they open promising new avenues for future research.

3.1. Other Views of the Economic System

The relationship between *public goods* and *information* stands in the center of Downs's (1972) approach. In modern societies social problems are taken to go through a cycle of public attention which is strongly influenced by the communications media. The duration of the cycle is variable but the sequence is given: (1) at the *preproblem stage* highly undesirable social conditions exist but have not yet captured widespread public attention; (2) usually due to some dramatic incidence, there is *alarmed discovery* of the problem and a euphoric *enthusiasm* about the possibilities for solution with no fundamental reordering of society; (3) the *high costs of significant progress* are realized, particularly that major sacrifices by large groups would be required; (4) the *intense public interest gradually declines,* partly because of cost, partly because the public becomes bored and the competing media turn to new issues. The average level of attention and public effort is, however, almost always higher after a social concern has gone through the cycle, mostly because of their institutionalization.

The relationship between the economy and polity takes quite a different form when a *planned* rather than a market *economy* is considered. In a collectivist economy, the planning authority has by necessity a lower time preference than consumers. The official plans stressing capital investment conflict with the population's desire for increases in or even maintaining the level of consumption goods. Social dissatisfaction arises and pressures are put on the planners to change allocation criteria. With the progressive economic and political difficulties, planners are forced to raise the output of consumption goods which removes the tensions. After some time the planning authorities' preferences regain control leading to a shift to investment and the start of a new cycle (Oliveira 1960). Generalizing, all the oscillation of economic activity in European socialist countries may be attributed to the conflict between the overambitious central plans and the ability to carry it out successfully (Bajt 1971). Communist China's cyclical fluctuations are also seen as the result of a vicious circle where economic progress leads to extreme stress in (Maoist) ideology, which in turn leads to economic crises, followed by a relaxation of ideology (Eckstein 1968).

3.2. Other Views of the Political System

According to the *Marxist* view, business cycles serve the interest of the capitalist class. Periodic recessions are essential to the maintenance of capitalist political and social control. The class *instinct* of the business community tells them that a regime of *continuous* full employment is contrary to their interest: The "sack" loses its role as a disciplinary measure and strikes for wage increases create political tensions. Business leaders are anxious to teach workers a lesson though they know that a recession means a cut in profits. They form a powerful coalition with the rentiers who as fixed nominal income receivers are harmed by the inflation accompanying the boom. The government is forced to create a recession. The concomitant fall in profits (and inflation) after some time leads the business community to demand an expansionary policy. The government obeys and reestablishes full employment (Kalecki 1943; for some empirical evidence see Feiwel 1974).

According to another Marxist view there is no conflict between the political and economic dimensions of class conflict in the state of full employment. The share of profit typically *falls* during the second half of an expansion. Capitalists need not rely on "class instinct" to realize that sustained full employment is unsound. A recession is a necessary condition for the first highly profitable phase of expansion, and puts an end to the unprofitable latter phase of the boom. A constant "reserve army" of unemployment is not sufficient to reestablish control over the workers. Those still employed feel threatened only when the rate of unemployment *increases,* which requires a policy of intermittent recessions. The government is completely subservient to capitalists' wishes: Its objective is to maximize corporate profits (Boddy and Crotty 1975).

The thinking of Marx—it may be claimed—manifests itself in post-Keynesian capitalism in a new way; it affects the choice of politico-economic regimes (Kolm 1970). In the period after the Second World War the dynamics of the Phillips curve in the United States have resulted in a clockwise movement in the inflation-unemployment plan. The governments cannot for political reasons tolerate high unemployment. They intervene quickly as soon as unemployment is sizeably increasing which leads to an inflation-unemployment *spiral* with a continually higher average level of inflation. In the median run there are only two possible steady-state solutions to this disequilibrium process: Either the government introduces rigid price and wage controls and the public sector takes the leading role in the economy which is a regime of socialism within a nation (*socialisme national*); or Pre-Keynesian unemployment is reestablished against the opposition of trade unions and workers which is a regime of authoritarian *national socialisme*.

4. Concluding Remarks

Discussion of the various politico-economic models has shown that there are a wide variety of possible approaches, and that in fact only some directions have so far been explored. Not surprisingly, the *formalized models* have taken the most narrow points of view. Nevertheless, they are able to give interesting insights into the interdependence between the economy and polity. Theorizing has (in contrast to some other areas of public choice) fortunately not remained purely abstract, rather, some approaches have devoted great attention to empirical testing.

It is easy to think of some of the directions in which the formalized models could be expanded in order to make them more realistic. Some suggestions are provided by the *nonformalized models* discussed in the preceding section. More institutions relevant for politico-economic interaction can be introduced, such as the central bank, public enterprises, interest groups, and trade unions. As a further step, an effort should be made to include areas of government activity not directly showing in the budget, such as the whole area of law making and (economic) regulations.

Politico-economic models have made an especially noteworthy contribution to the problem of *political business cycles* in providing a theoretical basis for this phenomenon.[3] Traditional business cycle literature (including textbooks) has completely disregarded this aspect and the theory of stabilization policy has assumed as a matter of course that the government should, and does, stabilize the economy. The *capacity* to do so has recently been questioned by monetarists (see, e.g., Brunner 1970), but politico-economic modeling provides a rationale for believing that governments are not only *unwilling* to stabilize the economy, but that they have *an interest* in *creating* (some types of) cycles. This throws up basic questions for the theory of economic policy (and beyond that for democratic theory) not to be considered here.

Some authors (Goodhart and Bhansali 1970; Nordhaus 1975; Lindbeck 1975; MacRae 1977) offer suggestions of what should be done against political business cycles: The electoral periods should be lengthened; economic policy should be taken out of the hands of politicians and given to nonpartisan institutions; the base of political participation should be broadened in the direction of indicative planning; economists and citizens should show a more critical view towards inflation, or the electorate should vote strategically by communicating a preference for deflation to government and a higher value of this goal (compared to other goals) in the election year. These suggestions do not, however, take sufficient account of the fact that the approach here discussed purports to construct closed models of both the economic and political systems. Most of the suggestions offered come from outside the politico-economic systems pictured, and thus belong to the realm of "constitutional" decisions. They would not emerge from within the politico-economic system itself. Some of the suggestions are, however, undemocratic, unrealistic, or do not seem to be politically feasible. An acceptable possibility of overcoming political business cycles is *social learning:* The voters must start realizing that the government produces cycles in order to improve its reelection chances. Such a learning process leads the electorate to punish governments behaving in this way. Once voters completely understand the relationship implied (rational expectations) the political business cycle breaks down.

Research on politico-economic interaction is in its infancy. The formalized models used to date must be characterized as *additive-interdependent:* A "pure" economic sector is amended to a "pure" political sector and the links of interdependence are studied. In reality, there are no such "pure" sectors; future research must endeavour to construct models in which the economic and the political sectors pervade and transform each other.

NOTES

I am grateful for helpful comments to the two formal discussants at the Namur Conference of ISPE, Gerald H. Kramer and Erich Streissler, and to Chris Goodrich, Gebhard Kirchgaessner, Werner W. Pommerehne, and Friedrich Schneider.

1. This is partly due to multicollinearity between the economic variables. It has been tested for both countries that the growth of income coefficient is statistically significant if one of the correlated independent variables is in turn omitted. The relative size and significance of the other coefficients remain essentially unaffected.
2. It has been checked that the policy on the expenditure side is not counteracted by actions on the tax side.
3. For mainly empirical observations see, e.g., Akerman 1947; Averch, Koehler, and Denton 1971; Tufte, 1974; and Ben-Porath 1975.

REFERENCES

Akerman, J. 1947. "Political Economic Cycles." *Kyklos* 1:107–17.

Arcelus, F., and Meltzer, A. H. 1975. "The Effect of Aggregate Economic Variables on Congressional Elections." *American Political Science Review* 69:1232–39.

Attali, J. 1972. *Analyse économique de la vie politique.* Paris: Presses Universitaires.

Averch, H. A.; Koehler, J. E.; and Denton, F. H. 1971. *The Matrix of Policy in the Phillipines.* Princeton, N.J.: Princeton University Press.

Bajt, A. 1971. "Investment Cycles in European Socialist Economies: A Review Article." *Journal of Economic Literature* 9:53–63.

Ben-Porath, Y. 1975. "The Years of Plenty and the Years of Famine: A Political Business Cycle." *Kyklos* 28:400–403.

Bernholtz, P. 1972. *Grundlagen der Politischen Ökonomie*. Vol. 1. Tübingen: J. C. B. Mohr.

Bloom, H. S., and Price, H. D. 1975. "Voter Response to Short-run Economic Conditions: The Asymmetric Effect of Prosperity and Recession." *American Political Science Review* 69:1240–54.

Boddy, R., and J. Crotty. 1975. "Class Conflict and Macro-Policy: The Political Business Cycle." *Review of Radical Political Economics* 7:1–19.

Breton, A. 1974. *The Economic Theory of Representative Government*. Chicago: Aldine.

Brunner, K. 1970. "The 'Monetarist Revolution' in Monetary Theory." *Weltwirtschaftliches Archiv* 105:1–29.

Davis, O. A.; Dempster, M. A. H.; and Wildavsky, A. 1966. "A Theory of the Budgetary Process." *American Political Science Review* 60:529–47.

Downs, A. 1957. *An Economic Theory of Democracy*. New York: Harper.

Downs, A. 1972. "Up and Down with Ecology." *Public Interest* 28:38–50.

Eckstein, A. 1968. "Economic Fluctuations in Communist China's Domestic Development." In *China in Crisis*, edited by P. Ho and T. Tsou, pp. 702–30. Chicago: University of Chicago Press.

Fair, R. C. 1975. *On Controlling the Economy to Win Elections*. Cowles Foundation Discussion Paper 397.

Feiwel, G. R. 1974. "Reflections on Kalecki's Theory of Political Business Cycles." *Kyklos* 27:21–48.

Frey, B. S. 1977. "On the Political Economy of Public Services." In *The Economics of Public Services*, edited by M. S. Feldstein and R. P. Inman, pp. 415–34. London: Macmillan and Co.

Frey, B. S., and Garbers, H. 1972. "Der Einfluß wirtschaftlicher Variabler auf die Popularität der Regierung." *Jahrbücher für Nationalökonomie und Statistik* 186:281–95.

Frey, B. S., and Lau, L. J. 1968. "Towards a Mathematical Model of Government Behavior." *Zeitschrift für Nationalökonomie* 28:355–80.

Frey, B. S., and Ramser, H. J. 1976. "The Political Business Cycle: Comment." *Review of Economic Studies* 43:553–55.

Frey, B. S., and Schneider, F. 1978*a* "An Empirical Study of Politico-Economic Interaction in the U.S." *Review of Economics and Statistics* 60:174–83.

______. 1978*b*. "A Politico-Economic Model of the United Kingdom. *Economic Journal* 88:243–53.

______. 1979. "An Econometric Model with an Endogenous Government Sector." *Public Choice* 34:29–43.

Goodhart, C. A. E., and Bhansali, R. J. 1970. "Political Economy." *Political Studies* 18:43–106.

Goodman, S., and Kramer, G. H. 1975. "Comment on Arcelus and Meltzer: The Effect of Aggregate Economic Conditions on Congressional Elections." *American Political Science Review* 69:1255–65.

Hibbs, D. A., Jr. 1974. "Problems of Statistical Estimation and Causal Inference in Time Series Regression Models." In *Sociological Methodology 1973–74*, edited by H. L. Costner, pp. 252–308. San Francisco: Jossey-Bass.

Kalecki, M. 1943. "Political Aspects of Full Employment." *Political Quarterly* 14:322–31.

Kolm, S. C. 1970. "L'avenir du capitalisme américain." *Revue d'Economie Politique* 80:999–1028.

Kramer, G. H. 1971. "Short Run Fluctuations in U.S. Voting Behaviour, 1896–1964." *American Political Science Review* 65:131–43.

______. 1975. *A Dynamical Model of Political Equilibrium.* Cowles Foundation Discussion Paper No. 396.

Lepper, S. J. 1974. "Voting Behavior and Aggregate Policy Targets." *Public Choice* 18:67–82.

Lindbeck, A. 1975. "Business Cycles, Politics and International Economic Dependence." *Skandinaviska Enskilda Banken Quarterly Review* 2:53–68.

______. 1976. "Stabilization Policy in Open Economies with Endogenous Politicians." *American Economic Review Papers and Proceedings* 66:1–19.

MacRae, D. C. 1977. "A Political Model of the Business Cycle." *Journal of Political Economy* 85:239–63.

Meltzer, A. H., and Vellrath, M. 1975. "The Effects of Economic Policy on Votes for the Presidency: Some Evidence from Recent Elections. Contribution to a Conference on the Economic Analysis of Politics, NBER, New York, 1975.

Morris, J. M., and Giral, B. J. 1969. "Notas sobre a Estrutura de um Modêlo Econômico-Político." *Dados,* Publicação Semestral do Instituto Universitârio de Perquisas do Rio de Janeiro, pp. 129–40.

Mueller, J. E. 1970. "Presidential Popularity from Truman to Johnson." *American Political Science Review* 64:18–34.

Niskanen, W. A. 1975. *Economic and Fiscal Effects on the Popular Vote for the President.* Working Paper No. 25, Graduate School of Public Policy, University of California, Berkeley.

Nordhaus, W. D. 1975. "The Political Business Cycle." *Review of Economic Studies* 42:169–90.

Oliveira, J. H. G. 1960. "Cyclical Growth under Collectivism." *Kyklos* 13:229–55.

Okun, A. M. 1973. "Comments on Stigler's Paper." *American Economic Review Papers and Proceedings* 63:172–77.

Pommerehne, W. W. 1978. "Institutional Approaches to Public Expenditure: Empirical Evidence from Swiss Municipalities." *Journal of Public Economics* 9:163–201.

Rae, D. W. 1971. "An Estimate of the Decisiveness of Election Outcomes." In *Social Choice,* edited by B. Lieberman, pp. 379–92. New York: Gordon and Breach.

Rothenberg, J. 1965. "A Model of Economic and Political Decision-making." In *The Public Economy of Urban Communities,* edited by J. Margolis, pp. 1–38. Baltimore: Johns Hopkins University Press.

Stigler, G. J. 1973. "General Economic Conditions and National Elections." *American Economic Review Papers and Proceedings* 63:160–67.

Tufte, E. R. 1973. "The Relationship Between Seats and Votes in Two-Party Systems." *American Political Science Review* 67:540–54.

______. 1974. "The Political Manipulation of the Economy: Influence of the Electoral Cycle on Macroeconomic Performance and Policy." Mimeographed. Princeton University.

______. 1975. "Determinants of the Outcome of Midterm Congressional Elections." *American Political Science Review* 69:812–27.

Wittman, D. A. 1973. "Parties as Utility Maximizers." *American Political Science Review* 67:490–98.

Legislatures as Unions

Robert E. McCormick and Robert D. Tollison

Good fences make good neighbors; so the saying goes. But since the most fertile ground often lies along the fence row, the cost of neighborliness is sometimes too high. So it has been with the modern colonization by economists of subjects usually reserved for other social sciences. Not untypically, the conventional views held by other disciplines have been strongly challenged by the application of economic methodology. While it is interesting that economists tend to generate different conclusions about social processes from those accepted in other social sciences, it suffices to say here simply that we write in this tradition.

We address the problem of how state legislators are paid. Our explanation of legislative pay will seem familiar to economists. Nonetheless, it will contrast markedly with the explanations and approaches to the same problem offered by other expert observers of such matters. The following quotations provide a menu of competing hypotheses:

> Despite the fact that in recent years a few states have provided substantial salaries for their legislators, no public servant in relation to his responsibilities is more underpaid. (Maddox and Fuquay 1966, p. 135)

> Most states fail to pay their lawmakers anything approximating a living wage. (Straayer 1973, p. 93)

> To a large extent, legislators are paid according to the frequency of regular sessions. (Council of State Governments 1968, p. 45)

> Legislators in annual session States generally fare better than lawmakers in biennial States. (Council of State Governments 1972, p. 54)

> As many analysts have pointed out, the most significant variable in determining the size of legislative salaries appears to be state population. (Council of State Governments 1974, p. 59)

Our explanation of legislative pay is fueled by a completely different mental set than that implied in the initial two quotations. We also provide a more complete model of the determination of legislative pay with which the type of claims made by the last three sources can be evaluated.

In effect, we view legislators as participants in a labor market, and we try

Reprinted from *Journal of Political Economy* 86 (February 1978):63–78, by permission of The University of Chicago Press.

to explain differences in the legal pay of legislators by factors that affect the supply of and demand for their services. We present a model of the legislature as a labor union, where in some states the legislative wage is set in the constitution (the analogue to competition) and in others it is set by the legislators (monopoly). We test the implications of the model with respect to relative legislator wages in the two types of states and with respect to other aspects of the legislature as a union (e.g., size of the legislature). We also test an implication of the model which suggests that, where legislative pay is low, the market for legislator services clears by attracting more legislators, such as lawyers, for whom legislative service can be combined with other outside earning activities. All the implications of the model hold up quite well in empirical tests. We examine state legislators because legislative pay and procedures differ across states, yielding a natural cross section of data on such matters (Council of State Governments 1976). The implications of the model, as such, could be applied to any legislative setting.

Basically, we share Stigler's (1976) concern with modeling the central tasks of representation properly. He states that "the central task of representation is to give efficient representation to the collection of group interests that express the desires of citizens who compose the state" (p. 17). We pose a corollary question, namely, "What is the legal payoff to the representative for performing those tasks?"

In section 1 we present a model stressing the supply of and demand for legislator services under union and nonunion conditions. The model involves the solution of a unique problem of present value maximization. We perform an empirical test of the implications of the model regarding relative legislator wages using data for 1974 on state governments in section 2. In section 3 we test an inference of the model that more lawyers will be present in legislatures when legislative pay is low. Finally, we offer some brief concluding remarks in section 4 on the relation between the pay of legislators and the prospects for malfeasance.

1. No Man is Safe When the Legislature is in Session: Theory and Preliminary Implications

The wide range in legislative pay among the fifty states is illustrated in table 1. Biennial pay for legislators in 1974–75 ranges from $200 in New Hampshire to $64,140 in California. Stigler's (1976) remarks about the small range of variation in the size of legislatures are reversed for legislative pay. This is a quite wide range of variation in wages across states, and this article presents an explanation of this variation.

The supply of legislative services is analogous to the supply of any service where labor is extensively used in (roughly) fixed proportions to other inputs. The quantity supplied of legislative services (which we will measure in man-years per year) is therefore determined by the relative wage, the price of inputs other than labor, and technology. Each state has a separate supply

TABLE 1. Estimated Biennial Compensation of Legislators, 1974–75

State	Biennial Compensation	State	Biennial Compensation
New Hampshire	$ 200	Georgia	$18,432
Rhode Island	600	Kansas	18,928
Utah	3,200	Arizona	19,170
Wyoming	3,348	Tennessee	19,909
Arkansas	3,600	Oklahoma	19,920
New Mexico	3,600	New Jersey	20,000
Maine	4,250	Oregon	20,010
North Dakota	6,540	Delaware	21,050
Montana	6,954	Indiana	21,420
South Dakota	7,475	Iowa	21,580
Idaho	7,535	Minnesota	23,862
Nevada	8,260	Maryland	25,000
Vermont	8,430	Virginia	25,850
Nebraska	10,000	Mississippi	26,480
Washington	11,200	Florida	27,125
Kentucky	12,350	Massachusetts	27,776
West Virginia	12,600	Hawaii	28,960
Alabama	12,940	Pennsylvania	31,200
Connecticut	13,000	Wisconsin	31,356
South Carolina	14,400	Ohio	35,000
Colorado	15,200	Michigan	38,000
Missouri	16,800	Alaska	43,920
Texas	17,400	Illinois	49,424
North Carolina	17,635	New York	57,500
Louisiana	18,000	California	64,140

Source: Council of State Governments 1976, 37.
Note: Includes salary, daily pay, and unvouchered expense allowances. Excludes special session compensation, per diem business allowances, mileage and transportation, and all vouchered expenses. In instances where daily pay or expenses were provided, days in session were estimated on the basis of days in session in 1973–74.

function, but we do not expect the conditions of supply to vary greatly across states. Potential legislators are never a finite fraction of the available labor in a state, and the occupational composition of legislatures is highly similar across states (Jewell and Patterson 1966, 44–48). These positions are held primarily by members of professions that can capitalize readily on certain aspects of being a legislator. Lawyers thereby avoid the professional ban on advertising (at least until the recent Supreme Court decision), and often continue to draw a wage from their law firms while serving. Farmers can be legislators where sessions are held between growing seasons. The reason that banking, insurance, and real estate people gravitate to these offices is not hard to discern. Our theory will lead us to expect relatively more legislators, such as lawyers, who can combine legislative service with outside earning opportunities in states where the legislative wage is low, but we defer this discussion until section 3.

In each state there is some demand for legislative influence. The demand for legislative influence implies a derived demand for legislators.[1] The technical relationship between influence and legislators is not one of proportionality because an excessive number of legislators would dilute the influence of each and might not be able to pass any laws. In fact, as Stigler points out, the influence of a legislator is a monotonically decreasing function of the size of the legislature. We further expect that, given the lack of low-cost substitutes for legislative action within a state, the elasticity of the demand for representation with respect to the legislative wage rate must be close to zero over the relevant range. We make no a priori estimate of the income elasticity. Across states, in contrast to the relative invariability of supply in this market, we expect that the demand for representation will shift as a function of state income, population, budget size, and so forth.

With this background in mind, we note that wage determination takes essentially two forms among states. In some states legislative pay is set in the constitution and is quite difficult to change. A new wage would require the passage of a constitutional proposal. Such proposals typically emanate from the legislature under relatively strict voting and quorum rules and must be signed by the governor and passed in a statewide referendum. In other states, pay is set by a statute passed by both houses of the legislature and signed by the governor. These pay bills are subject to legislative consideration under normal voting and quorum rules and do not require a statewide referendum.[2]

We contend that legislative determination of pay by statute amounts to a strong form of union power. Unions typically achieve higher relative wages by restricting entry. In this case entry is somewhat more loosely controlled via constitutional limitations on the size of the legislature and on the procedures for gaining a seat, and legislators are given a direct hand in wage determination. We would expect to observe the impact of this monopoly power in higher relative wages for legislators in these states.

The conditions in the legislative labor market for a single state are depicted in figure 1. Each legislature is treated as a separate labor market. A measure of legislative output (Q_L) in terms of man-years per year is on the horizontal axis, and annual legal pay (W_L) as dollars per man-year is on the vertical axis. The competitive supply curve for successful applicants for these seats is given by S. This relationship represents the wage that must be forthcoming for a given level of output to persuade prospective legislators to run for and to accept office. Following our previous argument, we draw a completely inelastic demand curve over the relevant range for the services of legislators. In the absence of any contrary evidence, we assume that existing wages clear the market for the given constraint on legislative size in both union and nonunion states. That is, there is no excess supply.

In states where the legislative wage is constitutionally determined, some given wage, W_C, will prevail. Candidates will adjust to the given wage, and

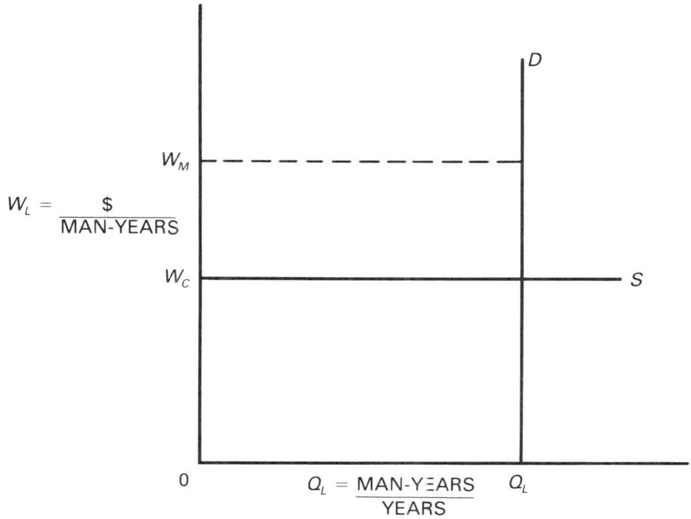

Fig. 1. Determination of legislative pay

supply or marginal opportunity costs will shift accordingly as more- or less-qualified individuals seek election, so that the market clears. In states that allow legislative control over pay, the wage is adjusted by legislators to maximize the present value of a seat. This wage is, for the moment, arbitrarily drawn in figure 1 at W_M. There are no free rents in this case because higher pay will be dissipated in competition for seats. If W_M is high, more able individuals will compete for legislative seats, and in the long run they will receive a competitive rate of return by having higher opportunity costs and/or by spending more to capture seats. Thus, there will only be gains from unexpected increases in wage rates.

The main issue confronting this theory concerns the forces which constrain the legislator from setting an infinite wage in figure 1. Since we argue that the demand for legislator time is completely inelastic over the relevant range, this pay problem reduces to a question of what limits the wage-setting ability of the legislature under these conditions.

Think of the problem in this way. Imagine that the Wish Fairy makes you the following proposition: You may make a wish today, but one year from now the fairy will return and (*a*) grant you your wish and allow you to make another one, or (*b*) deny your wish and disallow you any more wishes.[3] The fairy's decision is predicated on the premise that the higher the wish, the more likely is option *b* (rejection at the polls). The question facing the typical legislator under these conditions, then, is what wage to wish for when the wage goes into effect after the next election. That is, how does he maximize

$$\text{present value } (PV) = \int_0^T We^{-rs}ds, \quad (1)$$

subject to the constraint that $T = T(W)$, $(\partial T/\partial W) < 0$?[4] Or in words, how does he maximize the present value of this stream of wishes subject to the constraint that the higher the wish, the shorter the stream?

We can rewrite (1) as

$$PV = W\left(-\frac{1}{r}e^{-r\cdot T(W)} + \frac{1}{r}\right). \tag{2}$$

The first-order conditions for maximum present value with respect to W are thus

$$\frac{\partial PV}{\partial W} = e^{-r\cdot T(W)}\left(W\frac{\partial T}{\partial W} - \frac{1}{r}\right) + \frac{1}{r} = 0. \tag{3}$$

The result given by (3) merely states that the present value of the flow of services from the wish is maximized where W is chosen so that (3) holds. To solve for an optimum W, it is necessary to specify a functional form for $T(W)$.

An economically interesting case is

$$T(W) = \log\frac{a}{W}, \tag{4}$$

where a is some shift parameter, the determinants of which we will discuss presently. Two general properties of this function are useful. First,

$$\frac{\partial T}{\partial W} = -\frac{1}{W} < 0. \tag{5}$$

Second, the higher W, the slower $T(W)$ declines, since $(\partial^2 T/\partial W^2) = (1/W^2) > 0$.

By inserting this functional form in (3), we can solve for the optimum W. Thus,

$$\hat{W} = e^{\log a} - \frac{\log[1 - \log(1 + r)]}{\log(1 + r)}.\text{[5]} \tag{6}$$

So the optimum wage to set under the terms of the problem facing the typical legislator is given by equation (6). For illustration, we discuss two economic properties of this result.

First, as the discount rate increases, the optimum wage increases. That is, it can easily be shown that

$$\frac{\partial(\log \hat{W})}{\partial r} = \left\{\left[\log(1 + r) - \frac{r}{1 + r}\right]\Big/ r^2\right\} > 0. \tag{7}$$

As the terms of this pay problem make clear, the major influence on the durability of the wage payment is the prospect for reelection, which depends on factors such as closeness of party rivalry, age of the legislator, and so forth.

Second, the shift parameter, a, can be stated as a function of certain aspects of legislatures. In general, the change in the optimum W for a change in any of the arguments of a will have the same sign as the change in a for the change in any of its determinants. For example, as we argue below, the number of representatives (R) should affect the success of the legislative union in a predictable way. That is, a larger number of legislators will frustrate the success of the wage cartel. Thus, from equation (7) we expect that

$$\frac{\partial(\log \hat{W})}{\partial R} = \frac{1}{a}\frac{\partial a}{\partial R} < 0. \quad (8)$$

In our test of the model below, we employ this general interpretation of a to derive testable implications about aspects of legislatures that are likely to be important in the wage-setting process.

To recap somewhat, the economic analogue to the Wish Fairy problem is not hard to draw. We know that entry is not entirely barred in legislatures and that tenure extending beyond the present term is not guaranteed. This means that the present value of a seat will be inversely related to the wage rate after some point, because higher wages will attract new entrants and alienate voters, both of which dampen reelection prospects and offset the effect of increasing the wage on the present value of seats. Incumbents must thus trade off union wage gains and other benefits from being in office against the extra costs associated with increased competition to retain seats. This is precisely the economic content of the Wish Fairy problem, where legislative pay bills apply after the next election. There is thus a determinate upper bound on the monopoly wage in our problem.

As a result of monopoly power in this labor market, then, wages in states where legislators can set their own wage will be higher on average (W_M in fig. 1) relative to states where the wage is set in the constitution (W_C). The legislative union predictably will have a substantial impact on relative wages because the demand for legislator services will be quite inelastic, as we posited earlier. This condition follows from the rules of derived demand in two related senses. First, there is only one legislature per state, so there is not a nonunion sector from which to buy output. Second, there are in general poor substitutes for the services of legislators (e.g., laws).

Furthermore, two aspects of legislatures which are related to the wage-setting process can be treated within the interpretation of the shift parameter, a, in our model.

First, the size of the legislature is analogous to the size of a cartel. A larger number of legislators should thus influence the success of the wage cartel in a negative manner. This is our expectation, although we recognize following Stigler (1976) that the range of variation in legislative sizes is not large and that as a result we may not be able to detect empirically the effect of the number of legislators on the wage-setting process.

Second, since members of this union must stand for reelection, they are not guaranteed lifetime tenure as union members. The relationship between tenure and pay is twofold: higher pay promotes entry, and incumbents pay themselves more. Where there is free competition in entry into legislatures, we expect that tenure will be lower at higher rates of pay. Where there are monopolistic restrictions on entry (e.g., gerrymandering by incumbents or by the judiciary), we expect that tenure will be longer at higher rates of pay. We argue, following Crain (1977), that the latter case is more likely to predominate in state legislatures and that therefore $[\partial(\log \hat{W})/\partial T] = (1/a)\ (\partial a/\partial T) > 0$. In other words, we expect that tenure will be longer at higher rates of pay.

The conceptual experiment in figure 1 consists of converting a state where the legislative wage is set in the constitution to one where the wage is set by statute. We contend that the conditions of supply in this market are relatively homogeneous across states, but that we can observe demand differences across states. We can thus estimate a locus of market-equilibrium points over states, which can be interpreted as a Marshallian supply curve of labor, that is, the wage per man-year that is necessary to generate specific quantities of legislative services. This gives us an empirical means of testing the union metaphor and its implications with respect to the relative pay of legislators.

2. No Man is Safe When the Legislature is in Session: A Test of Relative Wage Implications

A test of the implications of our model regarding relative legislator wages in union and nonunion states is summarized in equation (9) and explained below.

$$\text{wage per man-year} = \begin{array}{c} f\,(\text{man-years per biennium, pay} \\ \text{method, date of state constitution,} \\ \text{turnover, no. representatives}) \end{array} \qquad (9)$$

The dependent variable, wage per man-year, is the annual wage of a legislator. Annual pay is measured as the average of a two-year period to overcome problems of annual versus biennial sessions. Biennial legislators would thus receive in one year twice the amount of this wage.

As in the case of other labor markets, the marginal product of labor will play a decisive role in wage determination. The practical problem for empirical purposes is to define the marginal product of a legislator (a task that continues to elude GNP accountants). We chose the number of legislators times the duration of the legislative session, which is simply man-years per biennium. As a supply variable, this measure picks up the duration of service. For example, in those cases where one legislator worked twice as long as the other at the same annual wage, his wage per man-year would be one-half of his counterpart. In principle, this measure of legislative output regressed against a measure of pay is analogous to an aggregate supply curve of legislative services across states.[6]

A dummy variable for pay method provides a direct test of the unionization hypothesis since it measures the degree of union power on average. It is anticipated that the dummy variable will have a positive sign. That is, states where legislators can set their own wage should exhibit higher wages.

The date of the state constitution is entered to check for the unionization effect in the following sense. The trend in more recent state constitutions is toward more effective cartelization of the political process. This variable may thus capture an effect on wages independently of the degree of union power. We expect newer constitutions to reflect higher wages, and since the date of the state constitution is entered as the year of adoption, we expect the sign on this variable to be positive.

Our measure of union tenure is turnover in state senates and houses.[7] Turnover is defined as the number of new legislators in 1974 divided by the size of the chamber. Since lower turnover implies longer tenure for the average legislator, we expect the relationship between turnover and pay to be negative. Such a finding would support the argument that tenure is longer at higher rates of pay due to entry restraints.

The size of the senate or house is entered to check for the effect of numbers on union success. We expect that larger legislatures will be more difficult to organize and discipline as a wage cartel.

Conventional multiple-regression procedures were used to estimate the model. We present the results of only the logarithmic specification of the model because it offers a slightly better fit than the linear form, and we can thus economize in the presentation of results. The coefficients in equation (10) are estimated from 1974 data on the variables across states in the United States (Council of State Governments 1976).[8] A copy of the data is available from the authors on request.

Fitting the model by ordinary least squares yields the prediction equations for legislative compensation given in table 2. The results in table 2 can be interpreted as the wage necessary to fill the legislature for a given amount of output, that is, a quasi–supply curve of state legislators for the United States as a whole. There are two prediction equations, one for state houses of representatives and one for state senates.

The output variable, man-years per biennium, turns out to be a useful predictor of legislative wages. The elasticity of wages with respect to this measure of output is .71 in the senate equation and .65 in the house equation. This means that a 100 percent increase in output requires a 65–71 percent increase in pay and that this relationship is quite inelastic.

Direct evidence on union power can be found by examining the dummy

TABLE 2. Log Compensation of Legislators (1974)

Independent Variables	House		Senate	
Man-years per biennium	0.65	(2.85)*	0.71	(3.38)*
Pay method	1.09	(3.86)*	1.25	(4.58)*
Date of state constitution	11.56	(2.60)*	12.93	(3.03)*
Turnover	−0.06	(−0.20)	−0.41	(−2.17)*
No. representatives	−0.46	(−1.27)	−0.61	(1.43)
Intercept	−82.37	(−2.44)*	−92.97	(−2.87)*
R^2	0.53		0.58	
$F_{5,36}$	8.02*		9.75*	

Source: Calculated from Council of State Governments 1976.
**t*-values significant at the 5 percent level or better.

variable for pay method. This variable appears at high levels of statistical significance, and in order to examine its impact more closely we convert the results into dollar terms. This is done in the following manner. Using the estimated coefficients in table 2 and the actual mean values of the other independent variables (calculated over all states), we let pay method take on the values 0 for constitutional states and 1 for union states and observe the change in ln wage.[9] We convert this change to dollars by taking anti-logarithms. This procedure yields an estimate of an average effect of pay procedure in dollar terms, holding constant the levels of the other independent variables across states.[10] For the house equation this procedure predicts a wage of $5,802 for constitutional states and $17,257 for pay-by-statute states. This represents a 197 percent increase in legal pay. The results for the senate equation are analogous. The predicted senate wage is $5,170 in constitutional states and $18,045 in union states. This represents a 249 percent increase in legal pay. As we expected, then, given the extreme degree of inelasticity of demand in this labor market, the legislative union is astonishingly powerful. Compare these results, for example, to Lewis's (1963) finding that unionization in the United States led, on average, to a 10–15 percent excess of union over nonunion wages (as a percent of nonunion wages) as of the late 1950s.

The variable on the date of the state constitution has the expected sign and appears at high levels of statistical significance. Since we interpret this variable as more recent implying greater cartelization, the effect on wages is probably strengthened by the fact that, even in states where the legislative wage is set in the constitution, a new wage and other cartel measures (such as entry restrictions) can be suggested by the legislature when the constitution is changed.

The negative coefficients on turnover support the argument that tenure is longer at higher rates of pay (remember that lower turnover implies longer tenure), and the results are statistically strong in the senate equation. We have some evidence, then, that turnover measures the effects of monopolistic restrictions on entry.

We find the expected negative signs on the coefficients on the number of representatives at reasonable levels of statistical significance (at the 16 and 22 percent levels, respectively). Larger legislatures thus tentatively appear to frustrate the operations of the wage cartel.

Finally, we note that the model explains over half of the variation in legislative pay across states for both senates and houses and that this specification holds up remarkably well for other recent cross sections taken from the *Book of the States* (see Council of State Governments, various years).[11]

3. No Man is Safe When the Legislature is in Session: The Incidence of Lawyers as Legislators

Where pay is fixed in the constitution and is therefore low, the market for legislators presumably clears by attracting more legislators, such as lawyers, for whom legislative service can be combined with other outside earning activities. This implies that there should be larger fractions of lawyers in legislatures where rates of wage pay are lower, for then the outside benefits are a larger fraction of total pay. However, two other considerations confound this effect. The typical labor supply argument that, in a given state, more lawyers will seek to become legislators where wage pay is higher (especially those not willing or able to procure outside earnings) has the opposite effect. More important, as the tentacles of state government extend to increasing facets of state life, the potential outside gains to legislator-lawyers increase. State expenditures are, however, a proxy for the largesse of government and are highly correlated with legislative pay.[12] Consequently, increasing outside earning potential for legislator-lawyers is coincident with a high legislative wage, and thus the second confounding effect is that increasing legislative wage pay should lead to an increased fraction of lawyers (because of higher outside pay). Empirically, however, we find that the argument that more lawyers will be in legislatures where the legislative wage is low dominates the two confounding effects. The following model is employed for our test.

$$\frac{\%\text{ lawyers in state legislatures}}{\%\text{ lawyers in state population}} = \begin{array}{c} f\,(\text{associate lawyers'} \\ \text{average income} - \text{legis-} \\ \text{lative wage, legislative} \\ \text{wage, voter turnout}) \end{array} \tag{10}$$

The dependent variable adjusts the percentage of lawyers in state legislatures by the percentage of lawyers in the state population. The first independent variable is a measure of the opportunity costs to a (young) lawyer for serving in the legislature. We expect a negative sign, since higher opportunity costs should be associated with a smaller percentage of a state's lawyers in the legislature. Legislative wage is the annual wage pay of legislators and provides a direct test of the outside earnings hypothesis. We expect a negative sign, since, other things being equal, we expect more legislator-lawyers

TABLE 3. Adjusted Percentage of Lawyers in State Legislatures (1974)

Independent Variables		
Associate lawyer's average income − legislative wage	−0.011	(−2.71)*
Legislative wage	−0.0067	(−1.62)*
Voter turnout	−11.48	(−6.31)*
Intercept	887.6	(9.22)*
R^2	0.57	
$F_{3,44}$	19.12*	

Sources: Calculated from *Census of Selected Service Industries* 1975; Council of State Governments 1976; Insurance Information Institute 1976; and *Statistical Abstract of the United States* 1976.

**t*-values significant at the 8 percent level or better.

where legislative pay is lower. Finally, voter turnout is entered in equation (10) to check a simple monitoring hypothesis, namely, that higher turnouts, measured as the percentage of voting-age population casting votes, reflect greater concern among voters about the outside earning activities of legislators. We therefore expect a negative sign.

We estimate the model by ordinary least squares for state senates and houses combined.[13] Table 3 presents the results.

The results are as expected for the measure of lawyers' opportunity costs and for voter turnout. The sign on legislative wage is negative, reflecting the point that the relative outside earnings hypothesis overwhelms the other confounding considerations. The individual coefficients are all highly statistically significant, and the model explains a great deal of the variation in the adjusted percentage of legislator-lawyers across states.[14]

4. No Man Is Safe When the Legislature Is in Session: Wage Pay and Malfeasance

We find that the union metaphor is a useful means of analyzing and explaining legislative pay. Our metaphor, in effect, stresses a monopoly aspect of politics, and in this regard we should never forget what Knight (1951) said in his presidential address to the American Economic Association: "Most of the evils inherent in the market organization plainly inhere still more in political campaigning, legislative debates, and administration, perhaps even judicial trials. Especially the tendency to centralization and concentration of power—which can only go so far until voting and political discussion will be empty forms if the boss allows them to go on at all" (p. 28).

Nonetheless, our discussion begs the question of why states differ in their method of setting legislative pay. Recent theories of the control of politicians and other public (and private) employees who must be "trusted" suggest an answer (Barro 1973; Becker and Stigler 1974).

Becker and Stigler (1974) stress that the way to control individuals in positions of trust, such as legislators, "is to raise the salaries of enforcers above what they could get elsewhere, by an amount that is inversely related to the probability of detection, and directly related to the size of bribes and other benefits from malfeasance. A difference in salaries imposes a cost of dismissal equal to the present value of the difference between the future earnings stream in enforcement and other occupations. This cost can more than offset the gain from malfeasance'' (p. 6). Or, put somewhat differently, they argue that ''trust calls for a salary premium not necessarily because better quality persons are thereby attracted, but because higher salaries impose a cost on violations of trust'' (p. 12). Our results suggest that outside earning activities will be more important to politicians where legislative pay is lower, as in states where their pay is set in the constitution. In higher-pay states, individuals who will find it less in their self-interest to seek outside earnings (e.g., bribes) will be attracted to legislative service. In other words, politicians will steal less if they are paid more, and voters may view legislative determination of pay as a method of controlling malfeasance among politicians.

NOTES

We are grateful to Raymond Battalio, Mark Crain, Roy Gilbert, John Kagel, Thomas Saving, Richard Wagner, and an unidentified referee of the *Journal of Political Economy* for helpful comments on earlier drafts of this paper. George Stigler and Arleen Leibowitz deserve special thanks for help. The usual disclaimer applies.

1. Stigler (1976) notes some other analogies between characteristics of consumer demand for privately produced goods and citizen demand for legislation.
2. There is also some use of pay commissions among states. These commissions are appointed by the legislature, and no elaborate theory of regulation is needed to explain why we treat these states as cases where the legislature sets the wage.
3. We rule out political comebacks for analytical simplicity.
4. We employ the continuous form of the present value function as an approximation to the discrete case for mathematical simplicity.
5. This result holds for $r > 0$, i.e., when the discount rate is positive, and for $a > e$ and $a > W$.
6. As a practical matter, however, other available proxies for the marginal product of a legislator (e.g., bills introduced) are highly correlated with man-years per biennium, and our results are not sensitive to the use of this particular definition.
7. Turnover in unions is not an unheard consideration (Stigler 1966, 267–68).
8. Due to the lack of data on one or more variables for 1974, Kansas, Louisiana, Minnesota, Mississippi, Nebraska, New Hampshire, South Carolina, and Virginia are omitted from this test. We are thus analyzing forty-two state legislatures.
9. This is equivalent in logarithms to letting pay method take on the values of 1 and e (i.e., ln pay method = 0 and 1), and observing the change in ln wage.
10. We chose to estimate the dollar results in this manner in order to present the ''average'' effect of unionization in the labor market. This obviously is not the only way to estimate the effect of unionization. It all depends on what is held in the pound of *ceteris paribus* in terms of the mean values of the other independent variables. For example, we could use values for only constitutional states and

predict the effect of unionization of a "typical" constitutional state, or we could use values for a single constitutional state and estimate the effect of unionizing that particular state. The reader can easily derive such estimates, but we would happily make them available upon request.

11. Two additional aspects of our results should be reported. First, the inclusion of a variable (size of majority) to measure the degree of competitiveness among parties in our estimating equations adds nothing to the analysis. Such a variable does not affect the other results and shows no statistical credibility in its own right. We take this as evidence that parties do not play a prominent role in determining legislative wages and also as additional evidence that the appropriate analogue to competition in politics is not party competition but competition among incumbents and potential entrants. Second, governors must sign legislative-pay bills, and we expect that they will therefore be cut in on union wage gains. We did not tackle this problem rigorously, where, e.g., the Wish Fairy problem is extended to cover the case where, by analogy, the husband (legislator) and wife (governor) have to optimize the stream of wishes jointly. We did find empirically that the pay of governors is related to the method of pay determination, as in the case of legislators, but at a substantially lower order of magnitude. For example, the difference in relative gubernatorial pay due to union power was 18 percent in 1971, which is much smaller than the differential we found for legislators. It is possible, however, that governors secure favors from legislators for signing pay bills that do not show up in their legal pay. Thus, if governors are rent extractors as a group, they may be receiving payments in kind.
12. This is consistent with our earlier observation that man-years per biennium is highly correlated with state expenditures.
13. Nebraska and Wyoming are excluded from this test due to lack of data on one or more variables for 1974.
14. We note two additional aspects of our results in this section. First, the outside earnings hypothesis continues to overwhelm the confounding effects if voter turnout is excluded from the model. The general explanatory power of the model falls, but the direction and statistical credibility of the coefficients on the measure of lawyers' opportunity costs and legislative wage remain essentially unchanged. Second, we note but do not report here that the percentage of similar occupations in state legislatures, such as real estate professionals, can be readily explained by a similar model.

REFERENCES

Barro, Robert T. "The Control of Politicians: An Economic Model." *Public Choice* 14 (Spring 1973): 19–42.

Becker, Gary S., and Stigler, George J. "Law Enforcement, Malfeasance, and Compensation of Enforcers." *Journal of Legal Studies* 3 (January 1974): 1–18.

Census of Selected Service Industries. 1972 Subject Series. *Legal Services* (SC72-S-4). Washington, D.C.: Government Printing Office, December 1975.

Council of State Governments. *Book of the States 1968–1969.* Chicago: Council of State Governments, 1968.

———. *Book of the States 1972–1973.* Lexington: Iron Works Pike, 1972.

———. *Book of the States 1974–1975.* Lexington: Iron Works Pike, 1974.

———. *Book of the States 1976–1977.* Lexington: Iron Works Pike, 1976.

Crain, W. Mark. "On the Structure and Stability of Political Markets." *Journal of Political Economy* 85, no. 4 (August 1977): 829–42.

Insurance Information Institute. *Occupational Profile of State Legislators.* New York: Insurance Information Inst., 1976.

Jewell, Malcolm E., and Patterson, Samuel C. *The Legislative Process in the United States.* New York: Random House, 1966.

Knight, Frank H. "The Role of Principles in Economics and Politics." *American Economic Review* 41 (March 1951): 1–29.

Lewis, H. Gregg. *Unionism and Relative Wages in the United States: An Empirical Inquiry.* Chicago: University of Chicago Press, 1963.

Maddox, Russell W., and Fuquay, Robert F. *State and Local Government.* 2d ed. Princeton, N.J.: Nostrand, 1966.

Statistical Abstract of the United States. Washington, D.C.: Government Printing Office, 1976.

Stigler, George J. *The Theory of Price.* New York: Macmillan Co., 1966.

———. "The Sizes of Legislatures." *Journal of Legal Studies* 5 (January 1976): 17–34.

Straayer, John A. *American State and Local Government.* Columbus, Ohio: Merrill, 1973.

Burden Sharing, Strategy, and the Design of NATO

Todd Sandler and John F. Forbes

War is a matter not so much of arms
as of expenditure, through which
arms may be made of service.
—*Thucydides,* History I

The theory of public goods played a fundamental role in the economic studies that predicted burden-sharing and suboptimality problems for military alliances.[1] The "purely public" deterrence model showed that disproportionate burdens were shouldered by large rich allies, and defense expenditures were suboptimal owing to noncooperative behavior (Olson and Zeckhauser 1966, 268–71). Later analyses considered both the deterrent and protective (i.e., damage-limiting) aspects of defense and, in so doing, stressed the impure public good properties.[2] The joint product model (Sandler 1977) is the most comprehensive model of alliance behavior, because it includes private, impure public, and pure public outputs of defense expenditures. Moreover, this model degenerates to the deterrence or the impure public models as special cases.

Changes in the seventies no longer allow for the straightforward application of the pure public good model to alliance behavior. The change in NATO's military strategy, the development of new weapon systems, and the increase of disputes exogenous to the East-West split favor the application of the joint product model, since rivalry in consumption, multiple outputs, benefit exclusion, *and* private benefits are increasingly characterizing modern alliances. These strategic developments concern the doctrine of flexible response, the deployment of tactical nuclear weapons (TNW), and the Strategic Arms Limitation Talks (SALT).[3] New weapon technologies involve multipurpose "Precision-guided munitions" (PGM) which blur the traditional distinctions between conventional, theater nuclear, and strategic weapons (Burt 1976, 23).

This article utilizes the joint product model to examine defense burden sharing and NATO's structure with respect to current strategic, diplomatic, and technological developments. In particular, we show that the unintegrated ("loose") structure of NATO, where allies act with little loss of autonomy, is justifiable from an economic viewpoint due to these developments, because

First published in *Economic Inquiry* 18 (July 1980): 524–44, Journal of the Western Economic Association.

the proportion of excludable benefits *and* the recognition of common interests are increasing in NATO. Even though allies use their discretion to purchase most weapons across markets, *defense burdens are* hypothesized to be approximately *shared according* to private and public *benefits* received. Any discrepancy is attributable to either the provision of strategic nuclear weapons or the pursuit of private benefits yielding jointly produced public benefits; hence, burden sharing is *independent* of the ally's industrial size. Empirical evidence supports our theoretical predictions and discriminates between the joint product and the deterrence models.

Five reasons make this study of general interest. First, the study casts doubt on the classic case for a nonmarket allocative structure (i.e., defense expenditures). Second, ability-to-pay *and* benefit measures are used to analyze burden-sharing behavior within an international organization. Third, the joint product methodology can be profitably employed to examine other international and national organizations. Fourth, this study presents an up-to-date view of American and Western European defense policy. Finally, the analysis *alters conventional wisdom* regarding alliance behavior by enriching and extending the theory and empirical support.

The paper contains six additional sections. The joint product model and its implications are reviewed in section 1, while current developments in strategy and technology are discussed in the next section. Section 3 analyzes NATO's structure. Benefit proxies for burden sharing, the statistical results, and the conclusions are presented in the remaining sections.

1. The Joint Product Model

Deterrence, Protection, and Publicness

By relying on the *threat of punishment,* deterrence *forestalls* hostility through an interalliance information flow of threats and counterthreats.[4] If the *sole* purpose of a weapon is to convey a credible retaliatory threat on behalf of an alliance (e.g., assured destruction), then the weapon is purely deterrent (*DW*) (e.g., Trident submarines, B-1 bombers). The other major component of defense involves an arsenal's damage-limiting abilities used when deterrence fails and war begins. Purely protective or damage-limiting weapons (*PW*) are deployed to deny an enemy its military objective. Antiballistic missiles, antitank guided weapons, and aircraft shelters represent *PW*. Since many weapons (e.g., multipurpose aircraft, cruise missiles) can satisfy both deterrent and damage-limiting purposes, these weapons are classified as mixed defense weapons (*MW*). The mixture of protective and deterrent components can be used to distinguish *MW* along a continuum with *PW* and *DW* located at the poles. While strategic nuclear weapons are best characterized as *DW*, conventional and tactical nuclear weapons are either *PW* or *MW* depending upon the weapon's design and purpose.

How well a weapon fulfills the publicness requirements of nonrivalry and nonexcludability depends in large part on the weapon's classification. Whenever an alliance's commitment to retaliate against aggressive acts directed at any ally is *credible,* then the punishment threat of *DW* provides nonrival benefits to the entire alliance. That is, additional nations can join the alliance without diminishing the deterrence provided to the existing allies. Furthermore, if an attack upon any ally inflicts unacceptable damage on the other allies in terms of fallout, or the loss of foreign investment interests and/or military personnel, then deterrence is nonexcludable, and *DW can* satisfy both characteristics of publicness. Nevertheless, it is doubtful whether deterrence as provided by strategic nuclear weapons is fully nonexcludable, because control of these weapons remains essentially in U.S. hands and the resulting damage to American interests from an attack on European allies may be within acceptable limits.

Many of the benefits derived from *PW* are impurely public owing to elements of rivalry *and* exclusion. When an arsenal of *PW* is required to protect a larger front or boundary as a new ally joins, a *thinning of forces* results from a spatial rivalry which detracts from the protection of the existing allies. This thinning effect depends on the allies' relative locations, the enemy's position, and the topographical characteristics of the front. Insofar as damage-limiting forces can be withdrawn and deployed elsewhere, many benefits of *PW* are subject to exclusion at the will of the provider. When a strong protective force reduces the probability that an opposing army will win, *PW* also provide some purely public benefits to the other allies in the form of deterrence. *MW* embody both deterrent and protective capabilities. Consequently, these weapons exhibit different properties of publicness (especially rivalry) in accordance with their utilization. A formal analysis must treat *MW* and *PW* as producing joint outputs which may be private, pure public, or impure public in nature.

The thinning phenomenon of *PW* and *MW* has important implications for sharing arrangements that determine alliance size, user fees or tolls, and defense provision. If an alliance depends on an arsenal of *PW* (e.g., a conventional war alliance), size restrictions must be based on thinning considerations. A potential ally should be permitted to join whenever its total benefits from membership equal or exceed the thinning costs imposed on the other allies. The price or user charge for a *unit* of defense is determined at the margin by the sum of thinning costs inflicted on the allies. Total charges should differ between allies depending upon their defense utilization rates as determined by their *exposed border* length. Exposed border consists of a country's perimeter less shared perimeter or border with a friendly country. For optimal provision, the sum of the allies' incremental benefits from force concentration (thickening) resulting from an expansion of the arsenal must equal the incremental costs of the new weapons. When utlilization and thinning are measured in an agreed way, the proposed toll scheme can finance optimal provision.[5] In the absence of a sharing arrangement, allies would purchase their weapons and deploy them as they see fit along their borders. Efficiency incentives would induce allies to negotiate subsequent sharing and standardization schemes so that weapons are optimally distributed and interoperable. Hence, rivalry and exclusion aspects of *PW* can *partially circumvent* free rider problems, since markets and sharing arrangements provide some means to share burdens and to approach efficiency based on utilization. Markets will not, however, work perfectly unless the common-interest aspects associated with the pure public outputs of *PW* and *DW* are recognized by the allies.

Alliances are classifiable along a spectrum where placement is determined by the ratio of *PW* to the sum of *PW* and *DW* in the arsenal (see fig. 1). *MW* must be separated into their deterrent and protective components when making the placement. By utilizing the ratio of protective to deterrent elements, *MW* can be transformed in value terms into *PW* and *DW*.

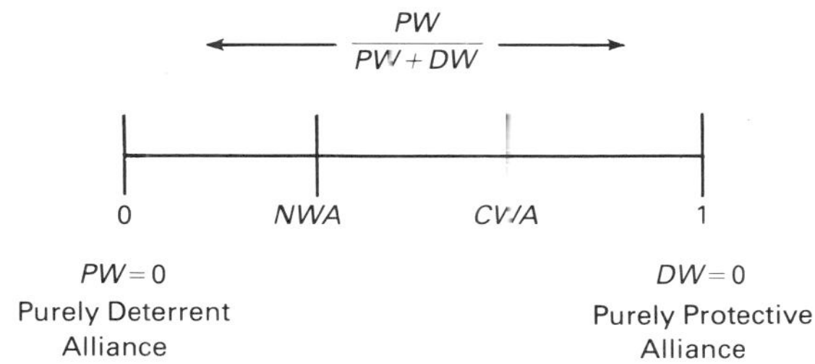

Fig. 1

Diverse alliance types occupy different locations along the continuum; e.g., conventional war alliances (*CWA*) are nearer to the right pole than nuclear war alliances (*NWA*). The right pole corresponds to a purely protective alliance, whereas the left indicates a purely deterrent one. The further an alliance lies on the right, the stronger is the thinning effect *and* the greater is the proportion of excludable benefits.

Defense and Joint Products

In addition to deterrence and damage-limiting protection, alliance-wide expenditures yield benefits that are private between allies, but public within an ally. For example, armed forces can maintain domestic order (e.g., Britain in Northern Ireland), provide foreign exchange to a host nation (e.g., Germany), or facilitate the development of an arms industry (e.g., United States). Expenditures on *DW* and *PW* yield private benefits such as augmented national prestige (for *DW*) and protection of coastal waters (*PW*); however, *PW* probably provide relatively more private benefits, since they can be used for intracountry purposes (e.g., national guard). Modern *DW* primarily include strategic weapons which do not readily serve intracountry threats and purposes. Thus, the right side of the spectrum is hypothesized to include a larger proportion of private benefits.

We assume that a general defense good (or an arsenal) produces deterrence, protection, and one or more private goods in fixed proportions.[6] If the general defense good is optimally provided, the incremental benefits of *all* of the joint outputs must be summed together and equated to the incremental cost of production. Moreover, the incremental benefits from deterrence and damage limitation must be summed over all allies, while those of the private good do not require summing; i.e., only one ally receives each unit. Size considerations for the alliance are solely based on the thinning costs arising from collective utilization of the damage-limitation joint product. This follows because the private goods are not shared and deterrence can be shared at zero costs. Thus, the previously given size requirements still hold. Pricing of the general defense good is related to the marginal value of the private benefits, the marginal thinning costs of protection, and the marginal value of the excludable benefits of deterrence.

The joint product model's implications for NWA are significantly at odds with those of the deterrence model. For the joint product model, *alliance size restrictions* should be determined by thinning. Secondly, defense preferences will be partially revealed and, consequently, efficient provision can be market financed *whenever* private and excludable public outputs are a *substantial* proportion of the jointly produced outputs. Thirdly, the ratio of excludable outputs *to* the sum of excludable and nonexcludable outputs indicates the extent of suboptimality; as the ratio approaches 1, suboptimality is reduced, because free riding declines. An unequal burden will fall on those allies, *regardless of income levels,* who are either providers of *DW* (e.g., Britain, France, United States) *or else* significant purchasers of private and/or excludable public outputs yielding alliance-wide deterrence (e.g., Britain, Germany, United States). In contrast, a deterrent alliance requires *no size restrictions.* Furthermore, allies reveal *false preferences* in the market, and disproportionate burdens are imposed *on the large rich allies.* Finally, the relative economic sizes of the allies determine suboptimality (Olson and Zeckhauser 1966).

2. Strategy, Technology, and the Alliance Spectrum

During the 1950s and early 1960s, NATO was near the left pole of the spectrum, because it relied upon strategic weapons due to the USSR's unbeatable conventional forces in Europe (Iklé 1973; Quester 1970). Current changes in strategy, diplomacy, and technology are significantly shifting NATO's position toward the protection end. For example, the current strategy of limited nuclear response increases the need for conventional forces, especially during the initial "testing" stages of an escalation (Davis 1975; Iklé 1973). This strategy introduces flexibility into NATO's nuclear employment plans by providing for a sequence of measured responses toward aggression so that general nuclear war can be avoided and deterrence restored when provocation requires a military response. With this strategy, strong conventional and tactical nuclear forces are essential if aggression in Europe is to be thwarted immediately by a show of intention.

Recent technological improvements in TNW and PGM allow NATO to overcome partially the pact's conventional superiority[7] owing to NATO's technical advantage in these weapon systems (Burt 1976; Canby 1974; Heisenberg 1973). Ultraaccurate guided munitions can be effective in counteracting the 3 to 1 tank disparity between the two sides. Development of these weapons adds credibility to the doctrine of flexible response, because NATO can defend itself without resort to an assured destruction response. By placing limits on strategic weapons, SALT also increased the importance of conventional forces and TNW. Current strategic and technological developments augment the importance and need for *PW*.[8] Therefore, thinning considerations are becoming more prevalent, and benefit exclusion more feasible; hence, *allies can rely on markets* to supply defense more effectively than previously supposed.

These changes in the international situation are not only increasing the importance of thinning and excludability, but they also are augmenting the perceived common interests of the European allies. Flexible response brings the initial stages of a war onto European soil. Until the seventies, there was little reason for the European allies to build up conventional forces, since *any* war would be fought in minutes with an exchange of nuclear warheads. Additionally, the technological advantage of NATO in precision weaponry augments common interests by giving the Europeans an alternative to nuclear exchange by the superpowers. SALT and détente are bringing the European allies closer together also, because they are apprehensive about arms agreements between the U.S. and Russia which they are not consulted about. As common interests are recognized, the positive externalities of defense will become internalized. Thus, the increased perception of common interests and the increased privateness of defense should make the European allies more willing to contribute toward NATO's defense.

The trend in NATO toward a larger proportion of *PW* is difficult to show empirically, primarily because detailed weapon expenditure information is classified; however, this trend is indicated by computing the ratio of non-U.S. defense expenditures in NATO *to* total NATO defense expenditures. If this ratio increases, the proportion of conventional forces is hypothesized to have increased, since the major contributor of strategic forces is the U.S. Moreover, there is no evidence that France and/or Britain have significantly increased their strategic forces expenditures. The average annual ratios for non-U.S. expenditures in NATO were .25 for 1949–1960; .26 for 1961–1970; and .34 for 1971–1977.[9] This upward movement in the 1970s is indicative of a larger share of *PW*, especially since the U.S. strategic forces budget showed no upward trend during the 1970s and actually declined by 5.5 percent a year in real terms (Department of Defense 1976, 41–43).

3. The Design of NATO

NATO operates as a "loose" or unintegrated structure in which sovereign nations maintain both policy independence and discretionary power over military expenditures.[10] Any action of the decision-making body of NATO (i.e., the North Atlantic Council) must be unanimous. Articles 4 and 5 of the treaty mandate consultation in the event that one of the allies or its property is attacked, but the commitment of the allies is left unspecified. The unintegrated nature of NATO is reflected in the expenditures on commonly funded projects reported in table 1. The three major areas of common funding include the civil budget financing NATO headquarters, its staff, and committees; the military budget supporting NATO's military structure, its staff, and committees; and NATO infrastructure (e.g., pipelines, communication networks, airfields). The figures for the civil and military budgets are unclassified, but have been buried in classified documents and have heretofore been unavailable. In table 1, all years indicate that less than *1 percent* of NATO's defense expenditures *is jointly financed;* hence, *over 99 percent of NATO expenditures is at the discretion of the allies and is transacted across markets.*

Should NATO be more tightly integrated? This question can only be answered by computing the net benefits from increased integration. Benefits in terms of efficiency gains, scale economies, and political and military consultation must be matched against communication, planning, interdependen-

TABLE 1. NATO Common Funding Expenditures 1968–78 (in millions of dollars)

Year (1)	Civil Budget[a] (2)	Military Budget[c] (3)	Infrastructure[d] (4)	Total Common Funding (5)	NATO Expenditures[e] (6)	Common Funding Percentage of NATO Expenditures (7)
78[a]	233.956[b]	850.328	283.333	1367.6		
77[a]	202.240[b]	717.152	300.000	1219.4	165,352	0.7
76	173.728	598.871	381.493[f]	1154.1	146,562	0.8[f]
75	174.436	611.213	180.539	966.2	145,955	0.7
74	132.900	480.422	281.819	895.1	132,919	0.7
73	113.608	457.360	232.828	803.8	119,933	0.7
72	97.376	391.436	137.766	626.6	112,212	0.6
71	74.168	382.672	175.178	632.0	103,862	0.6
70	68.884	308.052	61.336	438.3	103,279	0.4
69	63.472	259.343	134.255	457.1	105,171	0.4
68	55.148	241.957	92.600	389.7	103,914	0.4

[a]The classified sources for each year are as follows: BC-D(71)54 for 1968; BC-D(71)62 for 1969; BC-D(71)72 for 1970; BC-D(72)27 for 1971; BC-D(73)16 for 1972; BC-D(74)11 for 1973; BC-D(75)11 for 1974; BC-D(76)11 for 1975; and BC-D(77)7 for 1976.

[b]These figures are projected estimates and are extracted from the report on the 1978 civil budget, C-M(77)95.

[c]The source for 1975–78 is the files of the Military Budget Section of the U.S. Mission to NATO. The figures for 1968–74 come from the NATO Sub-Registry Financial Statements.

[d]These data are converted from that given in *NATO Infrastructure Program*, U.S. Mission to NATO, February 1977. To derive NATO's infrastructure expenditures from U.S. obligations, we used the following U.S. shares of the total: 1968–70, 33%; 1971–73, 32%; 1974–75, 31%; 1976–77, 30%; and 1978–79, 28%.

[e]All the figures for these years are projected estimates.

[f]The figures for 1976 are for the period from July 1975 to 30 September 1976, because the start of the U.S. fiscal year was moved from July to October.

[g]See the source in note 10.

cy, and decision-making costs that increased cooperation entails (Sandler and Cauley 1977). If the presence of common-interest awareness and private benefits induce preference revelation, as argued here, minimal gains in allocative efficiency can be achieved by further integration. Moreover, scale economies in weapons production are, essentially, being exploited through the market when large-scale producers sell weapons to allies and nonallies (Stanley and Pearton 1972; Facer 1975). Some additional scale economies may arise as European allies form consortia for the purpose of common weapon procurement (e.g., Roland Missiles, Alpha Jets). Facer (1975, 36–48) has shown that most common weapon procurement programs involved only two or a few of the NATO allies and that a cost premium resulted due to international cooperation. These premiums must be weighed against the benefits from common procurement, which include savings in research and development costs, scale economies, and the elimination of duplicate efforts; however, as yet there is little concrete evidence specifying the net benefits from common procurement.

Without this evidence, the major offset to the costs of increased integration must come from the benefits of *political and military consultation* (e.g., increased deterrence from a unified stand against an opposing alliance, increased force efficiency from an integration and interoperability of armies, better intelligence from shared information). In a recent report, the Department of Defense (1977*b*) indicated that significant efficiency gains are expected from standardization of weaponry, logistics, training, and doctrine, but the report also stated (p. 2) that only modest progress has been made regarding standardization due to political, economic, and military obstacles. One major obstacle concerns the unwillingness of allies to sacrifice autonomy over their military forces. Unless the political and military benefits outweigh the costs of increased cooperation, NATO's unintegrated structure probably will be maintained.

Positions along the alliance spectrum can be related partially to the desired degree of integration in NATO. Deterrent alliances can achieve significant efficiency gains by integrating, because the publicness of *DW* leads to nonrevelation of preferences and free rider behavior. These efficiency gains may offset costs of increased integration. In contrast, protective alliances can better utilize markets to allocate defense expenditures between allies and, consequently, less integrated alliances are desirable, because significant efficiency gains cannot be matched against integration costs.

The desired degree of NATO integration depends upon the awareness of common interests and the ratio of excludable to nonexcludable outputs as determined by the spectrum position. If this awareness and ratio increased in the seventies, then integration becomes less essential as preferences are revealed via markets.

4. Benefits and Burden Sharing in NATO

Previous NATO burden-sharing studies have invariably employed an ability-to-pay measure, usually that of GNP or per capita GNP. For example, van

Ypersele de Strihou (1967*b;* 1968) computed burden-sharing assessments using the British tax rates applied to per capita GNP and found that the large rich nations overcontributed and the small European countries undercontributed. Even though different ability-to-pay measures and/or tax rates were applied, similar results were shown by others.[11]

Table 1 raises doubts about some NATO burden-sharing studies (e.g., Price 1967) which, by only examining NATO's civil budget (accounting for less than 0.2 percent of NATO's total defense expenditures), could indicate little about overall burden sharing. Moreover, studies (Beer 1972, 24–25; Olson and Zeckhauser 1966, 276–79; Väyrynen 1976, 301–3) arguing that small countries' overpayment to infrastructure could compensate for large countries' overpayment to defense ignored the relative magnitude of NATO's infrastructure expenditures (i.e., less than 0.3 percent of NATO's annual defense expenditures).

By utilizing the ability-to-pay approach, all previous NATO burden-sharing studies have focused on the revenue side and have left the expenditure side dangling. We propose an improved approach including both benefits proxies and an ability-to-pay measure. Proxies for individual countries' share of total defense benefits are employed and compared with their actual share of NATO's total defense expenditures. According to the theory, the difference between actual and predicted burdens (i.e., those based on benefit proxies) should decrease in recent years due to strategic and technological changes.

What benefits do allies gain from deterrence and damage limitation? In the worst scenario, conflict could escalate into an assured destruction exchange in which both sides are annihilated. Defense benefits consist of what would be saved; *lives* and *industry*. Population size and gross domestic product (GDP) can serve as proxies for the excludable benefits derived from defense.

Since the benefits from *PW* depend crucially on thinning, which is determined by the length of perimeter needing protection, exposed border is included as an additional benefit proxy. This proxy also serves as a user fee measure.

5. Statistical Results

Investigating the empirical relationship between NATO defense expenditures and benefits-received or ability-to-pay indices raises problems of definition, measurement, and methodology. Although international comparisons of defense expenditures are often ambiguous due to variation in national definitions of defense expenditure, inconsistency between NATO allies is largely eradicated owing to the adoption of a common definition of defense expenditure.[12] Furthermore, the usual problems associated with comparing real product levels in different countries are inherent, but often intractable or ignored, in the existing valuation and comparison of ally defense expenditure.[13]

The choice of statistical methods in testing the hypotheses of the joint product and deterrence alliance models is constrained by the composition and characteristics of NATO data. Several studies (Beer 1972; van Ypersele de Strihou 1967*b;* 1968) exploited parametric methods using Pearson product moment correlations and ordinary least squares regression. Path analysis and generalized least squares regression were used by Shaffer (1975) in a time series study of the interrelationship between individual ally defense effort, aspects of the internal alliance setting, and external influences such as alliance threats. However, given our interest in examining the distribution of defense burdens and benefits between allies at specific points in time, parametric procedures are inappropriate due to the nature and limitations of NATO data.[14] Therefore, following Olson and Zeckhauser (1966), we utilize distribution-free inferential methods in our statistical analysis.

Traditionally, the ratio of defense expenditures to GNP at factor cost valued in national currencies has been used to measure each ally's defense burden. This approach, while lending itself readily to applications of the ability-to-pay principle, does not facilitate a comparison of relative defense expenditures and benefits received. Defense expenditures expressed as a percentage of GNP measure the burden of defense *within* an ally as opposed to the burden shared *between* allies. Thus, in addition to the conventional empirical measure of ability to pay, this study uses a relative burden measure derived by calculating each ally's share of total NATO defense expenditure (see columns 6 and 10 in table 3).

An empirical test, which discriminates between the "purely public" or deterrence model and our joint product model, emerges from examining the relationship between the size of a nation's GDP and the percentage of GDP spent on defense. The deterrence model suggests that there should be a systematic and significant positive relationship between the size of GDP and the "defense effort" within an ally, measured by the percentage of GDP spent on defense, since, *ceteris paribus,* "the larger a nation is, the higher its valuation of the output of an alliance" (Olson and Zeckhauser 1966, 274). Our joint product model predicts that as an alliance moves toward the protective pole, there will be less of a systematic relationship between the size of GDP and "defense effort." An ally's "defense effort" should be unrelated to its size, since an increase in the incidence of private and/or excludable public benefits should stimulate preference revelation and generate, as well as maintain, an increase in "defense effort" irrespective of the industrial size.

To test the implications of both models the following hypotheses are used:

H_1: Within NATO, there is a significant positive correlation between the absolute size of an ally's GDP and its ratio of defense expenditure to GDP.

H_0: There is no significant correlation between the variables in H_1.

The hypotheses are tested for individual years over a sixteen-year period (1960–75) using Kendall's rank correlation coefficient (τ), a measure of association between random variables from any bivariate population. A generalized Kendall partial rank coefficient is also used to measure the linear dependence of GDP and the ratio of defense expenditure to GDP, holding selected variables (viz., per capita GDP and exposed border) constant.[15] Results of the correlations are presented in table 2.[16]

Generally, between 1960 and 1966, the correlation results do not support H_0 and, thus, suggest the positive relationship between ally size and "defense effort" predicted in the deterrence model. However, beginning in 1967, the strength of the correlations tends to decline, and the null hypothesis of independence is rejected only once thereafter. The declining trend in the correlations suggests a gradual shift in NATO away from a purely deterrent alliance in the early 1960s toward a more conventional or protective alliance structure.

If, as argued here, ally defense expenditures are related to benefits received, we should expect an association between defense burdens and benefit proxies. More specifically, the residuals between actual defense burdens and predicted defense burdens based on benefits should decrease over time as common-interest awareness *and* the ratio of excludable outputs to the sum of excludable and nonexcludable outputs increases.

TABLE 2. Kendall Rank Correlation Results for Hypothesis 1

Year	τ_{12}	$\tau_{12,3}$	$\tau_{12,34}$
1960	.3186 (1.587)	.3761* (1.874)	.2589 (1.290)
1961	.2747 (1.368)	.3315* (1.651)	.2317 (1.154)
1962	.3406* (1.697)	.3880* (1.933)	.3039 (1.514)
1963	.3626* (1.806)	.4094* (2.040)	.3340* (1.664)
1964	.3406* (1.697)	.3934* (1.960)	.3094* (1.541)
1965	.3186 (1.587)	.4086* (2.036)	.3442* (1.715)
1966	.3186 (1.587)	.4086* (2.036)	.3538* (1.763)
1967	.2307 (1.149)	.3220 (1.604)	.2449 (1.220)
1968	.1428 (0.711)	.2600 (1.295)	.1823 (0.908)
1969	.0769 (0.383)	.1792 (0.893)	.0763 (0.380)
1970	.0989 (0.493)	.2130 (1.061)	.1057 (0.527)
1971	.1648 (0.821)	.3047 (1.518)	.2153 (1.073)
1972	.1868 (0.931)	.3180 (1.584)	.2249 (1.120)
1973	.2088 (1.040)	.3332* (1.660)	.2428 (1.210)
1974	.1868 (0.931)	.3180 (1.584)	.2318 (1.155)
1975	.0989 (0.493)	.2516 (1.253)	.1398 (0.696)

Sources: See table 3.

Note: τ_{12} = Zero order Kendall τ of GDP and ratio of defense expenditure to GDP.

$\tau_{12,3}$ = First-order Kendall partial τ of GDP and ratio of defense expenditure to GDP with per capita GDP held constant.

$\tau_{12,34}$ = Second-order Kendall partial τ of GDP and ratio of defense expenditure to GDP with per capita GDP and exposed border held constant. Numbers in parentheses are z-values (see n. 16). * indicates significantly different from zero at the 95 percent confidence level. Critical values for the one-tailed z test are 1.645 (95 percent confidence level) and 2.326 (99 percent confidence level).

Table 3 presents ally percentage shares of NATO's defense expenditure for 1960 and 1975, in columns 2 and 7 respectively.[17] In addition, the allies' shares of the overall population, GDP, and exposed border of NATO are depicted for 1960 and 1975.[18] Given an aggregate measure of ally benefits, actual defense shares can be compared with those based upon the three benefit proxies. Myriad weighting methods conceivably could be used to aggregate the various benefit measures. However, given our lack of knowledge regarding the appropriate specification of the allies' utility functions, we weight the individual indices equally in the absence of an alternative weighting formula of unquestionable superiority. Columns 6 and 10 of table 3 are arithmetic means of the population, GDP, and exposed border shares for the respective years, and represent composite benefit measures for predicted ally defense burdens which can be juxtaposed against actual defense burdens.

An examination of table 3 reveals that the United States overcontributed in 1960 relative to average benefits, whereas the remaining allies undercontributed. The ordering of allies, based on a comparison of relative defense burdens and benefits, corresponds to earlier studies using ability-to-pay assessments (e.g., van Ypersele de Strihou 1967*b*, 301).

Table 3 also indicates that the period between 1960 and 1975 resulted in notable changes in NATO burden sharing. While average relative benefits remained largely unchanged, relative defense contributions appear to have shifted in the seventies. Although the United States still overcontributed, approximately 6 percent of the total NATO defense expenditure was shifted onto the European allies, an increased European defense burden which represents approximately 27 percent of the European relative defense contribution in 1960. The shift is small in absolute magnitude, but it is still noteworthy, since no other period in NATO showed *any* measurable change in burden sharing. With the exception of Canada, the absolute value of the residuals between predicted and actual defense shares declined for *all* allies.[19] As the joint product model suggests, the providers of *DW*s and the recipients of private benefits (e.g., Britain, France, Germany, and the United States) either overcontributed or contributed roughly in accordance with relative benefits. The overcontribution of the United States (+26.3 percent) is closely predicted by our model; i.e., the U.S. expenditure on deterrent strategic weapons was approximately 30 percent of its defense budget (Department of Defense 1977*a*, 85), which translates into 20.1 percent of the total 1975 NATO defense expenditures. Canada emerged as the greatest undercontributor, which is to be expected, since the United States would have great difficulty in excluding Canada from its deterrent umbrella. The negative residual between Canada's assessed share and actual defense contribution (−7.56 percent) is more than compensated by the excess contribution of the United States. Thus, the redistribution of the NATO defense burden between the North American and European allies generally is consistent with our model's prediction that as the alliance shifts toward the protective pole, allies are more apt to reveal preferences and share defense burdens voluntarily.

TABLE 3. Relative Defense Burdens and Benefits in NATO Using Population, GDP, and Exposed Borders as Proxies: 1960, 1975

Country (1)	1960 Defense Burden[a] (2)	1960 POP[b] (3)	1960 GDP[c] (4)	Exposed Border[d] (5)	1960 Average Benefit Share[e] (6)	1975 Defense Burden[a] (7)	1975 POP[b] (8)	1975 GDP[c] (9)	1975 Average Benefit Share[e] (10)
Belgium	0.64	1.92	1.40	0.14	1.15	0.98	1.77	1.58	1.16
Canada	2.64	3.76	4.39	20.02	9.39	2.26	4.12	5.33	9.82
Denmark	0.33	0.96	0.86	2.23	1.35	0.46	0.91	0.89	1.34
France	6.34	9.59	7.18	4.44	7.07	7.01	9.52	8.70	7.55
Germany	5.38	11.64	10.29	2.75	8.23	8.09	11.16	10.56	8.16
Greece	0.26	1.75	0.42	5.84	2.67	0.85	1.63	0.66	2.71
Italy	2.06	10.54	4.75	9.09	8.13	2.90	10.07	5.29	8.15
Luxembourg	0.01	0.07	0.07	0.00	0.05	0.01	0.06	0.06	0.04
Netherlands	0.88	2.41	1.67	0.92	1.67	1.39	2.46	1.90	1.76
Norway	0.28	0.75	0.61	5.67	2.34	0.45	0.72	0.71	2.37
Portugal	0.20	1.86	0.30	1.50	1.22	0.48	1.70	0.40	1.20
Turkey	0.49	5.78	0.65	10.72	5.72	1.26	7.23	0.96	6.30
United Kingdom	7.25	11.04	8.15	9.27	9.49	6.86	10.11	6.89	8.76
United States	73.24	37.93	59.26	27.42	41.54	66.98	38.53	56.08	40.68
NATO–Europe	24.12	58.31	36.35	52.56	49.07	30.76	57.35	38.59	49.50
NATO–North America	75.88	41.69	63.65	47.44	50.93	69.24	42.65	61.41	50.50

Source: [a]*World Armaments and Disarmaments: Stockholm International Peace Research Institute Yearbook 1976* (London: MIT Press, 1976). Defense expenditures are valued in U.S. dollars at 1970 prices and 1970 exchange rates.

[b]*National Accounts of OECD Countries*, Vol. 1 "Main Aggregates" (Paris: OECD/OCDE, 1975). Population figures are midyear estimates.

[c]*Ibid.* GDP = Gross Domestic Product in purchaser's values in U.S. dollars, 1970 prices and 1970 exchange rates.

[d]*The Times Atlas of the World: Comprehensive Edition* (London: Times News-Limited, 1972). Exposed borders are derived from chartodometer estimates.

[e]See text.

Note: Figures represent percentage shares.

Area protected could be included as an additional benefit proxy reflecting resource wealth and option value. Moreover, area serves as a user fee measure for some defense benefits (e.g., national guard, monitoring purposes). When area is included as a proxy (see table 4), the results for 1960–1975 are almost the same as those reported previously; i.e., no shift in burdens occur until the seventies. The closeness of fit between actual and expected burdens *is*, however, *better* owing to the additional proxy. Furthermore, the North American allies only overcontributed by half of that shown in table 3 for 1975: some 9.5 percent. The fit for any set of proxies will not be perfect, because the publicness elements of defense can never be eliminated fully. Nevertheless, our proxies are an improvement over previous investigations, since ability-to-pay, benefit, and user fee measures are used here.

6. Summary and Policy Implications

By increasing both the relative proportion of PW and the common-interest awareness of allies, current strategic and technological developments in NATO are allowing markets to distribute defense burdens more efficiently than previously supposed. These developments favor the application of the joint product model over the deterrence model, because NATO's current arsenal jointly provides deterrence, damage limitation, and private benefits.

TABLE 4. Relative Defense Burdens and Benefits in NATO Using Area, Population, GDP, and Exposed Borders as Proxies: 1960, 1970, 1975

Country	Area[d]	1960 Defense Burden[a]	1960 Average Benefit Share[e]	1970 Defense Burden[a]	1970 Average Benefit Share[e]	1975 Defense Burden[a]	1975 Average Benefit Share[e]
Belgium	0.14	0.64	0.90	0.72	0.90	0.98	0.90
Canada	45.09	2.64	18.32	1.95	18.48	2.26	18.64
Denmark	0.19	0.33	1.33	0.35	1.06	0.46	1.06
France	2.47	6.34	5.92	5.67	6.17	7.01	6.28
Germany	1.12	5.38	6.45	5.92	6.56	8.09	6.40
Greece	0.60	0.26	2.15	0.45	2.17	0.85	2.18
Italy	1.36	2.06	6.44	2.40	6.48	2.90	6.45
Luxembourg	0.01	0.01	0.04	0.01	0.03	0.01	0.03
Netherlands	0.18	0.88	1.30	1.06	1.35	1.39	1.37
Norway	1.47	0.28	2.13	0.37	2.13	0.45	2.14
Portugal	0.42	0.20	1.02	0.42	0.98	0.48	1.00
Turkey	3.53	0.49	5.17	0.55	5.41	1.26	5.61
United Kingdom	1.10	7.25	7.39	5.60	6.97	6.86	6.84
United States	42.32	73.24	41.73	74.52	41.32	66.98	41.09
NATO–Europe	12.59	24.12	39.95	23.53	40.20	30.76	40.27
NATO–North America	87.41	75.88	60.05	76.47	59.80	69.24	59.73

Sources: a, d, e: see table 3.
Note: Figures represent percentage shares.

A rank correlation test supports the joint product model and discriminates between it and the deterrence model. If the deterrence model is applicable, then a significant relationship between industrial size and defense effort should be present; however, after 1966 the relationship is not statistically significant. This result is in agreement with the joint product model which predicts that defense efforts should be related to the distribution of excludable benefits *rather than* size, as the alliance shifts toward the protective pole in the late sixties and the seventies. Our statistical analysis indicates that defense shares are related to the benefit proxies chosen. The theoretical model accurately predicts the overcontributors: those allies providing DW and those receiving large private benefits.

The burden-sharing results suggest that the group of European nations is beginning to pay more of their share (especially when area is also a proxy). Hence, the European Defense Improvement Program (EDIP) appears to be achieving its objectives of increasing European defense expenditures. *However,* we would argue that the change in the alliance's orientation toward PW and *not* the EDIP (started in 1971) caused the desired result. If current strategic and technological developments continue to increase common-interest recognition among allies and the proportion of excludable benefits, then this burden-shifting trend should continue into the eighties. Nevertheless, a program to increase Canadian defense expenditures seems appropriate.

Our model and findings support NATO's unintegrated structure whereby sovereign nations decide their defense expenditures via market transactions. Arguments for a more integrated alliance *must rest on political and military benefits,* because many scale economies are exploited and efficiency gains are small due to the large portion of excludable benefits. Nonetheless, standardization agreements may warrant some increase in NATO's degree of integration. As strategy and technology change in the future, the structure of NATO must be reexamined in order to determine whether integration should be altered.

NOTES

The paper was written when Sandler was on leave at the Department of Economics and Related Studies at the University of York, U.K. He gratefully acknowledges the support of a NATO Postdoctoral Fellowship in Science. We thank T. J. Loveland from the U.S. Mission to NATO who provided data on NATO's civil and military budgets. Comments by Jon Cauley, Ann Chamberlain, Shelby Gerking, Donna Lake, James R. Marsden, Mancur Olson, Kate Ranta, William Schulze, V. Kerry Smith, and an anonymous referee significantly improved the paper. All views expressed and any remaining shortcomings are solely those of the authors.

1. The relevant literature consists of Beer (1972), Frohlich (1974), Loehr (1973), Olson (1965), Olson and Zeckhauser (1967), Russett (1970), Russett and Sullivan (1971), Sandler (1975, 1977), Sandler and Cauley (1977), van Ypersele de Strihou (1967*a*, 1967*b*, 1968), Väyrynen (1976), and Wagner (1975).

2. A pure public good (e.g., a cleaner environment) is totally nonrival in consumption, since its consumption by one individual does not detract in the slightest from the consumption possibilities available to other persons. Moreover, the benefits of a pure public good are nonexcludable, i.e., once it is provided, the good is available to everyone. In contrast, a private good (e.g., a piece of food) is totally rival and its benefits are excludable Impure public goods exhibit varying degrees of rivalry and/or excludability.
3. These strategic developments are discussed by Burt (1976), Canby (1974), Davis (1975), Grey (1975), Heisenberg (1973), Iklé (1973), Nerlich (1975), and Rosecrance (1975). Flexible response permits an alliance to react to an enemy's challenge in multiple ways (e.g., limited nuclear war) so that a full nuclear exchange is but one option.
4. On the distinction between deterrence and protection, see Canby (1974), Heisenberg (1973), Iklé (1973), McGuire (1967), Rosecrance (1975), Sandler (1977), Schelling (1966), van Ypersele de Strihou (1967*a*, 1967*b*, 1968), and Väyrynen (1976).
5. Self-financing fails whenever increasing returns (i.e., falling average costs) occur. In this case, tolls must be based on average rather than marginal costs or else subsidies must be arranged.
6. Fixed proportions indicate that the units of each of the jointly produced outputs are in a fixed relationship with respect to the units of the general defense good. Any fixed proportion relationship can be accommodated by judicious choice of the units of the jointly produced outputs (Samuelson 1969, 28–30).
7. Fischer (1976) calculated the following Warsaw Pact/NATO ratios to show the pact's conventional superiority: active combat units 2.1/1, groundforce manpower 1.09/1, and combat aircraft in Central Europe 2.1/1.
8. The current switch from *DW* to *PW* is in line with the policy of assured destruction and damage limitation first put forth by McNamara (House Committee on Appropriations 1965, 32–35. Once the objectives of assured destruction are reached, McNamara indicated that defense expenditures should be increasingly redirected toward damage limitation. The stockpile of *DW* is enabling NATO to follow McNamara's advice.
9. The ratios for 1949–1973 were computed from data given by NATO (1976, 296–97), while the ratios for 1974–1977 were computed from data listed in NATO (1977).
10. For an institutional description of NATO, see NATO 1976.
11. See Beer (1972), Olson and Zeckhauser (1966), Peacock (1972), Price (1967), and van Ypersele de Strihou (1967*b*; 1968). Important articles on burden sharing in international organizations include Kravis and Davenport (1963), and Pincus (1965).
12. The standard NATO definition of defense expenditure is outlined in Jordan 1967, 217–8.
13. International comparisons of defense expenditures are invariably based on converting the money value of defense expenditure to U.S. dollars via official or prevailing exchange rates. Although errors are introduced into comparisons based on this method due to the inequality of official exchange rates and purchasing power parities, defense expenditure comparisons using more accurate repricing or adjusted exchange rate methods are generally not feasible. Binary repricing schemes between pairs of countries, for example, are constrained by the problem of repricing unique defense goods (e.g., U.S. intercontinental ballistic missiles)

and variation in empty good categories or zero expenditure on specific categories of defense goods across countries. For a cogent summary of the problem of international defense expenditure comparisons, see Stockholm International Peace Research Institute 1976, 285–87.

14. Insufficient knowledge regarding the specific distribution function of the population from which NATO data is drawn is the primary justification for using distribution-free procedures. A preliminary investigation using the Shapiro-Wilk test, an omnibus test which detects deviation from normality due either to skewness or kurtosis (Shapiro and Wilk 1965; Shapiro, Wilk, and Chen 1968) revealed that the assumption of normally distributed NATO data is violated for GDP, defense expenditures, and defense expenditures/GDP ratio in the original data metric and in a logarithmic transformation. Moreover, the number of NATO allies dictates a cross section sample size of $n = 14$ (since Iceland does not contribute) which may jeopardize the asymptotic properties of regression techniques.
15. See Somers (1959) for a theoretical exposition and discussion of the generalized Kendall partial rank correlation coefficient.
16. It is well known that the zero order Kendall rank correlation coefficient is asymptotically normally distributed under the null hypothesis of independence as the sample size $n \rightarrow \infty$ and that for $n > 10$ the normal distribution provides an accurate approximation (Kendall 1970; Jirina 1976). Although to the best of our knowledge, the exact distribution of the Kendall partial rank correlation coefficient remains untabulated, it has been shown, using a Monte Carlo simulation, that the normal distribution provides a satisfactory approximation for the Kendall partial rank coefficient frequency distribution (Hoflund 1963).
17. The tables for 1965 and 1970 are virtually identical to that of 1960 and have been deleted. They are available from the authors.
18. The data of these tables can be easily arranged so that each ally is ranked with respect to relative defense burdens and benefits. With the data suitably transformed, Kendall's coefficient of concordance (W), a nonparametric analysis of variance technique, is used to test the null hypothesis that the defense burden and benefit rankings for NATO allies are independent. The value of W for 1960, 1965, 1970, and 1975 is .7951, .7978, .7967, and .8000, respectively. As all values are significant at the 99 percent confidence level, we reject the null hypothesis of independence and conclude that relative defense burdens in NATO are significantly related to relative benefits. The values of W are virtually identical when area rather than exposed border is used as a land proxy.
19. The coefficient of inequality (U) suggested by Theil (1966) is used to measure the magnitude of the overall residual error between predicted and actual defense burdens. As the value of U is bounded by 0 and ∞, smaller values of U indicate a closer correspondence between predicted and actual burdens; hence if $U = 0$, predicted and actual burdens are equivalent for all allies. The value of U based on the estimated residuals declines from .4556 in 1960 to .4177 in 1975, thus suggesting that a shift in burden sharing has occurred, reducing the residual error between predicted and actual defense burdens.

REFERENCES

Beer, Francis. "The Political Economy of Alliances: Benefits, Costs, and Institutions in NATO." *Sage Professional Papers in International Studies*. Beverly Hills, Calif.: Sage Publications, 1972.

Burt, Richard. *New Weapons Technologies: Debate and Directions. Adelphi Papers.* no. 126. London: International Institute for Strategic Studies (IISS), 1976.

Canby, Steven. *The Alliance and Europe: Part IV Military Doctrine and Technology. Adelphi Papers.* no. 109. London: IISS, 1974.

Davis, Lynn. *Limited Nuclear Options: Deterrence and the New American Doctrine. Adelphi Papers.* no. 121. London: IISS, 1975.

Department of Defense. *Annual Defense Department Report FY 1977.* Washington, D.C.: Department of Defense, 1976.

Department of Defense. *Annual Defense Department Report FY 1978.* Washington, D.C.: Department of Defense, 1977*a*.

Department of Defense. *Rationalization/Standardization Within NATO, Third Report.* Washington, D.C.: Department of Defense, 1977*b*.

Facer, Roger. *The Alliance and Europe: Part III Weapons Procurement in Europe—Capabilities and Choices. Adelphi Papers,* no. 108. London: IISS, 1975.

Fischer, Robert. *Defending the Central Front: The Balance of Forces. Adelphi Papers.* no. 127. London: IISS, 1976.

Frohlich, Norman. "Self-Interest or Altruism, What Difference." *Journal of Conflict Resolution 18* (1974):55–73.

Gibbons, J. D. *Nonparametric Statistical Inference.* New York: McGraw-Hill, 1971.

Grey, Colin. "Deterrence and Defense in Europe: Revising NATO's Theater Nuclear Posture." *Strategic Review,* 1975, pp. 1–9.

Heisenberg, Wolfgang. *The Alliance and Europe: Part I Crisis Stability in Europe and Theater Nuclear Weapons. Adelphi Papers* no. 96. London: IISS, 1973.

Hoflund, Olle. "Simulated Distribution for Small n of Kendall's Partial Rank Correlation Coefficient." *Biometrika 50* (1963): 520–22.

House Committee on Appropriations. *Department of Defense Appropriations for 1966, Hearings, Part 3.* Washington, D.C.: U.S. Government Printing Office, 1965.

Iklé, Fred. "Can Nuclear Deterrence Last Out the Century?" *Foreign Affairs 51* (1973): 267–85.

Jirina, Miloslav, "On the Asymptotic Normality of Kendall's Rank Correlation Statistic." *Annals of Statistics 4* (1976): 214–15.

Jordan, Robert. *The NATO International Staff/Secretariat 1952–1957: A Study in International Administration.* London: Oxford University Press, 1967.

Kendall, M. G. *Rank Correlation Methods.* London: Griffin, 1970.

Kravis, Irving, and Davenport, Michael. "The Political Arithmetic of International Burden-Sharing." *Journal of Political Economy 71* (1963): 309–30.

Loehr, William. "Collective Goods and International Cooperation: Comments." *International Organization 27* (1973): 421–30.

McGuire, Martin. "The Structure of Choice Between Deterrence and Defense." in *Issues in Defense Economics,* edited by Roland McKean, 129–49. New York: National Bureau of Economic Research, 1967.

NATO Information Service. *NATO Facts and Figures.* Brussels: NATO Publications, 1976.

NATO Press Service. *Financial and Economic Data Relating to NATO Defense.* M-DPC-3(77)18. Brussels: NATO Press Service, 1977.

Nerlich, Uwe. *The Alliance and Europe: Part V Nuclear Weapons and East-West Negotiations. Adelphi Papers,* no. 120. London: IISS, 1975.

Olson, Mancur. *The Logic of Collective Action.* Cambridge, Mass.: Harvard University Press, 1965.

Olson, Mancur, and Zeckhauser, Richard. "An Economic Theory of Alliances." *Review of Economics and Statistics 48* (1966): 266–79.

Olson, Mancur, and Zeckhauser, Richard. "Collective Goods, Comparative Advantage, and Alliance Efficiency." *Issues in Defense Economics,* edited by Roland McKean, 25–48. New York: National Bureau of Economic Research, 1967.

Peacock, Alan. "The Public Finance of Inter-Allied-Defense Provision." in *Essays in Honour of Antonio de Vito de Marco,* edited by Cacucci, 371–84. (*Bari, Italy: 1972*).

Pincus, John. *Economic Aid and International Cost Sharing.* Baltimore, Md.: John Hopkins Press, 1965.

Price, James. "The 'Tax' Burden of International Organizations." *Public Finance 22* (1967): 496–513.

Quester, George. *Nuclear Diplomacy.* New York: Dunellen Co., 1970.

Rosecrance, Richard. *Strategic Deterrence Reconsidered. Adelphi Papers,* no. 116. London: IISS, 1975.

Russett, Bruce. *What Price Vigilance? The Burden of National Defense.* New Haven, Conn.: Yale University Press, 1970.

Russett, Bruce, and Sullivan, John. "Collective Goods and International Organizations." *International Organization 25* (1971): 845–65.

Samuelson, Paul. "Contrast Between Welfare Conditions for Joint Supply and for Public Goods." *Review of Economics and Statistics 51* (1969): 26–30.

Sandler, Todd. "The Economic Theory of Alliances: Realigned." in *Comparative Public Policy: Issues, Theories and Methods,* edited by C. Liske et al., 223–39. New York: John Wiley and Sons, 1975.

Sandler, Todd. "Impurity of Defense: An Application to the Economics of Alliances." *Kyklos 30* (1977): 443–60.

Sandler, Todd, and Cauley, John. "The Design of Supranational Structures: An Economic Perspective." *International Studies Quarterly 21* (1977): 251–76.

Schelling, Thomas, *Arms and Influence.* New Haven, Conn.: Yale University Press, 1966.

Shaffer, S. M. "The Influence of Threat and Alliance Setting on National Defense Expenditures: NATO, 1950–1969." Ph.D. diss., University of Michigan, 1975.

Shapiro, S. S., and Wilk, M. B. "An Analysis of Variance Test of Normality (Complete Samples)." *Biometrika 52* (1965): 591–611.

Shapiro, S. S.; Wilk, M. B.; and Chen, H. J. "A Comparative Study of Various Tests for Normality." *Journal of the American Statistical Association 63* (1968): 1343–72.

Somers, Robert. "The Rank Analogue of Product-Moment Partial Correlation and Regression, with Application to Manifold, Ordered Contingency Tables." *Biometrika 46* (1959): 241–46.

Stanley, John, and Pearton, Maurice. *The International Trade in Arms.* London: Chatto and Windus, 1972.

Stockholm International Peace Research Institute. *World Armaments and Disarmaments: Stockholm International Peace Research Institute Yearbook 1976.* London: MIT Press, 1976.

Theil, Henri. *Applied Economic Forecasting.* Amsterdam: North-Holland Publishing Company, 1966.

van Ypersele de Strihou, Jacques. "Comments." in *Issues in Defense Economics,* edited by Roland McKean, 58–63. New York: National Bureau of Economic Research, 1967*a*.

———. "Sharing the Defense Burden Among Western Allies." *Review of Economics and Statistics 49* (1967*b*): 527–36.

———. "Sharing the Defense Burden Among Western Allies." *Yale Economic Essays 8* (1968): 261–320.

Väyrynen, Raimo. "The Theory of Collective Goods, Military Alliances and International Security." *International Social Science Journal 38* (1976): 288–305.

Wagner, R. Harrison. "National Defense as a Collective Good." in *Comparative Public Policy: Issues, Theories and Methods*, edited by C. Liske et al., 199–221. New York: John Wiley and Sons, 1975.

6 Constitutional and Philosophical Issues

A General Social Dilemma: Profitable Exchange and Intransitive Group Preferences

Peter Bernholz

During the last few years two seemingly unrelated developments have aroused attention among many economists, political scientists, and sociologists. The first is a general proof that the possibility of a profitable exchange of a majority of votes in a system of majority voting implies cyclical or at least intransitive group preferences and vice versa, if separable individual preferences are present (Bernholz 1973, 1974*a;* Oppenheimer 1972; Miller 1977; Schwartz 1977). The second is the proof first given by Sen that minimal liberalism and Pareto optimality may lead to a contradiction (Sen 1970). This implies, however, that with independent decisions by some individuals an outcome results which is not Pareto-optimal. As a consequence, these individuals could agree on profitable exchange to reach a Pareto-optimal outcome. Thus again, if a profitable agreement among some members of a group is possible, cyclical group preferences are present.

This result is preserved if a definition of minimal liberalism, which seems more adequate than Sen's, is accepted. Whereas in the latter definition at least two different individuals have the right to decide among two different pairs of outcomes, the former definition gives the right to individuals to decide among the alternatives of different issues or characteristics of outcomes (Bernholz 1974*b,* 1975; Gibbard 1974; Breyer 1978).

It has been shown that the logrolling theorem stated above is not only true for simple majority voting but also for all kinds of qualified majority voting up to near-unanimity (Bernholz 1974*a;* Oppenheimer 1972). The relation between the logrolling theorem and the paradox of liberalism, moreover, has soon been recognized (Bernholz 1976). The most general proof until now of the logrolling theorem including liberalism and all other kinds of social organization or allocations of rights to make decisions in a society, which will be discussed below, has been given by Schwartz (1977) for the case of separable individual preferences. But it is not clear from Schwartz's paper what kinds of assignments of rights are included and what the logrolling theorem means for the corresponding social organizations.

Let us sum up. It has been suggested by the developments sketched above that whenever a situation (outcome) results from the independent decisions of the subgroups who have the right to decide different issues which can be overturned by and to the benefit of a winning coalition of these subgroups,

First published in *Zeitschrift für Nationalökonomie* 40, nos. 1–2 (1980): 1–23.

then intransitive social preferences are present, if individual preferences are separable (compare sec. 2c). The very general meaning of this result as a social dilemma has, however, not been grasped until now and it is still confined to the assumption of separable individual preferences. It is the task of the present discussion to remove the latter assumption and to clarify the meaning of the general theorem.

Next, there is a close relationship between Arrow's General Impossibility Theorem and our results, as will be shown in section 3. For our assumptions fulfill Arrow's conditions. Thus the relations stated in this paper can be looked at as a substantive interpretation of Arrow's theorem.

Finally, it will be shown that the "paradox" proved by Sen for liberalism appears to be true for nearly all the decentralized social organizations considered.

1. Generalization of the Results Obtained for Majority Voting to a General Class of Decision Rules and Assignments of Rights

a. Definitions and Notation

In the following section, we consider a set V of $m \geqq 2$ individuals with weak, ordinal, complete and transitive preferences and a set M of $n \geqq 2$ issues M_i ($i = 1, 2, \ldots, n$). Each issue M_i comprises a finite number $m_i \geqq 2$ of alternatives. An outcome $x \in U$ is an n-dimensional vector with one and only one component (alternative) out of each issue. Consequently $U = M_1 \times M_2 \times \ldots \times M_n$. Note that there are $m_1 \cdot m_2 \cdot m_3 \cdot \ldots \cdot m_n$ outcomes.

For each issue M_i, there is a nonempty set $V_i \subseteq V$ of individuals, who have the right to decide according to some nonstochastic decision rule d_i for society among the alternatives of M_i. Note that only one decision rule d_i is used for issue M_i. Otherwise contradictory results might be reached for M_i.

Decision rule d_i ($i = 1, 2, \ldots, n$) can be any decision rule having the following properties: Assume that $x, y \in U$ are any two outcomes differing only in issue M_i ($i = 1, 2, \ldots, n$), and that we have any combination of individual preference orderings over them, namely $x R_j y$, $y R_j x$ or $x R_j y$ *and* $y R_j x$ for all $j \in V - V_i$. Then

a) there exists at least one $L_i \subseteq V_i$ ($L_i \neq \emptyset$) for any given combination of individual preferences over x and y for all $s_i \in V_i - L_i$ such that if for all $j_i \in L_i$ $x P_{ji} y$ is true, society prefers x to y, i.e. $x P y$;

b) if $L_i \subset V_i$ then a) is true for $L_i \cup \{g\}$, $g \in V_i - L_i$, if the same combination of individual preferences is given for all $s_i \in V_i - (L_i \cup \{g\})$ and if $x P_{ji} y$ for all $j_i \in L_i$ and $x P_g y$;

c) L_i and $L_i \cup \{g\}$ can bring about x as against y by using d_i, if only a decision is made concerning these outcomes.

Each L_i for all of whose members $x P_j y$ is true and which for a given decision rule d_i implies $x\,P\,y$, will be called a winning coalition C_i. Obviously there may be quite a number of winning coalitions C_i, C_i', C_i'', . . . for any pairs of alternatives.

It is obvious from the above that there may exist winning coalitions which are able to decide among z and v in their favour, $z, v \in U$, if these outcomes are different in exactly h well-determined issues, $1 \leqq h \leqq n$. We call such a coalition an h-issue coalition C^h. C_i, C_i', C_i'' are one-issue coalitions. C^h is composed out of h one-issue coalitions, e.g. $C^h = C_1 \cup C_2 \cup C_3 \cup \ldots \cup C_h$. There may be quite a number of such C^h coalitions, which may refer to the same issues and pairs of alternatives, but also to different pairs of alternatives and to different bundles of h issues. For our purpose we need, however, not make a notational difference between them. We will sometimes write ${}^rC^h$ ($r = 1, 2, \ldots$) to point out that different h-issue coalitions exist.

Let us stress that the above assumptions allow a wealth of different institutional arrangements of society. If d_i provides for majority rule among V_i for all i and if $V_i = V$, then we have a society in which all issues are decided by a majority of all voters. The other extreme case, "pure liberalism," would be present, if $V_i = \{j_i\}$, $j_i \in V$, and if each individual j_i would have the right to decide at least one issue (thus $m \leqq n$). The meaning of d_i would, of course, be quite obvious in this case. As an additional case, $V_1 = V_2 = \ldots = V_n = \{j\}$ would be a pure dictatorship.

But there can be, too, all possible combinations of allocations of issues to different subgroups V_i and of different decision rules. E.g., there may be issues $M_1, \ldots, M_m$ each of which has been allocated to a different individual of society according to the principle of liberalism; issues $M_{m+1}, \ldots, M_r$ may be decided by majority rule with $V_{m+1} = V_{m+2} \ldots = V_r = V$; M_{r+1} may be decided by a set of bureaucrats $V_{r+1} \subset V$ according to some decision rule d_{r+1}; M_{r+2} by a set of shareholders deciding $V_{r+2} \subset V$ according to a decision rule d_{r+2}, stating that all shareholders owning a majority of shares form winning coalitions C_{r-2}, C'_{r-2}, C''_{r+2}, . . . etc. Note, however, that we do not allow d_i to be a chance mechanism, since we have confined our analysis to nonstochastic decision rules.

We conclude by completing our definitions concerning social preference relations. Let us reçall first that "society prefers x to y", $x\,P\,y$, if there exists at least one winning coalition C for all of whose members $j \in C$ $x\,P_j\,y$ holds.

Next, let us assume that for the moment only 1-, 2-, . . . , h-issue coalitions are allowed. Then, if some x and y are different in $k > h$ issues no k-issue coalition can be formed. This means, of course, that there exists no subset of society $V^k \equiv V_1 \cup V_2 \cup \ldots \cup V_k \subseteq V$ having the right to decide among x and y.

As a consequence there can be no winning k-issue coalition C^k, too, whatever the preferences of the members of V. Society is not able or willing to form collective preferences or to make collective decisions between x and y. Thus we will say that no social preference relation exists between x and y, if no k-issue coalitions are allowed. The social preference relation is incomplete, since there is no social preference relation between all possible pairs of outcomes in U.

Finally, let some x and y differ only in at most h issues and let 1-, 2-, . . . , h-issue coalitions be allowed. Then $x\,R\,y$, "society prefers x to y or is indifferent between them," if there is no winning coalition whose members prefer y to x, i.e. if $y\,Px$ does not hold, with $x, y \in U$ and different in at most h issues. We may also say that there exists a blocking coalition preventing y. If neither xPy nor yPx are valid, i.e., if neither a winning coalition for x against y nor for y against x exists, again with $x, y \in U$ and different in at most h issues this will be expressed by $x\,I\,y$, "society is indifferent between x and y." This could, e.g., easily happen if x and y were different only in issue M_i and if d_i would prescribe a two-thirds majority of the members of V_i for a valid decision. Again, $x\,R\,y$ is written if either $x\,P\,y$ or $x\,I\,y$ is true. Thus either a winning coalition preferring x over y exists or no winning coalition preferring x over y or y over x is present. Obviously, if $x\,R\,y$ and $y\,R\,x$ are both true, then $x\,I\,y$.

b. Representation by a Digraph[1]

A finite directed graph (or finite digraph) consists of a finite number of points or vertices, part or all of which are connected by directed lines (arrows). If each pair of points is connected by at least one arrow one speaks of a complete digraph. In our case there are $m_1 \cdot m_2 \cdot \ . \ . \ . \ \cdot m_n$ points, namely all possible outcomes. The directed lines represent the R-relations between outcomes. If, e.g., $x\,R\,y$, then an arrow leads from x to y (see fig. 1). If for $u, v \in U$, $u\,R\,v$ and $v\,R\,u$ is true u and v are connected by an arrow from u to v and by another one from v to u. Two arrows between two vertices in opposite directions thus symbolize the indifference relations, here $u\,I\,v$. From this, if $x, y \in U$ are only connected by one arrow leading from x to y then $x\,P\,y$ holds.

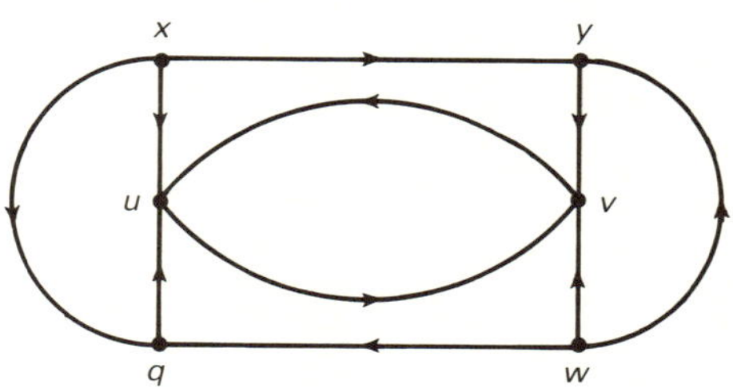

Fig. 1

Next we define what we call a digraph D_h $(1 \leqq h \leqq n)$. Assume that only $C^1=$, $C^2=$, . . . , C^h-issue coalitions are allowed or considered. Then, for $h < k \leqq n$ no arrows exist between outcomes (points) x and w which are different in k, i.e., in more than h issues. For there are no k-issue coalitions possible. Thus no R-relation and no directed line is present between x and w.

It follows from this definition that only digraph D_n is a complete digraph. All other digraphs D_h ($1 \leqq h < n$) are incomplete digraphs, since not all pairs of outcomes are connected by arrows. Moreover, each digraph D_h is a subgraph of each digraph D_k for $h < k$, since a digraph D_h has the same $m_1 \cdot m_2 \cdot \ldots \cdot m_n$ outcomes (points) as a digraph D_k and only part of the arrows present in the latter. The digraph in figure 1 can be interpreted as a digraph D_1, if we define $x = (x_1, y_1)$, $u = (x_2, y_1)$, $q = (x_3, y_1)$, $y = (x_1, y_2)$, $v = (x_2, y_2)$ and $w = (x_3, y_2)$ as two-dimensional vectors. Since only one-issue coalitions are allowed, no directed lines between points which are different in two issues are present. Thus there are no arrows between, e.g., x and w and u and y. The digraph is incomplete. The complete digraph corresponding to the digraph D_1 of figure 1 is given by the digraph D_2 of figure 2, because $n = 2$ in this case. One sees at once that the digraph D_1 is a subgraph of the complete digraph D_2. The digraph D_2 is only possible if C^2 coalitions are allowed.

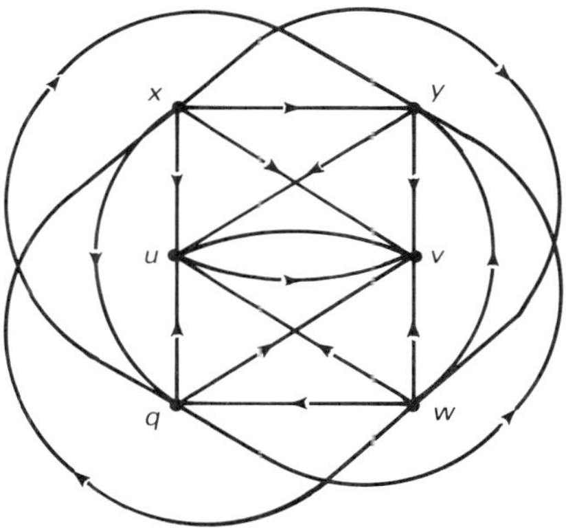

Fig. 2

It is important to realize that the fact that not all pairs of points are connected by arrows in a digraph D_h ($1 \leqq h < n$) does not mean that there is any point which is not related to some other points by at least one arrow. For each outcome there are always some outcomes which are different from the former in at most h issues. Thus there are no isolated points in the digraphs D_h even if $h = 1$. In the language of graph theory all digraphs D_h are weakly connected digraphs (Harary, Norman, and Cartwright 1965, 51).

Assume now that a sequence of arrows exists which leads from one point, say x, to another, v (compare e.g., fig. 1). Then we say that v is R-reachable from x. Obviously, this is only the case if $x R \ldots R v$ is true. The set of all outcomes which are R-reachable from some x in the digraph D_h ($1 \leqq h \leqq n$) will be called $F_h(x)$.[2] By definition we include x in this set. For the digraph D_1 of figure 1, we have $F_1(x) = \{x, u, q, y, v\}$, for the digraph D_2 of figure 2 $F_2(x) = \{x, u, q, y, v, w\}$.

We will further say that v is P-reachable from x if, as in figure 1

$$x\ P\ .\ .\ .\ .\ P\ v$$

is true. The set of all points in D_h which are P-reachable will be denoted by G_h (x). Obviously $G_h(x) \subseteq F_h(x)$.

We are now able to define the set of h-stable outcomes (points) and the corresponding subgraph $D_h{}^*$. Intuitively speaking this set $S_h \subseteq U$ comprises all $x \in U$ which are not P-reachable from any y outside S_h, $y \in U - S_h$, whereas y is P-reachable from at least one x belonging to S_h. More formally, for x, $y \in U$

$$U - S_h = \{y|\exists x\colon y \in G_h(x),\ x \notin G_h(y)\},$$

S_h is the complementary set to $U - S_h$. S_h may be called the general Condorcet set[3] in the case that no coalitions over more than h issues are allowed or considered.

Note that all $y \in U - S_h$ are unstable, since they are directly or indirectly dominated via P-relations by at least one $x \in S_h$. By contrast any $x \in S_h$ can at most be directly or indirectly dominated by other $z \in S_h$. S_h is thus the set of outcomes directly or indirectly dominating all other outcomes, if no k-issue coalitions $(h < k)$ are allowed.

The formal definition implies that no $z \in S_h$ is P-reachable from any $y \in U - S_h$. For assume that this were not true, then $z \in G_h(y)$. Moreover, we have from the definition $y \in G_h(x)$ and $x \notin G_h(y)$. Thus $z \in G_h(x)$. Now, if $x \in G_h(z)$ were valid then $x \in G_h(y)$, contrary to assumption. But if $x \notin G_h$ (z), then $z \in U - S_h$, since $z \in G_h(x)$, again contrary to assumption.

In figure 1 $S_h = \{x, w\}$, for $h = 1$. In figure 2 $S_h = \{w\}$ for $h = n = 2$. Finally in figure 3 $S_h = \{a, b, c, d\}$. Here h is not specified, but $h < n$, for the h-digraph is not complete.

The subgraph of the digraph D_h corresponding to S_h is the digraph comprising as points all elements of S_h and all directed lines (arrows) connecting them directly. It will be called digraph $D_h{}^*$.

c. The Formation of k-Issue Coalitions as a Reason for Intransitive or Cyclical Social Preferences

In this section we intend to prove some results, of which the logrolling theorem for separable individual preferences and the paradox of liberalism are just special cases (see sec. 2).

We begin by demonstrating the validity of the following.

LEMMA 1. *Each element of* $\mathrm{S_h}$ *is either a member of a social preference or indifference cycle within* $\mathrm{D_h}^*$ *or is an isolated point of the digraph* $\mathrm{D_h}^*$ *representing the elements of* $\mathrm{S_h}$ *and the* R*-relations between* *them. For* h = n *all elements of* S_h *are members of social preference or indifference cycles containing all other members of* S_h.

The proof follows directly from the definition of $U - S_h$. Assume $x, z \in S_h$. Then, if $x \in G_h(z)$ we must also have $z \in G_h(x)$. Otherwise $x \in U - S_h$, contrary to assumption. Further, if $x \notin G_h(z)$ for all $z \in S_h$ excluding x, then all $z \notin G_h(x)$. Otherwise, $z \in U - S_h$, contrary to assumption.

Thus either if $x \in G_h(z)$ $xP \ldots Pz$ or $xI \ldots Iz$ must hold with all outcomes in the chain belonging to S_h for some z; or if $x \notin G_h(z)$ x must be an isolated point in D_h^*.

Finally, if $h = n$ we have a complete digraph. Thus, we have at least one arrow connecting each pair of points, including $x, z \in S_n$. There is thus at least one arrow between all elements of S_n. But then $x \in G_n(z)$ and $z \in G_n(x)$ or $xI \ldots Iz$ from the above argument and thus x and z are members of a social preference or indifference cycle. This completes the proof.

We now proceed to prove:

THEOREM 1. *Assume that a nonempty set* $S_h \neq U$ *of* h-*stable outcomes exists and that* y, v, w $\in$ U *are outcomes such that* y *differs from* x $\in$ S_h *and* v, w *differ from each other in exactly* k *issues* ($1 \leqq h < k \leqq n$). *Then at least one cycle of intransitive social preferences, including* x $\in S_h$ *and* y $\in U - S_h$, *exists if*

a) for x $\in S_h$ *and* y $\in (U - S_h) \cap F_h(x)$, *a* C^k *coalition exists who prefers* y *to* x, *such that* y P x;

or if

b) for x $\in S_h$ *with* y, v $\notin F_h(x)$ *and* w $\in F_h(x)$, y $\in F_h(v)$, *two* C^k *coalitions exist, namely* ${}^1C^k$ *who prefer* y *to* x *so that* y Px, *and* ${}^2C^k$ *who prefer* w *to* v *so that* w Pv.

Let us observe that the social intransitivities mentioned in the theorem are a consequence of the possibility and usefulness to form winning coalitions over k issues, i.e., of an agreement concluded by k one-issue coalitions C_i to coordinate their decisions, an agreement which would be favorable to all their members.

The proof of theorem 1 is trivial. Let us turn first to part *a*. Since $y \in F_h(x)$ and $y\,Px$, we have

$$y\,P\,x\,R \ldots R\,z\,R \ldots R\,y.$$

Note that $z \in S_h$ is possible.

Next we prove part *b*. Here $y \in F_h(v)$, $y\,P\,x$, $w\,P\,v$ and $w = F_h(x)$. Thus $y\,P\,x\,R \ldots R\,w\,P\,v\,R \ldots R\,y$.

Moreover, since $y \notin F_h(x)$ two coalitions ${}^1C^k$ and ${}^2C^k$ are necessary to bring about intransitivity of group preferences involving x and y.

It is important to realize that in all cases in which $F_h(x) = U$, i.e., in which the digraph D_h^* has no isolated subgraphs, only part *a* of theorem 1 is applicable. This includes the special case in which x is the only element of S_h. We may call it the general Condorcet solution for the case that only h-issue coalitions are allowed. It is obvious, moreover, that in this case cyclical social preferences are present, whenever it is profitable for a C^k coalition to form an agreement to realize $y \neq x$, $y \in U$, instead of x. For if x is the only element of $S_h \subset U$ then $y \in G_h(x)$ for $y \in U - S_h$.

Let us illustrate theorem 1 by looking at the digraphs of figures 1 and 2. We recall that figure 1 is a digraph D_1 which is a subgraph of the complete digraph D_2 of figure 2. $S_1 = \{x, w\}$, $w \notin F_1(x)$ in figure 1. Allowing C^2 coalitions gives us for adequate individual preference orderings and assignments of rights figure 2. Here we observe that a two-issue coalition ${}^1C^2$ exists such that $v\ P\ x$. Further $v \in F_1(x)$. Thus as asserted in theorem 1*a* we have:

$$v\ P\ x\ P\ y\ P\ v.$$

Next look at figures 3 and 4. Figure 3 shows the digraph D_h, which is a subgraph of the digraph D_k of figure 4. Since the latter digraph is not complete $k < n$. The possibility to form $(h + 1)=$, $(h + 2)=$, . . . , k-issue coalitions has led to two new arrows in figure 4 as compared to figure 3, namely from j to b, such that $j\ P\ b$, and from c to f, such that $c\ P\ f$. Since $j \in F_h(f)$ and $c \in S_h \cap F_h(b)$ we have, as asserted in theorem 1*b*:

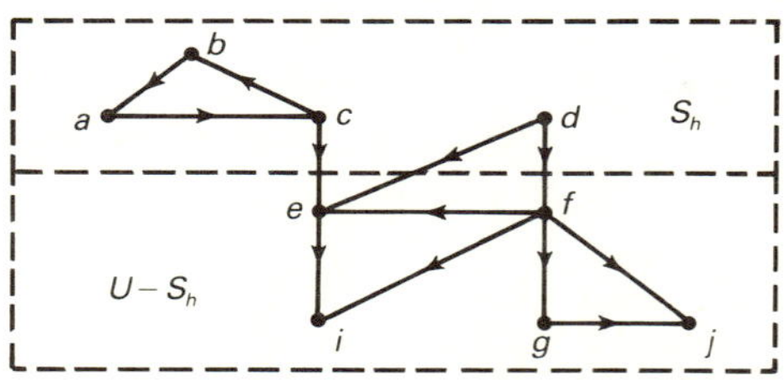

Fig. 3

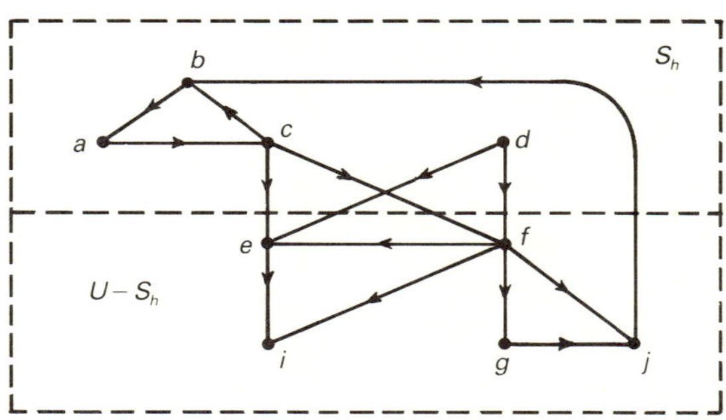

Fig. 4

$j\ P\ b\ P\ a\ P\ c\ P\ f\ P\ g\ P\ j.$

To conclude this section we turn to prove

THEOREM 2. *If the digraph* D_h *describing the situation in the absence of* (h + 1)=, (h + 2)=, . . . , k-*issue coalitions does not contain any social preference cycles, but if this is the case for the digraph* D_k, *then this is a consequence of the formation of one or more* (h + 1)=, (h + 2)=, . . . , k-*issue winning coalitions benefiting all of their members.*

Again the proof is trivial. The only difference between the digraph D_k and its subgraph, the digraph D_h, is the fact that the digraph D_k contains one or more additional arrows between outcomes which are not connected in the digraph D_h. These arrows are in our interpretation of the digraphs the result of the possibility to form winning coalitions over more than h issues, or—in the case of social indifference—the impossibility to form such coalitions, i.e., the fact that blocking coalitions are possible. But social preference cycles as against intransitive social preferences can only be the result of winning but not of blocking coalitions over more than h issues. This completes the proof.

2. Interpretation of Results[4]

a. The Paradox of Liberalism

It is important to get an intuitive feeling of the meaning of the above results. We begin by showing with the help of an example that the paradox of a Paretian liberal found by Sen (1970) is just a special case of theorem 1*a*. In doing so we will follow the idea that under liberalism individuals have the right to decide certain *issues* for society.

In the example let us consider a society of three individuals $V = \{1, 2, 3\}$, who have to decide three issues M_i $(i = 1, 2, 3)$, each with two alternatives: $M_i = \{x_i, \bar{x}_i\}$. Each individual has the right to decide one issue, namely individual i issue M_i: $V_i = \{i\} \subset V$, $(i = 1, 2, 3)$. Obviously $U = \{x_1x_2x_3)$, $(\bar{x}_1x_2x_3)$, $(x_1\bar{x}_2x_3)$, $(x_1x_2\bar{x}_3)$, $(\bar{x}_1\bar{x}_2x_3)$ $(\bar{x}_1x_2\bar{x}_3)$, $(x_1\bar{x}_2\bar{x}_3)$, $(\bar{x}_1\bar{x}_2\bar{x}_3)\}$. Individuals have the following strong, complete, and transitive preference orderings.

TABLE 1

1	2	3
$\bar{x}_1x_2\bar{x}_3$	$\bar{x}_1\bar{x}_2\bar{x}_3$	$\bar{x}_1\bar{x}_2x_3$
$x_1\bar{x}_2\bar{x}_3$	$\bar{x}_1x_2\bar{x}_3$	$\bar{x}_1\bar{x}_2\bar{x}_3$
$\bar{x}_1\bar{x}_2\bar{x}_3$	$\bar{x}_1x_2x_3$	$x_1x_2x_3$
$\bar{x}_1\bar{x}_2x_3$	$x_1x_2x_3$	$\bar{x}_1x_2x_3$
$x_1x_2x_3$	$x_1\bar{x}_2x_3$	$\bar{x}_1x_2\bar{x}_3$
$x_1\bar{x}_2x_3$	$x_1x_2\bar{x}_3$	$x_1x_2\bar{x}_3$
$\bar{x}_1x_2x_3$	$x_1\bar{x}_2\bar{x}_3$	$x_1\bar{x}_2\bar{x}_3$
$x_1x_2\bar{x}_3$	$\bar{x}_1\bar{x}_2x_3$	$x_1\bar{x}_2x_3$

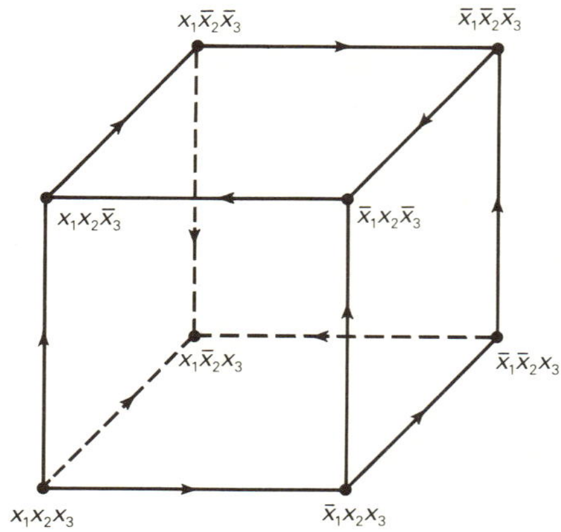

Fig. 5

The resulting digraph D_1 is given by figure 5. The digraph has been drawn in three dimensions to depict the three issues each with two alternatives.

The digraph D_1 contains only one one-issue stable solution $S_1 = \{x_1x_2x_3\}$. Consequently, $(\bar{x}_1\bar{x}_2\bar{x}_3) \in F_1\ (x_1x_2x_3)$. If we now consider the possibility of two- and three-issue coalitions, we find that $C^3 = \{1, 2, 3\}$ prefer $(\bar{x}_1\bar{x}_2\bar{x}_3)$ to $(x_1x_2x_3)$: $(\bar{x}_1\bar{x}_2\bar{x}_3)\ P\ (x_1x_2x_3)$. Thus an arrow has to be drawn from $(\bar{x}_1\bar{x}_2\bar{x}_3)$ to $(x_1x_2x_3)$. As a consequence we have, e.g.,

$$(\bar{x}_1\bar{x}_2\bar{x}_3)\ P\ (x_1x_2x_3)\ P\ (\bar{x}_1x_2x_3)\ P\ (\bar{x}_1\bar{x}_2x_3)\ P\ (\bar{x}_1\bar{x}_2\bar{x}_3).$$

Now realize that a three-issue coalition has to comprise with liberalism all three members of society. Thus $(\bar{x}_1\bar{x}_2\bar{x}_3)$ is Pareto-better than $(x_1x_2x_3)$. It follows that the cycle can be interpreted as a contradiction between pure liberalism, where each individual would decide his own affairs independently, and which would give $(x_1x_2x_3)$ as a solution, and the Pareto principle.

It is obvious, however, that this interpretation is somewhat doubtful. If individual i has the right under liberalism to decide issue M_i, why should he not have the right to make agreements with the other individuals as to their decisions if this is preferable? But then they can agree to decide in favour of the Pareto-optimal outcome $(\bar{x}_1\bar{x}_2\bar{x}_3)$ as against $(x_1x_2x_3)$. The real problem is, therefore, why the individuals either do not enter into such an agreement or why they violate it. In our example it is obviously to the advantage of 1 and (or) of 3 to break the agreement in the hope that the other may keep it or in the fear that the other may break it if one honours it oneself. For $(x_1\bar{x}_2\bar{x}_3)\ P_1\ (\bar{x}_1\bar{x}_2\bar{x}_3)$, $(\bar{x}_1\bar{x}_2x_3)\ P_3\ (\bar{x}_1\bar{x}_2\bar{x}_3)$ and $(\bar{x}_1\bar{x}_2\bar{x}_3)\ P_1\ (\bar{x}_1\bar{x}_2x_3)$, $(\bar{x}_1\bar{x}_2\bar{x}_3)\ P_3\ (x_1\bar{x}_2\bar{x}_3)$. Even 2 will be reluctant to conclude and to keep the agreement, since he has to fear its violation by the others, for $(x_1x_2x_3)\ P_2\ (x_1\bar{x}_2\bar{x}_3)\ P_2\ (\bar{x}_1\bar{x}_2x_3)$. All possible participants find themselves thus in a dilemma, which is certainly related to the allocation of rights to make decisions, but which is in no way a special trait of liberalism. On the contrary, as we could suspect from our theorems, this kind of dilemma is a general problem of a decentralized social system and may happen with any kind of such a social organization (see sec. 4). This will become clearer when we turn to the example of logrolling in the next section.

Concluding this section let us mention that $F_1\ (x_1x_2x_3) = U$. Since, moreover, $S_1 = \{x_1x_2x_3\}$, theorem 1*a* applies, if any C^k $(k > 1)$ coalition is present. This is the case in the present example.

b. Simple Majority Logrolling

Let us again consider a society of three individuals $V = \{1, 2, 3\}$, who have to decide three issues M_i $(i = 1, 2, 3)$, each with two alternatives: $M_i = \{x_i, \bar{x}_i\}$. But now all individuals together have the right to decide each issue M_i, i.e., $V_i = V$ $(i = 1, 2, 3)$, by simple majority voting. The individual preferences are presented in table 2 and the resulting social preferences are again given by figure 5.

In this example, too, $S_1 = \{x_1x_2x_3\}$ and $F_1\ (x_1x_2x_3) = U$. Thus cyclical group preferences result, since $C^3 = \{1, 2, 3\}$ prefer $(\bar{x}_1\bar{x}_2\bar{x}_3)$ to $(x_1x_2x_3)$. As a consequence we could speak of a "contradiction of the Pareto principle and of majority voting of all members of society", if separate votes would be taken on the three issues and if no agreement among them concerning their voting behavior were allowed. Thus Sen's paradox is not a special feature of liberalism. All members of society prefer $(\bar{x}_1\bar{x}_2\bar{x}_3)$ to $(x_1x_2x_3)$. But without logrolling $(x_1x_2x_3)$, which is not Pareto-optimal, will be the outcome.

On the other hand, as in the example given in section 2a for liberalism, it is not at all sure that a logrolling agreement will be concluded or kept if it has been concluded. For majority $C_1^2 = \{1, 2\}$ prefer $(x_1\bar{x}_2\bar{x}_3)$ and majority $C_2^2 = \{2, 3\}$ prefer $(\bar{x}_1\bar{x}_2x_3)$ to $(\bar{x}_1\bar{x}_2\bar{x}_3)$. Thus voters 3 and 1 cannot be sure that the voting agreement will be kept, and that not $(x_1\bar{x}_2\bar{x}_3)$ or $(\bar{x}_1\bar{x}_2x_3)$ will be the outcome instead of $(\bar{x}_1\bar{x}_2\bar{x}_3)$, if one of them sticks to the voting agreement and the others do not. But $(x_1x_2x_3)\ P_3\ (x_1\bar{x}_2\bar{x}_3)$ and $(x_1x_2x_3)\ P_1\ (\bar{x}_1\bar{x}_2x_3)$. This dilemma is, of course, nothing else than the cyclical group preferences present.

TABLE 2

1	2	3
$x_1\bar{x}_2\bar{x}_3$	$x_1x_2\bar{x}_3$	$\bar{x}_1x_2x_3$
$\bar{x}_1\bar{x}_2\bar{x}_3$	$x_1\bar{x}_2\bar{x}_3$	$\bar{x}_1\bar{x}_2x_3$
$x_1x_2x_3$	$\bar{x}_1\bar{x}_2x_3$	$\bar{x}_1\bar{x}_2\bar{x}_3$
$\bar{x}_1x_2x_3$	$\bar{x}_1\bar{x}_2\bar{x}_3$	$\bar{x}_1x_2\bar{x}_3$
$\bar{x}_1\bar{x}_2x_3$	$\bar{x}_1x_2\bar{x}_3$	$x_1\bar{x}_2x_3$
$\bar{x}_1x_2\bar{x}_3$	$x_1x_2x_3$	$x_1x_2x_3$
$x_1x_2\bar{x}_3$	$\bar{x}_1x_2x_3$	$x_1x_2\bar{x}_3$
$x_1\bar{x}_2x_3$	$x_1\bar{x}_2x_3$	$x_1\bar{x}_2\bar{x}_3$

c. Separable Individual Preferences

In the introductory section we mentioned that the logrolling theorem, which is a special case of theorems 1 and 2, has been derived with the help of the assumption of separable individual preferences in earlier articles. It is therefore useful to make clear the role of this assumption in these proofs. We do so by proving the following.

> THEOREM 3. *If separable individual preferences are present then the digraph* D_h^* *does not contain any subgraphs which are not* R*-reachable from each other, i.e., digraph* D_h^* *is a strongly connected digraph.*[5]

Before proving the theorem, let us shortly discuss its meaning. If the digraph D_h^* has no isolated subgraphs, then all points (outcomes) belonging to it have to be members of preference or indifference cycles within the digraph D_h^*. This follows directly from Lemma 1. Because of this only part *a* of theorem 1 and not part *b* is applicable in the case of separable individual preferences. We can, therefore, conclude that whenever separable individual preferences are present, and if a nonempty digraph D_h^* exists, intransitive social preferences will result including at least one member of $U - S_h$ and all members of S_h, if a C^k coalition exists who prefer one outcome $y \in U - S_h$ to another one $x \in S_h$. For the special case of simple majority voting on all issues by all members of society this means that a logrolling situation in which a majority prefer some $y \in U - S_h$ to some $x \in S_h$ implies intransitive group preferences. This allows, of course, the possibility of cyclical group preferences. Note that the consequences just mentioned are not confined to majority voting. As already realized by Schwartz (1977), they are valid for all the combinations of allocations of rights and decision rules which we have allowed in section 1a.

We turn now to the proof of theorem 3 and define first separable individual preferences.

Let y, y^*, z, $z^* \in U$ be such that

$$y = (y_1, y_2, \ldots, y_{i-1}, y_i, y_{i+1}, \ldots, y_n)$$
$$y^* = (y_1, y_2, \ldots, y_{i-1}, y_i^*, y_{i+1}, \ldots, y_n)$$

and

$$z = (z_1, z_2, \ldots, z_{i-1}, y_i, z_{i+1}, \ldots, z_n)$$
$$z^* = (z_1, z_2, \ldots, z_{i-1}, y_i^*, z_{i+1}, \ldots, z_n).$$

Then separable individual preferences are present, if $y\, R_j\, y^*$ implies $z\, R_j\, z^*$, $j \in V$ and for all y_p, z_p with $q \neq i$.

Next let us define $y^a \in U$ as those outcomes which are identical with y in the first α issues and with x in the last $n - \alpha$ issues. Therefore

$$y^1 \equiv (y_1, x_2, \ldots, x_n)$$
$$y_2 \equiv (y_1, y_2, x_3, \ldots, x_n)$$
$$\vdots \qquad \vdots$$
$$y^{k-1} \equiv (y_1, y_2, \ldots, y_{k-1}, x_k, \ldots, x_n).$$

We state first that theorem 3 is trivally true, if S_h contains only one element. Next, all outcomes in S_h differing in not more than h issues are obviously connected by at least one arrow in $D_h{}^*$, since 1-, 2-, . . . , h-issue coalitions are allowed.

Consider now two outcomes x, $y \in S_h$, which are different in k components ($1 \leqq h < k \leqq n$). Without loss of generality we can assume that x and y differ in the first k outcomes. Thus, let

$$x \equiv (x_1, x_2, \ldots, x_k, x_{k+1}, \ldots, x_n)$$
$$y \equiv (y_1, y_2, \ldots, y_k, x_{k+1}, \ldots, x_n)$$

We assume next that x, $y \in S_1$ are any points belonging to digraph $D_1{}^*$. If we can show, as will be done below, that the assumption of separable individual preferences implies $y = F_1\,(x)$, then $x = F_1\,(y)$ must be true, too, because of Lemma 1. As a consequence no x, $y \in S_1$ belong to isolated subgraphs of $D_1{}^*$ and theorem 3 is valid for the case $h = 1$. Finally we will demonstrate that the result can be generalized to the case $h > 1$, i.e., for the digraph $D_h{}^*$.

Let us begin by proving $y = F_1\,(x)$. We observe first that if for all members of some C_i coalition $y\ R_j\ y^*$ is valid then $z\ Rj\ z^*$ is true for the same members because of the assumption of separable individual preferences. But since C_i is a winning coalition for issue M_i it follows at once that we get $y\ R\ y^*$ and $z\ R\ z^*$ for society. The former relation implies the latter.

Now consider ${}^{\alpha}y \in U$, where

$${}^{\alpha}y \equiv (x_1, x_2, \ldots, x_{\alpha-1}, y_{\alpha}, x_{\alpha+1}, \ldots, x_n)\ (\alpha = 1, 2, \ldots, n),$$

and note that ${}^{\alpha}y$ differs from x only in one component, namely component α. Consequently there must be an arrow between x and ${}^{\alpha}y$. From this and since $x \in S_1$, if ${}^{\alpha}y \in U - S_1$ then

$$x\ R\ {}^{\alpha}y. \tag{1}$$

Further, if ${}^{\alpha}y \in S_1$, either the same relation holds or if ${}^{\alpha}y\ R\ x$,

$$x\ R \ldots R\ v\ R\ w\ R \ldots R\ {}^{\alpha}y, \tag{2}$$

because of Lemma 1. Here all elements belonging to this indirect relation between x and y are elements of S_1, e.g. v, $w \in S_1$. It is important to realize that v and w can only be different in one issue, since they belong to S_1.

From (1) we get for $\alpha = 1$

$$x \; R \; y^1. \tag{3}$$

Similarly from (2)

$$x \; R \; . \; . \; . \; R \; y^1 \text{ if } {}^1y \; R \; x. \tag{3a}$$

Next from (1) for $\alpha = 2$ we conclude by using the assumption of separable individual preferences:

$$y^1 \; R \; y^2. \tag{4}$$

Similarly from (2) for $\alpha = 2$ and using the same assumption,

$$y^1 \; R \; . \; . \; . \; R \; v^1 \; R \; w^1 \; . \; . \; . \; R \; y^2, \text{ if } {}^2y \; R \; x. \tag{4a}$$

This conclusion has to be explained in detail. First note that

$$\begin{aligned} v &\equiv (v_1, v_2, \ldots, v_n) \\ v^{\alpha - 1} &\equiv (y_1, y_2, \ldots, y_{\alpha - 1}, v_\alpha, \ldots, v_n) \\ w &\equiv (w_1, w_2, \ldots, w_n) \\ w^{\alpha - 1} &\equiv (y_1, y_2, \ldots, y_{\alpha - 1}, w_\alpha, \ldots, w_n). \end{aligned}$$

Since we consider the digraph D_1 it follows that w is different from v in only one component. The same is true for all neighboring outcomes in (2). Now by replacing the first $\alpha - 1$ components in v and w by $y_1, y_2, \ldots, y_{\alpha - 1}$ either leaves the component in which w and v differ unchanged in $w^{\alpha - 1}$ and $v^{\alpha - 1}$. Then $w^{\alpha - 1}$ and $v^{\alpha - 1}$ differ in the same single component as w and v and it follows from the assumption of separability that $v \; R \; w$ implies $v^{\alpha - 1} \; R \; w^{\alpha - 1}$. Or the only component in which w and v differ is replaced by the same y_i to get $w^{\alpha - 1}$ and $v^{\alpha - 1}$. Then $v^{\alpha - 1} = w^{\alpha - 1}$, $v^{\alpha - 1} \; I \; w^{\alpha - 1}$ and, therefore, $v^{\alpha - 1} \; R \; w^{\alpha - 1}$ holds.

As a consequence, we get from (2)

$$y^{\alpha - 1} \; R \; . \; . \; . \; R \; v^{\alpha - 1} \; R \; w^{\alpha - 1} \; R \; . \; . \; . \; R \; y^\alpha. \tag{2a}$$

Setting $\alpha = 2$, (4a) follows.

Moving on to $\alpha = 3$ we derive from (1) and (2a) respectively

$$y^2 \; R \; y^3 \tag{5}$$

or

$$y^2 \; R \; . \; . \; . \; R \; v^2 \; R \; w^2 \; R \; . \; . \; . \; R \; y^3 \tag{5a}$$

for ${}^{3}y\ R\ x$ etc. for $\alpha = 4, 5, \ldots$ until we finally get

$$y^{k-1}\ R\ y \tag{6}$$

or

$$y^{k-1}\ R \ldots R\ v^{k-1}\ R\ w^{k-}\ \ R \ldots R\ y \text{ for } {}^{k-1}y\ R\ x. \tag{6a}$$

Putting our results together we have

$$x\ R \ldots .\ R\ y. \tag{7}$$

Thus $y \in F_1\ (x)$ and because of Lemma 1 $x \in F_1\ (y)$. x and y do not belong to isolated subgraphs of the digraph $D_1{}^*$.

Until now we have only shown that no pair of outcomes $x, y \in S_1$ belongs to isolated subgraphs of the digraph $D_1{}^*$. But is the same true for the digraph $D_h{}^*$ $(1 < h \leqq k)$? It is easily shown that this is in fact the case. We have just demonstrated that for each $y \in S_1$ we have $y \in F_1\ (x)$ for all $x \in S_1$. But then, following from the definition of h-stability for all $z \in U - S_1$ we have also $z \in F_1\ (x)$ for all $x \in S_1$. Thus each point (outcome) is R-reachable from x. But this cannot change if h-issue coalitions are allowed $(h > 1)$. For this results only in a number of new arrows between the points. Thus if $x, y \in S_1$ are also members of S_h then they are not isolated as before. And if for some $z \in U - S_1$ we have $z \in S_h$, then this can only be the case through a C^k coalition for whose members $z\ P_j\ y$ is valid for some $y \in S_1$. For since $z \in F_1\ (y)$ it is only possible that $z \in S_h$ according to the definition of h-stability, if $y \in F_h\ (z)$. But then $z \in F_h\ (x)$ for all $x \in S_h$, because $y \in F_1\ (x)$. This completes the proof of theorem 3.

3. Relation to Arrow's General Impossibility Theorem

It has been shown in section 1 that if intransitive social preferences are absent in the digraph D_1 but present in the digraph D_n, this is the consequence of the possibility of 2-, 3-, . . . , n-issue coalitions benefiting all of their members (see theorem 2). The presence of intransitive social preferences in the digraph D_n can be interpreted as a contradiction between the assumptions if transitivity of the complete weak social preference ordering represented by the digraph D_n is postulated.

Apart from the case of intransitive social preferences in the digraph D_1 our results can thus be looked at as a substantive interpretation and a proof of Arrow's General Impossibility Theorem (Arrow 1963), since the existence of a C^n coalition can be shown for all social organizations considered (see section 4). For it is obvious that, excluding dictatorship, all conditions postulated by Arrow are fulfilled by our assumptions, as will be demonstrated. But if this is true, then the impossibility of a nondictatorial transitive social preference ordering for all possible combinations of individual preference orderings is only a consequence of the possibility to form 2-, 3-, . . . , n-issue coalitions benefiting all of their members in a decentralized social system, i.e., of the possibility to conclude agreements among C_i coalitions furthering the interests of all of their members. But if such C^h ($h = 2, \ldots, n$) coalitions are not allowed, non–Pareto-optimal outcomes may result as has been shown for the examples of sections 2a and 2b. With this prohibition of C^h coalitions one could therefore speak of a contradiction between Pareto–optimality and liberalism as has been done by Sen. But obviously such a restriction is not a trait of liberalism alone, but more generally for all forms of decentralization.

Let us show now that Arrow's conditions are fulfilled by our assumptions. In doing so we will, however, rely on the somewhat changed formulation used by Luce and Raiffa (1957, 333–40) and adapt it to the notation used above. We shall denote by a *profile of preference orderings* for the individuals of society an m-tuple of orderings, $(R_1, R_2, \ldots, R_m)$, where R_j is the preference ordering for individual $j \in V$ for some $x, y \in U$.

We discuss first

CONDITION 1.

a) *The number of outcomes in* U *is greater than or equal to three.*
b) *The social preference ordering is defined for all possible profiles of individual orderings; it is a weak, complete and transitive ordering.*
c) *There are at least two individuals.*

Conditions 1*a* and 1*c* are obviously met by our assumptions. Moreover, we have put no restrictions on possible individual preference orderings. With all h-issue coalitions allowed ($1 \leqq h \leqq n$), i.e., for the digraph D_n, our assumptions imply a weak and complete social preference ordering. Thus condition 1*b* is fulfilled with the exception of transitivity of the social preference ordering. But since, as will be seen, conditions 2 to 4 below are implied by our assumptions, intransitivity is a possible consequence of nondictatorship. This is the only reason why we did not include transitivity among our assumptions. If we do so condition 1 is fulfilled and the contradiction proved by Arrow is present in our system.

Let us turn to the condition of the positive association of social and individual values.

CONDITION 2. *If the social preference relation asserts that* x *is preferred to* y *for a given profile of individual preferences, it shall assert the same when the profile is modified as follows:*

a) *The individual paired comparisons between outcomes other than* x *are not changed.*
b) *Each individual paired comparison between* x *and any other outcome either remains unchanged or it is modified in* x*'s favor.*

Condition 2 is obviously fulfilled by our assumptions of section 1, for $x\ P\ y$ is only dependent on the fact that $x\ P_j\ y$ is valid for all members $j \in C$ of the corresponding C coalition. And if some individual $s \notin C$ changes his preference ordering from $y\ R_s\ x$ to $x\ P_s\ y$ we get either a coalition $C' = C \cup \{s\}$ which is according to our assumption still a winning coalition, so that $x\ P\ y$ holds, or $s \notin C_i$ for all possible C_i out of which some C'' can be formed. Then the change of his preference ordering has no consequences at all. The same is true if several members of $V - C$ change their preference orderings.

Let us now discuss the condition of the independence of irrelevant alternatives.

> Condition 3. *Let* U$_1$ *be any subset of outcomes in* U. *If a profile of orderings is modified in such a manner that each individual's paired comparisons among the outcomes in* U$_1$ *are left invariant, the social orderings resulting from the original and modified profiles of individual orderings should be identical for the outcomes in* U$_1$.

This condition is obviously fulfilled by the assumptions of section 1, for if $x\ P_j\ y$ for all $j \in C$, $x, y \in U_1$, with C being a winning coalition for x against y, we have $x\ P\ y$. And this relation is not changed if $v\ P_s\ w$ is changed into $w\ R_s\ v$ for some $s \in V$ and for some $v, w \in U - U_1$.

Next we turn to citizen's sovereignty.

> Condition 4. *For each pair of* x *and* y, *there is some profile of individual orderings such that society prefers* x *to* y.

Condition 4 is also fulfilled by our assumptions. If x and y are different only in issue M_i, then there exists for all profiles of individual orderings referring to all individuals $s \in U - V_i$ a $L_i \subseteq V_i$ such that $x\ P\ y$ if for all $j \in L_i$ $x\ P_j\ y$. But if this is true then there must be, moreover, a C^h composed out of h C_i coalitions such that $x\ P\ y$, if x and y are different in h issues $(1 < h \leqq n)$, and if $x\ P_j\ y$, $j \in C^h$.

Finally we have the condition of nondictatorship.

> Condition 5. *There is no individual with the property that whenever he prefers* x *to* y *(for any* x *and* y*) society does likewise, regardless of the preferences of other individuals.*

Condition 5 is not one of our assumptions. But it is easy to see that without it no contradiction among the conditions can result. Or put within the framework of our discussion no social intransitivity can be present. For according to our assumptions individual preference orderings are weak, complete, and transitive. Thus, if the preference orderings of one individual determine social preference relations, the social preference relation must be transitive, too. Thus we have to assume nondictatorship to get social intransitivity and a contradiction between the conditions.

4. Proof of the Possibility of Cyclical Social Preferences

We have still to show that our assumptions together with the assumptions of nondictatorship and transitivity of social preferences lead to a contradiction for all assignments of rights and decision rules considered. This will be done by showing that there exists at least one profile of individual preferences allowing the formation of $C_1, C_2, \ldots, C_n$ coalitions and a C^n coalition which imply cyclical social preferences, given the other assumptions.

Let us first state

THEOREM 4. *Assume that any assignment of rights and any decision rules allowed in section 1 are present and that there exists at least one collection of winning coalitions* $C_1, C_2, \ldots, C_n$ *such that*

$$C_1 \cap C_2 \cap \ldots \cap C_n = \varnothing. \tag{8}$$

Then there exists at least one profile of individual preferences which implies cyclical social preferences.

What is the meaning of the additional assumption? Obviously, if $C_1 \cap C_2 \cap \ldots \cap C_n \neq \varnothing$ would hold for all possible combinations of one-issue winning coalitions, there would be one or more individuals able to block all decisions favoring any outcome preferred by all other members of society to any other. These individuals would be members of a kind of veto-oligarchy, each of whose members were able to prevent any decision of society opposed to their interests. The additional assumption thus implies that there is at least one collection of winning coalitions without members who are "blocking dictators." Note that this assumption is weaker than nondictatorship which is implied by it.

To prove the theorem assume the following individual preferences:

$$\begin{aligned}
&xP_{j2}\, y \text{ for all } j_1 \in C_1,\\
&yP_{j_l}\, x \text{ for all } j_1 \in V - C_1;\\
&yP_{j2}\, u \text{ for all } j_2 \in C_2,\\
&uP_{j2}\, y \text{ for all } j_2 \in V - C_2:\\
&\vdots \qquad \vdots\\
&wP_{j_n}\, z \text{ for all } j_n \in C_n,\\
&zP_j\, w_n \text{ for all } j_n \in V - C_n.
\end{aligned} \tag{9}$$

Because of (9) we get

$$xPyPuP \ldots . PwPz. \tag{10}$$

Moreover, since because of (8) nobody can belong to all C_i ($i = 1, 2, \ldots, n$) in (9), everybody has to belong to at least one $V - C_i$. Thus

$$(V - C_1) \cup (V - C_2) \cup \ldots \cup (V - C_n) = V. \tag{11}$$

But from this and (9) it follows that for no $j_i \in V$

$$xR_{j_i}\ yR_{j_i}\ uR_{j_i} \ldots R_{j_i}\ w\ R_{j_i}z \tag{12}$$

is valid.

Now assume

$$zP_{j_i}\ x \text{ for all } j_i \in C^n \tag{13}$$

and thus

$$zPx. \tag{14}$$

Since (12) is not valid for any $j_i \in C^n \subseteq V$, (13) does not lead to a contradiction with the assumption of transitive individual preferences. Consequently C^n exists, since it could contain up to all members of society. It can be formed, e.g., as $V_1 \cup V_2 \cup \ldots \cup V_n$.

But from (10) and (14) we get cyclical social preferences. This completes the proof.

Finally let us show that Sen's result for liberalism can be generalized to the set of organizations of society considered and for which (8) is valid. For assume that

$$C^n = V. \tag{15}$$

Next let us follow the same procedure as in (9) to (14). Because of (10) x would be the outcome if no agreement to decide in favor of z among some $C_1', C_2', \ldots, C_n'$ forming C^n would be made. But clearly, because of (13) and (15) z is Pareto-better than x. Thus we may speak of a contradiction of the respective kind of organization of society and the Pareto principle.

Note that the case of liberalism with $C_i = V_i = \{j_i\}$, $j_i \in V$, $i = 1, 2, \ldots, n$ and $V_1 \cup V_2 \cup \ldots \cup V_n = V$ fulfills (8) and (15).

It is important to realize that if each $j_i \in V$ belongs to at least one V_i then assumption (8) implies $n \geqq m$ for some but not all kinds of organizations of society. This is true for the case of liberalism just stated, but it is also true, if $V_i = V$ for all i and if $m - 1$ members of society have to agree to get a decision in favor of one of two alternatives out of any issue.

On the other hand, with simple majority voting of all members of society on all issues $n \geqq 3$ is sufficient to bring about Sen's contradiction irrespective of the size of $m \geqq 3$ (see example in sec. 2).

NOTES

I am grateful to valuable comments and critical remarks by F. Breyer, H. P. Bauer, H. J. Jaksch and M. Faber. An exchange of ideas with Thomas Schwartz extending over years has been helpful to develop the intuitive understanding of the problems discussed.

1. Compare Harary, Norman, and Cartwright 1965.
2. See Harary, Norman, and Cartwright 1965, 85.
3. The expressions *Condorcet solution* and *Condorcet set* refer to majority voting. Here we use them with the adjective *general* since they refer to the very general form of decision making we consider.
4. More examples with different forms of social organizations can be found in Bernholz 1978.
5. A digraph is strongly connected if every two points are mutually *R*-reachable (Harary, Norman, and Cartwright 1965, 51).

REFERENCES

Arrow, K. J. *Social Choice and Individual Values*. New York, 1963.

Bernholz, P. "Logrolling, Arrow-Paradox and Cyclical Majorities." *Public Choice* 15 (1973): 87–95.

______. "Logrolling, Arrow-Paradox and Decision Rules: A Generalization." *Kyklos* 27 (1974*a*): 49–62.

______. "Is a Paretian Liberal Really Impossible?" *Public Choice* 20 (1974*b*): 99–107.

______. "Is a Paretian Liberal Really Impossible? A Rejoinder." *Public Choice* 23 (1975): 69–73.

______. "Liberalism, Logrolling and Cyclical Group Preferences." *Kyklos* 29 (1976): 26–37.

______. "Cyclical Group Preferences, Logrolling, Pareto-Optimality and the Paradox of Liberalism." Institut für Sozialwissenschaften, Institut für Angewandte Wirtschaftsforschung, Diskussionpapier Nr. 29, Universität Basel, December, 1978.

Breyer, F. *Das Liberale Paradox*. Meisenheim a. Glan, 1978.

Gibbard, A. "A Pareto-Consistent Libertarian Claim." *Journal of Economic Theory* 7 (1974): 388–410.

Harary, F., R. Z. Norman, and D. Cartwright. *Structural Models: An Introduction to the Theory of Directed Graphs*. New York, London, and Sydney, 1965.

Luce, D., and Raiffa, H. *Games and Decisions*. New York, London, and Sydney, 1957.

Miller, N. R. "Logrolling, Vote Trading and the Paradox of Voting: A Game-Theoretical Overview." *Public Choice* 30 (1977): 51–75.

______. "A New Solution Set for Tournaments and Majority Voting." Paper read at the 1978 Annual Meeting of the American Political Science Association, New York, 1978.

Oppenheimer, J. A. "Relating Coalitions of Minorities to the Voters' Paradox or

Putting the Fly in the Democratic Pie." Paper presented to Southwest Political Science Association Meeting, San Antonio, Texas, 1972.

Schwartz, T. "Collective Choice, Separation of Issues and Vote Trading." *American Political Science Review* 72 (1977).

Sen, A. K. "The Impossibility of a Paretian Liberal." *Journal of Political Economy* 78 (1970): 152–57.

The Normative Purpose of Economic "Science": Rediscovery of an Eighteenth-Century Method

Geoffrey Brennan and James M. Buchanan

The necessity of abstraction is self-evident. By its very nature, intellectual activity involves coming to terms with a chaos of observations through the imposition of an order which is itself an artifact of the mental process. In this activity, a selective strategy must be used. Irrelevances must be blotted out, where these consist of observations that tend to disprove, qualify, or overly complicate the sought-for mental picture. Any theory is abstracted from the reality perceived by the senses, and theory derives its potential value precisely because it *is* so abstracted. From this perspective, it follows that any theory, any model, can, and indeed must, be able to tolerate a certain amount of dissonance with perception before it loses its relative superiority over potential alternatives.

This perspective suggests that there may well be many possible mental orders or constructs that can "explain" a particular set of "facts" within the tolerated range of "error." Which particular order chosen depends on many elements, including the tastes of the analyst, intellectual habits and fashions of the times, and the extent of congruence with the reality that is perceived (congruence that embodies predictive power as an important part). We leave as basically "mysterious" the causal linkage between changes in these elements and a switching of mental orders (paradigms).

In this essay, we are interested in one particular abstraction, one that is familiar to all economists. We are concerned with the model of man that is used in economic theory—the model of man that actually takes its name from the discipline, *homo economicus*. Our purpose is to develop a specific justification for that abstraction that has not been sufficiently recognized by our fellow practitioners. In the exposition that follows we shall argue three propositions.

1. The purpose for which a theory is to be used is itself an important consideration in choosing how it should be formulated (that is, what abstractions are acceptable).
2. The purpose for which *homo economicus* was used in classical political economy was largely that of comparing the properties of alternative socioeconomic arrangements (constitutions) and not that of explaining "scientifically" (making predictions about) the behavior of economizing actors.

First published in *International Review of Law and Economics* 1 (1981): 155–66.

3. There are important differences between choices that are made among alternative institutions and choices made within the structure of given institutions, differences that are relevant to the nature of the assumptions about human motivation that might be viewed as appropriate.

Our objective is to spell out these propositions in such a way as to demonstrate that, appropriately understood, they provide a justification for the usage of *homo economicus* for comparative institutional analysis, even if the *homo economicus* behavioral postulate may be somewhat less satisfactory than possible alternatives in some predictive sense. In the discussion, we shall necessarily emphasize the differences between "constitutional choice" (that choice among institutions) and "postconstitutional or in-period choice" (the choice among alternative options within given institutions).

Homo Economicus Defined in Empirical "Economic Science"

There is a necessary distinction to be drawn between the formal, but empty, economic theory that incorporates a pure "logic of choice" on the part of the actors, and the allegedly operationally scientific theory or "economic science" that embodies empirically refutable hypotheses.[1] There is a corresponding distinction between the motivational postulates attributed to the human agents in the two constructions, between man as a rational utility maximizer, with the arguments in the utility functions remaining unspecified, and man as a net wealth maximizer, which requires explicit specification of the arguments in utility functions, and the assignment of predominant weights to those arguments that may readily be transformed into monetary wealth.[2]

If we define *homo economicus* in the second of these two senses we have a basis for empirical scientific explanation. Man, as modeled, acts so as to maximize his own interests (or the interests of those for whom he acts) objectively defined, in his economic relationships with other persons. He need not be inherently self-interested in some personalized sense. As Wicksteed noted, "non-tuism" is all that is required here.[3] In the interaction behavior that is to be modeled, man is postulated to further that interest which he represents. His behavior in the economic relationship is not influenced by ethical or moral considerations that serve to constrain his pursuit of his objectively defined interest. *Home economicus*, by construction, is not predicted to act other than in furtherance of his interest, vis-à-vis that of his trading cohorts, as he evaluates such interest at the moment of choice. He must act so as to advance his own net wealth (or that of the party or parties that he represents in the economic interaction).

Armed with this behavioral postulate, we can test "economic theory" against real world observations, and, as the record shows, we can explain much of what we see. There are not clearly defined limits on this model of "economic man"; there is no delineation between "economic" behavior on the one hand and "noneconomic" behavior on the other. *Homo economicus* remains *homo economicus*.

It may be useful to list some extreme examples in which the basic economic or economizing model of interaction is extended to behavioral settings that may not normally be classified as "economic" in nature. For example, if a judge's behavior in his assigned occupational role is modeled strictly in *homo economicus* terms, his decisions on the bench must be explained somehow as falling within a wealth-maximizing calculus. Similarly, for elected politicians and for bureaucrats. Parents' behavior toward their own children may be "explained" as down payments on reciprocal care in their dotage. Conscientiousness on the job may be interpreted in terms of the quest for promotion in a hierarchy. Honesty in business dealing is interpreted as the best policy to increase sales over the long term.

Homo Economicus as Abstraction

The first point to be made is to reemphasize that the *homo economicus* construction *is* an abstraction from reality. Its purpose is that of allowing economists to impose intellectual order on the observed chaos of human interaction, without excessive distracting detail in dimensions of the analysis that are not centrally relevant. Critics of economics may, with some legitimacy, think that economists do not recognize their own construction. There seems little doubt that there are economists, some of them influential within the profession, who do act and talk as if they think of *homo economicus* in much more descriptive ways. There are many economists who appear to think that the rarified *homo economicus* construction is, if not a perfect image of real man, at least sufficiently close so that no great violence is done by assuming that real man is actually *homo economicus*. And, these economists would argue, *homo economicus* is surely the "best" model of man that is available. In short, these economists defend the use of *homo economicus* on empirical, "scientific" grounds.

The methodological position alluded to here has been articulated by George Stigler in his 1980 Tanner lectures at Harvard University.

> Do people possess ethical beliefs which influence their behaviour in ways not dictated by, and hence in conflict with, their own long-run utility-maximizing behaviour?[4] . . . This question of the existence of effective ethical value is, of course, an empirical question and in principle should be directly testable. . . . Let me predict the outcome of the systematic and comprehensive testing of behaviour in situations where self-interest and ethical values with wide verbal allegiance are in conflict. Much of the time, most of the time in fact, the self-interest theory . . . will win. . . . I predict this result because it is the prevalent result found by economists not only within a wide range of economic phenomena, but in the investigations of marital, child-bearing, criminal, religious and other social behaviour. We believe that man is a utility-maximizing animal . . . and to date we have not found it informative to carve out a section of his life in which he invokes a different goal of behaviour. (Lecture II, pp. 23–24)

Or, as Stigler closes the lectures, he remarks:

> I arrive at . . . the thesis that flows naturally and irresistibly from the theory of economics. Man is eternally a utility-maximizer—in his home, in his office (be it public or private), in his church, in his scientific work—in short, everywhere. He can and often does err: perhaps the calculation is too difficult, but more often his information is incomplete. He learns to correct these errors, although sometimes at heavy cost.
>
> What we call ethics, on this approach, is a set of rules with respect to dealings with other persons, rules which in general prohibit behaviour which is only myopically self-serving, or which imposes large costs on others with small gains to oneself. General observance of these rules makes not only for long term gains to the actor but also yields some outside benefits, and the social approval of the ethics is a mild form of enforcement of the rules to achieve this general benefit.[5]

In Stigler's conception, *homo economicus* literally does become a man for all seasons, and wealth maximization becomes the only game in town. Yet there is surely much behavior that cannot be explained, or explained without resort to fantastic mental contortions,[6] if we adhere strictly to the assumptions of the severe economic man construction.

As many persons have noted, and as Douglass North has emphasized, the scope for "free riding" in human interaction is so ubiquitous that if men genuinely were as economic theory depicts them, no sort of ordered society, whether market-dominated or not, would be possible. In this basic sense, the very existence of an ordered society casts doubt on the *homo economicus* model of behavior, if used as some all-inclusive explanatory hypothesis. For example, people vote, yet a proper income- or wealth-maximizing calculus would necessarily classify the voting act as irrational in large-number electorates. Economic theory cannot "explain" voting except in the tautological terms that the act of voting is a consumption activity, and must be so because people do it. Likewise, individuals exercise courtesy and compassion in circumstances where these traits yield no apparent benefits save those inherent in the acts themselves. People volunteer to fight for their tribe, community, or country and, in so doing, take on risks of death, when it would be conspicuously more self-serving to allow others to take on defensive roles. And, more importantly for North's ultimate purposes, no satisfactory account of history—and particularly judicial history—can ignore the influence of changing views about the world and what constitutes moral behavior in it, on the actual behavior of those who seem to have made the decisions that influenced the course of events.

We are not, of course, calling upon our fellow economists to drop *homo economicus* and assume, *volte face,* that persons are saints—that ethical, or generally noneconomic, considerations dominate human motivations in behavioral settings that may or may not be narrowly "economic." Nor do we want to suggest that a mere demonstration that some course of action is "best" on moral grounds will be sufficient to convince persons to act in accordance with such a norm. Our plea is the more modest one that calls upon our fellow economists to recognize that *homo economicus* has its own limit as a useful abstraction. We can only load the construction with so much, and we stand in danger of having our whole "science" collapse in an absurd heap if we push beyond the useful limits. The fact that the whole set of "non-economic" motivations are more difficult to model than the "economic" should not lead us to deny their existence.

We are not even suggesting that more effective predictions about behavior may be made by refining and tempering the abstraction of economic man. The loss of elegance and simplicity that would necessarily be involved in any such attempts might not be offset by marginal extensions in the accuracy of the "scientific" predictions. Our implied criticism of the overextended usage of the *homo economicus* abstraction in trying to explain human behavior "scientifically" lies in our conviction that "scientific prediction," in the sense normally indicated, is *not* what our whole exercise is about and that this application is not the usage for which the abstraction was intended.

We suggest here an alternative usage of the *homo economicus* abstraction that seems more acceptable in all respects. In one sense, we offer a *methodological,* rather than a predictive ("scientific") defense of the whole construction. Simply put, our claim is that *homo economicus* rightly belongs in the analytical derivation of normative propositions about appropriate institutional design. In other words, the model of human behavior that we might properly use in choosing among alternative institutions may be different from the model that would be more appropriate in making predictions about behavior within existing institutional structures.

At one level of analysis our claim is very simple: at another level, however, it requires a rather subtle understanding of the difference between constitutional and postconstitutional choice. Our argument is that the *homo economicus* construction supplies a postulate about human behavior that is in many ways uniquely suited for the comparative institutional analysis that underlies genuine constitutional choice.

Homo Economicus and Constitutional Choice

As a point of departure, let us agree that whatever model of man is to be used in evaluating alternative social orders—alternative rules of the economic/political/social game—it must be applied *uniformly* over all the possibilities to be compared. Simple requirements of methodological consistency require this. If we are to employ one set of behavioral postulates for one institution, and another set for another institution, no legitimate comparison of the two institutions can be made. The ultimate purpose of the exercise is to choose among alternative sets of rules—not among alternative "models of man." We must therefore make a prior selection of a single model of man. Otherwise it becomes analytically impossible to isolate the effects of the institutions as such; the whole analysis is muddied by the arbitrary change in behavioral assumptions midstream.[7]

This is a simple point, and stated in this manner seems totally unexceptionable. Yet we know that it has proved in economics to be a curiously elusive one. The model of political process implicitly assumed in most orthodox discussion of economic policy has made profoundly different assumptions about individual behavior from the corresponding assumptions made in market settings. It has only been in the last twenty years with the burgeoning of public choice that this grotesque asymmetry has been exposed, and the "benevolent despot" model of politics been seriously queried.

But what is more important, because it may be less obvious, is that the methodological requirement of uniformity in the behavioral postulate *remains* even if there is good empirical evidence and analytical presumption that behavior may be different between different institutions. This is so because those differences in behavior have to be *shown* to be attributable to differences in institutions; and if a different model of human behavior is adopted for each institution at the outset, the relevant results will be simply assumed, not analytically *derived*.

A simple example may illustrate here. Suppose it is widely recognized by individual participants that the invisible hand operates in market processes to transform purely self-interested behavior into behavior in the interests of others. Suppose it is also recognized that no corresponding process operates in majoritarian political institutions. Then individuals may well behave in a totally self-interested manner in the market, precisely because the consequences of such behavior are desirable, yet at the same time operate in an ostensibly more altruistic manner in the political mechanism because the consequences of contrary behavior are much more disastrous. A rational actor who is only mildly altruistic might be predicted to behave more altruistically in the political setting than in the market: he "conserves" his altruism in the setting where it is least productive, and "spends" it in the political mechanism where it is more productive. This is the essence of the "economizing" on the scarce resource, love—which economizing, Dennis Robertson reminds us, is the prime virtue of the freely operating market order.

Suppose for the purposes of argument that this behavioral asymmetry is observed. Then it may be tempting for the "scientific observer" simply to note the fact that political agents seem more altruistic than market agents, and model behavior in the two institutions accordingly. But this procedure precludes any proper *explanation* of why behavior may differ—an explanation which is possible only if we maintain the methodological assumption that human motivations are the same across institutions. Moreover, the "empirical" procedure may well lead to the conclusion that people would be more altruistic if we relied more heavily on political rather than market institutions to coordinate individual actions, whereas, of course, no such conclusion can be drawn from the model of behavioral choice as we have given it in the preceding paragraph. On the contrary, heavier reliance on political institutions may simply destroy the incentives to behave altruistically at all.

To recapitulate, then, the requirement of a uniform model of human motivations is fundamental to proper institutional analysis, and remains so even in the face of empirical evidence that might suggest behavioral asymmetry. This requirement establishes a need for a *uniform* model of man—but not necessarily for *homo economicus* as such. What additional arguments can we bring to bear to support the use of this *particular* model of human behavior?

Our central argument here is simple. The question we are interested in posing about any particular social order is whether the rules by which individual actions are coordinated are such as to transform actions undertaken by participants in their own *private* interests into outcomes that are in the interests of others. We know that this curious alchemy is in fact worked by the *market*—that the invisible hand operates, under certain more or less well defined conditions, to convert private interest into public interest. The prime task of comparative institutional analysis is to enquire whether other institutions do the same, and, if so, whether those institutions do so under more or less restrictive conditions. The only assumption required to make this task an interesting one is the assumption that some individuals behave in their narrowly defined private interest at least some of the time. Clearly, if we lived in a world in which all individuals were motivated solely by a concern for the public interest—for example, a world of pure Kantians or Benthamite utilitarians, for whom each individual's own utility counts in determining his behavior no more and no less than anyone else's—then we should hardly be interested in whether the institutional structure served to transfer private interest into public interest or not: no distinction between private and public interest would make sense.[8] In this sense, the minimal agreement that the "invisible hand" mechanism is, *ceteris paribus*, a *virtue* in any social order is tantamount to setting aside as remote the possibility that *all* people are motivated by the public interest *all* the time. Further and more importantly for our purposes, in establishing whether any particular social order has this particular virtue, we can usefully abstract from public motivations entirely. In order to show that private interest is transformed into collective interest, we begin naturally by assuming agents to be privately motivated. If they happen to be publicly motivated *in part*, results may or may not be better: but it simply does not bear on the analysis whether they are so motivated. What is crucial is that *such privately motivated behaviour as exists* is converted into public interest outcomes. To assume that private interest is all that makes men tick is simply to focus on what is relevant for the exercise in hand.

In short, then, the question of whether *homo economicus* is a good approximation to empirical reality determines the *significance* of the exercise of institutional comparison, but not the appropriate *method*. The invisible hand is doubtless a more spectacular virtue in a world where self-seeking behavior is more, rather than less, prevalent. But whether institutions other than the market may exhibit an invisible hand mechanism and under what circumstances, are matters that can only be established by examining the implications of self-seeking behavior within those institutions: to examine the implications of non–self-seeking behavior for such a purpose is manifestly absurd.

A simple example may help to elucidate here. Suppose you are hiring a builder to build you a house. In selecting from among available builders, you will take a number of things into account—his general competence, his conscientiousness, his honesty. The latter characteristic is important because you will not normally want to deal with a builder who you seriously believe is likely to fleece you. For empirical purposes, therefore, the assumption you will make about the said builder is that he is honest: you would not deal with him if you genuinely believed otherwise. But now you proceed to your lawyer's office to draw up a contract. And in this setting, the working hypothesis you make about the builder is quite different. For the contract-drawing exercise, you make the assumption that the builder *is* going to fleece you, not because you believe this necessarily is his objective but because this is the contingency against which you wish to guard. The nature of the exercise leads you, in other words, to make an assumption about human motivations that you believe may be (and certainly hope will be) a poor reflection of empirical reality.[9]

In constitutional design, and in comparative institutional analysis more generally, one's particular beliefs about what model of man is empirically most descriptive are less relevant in precisely the same way and for much the same reason. One calls forth the *homo economicus* assumption, not because it is necessarily the most accurate model of human behavior but because it is the appropriate model for testing whether institutions serve to transform private interest into public. It is as simple as that.

To avoid some possible misunderstanding, we should perhaps emphasize that, in the content of constitutional design, the notion of *homo economicus* can be broadened somewhat beyond the confines of the definition used widely in "economic science." For the purposes of predictive science, the elements in individual utility functions must be specified in clear, recognizable, and measurable terms. Application of the *homo economicus* construction for empirical or predictive purposes requires something like the assumption of net wealth maximization as a surrogate for maximization of consumption more broadly conceived. For the purposes of constitutional design, however, *homo economicus* can be seen to maximize almost anything at all, providing each individual conceives of others as operating without his interest in mind. That is, all that we require is that each individual, in choosing a set of rules, models the motivations of others vis-à-vis himself in such a way that *excludes* their inclusion of his own interests or well-being in their utility functions. *This* version of the *homo economicus* model in no sense rules out the possibility that each individual may be motivated by certain ethical or moral concerns, as long as we can take it that such ethical conduct on the part of anyone cannot be presumed to benefit everyone else. Burning people at the stake in order to secure for them better claims on eternal life is, for example, perfectly consistent with *homo economicus* assumptions at the constitutional level.

For the purposes of constitutional design, then, no specification of arguments in *homo economicus's* utility function is required: the narrowly defined *homo economicus* of predictive science and the more open-ended construction in which the utility function includes any arguments other than the well-being of the chooser become *methodologically equivalent*.

An example may be helpful here. Suppose that a person is considered to be examining the working properties of an institution that would grant some other persons (say, an appointed "governor") the power to tax, with accompanying coercive enforcement. So long as the potential chooser models the behavior of the "governor" so as to exclude his own (the chooser's) interests, the constitutional calculus remains the same whether the "governor" is modeled as using tax revenues for financing a private harem or for providing transfers to other persons in the community, or any other purpose in which the chooser expects to have no interest.

It may be useful to summarize the argument to this point. We have insisted that the model of man to be used in comparative institutional analysis, whatever its precise characteristics, must for analytic reasons be uniform across institutions. And we have insisted that such uniformity must be maintained even in the face of empirical evidence to the contrary. We have argued further that the specific model of human motivations to be used in comparative institutional analysis must emphasize private interest as the prime motivating force, because the specific issue we are interested in examining at this level is whether alternative institutional rules are such as to convert *private motivations* into publicly desired actions. To the extent that the assumption of public motivation is included in the behavioral model, we come close to simply assuming what we wish to prove. We have termed this model of man *homo economicus* consistent with classical usage: it is, however, somewhat less restrictive a model of man than the net-wealth–maximizing model used extensively in economic science.

This argument is, as we see it, complete. There is, however, a complementary line of reasoning that is worth mention here. It runs as follows. For the purposes of economic science, the model of man to be used is the one that gives the best "fit," the most reliable set of predictions about the effects of particular changes in parameters. What is required for such purposes is a model of the "average" or "representative" man. In constitutional choice analysis, however, we seek a model of man which is a "*weighted* average man," where the weights at stake involve the costs that various types impose on the social fabric.

Consider a simple example. Suppose we postulate a world in which half the individuals are Kantians and half are *homines economici*. Suppose that the citizenry in this world examining the costs and benefits of alternative restrictions on the behavior of a dictator whose identity, and hence personality type, is presumed unknown. Clearly, a truly Kantian dictator will impose relatively little in costs upon those who are subject to his rule. A purely self-interested dictator, on the other hand, can be expected to impose enormously high costs on his subjects. For this reason, in any rational constitutional calculus, the model of man presumed will be much closer to the self-interest model than mere empirics might indicate. And this does not presuppose any particular risk aversion on the part of the individual choosing constitutional restrictions. Clearly a risk-*neutral* individual will take into account the expected costs associated with dictators of different personality type; and the whole calculus will naturally be weighted toward a consideration of those cases in which most is at stake. The self-interest postulate takes on a significance in the constitutional setting, therefore, that it essentially lacks in its "scientific" or strictly predictive setting. *Homo economicus* is alive and well, and living in the analytical foundations of constitutional choice—his natural homeland.

Homo Economicus in Classical Political Economy

We consider our argument to be directly within the tradition of classical political economy. Modern economists can still learn much from the methods of the eighteenth-century philosophers, such as Mandeville, Hume, and, particularly, Adam Smith. Their reflections led them to the recognition that the peculiar alchemy of the market order allows the transformation of private interest into "public interest." Individuals with no concerns beyond their own net wealth could, by virtue of the invisible hand of the market, be induced to act as if they were furthering the interests of others than themselves. Adam Smith's butcher could be recognized to be acting in the interests of his customers without one whit of concern for their welfare. It is not required of Smith's butcher that he have no direct concern for his customers; he may well have had such concern. The significant thing is that we do *not* require him to have such a concern in his utility function; and we do not model him as having such a concern when we compare the market with alternative institutional arrangements.

It is in this cradle that *homo economicus* was nurtured. He was a creation for a purpose—this being the demonstration of the virtues of the free market as an institutional order. Smith makes it clear that *homo economicus* is not to be conceived as a generalized *description* of human nature. "Humanity does not desire to be great [or, we may add, to be rich] but to be loved."[10] And no one who has looked at the first pages of *The Theory of Moral Sentiments* can deny Smith's belief in the ubiquity of sympathy. Nonetheless, if one wishes to examine the extent to which a particular institutional order transforms private interest into public interest, it becomes entirely appropriate to focus on a model of man in which private interest predominates. To model man as publicly motivated in making such a comparison would be to assume away the problem that institutional design involves—the problem that was central to Smith's purpose.

In comparative institutional analysis, and ultimately in constitutional design, one calls forth *homo economicus*, not for its accuracy in prediction, but for its assistance in helping to identify and to classify patterns of outcomes attributable directly to institutional differences. The central contribution of the eighteenth-century philosophers lay in their demonstration that, even under strictly *homo economicus* assumptions about behavior, public interest is served by the market order. No such demonstration can be made with respect to alternative arrangements.

The imputation of *homo economicus* motivation to actors in political roles may seem to violate ordinary notions about descriptive reality more than the comparable imputation to actors in the marketplace. But this difference need not provide any justification for replacing the model used for institutional comparison. It may be that judges seek to 'uphold the law' most of the time, that most government employees try to further their own conceptions of "public interest" most of the time, and that elected politicians are genuinely concerned about promoting the "good society." But, even if this were admitted, institutional arrangements would surely be preferred which made these congruent with narrow self-interest on the part of the relevant actors. A model of human behavior in which the natural impulse toward self-interest, narrowly defined, predominates is a highly useful artifact in helping us to identify that set of arrangements that "economize on love."

John Stuart Mill stated the point well:

> The very principle of constitutional government requires it to be assumed that political power will be abused to promote the particular purposes of the holder; not because it is always so, but because such is the natural tendency of things to guard against which is the special use of free institutions.[11]

We might add that what goes for political power goes for market power also, but this point hardly seems necessary. The *market* aspects of this truth have long since been widely recognized and accepted, which makes the continuing neglect (perhaps even denial) of the political aspects even more surprising.

Homo Economicus and Public Choice

In our recent book, *The Power to Tax,*[12] we incorporated a theory of political process in which the *homo economicus* construction was allowed full play. Many of the modern developments in public choice theory can also be interpreted as variations on what might be called the *homo economicus* model of politics.

In developing our approach to taxation, and particularly in attacking the benevolent despot model of politics that has for so long monopolized orthodox economic policy debates, we have been subjected to understandable criticism. The argument has been consistently made that politics is simply not like our models of it, that the application of the *homo economicus* model to political processes does little more than expose our own disciplinary hubris. At the same time, some critics who are generally sympathetic to our approach have sought to defend our position on the grounds that politics is indeed "like that," like our models of it, and so, indeed, is every aspect of human behavior. Our growing reluctance to support this latter ("Stiglerian") defense of our position has been met with some shock and sometimes resentment from some of our colleagues. But the battle over the empirical status of *homo economicus* is *not,* in our view, the crucial issue at all. On empirical grounds, we are surely closer to Adam Smith than to our modern critics, whichever side those critics come from. We admit freely the possibility and indeed the likelihood of non–self-seeking behavior by human agents in all institutional settings. But like Adam Smith, we believe that *homo economicus* remains the appropriate model of behavior in the derivation of normative propositions about the institutions themselves.

There is no inconsistency here. Nor is there any retreat from positions we have taken earlier. The appropriate use of the narrowly "economic" model depends on a prior understanding of what the model is to be used for. And although *homo economicus* may be a useful tool in providing a superior set of hypotheses about political behavior—behavior within well-defined rules—than much of traditional political science has appeared to offer, this is not to argue that it is *the* most useful model of man for such explanatory or predictive purposes, or that there is not much that such a model fails to explain. The level of discourse at which the *homo economicus* construction seems uniquely appropriate is the constitutional level, and this may remain true even if the construction does not give precisely the "best" empirical fit.

NOTES

This paper was originally prepared for a Liberty Fund Conference on "Science and Freedom" held in San Antonio, Texas in March, 1981. We are grateful to participants in that conference—particularly David Levy, Brian Loasby, Richard McKenzie and Karen Vaughn—and to our colleague Bob Tollison for useful comments. Several improvements were also suggested by helpful referees. Remaining errors are our own responsibility.

1. *See* J. M. Buchanan, "Is Economics the Science of Choice?" In *Roads to Freedom,* ed. E. Streissler (Routledge and Kegan Paul, 1969), pp 47–64.
2. In making this two-part distinction, we are "passing over" the in-between postulate, one that involves specification of the arguments in the utility function of persons, but which does not assign weights. In this in-between setting, there remains scope for positive prediction; for example, if we know that some argument, *X,* is valued positively in the utility function, we can predict that more *X* will be chosen as the relative cost of *X* falls. However, note that *X* may be "giving to others" or anything else. In other words, we do not require net wealth maximization as a behavioral postulate in order to have a "scientific" economics. For further discussion, *see* J. M. Buchanan, "Professor Alchian on Economic Meth-

od,'' in his *Freedom in Constitutional Contract* (College Station: Texas A & M University Press, 1978).

3. P. H. Wicksteed, *The Commonsense of Political Economy* (London: Macmillan and Co., 1910).
4. By ''utility-maximizing'' behavior, Stigler means self-serving behavior, with some allowance for altruism within the family and among close friends. He is careful to distinguish this usage from the purely tautological use of utility maximization as in a pure logic of choice.
5. G. Stigler, ''The Economist as Preacher,'' three Tanner Lectures delivered at Harvard University, April 1980.
6. Our colleague, David Friedman, one time in conversation explained the fact that individuals marry those who love them, on the grounds that this procedure reduces monitoring costs in household production processes. This sort of explanation makes creative use of the *homo economicus* model, but its empirical accuracy may seem questionable and it also tends to shift the model toward a pure logic of choice, albeit in a novel manner.
7. We need not argue here that institutions do not affect tastes—although such an argument is implicit in much of the neoclassical tradition. Even where preferences can be shown to be endogenous (i.e., influenced by the institutional environment), the model of man upon which the institutions exercise their influences must be the same *at the outset*. In what follows, however, we ignore the question of the influence institutions may have on tastes *per se* and focus on the effects of rules on the costs and benefits to the individual of alternative courses of action.
8. Of course, institutions may still be compared, but by reference to other criteria. For example, even in this world of publicly motivated individuals there is the question of how those individuals obtain the *information* necessary to enable them to act in accordance with their assumed norms. Interestingly enough, the market has virtues in this area as well, a point emphasized strongly by Hayek. See F. A. Hayek, ''The Use of Knowledge in Society,'' *American Economic Review* 35 (1945): 519–30. With imperfect information, it is reasonable to expect that perceptions of the ''public interest'' will differ. Then one can and must distinguish between the explicit private pursuit of public interest, and the emergence of ''optimal'' outcomes as an ''unintended consequence'' of the interactions within the institutional structure.
9. It could of course be argued (as a referee has done) that the contract-drawing exercise is based on uncertainty about the morality of alternative builders and that contract drawing is a *cheaper* way of saving on transactions costs than acquiring additional information. Analogously, choosing the institutional structure to guard against the abuse of power may be looked on as a cheaper way of ensuring tolerable outcomes than acquiring information about which individuals are sufficiently benevolent to be entrusted with political power.
10. A. Smith, *The Theory of Moral Sentiments* (Indianapolis: Liberty Fund, 1976), p. 30.
11. John Stuart Mill, on *Representative Government* in *Essays on Politics and Society*, vol. 19, *Collected Works*, p. 505.
12. G. Brennan and J. Buchanan, *The Power to Tax: Analytic Foundations of a Fiscal Constitution* (Cambridge: Cambridge University Press, 1980).

Voting by Veto

Dennis C. Mueller

In his seminal discussion of public goods, Paul Samuelson (1954) both defined the necessary conditions for Pareto efficiency in the presence of a public good, and emphasized the problem of getting individuals to reveal their preferences for the good. Since all members of the community jointly consume a public good, a market mechanism cannot be relied upon for revealing preferences, and some form of nonmarket mechanism, or voting procedure, appears required. To date, no agreement exists in the literature over which voting procedure, if any, can be efficiently used to reveal individual preferences for public goods. The unanimity rule appears to be the logical choice. If all can be made better off through the provision of a public good, none should oppose. But unanimity has generally been rejected as a useful voting rule—first, because it seems to require a potentially lengthy and costly redefinition of the issue to be decided until one benefiting all members of the group is found; second, because it grants to *each* member a right to veto *every* issue proposed, thus encouraging strategic behavior and the endless defeat of all issues; and third, because the probability of the status quo's becoming the committee decision seems too high, as members favored under the status quo exercise their unlimited veto rights to maintain their positions.[1]

Nor is a plurality rule likely to result in Pareto-preferred outcomes. When fewer than all members of a committee can determine the committee's decision, it is likely that some (presumably among those who oppose) are made worse off by the decision. Thus, a decision which might be formulated in such a way so that all committee members would be better off is likely to pass under a plurality rule in a form in which some members are made worse off. A potentially Pareto-preferred decision seems again unobtainable.

The present essay proposes a voting rule that can, like unanimity, result in Pareto-preferred outcomes, wherever they appear possible, but has the potential for avoiding the other disadvantages of the unanimity rule. It is meant to deal with decisions of a public good type, improvements in allocative efficiency potentially beneficial to all. The bulk of the paper is devoted to a somewhat simpler problem, however, and that is how to distribute a bundle of known benefits, *B*, among the members of the committee. This problem might seem easily soluble under a variety of voting rules, particularly if the committee risked forfeiting the benefits if they did not agree to a division of them. But, it is also the kind of decision that can lead to an endless cycle of defeated proposals under some form of plurality rule, as each issue proposes a

First published in *Journal of Public Economics* 10 (August 1978): 57–75.

new division of the benefits among a coalition capable of defeating the previous winning coalition, but also capable of being defeated itself.[2] It is also the kind of decision which critics of unanimity have envisaged as resulting in the endless defeat of each issue proposed, as some voter(s) always vote against a proposed division, in the hopes of securing a more favorable division on some subsequent winning proposal. Thus, the problem of devising a voting rule to divide a given amount of known benefits is of some interest in and of itself. In addition, it can be regarded as a first approximation to the problem of reaching collective agreement on a public good, the division of the benefits among the voters being a representation of the relative distances moved along each voter's utility axis in choosing a point on the generalized Pareto frontier. The problem of revealing preferences on public goods is taken up in section 3.

Throughout the next three sections, we assume coalitions are not formed. Each voter acts independently to maximize his expected utility. What happens when coalitions are formed and the potential for redistribution under the procedure are discussed in section 4. Conclusions are drawn in section 5. We begin, however, by describing the rule and analyzing its properties for committees of two and three persons in section 1, and then extend the results to committees of n persons in section 2.

1. The Voting Rule—Two- and Three-Person Committees

A committee of two is to decide whether to accept a gift of B dollars or not, and if so, how to divide it. The status quo is to reject the gift, $S(0,0)$. The set of Pareto-optimal decisions is to accept the gift and divide it in the proportions $(x, 1 - x)$, $x \geqq 0$.

Now consider the following voting procedure. Each voter can propose one division of B. The issue set is then composed of the two voters' proposals and the status quo, $A = \{P, P', S\}$. An order of voting is picked at random. The voter randomly selected to vote first removes one issue from the set. The second voter removes another. The issue remaining is the committee decision.

Each voter makes two decisions: the proposal of one issue for inclusion in the issue set, and the removal of one issue from this set. The voting procedure can be conveniently analyzed by considering each voter's strategies at the two decision points.

It does not benefit a voter to propose an issue that makes the other voter worse off than under the status quo. If such an issue were proposed, the other voter would certainly remove it from the issue set. Thus, redistribution, other than of the Pareto-efficient kind in which both givers and receivers are better off, cannot be achieved by this rule.[3] Each voter can benefit by his choice of proposal only if he chooses one which the other voter prefers to the status quo. Then, given a choice between the status quo and one voter's proposal, the other can be expected to propose an issue benefiting the other voter and himself, perhaps, even more.

Suppose the voter's proposals are $P(B - 1, 1)$ and $P' (1, B - 1)$, and further, that the proposer of P' is chosen by lot to vote first. He rejects P and the other voter must choose between P' and S. Since he is somewhat better off under P', he rejects S making P' the committee decision. The advantage in position lies in voting first. The second to vote is forced to choose between the status quo and the other voter's proposal.

Before turning to the three-person case, two observations are in order. First, the voting outcome must be Pareto-optimal. Each voter has both an incentive to make a Pareto-optimal proposal, and to reject the status quo in favor of the other voter's Pareto-preferred proposal.[4] Second, the procedure is fair. Each voter has an equal chance of going first.

When there are three members of the committee, an additional procedural decision arises. The full sequence of veto voting in the second step can be revealed to all voters once it has been determined by lot, or it can be kept secret, revealed only through the course of voting. Let us consider first the case in which the complete sequence is revealed following its determination. Assume first that the voters have made proposals analogous to those in the two-person example $P(B - 2, 1, 1)$, $P' (1, B - 2, 1)$, $P'' (1, 1, B - 2)$, S, and that the order of voting is the proposer of the first issue, followed by the second, and then the third.

The advantage of voting first has now been greatly reduced. Voter 1's best strategy is to remove P', for if he does not, voter 2 will remove P, and P' will win. But in removing P' voter 1 assures himself of only a fifty-fifty chance that the second voter does not reject his proposal, voter 2 being indifferent between P and P''.

Voter 1 could ensure the final selection of his proposal if it contained higher benefits for voter 2 than 3's proposal. If voter 1 had proposed $P(B - 6, 3, 3)$ with P' and P'' as before, the second voter would be sure to pick P over P''. Thus, with 3 or more voters, the relative magnitudes of the payoffs to each voter are important as well as (indeed more so than) the order of voting.

To see this more clearly, assume the three proposals are

$$P_1(B - 6, 3, 3), \quad P_2(2, B - 4, 2), \quad P_3(1, 1, B - 2).$$

(The subscripts denote the rank order of the proposals based on the size of benefits to voters other than the proposer, a convention adopted again later.) There are six possible sequences in which the three voters can be drawn. Once the sequence is known, each voter can determine his best veto vote for bringing about either the selection of his own proposal, or if that is impossible, the selection of the other issue most favorable to him. Suppose, for example, the sequence of voting is 321. The best voter 3 can do is ensure the victory of 1's proposal. If voter 3 eliminated P_1, voter 2 would eliminate P_3, and P_2 would become the committee choice. The best 3 can do is eliminate P_2, leaving 2 to eliminate P_3, and P_1 to emerge as the committee decision. The greater attractiveness of P_1 to the other proposals results in its selection via the voting procedure in five of six possible orderings of the three voters. Only when the ordering 213 occurs will P_1 not become the committee decision, as voter 2 will eliminate P_1 and voter 1 P_3 leaving P_2 to emerge as the committee decision.

Thus, when there are three voters, the relative magnitudes of the benefits proposed for the other voters is more important than the order of voting. With two voters, a voter can ensure the victory of his issue when he votes first, by vetoing the other voter's proposal, and proposing an issue slightly better than the status quo. With three voters and the order of voting known, the least popular of the three proposals has no chance of winning, and the proposal with the highest benefits to other voters emerges as the committee decision five-sixths of the time.

This result does not hold for the alternative variant of the procedure in which the subsequent order of voting is not initially revealed to all voters. In general every proposal promising some positive benefits to all voters can have a positive chance of winning under this alternative to the procedure, although the proposal promising the most even benefits still has the highest probability of winning. Since discussion of this procedure is far more complicated, and the outcomes under it seem in every way inferior, we limit discussion throughout the rest of the essay to the variant in which the complete order of voting is announced before the veto voting stage begins.

2. The *n*-Person Case

Let us now examine the properties of the voting procedure more systematically for the general case. Assume there are n voters and therefore $n + 1$ proposals $P, \ldots, P^{n+1}$ including the status quo. Each proposal P^j is an n-element vector $p^j(x_1^j, x_2^j, \ldots x_n^j)$ designating payoffs to each of the n voters, where $B \geqq x_i^j \geqq 0$, for all i and j. At this point we shall place no constraints on the distribution of the x *within* any proposal. It simplifies the discussion without affecting the conclusions, however, to assume that each proposal promises a given voter a different payoff, i.e.,

$$x_i^j \neq x_i^k \text{ for all } i, \text{ and all } j \neq k.$$

This assumption allows us to determine a unique ordering of all proposals for each voter.

Obviously, in a choice between any proposal and the proposal he ranks last, a voter always eliminates the latter. Thus, W, the winning proposal, can never be the proposal ranked last out of the entire issue set by the voter who is last in the voting sequence. Call this proposal R_n.

By the same reasoning, W cannot be the proposal ranked last by the second last voter. Suppose the second last voter and the last voter rank the same issue last, then W cannot be the proposal ranked second last by the second last voter. The argument is similar to the above. The second last voter knows that R_n cannot win, since the last voter will always reject it. If the second voter is confronted with a trio of proposals containing R_{n-1}, the issue he ranks second last, he will reject it, since he must prefer whatever issue the last voter would leave from the remaining pair, R_n being certain to be eliminated. In this way we can work our way back through the n voters and associate a given issue R_i with each voter i in the sequence, which can be rejected as a possible winning proposal, and a given set of issues $E_i\{R_i, R_{i+1}, \ldots, R_n\}$, taken together, which can be eliminated as possible winning issues. The R_i and E_i for any voter i can be found by applying the following rule.

RULE 1. *Define* $E_{n+1} \equiv \{0\}$. *To find* R_i *for any* $i = 1, n$, *first remove the set* E_{i+1} *from the full set of* $n + 1$ *proposals.* R_i *is voter* i*'s lowest ranked proposal in the subset of remaining proposals,* $E_i \equiv \{R_i\} UE_{i+1}$.

THEOREM 1. W *cannot be* R_i *for* $i = 1, n$.

Proof is by induction. The proposition has been demonstrated above for the nth voter. Assume for the ith voter that no element of E_{i+1} can win. Let R_i be the lowest ranked proposal in the remaining set. Since no element in E_{i+1} can win, the eventual winner must be in this remaining set. If R_i would win, if voter i did not reject it, voter i will eliminate it from the set, since he prefers all other issues in the remaining set to R_i. Thus, R_i cannot win.

Now consider the decision by voter $i - 1$. We know from rule 1 that voter i prefers R_{i-1} to R_i. Thus, if both R_i and R_{i-1} are passed on to voter i, he will reject R_i, if it could win, leaving R_{i-1} to continue on as a possible winning issue. But voter $i - 1$ can ensure the victory of an issue he prefers to R_{i-1} by rejecting this issue. In the presence of R_i and the other issues in the initial set remaining after E_{i+1} is deleted, we know that voter i rejects R_i. Since W cannot be in E_{i+1}, it is in the set of remaining issues, all of which voter $i - 1$ prefers to R_{i-1}. Thus, voter $i - 1$ will always reject R_{i-1} if he believes it would win, and neither R_{i-1} nor R_i can win. But, since $E_i = \{R_i\}UE_{i+1}$, we have also shown that no element of E_i can be W.

E_1, the set of proposals eliminated as possible winners after considering the preference orderings of all n voters, is an n-element set. Since the entire set of proposals contains only $n + 1$ elements, we have the following theorem

THEOREM 2. *The voting procedure defines a unique winning proposal* W *for any set of initial proposals, and a given sequence of voting.*

Under the procedure each voter is effectively confronted with a choice between two proposals. The first voter must choose an issue to be eliminated from the entire set of $n + 1$ proposals. He knows, however, that $n - 1$ of these proposals, the E_2 set, cannot win even if all are left in the issue set passed on to the second voter. So the first voter's actual choice is between the two issues not in E_2. His best strategy is to reject the proposal he least prefers,

R_1, and pass the other along with E_2 on to the second voter. This voter knows that the $n - 2$ proposals in E_3 cannot win, and so must effectively choose between R_2 and the other proposal left in the choice set by voter 1. His best strategy is to reject R_2 and pass the remaining proposal, W, and E_3 on to the third voter. Eventually, the last voter is left with the choice between R_n and W.[5] Each voter can do no better than to eliminate the least preferred of the two proposals from which he has an effective choice. Honest voting at each step of the veto voting sequence is a Nash equilibrium.

To learn more of the properties of the winning proposal we must examine the incentives for formulating the proposals, in the issue proposal stage. The choices facing a committee member at this stage can be conveniently divided into the amount he assigns to himself, and the distribution of the remainder among the other $n - 1$ voters. It is obvious that a voter will never propose a less than proportionate division of the benefits for himself. If he did it would be possible that he preferred someone else's proposal to his own, and had to eliminate his own. But then he should have proposed a greater share for himself at the issue proposal stage. The decision at the issue proposal stage is thus the amount to assign to oneself above B/n, and the division of the remainder among the other voters.

An obvious strategy is to give each of the other voters an equal share, say x, of the benefits not assigned to oneself. Now consider proposing slightly more for some other voter i (say $x + a$), and slightly less for some other voter j $(x - a)$. Given the mechanics of the procedure, the proposal will be vetoed whenever it provides less benefits to a voter than the proposals remaining in this voter's effective choice set. Call these minimum amounts for voters i and j, r_i and r_j. An asymmetric division of the benefits improves a proposal's chances of winning only if equal division leads to i's rejection of the proposal $(x < r_i)$, while the asymmetric division does not $(x + a > r_i)$, and also does not induce j's rejection $(x - a > r_j)$. On the other hand, the proposal's chances of winning are lowered, when it would not have been rejected under the equal division strategy $(x > r_i$ and $x > r_j)$, but is with an asymmetric division $(x - a < r_j)$. The probabilities that a proposal's chances of winning become higher (Π_H) or lower (Π_L) under asymmetric division of benefits are thus

$$\begin{aligned} \Pi_H &= \Pi\,(x < r_i < x + a) \cdot \Pi\,(x - a > r_j), \\ \Pi_L &= \Pi\,(x - a < r_j < x) \cdot \Pi\,(x > r_i). \end{aligned} \tag{1}$$

The proposer must assume that other proposers are going through calculations similar to his, and it would be reasonable for him to assume that the amounts offered on their proposals fall symmetrically around his. The probability that the amount offered a given voter on any other proposal falls in a small interval above the average amount he proposes should equal the probability the amount offered falls in the same sized interval below the average he proposes.[6] Thus, $\Pi\ (x < r_i < x + a) = \Pi\ (x - a < r_j < x)$. But, again given the symmetry inherent in the game, the expected values of r_i and r_j must be equal, and $\Pi\ (x > r_j)$ must be greater than $\Pi\ (x - a > r_j)$. Distributing a given quantity of benefits asymmetrically over the other voters lowers the probability of a proposal's success.

The $n + 1$ proposals can now be ordered on the basis of the amounts proposed, equally, for the $n - 1$ individuals other than the proposer. Let P_1 be the proposal offering the largest amounts to the other voters; P_{n+1} the smallest. If the status quo is a zero payoff for all voters, $P_{n+1} = S$. If not, we can, for simplicity, assume that it takes the form of the other proposals ($B/n + e$ goes to one voter and the rest is evenly divided), and include it in the ordering at its appropriate position.

Now let us see which of the proposals emerge as winners under the procedure. It is again useful to begin with the decision of the last voter. If he has not proposed P_{n+1}, he ranks it last and $R_n = P_{n+1}$. If the voter n has proposed P_{n+1}, he ranks P_n last and $R_n = P_n$. Thus, E_n must be either P_{n+1} or P_n. These possibilities along with those for the other $n - 1$ voters are summarized in table 1. Since either the nth or the $(n - 1)$th voter must *not* have proposed P_{n+1}, this proposal must be ranked last by one of them, and therefore must be an element of E_{n-1}. In addition, the E_{n-1} set must contain either P_n or P_{n-1} depending on whether the $n - 1$th voter has not or has proposed P_n. If we continue to examine the possibilities for each voter, we see that the size of the two possible elimination sets continues to expand by one, and the list of possible winners (the last column of table 1) to contract by one, until after considering all of the options for the first voter only two possible winning issues remain, P_1 and P_2. When any voter, other than the proposer of P_3 votes second, $E_2 = \{P_{n+1}, P_n, \ldots, P_3\}$. The first voter is effectively constrained to a choice between P_1 and P_2. If any voter other than the proposer of P_2 votes first, P_1 will be the committee choice. When the proposer of P_3 is second, the first to vote is limited to a choice between P_1 and P_3. Since the first to vote cannot be the proposer of P_3 in this case, P_1 must be the winner whenever P_3's proposer is second in the voting order. Thus, P_2 is the committee decision only when its proposer votes first, *and* he is not followed by the proposer of P_3. In all other cases P_1 wins.

As an alternative way of seeing why this must be so, notice that P_1 generally wins because it is the *second* choice of $n - 1$ of the voters, who work for its victory in the absence of a chance of their proposal's winning. When the proposer of P_2 goes first, however, he can put his proposal in this position by eliminating P_1. It pays him to do so, unless he is followed by the proposer of P_3. If he eliminated P_1 when followed by the proposer of P_3, the latter could make P_3 a winner by eliminating P_2. Thus, in this case, the proposer of P_2 also works for the victory of P_1.

If all voters have an equal probability of occupying any position in the voting sequence, the probability of P_2's winning, $\Pi(P_2)$, is the probability that he does vote first *and* is *not* followed by the proposer of P_3, i.e.,

TABLE 1

Voter	Issue Eliminated (R_i)	Possible E_i	Possible Winning Issues
1	P_3 or P_2 or P_1	$E_1 = \{P_{n+1}, P_n, \ldots, P_2\}$ or $\{P_{n+1}, P_n, \ldots, P_3, P_1\}$	$\{P_2, P_1\}$
2	P_4 or P_3 or P_2	$E_2 = \{P_{n+1}, P_n, \ldots, P_3\}$ or $\{P_{n+1}, P_n, \ldots, P_4, P_2\}$	$\{P_3, P_2, P_1\}$
.			
.			
.			
$n-2$	P_n or P_{n-1} or P_{n-2}	$E_{n-2} = \{P_{n+1}, P_n, P_{n-1}\}$ or $\{P_{n+1}, P_n, P_{n-2}\}$	$\{P_{n-1}, \ldots, P_1\}$
$n-1$	P_{n+1} or P_n or P_{n-1}	$E_{n-1} = \{P_{n+1}, P_n\}$ or $\{P_{n+1}, P_{n-1}\}$	$\{P_n, P_{n-1}, \ldots, P_1\}$
n	P_{n+1} or P_n	$E_n = \{P_{n+1}\}$ or $\{P_n\}$	$\{P_{n+1}, P_n, P_{n-1}, \ldots, P_1\}$

$$\Pi(P_2) = \frac{1}{n} - \frac{1}{n(n-1)} = \frac{n-2}{n(n-1)}. \tag{2}$$

$\Pi(P_2)$ converges on zero as n approaches infinity. Thus, when the order of voting in the second stage is known to all voters, the probability that the proposal promising the most even distribution of benefits to all voters is chosen approaches 1.0 as the size of the committee becomes large.

This result clearly illustrates the relationship between the committee's size, and the importance of the issue proposal step relative to the order of voting in the veto voting step. With two voters, the nature of the issues proposed only ensures that a Pareto-preferred outcome is obtained; the order of voting determines how the gains are distributed. With n infinitely large, the order of voting is irrelevant; the benefits from collective action are distributed according to the most egalitarian of the proposals made.

The next question to consider is how egalitarian this distribution can be expected to be. In making a proposal each voter must decide the level of benefits, e, above the average benefit to award to himself. If his proposal wins he receives $(B/n + e)$, and if it loses $(B/n - d/(n-1))$, where d is the benefits above B/n the proposer of the winning proposal awards to himself. If the committee meets but once to decide a division of a single B, it is reasonable to assume that a given committee member assumes that the proposals of the other committee members are independent of his own. The probability of his proposal winning, $\Pi(e)$, can be assumed to be a decreasing function of e. The expected payoff if he loses, d, can be assumed fixed, and the individual's problem is to choose an e to maximize his expected utility $E(U)$, where

$$E(U) = \Pi(e)U\left(\frac{B}{n} + e\right) + (1 - \Pi(e))U\left(\frac{B}{n} - \frac{d}{n-1}\right). \tag{3}$$

Under reasonable assumptions about U and Π a maximum exists for a nonnegative e.

More can be said about the choice of e if we assume that the same committee meets repeatedly to make similar collective decisions. Under such circumstances, an individual can no longer assume that the choice of e by other voters is independent of his own. Since the proposal with the lowest e (or occasionally the second lowest e) wins, the contest for choosing the winning e resembles a Bertrand oligopoly game in which all the sales and profits in the market go to the firm with the lowest price. As in a Bertrand oligopoly situation, one expects the winning e (lowest price) to converge on zero. As in the oligopoly game, however, there remain some potential gains from successfully proposing a nonzero e. But, unlike in the oligopoly game, there are also some risks since the proposal of an $e > 0$, carries with it the risk of a loss of $d/(n - 1)$, should some other proposal promising $d > 0$ win.

A voter contemplating a choice between a long-run strategy of proposing a series of nonzero e's around some $\bar{e}$, versus always proposing $e = 0$, can, given the symmetric nature of the game, reasonably assume that his proposal will win $1/n$ proportion of the time. Due to this symmetry, he can also expect the average e he proposes on those occasions he wins to equal the average e proposed by others when they win, i.e. that $\bar{e} = \bar{d}$. Thus, his expected long-run gains, G, from a strategy of proposing a series of nonzero e's is

$$G = \frac{1}{n}\left(\frac{B}{n} + \bar{e}\right) + \frac{n-1}{n}\left(\frac{B}{n} - \frac{d}{n-1}\right) = \frac{B}{n} + \frac{\bar{e} - d}{n} = \frac{B}{n}. \tag{4}$$

But, when n is large, the voter can virtually ensure himself a payoff of B/n by proposing an $e = 0$, and making his proposal at least as good as P_1. With n very large, the latter strategy has the same expected value, over an obviously smaller spread of outcomes. Thus a risk-averse voter should always propose an $e = 0$. With one risk-averse voter, the egalitarian distribution of benefits occurs with probability $1 - [(n - 2)/n(n - 1)]$. With two risk-averse voters, it always occurs.[7]

An alternative way of viewing the problem of proposing a division of B under the veto voting procedure is as an n-person, constant sum, noncooperative game. Under the rules of the procedure this game is symmetric and has a Nash equilibrium.[8] It is also easy to see that the strategy of proposing an equal distribution of benefits is a Nash equilibrium, i.e. if $n - 1$ players propose an equal division, the nth player can do no better by proposing any other division. Indeed, the equal division of benefits is far more "robust" than implied by the Nash equilibrium concept. The equal division outcome will occur as long as any two voters propose it, making their proposals P_1 and P_2, and is impervious to the nature of the proposals by the other voters, so long as the assumption of no coalitions is maintained. Thus, even when the game of dividing B is played only once, a choice of $e = 0$ by only two voters is sufficient to ensure an equal division of B as the committee decision. These considerations lend further plausibility to the likelihood of the equal division of the benefits from collective action being the outcome to either the one-time-only committee decision, or of the "super game" played over and over again by the same players for similar stakes.

3. Determining the Allocation of Public Goods by Veto Voting

It is easiest to begin applying the rule to decide public goods by assuming that only one dimension of the public good is to be decided. Let us assume, therefore, that the quantity and characteristics of the public good are predetermined, and the committee must decide the distribution of tax shares. Consideration is limited to tax proposals varying with some generally held and objectively measurable characteristic, e.g., income, consumption, property value. Each voter is able to calculate his own tax under every proposal, and those of the other $n - 1$ voters. Each can determine his own ordering of the n

+ 1 proposals, and those of all other voters. Theorem 2 holds, and a unique winning proposal exists for any set of proposals and order of voting.

Suppose that a property tax is being used, and that all tax proposals are restricted to a combination lump sum charge, and proportional rate, i.e. that $t_i^j = a_i + b_i V^j$, where t_i^j is the tax on voter j for tax proposal i, and V^j is the value of voter j's property. Each tax proposal is uniquely defined by the two parameters a_i and b_i. These parameters must be chosen to satisfy the constraint that the entire tax revenue equals the cost of the public good, C, i.e.

$$C = a_i n + b_i \sum_{j=1}^{n} V^j. \tag{5}$$

Higher values of a_i are accompanied by lower b_i and imply lower progressivity under the tax. If we assume that S takes the form of the other proposals and satisfies (5), a unique ordering of the $n + 1$ proposals on the basis of their progressivity exists. Given the constraint of equation 5, an individual's tax under a more progressive tax scheme is higher or lower depending on whether his property is valued at above or below the *mean* property value of the community. All individuals with property values above the mean will rank tax proposals from most regressive (highest a_i) to least regressive. All individuals with property values below the mean have the reverse ranking.

It is easy to show that the winning proposal is the $(r + 1)$th most progressive tax schedule (i.e. with the $[r + 1]$th lowest a_i), where r is the number of voters with property values above the mean. If the distribution of property values is symmetric around the mean, $r = n/2$ and W is the proposal with the median degree of progressivity (the median a_i). If the distribution is positively skewed, $r < n/2$ and the amount of progressivity of the winning proposal exceeds that of the median proposal. The r voters with property values above the mean can eliminate only the r most progressive proposals, and the next most progressive proposal wins, it being preferred by all other voters.

These results are important in appraising the normative properties of the outcomes under the procedure. With the quantity and other characteristics of the public good fixed, the determination of the tax shares to finance the public good is a zero sum game. Different proposals make some better off and some worse off and Pareto-preferred proposals are infeasible. Some proposals may contain tax shares exceeding some individuals' gross benefits from the public good. These seem most likely to be at the two tails of the distribution, the most and least progressive of the proposals. Their elimination under the procedure increases the likelihood that it yields outcomes Pareto-preferred to the status quo.

Now consider the other extreme possibility. A public good is to be provided *free*, and the committee must decide the amount to accept. Assume that each committee member has a symmetric single-peaked preference for the good, which attains a maximum at a finite quantity. If each individual proposes his most preferred quantity of the public good, it is possible for all voters to determine a unique ranking of the proposals for each other voter. The conditions of theorem 2 are again satisfied, and the proposal with the median quantity of public good wins. If voter preferences are not symmetric, some errors in predicting the other voters' rankings might occur, but the tendency for the procedure to yield the median outcome would remain.

Before turning to the more complicated public goods case, it is important to consider whether it is in the interests of a voter to propose his most preferred quantity of public good. For simplicity we abstract from the complications that can arise when the proposer of the second best proposal votes first and assume a single, winning issue x_M, the median quantity proposed, in a community of n. Now add voter i to the committee with preferred quantity x_i. Consider first the case where $x_i > x_{M+1}$, and x_{M+1} is the next highest quantity to x_M proposed. The rejectors of quantities above x_M are voters preferring quantities equal to or less than x_M. The addition of x_i to the issue set causes a rearrangement of the vetoes of the committee. The individual who previously rejected x_{i-1}, the next smallest quantity to x_i, in a choice between it and still smaller x_M, now rejects x_i. The voter who rejected x_{i-2} rejects x_{i-1}, and so on until the voter who rejected x_{M+1} rejects x_{M+2}, leaving x_{M+1} uneliminated. Voter i will reject some quantity less than x_M causing the previous vetoer of this quantity to veto a higher quantity, and so on until the previous vetoer of the quantity just smaller than x_M is left to veto x_M. The introduction of voter i with proposal $x_i > x_{M+1}$ results in a shift in the committee outcome from x_M to x_{M+1}.

Now suppose $x_M < x_i \leqq x_{M+1}$. Voters who rejected x_{M+1} and higher quantities in favor of smaller x_M will continue to do so in the presence of x_i which is no greater than any of these other quantities. Voter i can reject a quantity smaller than x_M causing a rearrangement of the vetoes in the direction of higher quantities, and the elimination of x_M, x_i becomes the new committee decision.

Thus, if all other voters propose their most preferred quantities, a proposal by voter i of his most preferred quantity x_i, either shifts the committee decision to the next closest proposal (x_{M+1} if $x_i > x_{M+1}$, and x_{M-1} if $x_i < x_{M-1}$), or results in x_i's selection itself (when $x_{M-1} \leqq x_i \leqq x_{M-1}$). When $x_i > x_{M+1}$ or $x_i < x_{M-1}$, no other proposal strategy can do better. When $x_{M-1} \leqq x_i \leqq x_{M+1}$, no other strategy is as good. The proposal of a voter's most preferred quantity is a Nash-equilibrium.[9]

Now let us turn to the decision to provide a public good along with a tax to finance it. If the provision of the public good is potentially Pareto-preferred to the status quo, then collective benefits from its provision exist, and the question is how to divide these benefits. The question resembles the problem of dividing B discussed above. A voter can assume that the smaller the benefits he proposes for any individual (i.e. the higher his tax share or the further the quantity is from his preferred quantity), the higher the probability that this individual rejects the proposal. In deciding how much public good to propose and the distribution of tax shares, an individual must speculate on the public good quantities and tax shares the other proposals contain, and each voter's evaluation of them. Thus, an issue proposer is forced to make interpersonal utility comparisons of the benefits to other voters his proposal contains versus the benefits he expects the other proposals to contain. In the absence of information regarding the content of the other proposals (implicit or explicit coalitions of the type described in section 4), the most reasonable strategy is again to treat each individual symmetrically. By analogy with the division of *B* example, an individual can expect to minimize the probability of his proposal's rejection by promising equal increments in benefits to all other voters. Any asymmetric distribution of benefits, unless matched by the other proposals, must raise the probability of the discriminated-against voter's rejecting the proposal by more than it reduces the probability of rejection by those favored under an asymmetric distribution. By further analogy with the division of *B* example, we can expect an individual to propose for himself the same increase in utility from the provision of the public good as he proposes for everyone else. If he proposes more for himself than for others, his benefits should his proposal win are higher, but the chances of his proposal's winning are lower. Given the symmetric character of the game, the expected value of his benefits is the same for either proposal, but the risk attached to proposing greater benefits for oneself is higher. A risk averse voter should propose a fair sharing of the benefits from collective action.

The issue of interpersonal utility comparisons has now arisen. But, if we have learned one thing from the work on Arrowian impossibility theorems, it is that the fundamental distribution issues inherent in collective decision making cannot be solved without introducing interpersonal utility comparisons (see, e.g., Sen 1970, 123–25). If the distributional question is to be faced at all, the issue is not *if* interpersonal comparisons will be made, but *how*. Voting by veto follows the essentially democratic procedure of having each committee member make his own set of interpersonal utility comparisons, and then selects that one which emerges as most egalitarian in the eyes of the other committee members.

The information requirements for application of the procedure in the general public-goods–tax-share case are obviously rather demanding. The procedure is more applicable in committees in which each member has a good deal of knowledge about the preferences of the other members than in committees in which all members are essentially strangers. Citizens at a New England town meeting might be expected to know a fair bit about the wealth and tastes of each other, for example. More generally, one could envisage the procedure operating in a parliamentary committee in which each member represented a separate group of voters. Knowledge of the preferences of each committee member would then come from knowledge of the representative's constituency, and the platform upon which he won election. Incentives to deceive other committee members as to what one's preferences are would be constrained by the need to win election and "answer to the voters."

Even in such settings the problem of proposing a public-good–tax-share combination providing equal utility increments to all voters is a good deal more difficult than that of proposing a division of cash *B*. Voters will err, proposing tax shares which are too high for some, given their evaluations of the public good, and too low for others. But here again, the mechanics of the procedure work to eliminate those proposals with the most discriminatory provisions. The emergence of the proposal incorporating the "median view" of the pattern of utility functions in the community can be expected.

4. Coalitions and Redistribution

Coalitions that form before the proposals are made can agree to lower the benefits assigned to specific other voters, and divide the extra benefits among themselves. To succeed, however, a coalition must be at least one larger than the group from which it attempts to redistribute to survive the veto votes of this group. It must also promise benefits to all committee members not in either the discriminated-against group or the coalition itself at least as high as the next best proposal. Thus when the size of coalitions that can effectively form is small relative to the committee's size, a roughly even distribution of benefits across all members can be expected, although some small groups might be discriminated against, and Pareto-preferred outcomes cannot be assured.

When more than half of the committee forms a coalition, there is no way to prevent it from redistributing income away from the other members. In this regard, the procedure resembles majority rule, and a significant difference exists between the outcomes obtainable under this procedure, and the rule of unanimity. Under the unanimity rule each voter can be certain of protecting his interests in the face of coalitions of any size through his use of the unlimited veto the voting procedure gives him.

In addition to formal coalitions against specific groups, the appearance of tacit, informal coalitions against certain minorities is possible. An ethnic or religious minority may have traditionally received a smaller share of the benefits from collective action. Assigning this minority a less than equal share of these benefits may constitute a form of "Schelling point" proposal that many committee members automatically make. The outcomes under voting by veto are thus dependent on both the views of each voter as to what the other voter's preferences are, and their expectations of the form the other proposals will take. Equal division of *B* occurred as the likely equilibrium in the first example because no 'consensus' was assumed over a possible deviation from an equal division.

An implicit assumption underlying the arguments in favor of the voting procedure is, thus, that a basic value consensus exists among the committee members on the underlying distribution of income, property rights, and general scope of government activity. The view here is essentially Wicksellian.[10] Given general consensus on these basic issues, each individual enters into collective activity, as into voluntary exchange, to increase his own welfare. Each acts independently and treats all others individually and symmetrically while taking part in the collective choice process. No coalitions, either explicit or implicit, of one *group against another* exist.

5. Summary and Conclusions

Under the usual assumptions made about voting procedures, committee members are not charged with responsibility for proposing issues. Each simply reveals his preferences, honestly or otherwise, via a yes or no vote on the issues that somehow come before the committee. Under the unanimity rule this structure gives each individual an infinite number of vetoes against the issues proposed, raising the spectre of an endless rejection of issues as some voters attempt to increase their shares of the benefits at the expense of others. When less than unanimous agreement can decide an issue, outcomes leaving some worse off than under the status quo can occur. What is more, it is likely that no proposal is capable of obtaining the required majority against all others. The spectre of an endless chain of defeated issues again appears.

The voting rule described in this paper charges each voter with the responsibility for making one proposal, and limits him to a single veto over another issue. Nevertheless, the vetoes the other voters hold force the voter to consider and attempt to define the form of collective decision they prefer, both with respect to the status quo and the other proposals, while at the same time revealing the form of collective decision he prefers. Instead of being able to conceal his own preferences and ignore those of others, each voter is forced into a kind of proposal popularity contest in which he must seek out the preferences of the other voters and weigh their interests against his. The endless defeat of each issue is avoided by forcing a choice from among the *n* proposals the committee members make and the status quo.

The probability of the status quo emerging as the committee outcome under the unanimity rule looms large owing to the unlimited number of vetoes each individual possesses. In contrast, the status quo appears as "just another issue" under the present procedure, certain to be rejected if the issue to be decided is capable of yielding a Pareto-preferred outcome. In this way, the procedure resembles more closely a simple plurality rule. Its outcomes also resemble those of a plurality rule when the proposals are capable of ordering along a single dimension like the degree of progressivity, or the amount of public good. When this can be done, the committee decision is drawn toward the mean or median outcome as under majority rule. Last of all, the outcomes under the procedure can resemble those under majority rule whenever tacit or formal coalitions form a consensus over some attribute of the issue to be decided, like the degree of progressivity of a tax. An individual or small minority, which finds its views out of tune with those of the majority on a given aspect of the issue is unable to prevent the majority from having its way. In situations like this, non–Pareto-preferred outcomes are possible; redistribution of this type can take place, and outcomes from the procedure again resemble those under majority rule.[11]

Thus, the voting by veto procedure combines some of the best, to my mind, attributes of both the unanimity and majority rule. When no consensus among a majority of voters exists, and no coalitions are allowed, it should tend to produce Pareto-preferred outcomes with an equitable sharing of the benefits from collective action. The right of veto each individual possesses offers some protection against an indiscriminate reduction in welfare through a proposal, which singles him out for ill-treatment. Yet the minority cannot indefinitely block a majority which is in consensus on some basic attribute(s) of the issue. These features of the voting procedure seem to warrant further study of its potential as a democratic procedure for revealing individual preferences on public goods.

NOTES

Valuable suggestions for improvements were received from Steven Slutsky and a referee. Special thanks are due to my colleague Murat Sertel with whom I discussed the paper several times.

1. See Barry 1965, 242–50; Black 1958, 146–47; Buchanan and Tullock 1962, chap. 6; Rae 1975; and Samuelson 1969.
2. The literature on cycling is admirably reviewed by Amartya Sen.
3. This conclusion rests on the absence of coalitions among voters' assumption in cases where there are more than two voters (see sec. 4). On Pareto-efficient redistribution see Hochman and Rogers 1969.
4. Of course, each voter will want to offer the other the *minimum* amount above 0, and an existence problem exists unless B is something, like money, which is only finitely divisible.
5. It is not always necessary for the procedure actually to proceed by each voter eliminating the proposal associated with him by the rule. If voter $(i + j)$ would eliminate R_i, should voter i eliminate R_{i+j}, voter i is indifferent between the two actions. What is true is that the outcome from any alternative sequence of voting is *as if* each voter had eliminated the proposal assigned to him by the rule.
6. If anything this assumption is conservative. To win, a proposal must avoid being vetoed through each round of voting. On average the benefits promised to the other voters must be close to the highest of those proposed. A voter who thinks his proposal stands more than an even chance of winning must assume the other proposals' benefits are clustered below his, i.e., $\Pi\,(x - a < r_j < x) > \Pi\,(x < r_i < x + a)$ and the conclusion reached in the text, that $\Pi_L > \Pi_H$, is strengthened.
7. See Rothschild and Stiglitz 1970. With n very large, and $\Pi\,(P_2) \approx 0$, any degree of risk aversion is sufficient to produce a choice of $e = 0$. With small n, a given degree of risk aversion is necessary before the result holds.
8. Friedman (1971) proves the existence of a Nash-equilibrium for a game of this type defined under 3 conditions, all of which are satisfied by our voting by veto procedure.
    1. The strategy space of each player is compact and convex.
    2. His payoff functions are continuous and bounded on the strategy space.
    3. His payoff function, given a set of strategies by all other voters, is a quasi-concave function of his own strategy.

9. This conclusion is unaffected when the special cases dependent on the ordering of voters are considered. If the proposer of x_M votes first, he is in the position of the proposer of P_2 in the example considered above; P_1 is either x_j (if $x_i \leqq x_{M+1}$) or x_{M+1} (if $x_i > x_{M+1}$). The proposer of x_M can maintain the victory of x_M in the absence of x_i, by vetoing either x_i or x_{M+1} depending on $x_i \lesseqgtr x_{M+1}$. When this occurs, i is simply unable to improve the committee outcome no matter what he proposes. On the other hand, when x_i falls between x_{M+1} and x_{M+2}, x_i takes the form of P_2, and its proposer can bring about x_i's victory by vetoing $x_{M+1}(P_1)$, should he vote first. Thus voter i remains either better off, or no worse off, than under any alternative strategy if he chooses to propose his true, most preferred quantity.
10. See Buchanan's (1949) discussion of the Wicksellian approach, as well as Wicksell (1896).
11. Readers familiar with the Vickrey-Clark-Groves procedure for revealing preferences for public goods will also recognize parallels with the present rule (see, e.g., Groves and Loeb 1975). Most importantly, both rules charge the voter with revealing more information about his preferences than is contained in a yes-no vote, and build in incentives to ensure honest revelation of preferences. On the margin, the proposal (demand schedule) of a single voter is effective in determining the exact nature of the final outcome under both procedures, the other proposals having essentially cancelled each other out. But, the process of cancelling (adding up) is such that with large numbers of voters, the elimination of this, or any, voter does not significantly affect the outcome. There are other parallels, but we cannot pursue them here.

REFERENCES

Barry, B. 1965. *Political Argument.* London, Routledge and Kegan Paul.

Black, D. 1958. *The Theory of Committees and Elections.* Cambridge: Cambridge University Press.

Buchanan, J. M. 1949. "The Pure Theory of Government Finance: A suggested Approach." *Journal of Political Economy* 57:496–505.

Buchanan, J. M. and G. Tullock. 1962. *The Calculus of Consent.* Ann Arbor: University of Michigan Press.

Friedman, J. W. 1971. "A Non-Cooperative Equilibrium for Super-Games." *Review of Economic Studies* 38: 1–12.

Groves, T. J., and Loeb, M. 1975. "Incentives and Public Inputs." *Journal of Public Economics* 4:211–26.

Hochman, H. M., and Rogers, J. D. 1969. "Pareto Optimal Redistribution." *American Economic Review* 59: 542–57.

Rae, D. W. 1975. "The Limits of Consensual Decision." *American Political Science Review* 69: 1270–94.

Rawls, J. 1971. *A Theory of Justice.* Cambridge: Harvard University Press.

Rothschild, M., and Stiglitz, J. E. 1970. "Increasing Risk 1: A Definition." *Journal of Economic Theory* 2:225–43.

Samuelson, P. A. 1954. "The Pure Theory of Public Expenditure." *Review of Economics and Statistics* 36: 387–89.

______. 1969. "Pure Theory of Public Expenditure and Taxation." In *Public Eco-*

nomics, edited by J. Margolis and H. Guitton, pp. 98–123. New York, St. Martin's Press.

Sen, A. K. 1970. *Collective Choice and Social Welfare.* San Francisco: Holden-Day.

Wicksell, K. 1896. "A New Principle of Just Taxation." *Classics in the Theory of Public Finance,* edited by R. A. Musgrave and A. T. Peacock, pp. 72–118. New York: St. Martin's Press, 1958.

On Equalizing the Distribution of Political Income

Dennis C. Mueller, Robert D. Tollison, and Thomas D. Willett

The Problem

Individuals obtain utility from the consumption of both public and private goods. There has been considerable interest recently in how money income—the power to purchase private goods—should be distributed (Fair 1971, Thurow 1971). In this paper we explore the complementary question of how political income, or voting rights, should be distributed to obtain a desirable distribution of individuals' utility from public goods.

It is important to distinguish two concepts of equality in the discussion of public policy which we will employ to discuss the distribution of political income.[1] Ex ante equity refers to fairness in the sense that risks or opportunities before the fact are equalized. Ex post equity is fairness in the sense of actual outcomes of social processes involving risk and uncertainty. In most cases ex post equity is probably of greater importance than ex ante equity, although, as we shall discuss, equalitarians have curiously failed to extend considerations of equity in the distribution of political income to an ex post setting.[2] There are, however, cases where ex ante equity would be more important. For instance, this would be the case where equality of opportunity is the objective or where it may be more desirable to substitute a mechanism to achieve ex ante equity (or some combination of the two concepts) because ex post equity is impossible or too costly to achieve. We will argue that the lack of consideration of establishing equality in the ex post distribution of political income cannot be explained by either the impossibility of achieving such an outcome or the high costs of pursuing such a goal.

Political equality is generally thought to be more feasible and desirable than economic equality. Economic equality—for example, in Lerner's sense of complete ex post equality of utility distribution—is typically expected to generate serious excess burden and disincentive effects, since the generation of private income takes a large part of an individual's time, that is, the elasticity of supply is higher.[3] Thus, emphasis in achieving greater equality of the private income distribution focuses on a mix of mechanisms which trade off some degree of ex post inequality in private incomes against the disincentive effects on the total amount of private income generated. For example,

---

Reprinted from *Journal of Political Economy* 82 (March/April 1974): 414–22, by permission of The University of Chicago Press.

mechanisms such as fair employment laws can be viewed as generating greater ex ante equity, or equality of opportunity, while a progressive income tax can be viewed as generating greater ex post equality.

Discussion of the analogous problem of the distribution of political income has been characterized primarily by the discussion of generating mechanisms to achieve ex ante equality of opportunity to participate (e.g., one man, one vote). Perhaps the primary reason that this form of ex ante equality has been stressed in the literature and institutions of democracy is that it is considered a basic sort of right, or value judgment, which goes hand in hand with political democracy (Vlastos 1962, Tobin 1970).[4] A second important reason for one man, one vote could be that there are only minor disincentive effects associated with guaranteeing this form of political equality.[5]

Given the relative lack of disincentive effects associated with mechanisms for reallocating voting rights, it is interesting that the discussion of political equality has never seriously considered establishing an ex post equality of the distribution of political income.[6] In markets for private goods, each voter-consumer allocates his income so that the expected marginal utility from each dollar vote on a good is equal. Planned consumption at equilibrium prices is identical with actual consumption. In the absence of mistakes due to lack of sufficient information, this assures equality between expected and actual utility. These conditions are not likely to hold where public goods are allocated via one man, one vote majority rule. The utilities a voter expects from each vote may vary widely. And there can exist a large divergence between what he expects (hopes?) to receive in public goods as indicated by his voting decisions and what he actually receives after all votes are cast and counted.

These two characteristics of voting have been typically described as giving rise to problems of "minority rights" or the "tyranny of the majority." It is important to note, however, that these characteristics create *two separate problems,* and thus require separate remedies. Let us illustrate their differences with an example.

Suppose a community plans to build a town hall. A referendum is held on whether the building should be of Gothic or Greek architecture. Fifty-one percent of the voters have a slight preference for the Gothic style, the other 49 percent are strongly opposed. On a straight majority vote, the Gothics win even though their utility gain is far outweighed by the minority's loss. We can describe this as a situation violating the principle of ex ante equality. Each citizen's vote does not represent an equal potential utility change.

Consider next the case where each citizen's vote does represent an equal potential utility gain. Then a simple majority rule will maximize the net utility gain for the community on this decision. Suppose, however, the town grows and new public buildings are erected. Each time the town votes on the architecture of the next building, and each time the pro-Gothics win. Every decision will be *efficient* in the sense that the utility gains of the winners exceed the losses of the minority, but one might well regard the long-run outcome as *inequitable,* as all the utility gains accrue to the pro-Gothics (ignoring the utility losses both groups might experience from mixing Gothic and Greek revival buildings). Thus, even where there is full ex ante political equality, there is still the possibility of ex post inequality of the utility income derived from the political sector. A person consistently in the minority may receive ex post a far smaller share of the gains generated by public collective action, even where there is ex ante equality over all voters.[7] Indeed, we would expect considerable ex post inequality of political outcomes to be the general case, rather than the exception.

Can political systems be devised to achieve both ex ante and ex post equality of political income? In the following section we consider mechanisms which seek to achieve this objective.

Solutions

The problem created by differing intensities of preference among voters can be solved by introducing point voting. Since point voting has been discussed in detail elsewhere, we shall only briefly outline it here (Musgrave 1959, 130–31; Mueller, Tollison, and Willett 197_, 1975). To begin with, voters and issues must be grouped into polities such that in any given polity each voter has an "equal stake" (in terms of his potential aggregate utility change) in the *set* of issues decided by the polity.[8] That is, governmental units are broken up into, say, neighborhood, city, regional, and national jurisdictions, so that the integral of voters' utility distributions over the issue set to be decided by a given polity is approximately equal. Each member of a polity is given an equal number of vote points to be allocated over the set of issues to be decided by the polity. If the voters honestly allocate the vote points in proportion to their relative intensities of preference on all issues (i.e., they do not engage in strategic behavior), the point allocations will reflect each voter's marginal rates of substitution between issues.[9] If the equal-stake criterion is met, the total expected utility of each voter in a polity will be equal, and the outcomes obtained from aggregating the point-vote allocations will maximize the utility gains of the community from voting. The equal-stake criterion produces ex ante political equality for each voter over the set of issues, while point voting allows each voter to achieve ex ante equality on every issue by revealing his relative intensities of preferences over the issue set. Together they form a system for achieving ex ante political equality for each voter on every issue.

There are two contexts in which one can conceive of equalizing the distribution of political income ex post. First, one could adjust each individual's vote stock at the beginning of a voting period, depending upon his success over *all* previous periods. Suppose that in the first round an individual won on issues totaling 90 percent of his vote points, while the average voter won only 70 percent. If the initial stock were 100 votes, the individual would be given 80 votes at the start of period 2. If he again won on 90 percent, he would win on 72 vote points, and his tax for the next period would be two votes. He would thus have 78 votes for period 3, and as long as he continued to win on 90 percent of his vote point allocations, he would be winning on issues totaling 70 vote points, the average for the community. If, on some round, either his tastes or the community's changed so that he only won on half of his allocations, his total successful allocations would fall to 39. In the next round his cumulative overall tax would be $20 + 2 - 31 = -9$, and he would receive 109 votes. If he continued to win on only 50 percent of his vote-point allocations, his vote holdings would continue to rise until he began receiving 140 vote points, assuming the average voter was still winning on 70 vote points.[10]

This procedure is a compromise between the ex ante equalitarian condition embodied in the equal-stake criterion, and a full ex post equality of political income as described below. The stability of voter preferences, and therefore of voter winning percentages, is relied upon to adjust their vote holdings so that each voter's expected successful vote allocations, based on past outcomes, are the same for the coming round. (If the voters' winning percentages are not stable over time, there is no long-run tyranny of the majority problem, and hence no need to adjust individual vote stocks.) In the above example, the voter would continue to get 78 votes as long as his winning percentage stayed at 90, because he would then continue to win on issues totaling 70 vote points, the community's average. No adjustments would ever be made, however, for the 22 "extra" vote points he won in the first two rounds. He is always "ahead of the game" by that amount. Alternative tax subsidy schemes could be designed to achieve equal *cumulative* ex post political income, but these would have the serious disadvantage of requiring a constant potential total utility gain for each voter from period to period.[11]

No such restrictive assumption is required for the lagged vote-tax scheme, since its goal is merely to equate each voter's expected winning number of vote points in the coming period. By basing these expectations on each voter's past history of successes, and taking into account the stability of these winning percentages, individual vote stocks could be adjusted to bring ex ante and ex post political income into equality over time.[12] The voter who has done badly in the past can only write these losses off, and console himself with the knowledge that he may expect a more equal share of public-goods pie in the future, whatever the size of that pie might be.[13]

Alternatively, one might decide to equalize the realized utility gains over the set of issues a polity decides at any point in time, by a system of taxes and subsidies on voting rights and a sequential, nonbinding series of votes on issues. Such a system could achieve *full* ex post equality of political income. Initial votes would be tentative, subject to the vote-income distribution that resulted from voting. As an example, suppose that after the initial vote the set of outcomes would be such that each voter would have on average decisions corresponding to 70 percent of their vote-point allocations satisfied. If a particular voter won on a set of issues corresponding to 90 percent of his vote-point allocations after the first round, then his total vote holdings would be reduced for the second round of voting. Thus, vote stocks would be adjusted by taxing abnormally high winners (say a tax of 20 votes on the 90 percent winners) and subsidizing losers, after which the vote points would be cast again. Over a series of recontracts with adjusted stocks of vote points, the gains from winning and losing would be equalized. To avoid excessive recontracting under this scheme, one might be satisfied with bringing everyone within five or ten points of the average utility gain.[14]

Thus, as is illustrated by these examples, operational systems of vote taxation that attain greater equality of political income can be devised and applied in representative democracies. The importance of such a mechanism in a well-working model of representative democracy lies in its ability to reduce or eliminate the potential for a tyranny of the majority problem to persist over a long period of time.

Summary

This paper has discussed possible mechanisms for achieving ex ante and ex post equality of political income. While any of the structural reforms could be implemented separately, it makes the most sense to combine them. Indeed, the equal-stake criterion is to some extent a necessary condition for the implementation of a redistributive vote tax. A voter's winning percentage on an issue set cannot be regarded as an index of his political income unless each vote has an equal value ex ante to all voters.[15]

The idea of the state arising from a "social contract" formed by all citizens to achieve collective ends can imply the concepts of both ex ante and ex post political income equality. Of the two, only ex ante equality has received attention in the literature. Yet, to those who embrace the equalitarian ethic, the ex post equality of political income should be of even greater importance than ex ante equality of voting rights. This paper argues that the attainment of ex post equality of the political income distribution is conceptually plausible and quantitatively important.

Further, a policy of vote taxation does not appear to be subject to as serious disincentive effects as taxation to obtain complete equality of ex post private economic income. This follows by analogy to elasticity conditions where voting takes very little time as opposed to the length of the work week, for example, and attempts to equalize realized private income.

There do not appear to be any functional equivalents under present democratic systems to achieve ex post equality of political income.[16] Indeed, taking the United States as an example of a two-party, geographic-based democratic system, one could argue that there are perverse mechanisms, such as monopolistic systems of committee power and the like, which tend to lead to greater inequality of realized utility for many voters. Many voters from lower income-education classes do not vote under the present system, which, although it does not mean that these voters do not receive political incomes, does mean that the equalization of political income would be a difficult task without also implementing a thorough reform of public choice mechanisms to insure efficient revelation of *all* voter preferences in polities defined on the equal-stake criterion.

NOTES

We are grateful to James M. Buchanan for useful comments. Any remaining errors are our responsibility.

1. For an extended treatment of the two concepts of equity, see Pauly and Willett 1972 and the references cited there.
2. Note, however, the following quotation from a paper by Kolm (1971, p 8): "Les Américains ne s'intéressent pas à la justice sociale, du moins au sens où l'entendons en France (Léon Walras écrivait dé jà: 'La justice est une idée gréco-latine et française"). En particulier, la notion d'égalitarisme dans les résultats—plutôt que dans les chances—a beaucoup moins d'attraits pouveux que pour nous."
3. For Lerner's proposal and some discussion of it, see Lerner (1935; 1980), Breit and Culbertson (1970; 1972), Morrison and Higgins (1971), McCain (1972), and McManus, Walton, and Coffman (1972).
4. Tobin (1970, 269) also argues that "obviously an equalitarian distribution of the vote can be enforced without any loss of efficiency. The aggregate supply of votes is intrinsically inelastic." This is an overstatement of the issue, since although voting can be enforced or subsidized and in the extreme all would vote, this does not guarantee that votes are of any given level of informational quality. We have discussed elsewhere some ways out of this dilemma. See Mueller, Tollison, and Willett (1971; 1972; 1975).
5. For example, an alternative distribution of the right to participate in the political process might be to give votes proportional to years of formal education, i.e., some sort of scheme of weighted voting rights (Vlastos 1962). Counteracting the need for this sort of system, however, are such factors as the effect of education on one's perception of his "obligation" (elasticity) to participate in politics which tend to lead to very few observed disincentive effects for educated voters under a system of full, ex ante political equality with everyone voting and weighted equally. Thus, on practical grounds political equality of this sort could be defended. For empirical evidence on this point, see Milbrath (1965). For a discussion of the economic theory of voting behavior, see Tollison and Willett (1973).
6. Braybrooke (1968) is a partial exception. In his proposed tests for whether actual governmental systems conform closely enough in practice to the theoretical norms of democratic theory to be approximately labeled democracies, Braybrooke suggests the criteria that no voter be in the minority more than 90 percent of the time and that not more than 10 percent be in the minority more than two-thirds of the time (p. 171).
7. The point here is similar to Arrow's (1971) discussion of input and output equalization for public expenditures. Also, evidence from simulation studies of the gains from trade from vote trading indicate that the quantitative importance of the problem of political income distribution may be significant (Mueller, Philpotts, and Vanek 1972).

8. For analytical discussion of the equal-stake criterion, see Mueller (1971).
9. Mueller (1973) discusses the conditions under which point voting proceeds honestly.
10. One might think at first glance that the tax would not have to be the integral of all past deviations from the median, but just the divergence since last period. But such a system does not converge to the median, since the voter is only taxed the incremental divergence of winning or losing votes from the median in the immediately preceding period. In the above example the individual's tax at the end of two periods would only be two votes, allowing him a total of 98 votes as opposed to 78 votes where the integral of differences over all past votes is taken.
11. This problem could possibly be handled by introducing equal increments of votes: say each voter in the polity gets 10 additional votes in the period in which a new public-good issue (of importance roughly equal to 10 percent of the normal total) is introduced. Then the vote-tax system can continue, and "new money" in the form of the extra votes will keep "purchasing power" proportionate to total income. Such a solution would follow, of course, if voting periods were time dependent. An alternative way to meet this problem is to make voting periods not time dependent, but dependent on the total value of issues, e.g., vote every x issues worth of political income. However, the problem of holding the total utility gain constant for each voter from period to period would involve gains and losses analogous to the windfall gains and losses that accrued in the first few periods to above average winners and losers. That is, changes in the size of the pie would create additional gains and losses until the lagged vote-tax system equated expected voters' winnings over a longer run. To handle either of these problems neatly would probably make the vote-tax system unduly complicated and also raise additional conceptual problems.
12. Of course, where there are strong differences in preferences on an issue (i.e., an intense majority facing an intense minority), the system of political taxation may never succeed in equalizing income. For that matter, the equal-stake criterion may not be satisfied. Such issues should rationally be decided under conditions of equal ignorance about the future in a constitutional period, and if agreement cannot be reached there, then separate states should be set up. See, in particular, Mueller (1971, 1973) and Mueller, Tollison and Willett (1971; 1972; 1974; 1975).
13. Problems exist in applying the lagged vote-tax system to a representative body. If the legislators represent geographic units, a newly elected member could simply inherit the stock of vote points of his predecessor. This would introduce a certain amount of instability if newly elected representatives had significantly different tastes than their predecessors. Redistricting would also cause problems, as would a proportional representation scheme as discussed in Mueller, Tollison, and Willett, (1971; 1975). These problems vanish if immediate recontracting is employed.
14. The recontracting procedure can be simplified by the use of a computer. The voter need reveal only once the percentage of his vote stock he assigns to each issue (i.e., his relative intensities over the issue set). The computer can then adjust stocks to bring each voter's realized gains into equality.
15. It should also be noted that the application of the vote-tax system relaxes the problem of assuming that identical tastes obtain for the distribution of public goods in models of simultaneous determination of optimal distribution and opti-

mal allocation with both private and public goods. See, e.g., Winch (1969; 1970) and Roberts (1970).

16. Approximations in the private sphere can be found in the way competition is set up in some sports. Perhaps the handicapping system in golf is the best example corresponding to the vote tax. However, such institutions as the player draft in professional sports show much the same purpose as the vote tax in the sense that successful teams are penalized after the season with lower draft picks in an effort presumably to make next season's competition more equal ex ante. The ability of teams to trade personnel and their lack of ability to forecast perfectly future players' performance hinders the attainment of full ex ante equality (in the sense that each team becomes equally likely to win the title) over time in such sports (thus the Green Bay Packers, Boston Celtics, and so forth). However, there do not appear to be any equivalent reasons to think that the vote tax would operationally generate long winning or losing streaks. Indeed, it is to avoid such winning streaks in the political process that one would advocate a vote tax.

REFERENCES

Arrow, K. J. "Equality in Public Expenditure." *Quarterly Journal of Economics* 85, no. 3 (August 1971): 409–15.

Braybrooke, D. *Three Tests for Democracy.* New York: Random House, 1968.

Breit, W., and Culbertson, W. P., Jr. "Distributional Equality and Aggregate Utility: Comment." *American Economic Review* 60, no. 2 (June 1970): 435–41.

———. "Distributional Equality and Aggregate Utility: Reply." *American Economic Review* 62, no. 3 (June 1972): 501–2.

Fair, R. C. "The Optimal Distribution of Income." *Quarterly Journal of Economics* 85, no. 4 (November 1971): 551–79.

Kolm, S. C. "Justice et équité." Mimeographed, Paris: CEPREMAP, 1971.

Lerner, A. P. *The Economics of Control.* New York: Macmillan Co., 1935.

———. "Distributional Equality and Aggregate Utility: Reply." *American Economic Review* 60, no. 2 (June 1970): 442–43.

McCain, R. A. "Distributional Equality and Aggregate Utility: Further Comment." *American Economic Review* 62, no. 2 (June 1972): 497–500.

McManus, M.; Walton, G. M.; and Coffman, R. B. "Distributional Equality and Aggregate Utility: Further Comment." *American Economic Review* 62, no. 2 (June 1972): 489–96.

Milbrath, J. *Political Participation.* Chicago: Rand-McNally, 1965.

Morrison, C. C., and Higgins, R. S. "On Distributional Equality." *Southern Economic Journal* 38, no. 4 (October 1971): 260–62.

Mueller, D. C. "Fiscal Federalism and Constitutional Democracy." *Public Policy* 19 (Fall 1971): 567–94.

———. "Constitutional Democracy and Social Welfare." *Quarterly Journal of Economics* 87, no. 1 (February 1973): 60–80.

Mueller, D. C.; Philpotts, G.; and Vanek, J. "The Social Gains from Exchanging Votes." *Public Choice* 13, no. 2 (Fall 1972): 55–79.

Mueller, D. C.; Tollison, R. D.; and Willett, T. D. "Solving the Intensity Problem in Representative Democracy." Mimeographed. Cornell University, 1971.

———. "Representative Democracy via Random Selection." *Public Choice* 12, no. 1 (Spring 1972): 59–68.

———. "A Normative Theory of Representative Democracy." In *Democratic Representation and Apportionment: Quantitative Methods, Measures, and Criteria,* edited by L. Papayanopoulos, pp. 5–19. New York: New York Academy of Sciences, 1973.

———. "The Utilitarian Contract: A Generalization of Rawls' Theory of Justice." *Theory and Decision* 4 (February/April 1974): 345–67.

———. "Solving the Intensity Problem in Representative Democracy." In *Economics of Public Choice,* edited by R. D Leiter and G. Sirkin, pp. 54–94. New York: Cyro Press, 1975.

Musgrave, R. *The Theory of Public Finance.* New York: McGraw-Hill, 1959.

Pauly, M. V., and Willett, T. D. "Two Concepts of Equity and Their Implications for Public Policy." *Social Science Quarterly* 53 (June 1972): 8–19.

Roberts, D. J. "Pareto, Public Goods, and Politics." *Canadian Journal of Economics,* no. 3 (November 1970), pp. 615–16.

Thurow, L. "The Income Distribution as a Pure Public Good." *Quarterly Journal of Economics* 85, no. 2 (May 1971): 327–36.

Tobin, J. "On Limiting the Domain of Inequality." *Journal of Law and Economics* 13 (October 1970): 263–79.

Tollison, R. D., and Willett, T. D. "Some Simple Economics of Voting and Non-Voting." *Public Choice* 16 (Fall 1973): 59–71.

Vlastos, G. "Justice and Equality." In *Social Justice,* edited by R. B. Brandt. New York: Prentice-Hall, 1962.

Winch, D. M. "Pareto, Public Goods and Politics." *Canadian Journal of Economics,* no. 2 (November 1969), pp. 492–508.

———. "Pareto, Public Goods, and Politics: Reply." *Canadian Journal of Economics,* no. 3 (November 1970). pp. 616–17.

Why Governments Fail: An Inquiry into the Use of Instruments of Evil to Do Good

Vincent Ostrom

In addressing the topic of "why governments fail" I shall emphasize the obvious. The very nature of government involves the legitimate use of force in ordering human relationships. The use of force in human relationships is of the nature of an evil. The use of instruments of evil as a necessary means to realize the advantage of ordered social relationships creates a fundamental moral dilemma that can be appropriately characterized as a Faustian bargain. A reasonable expectation, given the Faustian bargain, is that governments will fail. To ignore the moral dilemma is to set a course that inevitably leads to human tragedy.

In examining the Faustian bargain inherent in human societies, I shall draw upon two analytical traditions that attempt to cope with this problem. One is Thomas Hobbes's explanation of the nature of political phenomena. In drawing upon Hobbes's analysis, I shall emphasize the relationship of political organization to human well-being and show how instruments of evil are necessary to the realization of the common good. Hobbes's solution turns upon a sovereign's accountability to God, and fails if a sovereign neglects his responsibility to God.

I shall then turn to American efforts to devise an alternative solution where the exercise of governmental authority is subject to a rule of constitutional law. The Faustian bargain remains an integral part of this solution but the constraints inherent in a system of constitutional law may place some limits upon those who would use the coercive powers of government to their own advantage. But such constraints will have the desired effect only if citizens in a democratic society have a critical self-awareness of what they are doing and exercise their prerogatives of constitutional choice so as to maintain appropriate limits. Under these circumstances, the normal expectations of tragedy can be ameliorated somewhat. Attention will be given in conclusion to some factors that detract from developing a critical self-awareness among citizens about problems of constitutional choice in a democracy.

Hobbes's Leviathan

Some of the puzzles or paradoxes inherent in the human condition are best highlighted in Hobbes's analysis of the basic logic inherent in the organization of human societies. Hobbes proceeds on the assumption that commonwealths are artifacts ("artifices" is his term) and that human beings are both the material (matter) of which commonwealths are made and the artisans (artificers) that create and organize commonwealths. Like a modern economist, Hobbes treates the individual as the basic unit of analysis and devotes the first several chapters of *Leviathan* to human nature. His development of a theory of governmental organization involves three major steps.

Elements in a Theory of Governmental Organization

The first step is to try to conceptualize a situation that is devoid of all of the constitutive elements of a commonwealth except for human beings. Without rules or any of the other constitutive elements of political organization, Hobbes anticipates that human beings will experience a state of war of each individual against every other individual, where "the life of man" would be "solitary, poor, nasty, brutish, and short" (82). Since Hobbes has posited that the object of each individual is "some good to himself" (86), a puzzle or paradox is created: people seek their own good but realize misery instead. An unconstrained pursuit of self-interest yields the misery of war. Hobbes then anticipates that human beings can have recourse to reason to avoid the miseries of war.

The second step is to conceptualize peace as an alternative to war and proceed from the imagined consequent to identify the causes so that the conditions necessary to the realization of peace might be specified. In doing so, Hobbes formulates his laws of nature. Since these specify rules for the ordering of human relationships that will lead to peace, they can be viewed both as logically necessary conditions for peace and as moral precepts. The rules imply that some forms of behavior are foreclosed and other forms of behavior are allowed. Language is used to partition behavioral space by moral criteria. These criteria distinguish admissible from inadmissible patterns of conduct. Since human beings are creatures that use language, they can use words formulated as rules to order their relationships with one another.

Hobbes views his natural laws to be generally consistent with the Golden Rule: "*Do not that to another, which thou wouldst not have done to thyself*" (103). He suggests that the Golden Rule can be used to make his laws of nature intelligible even to those of the "meanest capacity."

> [H]e has no more to do in learning the laws of nature, but, when weighing the actions of other men with his own, they seem too heavy, to put them in the other part of the balance, and his own in their place, that his own passions, and self-love, may add nothing to the weight; and then there will be none of these laws of nature that will not appear unto him to be very reasonable (103).

This capacity of an individual to take on the perspective of another and potentially to function as an impartial observer is related to Hobbes's presumption that an underlying "similitude of thoughts and passions" (6) characterizes all mankind. Men vary in the objects of their thoughts and passions. But there is an underlying similitude of thoughts and passions that enables one person, by first coming to understand oneself, to understand how others think and feel. To the extent that human beings share an underlying similitude of thoughts and passions, grounds exist for the development of common elements of understanding and agreement among human beings. Those characteristics that are shared in common by all mankind are the universal characteristics of human nature.

Hobbes's laws of nature are derived from these presuppositions. He anticipates that each individual would, on prudent, self-interested grounds, prefer peace to war. Thus, each human being would have an individual preference for living a life in accordance with the moral precepts inherent in the laws of nature, rather than to endure the miseries of war. "The laws of nature are immutable and eternal" (104) because the vices of injustice, ingratitude, arrogance, pride, iniquity, etc., can never be a lawful basis for governing human relationships.

The third step in Hobbes's analysis is the most difficult one. While everyone would prefer peace to war, no one would act in conformity with the laws of nature unless others did so too. The problem then is how to bind men to their words so that the rules implied by the laws of nature can be made effective in ordering human relationships. Universal acceptance of the laws of nature as good is not sufficient. It is necessary to have recourse to "the terror of some power to cause them to be observed" because the laws of nature are contrary to some passions that carry human beings "to partiality, pride, revenge, and the like" (109). "[C]ovenants, without the sword, are but words, and no strength to secure a man at all" (109). This poses a serious dilemma in organizing human social relationships. Instruments of evil—the terror of the sword—are necessary for realizing the common good of peace.

Hobbes's resolution is for each individual to recognize that the advantage of a rule-ordered society requires recourse to some human agents who are authorized to function as rulers and others as ruled. Rules necessarily imply both rulers and ruled. Hobbes's basic covenant for the creation of a commonwealth, thus, requires each to surrender his natural right to govern himself to a ruler or assembly of rulers who exercise the basic prerogatives of rule, including the terror of the sword to bind men to their word. For there to be a single system of rules, Hobbes reasons that there must be a single source of rules. Those who are the source of rules cannot themselves be held accountable to law. Those who rule exercise an unlimited and undivided authority to govern.

In Hobbes's formulation, civil law embodies the prinicples of the laws of nature; and civil law becomes the measure of right and wrong, justice and injustice, and lawful and unlawful. By definition, then, those who exercise sovereign prerogatives can do no injustice, nor commit a wrong under law. While sovereigns cannot commit an injustice in Hobbes's theory, he does recognize that they can commit "iniquities" (116).

Hobbes's commonwealth thus depends upon a radical inequality between sovereigns, as those who exercise the prerogatives of rule, and subjects, as those who are bound by rules as the necessary condition for deriving the benefits of a rule-ordered society. Again, rules imply rulers and ruled. Those who rule wield the sword of justice. The advantages of law depend upon the potential use of instruments of evil in the enforcement of law.

The Faustian bargain inherent in the potential use of instruments of evil as necessary conditions for deriving mutual advantages in a system of law creates extraordinary opportunities for those who exercise the prerogatives of rule to exploit others and to dominate the allocation of values in a society. Hobbes recognizes this possibility, but he considers a willing acceptance of these burdens on the part of subjects as the price of peace. He sees no way that rulers can be held accountable to others without the creation of some new sovereign who would exercise ultimate authority. As a result, he contends that sovereigns can be responsible to none but God. We need then to consider Hobbes's conception of God and how an accountability to God might affect the use of instruments of evil to do good.

The Metaphysical Key to Hobbes's Commonwealth

Hobbes considers the "general inclination of all mankind" to be "a perpetual and restless desire for power after power, that ceaseth only with death" (64). Power is defined as "present means to attain some future good" (56). Human life is thus marked by a continual striving for present means to attain some future good that goes on without end and ceases only with death.

Among the manifestations of this continual striving is an "anxiety for the future time," which

> disposeth men to inquire into the causes of things; because the knowledge of them, maketh men better able to order the present to their best advantage.
>
> Curiosity, or love of knowledge of causes, draws a man from the consideration of the effect, to seek the cause; and again, the cause of that cause till of necessity he must come to this thought at last, that there is some cause, whereof there is no former cause, but is eternal; which is it men call God. (68)

Love of knowledge thus leads human beings to conceptualize God as eternal being. Man can conceive of God as eternal being, but there is no way that God can be directly perceived by humans as an observable being. The meaning of God can either be discovered by "the natural dictates of right reason" (233–34) or by revelation and the teaching of the prophets. True religion for Hobbes is one where revelation and prophetic teachings are consistent with the dictates of right reason.

Hobbes explicitly views his laws of nature or articles of peace as being "Divine laws" (235). If God is an eternal being ruled by covenant, then those rules would be "immutable and eternal" (104) and serve as a basis for governing relationships among all who acknowledge an eternal providence (233). The question then is what accountability to God implies when Hobbes indicates that a sovereign is accountable to none but God. This is the central issue addressed in Hobbes's chapter on the Kingdom of God by Nature.

In developing his argument, Hobbes turns to the common meaning of the terms used to express the concepts of worship and culture in Latin. He suggests that the education of children in the sense of "a *culture* of the mind" (235) provides the proper referent for the relationship of sovereigns to subjects. Hobbes then observes:

> where men's wills are to be wrought to our purpose, not by force, but by compliance, it signifieth as much as courting, that is, a winning of favour by good offices; as by praise, by acknowledging their power, and by whatsoever is pleasing to them from which we look for any benefit. And this is properly *worship;* in which sense *Publicola,* is understood for a worshipper of the people; and *cultus Dei,* for the worship of God. (235–36)

"Courting" in the sense used by Hobbes might be translated to mean "loving care." The proper attitude of one who cultivates the minds of children is one of loving care. This, to Hobbes, means worship.

The conclusion that Hobbes draws from a somewhat more elaborate argument is that "obedience to his [God's] laws, that is, in this case, the laws of nature, is the greatest worship of all" (239). Adherence to the natural laws is the highest form of Divine worship. In turn, the neglect of God's laws "is the greatest of all contumelies" (240). Hobbes then concludes, "And these are the laws of that divine worship, which natural reason dictateth to private men" (240).

Hobbes goes on to conclude his chapter on the Kingdom of God by Nature by warning of the natural punishments which will follow from a neglect of God's law.

> There is no action in this life, that is not the beginning of so long a chain of consequences, as no human providence is high enough, to give a man a prospect to the end. And unpleasing events; in such manner, as he who will do any thing for his pleasure, must engage himself to suffer all of the pains annexed to it; and these pains, are the natural punishments of those actions, which are the beginning of more harm than good. And hereby it comes to pass, that intemperance is naturally punished by diseases: rashness, by mischances; injustice, with the violence of enemies; pride with ruin; cowardice, with oppression; negligent government of princes, with rebellion; and rebellion, with slaughter. For seeing punishments are the consequent to the breach of laws; natural punishments must be naturally consequent to the breach of the laws of nature; and therefore follow them as their natural, not arbitrary effects. (240–41)

We can conclude from Hobbes's analysis that instruments of evil can be used to gain the advantages of peace and the other benefits of human organization *only so long as those who exercise the prerogatives of rule do so with loving care for their subjects and adherence to the moral precepts of the natural laws as the highest form of worship owing to God as eternal providence.*

Moral virtue, in Hobbes's theory of government, derives critically from the virtue of those who exercise sovereign authority. Once virtuous sovereigns exist, law can be used as the measure of value. Virtue accrues to subjects by learning to order their relationships with one another by reference to law. But if moral virtue is abandoned by those who exercise the prerogatives of rule, bad laws become "traps for money" (228) and rulers can use their prerogatives to exploit others. Those who have greatest confidence in their capacity to do good suffer false pride and can produce the greatest evil. Instruments of evil come to dominate human relationships and the human condition assumes tragic proportions. A basis no longer exists for reciprocity to occur among members of human communities on mutually beneficial terms. Peace and concord give way to oppression and tyranny. These are the natural punishments that flow from a neglect of moral virtue that is consistent with prudent self-interest.

Efforts to Limit the Exercise of Governmental Prerogative by a Rule of Law

If the lot of mankind is the negligent government of princes, then Hobbes's quest for peace can be expected to yield oppression and tyranny instead. This circumstance leads to the question of whether human beings might again have recourse to reason and search out an alternative to Hobbes's theory of sovereignty. A revolution, or a rebellion in Hobbes's terms, would not suffice. A successful revolution would merely replace an existing sovereign with a new sovereign. When successful revolutionists demand unlimited authority to accomplish the tasks of the revolution, they are making a claim for unlimited sovereign authority. If people acquiesce in that claim a new sovereign is created; and that new sovereign confronts anew the dilemma inherent in using instruments of evil to do good.

The struggle from the sixteenth century onward, especially in Europe and North America, has been one of finding an alternative to unlimited exercise of sovereign authority. While there are venerable traditions in Switzerland, the Netherlands, Great Britain, France, and elsewhere in Europe, I shall draw upon efforts in the United States of America to fashion a solution in which no one would exercise absolute authority and everyone would exercise some fundamental authority in the governance of society. In this arrangement, all exercise of governmental authority is subject to a rule of law. Government, as the legitimate use of coercion to enforce law, is necessary to gain the benefits of an organized society. The question is whether recourse to a rule of law that applies to the conduct of government might reduce the tendency to use instruments of evil to exploit others and dominate the allocation of values in a society. To explore this question requires one to specify the conditions that would apply to a system of government where rules of law might be enforced against those who govern. Rather than presuming that governmental authority is indivisible, the American theory of constitutional choice presumes that authority can be allocated and distributed in a complex structure of authority relationships. Several basic distinctions are made for developing such a system of allocated and distributed authority.

The Structure of Constitutional Rule

Perhaps the most basic distinction is that made between a constitution as fundamental law and ordinary law. A constitution applies to the organization and conduct of government. Ordinary law applies to patterns of social relationships that would normally characterize relations among subjects. These distinctions, in turn, depend upon distinctions between constitutional decision making and governmental decision making. Effective limits cannot be maintained if a government is free to alter the basic law that applies to its own organization and conduct. As a result, special prerogatives are reserved to the people to decide matters pertaining to a constitution as fundamental law. But a government can exercise authority to enact and revise ordinary law subject to the terms and conditions of basic constitutional law.

Once the distinction between a constitution and ordinary law, and between constitutional decision making and governmental decision making, is established, it is then possible for a people in a democratic society to decide upon the basic allocations of authority that are specified in the terms of a constitution itself. Three different types of provisions can be viewed as having an important place in establishing limits upon the exercise of governmental authority.

The first of these limits pertains to the formulation of the basic authority of persons and citizens together with the implied correlative limits upon the authority of government. If citizens are to exercise basic prerogatives of government then their capacity to maintain an open public realm for discussions, debates, and deliberation about public affairs, free from dominance by governmental authorities, is essential. Freedom of speech, press, and assembly become essential prerogatives accruing to individuals in a democracy with correlative limits upon the authority of government. Similarly, persons and citizens require an individual authority to exercise autonomy in the governance of their own affairs: individuals in a democracy are first their own governors. Authority pertaining to rights of property, contract, and voluntary association are, thus, fundamental prerogatives of persons in a democratic society. In addition, the right of both citizens and persons to make enforceable claims upon officials exercising governmental prerogatives is essential in assuring due process of law. Procedural rights specify the liability of officials to conform to rules governing official conduct so as to fulfill the procedural requirements for doing justice.

Another method of distributing authority in a democratic constitution is to allocate the prerogatives of government among different types of decision structures. In the American experience this is typically done by distinguishing legislative, executive, and judicial functions, and assigning authority so that each decision structure is subject to limits exercised by other decision structures. This system of reciprocal vetoes gives rise to what is characterized as a system of checks and balances. Governmental action requires the concurrence of the different decision structures. Each decision structure is constrained by the limits imposed by the others. The realm of feasible actions is bounded by limits; and, so long as the different decision structures act within the constraints of constitutional law, a system of government can be conceived where no one structure is allowed to dominate the rest and all forms of governmental actions occur within the constraints of fundamental law.

A third type of limit specified in American constitutions is provision for the direct or indirect participation of citizens within the different decision structures of government. The election of legislative, executive, and judicial officials allows for the direct participation of citizens in selecting the basic personnel of government and for the indirect representation of citizens in the councils of government. Among the states, provision for citizen participation in the affairs of local units of government is even more extensive than was provided for in state governments themselves. In addition, direct citizen participation in the operation of the judiciary occurs in the organization of trial juries and grand juries. A decision to use the coercive authority of the community thus allows for the direct participation of citizens in making such decisions. The exercise of punishment associated with the violation of law depends upon the right of each person charged with a crime to the right of a trial by jury. Citizens have a direct role in scrutinizing the charges made by officials before coercive sanctions can be imposed.

Grand juries provide further opportunity to scrutinize the grounds for levying criminal charges and more generally inquiring into the discharge of public trust by public officials. Grand juries are entitled to initiate their own investigations into the discharge of responsibilities by public officials and can return indictments for misfeasance or malfeasance in office when evidence exists to support such charges.

Amplifying Limits through Principles of Federalism

The most difficult problem in fashioning a system of government that is subject to a system of constitutional law arose in the development of a government that applied to the United States of America as distinct from the several states. The first efforts to establish such a government drew upon principles of confederation in which the several states were represented in a Congress that was vested with authority to act on behalf of the several states in formulating measures that would apply to continental defense, interstate and foreign commerce, and other matters of joint interest.

After a period of initial experience with principles of confederation, the conclusion was reached that those principles were based upon a fundamental error in conceptualizing the nature of government. A new effort was made to fashion an alternative structure based upon principles that have come to be identified with a federal system of government as distinguished from a confederation. The crucial point at issue is whether Congress as a government could govern other governments, or whether it was necessary to create a concurrent system of government, which included executive and judicial as well as legislative instrumentalities that could then act in relation to the person of individuals. The conclusion was reached that justice could not be done unless the authority of magistrates relates to the person of individuals. The use of collective sanctions does not discriminate between wrongdoers and those who are innocent of wrongdoing. The requirements of justice thus depend upon the organization of governments that relate themselves to the person of individuals as responsible actors. The sword of justice must apply to persons in their individual capacities rather than to collectivities.

Federalism permits the concurrent application of principles of constitutional rule; and the integrity of a federal system can be maintained only so long as all units of government are subject to an enforceable system of constitutional law. Under these circumstances, people can participate in the organization and governance of diverse communities of interest without having a single unit of government that exercises sovereign authority. Rather, people can participate in diverse units of government, each of which exercises limited authority.

Principles of federalism are potentially subject to indefinite extension. Under those circumstances, all human relationships might potentially be subject to law. Hobbes's theory of sovereignty, by contrast, implies that relations among sovereigns cannot be constrained by law. The human lot, under those conditions, is limited to one where islands of peace might be attained within commonwealths. Relationships among commonwealths themselves would remain under a continued threat of war.

The rather ingenious constitutional paraphernalia of the American system of government is extended to a point where no one exercises unlimited authority. No one is allowed to be a judge of his own cause in relation to the interests of others. All who exercise authority are subject to limits. Under these circumstances, those who exercise the prerogatives of government can be subject to the limits of an enforceable system of constitutional law.

Institutional Failure in Constitutional Orders

But this ingenious constitutional apparatus continues to be subject to institutional failure. Wherever majorities can dominate access to instrumentalities of government they can use those instrumentalities to exploit others. Systematic exclusion of blacks from the offices of persons and citizens permitted one of the most oppressive tyrannies known to mankind in the form of that peculiar institution of American slavery. The extension of legal personality and citizenship, following the American civil war, failed to prevent ruling coalitions from forming to continue the exploitation of blacks in many American communities.

Traditions of machine politics and boss rule developed where those who controlled elections could dominate all relevant decision structures and exploit the coercive powers of government to their own advantage. In the course of doing so, the power of eminent domain and the granting of public franchises enabled a generation of robber barons to gain control over public utilities as natural monopolies and capture a lion's share of the economic rent inherent in nineteenth-century economic development. Similarly, in the contemporary scene, control over the supply of money and credit enables some to usurp the prerogatives of government and impose the costs upon others through an increasing rate of inflation.

The use of instruments of evil to do good continues to plague even societies organized according to constitutional principles of limited and federal government. The question remains whether people in a democratic society can have recourse to the appropriate knowledge and processes for decision making so as to correct the problems of institutional failure when these become manifest in human relationships. Can oppressed minorities, such as American blacks, have recourse to appropriate decision-making processes so that remedial actions under universal standards of law can be taken despite their minority status? Can the rig of the political game be changed to reduce the dominance of political bosses? These questions point to the essential importance of citizens being able to act in a way that imposes limits upon officials and to make constitutional changes to reestablish limits when prior limits no longer suffice.

The Moral and Metaphysical Foundations of Constitutional Choice

We are thus confronted with the question of whether citizens in a democracy can organize the conduct of moral and political inquiry under circumstances where they can take account of each other's interests and do so in a way that is consistent with the responsibility of Hobbes's sovereign to God as eternal being. Citizens in a democracy, if they are ultimately responsible for maintaining the limits of constitutional rule, must be accountable to the same moral and metaphysical standards as Hobbes's sovereign.

Hobbes proceeds on an assumption that unity of a commonwealth derives from having one sovereign whether that sovereign is one man or an assembly of men. A multitude can function as an organized society for Hobbes only as it derives unity from the exercise of authority by a single sovereign representative. But for a democracy to function there must be an agreement upon the basic constitutional terms and conditions for doing so. Unity must derive from the represented. The measure of what is right and wrong, just and unjust, lawful and unlawful comes not from the ordinary law but from measures that citizens can use in evaluating the conduct of officials in the discharge of their governmental responsibilities. Can we imagine circumstances where citizens in a democracy will have opportunities for the conduct of moral and political inquiry that are conducive to the exercise of prerogatives of constitutional choice so that the discharge of governmental prerogatives conforms to appropriate moral precepts?

Such a possibility might be derived from Hobbes's basic presupposition that human beings are potentially self-knowing creatures that share a similitude of thoughts and passions characteristic of all mankind. By reflecting upon the way one thinks and feels, one can come to an understanding of oneself as an autonomous creature and use one's reflective knowledge to order one's life in a way that enables one to become a responsible being, both in relating to other human beings and to other forms of being. In doing so, one might come to understand how others think and feel without knowing the particular idiosyncrasies of their thoughts and passions. A limited ground exists for making intersubjective comparisons about what it means to be human.

Such a method of inquiry enables potentially self-knowing creatures to become aware of their own essential values in considering their relationships with others. On the basis of such inquiries, informed by the responses of others, human beings may develop appropriate measures for informing human choice and in evaluating human actions. If there is a basic similitude of thoughts and passions characteristic of all mankind, such modes of inquiry should permit people who share a community of interest with each other to reach general concurrence about the criteria of choice that have fundamental meaning to each and every person. Common understanding, if properly grounded, gives rise to common agreement.

If human beings can develop appropriate measures to serve as criteria of choice and for the evaluation of human actions, we might follow Hobbes further in anticipating how appropriate rules of conduct might be derived from natural dictates of right reason. The measure here is to contemplate how God might rule by covenant. Such rules would then be universal rules that would be consistent with the criteria of choice that take account of the basic values derived from the similitude of thoughts and passions characteristic of all mankind. Such rules would, if properly understood, serve as the basis for ordering human relationships that would be consistent both with the prudent interests of fallible creatures and with a universal order.

Moral virtue in a democratic society thus depends upon citizens having knowable grounds for establishing measures that can both be used as criteria of choice and standards for evaluating human actions. Such measures should serve as criteria of choice in devising rules of law that are applicable to the contingencies found in existential situations and for evaluating actions that flow as a consequence of using such rules to order relationships among human beings. Such measures should be applicable to both rulers and ruled. To be appropriate such measures of value should provide the basis for maintaining reciprocity among members of human communities on mutually beneficial terms. Self-interest rightly understood, to paraphrase Tocqueville, depends upon a shared understanding of moral virtue that is consistent with prudent self-interest.

If decision processes are organized so as to facilitate the testing of intersubjective comparisons, we can have some measure of confidence in their "objective" character. We continuously rely upon human beings to judge good wines, talented singers, the power and gracefulness of ballet dancers, and the skill of gymnasts. Citizens, if provided with the appropriate circumstances, can learn to recognize a wrong or an injustice when they see it. Fallibility also requires that such judgments be carefully scrutinized by others so that no one is allowed to judge his own cause. "[M]an can transcend his own subjectivity by striving passionately to fulfill his personal obligations to universal standards" (M. Polanyi, *Personal Knowledge* Chicago: University of Chicago Press, 1958). Only by striving passionately to develop appropriate measures for evaluating human action can we aspire to standards that can apply to rulers and ruled alike.

The viability of a democratic society depends upon a shared understanding of the meaning that is attributed to the basic value terms inherent in rule-ordered relationships. Citizens are responsible for understanding the terms that are embodied within the framework of fundamental law. As both subjects and citizens, individuals in a democratic society are required to know when obedience is proper and when disobedience is essential to maintain the limits of an enforceable system of constitutional law. Otherwise, the usurpation of authority by officials will threaten the viability of any democratic society. If citizens as subjects acquiesce in the usurpation of authority by officials, unlimited prerogatives will prevail and a democracy will cease to exist.

Thus, citizens need to know the basic criteria of choice that pertains to the proper exercise of governmental authority. Without such criteria of choice, to paraphrase Hobbes, one does not know, when commanded by officials, whether it is contrary to fundamental law or not. In such a circumstance, a citizen by "too much obedience" (232) can offend against the fundamental law.

We might look upon democracies as a way of life in which citizens are the basic artisans responsible for the governance of such societies. The language of artisanship is always thoroughly permeated with the use of value terms. The opportunities for political artisanship extend to all forms of association in the organization of collective endeavors and are not limited to constitutional decisions that apply only to national governments. So long as basic principles of organization can be reiterated in the organization of diverse associations and consistent measures can be used as criteria of choice across associations, we can have recourse to general principles of organization that can be applied to attain complex structures that take account of diverse communities of interest. So long as citizens are experienced in the skills of political artisanship, and share a knowledge of political artisanship, we can have some confidence that the basic principles of constitutional choice can be articulated in the way that citizens can use in the organization and conduct of their everyday lives.

Conflict over basic matters of governance may, if appropriately presented in a language of constitutional choice, provide the occasions for a continuing inquiry about recurrent issues of institutional weakness or institutional failures that require the attention of citizens as constitutional decision makers. So long as the political process is organized to facilitate basic constitutional inquiry, we might assume that citizens in a democracy can acquire capabilities to address and solve new problems over time.

Threats to the Maintenance of Constitutional Order

We are, however, also confronted with the circumstance that a universal characteristic of human beings is their capability for learning. They enter into being, not as fully equipped omniscient observers endowed with perfect information, but as creatures that only have a potential for learning. When amplified with the development and use of language, human beings acquire extraordinary potential for learning, but those potentials are unlikely to be exhausted. So long as human beings have potentials for new learning, they can never escape the burden of being fallible.

The problem of maintaining ordered social relationships is always subject to the basic limitation and tension that the human condition is itself subject to transformation in light of new knowledge and new patterns of development that occur as a result of new knowledge. The referent to which the language of rule-ordered relationships applies is itself subject to change. What is "interstate commerce" in the meaning of the U.S. Constitution, for example, is quite different today than when that term was first specified in 1787. This circumstance greatly increases the ambiguities associated with the use of language in rule-ordered relationships.

The language appropriate to citizenship in a democratic society can also be easily corrupted. The cult of modernity leads the "modern" intellectual to reject the terminology of an earlier generation as archaic. Value terms in particular are apt to be identified as meaningless. With the rejection of value terms as meaningless comes a denial of the artifactual nature of political and social phenomena and a demand that methods of the natural sciences be applied to the study of such phenomena. Value terms are at the core of rule-ordered relationships, and rule-ordered relationships are at the core of political order and social relationships. An intellectual tradition that rejects value terms as meaningless cuts itself off from the essential nature of political and social phenomena. If citizens were to accept epistemological positions taken by many modern scholars, they would be devoid of the appropriate moral and metaphysical grounds for functioning as intelligent constitutional decision makers.

While we can conceptualize the possibility that citizens might develop the appropriate conditions of moral and political inquiry for exercising constitutional choice, we also must recognize that human beings continually strive to test the limits of their capabilities. Under these circumstances we need to recognize that the use of instruments of evil to do good is always problemmatical. Human beings can aspire to creating the conditions of life where prudent self-interest is consistent with universal standards of freedom, justice, and mutually productive relationships. But these conditions depend upon potential recourse to the coercive power of the sword. If human beings become critically aware of the burden of being fallible, they might learn how to make only very limited use of instruments of evil to do good. In that case, human beings would learn to live with the conditions where both rulers and ruled are subject to the rule of law and are held accountable to the same standards of evaluation.

NOTE

This paper was prepared for presentation at an international symposium on Anatomy of Government Deficiencies held in Diessen am Ammersee (Bavaria), July 22–25, 1980. It draws heavily upon work that I am currently doing on a book-length manuscript entitled *Leviathan and Democracy*. References are to the Michael Oakshott edition of Hobbes's *Leviathan* (Oxford: Basil Blackwlll, 1960).

7 Future Directions and Prospects

Constitutional Restrictions on the Power of Government

James M. Buchanan

My title is indeed comprehensive, and it should be evident that I cannot, in the space of one article, do more than offer highly selected comments. Nonetheless, I should defend both my title and my own efforts, here and elsewhere, to call attention to constitutional matters. I use this inclusive term to embody constitutional history, constitutional law, constitutionalism as an approach to political philosophy, and, in particular, constitutional challenges that the United States faces in the 1980s.

I have often suggested that what is now needed is widespread adoption of a genuine "constitutional attitude," a proclivity or tendency to examine issues from a constitutional perspective, as opposed to the pragmatic, short-run, utilitarian perspective that seems to characterize modern academic scholarship as well as day-to-day political discussion and action. As I compare the political discourse of our time, the late twentieth century, with that of the late eighteenth century, when the American Founding Fathers were doing their work, the distinctive difference lies in our century's loss of an earlier "constitutional wisdom."

There are, of course, very good reasons why the American Founders, and especially Madison, Hamilton, and Jay, adopted a constitutional perspective in the 1780s. They were actively engaged in Constitution making, and they were trying to articulate the set of ideas that would convince the wider public that a draft document would work. As we all know, subsequent generations of Americans, including our own, have been beneficiaries of their genius, both with respect to basic design and to their persuasive powers. We still live in the "building" that they constructed for us, and I think that this metaphor is of considerable advantage in thinking about my whole subject matter.

Once constructed and in place, the "building" stood the test of time. It has been added to, changed, twisted out of recognition in some respects, allowed to fall down here and there, deliberately torn down in parts, but perhaps it still remains recognizable as the same "building" that emerged in 1789. These modifications in the structure have been allowed to take place, however, almost without conscious attention to the "grand design" of the architects. The changes have been essentially pragmatic responses to particular situations as these arose. It should not be surprising therefore, that what we

First published as *Constituional Restrictions on the Power of Government*, The Frank M. Engle Lecture in Economic Security (Bryn Mawr, Pennsylvania: The American College, 1981).

now see appears jerry-built and distorted, considerably out of line, strongly tilted, and apparently liable to collapse unless shoring up efforts are commenced, and soon.

Only within the decades of the 1960s and notably the 1970s has there been an emerging awareness that the very bases of our socioeconomic-political-legal order are seriously in disarray. For more than a century, and indeed since the debate prior to the Civil War, political leaders, social philosophers, social scientists, constitutional lawyers, and the public generally forgot the simple principles, apparently secure in the false presumption that the American constitutional structure was permanently emplaced and not subject even to potential collapse. I shall discuss the signs of this new awareness later, but before I do so, it is necessary to lay out in some detail the fundamental meaning of a *constitution*.

Constitutional and Postconstitutional Choice

I have continued to be surprised that my economist colleagues, all of whom are sophisticated and competent social scientists, seem to have no inkling as to what a "constitution" is, and that they go about their own chores as if the whole subject remains irrelevant and unimportant. I could extend this category beyond economists, to include most modern social scientists, and even to many of those who lable themselves as constitutional lawyers. It should not be necessary here to go over what must be very elementary precepts were it not for what I can only label as gross illiteracy on the part of so many who should but do not know them. And perhaps I should stress that it is "knowledge" not "values" or "beliefs" that I refer to here.

What a Constitution Is

Put in its simplest if possibly confusing terms, "a constitution" is the "higher law." This terminology is helpful because it suggests a two-stage or two-level legal structure. There are laws that lay down the rules within which ordinary laws are made. The political constitution is the first set of laws here, the higher laws, the basic rules for political order and political decision making. Professor Hayek, in the very title of his three-volume work, distinguishes between the terms *law* and *legislation*.[1] These may be translated, in my terms, as *constitutional law* and *ordinary legislation*.

On many occasions, and in several places in print, I have used the analogy with games since I think this allows us to present the basic distinction most clearly. Consider a poker game. Participants must initially agree on the set of rules that will define the game to be played. This agreed-on set of rules becomes the constitution of the game. Play takes place within these rules, and this play may be termed *postconstitutional*. As such, it is explicitly constrained by the rules chosen, constrained externally to the actual play itself.

There are two quite distinct stages or levels of choice involved here, and these choices have quite different features. First, there is the choice of the rules themselves, *constitutional choice*. Second, there is the choice among the strategies of play within the rules that define the game. I call this choice of strategy *postconstitutional choice*.

We may think of a single person as he or she tries to establish criteria for evaluating alternatives for choices in these different settings, with the knowledge that he or she is participating in a collective or group decision process. In constitutional choice, the individual cannot know precisely what his or her own position will be, or precisely how the cards will fall in the poker game analogy. In his or her own self-interest, the person will be led to evaluate alternative rules on something like the "fairness" criterion.[2] For choices made within the constraints of established rules, however, the individual will be able to identify his or her position. He or she will, therefore, aim at maximizing the individual payoffs to be gained, whatever these payoffs might be. Here the appropriate model is one of a maximizing strategy.

Constitutional Rules

Let me now return to the political constitution and apply these basic notions. A political constitution is the set of rules that define the socioeconomic-political game that we all must play. These rules define the relative spheres for private and governmental action, and they impose external constraints on the procedures through which political action takes place.

The central confusion in the discussions of politics has been in the failure to recognize that two levels of evaluation and choice exist and that these are quite different from each other, requiring different types of analysis on the part of social scientists. The analysis-evaluation of alternative constitutional rules and arrangements must have as an input some models or predictions as to how choices will be made within or under the alternative sets of rules that might be laid down in the constitution. Modern social scientists have failed to recognize that reform or improvement must have as its direct object change in the rules or constraints within which political decision makers are allowed to operate. They have not been concerned at all with genuine constitutional reform. Instead, modern social scientists have tended to focus on the particulars of policy alternatives or options.

Constitutionalism and Public Choice

These scholars have proceeded as if they are offering advice to some benevolent despot, who is presumed to stand ready and willing to promote "the public interest" once it is enlightened as to what such "interest" is by the expertise of those who are doing the advising. Such a procedure is absurd on its face. Government politics is not a single-minded decision-making entity. And even if government were such, we surely could not model it to be benevolent. Government as it exists is, of course, an extremely complex interaction process that involves literally thousands of persons, who participate in many different roles and capacities. Out of this process particular outcomes emerge. Of what use is the "advice" of the economist to the effect that this or that policy A is more or less "efficient" than policy B? Persons who participate in political decision making are no different from the rest of us. They respond to the rewards and penalties that the "rules of the game" confront them with, and such persons would indeed be foolish if they took the advice of their economist advisers very seriously.

Public Choice Analysis

"Public choice," the new subdiscipline that applies essentially economic methods of analysis to the behavior of persons in political decision-making capacities, involves the study of the whole interaction process. As such, the analysis in public choice is positive rather than normative. It does not advance propositions that politicians, bureaucrats, or voters "should" or "should not" adopt.

Nonetheless, there are important reform implications that emerge from the whole body of public choice analysis, and these implications are those that tie us back into the main theme of this essay. Public choice analysis, which has as one of its central elements the critical distinction between constitutional and postconstitutional choice, strongly implies that reform or improvement in political outcomes or results is to be sought through possible changes in the rules, in the set of constraints within which political decisions are made, in the *Constitution,* and not in changes in day-to-day policy that temporary politicians may be somehow persuaded to follow.

A somewhat different way of constrasting the constitutional perspective with the standard one taken in most discussions on politics is to note that, with constitutional-institutional reform, there is little or no concern with replacing "bad," "evil," or "incompetent" politicians with others who may be "good," "kind," or "competent." The emphasis in constitutional reform is neither on persuasion nor on selection of "better" persons to act as agents in governing roles. The emphasis stays precisely where it was with the Founding Fathers: on setting up rules or constraints within which politicians must operate, rules that will make it a relatively trivial matter as to the personal characteristics of those who happen to be selected as governors. This emphasis is strictly eighteenth-century in spirit, and it is present in Adam Smith's great treatise on economics, *The Wealth of Nations* (1776), as well as in *The Federalist Papers.*

Can Government Be Constrained?

Critics of the constitutional perspective, for three centuries, have made several arguments. Perhaps the most important of these, and surely one that warrants our consideration here, is the charge that constitutions do not and cannot constrain sovereign governments. If this charge is valid, all discussion of constitutional constraints is mere fancy, an illusory and escapist exercise in futility.

Hobbes's View

The position was taken by Thomas Hobbes, who published his book *Leviathan* in 1651. Hobbes argued that persons value the security of life and property so highly that they will assent to the establishment of a sovereign governmental power. They will do so, however, in the full knowledge that, once established, persons can exert no subsequent control over the activity of the sovereign. Government can do as it pleases, once it has attained a position of authority and power. There is no enforcing agent or agency that can require the sovereign to abide by the rules that might be laid down in some conceptual contract, some constitution.

In this Hobbesian perspective, the only constraints on the range and extent of the activities of the sovereign must be self-imposed. Those persons who are in positions of governmental authority may voluntarily choose to restrict their behavior, but they recognize no externally imposed limits in so doing.

I suggest that this rejection of the efficacy of constitutional constraints on government belies the whole tradition that embodies the American political experience. The Founding Fathers did not conceive their own efforts to be illusory; they thought that the framework of rules laid down would, and could, limit the scope of governmental power. And two centuries of history corroborate this hypothesis, despite the record that also exhibits failure, erosion, and explicit violation of constraints that the Founders sought to incorporate into our basic "higher law." I need not list the many aberrations in our constitutional history, aberrations from the basic structure of governance as conceived by our Founders.

I shall assert, however, that, even in the 1980s, government is limited by the Constitution, and not by the mere self-impositional behavior of those who act in the name and the authority of government. There are things that government dare not do, even in our era where governmental power seems almost ubiquitous. We may, of course, readily point to areas of activity where government intrusion into our lives and liberties seems unlimited. I shall treat some of these in more detail later, but my primary emphasis at this point is to state categorically that the United States, even in the 1980s, is not "beyond law," beyond some "constitutional limits."

The Electoral Fallacy

Acceptance of the general proposition that government can be constitutionally limited, and that, in the United States, government remains subject to constitutional constraints, need not embody the "constitutional attitude" nor reflect the genuine "constitutional wisdom" that seemed characteristic of eighteenth-century political thought. Many modern scholars, along with practicing politicians and members of the public, will acknowledge that basic individual rights, such as those summarized in the first ten amendments, the Bill of Rights, should be and must be accorded constitutional status; that is, such rights should not be embodied in the "higher law" of the land and should not be subject to change by temporary majority coalitions in the Congress, acting with the assent of the president.

Such acknowledgment of the constitutional status of basic individual rights may, however, be accompanied by an acceptance of or acquiescence in, and even support for, almost any decision that is reached through constitutionally sanctioned means or processes. So long as individuals possess freedom of speech, press, and assembly; so long as each person has the right to vote; so long as candidates and parties are chosen in free and open elections conducted on agreed-on rules; and so long as agents or representatives are chosen for specifically limited terms of office—if these conditions are guaranteed constitutionally, the results, whatever these might be, are themselves to be treated as "constitutionally legitimate." Or so the standard argument goes to the extent that it is articulated at all.

The whole argument is, I suggest, based on a set of elementary misconceptions or errors. At a fundamental philosophical level, the argument embodies an exclusive evaluation of process and procedures quite independently of the end-states or results that such procedures may generate. In many of my own writings, I have strongly supported arguments for process evaluation, largely because institutional procedures or rules are the normal objects for choice. However, the choice or selection among different processes or procedures must remain empty unless it is somehow informed by predictions of outcome or end-state patterns that will be generated under alternative rules. To judge a set of procedural rules to be desirable it is necessary to establish at least some proof, within reasonable tolerance, that such rules will "work," that is, will produce end-states that are valued in themselves. To argue that any collective outcome or decision reached by a majority of the community's members (or by some majority of their representatives, themselves elected by simple majorities in defined constituencies) is acceptable merely because it is reached by procedures that are independently evaluated to be desirable is an unwarranted logical step. Procedures themselves must be adjudged in accordance with predicted end-state patterns. Hence, simple majority rule, political equality, and periodic elections are to be judged acceptable only if there is independent argument to the effect that such institutions will generate a pattern of end-states that may be judged acceptable independently of procedures.

To put my point in a somewhat different way, I am suggesting that there is nothing sacred in the ordinary institutions of political democracy, nothing that should prevent us from taking a continuing critical look at these institutions to try to understand as best we can just what patterns of results they seem most likely to generate. To assume the opposing stance, to refuse to look at such results, to retain an implicit and blind faith in the efficacy of such institutions is to be trapped in what I shall call "the electoral fallacy."

Models of Politics

In order to evaluate alternative political rules and institutions, it is necessary to undertake positive analysis of how they work. It is necessary to model politics and political behavior. Such modeling is much of what "public choice theory" is all about. And what can such modeling tell us? What does it tell us?

Major scientific advances have been made in our understanding of governmental-political processes in the decades since World War II. One of the most shocking proofs, at least to many scholars, was a rediscovery of an earlier demonstration to the effect that simple majority voting does not, on many occasions, result in a stable set of outcomes. A majority may be found that will support almost any choice in a set; there may be no unique majority motion or candidate. Among a set of three options—A, B, and C—a majority may be found to support A over B and B over C, then choose C over A. To expect institutions of majority voting to yield "rational" outcomes was shown to be folly. Political decision rules that incorporate the evaluations of more than one person are inherently unstable, capricious, nonrational.

This proof, associated with the work of Duncan Black and Kenneth Arrow in the early 1950s, shocked those who placed implicit faith in democratic electoral process unbounded by constitutional constraints. But what if actual governments are not so simple as these elementary majority-rule models imply? What if actual politics, as it really works, is not properly modeled as simple majority voting, but instead is best interpreted in terms of the behavior of a monolithic decision maker, a "ruler." Would not decisions in such cases be consistent, stable, and rational? Would not all problems of cyclical rotation, inconsistency, and nonrationality then disappear? Indeed so, but what arguments are then to be put into the objective or utility function of the decision makers? Unless we somehow can justify a "benevolent despot" presumption here, we find it even more necessary to reexamine the appropriateness of extending constitutional limits beyond the basic protections of rights of speech, press, assembly, and voting. Otherwise, what is to prevent government from taking all that is of economic value for its own purposes?

If models of genuinely democratic politics (one man, one vote majority models) are demonstrated to generate nonconsistent patterns of outcomes, and if nondemocratic models (monolithic bureaucracy, dictatorship, one-party states, etc.) dare not embody a benevolence presumption, the argument for some reexamination of constitutional constraints or limits is surely in order. If all politics is flawed, what sort of constitutional constraints can be invented to keep government within tolerable bounds?

The Power to Take and the Power to Tax

I posed the question above: What is to prevent government from taking all that is of economic value from citizens? A preliminary answer to this question is provided in the set of basic rights laid out in the United States Constitution. Government cannot explicitly "take" property without "due process of law," and without appropriate compensation. There are, of course, notable exceptions, and there have been many violations of the taking prohibition that have been allowed to go unchallenged by the courts. Nonetheless, there do exist constitutional limitations on the taking power of government, and these limitations are acknowledged.

But what about the closely related power to tax? If government cannot arbitrarily "take" property from a person, it may accomplish roughly the same purposes by *taxing*. The essential legal difference between "taking" and "taxing" is that, in the latter, there is some acknowledged requirement of uniformity, generality, or nondiscrimination, at least within broad ranges. The difference can perhaps be illustrated by the existing constitutional limits on the government's power to tax in the United States. Neither the federal government, the state government, nor the local government can single out a particular person by name, by clan, by religion, by race, by sex, or any other arbitrary designation, and levy on that person a particular tax. Such arbitrary treatment would be held unconstitutional. Grounds for differentiation in taxation must be nonarbitrary and must somehow be seen to emerge from reasonable argument. Hence government cannot tax away a substantial part of the economic value earned or owned by a person *unless it also treats like persons similarly*. The proviso for uniformity, generality, or equity is very important for my purposes in this discussion because, properly understood, it points up a glaring omission in existing constitutional limits on governmental powers to exact economic resources from the citizenry. *There is no constitutional limit on the aggregate power of government to tax,* provided only that the uniformity-equity precepts are honored. That is to say, if government treats all persons in comparable situations similarly (say, all persons with incomes over $20,000), then it becomes constitutionally permissible for taxes to be levied confiscatorily. There would be nothing unconstitutional in a coercive tax measure that imposed 100 percent marginal rates on all incomes above some designated figure, say, $25,000 per year, with all incomes below this level totally exempted from taxation.

Before 1913 and the passage of the Sixteenth Amendment no such tax arrangement would have been constitutional, but even then there would have been no barrier against the levy of, say, a 90 percent rate of tax on all incomes. In either case, the point is clear. There are no constitutional constraints on government's power to raise revenues via taxes.

Only in the 1970s did it come to be recognized, grudgingly by some, that the failure to include such absolute limits on the power to tax reflects a rather obvious deficiency in the "law of the land," the United States Constitution, a deficiency that cries out for remedy. It is, of course, easy to understand why the American Founding Fathers did not include any such limit. They could scarcely imagine, two centuries ago, that the central government would come to be the dominant economic force that it has grown to be, and that the rate of growth in government's share in the economy, and hence in real taxes, would increase more than proportionately with the nongovernmental sector.

The Fiscal Challenge of the 1980s

The challenge of the 1980s lies in constitutional reform. Can our society reform itself by imposing fiscal constraints on government's power to tax, and, by inference, on its power to spend monies for governmental purposes, including transfers to those persons and groups who do not pay taxes but who hold rights to the franchise? Alongside such fiscal constraints that may be discussed, there is the accompanying set of issues involving possible constitutional limits on the obtrusive regulatory interferences of modern governmental agencies. But in the remainder of this article I shall concentrate attention on fiscal constraints, both because these are easier to analyze and because my own research in the last two years has been largely on the "fiscal constitution," broadly defined.[3]

Is Constitutional Reform Possible?

First of all, it is necessary to examine the conceptual possibility of such constitutional reform. Is it idle fancy to think that such fiscal limits might be incorporated in the Constitution? In 1977 many persons might have thought so, but in 1978 California voters did overwhelmingly approve Proposition 13. And further, in 1979 thirty state legislatures did pass resolutions calling on the Congress to authorize a constitutional convention to consider a balanced-budget amendment. Given sufficiently broad citizen-taxpayer support, existing and long-established procedures will allow genuine constitutional changes to be made.

Will the Public Back It?

Second, however, we come back to the electoral issue, discussed above. If it is possible to generate broad-based citizen support for constitutional reform, why is it not possible that the ordinary checks of the democratic electoral process will produce similar results, thereby making resort to constitutional change unnecessary? In other words, if taxpayers-citizens want to turn things around, why won't they throw the big spenders out and replace them with politicians and parties that promise and deliver lower taxes and reduced rates of government growth?

I do not want to deny that some such effect has happened since 1978; politicians of all persuasion did get the Jarvis-Gann message. But to depend on electoral feedbacks to reverse the long-continuing trend of public sector expansion would, I think, be a dangerous delusion. In saying this, I am referring to what I consider to be fundamental biases in the taxing and spending process in American politics, biases that insure a continuation of pressures for increased real tax rates, almost independently of just what politicians or parties hold electoral offices. Several of these biases deserve further discussion.

Pressure Groups

As our representative democracy works in the context of our legal-constitutional history, prospective beneficiaries of governmental spending programs bring concentrated pressures to bear on elected representatives. There are no constitutional requirements that benefits from spending programs shall be uniformly or generally distributed; the spending side of the account differs categorically from the taxing side in this important respect. Arbitrary discrimination in providing governmental benefits is constitutionally permissible; hence, the beneficiaries of a program can be sufficiently concentrated to allow for carefully orchestrated efforts. Offsetting these pressure groups, the program costs will tend to be spread out among all taxpayers, no one group of which has much incentive to oppose a particular program. Congressmen respond, quite straightforwardly, to pressures from their constituents, and we should not then be surprised when we see them devote more interest to spending projects in their own districts than to the level of real tax rates imposed on taxpayers throughout the economy.

Once a spending program is established, once it gets across the commencement threshold, the specific beneficiaries become an even more intensive pressure group for maintenance and expansion of rates of outlay. It becomes almost impossible, politically, to cut off program benefits, once these have been commenced, and once recipients come to treat benefits as entitlements.

This basic bias is accentuated by the role of the bureaucracy, which introduces nondemocratic elements in the whole process. Spending programs are often invented by imaginative entrepreneurs in the bureaucracy, who then are led to organize the beneficiary groups and to manipulate the agenda for political action so as to insure program continuation and expansion.

Nontax Sources of Revenue

The bias discussed above is inherent in the structure of democratic decision making so long as there is a basic asymmetry between the legal constitutional norms applied to the taxing and the spending sides of the fiscal account. A quite different bias toward spending emerges from potential governmental access to nontax sources of revenue raising. Even with the decision bias noted above, spending rates would be lower if all programs were required to be tax-financed. Government, however, may have access to both debt issue and money creation as alternative revenue sources. These allow the government to spend without taxing, which is almost the ideal setting for elected politicians. By creating deficits, goverment is allowed to finance desired programs that provide benefits to potential voters without overt increases in rates of tax.

This bias is important only for governments that have money-creation power; without such power any public debt issued must be borrowed quite like ordinary borrowing. Even for central governments, however, the deficit-spending bias has become important only in the post-Keynesian era, during which Keynesian economics has offered politicians academic-intellectual excuses for pursuing their own interests. Keynesian teachings provided an apologia for deficit creation, producing rapidly increasing public debt accompanied by accelerating inflation generated by use of the printing press.[4] Inflation, in its own turn, increased real rates of taxes on incomes, which, in turn, allowed revenues to be available for increased real rates of governmental outlay. Politicians have been allowed to play out their roles in an ideal setting, to spend without taxing; and, even more surprising in many respects, they have been largely successful in blaming the predictable inflation on the evil machinations of businessmen and labor leaders. The response of the public to the inflation of the 1970s scarcely provides much ground for expecting reforms in this pattern by way of ordinary electoral (i.e., nonconstitutional) channels.

Inflation Expectations

Inflation, like particularized spending programs, cannot readily be "turned off" once inflationary expectations come to be incorporated in contracts. In short-run terms, there is a trade-off between any reduction in the rate of inflation and economic prosperity. To try to reduce an inflation rate of 15 percent to, say, 10 percent, after the 15 percent rate has come to be expected or anticipated, exerts economic effects that are equivalent to the imposition of a 5 percent deflation on an economy adjusted to monetary stability. Politically it becomes almost impossible for a government to get a continuing inflation under control without major disruption, despite the government's direct role and responsibility in creating the inflation in the first place. There is a bias toward inflationary financing almost independently of the form of government itself, whether this be pure democracy, representative democracy, or dictatorship.

This deficit spending–inflation bias, along with the structural bias discussed earlier, suggests that genuine reform must be sought *constitutionally* rather than *electorally*. That is to say, politicians who find themselves in responsible official positions will almost necessarily find it impossible to impose fiscal constraints, regardless of ideological persuasion. If fiscal constraints on government are to be imposed at all, there must be change in the set of things governments are allowed to do; there must be change in the basic rules, the Constitution.

Procedural and Quantitative Constraints

If we acknowledge that additional fiscal and monetary constraints on government are desired and, further, that these constraints must be implemented constitutionally, we are still confronted with issues concerning specific forms of limits.

More Than a Simple Majority

There are two broad types. The first includes what I have called *procedural* constraints. By these, I refer to possible constitutional changes in the rules for making decisions politically. If simple majority voting rules in legislatures, in Congress, are predicted to generate undesired results on the side of an excessive rate of growth in real tax and spending rates, these rules may be changed so as to require majorities larger than simple majorities for approval of any fiscal measure. Alan Greenspan has proposed that all spending authorizations require two-thirds majorities in each house of Congress. One of the important, and sometimes overlooked, parts of California's Proposition 13 is the requirement that new taxes must have the approval of two-thirds majorities in the state legislature.

Linkage of Taxing and Spending

A somewhat less dramatic procedural change would be one that required more direct linkage between taxing and spending decisions. Legislatures might be required to keep their own accounts in better balance, and to indicate just how revenues sufficient to finance each item of spending are to be raised before the item of spending is approved. This requirement may, but need not, take the form of imposing a balanced-budget constraint, requiring that anticipated tax revenues match anticipated outlays, essentially closing off the debt and money-creation options as revenue-raising devices. The balanced-budget proposal, as a constitutional amendment, was demonstrated in 1979 to have widespread appeal to the public generally. If finally incorporated as an explicit amendment to the United States Constitution, it might do much toward eliminating the proclivity of government toward excessive rates of growth in spending and close up, so to speak, the deficiency on the fiscal constitution noted earlier.[5]

Quantitative Limits on Taxing and Spending

Additional procedural constraints could be mentioned, but my purpose here is not to list all potential constitutional changes. The general set of procedural constraints should, however, be compared with what I have called *quantitative* constraints, perhaps best exemplified by the proposed constitutional amendment that would relate the rate of growth in federal outlays directly to the rate of growth in national product, an amendment widely discussed in 1979. Variants on this sort of constraint have been introduced in several state constitutions. An additional example of a quantitative constraint is Proposition 13's explicit limit on the rate of tax on real property in California. The quantitative constraints have the advantage of being more specific than the procedural ones, but, like the other side of this same coin, they reduce the flexibility of governmental response to uncertain circumstances somewhat more than procedural requirements.

A Fiscal-Monetary Constitution

It should be evident that I could go on to elaborate this discussion of alternative proposals for elements of a fiscal constitution at some length. But this elaboration would hardly be appropriate in the more general discussion of constitutional limits that I have undertaken here. Let me summarize my previous discussion in a set of statements. I have argued that government can be constitutionally constrained. I have argued that there is a flaw in our existing Constitution that allows for excessive rates of growth in real taxes, real public spending, and in the relative size of the governmental sector. I have argued that observed rates of growth in governmental outlays can be scientifically adjudged to be excessive due to biases in the processes of democratic decision making, as these are legally defined in the United States. Finally, I have argued that there are essentially two separate ways of imposing desired limits to deal with the problem discussed.

I do not, however, want to leave my discussion at such a level of generality. I think that the arguments I have advanced should clearly demonstrate the desirability of changes in our Constitution. This much may be granted, however, without necessary agreement on the specific proposals to be adopted.

In order to end on a positive note, I want to lay out my own set of proposals for constitutional change. Both at the level of academic scholarship and in testimony before committees of federal and state legislatures, I have supported the proposed constitutional amendment that would require the federal government to balance its budget accounts. I have suggested that a four-year phase-in period might be needed to avoid sudden and unanticipated shifts in rates of real taxes and spending. Accompanying this budget-balance amendment, I should also support the adoption of a monetary growth rule. Such a rule would require that the Federal Reserve authorities increase the supply of base money in the economy between 3 and 5 percent annually, with specified penalties for violations of these targets. Note that, with a budget-balance rule in place, there would be much less political pressure on the monetary authorities to exceed defined money-growth targets. The two rules suggested, the fiscal and the monetary, are closely complementary.

The enactment of such constitutional amendments would have major symbolic value, over and beyond the directly constraining effects that are incorporated in them. The enactment of such changes would modify dramatically both domestic and foreign expectations about the future activities of American governments in the third century of our constitutional history. My personally idealized scenario calls for the "constitutional dialogue," which did genuinely commence in the late 1970s, to accelerate in the early 1980s, so much so that the 1980s will become the "decade of constitutional reexamination and reevaluation." The scenario then calls for these efforts to be crowned with success well before we celebrate the bicentennial of the Constitution itself, a celebration that could then take place in confidence and hope.

NOTES

1. F. A. Hayek, *Law, Legislation, and Liberty*, 3 vol. (Chicago: University of Chicago Press, 1979).
2. The fairness criterion for evaluating alternative rules has been made familiar to social scientists and social philosophers through the work of John Rawls. See *A Theory of Justice* (Cambridge, Mass.: Harvard University Press, 1971). For a similar evaluative procedure, strictly related to constitutional choice, see James M.

Buchanan and Gordon Tullock, *The Calculus of Consent* (Ann Arbor: University of Michigan Press, 1962).

3. See Geoffrey Brennan and James Buchanan, *The Power to Tax: Analytical Foundations of a Fiscal Constitution* (Cambridge: Cambridge University Press, 1980).
4. For an elaboration of this argument, see James M. Buchanan and Richard E. Wagner, *Democracy in Deficit* (New York: Academic Press, 1977).
5. Although it was legislative rather than constitutional, the Budget Reform Act of 1974 represents an attempt by Congress to introduce procedural changes in its own fiscal decision processes so as to remove acknowledged biases toward excessive spending. This act does not require budget balance, but, by means of the Budget Resolutions, it does require Congress to consider simultaneously both sides of the budget account. The act's history is too short to allow for much evaluation of its effect. And, of course, its legislative basis means that any Congress could disregard its precepts.

Contributors

James T. Bennett, George Mason University
Peter Bernholz, University of Basel
Geoffrey Brennan, Center for Study of Public Choice, George Mason University
James M. Buchanan, Center for Study of Public Choice, George Mason University
W. Mark Crain, Center for Study of Public Choice, George Mason University
Thomas J. DiLorenzo, George Mason University
Robert B. Ekelund, Jr., Auburn University
Roger L. Faith, Arizona State University
John F. Forbes, University of Glasgow
Bruno S. Frey, University of Zurich
Dwight R. Lee, Center for Study of Public Choice, George Mason University
Robert E. McCormick, Clemson University
Dennis C. Mueller, University of Maryland
Vincent Ostrom, Indiana University
Thomas Romer, Carnegie-Mellon University
Howard Rosenthal, Carnegie-Mellon University
Todd Sandler, University of Wyoming
T. Nicolaus Tideman, Virginia Polytechnic Institute and State University
Robert D. Tollison, Clemson University
Gordon Tullock, Center for Study of Public Choice, George Mason University
Richard E. Wagner, Florida State University
Thomas D. Willett, Claremont Graduate School